FUTURE DIRECTIONS IN EXERCISE AND SPORT SCIENCE RESEARCH

James S. Skinner, PhD
Charles B. Corbin, PhD
Daniel M. Landers, PhD
Philip E. Martin, PhD
Christine L. Wells, PhD
Arizona State University
Editors

Human Kinetics Books
Champaign, Illinois

Library of Congress Cataloging-in-Publication Data

Symposium on Future Directions in Exercise/Sport Research (1986 : Tempe, Ariz.)
Future directions in exercise and sport science research / edited by James S. Skinner . . . [et al.].
p. cm.
"Proceedings of the Symposium on Future Directions in Exercise/Sport Research, held in Tempe, Arizona, January 1986"—T.p verso.
Bibliography: p.
ISBN 0-87322-174-5
1. Sports sciences—Research—Congresses. I. Skinner, James S., 1936- . II. Title.
GV557.5.S95 1986
613.7'1—dc19 88-26637
CIP

Proceedings of the Symposium on Future Directions in Exercise/Sport Research, January 9-12, 1986, Arizona State University, Tempe, Arizona.

Developmental Editor: Joanne Fetzner
Production Director: Ernie Noa
Managing Editor: Kathy Kane
Copyeditor: Claire Mount
Assistant Editors: Holly Gilly and Valerie Hall
Typesetter: Yvonne Winsor
Text Design: Keith Blomberg
Text Layout: Denise Peters
Printed By: Braun-Brumfield, Inc.

ISBN: 0-87322-174-5

Printed in the United States of America

10 9 8 7 6 5 4 3 2 1

Human Kinetics Books
A Division of Human Kinetics Publishers, Inc.
Box 5076, Champaign, IL 61820
1-800-DIAL-HKP
1-800-334-3665 (in Illinois)

Contents

Preface

In the rapidly growing and diversified fields of exercise and sport science, research is conducted in such varied disciplines as biomechanics, exercise physiology, motor development and learning, and sports psychology. Especially in a young field, it is essential to periodically examine these subdisciplines within the field, to redefine the scope of the research, and to identify needed research for the future.

Forty-three leading scientists representing several subdisciplines were invited to participate in the Symposium on Future Directions in Exercise/Sport Research in January 1986 at the official opening of the Exercise and Sport Research Institute at Arizona State University. These proceedings include chapters by 37 of the 43 invited speakers at this unique symposium. Recent research results in the areas of biomechanics, exercise physiology, motor development and learning, and sports psychology are reviewed, evaluated, and positioned within the broad area of exercise and sport science research. Further, in accordance with the goals of the symposium sponsors, the research needs of the future are identified. An interdisciplinary approach is encouraged throughout this volume, as these scientists look to the future of exercise and sport science research.

Acknowledgments

The Exercise and Sport Research Institute has been very fortunate to obtain unusually generous backing from the Arizona State University administration and from The Quaker Oats Company and Gatorade Thirst Quencher. Gatorade's generous support of this symposium has provided the opportunity for many researchers and graduate students to exchange ideas with some of the best scientists in their respective fields. We feel a deep commitment to acknowledge that support and to be worthy of it. We hope to repay their trust and extend those benefits to the public and to our profession by making a significant contribution to the knowledge in the various aspects of exercise science. The symposium and this book are just the beginning.

James S. Skinner
Charles B. Corbin
Daniel M. Landers
Philip E. Martin
Christine L. Wells

Acknowledgments

Contributors

Future Directions in Exercise and Sport Science Research
Edited by James Skinner

Elizabeth A. Aaron
John Rankin Laboratory
of Pulmonary Medicine
University of Wisconsin-Madison
504 N. Walnut St.
Madison, WI 53705

Thomas P. Andriacchi, PhD
Department of Orthopedic Surgery
Rush-Presbyterian-St. Luke's Hospital
1753 W. Congress Parkway
Chicago, IL 60612

Per-Olof Åstrand, MD
Department of Physiology III
Karolinska Institute
Lindingovagen 1
S-114 33 Stockholm
Sweden

Dr. Oded Bar-Or
Department of Pediatrics
McMaster University
1200 Main Street West
Hamilton, Ontario, Canada L8N 3Z5

Ian C. Bruce
Department of Exercise Science
N420 Field House
University of Iowa
Iowa City, IA 52242

Peter R. Cavanagh, PhD
Center for Locomotion Studies
The Pennsylvania State University
University Park, PA 16802

Dr. Robert W. Christina
Department of Physical Education
The Pennsylvania State University
University Park, PA 16802

Charles B. Corbin, PhD
Department of Health
and Physical Education
Arizona State Uiversity
Tempe, AZ 85287

Jerome A. Dempsey
John Rankin Laboratory
of Pulmonary Medicine
University of Wisconsin-Madison
504 N. Walnut St.
Maidson, WI 53705

Charles J. Dillman, PhD
Director, Sports Science Program
United States Olympic Committee
1750 East Boulder Street
Colorado Springs, CO 80909

Barbara L. Drinkwater, PhD
Department of Medicine
Pacific Medical Center
1200 12th Avenue S.
Seattle, WA 98144

Deborah L. Feltz
School of Health Education, Counseling
Psychology, and Human Performance
Michigan State University
East Lansing, MI 48824

Henrik Galbo
Department of Medical Physiology B
The Panum Institute
Blegdamsvej 3C
2500 Copenhagen N
Denmark

Carl V. Gisolfi, PhD
Department of Exercise Science
N420 Field House
University of Iowa
Iowa City, IA 52242

Philip D. Gollnick
Dept. of Veterinary and Comparative
Anatomy, Pharmacology, and Physiology
College of Veterinary Medicine
Washington State University
Pullman, WA 99164-6520

Robert J. Gregor
Human Biomechanics Laboratory
Department of Kinesiology
University of California, Los Angeles
Los Angeles, CA 90024

William L. Haskell, PhD
Stanford University School of Medicine
Stanford, CA 94035

James G. Hay, PhD
University of Iowa
Department of Exercise Science
Iowa City, IA 52242

Kathe G. Henke
John Rankin Laboratory
of Pulmonary Medicine
University of Wisconsin-Madison
504 N. Walnut St.
Madison, WI 53705

Michael Kjaer
Department of Medical Physiology B
The Panum Institute
Blegdamsvej 3C
2200 Copenhagen N
Denmark

Paavo V. Komi
Department of Biology of Physical Activity
University of Jyvaskyla
Seminaarinkatu 15
SF 40100 Jyvaskyla 10
Finland

Daniel M. Landers
Exercise and Sport Research Institute
Department of Health
and Physical Education
Arizona State University
Tempe, AZ 85287

Kari J. Mikines
Department of Medical Physiology B
The Panum Institute
Blegdamsvej 3C
2200 Copenhagen N
Denmark

Doris I. Miller
Faculty of Physical Education
University of Western Ontario
London, Ontario, Canada N6A 3K7

William P. Morgan
Sport Psychology Laboratory
University of Wisconsin-Madison
Unit 2 Gymnasium
2000 Observatory Drive
Madison, WI 53706

Richard C. Nelson, PhD
Exercise/Sport Science Department
Pennsylvania State University
Biomechanics Lab
University Park, PA 16802

Benno M. Nigg
Biomechanics Laboratory
Faculty of Calgary
Calgary, Alberta, Canada T2N 1N4

Robert W. Norman
Department of Kinesiology
University of Waterloo
Waterloo, Ontario, Canada N2L 3G1

G. Lawrence Rarick
Department of Physical Education
University of California, Berkeley
103 Harmon Gymnasium
Berkeley, CA 94720

Mary Ann Roberton
Department of Physical Education
and Dance
University of Wisconsin-Madison
Madison, WI 53706

Glyn C. Roberts, Professor
Institute for Child Behavior
and Development
51 Gerty Drive
Champaign, IL 61820

Richard A. Schmidt
Motor Control Laboratory
Department of Kinesiology
University of California, Los Angeles
Los Angeles, CA 90024

James S. Skinner
Department of Health
and Physical Education
Arizona State University
Tempe, AZ 85287

Everett L. Smith, PhD
Director, Biogerontology Lab
Department of Preventive Medicine
University of Wisconsin
504 Walnut Street
Madison, WI 53705

Ronald E. Smith
Department of Psychology NI-25
University of Washington
Seattle, WA 98195

George E. Stelmach
Professor and Director
Motor Behavior Lab
University of Wisconsin-Madison
2000 Observatory Drive
Madison, WI 53706

Richard M. Suinn, PhD
Department of Psychology
Colorado State University
Fort Collins, CO 80523

Jerry R. Thomas
Professor and Chair
Department of Health
and Physical Education
Arizona State University
Tempe, AZ 85287-0701

Charles M. Tipton, PhD
University of Arizona
Department of Exercise
and Sport Sciences
Tucson, AZ 85721

Christine L. Wells, PhD
Exercise and Sport Research Institute
Department of Health
and Physical Education
Arizona State University
Tempe, AZ 85287

Jack H. Wilmore
Department of Physical
and Health Education
The University of Texas at Austin
Bellmont Hall 222
Austin, TX 78712

David A. Winter, PhD
Department of Kinesiology
University of Waterloo
Waterloo, Ontario, Canada N2L 3G1

Ronald F. Zernicke
Department of Kinesiology
University of California
Los Angeles, CA 90024

Keynote Lecture: Exercise and Sports for All—Our Biological Heritage

Per-Olof Åstrand

Before I discuss the future of exercise and sport, I will present a brief sketch of our evolutionary history to remind us that it has taken us a long time to become the way we are. Many of the biological processes involved are in fact thousands of millions of years old. Thus, a comprehensive textbook of biochemistry written some 1,500 million years ago would no doubt still be up to date in its treatment of the functions of the cell.

It is assumed that our solar system was created some 4,600 million years ago (Dickerson, 1978). Evidently, the atmosphere surrounding our planet at that time did not contain oxygen. This was a prerequisite for the evolution of life from non-living organic matter. Without atmospheric oxygen, the ultraviolet radiation from the sun, in the absence of high-altitude ozone, reached the surface of the earth. This radiation then provided the energy for the photosynthesis of organic compounds from such molecules as water, carbon dioxide, and ammonia. The process that enabled living organisms to capture solar energy for the synthesis of organic molecules (e.g., glucose) can be clearly traced in fossils that are about 3,500 million years old. Similarly, the familiar anaerobic fermentation (i.e., glycolysis) is probably the oldest energy-extracting pathway found in life on earth. Those who are interested in additional reading on this subject should refer to British Museum (1980) and ''Evolution'' (1978).

The ancient organisms split water by photosynthesis, gradually releasing free oxygen into the atmosphere. It may have taken some 2,000 million years to create an atmosphere in which one out of every five molecules was oxygen. As oxygen became toxic for many of the original oxygen producers, new metabolic patterns were developed (i.e., aerobic energy yield) that utilized oxygen as a hydrogen acceptor.

Note. Parts of this chapter summarize chapter 1 in *Textbook of Work Physiology*, by P. Åstrand and K. Rodahl (1986), New York: McGraw Hill.

A new milestone in the biological evolution was reached approximately 1,500 million years ago when the unicellular organism *with a nucleus*, the eukaryote, was developed (Vidal, 1984). The energy-absorbing and energy-yielding processes typical for our cell activities today are merely copies of events that occurred thousands of millions of years ago, such as the ATP-ADP system. Actually, ATP is the principal medium for the storage and exchange of energy in almost all living organisms. The store of ATP is, however, very limited because it is a heavy fuel. Within 24 hours, a man will spend energy equivalent to the energy stored in ATP weighing 50% to 100% more than his own body weight, depending on how physically active he is. A very rapid resynthesis of ATP is therefore necessary, and the *anaerobic* processes, which are several thousand million years old, are supplemented by the *aerobic* energy yield taking place inside the mitochondria.

Thus, over thousands of millions of years of evolution, a unicellular living organism was created. By some sort of trial and error, the fundamental biological principles for maintaining life were developed. They are still in efficient operation.

The evolution was now ready for the next major step, the creation of larger animals. That stage probably began 700 million years ago (Valentine, 1978). In this evolution of larger animals, the individual cell retained its original size (i.e., the same size as the unicellular organism living more than 1,000 million years ago), but more cells were grouped together to increase the size of the organism.

As an inevitable consequence of grouping thousands of millions of some 200 different types of cells together in one organism (the human being), the individual cell lost its intimate contact with the external environment. This problem was solved by bathing each cell in water (i.e., the interstitial fluid). Like the amoeba, each cell in our body (with some exceptions) is surrounded by fluid, the composition of which is basically very similar to that of the ancient oceans. The organism brought the sea water with it, so to speak, in a bag made of skin.

In the course of the diversification of the multicellular organisms, which occurred over the last 700 million years, new types of organisms appeared and dispersions took place within already established groups. It should be noted that the history of the mammals covers the last 220 million years, if not more. The first primates (the order including man) can be traced back some 60 to 70 million years to a period when the dinosaurs still dominated the scene. With the extinction of the dinosaurs, there was a mammalian dispersion into vacant niches. Another evolutionary explosion occurred, with a dispersion of flowering plants, birds, and mammals.

What then are the mechanisms that underlie the origin of species and the evolutionary relationships among them (i.e., Darwinism)? Lewin (1980) summarized the current views held by different researchers in this field. According to the modern synthesis, evolution is a consequence of the gradual accumulation of genetic differences due to point mutations and rearrangements in the chromosomes. The direction of an evolutionary change is determined by natural selection, promoting the variants that are best fitted to their environment. The fact remains, however, that fossils, on the whole, do not document a smooth transition from old morphologies to new ones. This was also discussed by Darwin. For millions of years, species remain unchanged in the fossil record, suddenly to be replaced by something that is substantially different but clearly related (Lewin, 1980).

Because the accumulation of small genetic changes cannot exclusively explain the development of new species, a new theory called *punctuated equilibrium* has been advanced. According to this theory, individual species may remain virtually unchanged for long periods of time. They are then suddenly punctuated by abrupt events in the environment, and a new species arises from the original stock. It is conceivable, however, that future fossil records may fill many of the gaps and provide some of the missing links. It may have been only 5 or as many as 20 million years ago that the family tree of primates developed a branch, the hominids, which finally resulted in *Homo sapiens sapiens*, the only surviving hominid. Not until about 4 million years ago do the African fossils reveal the presence of the hominid genus *Australopithecus*. The pelvis permitted an upright posture and bipedal gait with the arms free. There are archaeological records of tools, pebble choppers, and small stones that are probably more than 3 million years old (Lewin, 1981). Toolmaking was thus established before there was a marked brain expansion in the hominid stock. Although a few varieties have been identified, the *Australopithecus* was a relatively homogeneous genus that survived for more than 2 million years. The next well-identified member of our family tree may have been the first true man. *Homo habilis* existed from 2.3 to 1.5 million years ago. He was replaced by *Homo erectus*, who had a modern pelvis and moved with a striding gait. He lived as a hunter and food gatherer and had a wide geographical range. His body height was probably 150 to 160 cm. He made use of fire, as evidenced by a hominid occupation site 1.4 million years old.

The general public is probably most familiar with the Neanderthal man *(Homo sapiens neanderthalensis)*, who from archaeologic findings appears to have been well established more than 100,000 years ago (Trinkaus & Howells, 1979). These were skilled hunters of large and small game, forming bands similar to those of more recent hunting people, and were probably linked into tribal groupings, or at least groups with a common language. They formed a human population complex extending from Gibraltar across Europe into East Asia. The Neanderthal population was as homogeneous as the human population of today. On the average, the brain encased in the Neanderthal skull was slightly larger than the brain of modern man. Although the Neanderthals had the same postural abilities, manual dexterity, and range and character of movement as modern man, they had more massive limb bones and a larger muscular mass and power. The departure of the Neanderthals occurred some 35,000 years ago. When they disappeared from the scene anatomically, modern man, *Homo sapiens sapiens*, was already in existence. No one knows why modern man came to the fore while the Neanderthal disappeared. Most likely, a human being living 50,000 years ago had the same potential for physical and intellectual performance, playing a piano or constructing a computer, as anyone living today. So, from all indications, *Homo sapiens sapiens* has remained biologically unchanged for at least 50,000 years. By 30,000 years ago, modern man had spread to nearly all parts of the world. It was not until some 10,000 years ago that the transition from a roaming hunter and food gatherer to a stationary farmer began.

To illustrate the evolutionary time scale, let us compare the 4,600 million years our planet has existed with a 460-km journey (Table 1). Life began after the first 100 km of the trip had been covered. It took another 200 km before the unicellular organism with a nucleus was born. Multicellular animals were living when we arrived at the 400-km mark. An evolutionary radiation of the mammalian stock began somewhere around the 453-km mark. The first hominid appeared approximately 6 km later. The *Australopithecus*, however, joined the journey 200 to 450 m from the end, and the Neanderthals disappeared just about 3.5 m from the finish line, where they were replaced by modern man. The cultivation of land and keeping of livestock occurred 1 m from our present position. A 100-year-old person today has merely covered a distance of 0.01 m or 10 mm of the 460-km journey.

The purpose of this brief summary has been to present an outline of our genetic background. Many structures and functions are common to different species in the animal kingdom. For instance, there appears to be no fundamental difference in structure, chemistry, or function between the neurons and synapses in man and those of a squid, a snail, or a leech (Kandel, 1979). Therefore, we can learn a great deal from studying different species. It is remarkable that all living organisms have a genetic

Table 1 Our Biological Evolution

Progress (in km)	Evolution	Years ago
0	The earth is created	4,600,000,000
110	Biochemical processes developed that can trap solar energy	3,500,000,000
310	Single-celled organisms with a nucleus appear	1,500,000,000
390	Multicellular organisms appear	700,000,000
453	Modern mammals appear	70,000,000
459	Hominid branch begins to develop	10,000,000
459.6	Australopithecus appears	4,000,000
459.99	Neanderthal man appears	100,000
459.999	Agriculture introduced	10,000
459.999.99	Present 100-year-old man born	100

code based on the same principle. Data indicate, for instance, that man and the chimpanzee share more than 99% of their genetic material (Washburn, 1978). However, minimal genetic changes can affect major morphological modification. Consequently, one should be careful when extrapolating findings from one species to another, because over millions of years many species undergo minor or major modifications in their physical and other characteristics. In general, however, evolution is a very conservative process. For example, all vertebrates, including the hominids, have backbones. Backbones are complicated in design and are quite similar in all animals that have them. This supports the hypothesis that backbones have evolved only once, that is, all vertebrates share a common ancestor with a backbone.

In general, vertebrate locomotion is genetically programmed. Fish can swim and birds can walk as soon as they hatch. Many species of mammals are well developed at birth. Thus, some are able to walk or run as soon as they are born, and some of them are able to attain a speed of 35 kph when they are only a few days old. Evidently, survival may depend on their ability to get away. In the case of man, who is utterly helpless at birth and entirely dependent on the parents' care, it may be to his advantage not to be able to remove himself very far from his parents until he is mature enough to stand on his own feet.

The evolutionary process continues, and the more recent mammalian history has seen a wave of extinction, particularly severe for large mammals, including the hominids. Extinctions are a measure of the success of evolution in adapting organisms, because particular adaptations provide entry into a relatively empty niche. In the balance between existence and extinction, the odds are not too favorable. It has been estimated that 2,000 million species have appeared on earth during the last 700 million years, but the number of multicellular species now living is only a few million (i.e., only 0.1% to 0.2% have survived).

The cortex of the human brain mirrors man's evolutionary success. For just as the proportions of the human hand, with its large opposable and muscular thumb, reflect successful adaptation for life in trees and later for the use of tools, so does the anatomy of the human brain reflect a successful adaptation for manual and intellectual skills.

Just as upright walking and toolmaking were the unique adaptations of the earlier phases of human evolution, the physiological capacity for speech was the biological basis for the later stages. Indeed, it is by language that human social systems are mediated. Speech is the form of behavior that differentiates man from other animals. The passing down of knowledge and experience by language from one generation to the next has enabled man, biologically unchanged for tens of thousands of years, to accelerate progress. In addition, it has enabled humans to apply their endowed intellectual resources in a technical revolution leading to entirely new and complex tools, weapons, shelters, boats, wheeled locomotion, exploratory voyages, and the attainment of the impossible: space travel. Nevertheless, in the midst of these splendid achievements, there are those who now wonder whether the evolution of the human brain has gone too far. Although its ability to conceive, invent, create, and construct is astonishing, it remains to be seen whether or not it has retained or developed equally well its capacity for ethical conduct or responsible application of its endowed potential. When our ancestors roamed around in small bands, any destructive consequence of their activity was quite limited. Because of social developments and technical innovations, however, basically the same brain is now capable of self-destruction.

Like all higher animals, man is basically designed for mobility. Consequently, our locomotive apparatus and service organs constitute the main part of our total body mass. The shape and dimensions of the human skeleton and musculature are such that the human body cannot compete with a gazelle in speed or an elephant in sturdiness, but it is indeed outstanding in diversity. The basic instrument of mobility is the muscle. It is a very old tissue. As already mentioned, the earliest animal fossils were the burrowers living some 700 million years ago. By muscle force, these animals could dig into the seabed. They retained the metabolic pathways developed when the air had no oxygen (i.e., the anaerobic energy yield). Now, the pyruvic acid formed in our muscles under anaerobic conditions is removed by the formation of lactic acid. One old-fashioned alternative could have been the transformation of the pyruvate into ethyl alcohol. There may be those who now regret that the skeletal muscles did not select this alternative route. Had this occurred, producing pyruvate by exercising to exhaustion or running uphill might have been a very popular endeavor!

At any rate, the skeletal muscle is unique in that it can vary its metabolic rate to a greater degree than any other tissue. In fact, active skeletal muscles may increase their oxidative processes to more than 50 times the resting level. Such an enormous variation in metabolic rate must necessarily create serious problems for the muscle cell, because although the consumption of fuel and oxygen increases 50-fold, the rate of removal of heat, carbon dioxide, water, and waste products must be similarly increased. To maintain the chemical and physical equilibrium of the cell, there must be a tremendous increase in the exchange of molecules between intracellular and extracellular fluid (i.e., fresh fluid must continuously flush the exercising cell). When muscles are thrown into vigorous activity, the ability to maintain the internal equilibriums necessary to continue the exercise is entirely dependent on those organs that service the muscle's circulation. Food intake, digestion and handling of substrates, kidney function, and water balance are also very much affected by variation in metabolic rate.

Almost 100% of the biological existence of our species has been dominated by outdoor activity. Hunting and foraging for food and other necessities have been conditions of human life for millions of years. We are adapted to that style of life. This applies to our emotional, social, and intellectual skills. After a brief spell in an agrarian culture, we have ended up in an urbanized, highly technological society. There is obviously no way to revert to our natural way of life, which was not without its problems. With insight into our biological heritage, however, we may yet be able to modify our current lifestyle. Knowledge of the function of the body at rest, as well as during exercise under various conditions, is important as a basis for an optimization of our existence.

Children definitely are spontaneously physically active. Unfortunately, in our modern society, we discourage them in this activity by furnishing houses and apartments to fit the parents' needs, keeping them indoors in schools and doing homework for many hours, creating heavily overpopulated "concrete deserts," and producing TV programs to capture their attention. Children should keep quiet and stay clean and neat! Vigorous physical activity is an asocial behavior in too many circumstances. From the time of puberty, human nature has an inclination toward physical laziness. There is no appetite center for physical activity.

Some years ago, I visited the Bushmen in the Kalahari Desert, probably the last remaining Stone-Age people. They followed the lifestyle of the true hunters and food gatherers. Gathering sufficient food meant trudging long distances, for the men in their hunting efforts, and the women and children in their collection of berries, melons, roots, and various plants. This walking, stopping, and squatting to dig, and walking again, is physically demanding. When the women gather enough and return home, they still have to collect and carry firewood for the cooking and the night fire. Most of the year, the game and food plants are not found in any abundance. To get enough to eat, the Bushmen have to exercise for hours almost every day. The driving factor for the habitual physical activity is hunger and thirst, not a particular love for exercise. I never saw an adult Bushman out jogging, but the walking was fast! The Bushmen are well trained with emphasis on endurance.

It is quite evident that the major adaptations for our survival were consonant with regular physical activity, but what about the future? The next few days will be very exciting. I have the privilege of presenting some concluding remarks, and I hope that I am, at that stage, better prepared to speculate on the future beyond Sunday, January 12, 1986! For now, I postulate that there is unanimous agreement among the experts that regular physical activity is necessary for optimal functioning and physical fitness. We can list dozens of positive effects on structures and organ function; these effects will be positive today and tomorrow. Whether they are positive a week or a month from now if the training is interrupted, I do not know. The physical endowment, the initial fitness level, and the type and intensity of activities are decisive factors in determining the end results of the efforts. Certainly, various diseases and physical handicaps can interfere with the effects of a training program. A challenge for the future is to learn more about the chain of events triggering the acute and chronic effects of training, including individualized threshold rates of exercise, its duration, and its frequency—in other words, a cost-benefit analysis. It is an axiom that exercise can also induce injuries and other harmful effects. What about early warning signals? What is *overtraining* and how can we diagnose it?

In asking physicians if scientific data prove that habitual physical activity is beneficial, I discovered that they concentrate on the question of whether or not such activity is effective in the primary and secondary prevention of various diseases. The epidemiological studies are very complicated, and data are inconclusive. For this reason, a majority of physicians do not actively recommend exercise, and, I shall add provocatively, too many of them know too little about exercise physiology. In the last decade, epidemiologists in the area of coronary heart diseases have begun to include sedentary lifestyle as an independent risk factor. However, there is still a long way to go in such analyses. We are facing an enormous educational task. For instance, by exposing the cardiologist who does not believe that physical inactivity is a risk factor for cardiovascular diseases to general information about exercise physiology, we may be able to persuade him or her to prescribe exercise because of its many positive effects on body structures and functions. Many physicians are not so demanding of scientific proof that their recommendations are justified for a particular patient when they prescribe pills and traditional treatments as they are when it is a question of influencing that patient's lifestyle.

Second, how can we advise the descendants of the hunters and food gatherers to cope with a completely new environment, with a minimum of instructions in the genetic code? Although body structure and functions inevitably deteriorate with age, to what extent can such changes be delayed by lifestyle patterns? Another demanding issue is the fact that we must recognize that there are health problems that we must learn to live with and that no medical experts and treatments can eliminate. Which of these problems are inevitable?

Finally, from a physiological-medical point of view, we were not born equal. From a biological and physiological viewpoint, classifying individuals by chronological age is a very poor guideline for evaluating their potential to learn, mature, perform physically and mentally, or deteriorate physically and mentally. Can we find better alternatives?

References

British Museum. (1980). *Man's place in evolution*. Cambridge: Cambridge University Press.

Dickerson, R.E. (1978). Chemical evolution and the origin of life. *Scientific American*, **239**(3), 62-78.

Evolution. (1978). *Scientific American*, **239**(3).

Kandel, E.R. (1979). Small systems of neurons. *Scientific American*, **241**(3), 60-70.

Krogh, A. (1941). *The comparative physiology of respiratory mechanisms*. Philadelphia: University of Pennsylvania Press.

Lewin, R. (1980). Evolutionary theory under fire. *Science*, **210**, 883-887.

Lewin, R. (1981). Ethiopian stone tools are world's oldest. *Science*, **211**, 806-807.

Trinkaus, E., & Howells, W.W. (1979). The Neanderthals. *Scientific American*, **241**(6), 94-105.

Valentine, J.W. (1978). The evolution of multicellular plants and animals. *Scientific American*, **239**(3), 104-117.

Vidal, G. (1984). The oldest eukaryotic cells. *Scientific American*, **250**(2), 32-41.

Washburn, S.L. (1978). The evolution of man. *Scientific American*, **239**(3), 146-154.

PART I

Future Directions for Diverse Populations

SECTION A:
PERSONS OF AVERAGE HEALTH AND FITNESS

Biomechanics for Better Performance and Protection From Injury

Richard C. Nelson

Biomechanics within physical education and sport science began to emerge in the U.S. in the late 1960s. It grew out of both the traditional kinesiology courses and content and the realization that all questions dealing with human movement could not be answered by exercise physiologists. This development was highlighted by the organization of the first professional meeting in the U.S. in which the term *biomechanics* appeared in the title. This occurred in 1970 under the direction of Dr. John Cooper at the University of Indiana. At this meeting I had the privilege of presenting an introductory paper entitled "Biomechanics of Sport: An Overview" (Nelson , 1971). In this paper I described the status of sport biomechanics at that time and outlined predictions for the future. I presented a similar paper a year later in Rome at the Third International Seminar on Biomechanics (Nelson, 1973).

Now, some 15 years later, I again have the opportunity to review the present state of sport biomechanics and to speculate on its future. In a sense, this represents an examination of a 30-year period from a platform positioned at the midpoint. The first step will be to restate these early predictions, which will then be compared with the present status of sport biomechanics. Finally, an attempt will be made to look ahead with predictions and recommendations for sport biomechanics research by the year 2000.

Early Predictions

The following summary contains the main points derived from the "Future Directions" sections of the previously cited papers. It should be remembered that these predictions were made about 15 years ago.

1. The number of graduate and research programs will increase significantly.

2. An increase in the number of professional and scientific meetings at the national and international level will occur, including those devoted to specific sport specialties.
3. Application of biomechnics to the training and development of elite athletes will be greatly expanded.
4. The number of academic positions for sport biomechanists will increase dramatically.
5. International exchanges among American and foreign biomechanists will be established.
6. An International Society of Biomechanics will be founded.
7. A North American Society of Sport Biomechanics will be founded.
8. Biomechanists will conduct cooperative research with exercise physiologists and motor learning specialists.
9. An *International Journal of Sport Biomechancs* will be published.
10. Mathematical modeling and computer simulation techniques will be used extensively by sport biomechanists.
11. Sport biomechanics will become an important topic on the programs of future Olympic Scientific Congresses.
12. The term *kinesiology* will become extinct.
13. An Olympic Film Archives will be established using high speed films taken during the Summer and Winter Olympic Games.
14. Major advances will occur in electronic recording techniques and computer applications.

Present Status of Sport Biomechanics

It is evident that a number of the early predictions have in fact come true. There has been an increase in the number of biomechanics laboratories and graduate programs, but this growth has been relatively modest in the U.S. In fact, the number of highly qualified PhD graduates being produced has stayed relatively constant over the past few years.

The number of new academic positions in the U.S. has remained relatively constant at approximately 10 each year. Specialization by laboratories has occurred to the extent that graduate students may now select the program that best meets their needs and interests. Extensive international exchanges and contacts have been established among sport biomechanists from countries throughout the world. Remarkable improvements in instrumentation and recording methods have evolved in combination with exceptional advances in computer technology. The level of measurement sophistication available today is well beyond anything envisioned 15 years ago. Measurement techniques used at that time were limited to motion photography, stroboscopic methods, and very modest use of digital computers.

Other predictions that were reasonably accurate include the formation of the International Society of Biomechanics (ISB) in 1973 and the increase in the number of national and international meetings dealing with biomechanics. Beginning in 1976 at the Olympic Scientific Congress in Quebec

City, sport biomechanics has become an integral part of all subsequent Olympic Congresses. *The International Journal of Sport Biomechanics* (IJSB) was launched in 1983 with the first issues published in 1985. Increased emphasis on the application of biomechanics to the training and development of elite athletes has occurred within the U.S. Olympic Sports Medicine and Science programs as well as in selected national sport federations. An Olympic Film Archives has been established under the direction of the Medical Commission of the International Olympic Committee. High-speed films taken of track and field, weight lifting, and gymnastics during the 1984 Los Angeles Olympic Games represent the first contribution to the Archives. Films taken at future Olympic Games will be added to this collection,thereby providing a permanent record of Olympic performances. Duplicates of these films will be available to sport biomechanists from countries throughout the world.

On the basis of the preceding evaluation, it would appear that the 1970 predictions were quite accurate. However, with the exception of two or three very specific cases, most of the predicted events would be typical of any scientific discipline. Such things as increased number of programs, development of new labs, international exchanges, advances in technology, new societies, and greater job opportunities represent what could be called generic features of any emerging discipline. The formation of the ISB was easily predicted because in 1971 a committee had already been formed to found such an international organization. Regarding the publication of the IJSB, since I am the editor of this journal, its establishment could be considered a self-fulfilling prophecy.

A number of predictions were not accurate, and significant developments occurred that had not been anticipated. The term *kinesiology* was expected to disappear but in fact it has continued to be used within physical education and sport science in the U.S. This is difficult to understand in light of the fact that the few countries using the term in 1970 have since abandoned it in favor of *biomechanics*. It is surprising that in spite of the lack of acceptance of the term within physical education, biomechanics has become a household word in America. This has resulted from the media coverage of sports medicine topics and the heightened interest in the Olympic Games. The emergence of a North American Society of Sport Biomechanics, which would have paralleled similar societies in sport psychology, sport sociology, and sport history, did not occur.

The emergence of industrial research and development programs in biomechanics in recent years was not anticipated. Biomechanists have become of major importance to new product development in sports equipment industries. Well-equipped and technically staffed laboratories have been developed. In fact, the most significant improvements in lab facilities have occurred in industry. Primary funding of research programs in the leading university biomechanics laboratories has come from private companies. The possibility of generating outside research funds from the private sector was not seriously considered 15 years ago.

Another completely unanticipated role for biomechanics has been in the area of expert witness testimony in product and personal injury liability cases. This activity receives very little publicity because documents prepared and testimony given in court are generally not available. However, based on my experience and that of a few colleagues, it is evident that biomechanics is playing an increasingly more important role in the settlement of these cases. This activity will continue to expand in the future, and it would seem advisable to establish some mechanism for discussion and interaction among persons who represent biomechanics as expert witnesses in such cases.

In summary, it can be said that the predictions made in 1970 were reasonably accurate with respect to the traditional aspects of a developing science. However, a number of unforeseen developments occurred, especially in the area of technical advances, sources of funding and applications. Since biomechanics has matured as a discipline, the predictions for the future will be even more difficult. With this in mind the following attempt to look ahead to the year 2000 is presented.

Biomechanics and Human Existence

Before outlining my predictions for the next 15 years, I think it's appropriate to reflect on the present state of human existence. The physical aspects of life can be described as a continuous interaction between human beings and their environment. In fact, it is impossible to exist without some physical contact with the environment. The interactions that we experience in our daily lives range widely from lying in bed to walking, running, cutting wood, typing, playing tennis, shoveling, driving an auto, telephoning, and doing numerous other activities. In its broadest interpretation, the science of biomechanics is concerned with these interactions between the human organism and the environment. The vast majority of research to date has focused on such interactions. Two basic purposes that underlie virtually all of this work have been (a) to improve human performance (efficiency) and (b) to minimize or prevent injury. Improving performance may involve increasing productivity in an industrial setting or reducing the competitive time of an elite runner. The second purpose, to reduce injury, has been strongly emphasized in biomechanics research. Examples include the efforts to improve the working environment in industry and the attempts to upgrade the protective equipment in sports. In many cases the efforts to reduce injury coincide with the interest in maintaining or improving performance.

If the overall purpose of biomechanics research is to help people perform better and more safely, then how can this best be achieved? One approach has been to modify the environment to provide for a more accommodating interaction based on the physical capabilities of the participants. The second strategy has been to modify the physical status of the participants so they are better able to adjust to the demands of the activity. In many instances, both approaches have been used. The vast majority of the research in sport biomechanics conducted to date has concentrated on modifying the environmental components with which people come in contact and studying the kinematics and kinetics of human movement in an effort to better understand how we move and how we might move more efficiently. The examples that follow will serve to illustrate these concepts.

In 1978, the U.S. Army through its Natick Research and Development Command published a request for proposals (RFP) for biomechanical studies of load-carrying behavior. The Biomechanics Lab at Penn State was awarded an initial contract and subsequent contracts that eventually spanned 5 years of experimental work (see Nelson & Martin, 1982). The interest on the part of the Army was motivated by the need for an improved load-carrying system and also by the influx of female soldiers, who at that time totaled over 100,000. This represents a classic example of the conflict between the physical capabilities of the participants and the frame-pack system they were required to carry under a variety of physically demanding conditions. Two alternatives became apparent: (a) modify the load-carrying system and/or (b) improve the physical capabilities of the military personnel to meet the needs of the activities, even though the load-carrying system was in many cases inadequate.

The results of the numerous experiments indicated that certain combative movements were extremely difficult for most of the female subjects and that optimum frame length and load distribution were dependent upon both gender and the type of movements being performed. Unfortunately, the U.S. Army has a one-size-fits-all load-carrying sytem with a 20-in. long frame and standard-sized packs. Such a system will never be able to provide all soldiers with optimum conditions under which they will be able to perform effectively and relatively free from injury. The solution, which has not as yet been adopted by the Army, is to develop an adaptable frame-pack system that can be adjusted to fit each individual regardless of body size and to meet the specific demands of the movements being made.

The second example is drawn from a current project of mine that is being conducted in an industrial setting. The company being assisted manufactures glass screens for television sets. Until 1984 the units being handled by the workers ranged from 13 to 21 in. in width and from 15 to 23 lb. As a result of foreign competition the company shifted its production to larger screens of 25 to 27 in. and 32 to 35 lb. The factory employs about 600 assembly line workers who are divided into four groups to cover three shifts per day because the factory runs continuously. The majority of the workers have been employed for 10 years or more. As the larger units were cycled into the process, the workers began to complain to the point of turning down overtime if the work involved handling the heavier units. In addition, the number and severity of injuries to the workers began to increase steadily. In fact, the annual health costs doubled in 1 year as a result of the change in the product being manufactured.

This scenario points out the critical nature of the interaction of people with their environment. These workers have encountered problems that have led to reduced performance and increased injuries. It represents an ideal situation for the application of biomechanics research and current knowledge. A solution to the problem is being sought through changes in the workplace and improvement in the physical capacity of the workers and their assembly line movement skills. The two purposes of biomechanics, namely, to improve performance and reduce injury, are clearly observed in this example.

The final example is drawn from sports. Cross-country sking is presently undergoing a revolution caused by the advent of the new skating style officially identified as free technique. For the current season (1985-86) the International Ski Federation has ruled that World Cup events must be either free technique or classical (diagonal-stride technique), but they cannot be mixed. The new style has proven to be faster, and virtually all world-class skiers are capable of using it. Although the skating technique differs greatly from the classic style, the equipment being used by the skiers has undergone very little modification to date. The skiers have learned to perform the skating technique with considerable success despite the fact that the equipment is not ideally suited to the task. This has created a situation in which athletes perform under conditions that prevent them from reaching their highest level of performance and that subject them to greater possibility of injury. The solution to this problem will be found through biomechanics research in which the skis, boot-binding interface, and poles will be modified to meet the specific requirements of the new skating technique.

Predictions for the Year 2000

It is my opinion that biomechanics will continue to focus on the two themes previously stated, namely, improving human performance and protecting against injury. These goals will most likely be achieved through modifications in the contact elements within our daily activities and through continued study of the human body in motion. This combination of modifying the environment and improving our adaptability will form the basis of future research in human biomechanics.

Future research will also place much greater emphasis on the individual characteristics of people. This will require that physical performance components be routinely assessed so that objects used in daily activities can be designed according to size, shape, weight, and other requirements. Such an approach will provide for a much more effective interaction. It is anticipated that such things as tools, clothing, shoes, gloves, chairs, and sports equipment will be sufficiently adaptable so as to provide for optimum conditions.

Biomechanics will play an increasingly important role in the evaluation, treatment, and prevention of injuries, especially those in sports. Specialists from this field will become regular members of sports medicine clinics. The high-tech instrumentation systems presently available will prove extremely useful in the quantification of movement patterns of patients undergoing physical therapy and rehabilitation.

Industrial research and development programs using biomechanists will certainly expand in the future. It will become increasingly important that products commonly used in our daily activities and sport participation be designed on the basis of sound biomechanical principles. The motivation for this will come from groups such as the National Institute of

Occupational Safety and Health (NIOSH), the Consumer Products Safety Commission, and the ever-increasing number of personal injury and product liability cases. It is conceivable that suits will be filed against manufacturers of products on the grounds that the product did not properly fit the plaintiff.

Biomechanists will assume an increasingly important role as consultants and expert witnesses in product and personal injury liability cases. The reason for this is that biomechanics is ideally suited to assessing the conditions of accidents because an understanding of the physical capabilities of human beings can be effectively integrated with a detailed understanding of the environmental conditions in these accidents.

Investigations of the elderly should and most likely will receive greater attention from researchers in this field. There are two reasons for this: (a) the increase of this segment of our population, and (b) the changing attitudes in the country toward a more active lifestyle for these people. Again, the assessment of physical capacities with respect to the activities and environmental components will form the basis for this work. The movement characteristics of the elderly will provide the basis for modifying the objects they contact in their daily lives.

The concept of individualization mentioned earlier will lead to the development of new exercise machines. In fact, units such as the Nautilus and Universal Gyms will disappear by the year 2000 to be replaced by compact, computer-controlled units that will be able to provide the precise resistance pattern desired by the participant. Exercise prescriptions will be available for recreational athletes that will provide the exact adaptation necessary for improving or maintaining performance. The concept of *general strength training*, for example, will no longer be acceptable.

Conclusion

The science of biomechanics within physical education and sport science has developed at an extremely rapid rate over the past 15 years. The enthusiasm and excitement about biomechanics will most likely continue over the next 15 years. It will be essential, however, that emphasis be shifted toward the needs of the *average* person if biomechanics is to make a significant contribution to the enrichment of the lives of the total population of our society.

References

Nelson, R.C. (1971). Biomechanics of sport: An overview. In J.M. Cooper (Ed.), *Biomechanics* (pp. 31-37). Chicago: The Athletic Institute.

Nelson, R.C. (1973). Biomechanics of sport: Emerging discipline. In S. Cerquiglini, A. Venerando, & J. Wartenweiler (Eds.), *Biomechanics III* (pp.336-341). Basel, Switzerland: S. Karger.

Nelson, R.C., & Martin, P.E. (1982). *Phase 1: Effects of gender and load on combative movement performance.* And *Phase 2: Effects of gender, load and pack on easy standing and vertical jump performance.* (Report DAAK60-79-C-0131). Natick, MA: U.S. Army Natick Research and Development Command.

Exercise Prescription for Health and Fitness

Jack H. Wilmore

The assigned task in writing this chapter was to summarize the state of the art and project future directions in exercise and sport research for persons of average health and fitness, focusing on the area of exercise physiology. Fortunately, this assignment was limited to persons of average health and fitness, with Haskell and Costill covering the topics of exercise physiology for those of below-average and above-average health and fitness, respectively. Still, it was necessary to further limit the discussion in this chapter to stay within the allotted space, avoid redundancy with material presented in other chapters, and avoid a superficial discussion of too many topics. Finally, it was necessary to limit discussion in this chapter to an area within which I felt comfortable and had a reasonable level of expertise. In short, the focus of this chapter will be on the *prescription of exercise for health and fitness,* with apologies to my colleagues who are conducting research in those additional areas within the field of exercise physiology not discussed in this chapter.

Selection of the topic on the prescription of exercise for health and fitness seemed particularly appropriate for this section of the book dedicated to persons of average health and fitness. First, considerable interest in physical fitness has been generated by the mass media, and Americans are supposedly in the middle of a physical fitness boom. However, Kirshenbaum and Sullivan (1983) have recently questioned the existence of the fitness boom, contending that those involved are basically limited to a small segment of the total population (i.e., high income, executive level, white, college-educated, and young to middle-aged). The results of the Pacific Mutual Life Insurance Company survey (Harris, Louis, & Associates, 1978) confirm the demographics of the fitness boom as critiqued by Kirshenbaum and Sullivan. Further, four additional national surveys reported that only between 15% and 36% of the adult population participate in regular vigorous activity (General Mills, 1979; Harris, Louis, & Associates, 1979, 1983; and Miller Brewing Co., 1983). Most recently, Caspersen (1987) has estimated that only 7.5% of adult Americans meet the American College of Sports Medicine guidelines for cardiorespiratory fitness development and maintenance (ACSM, 1978).

Second, even though the percentage of those participating in vigorous physical activity is relatively low in the American adult population, there is increased awareness in the general population of the importance of regular physical activity with respect to its health-related benefits. It is now clearly established that exercise training is associated with significant reductions in blood pressure at rest and during steady-state exercise (Tipton, 1984), enhanced cardiac performance (Dowell, 1983), increased high-density lipoprotein cholesterol and decreased low-density lipoprotein cholesterol (Haskell, 1986), reduced levels of body fat and increased levels of lean tissue (Wilmore, 1983), and a reduced risk for a subsequent infarction in post-myocardial infarction patients (May, Eberlein, Furberg, Passamani, & DeMets, 1982). Further, exercise training is associated with a more positive psychological state (Dishman, 1985), reduced risk for osteoporosis (Montoye, 1984), and is recognized as an important therapeutic modality in the treatment of both diabetics (Bjorntorp & Krotkiewski, 1985) and hemodialysis patients (Harter & Goldberg, 1985).

The increased awareness of the health-related benefits of exercise training among the public coupled with the mass media's promotion of an active lifestyle places a responsibility on exercise scientists and clinicians to provide the general population with guidelines for exercise training that will minimize the potential risks and maximize the benefits associated with increasing levels of physical activity. The American College of Sports Medicine (ACSM) has been responsive to this need with its *Guidelines for Graded Exercise Testing and Exercise Prescription* (ACSM, 1975, 1980, 1986) and its position statement, *The Recommended Quantity and Quality of Exercise for Developing and Maintaining Fitness in Healthy Adults* (1978). Likewise, the American Heart Association (AHA) published *Exercise Testing and Training of Apparently Healthy Individuals: A Handbook for Physicians* (AHA, 1972). These guidelines have served a most useful purpose since they were initially published, assisting hundreds of thousands of individuals in the development of safe and sound exercise programs. As with any set of guidelines, however, there are new pieces of scientific information, new theories, and new ways to look at old data that need to be continuously analyzed, critically evaluated, and then compared with the original knowledge base used in establishing the guideline. Frequently, following such a process, guidelines need to be altered to reflect the expanding knowledge base. This chapter attempts to conduct such an analysis and critique of the present guidelines for exercise prescription, pointing to several areas where there may be a need to alter existing guidelines and suggesting areas where additional research is needed.

In the prescription of exercise for the healthy adult population, the initial step involves obtaining medical clearance. Once an individual is declared medically fit to participate in an exercise program, he or she is then provided with an individualized exercise prescription, specifying the *mode* or type of activity, the *intensity* of exercise, the *duration* of each exercise session, and the *frequency* or number of exercise sessions per week. Typically, the individual's past medical history; present medical, health, and fitness status; and activity/sport interests and proficiencies form the basis of this individualized exercise prescription. Each of the above factors will be briefly discussed.

Medical Clearance

There is little disagreement as to the advisability of having medical clearance prior to receiving an exercise prescription and initiating an exercise program. There are certain individuals who either should not be exercising at all (ACSM, 1986) or who are considered to be at high risk and should exercise only under close medical supervision. The appropriate medical clearance will identify these high-risk individuals. The basic question to be asked is, What constitutes an appropriate medical clearance?

Ideally, medical clearance would include a complete risk factor analysis for cardiovascular disease, which would consist of a thorough family history; past and present medical and physical activity history; smoking, alcohol, and substance abuse history; screening for blood pressure, blood lipids, and selected constituents of the plasma and urine; and a thorough physical examination as outlined in the ACSM guidelines (1986). Also, a resting and exercise or stress electrocardiogram (ECG) is considered to be an integral part of the overall medical clearance.

The inclusion of each of the above tests or parameters in a general medical screening for clearance into an exercise program is certainly desirable from the viewpoint of early disease detection and health promotion. However, it is important to consider how comprehensive a medical clearance must be to allow participation in an exercise program with *reasonable* assurance that the risk to the participant will be minimal. Two factors mitigate against a blanket policy for such a comprehensive examination: availability of qualified personnel and facilities to conduct such an examination and the ability of the participant to bear the costs associated with such an examination.

Implicit in the AHA (1972) and ACSM (1986) guidelines are recommendations that a physical examination including an exercise electrocardiogram be administered prior to prescribing exercise. Although a great deal of useful information can be derived from both the exam and the exercise test, are they really justified recommendations (i.e., will the ultimate yield of truly abnormal test results justify the associated costs)? Whereas a screening-type physical examination will cost the individual between $50 and $100 with his or her own personal physician, the exercise test will generally cost between $150 and $350 depending on the price structure within the community and the extent of the test (e.g., single lead vs. 12-lead, 12-lead with oxygen uptake measurements, etc.). If a mass test is conducted, it is possible to reduce these costs by approximately 50%, and in some cases less.

It is presumed that the exercise test is recommended by the AHA and the ACSM for the primary purpose of disease detection. It is now widely recognized that the sensitivity, specificity, and predictive accuracy of exercise testing for the detection of coronary artery disease (CAD) is relatively low in an asymptomatic population (Uhl & Froelicher, 1983). *Sensitivity* is defined as the percentage of individuals with identifiable CAD who demonstrate an abnormal exercise test (i.e., accuracy of correctly identifying those with CAD by the results of the exercise test). *Specificity* refers to the percentage of individuals without disease who demonstrate a normal exercise test (i.e., accuracy of correctly identifying those without CAD by the results of the exercise test). *Predictive accuracy* refers to the percentage of abnormal or positive tests that are truly positive (i.e., CAD is present). These relationships can be expressed mathematically as follows:

$$\text{Sensitivity} = [TP/(TP + FN)] \times 100$$
$$\text{Specificity} = [TN/(TN + FP)] \times 100$$
$$\text{Predictive accuracy} = [TP/(TP + FP)] \times 100$$

where TP = true positive (CAD + abnormal test), FN = false negative (CAD + normal test), TN = true negative (no CAD + normal test), FP = false positive (no CAD + abnormal test), and a test is considered positive on the basis of changes in the S-T segment on the electrocardiogram. According to Uhl and Froelicher (1983), the exercise electrocardiogram

Table 1 Comparison of Predictive Accuracy of Exercise Testing Between Populations With 5% and 50% CAD Prevalence

Population subgroups	N (%) of subjects	N (%) abnormal exercise ECG	N (%) normal exercise ECG
5% Prevalence			
Normal	950 (95)	95 (10% FP)	855 (90% TN)
CAD	50 (5)	25 (50% TP)	25 (50% FN)
Total	1,000 (100)	120 (12%)	880 (88%)
Predictive accuracy = [25/(25 + 95)] = 20.8%			
50% Prevalence			
Normal	500 (50)	50 (10% FP)	450 (90% TN)
CAD	500 (50)	250 (50% TP)	250 (50% FN)
Total	1,000 (100)	300 (30%)	700 (70%)
Predictive accuracy = [250/(250 + 50)] = 83.3%			

has a sensitivity of approximately 50% and a specificity of approximately 90%, and the predictive accuracy varies according to the prevalence of disease in the population. This latter point is illustrated in Table 1, where a 50% sensitivity and a 90% specificity are assumed, and a CAD prevalence of 5% is compared to one of 50% for a population of 1,000.

The table illustrates Bayes' theorem, that is, the predictive accuracy of a test depends not only on its sensitivity and specificity, but also on the prevalence of the disease in the population tested (i.e., the pretest likelihood that disease is present, Laslett & Amsterdam, 1984). In short, for asymptomatic, middle-aged adults the predictive accuracy of the test is likely to be low. Unfortunately, this is not new information. Redwood, Borer, and Epstein (1976) presented similar information and argued that the exercise test is of limited diagnostic value in symptomatic patients because the diagnosis is virtually established by their symptoms alone. Further, they go on to state that "most importantly, the test is of very limited diagnostic value when applied to asymptomatic subjects because of the large percentage of false positive results that occurs in this population" (p. 706).

Laslett and Amsterdam (1984), in summarizing their review of this area, state, "because of the inefficiencies of testing for coronary disease in people at low risk for having this disease, those who are asymptomatic, relatively young, and without coronary risk factors probably should not undergo stress ECG testing unless public safety demands it" (p. 1746). Uhl and Froelicher (1983) suggest a three-step approach to screening for asymptomatic coronary heart disease in men over 35 years of age. The first step would be to obtain a history of angina; a CAD risk factor analysis, including HDL-cholesterol; and a resting electrocardiogram. If the subject is considered at risk on the basis of this first step, then a maximal exercise test is recommended. They conclude by stating that good clinical judgment must be exercised to avoid the iatrogenic complication of producing "cardiac cripples" by mislabeling healthy people.

Finally, Malinow, McGarry, and Kuehl (1984) conducted a 10-year retrospective survey of YMCAs in the United States, observing rates of 1 event/3 million and 1 event/2 million person-hours for sudden death and cardiac arrests, respectively. They concluded that, based on the uncertainties associated with positive and negative results from graded exercise tests in populations with a low prevalence of disease, it would be impractical to use graded exercise testing to prevent significant cardiovascular complications during exercise in asymptomatic individuals.

What do these results and interpretations mean with respect to the future? First, it is important to point out that an exercise test provides considerable information of importance to the prescription of exercise above and beyond changes in the S-T segment of the electrocardiogram (e.g., arrythmia detection, maximal working capacity, and ratings of perceived exertion). However, only a small percentage of the total population would be able to afford such testing. A "recommendation" within a set of guidelines established by the AHA and the ACSM is tantamount to a "standard of practice" within the medical community, a fact that could have significant medical-legal consequences. More definitive guidelines need to be established by both the AHA and ACSM based on the information now available, recognizing the limitations of exercise testing for disease detection. Although this may require additional research of either a prospective or retrospective nature, it seems clear that clarification of existing guidelines can be undertaken immediately on the basis of the present knowledge base.

Components of the Exercise Prescription

Of the four major components comprising the exercise prescription, the most recent guidelines (ACSM, 1986) and position statement (ACSM, 1978) continue to reflect accurately the present state of the art, with several exceptions. Each of these will be briefly discussed.

According to the ACSM (1978), the intensity of training should be between 60% and 90% of maximal heart rate, or between 50% and 85% of maximal oxygen uptake. This guideline was established specifically for the purpose of developing and maintaining cardiorespiratory fitness. Gaesser and Rich (1984) have recently demonstrated a 17.2% increase in maximal oxygen uptake following 12 weeks of low-intensity training (e.g., 45% of the subject's maximal oxygen uptake). Thus training at even lower levels may, in fact, result in increased cardiorespiratory capacity.

Possibly of even greater significance, LaPorte et al. (1984) have challenged the importance of cardiorespiratory fitness relative to its role in reducing the risk for CAD. They make the astute observation that "high active groups" in epidemiological studies of physical activity and coronary heart disease generally do not achieve a sufficient intensity level of activity to produce a cardiovascular training effect. The important distinction is made between people who are active and those who are fit, indicating that activity, rather than fitness may be the more important factor with respect to health and disease prevention. In a related article (LaPorte, Dearwater, Cauley, Slemenda, & Cook, 1985) they conclude that cardiovascular fitness may not be the mediating link between activity and health. Further, they are critical of the fact that the U.S. population has been told that an activity program must be designed for aerobic conditioning to reap the health benefits. They contend that the epidemiological research does not support this conclusion, and that increased activity without increased cardiorespiratory fitness is clearly beneficial and perhaps more applicable for groups who could benefit the most from physical activity. Although this logic runs counter to current guidelines and thinking, it raises a most important and critical issue to be addressed in future research.

Clearly, the existing guidelines (ACSM, 1986) and position statement (ACSM, 1978) do not adequately address the issue of exercise prescription for maintaining fitness levels once the training program has elicited the desired change in cardiorespiratory fitness. Once optimal fitness levels have been achieved, is it necessary to continue the original conditioning program, or is it possible to alter the program by switching to different activities (e.g., individual, dual, or team sports vs. jogging or swimming) or reducing the intensity, duration, and frequency of activity? The most recent study by Hickson, Foster, Pollock, Galassi, and Rich (1985) would suggest that frequency can be reduced by two-thirds and intensity by one-third without affecting maximal oxygen uptake. They found, however, that intensity, when reduced by even one-third of the original training intensity, resulted in major decrements in maximal oxygen uptake over the course of 15 weeks. This area of maintenance exercise programs needs to be researched in considerably more depth before appropriate guidelines can be provided to the general population.

One last area that needs to be better researched concerns the means by which exercise intensity is monitored. The ACSM guidelines (1986) suggest that intensity be monitored either by the use of a training heart rate, or by assigning activities on the basis of the appropriate metabolic equivalent (MET), where 1.0 MET is equivalent to the resting metabolic rate. As an example, a 4.0-MET activity (e.g., table tennis) would be equivalent to four times the resting metabolic rate. Although the MET method for monitoring exercise intensity provides a useful guide for activity selection, it is not sensitive to changes in environment (e.g., heat and altitude) or to changes in the level of fitness. What might be a comfortable activity at sea level on a cool day may be impossible to perform at altitude or on a hot day. Further, as one becomes better conditioned, the same activity does not provide the same relative stress.

The use of an individually prescribed training heart rate or heart rate range for monitoring exercise intensity avoids the problems associated with the METs technique. Quite simply, with increasing altitude or temperature, the individual does less work to achieve the same heart rate response. As he or she becomes better conditioned, it will require more work to achieve the same heart rate; thus there is little need to alter the intensity prescription as the individual experiences improvements in cardiorespiratory fitness.

Most recently, researchers have attempted to use ratings of perceived exertion (RPE) to monitor exercise intensity. Chow and Wilmore (1984) found that subjects, when allowed to control their own speed on a treadmill, were able to maintain an exercise intensity within their exercise training heart rate range simply by using RPE. The subjects were unaware of their exercise heart rate, but had been given two practice periods where they were instructed in the use of the RPE technique. They were able to maintain an intensity that was nearly identical to a group that adjusted their treadmill speed on the basis of palpated pulse rate. The training heart rate range technique for monitoring exercise intensity has served well over the years, but it would be a distinct advantage to use perceptions of effort if further research supports its viability as an intensity monitoring technique.

Conclusion

It has been the purpose of this chapter to focus on one area within the total field of exercise physiology—the prescription of exercise for health and fitness. The intent was to summarize the state of the field and then to project future directions for research within this area. We are now living in an age where society places a high premium on health and physical fitness, yet the fitness boom is apparently affecting only a relatively small percentage of our total population. Dishman, Sallis, and Orenstein (1985) have concluded that only 15% of our adult population are believed to expend an energy equivalent (1,500 kcal per week) of known epidemiologic significance, and of those regularly engaged in either group or individual exercise, about 50% will discontinue activity at some time in the coming year.

As a profession, we are clearly missing the mark. Our future focus on research must identify ways to involve much larger segments of our population in regular physical activity, and to better understand those factors that affect compliance to a lifestyle of regular physical activity. Possibly, we have taken the fun out of physical activity in an attempt to become scientific in our approach to exercise prescription. The requirement of medical examinations and maximal exercise tests prior to allowing participation in exercise programs is portraying a rather negative image of physical activity. For some, the compulsive pulse rate monitoring, which has been the hallmark of exercise prescription for years, only adds to this negative image (i.e., exercise must be dangerous). In addition, previous practices of physical educators and coaches have also given a negative image to physical activity, where exercise was used as a form of punishment or discipline. It is not difficult to see that much of our effort in the future needs to be directed toward building a new image—one that portrays physical activity as fun and enjoyable!

References

American College of Sports Medicine. (1975). *Guidelines for graded exercise testing and exercise prescription*. Philadelphia: Lea & Febiger.

American College of Sports Medicine. (1978). The recommended quantity and quality of exercise for developing and maintaining fitness in healthy adults. *Medicine and Science in Sports*, **10**, vii-x.

American College of Sports Medicine. (1980). *Guidelines for graded exercise testing and exercise prescription* (2nd ed.). Philadelphia: Lea & Febiger.

American College of Sports Medicine. (1986). *Guidelines for exercise testing and prescription* (3rd ed.). Philadelphia: Lea & Febiger.

American Heart Association. (1972). *Exercise testing and training of apparently healthy individuals: A handbook for physicians*. New York: American Heart Association.

Bjorntorp, P., & Krotkiewski, M. (1985). Exercise treatment in diabetes mellitus. *Acta Medica Scandinavica*, **217**, 3-7.

Caspersen, C.J. (1987). Physical activity and coronary heart disease. *The Physician and Sportsmedicine*, **15**(11), 43-44.

Chow, R.J., & Wilmore, J.H. (1984). The regulation of exercise intensity by ratings of perceived exertion. *Journal of Cardiac Rehabilitation*, **4**, 382-387.

Dishman, R.K. (1985). Medical psychology in exercise and sport. *Medical Clinics of North America*, **69**, 123-143.

Dishman, R.K., Sallis, J.F., & Orenstein, D.R. (1985). The determinants of physical activity and exercise. *Public Health Reports*, **100**, 158-171.

Dowell, R.T. (1983). Cardiac adaptations to exercise. *Exercise and Sport Sciences Reviews*, **12**, 99-117.

Gaesser, G.A., & Rich, R.G. (1984). Effects of high and low-intensity exercise training on aerobic capacity and blood lipids. *Medicine and Science in Sports and Exercise*, **16**, 269-274.

General Mills, Inc. (1979). *Family health in an era of stress*. Minneapolis, MN: Author.

Harris, Louis, & Associates, Inc. (1978). *Health maintenance*. Newport Beach, CA: Pacific Mutual Life Insurance Co.

Harris, Louis, & Associates, Inc. (1979). *The Perrier study: Fitness in America*. New York: Perrier-Great Waters of France, Inc.

Harris, Louis, & Associates, Inc. (1983, October-November). Prevention in America: Steps people take—or fail to take—for better health. *Prevention Magazine*.

Harter, H.R., & Goldberg, A.P. (1985). Endurance exercise training: An effective therapeutic modality for hemodialysis patients. *Medical Clinics of North America*, **69**, 159-175.

Haskell, W.L. (1986). The influence of exercise training on plasma lipids and lipoproteins in health and disease. *Acta Medica Scandinavica*, **711**(Suppl.), 25-37.

Hickson, R.C., Foster, C., Pollock, M.L., Galassi, T.M., & Rich, S. (1985). Reduced training intensities and loss of aerobic power, endurance, and cardiac growth. *Journal of Applied Physiology*, **58**, 492-499.

Kirshenbaum, J., & Sullivan, R. (1983). Hold on there America. *Sports Illustrated*, **58**(5), 60-74.

LaPorte, R.E., Adams, L.L., Savage, D.D., Brenes, G., Dearwater, S., & Cook, T. (1984). The spectrum of physical activity, cardiovascular disease and health: An epidemiologic perspective. *American Journal of Epidemiology*, **120**, 507-517.

LaPorte, R.E., Dearwater, S., Cauley, J.A., Slemenda, C., & Cook, T. (1985). Cardiovascular fitness: Is it really necessary? *The Physician and Sportsmedicine*, **13**(3), 145-150.

Laslett, L.J., & Amsterdam, E.A. (1984). Management of the asymptomatic patient with an abnormal exercise ECG. *Journal of the American Medical Association*, **252**, 1744-1746.

Malinow, M.R., McGarry, D.L., & Kuehl, K.S. (1984). Is exercise testing indicated for asymptomatic active people? *Journal of Cardiac Rehabilitation*, **4**, 376-380.

May, G.S., Eberlein, K.A., Furberg, C.D., Passamani, E.R., & DeMets, D.L. (1982). Secondary prevention after myocardial infarction: A review of long-term trials. *Progress in Cardiovascular Diseases*, **24**, 331-352.

Miller Brewing Co. (1983). *The Miller Lite report on American attitudes towards sports*. Milwaukee, WI: Author.

Montoye, H.J. (1984). Exercise and osteoporosis. In H.M. Eckert & H.J. Montoye (Eds.), *Exercise and health* (pp. 59-75). Champaign, IL: Human Kinetics.

Redwood, D.R., Borer, J.S., & Epstein, S.E. (1976). Whither the ST segment during exercise? *Circulation*, **54**, 703-706.

Tipton, C.M. (1984). Exercise, training, and hypertension. *Exercise and Sport Sciences Reviews*, **12**, 245-306.

Uhl, G.S., & Froelicher, V. (1983). Screening for asymptomatic coronary artery disease. *Journal of the American College of Cardiology*, **1**, 946-955.

Wilmore, J.H. (1983). Body composition in sport and exercise: Directions for future research. *Medicine and Science in Sports and Exercise*, **15**, 21-31.

Scientific Issues and Research Trends in Sport Psychology

Ronald E. Smith

The past decade has been a highly significant one for scientific progress in the burgeoning area of sport psychology. Sport psychology has broadened its scope considerably as an interdisciplinary science. An increasing level of theoretical and methodological sophistication is evident in the sport psychology literature, and research reports are now beginning to appear with some regularity in established psychological journals (e.g., Allison & Ayllon, 1980; Horn, 1985; Kirschenbaum, Ordman, Tomarken, & Holtzbauer, 1982). The American Psychological Association (APA) has established a division of Exercise and Sport Psychology (Division 47), and the "Call for Papers" for a recent APA convention contained a request for submission of proposals for continuing education workshops in the area of sport psychology. The discipline seems ready to be embraced within mainstream psychology.

Kinesiologists have always appreciated the importance of psychological factors in sport performance. Now, an increasing number of psychologists are viewing sport as an unusually rich naturalistic laboratory for the study of psychological phenomena, the development and testing of scientific theories, and the application of psychological principles (cf. Goldstein, 1979; Martin & Hrycaiko, 1983; Smith, Sarason, & Sarason, 1986). The sport environment offers the researcher a microcosm of many other life situations, an opportunity to study involved and motivated subjects in a circumscribed environment, and the availability of behavioral measures having unquestioned ecological validity.

Although significant advances are occurring in studies of elite athletes, the bulk of contemporary sport psychology research is being performed on subject populations whose fitness and ability levels fall within the average range. These populations include youth sport participants and coaches, adults involved in recreational programs, and the ubiquitous college undergraduate. Because virtually every area of scientific psychology (e.g., learning, cognitive, physiological, social, developmental, clinical, quantitative) can relate in one way or another to important sport phenomena, sport psychology research is advancing on a wide variety of fronts, and no attempt will be made in this discussion to cover all of them. Instead, I shall focus on a few selected areas and attempt to delineate what I consider to be important current trends, unresolved empirical questions, and promising areas for future research.

Measurement Trends and Issues

Measurement is the *sine qua non* of any research enterprise. Without reliable and valid operational definitions and measures of the constructs that interest sport psychologists, we have nothing. Moreover, research directions in sport psychology, as in other areas, are dictated in part by the availability of good measures. For example, the development of sport-specific measures of anxiety by Martens and his co-workers (Martens, 1977; Martens, Burton, Vealey, Smith, & Bump, 1983) has helped stimulate a surge of research on the antecedents and consequences of competition anxiety.

Four major classes of variables are of interest to sport researchers: situational factors, cognitive processes, physiological responses, and overt behaviors. There have been triumphs as well as disappointments in the development and application of self-report, physiological, and behavioral measures. On the physiological front, one truly noteworthy advance has been made by Landers and his associates in studying psychophysiological correlates of performance in elite athletes, such as rifle shooters and archers (Hatfield & Landers, 1983; Hatfield, Landers, & Ray, 1987). Both cardiovascular and EEG measures have been found to be related to performance, and these findings have inspired the use of biofeedback techniques in an attempt to train athletes to regulate their behavior.

One of the psychometric disappointments of recent years in the cognitive processes domain is Nideffer's (1976) Test of Attentional and Interpersonal Style (TAIS). There are few psychological processes as important to athletic performance as attention, and Nideffer has advanced an intuitively appealing model of attentional processes. The model posits two orthogonal dimensions of breadth (wide-narrow) and direction (internal-external) of attention. The model not only is consistent with basic dimensions of attention identified in laboratory research, but also seems to incorporate the kinds of task demands that are required of athletes in a wide variety of sport situations. The TAIS was developed to measure individual differences and deficits in attentional style, its items being written on an intuitive basis. Although used with varying degrees of success by a number of sport researchers (e.g., Vallerand, 1983; VanSchoyck & Grasha, 1981), only recently has the basic factor structure of the TAIS been examined by means of factor analysis of its 52 attentional items. Robl (1983) found no support for the dimensional structure specified by the attentional model. Instead, she found a factor that she called "ineffective," consisting of 8 items, and a second factor, comprised of 3 items, that she called "effective." Two other factors, each comprising 2 items, appeared, but they were uninterpretable. Together, the 4 factors accounted for only 33% of the variance on the test. Attempts to write new items to fit the dimensional structure specified by Nideffer were also unsuccessful. These results raise something of a dilemma. Is the model, which seems so tenable on an intuitive level, wrong, or have we simply not found a way to measure the variables of interest? Because of the clear theoretical and practical import of this question, more research in this area is clearly needed. Although the TAIS may have considerable practical utility in identifying athletes who report attentional difficulties, its construct validity as a measure of the basic model's dimensions is in serious question.

Behavioral and cognitive-behavioral theories have influenced sport psychology in numerous ways during the past decade, and they have now emerged as an important wave of the future as well. From a measurement perspective, the use of behavioral assessment approaches in sport has been a significant advance. In a sense, sport psychologists have always relied on behavioral measures when they assessed performance; indeed, it is the ready availability of these measures that has attracted many psychologists to sport research. More recently, however, behavioral assessment methodology has been applied to the measurement of other classes of behavior as well. This has made it possible to study both situational factors, such as the behavior of coaches and parents, and outcome behaviors, such as social responses (Horn, 1985; Rushall, 1977, 1981; Smith, Zane, Smoll, & Coppel, 1983). When used as a way of defining situational variables (e.g., the level of social support provided by a coach or teammates), behavioral codings may be used in conjunction with self-report measures of the same variable, because responses to situations are a function of not only the objective characteristics of the situation, but also, and more proximally, the subject's perception of the situation. Thus it has been shown that behavioral measures of coaching behaviors together with player ratings of the frequencies with which those behaviors occur account for more variance in players' attitudes toward the coach than does either class of predictor variable considered alone (Smoll, Smith, Curtis, & Hunt, 1978). In this illustrative area of research on coaching behaviors, future research might profitably combine behavioral assessment with self-report instruments, such as Chelladurai and Saleh's (1980) Leadership Scale for Sports. One of the advantages enjoyed by the sport researcher is that the behaviors of interest frequently occur in a public setting where they can be coded. This is not always the case in other research areas, such as marital interactions.

This is not to say that behavioral measures are the be-all and end-all of assessment. Behavioral measures are subject to the same standards of reliability, content validity, and construct validity as self-report measures. In instances where the variable of interest is a subjective one such as satisfaction or attributions, self-report measures are clearly more appropriate than some sort of indirect behavioral measure that requires an inferential leap on the part of the researcher. However, because behaviors that can be observed and coded in the sport environment are often those in which we are directly interested, we are likely to see increasing application of behavioral assessment in sport psychology research.

Trends in Research on Children's Sports

Youth sports have long been an important part of our culture, and all indications are that the scope of organized athletics for children is continuing to expand. Sport participation is thought to be an important psychosocial experience for children by both proponents and critics of youth sport programs. The physical and psychosocial effects of participation will continue to be the focus of many researchers, whereas others will be interested in sports because they are a setting in which important developmental processes can be studied.

An answer to the basic question of how sport participation affects the psychosocial development of children continues to elude us. There are two important and related reasons. One is that we have not used the kind of research designs needed to answer the question. The other is that the question is the wrong one, because it implies that the effects of participation are uniform for children. Let us consider these points in turn.

More than a decade ago, Stevenson (1975) critically reviewed the existing body of literature on the psychosocial effects of sports participation on children. He correctly concluded that, despite numerous studies in the area, few firm conclusions involving causality could be drawn. For one thing, virtually all of the research has been cross-sectional in nature, with athletes being compared with non-athletes. When differences are found in such studies, one cannot ascertain whether the differences are the result or the cause of participation. There is a small scattering of short-term longitudinal studies in the literature (e.g., Schendel, 1968), but they are characterized by small sample sizes or a relatively brief time period. Thus we know little about developmental changes that occur as a result of sport participation.

The second problem is that the basic question must be expanded to ask, What kinds of children exposed to what kinds of athletic experiences in the presence of what kinds of significant adults show what kinds of effects? This question leads us to look for interactions among the personal characteristics of the children, the conditions under which they live, the kinds of sport experiences that they have (and the sequence in which they have them), and the many types of measurable outcomes that can occur.

Is it feasible or even possible to answer such a question? It is surely difficult, but if we are to try, we must adopt a different approach than the isolated one-shot study. What is needed is a nationally funded long-term longitudinal study involving the collaboration of several research centers. The starting point for the collection of data must be before the children are old enough to begin participating in sport, and the data must include characteristics of not only the children, but also the parents and other aspects of the child's life. A large number of outcome variables must be measured repeatedly at intervals of no longer than a year. Given a sufficiently large sample size, it would be possible at any given time to match sport participants with nonparticipants on potentially important characteristics and compare them on outcome measures. A study of this kind would have to extend from the early elementary years until late adolescence or early adulthood. Because social and cultural conditions would likely change during this extended period of time, and because subjects and significant others would have to be assessed repeatedly, a sequential longitudinal design (Schaie, 1965) would be the most appropriate approach to control for generational effects. The sequential design includes (a) a longitudinal study measuring the same people at different ages, (b) a cross-sectional study testing different age groups at the same time (does not control for the generational effect or other differences between groups), (c) a time-lag study repeating the cross-sectional study in different years (to control for the generational effect by comparing groups tested in different years), and (d) a control group to control for the effects of repeated testing. Although a study of this type would be extremely expensive and time consuming, the extraordinary amount of data it would generate would help provide answers to a myriad of developmental questions, and would allow the tracking of many different subgroups of children through their socialization process.

The great expense entailed in carrying out a truly meaningful longitudinal study brings up an important practical issue. Very few sport psychology projects have been supported by federal funding agencies, and the current climate does not favor the funding of psychosocial research (as we discovered when the branch of the National Institute of Mental Health that had funded our research on coaching behaviors was eliminated during a reorganization!). Nevertheless, we must continue to pursue federal funding aggressively if we are to carry out large-scale research projects in the area of sport psychology. We should be able to argue successfully for the relevance and advantages of the sport setting for studying theoretically meaningful research questions.

Beyond the broad question of how sports affect children is one of practical significance: How can we make sports a better environment for the learning of skills and for psychosocial development? In the recent past, several important lines of intervention have appeared that are relevant to this question.

At the technical skills level, the most important advance in recent years is the introduction of behavioral coaching, which involves the systematic application of behavioral principles to the teaching of skills (Allison & Ayllon, 1980; Martin & Hrycaiko, 1983; Rushall & Smith, 1979; Siedentop, 1976). Coaches are taught to systematically employ principles of behavior modification derived from operant conditioning to identify target behaviors and to increase or decrease them. Behavioral assessment is used to evaluate systematically the changes in target behaviors that occur. Specific procedures are prescribed both for developing new behaviors and for maintaining (or motivating) existing behaviors. Athletes are encouraged to self-monitor their own behavior and to work with the coach to establish specific goals. In a sense, the art of coaching becomes the science of coaching, as behavior change principles that have been validated in many other settings are systematically applied to the learning of athletic skills.

Behavioral coaching has been applied to a variety of sport settings and athletic populations with highly impressive results (Martin & Hrycaiko, 1983). In contrast to the robotic images of behavior modification subjects fostered by the early use of applied behavior analysis, its present application relies on shared goals established by athlete and coach, as well as mutual evaluation of methods used and results obtained.

To the present time, the major emphasis in behavioral coaching has been on the effectiveness of various techniques. Sport psychologists who are interested in developmental variables and individual difference variables would find this area to be a fertile one in which to relate such variables to the effectiveness of various techniques of behavioral coaching. In my judgment, because of the nomothetic assumptions of operant psychologists, the area of applied behavior analysis has always suffered from a lack of interest in the study of individual difference and cognitive variables that might interact with treatment effectiveness. Later, I shall provide several examples of the importance of individual difference variables in moderating the effects of intervention programs.

A second and related emphasis in youth sports is the development and evaluation of programs designed to help coaches create a more positive learning and social environment. Here, the emphasis is primarily on fostering positive attitudes toward the athletic experience rather than on increasing skill acquisition (although many of the principles are consistent with behavioral coaching and would be expected to enhance skill acquisition as well).

As in the case of behavioral coaching, intervention programs in this area should be based on firm scientific foundations. This is relevant to the relationship that is often cited between basic research and applied research. A program developed by our research team at the University of Washington illustrates this approach to program development and evaluation. In the first phase of the project, a behavioral assessment system was developed to observe and code coaching behaviors during practices and games (Smith, Smoll, & Curtis, 1978). In subsequent study of Little League Baseball coaches, 51 coaches were observed during several hundred games, and behavioral profiles were compiled based on more than 57,000 total behaviors. After the season, the coaches' players were intereviewed in their homes to obtain measures of liking for the coach, the sport, their teammates, and their experience in general. These outcome measures were related to coaching behaviors, and the obtained relationships were used as the foundation for a set of behavioral guidelines in an experimental training program administered to an experimental group of coaches the following year. The training program involved four elements: description of the previous year's findings and verbal presentation of the guidelines; modeling of several of the guidelines; feedback in the form of behavioral profiles for each coach and the setting of behavioral objectives; and instruction in self-monitoring of key behaviors in the guidelines.

During the season, the experimental group coaches and a control group that had received no instruction were observed and their behaviors coded. At the end of the season, the children who played for the two groups of coaches were again interviewed. The results of this assessment indicated that the children who played for the trained coaches liked the coach and their teammates more and that they showed a significant increase in self-esteem over the course of the season. Those who played for the untrained coaches showed no change in self-esteem (Smith, Smoll, & Curtis, 1979).

In recent years, several other coach training programs have been developed at Michigan State University and the University of Illinois. Research on the effects of these programs should provide additional information on how coaches can most effectively be prepared to enhance the athletic experiences of children. It is important, however, that researchers move beyond global outcome studies to identify the effective ingredients of the interventions. In psychotherapy research, these are called dismantling studies. For example, our training program involved four separate components. At this point, we do not know which of those components or combination of components produced the positive effects. We are now planning a follow-up study in which groups of coaches receive didactic instruction on the guidelines plus different combinations of the other three components. This kind of research should allow us to develop a more potent (and, perhaps, more economical) program by accentuating the components that are most important. We hope that other investigators will be doing similar studies, as well as projects examining the effects of possible moderator variables such as the nature of the sport, the level of experience of the coach, and coach personality variables.

Parents of young athletes are another potential target group for basic research and intervention programs. There is no reason why parallel programs for coaches and parents cannot and should not be developed. In the case of parents, the effects of guidelines that are designed to increase social support for the child, to increase positive motivation while decreasing anxiety or fear of failure, and to communicate healthy viewpoints on dealing with success and failure might be expected to generalize to other areas of the parent-child relationship. An assessment of such effects should be built into the evaluation of the program.

There are many other important frontiers of youth sport research, such as stress, social cognition, moral development, and aggression. These cannot be discussed here, but they will surely continue to be foci of sport psychology research. An encouraging development in these areas is an increasing tendency toward model testing using confirmatory factor analytic techniques such as LISREL (Joreskog & Sorbum, 1981). Interestingly, when models derived from other behavioral domains are applied to that of sport, the fits are less than perfect. For example, Weiss, Bredemeier, and Shewchuk (1985) found that sport motivation data derived from a revision of Harter's (1981) competence motivation measure did not fit the model derived by Harter in other settings. Findings like these support the arguments of those who have urged the development of our own sport-specific theoretical models rather than the extrapolation of theories derived from other behavioral domains to sport (e.g., Landers, 1983; Martens, 1979).

Psychological Skills: From Sport to Life

One of the truly burgeoning areas of activity in sport psychology involves the development and implementation of psychological skills training programs. These programs are designed to teach specific skills, such as concentration, arousal control, imaginal rehearsal, and goal setting, that are assumed to facilitate athletic performance. The widespread interest in such programs is reflected in a proliferation of how-to books (e.g., Gauron, 1984; Harris & Harris, 1984; Orlick, 1980); an increasing volume of experimental research on the effects of some of these approaches (e.g., Kirschenbaum, 1984; Seabourne, Weinberg, Jackson, & Suinn, 1985; Ziegler, Klinzing, & Williamson, 1982); and even the emergence of a new professional and scientific organization, the Association for the Advancement of Applied Sport Psychology. Although this enthusiasm for applied sport psychology has elicited justifiable concerns about ethical, competency, and training issues (e.g., Danish & Hale, 1981; Heyman, 1984; Nideffer, 1981), it also can (and, I believe, will) provide the impetus for significant theoretical and empirical advances in the field. As I indicated earlier, sport offers an ideal setting in which to study and apply psychological principles, and the intimate relationships that can be forged between basic and applied research are fully evident in this domain of behavior.

Much of the current interest in psychological skills training has arisen from attempts to enhance the athletic performance of elite competitors (e.g., Suinn, 1976). The United States Olympic Committee (1983) has established a board of prominent sport psychologists to help coordinate the delivery of psychological services to athletes and coaches. An increasing number of professional sport teams and collegiate athletic programs are receiving sport psychology consultation. I would not be surprised if, a decade from now, sport psychologist consultants were as much a part of elite athletic programs as strength coaches are now.

But what of the non-elite sport participant, the adult or child who participates on a recreational level? I would argue that psychological skills training is just as potentially valuable for the casual participant as for the elite athlete. This assertion is reinforced by my experiences in offering a course called "Psychological Skills in Athletics" at the University of Washington. The course is organized around the familiar athletic concept of *mental toughness*, which is conceptualized as a constellation of abilities that facilitate peak performance and consistency of performance. Included are arousal control skills, attention control procedures, ability to direct cognitive processes to the task at hand, goal-getting procedures, mental programming and rehearsal of skills, and so on. A requirement of the course is that students keep a journal of their activities relevant to the course and turn in an entry each week.

All of the 40 students in the course are involved in athletics of one form or another, and about a third of them are varsity athletes. Most of them have shown a good deal of commitment in reading the theoretical and research literature underlying the techniques and doing the homework assignments designed to help them learn and apply the skills. The most striking aspect of their journals, however, is the wide range of life situations in which they report successfully applying their developing skills. It is clear that the skills we teach athletes have application far beyond the sport setting; they are *life skills*, not simply athletic skills. The athletic setting is an unusually fine one in which to learn stress management, concentration, goal setting, and other skills for the same reasons that it is a good setting in which to do research: Subjects are highly motivated and involved, the target behaviors are easier to define, and progress (or lack thereof) is easier to evaluate than in many other settings.

So as not to belabor this point, let me cite just one additional example of the potential value of psychological skills training, this time for children. Proponents of youth sports frequently maintain that it is a setting in which children can learn to deal with stress. To the extent that this naturally occurs (and we ought to be doing more research to see how often and under which conditions it does), the child may learn skills that help him or her to deal more effectively with other life stressors. But why should we leave this to chance? The application of stress management training programs to preadolescent children with appropriate generalization training could provide them with a valuable set of psychological skills that can be applied later in life. We are in the beginning stages of a project in which we will apply our cognitive-affective stress management program (Smith, 1980) to child athletes and study the effects not only within sports but in other settings as well, from childhood into adolescence. Other psychological skills programs adapted for children could be studied in similar fashion.

At a 1978 sport psychology conference, John Salmela (1979) made a presentation entitled "Psychology and Sport: Fear of Applying." The theme of his talk should be quite obvious. I think it is safe to conclude that whatever trepidation might have existed a decade ago has been largely extinguished. Many sport psychologists have become more oriented toward intervention, and there are certainly enough intervention procedures to go around. For this reason, many of the same ethical and professional issues that exist in my parent discipline of clinical psychology are bubbling just beneath the surface. Some years ago, Paul Meehl, a leader in clinical psychology, was asked what he considered to be the most urgent issue confronting his field. He replied that it was the fact that the professional activities of many clinicians had become divorced from the research literature. On a day-to-day basis, they were using assessment and intervention techniques of unproven validity (and, in some cases, proven invalidity). We must be very certain that, in the years to follow, research and theory development in sport psychology keeps pace with application. Application can be the crucible in which we test models and develop ever more effective interventions. We need to pose more complicated questions about effectiveness than, "Does it work?" A more suitable question is, "For whom and under what conditions does it work?" This kind of question is much harder to answer, but the epistemic yield is much greater when we try.

I believe that a number of important issues will be the focus of research and theory development in the coming years. The cognitive-behavioral approach has already had a major influence on the development of intervention programs in sport psychology, and this influence will continue to be felt. I also believe, however, that mainstream cognitive psychology, which is concerned with many of the mental processes that are the targets of sport psychology intervention programs, will influence our thinking to a greater degree. For example, many of our intervention procedures involve the use of imagery, particularly visual imagery, and there is substantial evidence that imagery can be an effective performance enhancement technique under certain conditions (Feltz & Landers, 1983). Yet, our thinking about the role of imagery seems to be based on a mental photograph model that is being supplanted within cognitive psychology by one in which visual images are viewed as comprising multiple representational events of a visual, verbal, and affective nature and the parallel processing activities of visual and verbal representational systems (Anderson, 1978; Kosslyn & Pomerantz, 1977). For example, mental training programs frequently emphasize the importance of forming a vivid visual image. Yet, studies have shown that the vividness of imagery is frequently unrelated to behavioral improvement brought about by imagery techniques (Strossahl & Ascough, 1981). Perhaps the more sophisticated imagery models of cognitive psychology will help us to develop more effective imagery-based procedures.

Another area in which I expect advances to occur is that of attention and concentration training. As noted earlier, attentional processes are of paramount importance in all sorts of performance situations, and many people report attentional problems. Yet, we have done little empirical research in sport psychology on how athletes can be trained to achieve greater control over attentional processes. The centering technique that Nideffer (1981) uses may be a promising start, but we clearly need to evaluate it and other approaches, such as self-hypnosis. Nideffer's leadership in this important area is likely to stimulate further research and technique development.

All of the techniques I have discussed in this section involve attempts to train athletes in self-regulatory skills of various kinds. Kirschenbaum (1984) has presented a five-stage model of self-regulation that is a useful conceptual framework for the area of psychological skills training. The early phases of the model involve problem identification, goal setting, and planning behaviors that are instrumental to goal attainment. The usefulness of goal-setting procedures in facilitating behavior change has been repeatedly demonstrated in other areas of psychology. For example, Locke, Shaw, Saari, and Latham (1981) reviewed more than 100 studies performed with subjects ranging from schoolchildren to truck drivers and found significant positive effects in 90% of the studies. Coaches and athletes frequently speak of the importance of goals, and yet, as Gould (1986) has pointed out, only a few studies (e.g., Botterill, 1977; Burton, 1983) have been performed. Given the many parameters in terms of which goal-setting procedures can vary (e.g., general vs. specific, process vs. outcome, long-term vs. short-term, etc.), this is an area ripe for future research.

Let me conclude by reiterating the desirability of adopting a person X situation interactional model in our future research on intervention programs. Many of our intervention techniques are derived from the behavioral perspective, and behavior therapy research has tended to focus on the impact of situational factors (i.e., on techniques). However, if we expect to answer the theoretically and practically important question, Which technique for which person?, then we need to incorporate individual difference variables into our research designs. Doing so can help to identify subject populations that are likely to be helped by a particular technique (and, conversely, people who will not profit from them). Let me cite two examples from my own research to illustrate this point.

In our research on coaching behaviors and on the coach training program that we developed, we used a measure of general self-esteem with the children we studied. In all of our studies, we have found that low self-esteem children are most affected by how the coach behaves on social support and instructional dimensions. Moderate and high self-esteem subjects are less affected by differences in coaching behaviors (Smith, Smoll, & Curtis, 1978). Likewise, in assessing the effects of the training program on the attitudes of the children who played for the trained and untrained coaches, we found that the low self-esteem children were most affected by the training program (Smith, Smoll, & Curtis, 1979).

In a recent study, we applied our cognitive-affective stress management program to heavy social drinkers who were at risk for the development of alcohol addiction (Rohsenow, Smith, & Johnson, 1985). Because problem drinking often occurs under stress, we reasoned that the development of stress coping skills might reduce the need to drink under stress. We collected mood ratings and reports of alcohol consumption on a daily basis over a 6-month period preceding and following the program. As is often the case in treatment studies involving addictive behaviors, we found positive post-treatment effects in the treated subjects that decreased over the 6-month follow-up period. Fortunately, however, we had also administered a variety of personality and individual difference measures to the subjects. When follow-up change scores on the outcome measures were correlated with these measures, we found a cluster of individual difference factors that correlated highly with positive change. Briefly, those who maintained decreases in daily anxiety were those who were initially external in locus of control and low in social support and who had reported that they used alcohol to cope with negative moods. Continued improvement in alcohol consumption occurred in men who were low in social support and who reported few obsessive thoughts about drinking. Because these relationships were found only in the experimental group and not in the untreated control group, they appear to be factors that predict positive response to stress management training in this population. It is likely that the incorporation of theoretically relevant individual difference variables in outcome studies in sport psychology would similarly help us to identify personal factors that interact with our treatment manipulations.

Conclusion

One of the difficulties I had in preparing this discussion of future research trends in sport psychology with non-elite populations is that my crystal ball was, to borrow William James' description, a "blooming, buzzing confusion" of possibilities. In my need to be selective I have undoubtedly failed to mention many other promising research areas. This is, I think, a very healthy sign concerning our field, as it attests to the many exciting frontiers of research and application that lie before us.

References

Allison, M.G., & Ayllon, T. (1980). Behavioral coaching in the development of skills in football, gymnastics, and tennis. *Journal of Applied Behavior Analysis*, **13**, 297-314.

Anderson, J. (1978). Arguments concerning representations for mental imagery. *Psychological Review*, **85**, 249-277.

Botterill, C. (1977, November). *Goal setting and performance on an endurance task*. Paper presented at the Canadian Psychomotor Learning and Sport Psychology Conference, Banff, Alberta, Canada.

Burton, D. (1983). *Evaluation of goal setting training on selected cognitions and performance of collegiate swimmers*. Unpublished doctoral dissertation, University of Illinois, Urbana, IL.

Chelladurai, P., & Saleh, S.D. (1980). Dimensions of leader behaviors in sport: Development of a leadership scale. *Journal of Sport Psychology*, **2**, 34-35.

Danish, S.J., & Hale, B.D. (1981). Toward an understanding of the practice of sport psychology. *Journal of Sport Psychology*, **3**, 90-99.

Feltz, D.L., & Landers, D.M. (1983). The effects of mental practice on motor skill learning and performance: A meta-analysis. *Journal of Sport Psychology*, **5**, 25-57.

Gauron, E.F. (1984). *Mental training for peak performance*. Lansing, NY: Sport Science Associates.

Goldstein, J.H. (1979). *Sports, games, and play: Social and psychological viewpoints*. Hillsdale, NJ: Erlbaum.

Gould, D. (1986). Goal setting for peak performance. In J. Williams (Ed.), *Applied sport psychology: Personal growth to peak performance* (pp. 133-148). Palo Alto, CA: Mayfield.

Harris, D.V., & Harris, B.L. (1984). *The athlete's guide to sport psychology: Mental skills for physical people*. New York: Leisure Press.

Harter, S. (1981). A new self-report scale of intrinsic versus extrinsic orientation in the classroom: Motivational and informational components. *Developmental Psychology*, **17**, 300-312.

Hatfield, B.D., & Landers, D.M. (1983). Psychophysiology—A new direction for sport psychology. *Journal of Sport Psychology*, **5**, 243-259.

Hatfield, B.D., Landers, D.M., & Ray, W.J. (1987). Cardiovascular—CNS interactions during a self-paced, intentional attentive state: Elite marksmanship performance. *Psychophysiology*, **24**, 542-549.

Heyman, S.R. (1984). The development of models for sport psychology: Examining the USOC guidelines. *Journal of Sport Psychology*, **6**, 125-132.
Horn, T.S. (1985). Coaches' feedback and changes in children's perceptions of their physical competence. *Journal of Educational Psychology*, **77**, 174-186.
Joreskog, K.G., & Sorbum, D. (1981). *LISREL V; Analysis of linear structural relationships by the method of maximum likelihood*. Chicago: International Educational Services.
Kirschenbaum, D.S. (1984). Self-regulation and sport psychology: Nurturing an emerging symbiosis. *Journal of Sport Psychology*, **6**, 159-183.
Kirschenbaum, D.S., Ordman, A.M., Tomarken, A.J., & Holtzbauer, R. (1982). Effects of differential self-monitoring and level of mastery on sports performance: Brain power bowling. *Cognitive Therapy and Research*, **6**, 335-342.
Kosslyn, S., & Pomerantz, J. (1977). Imagery, propositions, and the form of internal representation. *Cognitive Psychology*, **9**, 52-76.
Landers, D.M. (1983). Whatever happened to theory testing in sport psychology? *Journal of Sport Psychology*, **5**, 131-151.
Locke, E.A., Shaw, K.N., Saari, L.M., & Latham, G.P. (1981). Goal setting and task performance. *Psychological Bulletin, 90*, 125-152.
Martens, R. (1977). *Sport Competition Anxiety Test*. Champaign, IL: Human Kinetics.
Martens, R. (1979). About smocks and jocks. *Journal of Sport Psychology*, **1**, 94-99.
Martens, R., Burton, D., Vealey, R., Smith, D., & Bump, L. (1983). *The development of the Competitive State Anxiety Inventory-2 (CSAI-2)*. Unpublished manuscript, University of Illinois, Urbana, IL.
Martin, G.L., & Hrycaiko, D. (1983). *Behavior modification and coaching: Principles, procedures, and research*. Springfield, IL: Thomas.
Nideffer, R.M. (1976). Test of Attentional and Interpersonal Style. *Journal of Personality and Social Psychology*, **34**, 394-404.
Nideffer, R.M. (1981). *The ethics and practice of applied sport psychology*. Ithaca, NY: Movement.
Orlick, T. (1980). *In pursuit of excellence*. Champaign, IL: Human Kinetics.
Robl, R.J. (1983). *Assessment of attentional style*. Unpublished master's thesis, University of Washington, Seattle, WA.
Rohsenow, D.J., Smith, R.E., & Johnson, S. (1985). Stress management training as a prevention program for heavy social drinkers: Cognitions, affect, drinking, and individual differences. *Addictive Behaviors*, **10**, 45-54.
Rushall, B.S. (1977). Two observation schedules for sporting and physical education environments. *Canadian Journal of Applied Sport Sciences*, **2**, 15-21.
Rushall, B.S. (1981). Coaching styles: A preliminary investigation. *Behavior Analysis of Motor Activity*, **1**, 3-19.
Rushall, B.S., & Smith, K.C. (1979). The modification of the quality and the quantity of behavior categories in a swimming coach. *Journal of Sport Psychology*, **1**, 138-150.

Salmela, J. (1979). Psychology and sport: Fear of applying. In P. Klavora & J.V. Daniel (Eds.), *Coach, athlete, and the sport psychologist* (pp. 13-21). Champaign, IL: Human Kinetics.

Schaie, K.W. (1965). A general model for the study of developmental problems. *Psychological Bulletin*, **64**, 92-107.

Schendel, J.S. (1968). The psychological characteristics of high school athletes and non-participants in athletics. In G.S. Kenyon (Ed.), *Proceedings of the Second International Congress of Sport Psychology* (pp. 147-155). Chicago: Athletic Institute.

Seabourne, T.G., Weinberg, R.S., Jackson, A., & Suinn, R.M. (1985). Effect of individualized, nonindividualized, and package intervention strategies on karate performance. *Journal of Sport Psychology*, **7**, 40-50.

Siedentop, D. (1976). *Developing teaching skills in physical education*. Boston: Houghton-Mifflin.

Smith, R.E. (1980). Development of an integrated coping response through congnitive-affective stress management training. In I.G. Sarason & C.D. Speilberger (Eds.), *Stress and anxiety*, (Vol. 7, pp. 265-280). Washington, DC: Hemisphere.

Smith, R.E., Sarason, I.G., & Sarason, B.R. (1986). *Psychology: The frontiers of behavior* (3rd ed.). New York: Harper and Row.

Smith, R.E., Smoll, F.L., & Curtis, B. (1978). Coaching behaviors in Little League Baseball. In F.L. Smoll & R.E. Smith (Eds.), *Psychological perspectives in youth sports* (pp. 173-201). Washington, DC: Hemisphere.

Smith, R.E., Smoll, F.L., & Curtis, B. (1979). Coach Effectiveness Training: A cognitive-behavioral approach to enhancing relationship skills in youth sport coaches. *Journal of Sport Psychology*, **1**, 59-75.

Smith, R.E., Zane, N.S.W., Smoll, F.L., & Coppel, D.B. (1983). Behavioral assessment in youth sports: Coaching behaviors and children's attitudes. *Medicine and Science in Sports and Exercise*, **15**, 208-214.

Smoll, F.L., Smith, R.E., Curtis, B., & Hunt, E. (1978). Toward a mediational model of coach-player relationships. *Research Quarterly*, **49**, 528-541.

Stevenson, C.L. (1975). Socialization effects of participation in sport: A critical review of the research. *Research Quarterly*, **46**, 287-301.

Strossahl, K.D., & Ascough, J.C. (1981). Clinical uses of mental imagery: Experimental foundations, theoretical misconceptions, and research issues. *Psychological Bulletin*, **89**, 422-438.

Suinn, R.M. (1976). Body thinking: Psychology for Olympic champs. *Psychology Today*, **10**(2), 38-44.

United States Olympic Committee. (1983). U.S. Olympic Committee establishes guidelines for sport psychology services. *Journal of Sport Psychology*, **5**, 4-7.

Vallerand, R.J. (1983). Attention and decision making: A test of the predictive validity of the Test of Attentional and Interpersonal Style (TAIS) in a sport setting. *Journal of Sport Psychology*, **5**, 449-459.

VanSchoyck, S.R., & Grasha, A.F. (1981). Attentional style variations and athletic ability: The advantages of the sport specific test. *Journal of Sport Psychology*, **3**, 149-165.

Weiss, M.R., Bredemeier, B.J., & Shewchuk, R.M. (1985). An intrinsic/extrinsic motivational scale for the youth sport setting: A confirmatory factor analysis. *Journal of Sport Psychology*, **7**, 75-91.

Ziegler, S.G., Klinzing, J., & Williamson, K. (1982). The effects of two stress management training programs on cardiorespiratory efficiency. *Journal of Sport Psychology*, **4**, 280-289.

Exercise and the Average Person: A Commentary

Charles B. Corbin

The charge to those preparing the preceding three papers was to discuss the research in exercise and sport science over the last 20 to 30 years and to try to make statements about future directions for research with specific reference to the average person. Though each paper focused on a different area of the sport and exercise sciences (Nelson on biomechanics, Wilmore on exercise physiology, and Smith on sport psychology, the latter including motor learning, control, and development), the assignment for each was most difficult. Some of the factors making the assignment difficult were the relative newness of the exercise/sport science discipline, the recent explosion of information in the discipline, the broad focus associated with studying the average person, and the diverse nature of the exercise/sport science disciplines.

Nelson pointed out that almost all of the symposium speakers in biomechanics received their terminal degrees within the last 10 to 15 years. In many cases PhD degrees in the exercise/sport science specialties were not offered prior to that time. Also, graduate education courses, specialized publications such as scientific journals, and synthesis publications such as textbooks have been available in most areas of exercise and sport science only since the 1950s and 1960s. For this reason much of the early research is from the parent disciplines rather than from the exercise/sport sciences. This makes it difficult to discern which of the various early research studies are most relevant to the emerging exercise and sport sciences. Likewise, the enormous recent growth of the knowledge base in the exercise/sport sciences makes it difficult to determine exactly which findings to summarize for a meeting such as this.

Particularly difficult is identifying what information is most important for the average person.[1] For the elite athlete, performance is critical, and for this reason performance is the topic of much of the research on this

[1]At least one of the speakers questioned whether there was such a person as the average person.

population. For the below-average person, effective functioning and health are critical. However, for the average person, there are many more topics on which emphasis could be placed, including: health; freedom from, prevention of, and rehabilitation from disease and injury; development of personal competence; and, as all of the speakers pointed out, the fun and enjoyment of regular exercise and sports involvement.

Though each speaker chose specific kinds of research findings around which to organize his comments, it is clear that for the average person, the emphasis has been on the process rather than the product. In this context, process refers to the qualitative rather than the quantitative aspects of exercise and sport. The elite athlete may be most concerned with how fast or how far he or she can run, whereas the average person may be more concerned with the benefits that may be received from the exercise or sport. For example, Smith talked of the need in youth sports to "foster positive attitudes" rather than "increased skill acquisition," and Wilmore spoke of the need to "portray physical activity as fun and enjoyable" rather than "negative or manual labor." Clearly each speaker had a concern for enhancing performance, even for the average person, but each emphasized the importance of continued research designed to improve the lives of those involved in sport and exercise. Nelson summarized it well when he suggested that if the exercise and sport sciences are to make a "contribution to the enrichment of the lives of the members of our society," a priority must be placed on the average person.

In addition to a general concern for quality lifestyles for the average person as we conduct research in the future, the speakers also pointed out the necessity of clearly identifying the benefits versus the risks of exercise and sport participation. Wilmore in particular was concerned that we more clearly identify the true risks associated with exercise involvement. As we study the contributions of exercise and sports to the healthy lifestyle, we also need to take objective looks at the risks associated with participation with reference to all three exercise sciences.

As noted earlier, a major problem with identifying future research directions in the exercise sciences is the great diversity of the exercise science subdisciplines. As would be expected, each speaker identified past research and future directions in his own subdisciplinary area. Unexpected was the unanimity of the speakers in their concern for interdisciplinary research. Conducting research in each subdiscipline can be likened to learning more about the pieces of a puzzle. However, it will take interaction and integration of this subdisciplinary research if important problems are to be solved in the future. In response to questions from the audience, all speakers agreed that the success of future exercise and sport science research depends on educating high-quality scholars in each of the subdisciplines (specialists) who are willing to work together with experts in the other subdisciplines to answer future exercise/sport science questions. It is in this interactive way that we can put together the pieces of the puzzles of the exercise/sport sciences. Interdisciplinary or cross-disciplinary research may be particularly important for those who study children and the older populations (a certain topic of expanded research in the future).

As would be expected from scholars of the quality of those presenting in this session, each warned of the need for sound theory building, effective measurement, and efficiency of methods. Smith was especially careful to point out the need for careful measurement in exercise/sport psychology where measurement is often less precise than in exercise physiology and biomechanics. The need for longitudinal research was also noted. These points are always worthy of mention. But in the final analysis the speakers have shown that the technology is present, or soon will be, to do quality research in the future. As important as knowing how to answer questions is learning how to ask the right questions.

In all areas of exercise/sport science, asking and answering questions with reference to individual differences is critical. When dealing with the average person this is especially important because there is such a wide range of normal when studying human movement. Nelson uses the example of designing backpacks for the military to illustrate how biomechanics can help accommodate individual needs. The unique characteristics of individuals relative to their readiness for cardiovascular exercise, as pointed out by Wilmore, also illustrates the importance of individual differences. Future research and applications of research must be aware of the individual nature of average people.

A potential problem for those conducting future research concerning average populations is the lack of funding sources. Recent developments have finally resulted in increasing funding for research among elite performers and funding for special below-average populations such as the diseased and handicapped. But funding is more difficult to obtain for normal populations. Some have suggested that it is easier to get funds to help people get well than it is to help them stay well. Creative approaches such as interdisciplinary research with normal but older people may be necessary if future funding is to be forthcoming.

In conclusion, Nelson, Wilmore, and Smith come from different subdisciplinary backgrounds. The content of their research reviews and the specifics of their suggestions for the future reflect their subdisciplinary interests. Nevertheless, their comments and responses reflect remarkable similarity. Each based his faith for the future of research in the exercise and sport sciences on the quality of the preparation of future scientists within specialized subdisciplinary areas and on the ability of these well-qualified scientists to ask and answer important questions in an interdisciplinary way. Though they all make reference to good scientific methodology, they agree that the tools are, or soon will be, available to accomplish the missions of exercise and sport science research. The extent to which we succeed will depend on the people who do the work, not the technology available to do it. For the average person, these scholars predict that future research will focus on helping people to become fully functioning healthy individuals. The focus will be on the process as well as the product, with attention given to both the benefits and the risks of sport and exercise involvement. As the exercise and sports scientists of the future learn more about the pieces of the puzzle and work with each other to put the puzzles together, the emphasis will be on *individual differences*, because no two average people are exactly the same.

SECTION B:

PERSONS OF BELOW-AVERAGE HEALTH AND FITNESS

Biomechanics and Orthopedic Problems: A Quantitative Approach

Thomas P. Andriacchi

The human musculoskeletal system adapts in many ways to changes in either its external or its internal stimuli. These adaptations can occur as morphological changes in bone (muscle atrophy or hypertrophy), as well as alterations in the control mechanisms for locomotion. In many cases, the stimulus for the adaptation is mechanical in nature. One type of adaptation is structural in nature and can be seen in bone when it changes both its density and architecture in response to alterations in mechanical stress. Another type of adaptation is dynamic in the sense that the adaptation appears only during activities such as walking. Stimuli such as pain, instability, or muscle weakness can cause dynamic changes in gait that reflect the nature of the disorder. For example, a particular type of gait, described as Trendelenburg, is associated with weakness of the hip abductor muscles. A biomechanical analysis of this gait indicates that the adaptation is associated with an avoidance of the need to stress the abductor muscles. Shifting the body weight over the center of the hip joint eliminates the need for the abductor muscles to balance the moment due to the offset of the body's weight.

An understanding of the cause and effect of functional adaptations is extremely important for the development of methods for training, rehabilitation, and treatment of functionally impaired individuals. The purpose of this paper is to examine some aspects of our current knowledge of biomechanical functional adaptations and to discuss the future needs in this area from both a developmental and a research viewpoint. Several specific examples related to orthopedic problems will be presented.

Time-Distance, Kinematic, and Kinetic Measure of Function—A Descriptive Evaluation of Abnormal Walking

The current state of the art in the analysis of human locomotion is descriptive in nature. Temporal (Grieve, 1968), kinematic (Lamoreux, 1971; Murray, Drought, & Kory, 1964), kinetic, and physiological parameters have been quantified during walking, running (Cavanagh,

Pollock, & Landa, 1977; Dillman, 1975), and other activities of daily living. There have also been a number of investigations describing quantitative changes in locomotion associated with functional disabilities or treatment modality (Chao, Laughman, & Stauffer, 1980; Murray, Brewer, & Zuege, 1972; Perry, Hoffer, Giovan, Antonelli, & Greenberg, 1974).

Time-distance parameters such as stride length, walking speed, and cadence are important measures of normal and abnormal walking (Perry, 1974). Stride length (distance between consecutive heel strikes on the same side) is one of the most easily attained and sensitive indicators of walking abnormalities. Changes in stride length have been associated with walking disabilities. As an example, stride length has been shown to increase in a characteristic and repeatable manner with walking speed for normal subjects. Patients with arthritic knees walk with a substantially shorter than normal stride length (Andriacchi, Ogle, & Galante, 1977). These changes can be evaluated by examining the relationship between stride length and walking speed. This relationship can be graphically and statistically compared (Figure 1). A change in walking ability

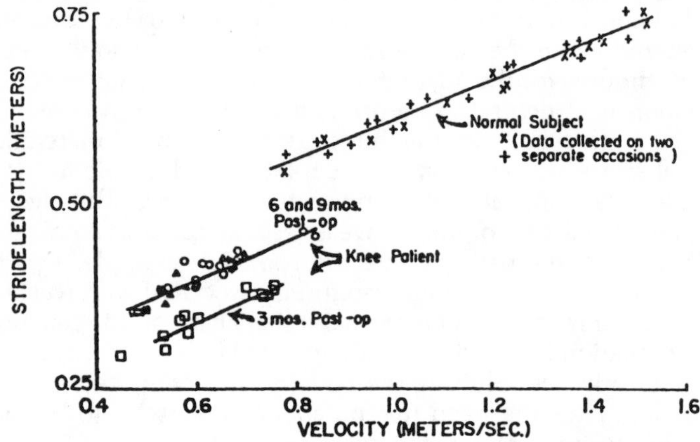

Figure 1. An illustration of the stride length-velocity relationship for a normal subject and patient with total knee replacement. The results indicate the increase in the patient stride length following surgery with velocity held as independent variables. *Note*. From "Walking Speed as a basis for normal and abnormal gait measurements" by T.P. Andriacchi, J.A. Ogle, and J.O. Galante, 1977, *Journal of Biomechanics*, **10**. Reprinted by permission.

following knee replacement surgery can be quantified as a change in the stride length to walking speed relationship between the 3rd- and 6th-month post-operative evaluations. This type of quantitative information is useful in demonstrating an objective change that can be associated with change in the clinical status of the patient. It is also important to note that the interrelationship between stride length and walking speed is an important consideration when attempting to evaluate comparisons among different observations. Length normalization, with respect to overall height or leg length, is also an important consideration when attempting to compare different individuals.

The time-distance parameters, although extremely efficient in evaluating quantitative changes in the overall characteristics of walking, do not provide specific information that can be related to the cause of the walking abnormality. Measurement of joint kinematics, in terms of relative segmental angles, is useful in identifying changes in pattern of motion related to a specific joint. This type of measurement is also useful because it identifies the phase of the walking cycle. Again, using the example of gait in patients with total knee replacements, it has been shown that these patients characteristically alter the normal knee flexion during the mid-portion of stance phase by maintaining a straighter than normal knee (Rittman, Kettlekamp, Pryor, Schwartzkopf, & Hillberry, 1981; see also Figure 2). This result occurs even in patients who are pain free and considered an excellent clinical result. Thus, some type of adaptation to the

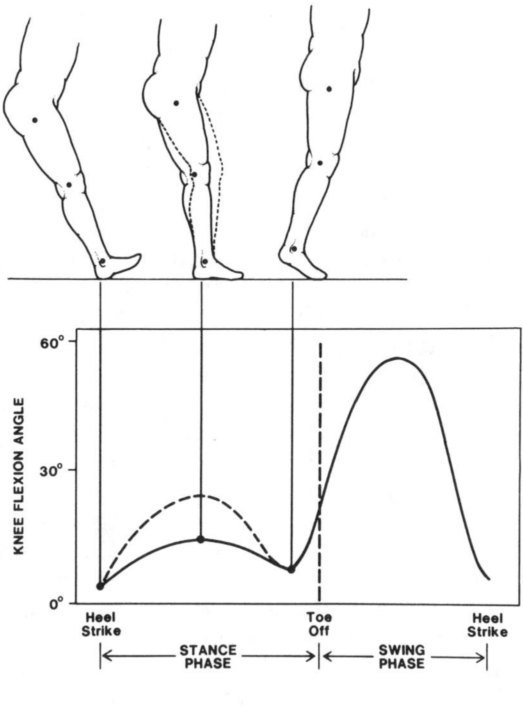

Figure 2. An illustration of the reduction in mid-stance knee flexion in patients with total knee replacement (solid line) compared to normal (dashed-line). (C) *Note.* From "The biomechanics of running and knee injuries" by T.P. Andriacchi, G.M. Kramer, and G.C. Landon. In *American Academy of Orthopaedic Surgeons Symposium on Sport Medicine, The Knee* (G. Finerman, Ed.). Copyright 1985 by C.V. Mosby. Reprinted by permission.

disease process or to the knee reconstruction occurs in these patients. The current state of the art in gait analysis gives us the capability to identify these adaptations in patients, but at present the identification of their cause is still beyond the scope of this field.

The net joint reaction moment during walking as a measure of function has received increasing attention in recent years (Andriacchi & Strickland, 1985; Bresler & Frankel, 1960; Cappozo, Figura, & Marchetti, 1976). Quantification of moments at the joint during locomotion provides information not available from measuring motion or temporal parameters. This information can be related to muscular function and indirectly to joint loading. Along the lines of the example of gait in patients with total knee replacements, it has been reported (Andriacchi, Kramer, & Landon, 1985; Simon, Trieshmann, Burdett, Ewald, & Sledge, 1983) that the moment at the knee joint is substantially different from normal.

A physical interpretation of the net joint-moment vector can be facilitated by resolving the vector into components in directions associated with flexion-extension, abduction-adduction, and internal-external rotation. At the knee joint, for example, the moment tending to flex or extend the knee must be balanced by internal flexor and extensor muscle groups. Obviously, the moment is not a direct measure of the muscle activity due to the redundancy of muscle group, as well as the potential for antagonistic muscle action. Nevertheless, an alteration in the moment pattern clearly reflects an alteration in the manner in which the muscles are functioning.

An analysis of the abnormal moments in post-operative patients with total knee replacements illustrates how the moments can be used to provide a physical interpretation of the walking abnormality. Recall that post-operative patients with total knee replacements walk with a shorter than normal stride length and with reduced mid-stance knee flexion. As previously noted, these abnormal gait characteristics occur in spite of pain-free gait and an excellent clinical result. A useful way to visualize the effect of the joint-reaction moment is to display the ground reaction force vector superimposed on the image of the leg (Figure 3). This analysis assumes that the mass and acceleration of the shank segment are negligible compared to the ground reaction force vector; this is a reasonable assumption for the knee joint during stance phase. During normal walking, the normal flexion-extension moment pattern is biphasic: the ground reaction force passes anterior to the knee joint at heel strike, producing an extension moment; at mid-stance, the ground reaction force vector passes posterior to the knee, producing a flexion moment; the cycle reverses again at approximately 70% stance phase following the final reversal just prior to toe-off. It has been reported (Andriacchi & Strickland, 1985) that more than 80% of the normal subjects studied use this oscillatory biphasic pattern. The abnormal gait seen in total knee replacements is associated with non-oscillatory moment patterns. Following total knee replacement, patients typically walk with either a pattern that maintains the ground reaction force vector anterior to the knee joint (extensional pattern in Figure 3) or a pattern that maintains the ground reaction force vector posterior to the center of the knee joint (flexional pattern). If one accepts the correspondence between the flexion-extension moment and the phasic

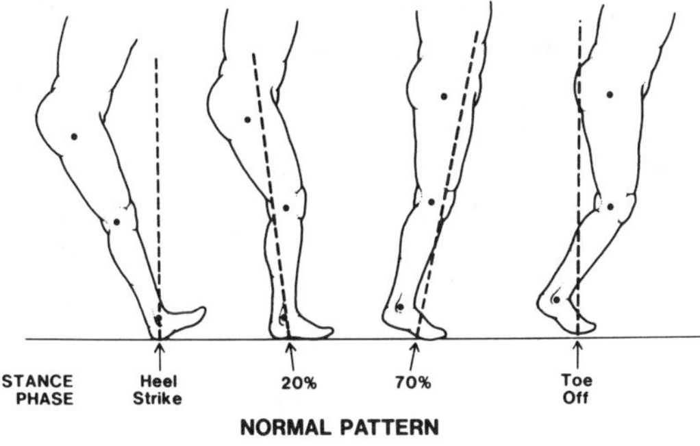

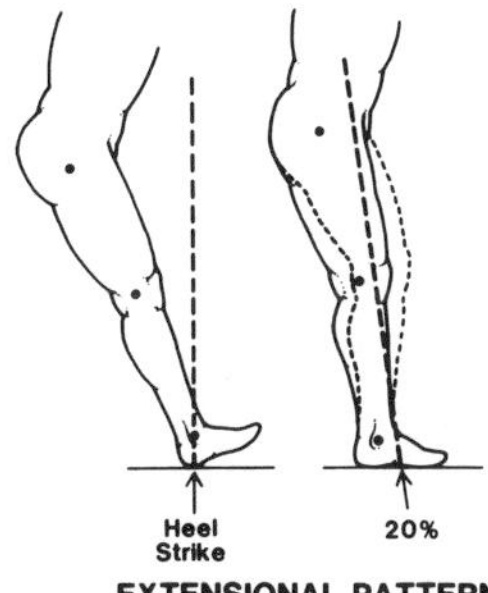

Figure 3. An illustration of the pattern of the leg with the ground reaction force superimposed on the leg. A vector passing anteriorly to the knee creates a moment tending to extend the joint. This figure illustrates the normal pattern and the "extensor" pattern seen in patients with total knee replacement. (C) *Note.* From "The biomechanics of running and knee injuries" by T.P. Andriacchi, G.M. Kramer, and G.C. Landon. In *American Academy of Orthopaedic Surgeons Symposium on Sport Medicine, The Knee* (G. Finerman, Ed.). Copyright 1985 by C.V. Mosby. Reprinted by permission.

on-off patterns of flexor and extensor muscle groups, these results suggest that there is abnormal phasing of the flexor and extensor muscle groups. It has been suggested that a loss of proprioceptive control following total knee replacement subtly alters the ability to control joint position during walking, thus altering the normal oscillatory moment pattern seen in normal subjects. At this point, this explanation is hypothetical. However, it demonstrates the added physical insight provided by examining the joint-reaction moment in attempting to interpret abnormal characteristics during locomotion.

Kinetic Analyses of Running—A Prediction of Potential Overuse Injury Mechanism

Another example of an application of joint kinetics is related to the analyses of the overuse injury occurring in middle- and long-distance runners.

The overuse injury results from cyclic loading at the joint with sufficient magnitude to produce injury when applied over a large number of cycles. This type of injury is differentiated from a traumatic injury in which the load is substantially higher and is of sufficient magnitude to cause injury during a single occurrence. The knee joint is the most frequent site of overuse injury patterns in middle- and long-distance runners (James, Bates, & Osternig, 1978). Other frequent sites of overuse injury of runners are the ilio-tibial band, Achilles tendon, and metatarsal heads (Table 1).

Table 1 A Comparison of the Maximal Loads During Running and Overuse Injury

Biomechanical variable[a]	Maximal load during running[b]	Overuse injury
Knee flexion moment	5×	Patello-femoral pain
Hip adduction moment	2×	Iliotibial band
Ankle dorsal flexion	2×	Achilles tendonitis
Metatarsal head forces	2×	Metatarsalgia

[a]Moments are described in directions acting on the limb (i.e., a flexion moment would be balanced by the extensor muscle group).

[b]Expressed as multiples of the maximal values during walking.

A comparison of the maximal loads that occur during running at a relatively slow pace (3 m/s) and walking (1.2 m/s) indicates that the moment tending to flex the knee has the largest increase over level walking. The increase is nearly a factor of 5 over level walking. As noted previously, the flexion moment must be balanced by the action of the extensor muscle groups internally. Thus, an increase in the magnitude of the flexion moment can be related to an increase in the quadriceps force, patello-femoral contact force, and joint compressive force. Therefore, there appears to be a correspondence between the frequency of injury patterns and the load component that shows the largest increase over level walking. Similarly, the large adduction moment at the hip would stress the ilio-tibial band, and the dorsal flexion at the ankle would stress the Achilles tendon. Clearly, structures that are more highly stressed during running are operating in a range where any perturbation (e.g., changes in distance, speed, or shoe style) may be sufficient to alter the delicate balance between healing and repair mechanisms associated with overuse injuries.

An understanding of the mechanics of abnormal locomotion is extremely important as a means for future improvement in treatment, as well as for injury prevention. In the case of patients with total knee replacement, gait analysis provides a way to quantify changes as a result of treatment. It also provides insight into the mechanics of post-treatment walking and the potential limitations associated with total knee replacement arthroplasty. In the case of the overuse injury pattern in runners, the information from gait analysis may be a useful starting point in attempting to evaluate methods for reducing these loads, with the assumption that a reduction in the high loads associated with overuse injury may also reduce the probability for overuse injury. This is an area that warrants further study. The use of gait analysis to evaluate disability, to plan treatment or rehabilitation, and to diagnose and treat disease requires a better understanding of the causes of biomechanical changes during locomotion. In particular, there is a need for understanding the causes and effects of functional adaptations. This is an area that is important for the future and will be illustrated in two examples in the next section.

Future Research

The mechanisms of functional adaptation during locomotion are not well understood. These mechanisms can be quite obvious, as in the case of an individual with cerebral palsy, or quite subtle, appearing as a slight limp in an individual with a ligamentous injury. In both extremes, the pattern of locomotion reflects adaptation to injury or disease and can be described in biomechanical terms. The biomechanics of this adaptation has important implications for understanding the injury or disease process, as well as for potential treatment modalities. The following two examples will illustrate these concepts.

The first example is associated with osteoarthritis of the knee joint. In many cases, arthritis develops in only one compartment, usually the medial one. This degenerative process is often associated with bowed legs (varus knees). It has been suggested (Maquet, 1980) that the varus deformity places an increased stress on the medial compartment of the knee and that this stress is associated with the symptoms and the degenerative process. Medial-compartment osteoarthritis is often treated by straightening out the bow-legged deformity using a procedure called a high tibial osteotomy. In this procedure, the tibia is cut and the limb is realigned. Again, the theory is that in the realigned position, the stresses will be lower on the medial compartment of the knee. The procedure is quite attractive because it is more conservative than other treatment modalities, such as total joint arthroplasty. The results, however, have been somewhat variable (Insall, Joseph, & Miska, 1984). The difficulty has been in the selection of patients best suited for this treatment.

The biomechanics of walking was used to study the possibility that dynamic loading during walking plays a role in the outcome of high tibial osteotomy. Patients who were candidates for this treatment were tested in the gait laboratory prior to treatment and at yearly intervals following treatment (Prodromos, Andriacchi, & Galante, 1985). The investigation focused on the dynamic peak adduction moment at the knee, with the assumption that the magnitude of this moment was related to the load

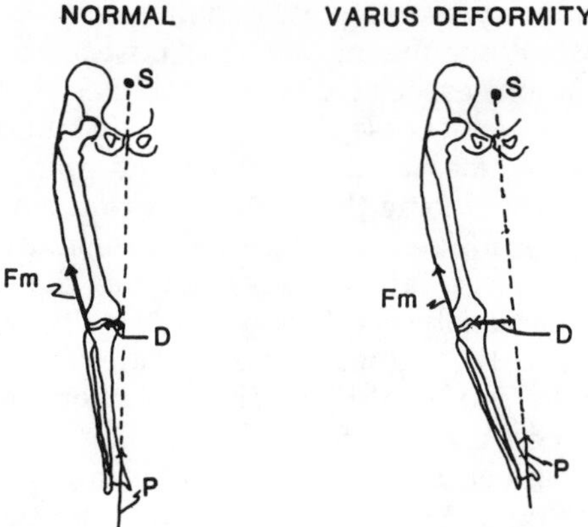

Figure 4. When using a static analysis, increasing the distance (D) will result in higher medial joint loads.

on the medial compartment of the knee (Figure 4). The initial hypothesis of this study was that patients with a large varus deformity would have a higher than normal adduction moment that could be associated with the offset of the ground reaction force to the center of the joint. The pre-operative gait analysis indicated that only about half of the patients had a higher than normal adduction moment (High Adduction Moment group) during walking, whereas the remaining patients had a normal or slightly below normal adduction moment (Low Adduction Moment group), in spite of a varus deformity at the knee. Following surgery in which the varus deformity was corrected in all patients, a 1-year post-operative gait analysis was conducted. It was found that the adduction moment was reduced in all patients. However, patients with a higher than normal adduction moment pre-operatively maintained a higher adduction moment post-operatively than did the patients in the Low Adduction Moment group (Figure 5). Patients in the pre-operative Low Adduction Moment group actually had a lower than normal adduction moment following high tibial osteotomy. The patients in the Low Adduction Moment group pre-operatively had better clinical results than the High Adduction Moment group at an average of 3.2 years following correction of the varus deformity. The average clinical score of the former group was 92 points (100 = perfect), whereas the latter group had a significantly lower score of 70 points.

The results of this study suggest that pre-operative peak adduction moments during walking are predictive of post-operative clinical results. This finding suggests that some type of dynamic adaptation occurred to reduce the peak adduction moment in patients with varus deformity at the knee. If this dynamic compensation did not take place, the varus deformity would increase the adduction moment. These findings also suggest that this mechanism of dynamic compensation continues after the varus deformity is surgically realigned, because patients with a lower

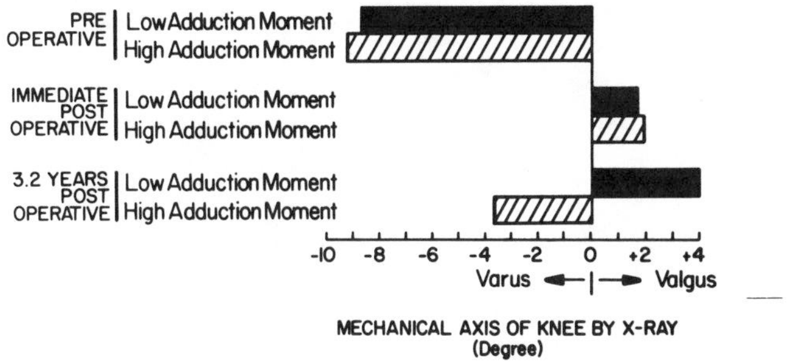

Figure 5. The patient group with the "High Adduction Moment" had a recurrence of the varus deformity at the 3.2 year follow-up. *Note.* From "A relationship between gait and clinical changes following high tibial osteotomy" by C.C. Prodromos, T.P. Andriacchi, and J.O. Galante, 1985, *Journal of Bone and Joint Surgery,* **67A**(8). Reprinted by permission.

pre-operative adduction moment continued to have a lower post-operative adduction moment. Further analysis of the patient groups (Low and High adduction moments) indicated no differences in deformity, pain, body weight, or other clinical parameters. It may be that proprioception, subconscious pain, or some other unconscious neuromechanism is responsible for this compensatory unloading gait in some patients but not in others. The observation of this phenomenon, although clinically relevant, is really only the first step toward understanding the control processes and adaptations in patients with walking disabilities. Future work is needed to identify the source of the signal producing the adaptive gait.

A final example of an adaptive mechanism involves the analysis of patients with complete tears of the anterior cruciate ligament (ACL) of the knee. Patients with an ACL-deficient knee typically have difficulties with movements involving a lateral thrust or rotatory loads at the knee joint. However, some patients are able to perform these activities. A group of these subjects was tested in the laboratory during a 90°-side-step cutting maneuver (Andriacchi et al., 1985). Normal control subjects were also tested during running and side-step cutting maneuvers. The major differences between loading at the knee during straight running and during cutting were the presence of larger external rotation moments during the mid-support phase and a large increase in the anterior shear on the tibia at the foot-strike position (Figures 6a and 6b). These types of loads tend to elicit the signs of instability associated with a torn ACL and are in similar directions to those applied during clinical tests for ACL-deficiency. Thus, it is reasonable that patients with a torn ACL would have difficulty with lateral cutting movement.

Each of the patients with an ACL-deficient knee was able to perform the lateral cutting test in the laboratory. However, these patients performed the cutting maneuver in a manner considerably different from normal, but similar to one another. They performed the cut with the body more flexed at the hip and knee and maintained the torso in a more erect

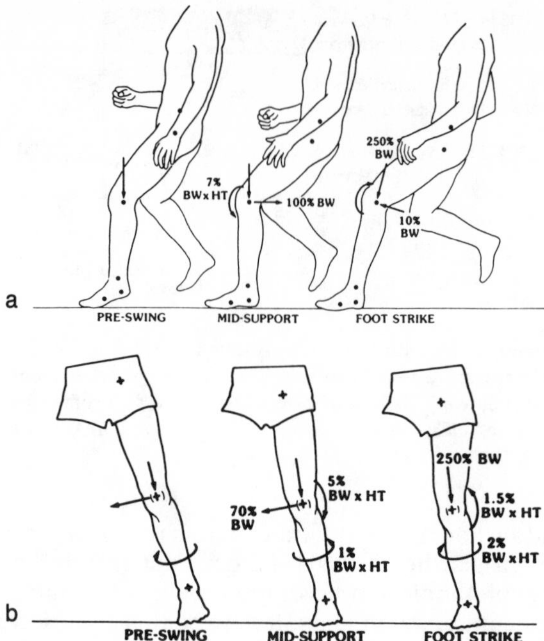

Figure 6. (a) Sagittal plane view of leg during foot strike, mid-support, and pre-swing phases of 90° side-step cut. Numbered values indicate occurrence of maxima.
(b) Frontal plane view of the leg during 90° side-step cut. Numbered values indicate occurrence of maxima. *Note*. From "The biomechanics of running and knee injuries" by T.P. Andriacchi, G.M. Kramer, and G.C. Landon. In *American Academy of Orthopaedic Surgeons Symposium on Sport Medicine, The Knee* (G. Finerman, Ed.). Copyright 1985 by C.V. Mosby. Reprinted by permission.

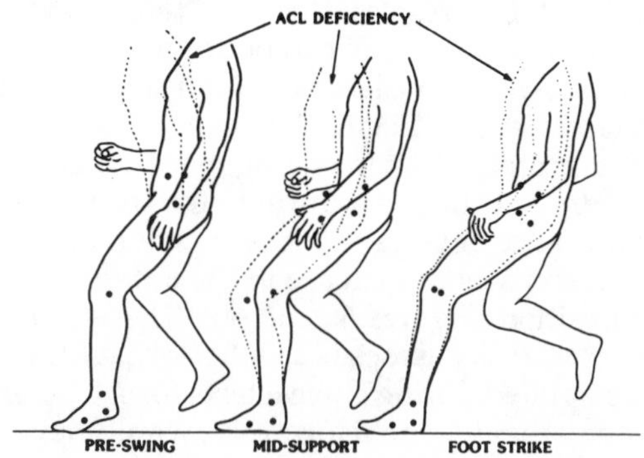

Figure 7. Different mechanisms used during cutting maneuver by patients with ACL insufficiency compared to normal. Patients with ACL insufficiency tended to cut with knee and hip more flexed. *Note*. From "The biomechanics of running and knee injuries" by T.P. Andriacchi, G.M. Kramer, and G.C. Landon. In *American Academy of Orthopaedic Surgeons Symposium on Sport Medicine, The Knee* (G. Finerman, Ed.). Copyright 1985 by C.V. Mosby. Reprinted by permission.

position (Figure 7). Using this body posture, the patients had a larger than normal hip and knee flexion moment during the cut.

The flexed limb posture used by these subjects may be associated with the role of the hamstring muscles in stabilizing the knee. By maneuvering with the knee in a more flexed position, the hamstrings are in a better position to stabilize the tibia and prevent abnormal anterior translation and internal rotation. This is another example of a subtle functional adaptation that is clinically relevant, but not well understood.

Conclusion

At present, the study and analysis of functional biomechanics in patients with subnormal function due to disease or injury are descriptive. Normal function can be quantified in terms of time-distance, kinematic, and kinetic variables. Functional adaptation can be identified. In addition, these adaptations can be interpreted from a biomechanical and functional viewpoint. However, studies of this nature are empirical and often quite time-consuming because relatively large numbers of subjects must be studied over a period of time to evaluate long-term clinical results. In many cases, it is difficult to extrapolate results from one study to another when a different patient group is involved. Thus, the ability of functional evaluation to provide meaningful widespread results requires either a tremendous data base of research on various clinical problems or additional basic research work in an attempt to understand the functional adaptations from a biological, neurological, and biomechanical viewpoint. Multidisciplinary projects requiring expertise in neurophysiology, biomechanics, gait analysis, anatomy, and physiology are needed. Once an underlying theory for understanding the cause and effect of functional adaptations evolves, functional evaluation can be an extremely useful tool in determining methods for rehabilitation, training, and treatment of individuals with functional disabilities.

References

Andriacchi, T.P., Kramer, G.M., & Landon, G.C. (1985). The biomechanics of running and knee injuries. In G. Finerman (Ed.), *American Academy of Orthopaedic Surgeons Symposium on Sport Medicine, The Knee* (pp. 23-32). St. Louis: C.V. Mosby.

Andriacchi, T.P., Ogle, J.A., & Galante, J.O. (1977). Walking speed as a basis for normal and abnormal gait measurements. *Journal of Biomechanics*, **10**, 261-268.

Andriacchi, T.P., & Strickland, A.B. (1985). Lower limb kinetics applied to the study of normal and abnormal walking. In N. Berme, A.E. Engin, & K.M. Correia Da Silva (Eds.), *Biomechanics of normal and pathological human articulating joints* (NATO ASI Series E, No. 93, pp. 83-102). Dordrecht, Holland: Martinus Nijhoff.

Bresler, B., & Frankel, J.P. (1960, January). The forces and moments in the leg during level walking. *Transactions of the American Society of Mechanical Engineers,* **48A**, 62.

Cappozzo, A., Figura, F., & Marchetti, M. (1976). The interplay of muscular and external forces in human angulation. *Journal of Biomechanics,* **9** (1), 35-43.

Cavanagh, P.R., Pollock, M.L., & Landa, J. (1977). A biomechanical comparison of elite and good distance runners. *Annals of the New York Academy of Science,* **301**, 328-345.

Chao, E.Y., Laughman, R.K., & Stauffer, R.N. (1980). Biomechanical gait evaluation of pre and post operative total knee replacement patients. *Archives of Orthopedic and Traumatic Surgery,* **97**, 309-317.

Dillman, C.J. (1975). Kinematic analyses of running. In J.H. Wilmore (Ed.), *Exercise and sport sciences review* (Vol. 3, pp. 193-218). New York: Academic Press.

Grieve, D.W. (1968). Gait patterns and the speed of walking. *Biomedical Engineering,* **3**, 119-122.

Insall, J.N., Joseph, D.M., & Msika, C. (1984). High tibial osteotomy for varus gonarthrosis. *Journal of Bone and Joint Surgery,* **66A**(7), 1040-1048.

James, S.L., Bates, B.T., & Osternig, L.R. (1978). Injuries to runners. *The American Journal of Sports Medicine,* **6**(2), 40-50.

Lamoreux, L. (1971). Kinematic measurements in the study of human walking. *Bulletin of Prosthetics Research,* **10**(15), 3-84.

Maquet, P. (1980). The biomechanics of the knee and surgical possibilities of healing osteoarthritic knee joints. *Clinical Orthopedics and Related Research,* **146**, 102-110.

Murray, M.P., Brewer, B.J., & Zuege, R.C. (1972). Kinesiologic measurements of functional performance before and after McKee-Farrar total hip replacement: A study of thirty patients with rheumatoid arthritis, osteoarthritis, or avascular necrosis of the femoral head. *Journal of Bone and Joint Surgery,* **54A**(2), 237-256.

Murray, M.P., Drought, A.B., & Kory, R.C. (1964). Walking patterns of normal men. *Journal of Bone and Joint Surgery,* **46A**, 335-360.

Perry, J. (1974). Clinical gait analyzer. *Bulletin of Prosthetic Research,* Fall, 188-192.

Perry, J., Hoffer, M.M., Giovan, P., Antonelli, D., & Greenberg, R. (1974). Gait analysis of the triceps surae in cerebral palsy. A preoperative and postoperative clinical and electromyographic study. *Journal of Bone and Joint Surgery,* **56A**(3), 511-520.

Prodromos, C.C., Andriacchi, T.P., & Galante, J.O. (1985). A relationship between gait and clinical changes following high tibial osteotomy. *Journal of Bone and Joint Surgery,* **67A**(8), 1188-1194.

Rittman, N., Kettlekamp, D.B., Pryor, P., Schwartzkopf, G.L., & Hillberry, B. (1981). Analysis of patterns of knee motion walking for four types of total knee implants. *Clinical Orthopedics and Related Research,* **155**, 111-117.

Simon, S.R., Trieshmann, H.W., Burdett, R.G., Ewald, F.C., & Sledge, C.B. (1983). Quantitative gait analysis after total knee arthroplasty for monarticular degenerative arthritis. *Journal of Bone and Joint Surgery,* **65A**(5), 605-613.

Exercise: Measurement, Dose-Response Relations, and Compliance

William L. Haskell

Those persons likely to benefit the most from an increase in physical activity appear to be individuals who are the least active and have the lowest levels of fitness. As baseline fitness and activity levels increase, the magnitude of the health and performance benefits derived from further increases in activity seem to be less and harder to achieve. That greater exercise training–induced increases in aerobic power and muscular strength are achievable by the very unfit than by the more fit is well documented, but the dose-response relationships for other health-related measures in initially low-fit persons as compared to the more fit have not been established. If the greatest potential for benefit from increased activity is in very low-fit persons, then it is surprising that more research has not been conducted (a) to improve methodologies for accurately quantifying their activity, (b) to better define health and performance benefits resulting from activity regimens capable of being performed by low-fit persons, (c) to determine the biologic mechanism of action for each benefit, and (d) to characterize the most effective and safe training programs for producing the desired changes in fitness and health status.

In this manuscript, below-average fitness is defined as a physical working capacity that is more than one standard deviation below the average for healthy, generally active persons of the same gender and age. Reasons why people are below average in fitness include very little habitual activity but not disabled, disabled due to neuromuscular trauma or disease, disabled due to chronic degenerative disease (coronary heart disease, chronic obstructive lung disease, cancer, diabetes, osteoarthritis, etc.), disabled due to acute or other chronic disorders that limit exercise tolerance, gross obesity, the aging process, and heredity. Being sedentary or very inactive is defined as routinely performing only activities that are less vigorous than brisk walking or having an energy requirement of less than 4 METS (1 MET is the energy used at sitting rest and corresponds to a $\dot{V}O_2$ of 3.5 $ml \cdot min^{-1} \cdot kg^{-1}$).

The primary objective of this manuscript is to review selected areas of research that would benefit or pertain most to persons with below-average health or fitness. Emphasis is placed on research opportunities that have biological/clinical implications for the very inactive but clinically healthy person or people with (or at high risk for developing) selected chronic degenerative diseases. Topics such as aging and the psychological benefits of exercise are extensively covered in other sections of this book.

Physical Activity Measurement

One of the major factors limiting our understanding of the relationship between physical activity and health status in low-fit persons is the lack of easily administered, valid, and reliable measures of routine or habitual activity. Techniques have not yet been developed that allow us to accurately characterize the physical activity patterns of physically inactive persons. In fact, we are not even sure which features of activity are most important to document in order to understand the relationship between activity and specific health benefits. For example, which descriptor of inactivity best defines its relationship to rate of bone calcium loss and osteoporosis or to insulin-mediated glucose uptake and the risk of adult-onset diabetes? When is it more important to define the length of time spent at a specific intensity of exercise, as compared to the total energy expended during an exercise training session or the total energy expenditure per day?

Measurement tools are needed so that we can establish baseline activity patterns in low-fit persons, accurately measure changes in their activity outside of supervised settings, and design activity recommendations that are effective yet safe. The validity and reliability of activity diaries or logs, time-based recalls, and frequency questionnaires need to be established (Laporte, Montoye, & Caspersen, 1985). Currently, there are no standardized questionnaires or diaries for which the psychometric characteristics have been established. Without such instruments, it has not been possible to meaningfully compare the results of various studies using different techniques to assess physical activity. In addition to questionnaires and diaries, attempts have been made to quantify activity using motion sensors attached to the body or continuous monitoring of physiological responses, primarily heart rate (Warnold & Lenner, 1977). For such techniques to be of value, they need to be valid and reliable, and they cannot significantly interfere with the activity pattern of the low-fit subject because of the weight, size, or other characteristics of the monitoring device.

Most physical activity questionnaires and diaries have been used to identify participation in more vigorous activities and to classify persons as either active or sedentary. Very little emphasis has been placed on the development of questionnaire methodology for characterizing the physical activity patterns of generally less active individuals. People tend to record or recall quite accurately the vigorous activities they perform but have a much more difficult time documenting the amount of time spent in light-intensity activities such as standing and walking (Taylor et al., 1984), both of which may be an adequate stimulus for selected health benefits. New techniques that facilitate the accurate recording of lower-intensity activities performed sporadically throughout the day need to be developed.

Possible approaches include the use of minaturized, voice-activated audiotape recorders with an internal timing device and alarm that would signal the person to describe what he or she has been doing during the most recent period of time. This technique would be useful in situations where it is inconvenient to write down information and would eliminate the problem of participants' forgetting the time spent in more routine activities.

So far, the development of either motion sensors or physiologic monitors has not met with great success in defining procedures for characterizing physical activity patterns. Motion sensors have been made quite small, unobtrusive, and inexpensive, and can be used to separate the very active person from the inactive (Klesges, Klesges, Swenson, & Pheley, 1985). However, these devices are not sufficiently sensitive to accurately quantify differences among relatively inactive persons. For example, they will not differentiate between walking on the flat versus walking up a grade or upstairs (Montoye et al., 1983). Also, all of these devices provide information only on the total amount of activity performed and not on time spent at various intensities of exercise. It may be that time or energy spent above a specific intensity may be more important for modifying health status than total energy expenditure.

Physiologic monitoring for the assessment of physical activity has been investigated for several decades using heart rate as the primary measure of interest (Dauncey & James, 1979). However, heart rate has been considered of questionable value because of the known influence of psychological stress, fatigue, and environmental temperature on resting values and the wide interindividual differences in heart rate response to any given intensity of exercise. Also, concern has been expressed that the heart rate response is different during dynamic versus isometric or heavy-resistance exercise. Although all of these concerns are valid, it does appear that the continuous monitoring of heart rate can be useful in describing the physical activity profile of persons performing a wide range of activity (Bradfield, 1971). New solid-state recording equipment permits continuous monitoring of heart rate for up to 5 days, and computerized analysis of these data allows for rapid, accurate interpretation (Taylor et al., 1982). If the person's heart rate–energy expenditure relationship is established in the laboratory, then heart rate data can be used to estimate absolute and relative exercise intensity. The development of greatly improved heart rate monitoring systems is possible as a result of the recent advances in solid-state electronics. Equipment can be developed that will enable continuous recording for weeks rather than days, will be small and light (<0.25 kg), and will provide data in a format that can be easily analyzed by general-use computers.

Due to inherent limitations of both motion sensors and heart rate monitoring to accurately quantify physical activity, an improved approach for the future may be to use monitors that simultaneously record motion and heart rate. Given the increased analysis capability of computers, it may be possible to analyze these simultaneous recordings in a way that would allow some of the major limitations of single variable systems to be overcome. For example, "meaningful exercise" might be identified as only those periods when both the motion sensor and heart rate have increased a specified amount above rest, thus reducing the likelihood that an increase in heart rate due to psychological stress would be classified as an increase in activity. The recording of heart rate would help discriminate between walking on the flat and walking upstairs, which would not be detected by the motion sensor alone. Ambulatory monitors capable of multichannel recording are now available and have been used for physical activity assessment (Taylor et al., 1982). Whereas the heart rate monitoring functions work quite well (Figure 1), improved motion sensors are required and computer analysis programs need to be developed for the simultaneous evaluation of multiple variables for quantifying physical activity.

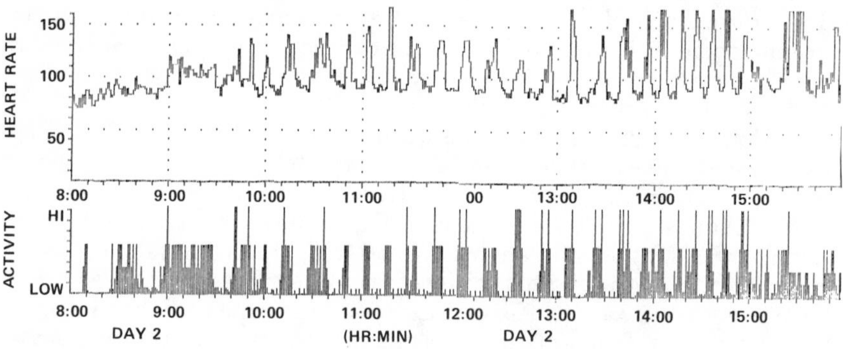

Figure 1. Recording of heart rate and body movement made using a solid-state, multichannel ambulatory recorder. Recording is from 8:00 a.m. until 4:00 p.m. with average heart rate (beats/minute) and activity recorded for each minute. During the day, the subject was alpine skiing a lift-served mountain with approximately a 3,000-ft descent. The recording demonstrates that discrete bouts of exercise throughout the day can be identified by heart rate or motion sensors.

So far, no one has identified a biochemical marker for physical activity. It would be of great benefit to be able to accurately determine the amount of activity that a person has performed in the recent past by the analyses of some relatively easily obtainable biologic indicator. Ideally, such an indicator would be available in urine, saliva, or venous blood, with the analytical procedure being sensitive to small differences in activity, easy to standardize, and inexpensive. Possible candidates for such a marker have included high-density lipoprotein cholesterol (HDL-C) or the HDL-C2 subfraction, enzymes (e.g., lipoprotein lipase), hormones (e.g., insulin), and such skeletal muscle characteristics as mitochondrial content or the activity of specific oxidative enzymes. The concentrations of all these measures are significantly modified by vigorous activity but they also are influenced by other personal traits or behaviors and thus are not sufficiently specific to be used as an activity marker. Of greatest promise appears to be the activity of specific enzymes in skeletal muscle, but the need to perform a muscle biopsy to obtain a sample makes this procedure impractical for most studies. Newer analytical techniques may allow for the noninvasive quantification of metabolic functions in specific tissues (e.g., positron emission tomography and magnetic resonance imaging) and could provide an opportunity to identify highly sensitive and specific biochemical markers for physical activity.

Exercise and Health-Dose Response Relationships

Most exercise training program recommendations for achieving health benefits are based on the relationships between the amount or intensity of activity and changes in maximal aerobic power (American College of Sports Medicine, 1986). Very few recommendations are based on information related to the specific health benefits or the clinical status of the person. Studies that have systematically evaluated the nature and magnitude of change produced by specific amounts of exercise have focused on changes in maximal aerobic power or physical working capacity. Even here, the information is mostly limited to data collected for relatively short periods of time (<16 weeks) and at intensities exceeding 60% of the participants' physical working capacity or maximal aerobic power. There is a major need to study the dose-response relationships for other biological and psychological measures, especially those associated with improved health status. This need is greatest in persons with below-average fitness or health and older persons because more readily collected data on younger, more active persons may not be applicable.

Can some health benefits from exercise be achieved without significant improvements in maximal aerobic power? The exercise required for a change in $\dot{V}O_2max$ may not be the same as that required for other health-oriented fitness measures. It may require more, less, or a different type of activity to most efficiently produce specific health benefits while minimizing risk of injury. For example, can low-intensity or resistive exercise significantly decrease bone calcium loss in post-menopausal women without producing a significant improvement in maximal aerobic power? Preliminary evidence indicates that bed rest will rapidly reduce glucose intolerance (Dolkas & Greenleaf, 1977) and plasma HDL-C concentrations (Nikkilä, Kuusi, & Myllynen, 1980). How much and what type of exercise is required to reverse these negative health consequences in very low-fit persons?

Most training studies have evaluated participants in supervised programs with exercise being performed at specified intensities for a continuous period of time. It is from these types of studies that currently existing recommendations were developed, with an emphasis placed on higher intensity exercise being performed continuously. Studies are needed to evaluate the effects of more varied activity regimens on different health-related measures. For example, what are the training effects in low-fit people whose exercise consists of four 10-min bouts per day, as compared to one bout of 40 min? The four shorter bouts might be more convenient for many low-fit, sedentary people and result in a significant increase in their health and fitness status. Information of this type would be extremely valuable if it led to a broadening of the exercise prescriptions being promoted. Such a diversification of exercise recommendations for low-fit people might significantly contribute to an increase in physical activity of the more than 80% of the United States population over age 18 who do not now perform sufficient activity to meet current recommendations (Figure 2).

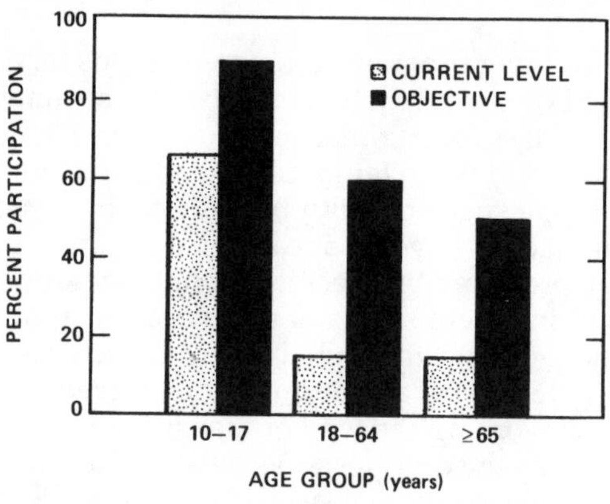

Figure 2. Current prevalence (1985) and 1990 national objectives for appropriate physical activity by age group. Appropriate exercise is defined as moderate to vigorous intensity exercise performed 20 min or more per session, three or more times per week.

A particular component of the exercise prescription that warrants further investigation is *intensity*. Most training changes occur when an exercise overload or stress is placed on the system. This overload can be either the intensity of exercise or the total amount of exercise performed. It is reasonably well established that with endurance-type exercise, the higher the intensity (up to about 90% $\dot{V}O_2max$), the greater the increase in physical working capacity, $\dot{V}O_2max$, and various hemodynamic and metabolic functions closely tied to oxygen transport and oxidative metabolism. Most often, exercise program guidelines recommend that exercise needs to be performed at 60% $\dot{V}O_2max$ (70% maximal heart rate) or above (American College of Sports Medicine, 1986). Although this intensity is well within the capacity of nearly everyone, many low-fit people do not like to exercise this vigorously or are concerned to do so due to fear of orthopedic or cardiac injury. We have demonstrated that training regimens that require no more than 55% of initial $\dot{V}O_2max$ will significantly increase the $\dot{V}O_2max$ of healthy men whose initial fitness is low (Gossard et al.,

1986). These results are consistent with previous studies on very sedentary young women (Edwards, 1974) and inactive men and women over age 60 (Badenhop, Cleary, Schaal, Fox, & Bartels, 1983). Additional results investigating the lower intensity thresholds for various health benefits of exercise should be given high priority. Such information is needed as the scientific basis for expanding exercise guidelines for low-fit persons.

Research Priorities for Persons With Selected Clinical Conditions Contributing to Below-Average Fitness

Most of the information available on the relationship between exercise and health is based on the biologic differences between more active persons and their sedentary counterparts (observational studies) or biologic changes produced by exercise training (experimental studies) and not on changes in the etiology of the disease or the clinical status of patients. Understanding the biologic changes produced by exercise training is important, but it does not have the same clinical significance as demonstrating a change in a disease process or in the clinical manifestations of the disease. It is equally important to determine if physical activity contributes to the primary prevention of major chronic disorders, as well as to the secondary prevention or to rehabilitation once the disorder becomes clinically evident. Most secondary prevention or rehabilitative efforts will need to take place in persons with below-average fitness and health.

Coronary Heart Disease (CHD)

Moderate or vigorous intensity physical activity on the job or during leisure time is associated with a reduced risk of CHD (Paffenbarger, Hyde, Wing, & Hsieh, 1986; Salonen, Puska, & Tuomilehto, 1982), as is an above-average physical working capacity (Peters, Cady, Bischoff, Bernstein, Pike, 1983). A question of major importance that still remains unanswered is, Will an increase in activity by unfit persons who are middle-aged or older lessen their risk of developing clinical manifestations of CHD? Given the difficulties of successfully completing a randomized controlled trial to answer this question, it is unlikely such a study will be conducted. The sample size would need to be large, high dropout rates are a major concern, and contamination by changes in other risk factors or medical management is likely. It may be that with further development of noninvasive techniques to accurately measure coronary artery narrowing, it will be possible to evaluate the effects of exercise training by serially measuring the progression of coronary atherosclerosis (Alderman, Berte, Harrison, & Sanders, 1981). An accurate and reproducible procedure would significantly reduce sample size and study duration compared to a study using CHD morbidity and mortality as end points. Noninvasive techniques such as ultrasound (or minimally invasive ones such as digital subtraction angiography) that permit serial measurements of coronary anatomy would allow for large-scale studies of risk modification including exercise alone or in combination with other behaviors.

An overall assessment of those studies that have investigated the effects of exercise training on recurrent myocardial infarction or CHD mortality in postinfarction patients suggests that exercise may be of some benefit (May, Eberlein, Furberg, Passamani, & DeMets, 1982). Definitive evidence is still needed on this question and is scientifically and logistically obtainable by conducting a large multicenter, collaborative trial enrolling higher risk myocardial infarction patients immediately after hospital discharge. Recruiting patients with a combined non-fatal reinfarction and CHD mortality rate of 10% per year, adequate power to detect a significant difference (alpha = .05, beta = .80, one-tailed test) could be obtained by recruiting 3,000 patients, if the exercise training reduced the event rate by 25% and all patients were followed for 3 years. Given the rapid growth of cardiac rehabilitation programs, despite significant skepticism regarding their clinical benefits, such a study should be given serious consideration.

It has been well established that the functional capacity of patients with CHD can be substantially increased by exercise training (Haskell, 1986). Especially in low-fit patients limited by myocardial ischemia, their symptom-free exercise tolerance is enhanced by even short bouts of training using moderate-intensity exercise; this improvement results primarily from a reduction in myocardial oxygen demand and not from an increase in myocardial oxygen perfusion (Sim & Neill, 1974). The hemodynamic effects of exercise training in these patients have been documented but there is still substantial controversy regarding what happens to intrinsic myocardial function. Newer cardiac imaging techniques provide unique opportunities for investigating this issue.

Congenital Heart Disease

Exceedingly little exercise training research has been conducted on patients with congenital heart disease. Very little is known about the risks or benefits of various exercise training regimens in patients with diagnosed congenital cardiac or vascular abnormalities, either before or after surgical correction. Many of these patients are very inactive and unfit due to unwarranted restrictions in their activity. It has been generally assumed that, because the structural abnormality would not be altered by training, the risks of exercise outweigh any potential benefits. However, these patients may benefit from training-induced changes in skeletal muscle metabolism, neurologic activity, and hormone sensitivity that contribute to an increase in functional capacity and health status independent of any effects on the congenital defect. Randomized studies of patients assigned to different exercise regimens with measures of cardiac function at rest and exercise are warranted. Training regimens studied should include heavy resistance and endurance-type exercise.

Systemic Arterial Hypertension

There is preliminary evidence that exercise reduces the incidence of systemic arterial hypertension (Paffenbarger, Wing, Hyde, & Jung, 1983) and that blood pressure is reduced in some hypertensive patients following exercise training (Duncan et al., 1985). Additional controlled trials of exercise versus placebo control or exercise plus other nonpharmacologic interventions (diet, weight loss, stress reduction) versus nonpharmacologic interventions without exercise in mild to moderate hypertensive patients seem justified. Can exercise training undertaken by very sedentary persons lower the incidence of age-related increases in blood pressure? Of special interest is the influence of exercise training on the ambulatory blood pressure of low-fit subjects who demonstrate a hyperreactivity to various physical or psychological stimuli. Hyperreactive persons (disproportionate increases in blood pressure and/or heart rate) identified by laboratory tests or ambulatory recording at home and at work would be randomized to exercise treatment or placebo control. Improved instrumentation for measurement of ambulatory blood pressure would enhance study validity and power and provide useful data on usual or operational blood pressures.

Diabetes

Substantial evidence exists that exercise training has profound effects on carbohydrate metabolism. Following exercise training, the plasma insulin concentration stimulated by a given glucose load is significantly reduced (Leon, Conrad, Hunninghake, Serfass, 1979; Seals, Hagberg, Hurley, Ehsani, Holloszy, 1984) or the amount of glucose taken up by tissues at any given plasma insulin concentration is substantially increased (Rosenthal, Haskell, Solomon, Widstrom, Reaven, 1983). These changes in the glucose-insulin interaction may be a training response but there is some evidence that they are primarily the response to a recent bout of exercise (Heath et al., 1983). Glucose tolerance is rapidly compromised in persons undergoing bed rest, suggesting a rapid decline in insulin sensitivity and glucose uptake with total rest (Dolkas & Greenleaf, 1977).

Many diabetic patients have very low levels of fitness due, in part, to medical restriction of their exercise. Although there is some evidence that these patients can reduce insulin requirements if they exercise regularly, there is no systematic study of the long-term clinical benefits of exercise training in these patients. Are the clinical complications of Type I or Type II diabetes decreased as a result of exercise training? If so, what is the optimal exercise regimen for promoting these benefits while minimizing risks? How can exercise best be combined with diet and weight management for both the primary and secondary prevention of Type II diabetes or its clinical complications?

Osteoarthritis and Osteoporosis

The increased participation in such weight-bearing activities as jogging and racquet sports by older persons has stimulated concern regarding the potential for musculoskeletal injury or damage. However, in a recent study at Stanford University comparing the prevalence of osteoarthritis signs and symptoms in long-term runners over age 50 versus sedentary controls, there was no evidence of any increased joint disease in these very active men and women (Lane, Bloch, Jones, Wood, & Fries, 1986). A major limitation of this study was the possibility that anyone with recurrent orthopedic pain discontinued their regular running and thus produced a major selection bias. Do the cardiovascular and metabolic benefits of exercise significantly outweigh the potential musculoskeletal hazards? In persons whose activity is minimally restricted due to osteoarthritis, does a controlled program of exercise delay or accelerate the progression of the disease or its clinical manifestations? Does exercise training modify the disease process or just increase the patient's tolerance to it? How can patients with severe osteoarthritis best benefit from exercise training, including increases in muscle strength, endurance, and flexibility? Can circuit programs of non-weight-bearing activities be devised that are effective, safe, and practical? Of particular concern is the older patient with both cardiac and orthopedic limitations.

Data from observational studies indicate that regular exercise contributes to bone mineral retention, especially in older women (Black-Sandler et al., 1982). Preliminary studies of increased activity by older women with low exercise capacities also have demonstrated a positive effect of relatively small amounts of exercise on bone density (Smith, Reddan, & Smith, 1981). Such data are extremely important when the prevalence of osteoporosis and fractures due to trauma in older persons are considered. However, no systematically collected data have yet been presented on the clinical consequences of osteoporosis following exercise training. Is bone structure sufficiently altered by exercise training in persons with low levels of fitness to reduce significantly the incidence or severity of fractures? Is a positive exercise effect enhanced by increased calcium intake? Studies in post-menopausal women are of particular importance because they are of greatest risk for skeletal disorders, they are the least active segment of the population, and they have received the least attention regarding the health effects of exercise.

Obesity

Persons who are substantially overweight due to obesity frequently have below-average fitness, especially if their $\dot{V}O_2max$ is expressed per kilogram of body weight. Overweight, inactive individuals can achieve weight loss by caloric restriction or by increased energy expenditure through exercise, with the best results probably occurring when both intake and expenditure are modified (Zuti & Golding, 1976). Substantial disagreement exists regarding the differential effects of exercise and caloric restriction on various metabolic processes, as well as regarding the relationship of weight loss to various health-related measures. For example, does exercise training that results in loss of body weight change the basal, resting, or post-exercise metabolic rate in low-fit persons when expressed per unit of body mass or lean body mass? What happens to basal metabolic rate when significant caloric restriction is combined with a major increase in exercise? Does this combined approach negate the caloric-sparing effect reported with large restrictions in caloric intake by obese subjects (Wolley, Wolley, & Dyrenforth, 1979)? What is the decay curve for post-exercise metabolic rate over 24 to 48 hr following exercise training sessions with different characteristics (especially high-intensity vs. prolonged duration)? Does this decay curve differ for lean versus overweight individuals?

It has been difficult to separate the effects of leanness from fitness on various health-related measures, including plasma lipid or lipoprotein concentrations, carbohydrate metabolism, and systemic arterial blood pressure. Statistical adjustments for differences in body weight, body mass index, or percent body fat in cross-sectional comparisons between very active and inactive populations have been inadequate. Preliminary experimental data suggest that certain, but not all, of the exercise effects on lipoprotein metabolism may be mediated through changes in energy balance. In some cases, the effect may be achieved by either increased energy expenditure in the very unfit or weight loss by caloric restriction in the obese. How much of an improvement in the lipoprotein profile can out-of-shape overweight persons make by significantly increasing their exercise habits, as compared to achieving leanness just by caloric restriction? The same question needs to be answered for glucose uptake and insulin sensitivity. Are the biologic mechanisms by which these changes are produced different for weight loss by caloric restriction versus exercise training?

Evolving Areas for Investigation

A great deal is yet to be learned regarding the relationship between physical activity and newly evolving disorders in the general population, but even more so in low-fit persons. As our understanding of the etiology of various diseases is improved, the probability that exercise may provide some protection against or help alleviate certain clinical manifestations of diseases not now considered exercise-related will likely be increased. This is not to suggest that exercise is any kind of health panacea, but just that some of the many biologic changes that are produced by exercise may favorably alter the underlying pathology of selected diseases or the body's capacity to adapt to this pathology. For example, the increase in sympathetic nervous system activity during exercise could alter the body's response to various neural or neuromuscular disorders. The increase in body temperature could influence primary immunologic functions, leading to increased resistance against various acute and chronic diseases, including viral infections (Simon, 1984) or malignant neoplasms (Vena et al., 1985). As the population ages, those disabilities that increasingly plague the elderly will warrant further investigation. Data are needed on the relationship of exercise to Alzheimer's disease. Is the incidence of this disorder altered by lifelong activity, or does exercise play a role in its treatment? Because the elderly remain the least active segment of our population (probably even when adjusted for their intrinsic functional capacity), substantial behavioral-oriented research is required to develop strategies that will keep large segments of the population physically active until their 70s and 80s. Of particular concern is the older person with a very low functional capacity due to any one of a number of chronic ailments who suddenly becomes bedridden due to an acute illness or injury. Unless an aggressive program of rehabilitation is initiated, it is very likely that this person will become permanently incapacitated due primarily to a reduction in activity below some critical threshold. Research defining the exercise parameters that most effectively alleviate this situation should be given high priority.

References

Alderman, E., Berte, L.E., Harrison, D.C., & Sanders, W. (1981). Quantitation of coronary artery dimensions using digital imaging processing. *Digital Radiography*, **314**, 273-278.

American College of Sports Medicine. (1986). *Guidelines for graded exercise testing and prescription* (3rd ed.). Philadelphia: Lea & Febiger.

Badenhop, D.T., Cleary, P.A., Schaal, S.F., Fox, E.L., & Bartels, R.L. (1983). Physiological adjustments to higher- or lower-intensity exercise in elders. *Medicine and Science in Sports and Exercise*, **15**, 496-502.

Black-Sandler, R., Laporte, R.E., Sashin, D., Kuller, L.H., Sternglass, E., Cauley, J.E., & Link, M.M. (1982). Determinants of bone mass in menopause. *Preventive Medicine*, **11**, 269-280.

Bradfield, R.B. (1971). A technique for determination of usual daily energy expenditure in the field. *American Journal of Clinical Nutrition*, **24**, 1148-1154.

Dauncey, M.J., & James, W.P.T. (1979). Assessment of the heart rate method for determining energy expenditure in man, using a whole-body calorimeter. *British Journal of Nutrition*, **42**, 1-13.

Dolkas, C.B., & Greenleaf, J.E. (1977). Insulin and glucose responses during bed rest with isotonic and isometric exercise. *Journal of Applied Physiology*, **43**, 1033-1038.

Duncan, J.J., Farr, J.E., Upton, S.J., Hagen, R.D., Oglesby, M.E., & Blair, S.N. (1985). The effects of an aerobic exercise program on sympathetic neural activity and blood pressure in patients with mild essential hypertension. *Journal of the American Medical Association*, **254**, 2609-2613.

Edwards, M.A. (1974). The effects of training at predetermined heart rate levels for sedentary college women. *Medicine and Science in Sports*, **6**, 14-19.

Gossard, D., Haskell, W.L., Taylor, C.B., Mueller, J.K., Rogers, F., Chandler, M., Ahn, D.K., Burnett, K., & DeBusk, R.F. (1986). Effects of low- and high-intensity home-based exercise training on functional capacity in healthy middle-aged men. *American Journal of Cardiology*, **57**, 446-449.

Haskell, W.L. (1986). Mechanisms by which physical activity may enhance the clinical status of cardiac patients. In M.L. Pollock & D.H. Schmidt (Eds.), *Heart disease and rehabilitation* (2nd ed., pp. 303-324). New York: Wiley.

Heath, G.W., Gavin, J.R., Hinderliter, J.M., Hagberg, J.M., Bloomfield, S.A., & Holloszy, J.O. (1983). Effects of exercise and lack of exercise on glucose tolerance and insulin sensitivity. *Journal of Applied Physiology*, **55**, 512-517.

Klesges, R.C., Klesges, L.M., Swenson, A.M., & Pheley, A.M. (1985). A validation of two motion sensors in the prediction of child and adult physical activity levels. *American Journal of Epidemiology*, **122**, 400-410.

Lane, N.E., Bloch, D., Jones, H., Wood, P., & Fries, J.F. (1986). Long distance running, osteoporosis and osteoarthritis. *Journal of the American Medical Association*, **255**, 1147-1151.

Laporte, R.E., Montoye, H.J., & Caspersen, C.J. (1985). Assessment of physical activity in epidemiologic research: Problems and prospects. *Public Health Reports*, **100**, 131-147.

Leon, A.S., Conrad. J., Hunninghake, D.B., & Serfass, R. (1979). Effects of a vigorous walking program on body composition, and carbohydrate and lipid metabolism of obese young men. *Journal of Clinical Nutrition*, **33**, 1776-1787.

May, G.S., Eberlein, K.A., Furberg, C.D., Passamani, E.R., DeMets, D. (1982). Secondary prevention after myocardial infarction: A review of long-term trials. *Progress in Cardiovascular Diseases*, **24**, 331-352.

Montoye, H.J., Washburn, R., Servais, S., Ertl, A., Webster, J.G., & Nagle, F.J. (1983). Estimation of energy expenditure by a portable accelerometer. *Medicine and Science in Sports and Exercise*, **15**, 403-407.

Nikkilä, E.A., Kuusi, T., & Myllynen, P. (1980). High density lipoprotein and apolipoprotein A-I during physical inactivity. *Atherosclerosis*, **37**, 457-462.

Paffenbarger, R.S., Hyde, R.T., Wing, A.L., & Hsieh, C. (1986). Physical activity, all cause mortality, and longevity of college alumni. *New England Journal of Medicine*, **314**. 605-613.

Paffenbarger, R.S., Wing, A.L., Hyde, R.T., & Jung, D.L. (1983). Chronic disease in former college students. Physical activity and incidence of hypertension in college alumni. *American Journal of Epidemiology*, **117**, 245-257.

Peters, R.K., Cady, L.D., Bischoff, D.P., Bernstein, L., & Pike, M.C. (1983). Physical fitness and subsequent myocardial infarction in healthy workers. *Journal of the American Medical Association*, **249**, 3052-3056.

Rosenthal, M., Haskell, W.L., Solomon, R., Widstrom, A., & Reaven, G.M. (1983). Demonstration of a relationship between level of physical training and insulin-stimulated glucose utilization in normal humans. *Diabetes*, **32**, 408-411.

Salonen, J.T., Puska, P., & Tuomilehto, J. (1982). Physical activity and risk of myocardial infarction, cerebral stroke and death. *American Journal of Epidemiology*, **115**, 526-537.

Seals, D.R., Hagberg, J.M., Hurley, B.F., Ehsani, A.A., & Holloszy, J.O. (1984). Effects of endurance training on glucose tolerance and plasma lipid levels in older men and women. *Journal of the American Medical Association*, **252**, 645-649.

Simon, H.B. (1984). The immunology of exercise. *Journal of the American Medical Association*, **252**, 2735-2738.

Sim, D.N., & Neill, W.A. (1974). Investigation of the physiological basis for increased exercise threshold for angina pectoris after physical conditioning. *Journal of Clinical Investigation*, **54**, 763-770.

Smith, E.L., Reddan, W., & Smith, P.E. (1981). Physical activity and calcium modalities for bone mineral increase in aged women. *Medicine and Science in Sports and Exercise*, **13**, 60-64.

Taylor, C.B., Coffee, T., Berra, K., Iaffaldano, R., Casey, K., & Haskell, W.L. (1984). Seven-day activity and self-report compared to a direct measure of physical activity. *American Journal of Epidemiology*, **120**, 818-824.

Taylor, C.B., Kraemer, H.C., Bragg, D.A., Miles, L.E., Rule, B., Savin, W.M., & DeBusk, R.F. (1982). A new system for long-term recording and processing of heart rate and physical activity in outpatients. *Computers and Biomedical Research*, **15**, 7-17.

Vena, J.E., Graham, S., Zielezny, M., Swanson, M.K., Barnes, R.E., & Nolan, J. (1985). Lifetime occupational exercise and colon cancer. *American Journal of Epidemiology*, **122**, 357-365.

Warnold, I., & Lenner, R.A. (1977). Evaluation of the heart rate method to determine the daily energy expenditure in disease. A study in juvenile diabetics. *American Journal of Nutrition*, **30**, 304-315.

Wolley, S.C., Wolley, O.W., & Dyrenforth, S.R. (1979). Theoretical, practical and social issues in behavioral treatments of obesity. *Journal of Applied Behavior Analysis*, **12**, 3-25.

Zuti, W.B., & Golding, L.B. (1976). Comparing diet and exercise as weight reduction tools. *The Physician and Sportsmedicine*, **4**, 49-57.

When Motivation Matters: The Need to Expand the Conceptual Model

Glyn C. Roberts

The area of sport psychology is one of the most diverse and complicated of all the sport sciences. The subspecialities of sport psychologists range from the neurophysiological (e.g., motor control) through the purely psychological (e.g., skill acquisition) to social psychological and personality areas (e.g., motivation). The area is further complicated because there are two types of sport psychologists. We have researchers who wish to understand and explain psychological phenomena in exercise and sport (academic sport psychologists), and we have professionally oriented practitioners who wish to use psychological skills and therapies to enhance performance in exercise and sport (applied sport psychologists). A concern many of us have in sport psychology is the rapidly developing gulf that is emerging between the academic and applied sport psychologists. The academic types argue that we cannot practice intervention strategies until we understand the pertinent psychological constructs. The applied types argue that there is a real need for intervention, and we had better satisfy that need by applying what knowledge we do have. (At this time, I do not want to discuss the controversy raging within applied sport psychology about whether we should employ a clinical model, a counseling model, or a human development model in the delivery of psychological services to exercise and sport participants.) The diversity and controversy in sport psychology may not be that surprising when we note that the field of psychology itself is equally as diverse and complicated and rife with controversial issues.

The complication in sport psychology comes primarily from the lack of a generally accepted conceptual paradigm that drives the research and applied efforts of sport psychologists. This is where psychology is at a disadvantage to many of the other sport sciences. In exercise physiology, for example, the paradigm is clear. The issue exercise physiologists face is the appropriate level of analysis in which to conduct research. Exercise physiologists are locked into a reductionist paradigm in that the important questions are approached from more and more fundamental levels of analysis; this means that the units of study are more and more basic. For example, knowledge of biochemistry and neurophysiology are essential if exercise physiologists wish to be on the cutting edge of current research in the field. In contrast, biomechanics is a little different in that it may be stated, somewhat unkindly I suppose, that it is an area replete with sophisticated measurement technologies in search of a question. Biomechanics typically follows an engineering model in its research activity. Sport psychology has the rather unique complication that it is a relatively new and emerging sport science that is currently developing its appropriate conceptual paradigm. In the meantime, sport psychology is going through a difficult adolescence.

In sport psychology, there are several conceptual paradigms vying for attention. The major problem is that the half-life of a conceptual paradigm in psychology (Kuhn, 1970) is about 10 years. Thus the mechanistic, behavioral-drive model that dominated the research efforts of sport psychologists in the sixties and early seventies has given way to a cognitive paradigm in the late seventies and the eighties. To be abreast of current psychological thought and theorizing, sport psychologists should be using cognitive models to understand psychological behavior in sport and exercise. Unfortunately, as is true of other applied areas in psychology, the half-life of a conceptual paradigm in sport psychology is typically 20 years, not 10. Consequently, we have sport psychologists operating in conceptual paradigms generally discarded by psychologists. A classic case is sport personality research. Some sport psychologists are still operating on trait and pseudo-mechanistic drive models when personologists in psychology have long recognized that such models are not particularly functional or useful in understanding behavior. Personologists in psychology are moving into other paradigms such as social cognition models. It is my plea that sport psychologists become better acquainted with the epistemological concerns of mainstream psychology.

As if this were not enough in itself, there is a further complicating factor for those not initiated in the conceptual canons of sport psychology—the preponderance of minitheories. Many psychologists pose minitheories to explain subsets of behaviors. In my own area of semicompetence, motivation, there are several minitheories that purport to explain a small subset of achievement behaviors, for example, Deci's (1975) theory to explain intrinsic motivation, Bandura's (1977) theory to explain self-efficacy, and Harter's (1981) theory to explain competence motivation. Investigators who are invested in these models either refuse or fail to recognize that these minitheories are part of a larger conceptual framework explaining motivation. When they use these conceptual and empirical paradigms from psychology, sport psychologists often fail to recognize that the research of others is pertinent to the question being asked. They develop a slavish allegiance to a particular minitheory. Thus, as a backdrop to the genuine advances that are made, there is a constant stream of random noise emitted from conceptually narrow perspectives, against which the true signal of advancement is sometimes difficult to discern.

As we can appreciate, this makes communication among sport psychologists difficult, let alone communication among sport scientists. To understand the work of sport psychologists, it is important that we realize the conceptual approach each sport psychologist takes. The basic assumptions underlying the psychological functioning of the individual differ among sport psychologists. Thus I believe it incumbent on sport psychologists to articulate the conceptual framework governing their research efforts.

The Emergence of Cognitive Science

The most evident way in which psychology has changed in the past 10 years is in the increasing dominance of the cognitive paradigm. There are, of course, many who would not accept this view and who continue to rage against the dying of the light of their particular paradigm. In the main, however, it is true that the cognitive paradigm is now dominant in psychology. To a cognitive theorist, thought governs action. The essential task is to study the way in which knowledge is acquired, represented, and used by humans. The emphasis is on the creation of models of knowledge to understand how cognitions, or thoughts, govern behavior. Thus cognitive theorists in sport psychology would eschew paradigms that are strictly behavioral, such as those by Seidentop (1976) or Rushall (1979, 1982), or are trait or drive based, such as those by Straub (1978) or Morgan (1980). Cognitive theorists believe that behavioral variance in sport and exercise is better captured by models that incorporate the cognitions and beliefs of individuals. In other words, the cognitions and beliefs individuals have mediate their behavior, and it is up to us as scientists to describe and explain what constellation of cognitions affects this or that behavior. As one wit put it recently, having lost it during the radical behaviorism era of Skinner and others, psychology has finally regained its mind!

When considering individuals who are low in health and fitness and wish they were not so, or who suffer performance decrements in physical activities of importance to them, then motivation matters. Consequently, I am limiting my comments to motivational issues. When we discuss motivation, we refer to those personality factors, social variables, and/or cognitions that come into play when a person undertakes a task at which he or she is evaluated, enters into competition with others, or strives to attain a standard of excellence, either self-imposed or externally imposed. The determinants of motivation are assumed to be evoked in such situations that drive achievement or motivate behaviors. The behaviors we typically assume to be under the influence of motivational constructs are behavioral intensity or effort (trying hard), persistence (keep trying hard), and choice of activity in which to engage.

Learned Helplessness and Attribution Retraining

When motivation matters, several lines of research are relevant. The first one I wish to discuss is the area called *learned helplessness*. Learned helplessness is the perception that one's responses and the occurrence of failure are independent; that is, one has no control over negative events. Helpless individuals believe failure is inevitable or insurmountable

(Dweck, 1980). In contrast, some people believe that their responses and the occurrence of outcomes are dependent; that is, one has control over positive and negative outcomes. These individuals are called *mastery oriented*, and they believe that successes may be repeated and mistakes rectified (Dweck, 1980).

In terms of behavior, failure has different effects on helpless versus mastery individuals. When helpless people experience failure, effort is curtailed, strategies deteriorate, and performance typically gets worse over time. Indeed, these individuals often fail to complete tasks performed successfully earlier and experience performance deterioration. When mastery people experience failure, the effects are completely opposite in that effort is escalated, concentration is intensified, alternative strategies are explored and developed, and performance is enhanced. These people persist in their behavior. Intuitively, one might argue that the best predictor of these diverse behaviors would be the level of ability of the performer; that is, high-ability people would be mastery oriented and low-ability people would be helpless oriented. This is not the case. High-ability people are often helpless in the face of failure, and low-ability people are often the persisters and try the hardest when failing. What distinguishes the helpless and mastery-oriented individuals are the cognitions these people hold about their successes and failures.

Research demonstrates that the cognitions held by helpless individuals are very different from those held by mastery-oriented individuals. The cognitions measured in these situations are typically causal attributions to success and failure. Helpless individuals hold stable attributions about their failures, such as perception of low ability, which implies that failure will continue in the future. Why try hard if failure is inevitable? Mastery individuals on the other hand hold unstable attributions about their failures, such as insufficient effort, bad luck, or an incorrect strategy, so that future success remains possible if more effort or a different strategy is employed (Dweck, 1975, 1980; Weiner, 1972, 1974, 1979).

The performance persisters and the performance deterioraters clearly have different constellations of cognitions. But do these cognitions cause the typical behavioral responses described above? Dweck (1975) argued that, if so, then it should be possible to change cognitions and alter the performance of individuals.

Dweck (1975) decided to alter the cognitions of helpless individuals to determine if she could instill the cognitions typical of mastery-oriented individuals. To do this, she identified a group of helpless children and obtained baseline data on their reactions to failure before having the children undergo one of two treatment conditions. Half of the children received a success-only treatment. Some psychologists argue that poor reactions to failure are the result of a lack of confidence because these children haven't had enough success experiences to know how to act appropriately. Given success experiences, confidence would rise and bolster the children so that when failure does occur, the children continually apply effort and try. This is a perception many coaches hold, and the argument is that nothing begets success like success. There are even data to support that thinking (Feather, 1966).

The other half of the children in Dweck's (1975) study received attribution retraining. The children were taught that failure was the result of a lack of effort, an unstable attribute, and not necessarily the result of low ability. The experimenter instructed the children how to interpret their outcomes, and failure was always attributed to a lack of effort.

The results of the study were very illustrative. The children in the success-only treatment soon became helpless again when failure occurred after the treatment phase. The success-only treatment did not imbue the children with the cognitions necessary to counteract failure. The attributionally retrained children had a very different reaction. By the end of the experiment, these children showed no impairment and even improved their performance in the face of failure. In other words, the cognitions given by the attributional retraining improved performance and made the children more mastery oriented. This finding has been replicated with other populations in other situations (e.g., Andrews & Debus, 1978; Storms & McCaul, 1976).

There are direct implications for exercise and sport behavior. We can easily determine the helpless versus the mastery players in sport. Sport is a very public affair where success and failure is evident to everyone. Helpless individuals are probably motivated to avoid such situations (Dweck, 1980; Halliwell, 1980), or they drop out or are cut by coaches. Those who do participate because of peer pressure or other reasons are likely to display the deteriorating performance syndrome when failure looks likely. Mastery individuals, on the other hand, seek out such environments and strive to demonstrate their ability (Roberts, 1982; 1984b). These individuals are the persisters in sport environments.

There are individuals involved in sport who are highly gifted in terms of ability and have never really had to face up to failure. They may perform very well until suddenly faced with failure, may reflect the success-only syndrome of Dweck's (1975) study, and deteriorate in performance as soon as failure appears likely. In other words, they become helpless. A classic case may be Evonne Goolagong. When things were going well, she appeared invincible. When things were starting off poorly, however, her skills deteriorated rapidly and she perceived herself as having no control (Dweck, 1980). Mastery-oriented athletes never give up, and they change strategies in order to succeed. Ivan Lendl is such an example. In a grand-slam tennis final match in Paris, he was two sets down and actually had a match point against him before he fought back and beat his then arch rival John McEnroe in five sets. Although it is easier to recall mastery-oriented elite athletes, there are helpless-oriented elite athletes and only their superior skills protect them.

The same may be stated for exercise participants. There are many people below average in health and fitness who truly believe that losing weight or gaining fitness is beyond their control. How many times have we heard of individuals who blame their own metabolism for gaining weight? These are the people who go on diets or exercise regimens continually but who drop out very quickly because they perceive a lack of control over events. Mastery-oriented individuals are those who are the persisters and continue with diets and/or exercise regimens. My point is that what differs between these individuals are their attributions for success and failure, and it is this cognitive set that governs their behavior.

We need much more research in the area of attribution retraining in exercise and sport environments. Although the work thus far has been less than satisfactory, the area has a great deal of potential for health and sport psychology, particularly for those who are low in health and fitness and who perceive a lack of control over their own behaviors. A caution is in order, however, because the relevant attributions for retraining are very likely to be situation specific. There is evidence (Roberts, 1984b) that attributions in sport are different from attributions in other achievement settings. Thus, when we borrow our conceptual paradigms, we need to ensure that our attribution retraining variables are relevant for exercise and sport participants. We need to undertake some fundamental research to determine the relevant attributions underlying motivated behavior in the setting of interest to us. We must focus our research on the specific exercise and sport settings so that when we apply our knowledge it is relevant to the context.

The Achievement Goals of Individuals and Goal Setting

When motivation matters, a second area of research is also pertinent. This research area deals with the achievement goals of individuals and how they affect achievement behavior in exercise and sport. The achievement goal approach argues that, to understand the behavior of individuals, one must understand the *subjective meaning* of achievement within the situation for the individual. This is the approach that more recent conceptualizations of achievement motivation have taken (Maehr & Nicholls, 1980; Roberts, 1982, 1984b). Whether an individual demonstrates motivation to achieve depends upon the subjective meaning of achievement for that individual. More importantly, individuals may have more than one achievement goal. Thus the cognitive perspective to motivation eschews the unitary construct approach to motivation that has been used in the past.

It has been argued that individuals may hold one of three achievement goals relevant to sport motivation (Roberts, 1984b). These achievement goals differ in the cognitions underlying them and in the behaviors that emanate from these cognitions. The first goal is called *competitive ability* (Roberts, 1984b) and describes those who are motivated to demonstrate high ability and who avoid demonstrating low ability in valued achievement contexts. The individual's focus of attention is on other people and how his or her ability compares to that of others. These individuals constantly evaluate whether ability has been demonstrated. If the assessment is one of high ability, they try hard and expect to do well in the future. If they perceive low ability, then they do not exert effort and are likely to drop out if success is not forthcoming (Ewing, 1981; Roberts, 1984b).

The second goal is called *sports mastery* (Roberts, 1984b) and describes those who also wish to demonstrate ability, but the focus is on performing well rather than demonstrating higher ability. These individuals wish to improve or master a skill and are referred to as being task-involved or intrinsically motivated. They exhibit those behaviors typical of what Dweck (1980) calls mastery-oriented individuals.

The third goal is called *social approval* (Maehr & Nicholls, 1980; Roberts, 1984b) and describes those who wish to obtain social approval from significant others. For children, the significant others are coaches, parents, and peers. For older individuals, significant others are coaches, spectators, and peers. These individuals are motivated, not because they want to master a skill or demonstrate higher capacity than others, but because they seek social approval.

The above are the three goals identified as the most relevant for the competitive sport experience and exercise setting (Roberts, 1982; 1984b), and the extant literature supports the same (Duda, 1981; Ewing, 1981, Pemberton, 1986; Roberts, 1984a). The most important point to note is that the constellation of cognitions underlying each goal differs (Burton, 1983; Duda, 1981; Ewing, 1981). For example, Ewing (1981) found that, when she investigated the achievement goals of individuals who were participants, nonparticipants, or dropouts from the high school competitive sport experience, the various groups had substantially different cognitive sets. Dropouts were competitive-ability-oriented and were constantly comparing their ability to that of others. Ewing argued that the individuals who dropped out did so because they were failing to meet their achievement goal of demonstrating ability in sport and were, as a consequence, losing motivation. Those who remained in the experience, the persisters, were social-approval-oriented and were trying to please others. Ewing argued that sitting on the bench, being involved, and being loyal met the achievement goal of these people, and this is why they remained within the experience. Thus the motivation of individuals seems to be dependent upon the achievement goal and whether the individual perceives he or she is meeting that goal.

In an exercise setting, Pemberton (1986) used the achievement-goal approach to attempt to understand the motivation of exercise adherence when compared to nonadherence. First, she found that exercise participants do have their own particular constellation of cognitions that is different from that of sport participants. Second, when she looked at whether she could account for a significant amount of the behavioral variance of exercise adherence, her results indicated that the achievement-goal approach accounted for somewhat more behavioral variance than the self-motivation construct of Dishman and Gettman's (1980) psychobiological approach. Much more research is needed to verify these findings and determine the relevance of the goal-oriented approach to exercise adherence.

The theory and research briefly reported above demonstrates that individuals who are lower in average health, fitness, and performance may be that way because they have a different set of cognitions than those who are higher in health, fitness, and performance. Further, it is these various constellations of cognitions that determine the perception of individuals about whether they can improve their own health, fitness, and performance in the future. It is this line of research that has given impetus to cognitive intervention strategies to enhance behavior. Several strategies have been proposed (Bandura, 1977; Dweck, 1980; Hill, 1984), but the one most advocated in exercise and sport is goal setting.

The goal-setting research literature has been primarily an empirical approach to performance enhancement. For example, Locke and his colleagues investigated various performance goals and their impact on subsequent performance (Locke & Latham, 1985; Locke, Shaw, Saari, & Latham, 1981). The research documented that specific difficult goals lead to better performance than do vague or easy goals; short-term goals facilitate achievement of long-term goals; and goals affect performance (a) by affecting effort, persistence, and direction of attention and (b) by motivating strategy development. Feedback regarding progress is necessary to enhance performance, and goals must be accepted by individuals if they are to affect performance (Locke & Latham, 1985). Although this empirical approach has demonstrated the efficacy of goal setting, it is the work within the attribution and achievement-goal paradigms that has given conceptual impetus to the goal-setting approach (Hall, 1988; Roberts & Hall, 1988). The achievement goal approach gives direction to the appropriate goal-setting procedures in that goal setting attempts to enhance mastery perceptions and those cognitions consistent with a mastery orientation (Hall, 1988; Roberts, 1984a).

This approach has been attempted in sport. Using college-age varsity swimmers at Big Ten institutions, Burton (1983) set up a goal-setting program that focused on enhancing mastery cognitions. The investigation tested two general hypotheses. First, does goal setting teach athletes to set appropriate goals? Second, do athletes who set effective goals have cognitions consistent with those of people who are mastery oriented?

Burton's (1983) results show that the first hypothesis was supported in that the swimmers who set goals focused on mastery goals that made them more realistic in their performance expectancies. Of importance in this context, Hypothesis 2 was supported in that swimmers who set goals demonstrated significantly more optimal cognitions than those who did not. In addition, swimmers who set goals (i.e., developed a mastery-goal orientation) actually performed better.

In a goal-setting study investigating weight loss, Bandura and Simon (1977) found that overweight clients in a weight loss clinic who set specific goals and kept a daily log of their food consumption consumed significantly less food and lost more weight than clients in a control group who neither set goals nor kept a log. A third group that kept daily logs but did not set goals did not differ from the control group. Even though the study did not measure mastery cognitions, it may be argued that setting goals gave clients the perception of control and mastery over events and contributed to the enhanced behavior.

The above research in learned helplessness and achievement-goal orientation demonstrates the application of the cognitive approach to understanding exercise and sport behavior, especially for those who are considered below average on dimensions of importance to us. Further, the intervention strategies that emanate from the cognitive approach, procedures that may be generically labeled *cognitive restructuring*, seem to hold more potential than conditioning and behavioral intervention approaches. Indeed, cognitive restructuring is currently under investigation in medical schools. Called *experimental psychopathology*, cognitive restructuring is being considered as an alternative to psychopharmacological approaches. This is not meant to suggest that cognitive restructuring will replace more traditional approaches. Rather, the cognitive approach may be another weapon to remedy or modify the individual's ongoing stream of behavior.

There is an obvious need for more research in this area, but the research must be directed at understanding *why* motivation ebbs. This is why we need to understand the conceptual underpinning of motivation so that when we apply our intervention strategies, they emanate from an understanding of the determinants of motivated behavior.

Even though I have focused on the cognitive underpinning of the determinants of motivation and achievement behavior, this is not meant to imply that other determinants do not influence motivation. Further, the ultimate conceptual paradigm may be very different in character from the ones we are currently using. It is imperative, therefore, that those who conduct research in these areas be tolerant and accepting of the positions of others. Who knows whether the ultimate paradigm will be psychobiological or cognitive, or involve some other constructs. Thus, in our research, we must be consistent with our own conceptual perspective, but be open to the research and efforts of others. To my knowledge, there is no one path to the truth.

Future Directions in Sport Psychology Research

My perception of the future directions in sport psychology research involving motivational issues is obvious from my comments thus far. But for sport psychology in general, I believe we need to come to grips with fundamental issues that will be critical in the years ahead. The first is conceptual, the second methodological.

There has been an assault on the conceptual undergirding of sport psychology. It has been argued that hypotheses should be formulated for their relevance to practical problems, rather than for their relevance to theory (Martens, 1979). The extent to which the pendulum has swung toward practical issues is evident in the recent upsurge in publications on applied aspects, on such socially relevant issues as anxiety and aggression; the publication of a new journal, *The Sport Psychologist*, that is devoted entirely to applied issues; and in the formation of a new professional organization devoted solely to applied sport psychology. The emphasis on practical versus conceptual relevance as the appropriate model for generating hypotheses is only a superficial and cosmetic modification that diverts our attention from the fundamental issue. Practically relevant hypotheses, no less than theory-driven hypotheses, are based upon simple linear processing and sequential cause-and-effect models that are inadequate to describe the complexity of the individuals' cognitive set and the multidimensionality of the exercise and sport environments we are trying to understand (McGuire, 1973). The conceptual models we erect to describe psychological functioning fail to capture the true complexities of bidirectional causality, the use of feedback mechanisms, and the constellation of cognitions that characterize individuals in exercise and sport. The problem with both theory-driven and practice-driven hypotheses currently tested in exercise and sport is that both fail to attend to the complexities with which the variables are organized in the individual and social systems.

Sport psychologists in the future must create conceptual models that incorporate the multivariate complexity of information processing, bidirectional causality, cognitions, and feedback loops, because such models are more likely to capture the individual and social reality of individuals in exercise and sport. We must eschew the simplistic linear processing models that use too few variables and emphasize the distinction between dependent and independent variables. In the real world, effects are the result of multiple causes in complex interaction. Thus sport psychologists must spend more time creating appropriate hypotheses that emanate from an understanding of the cognitive complexity of the individual. We need to describe, document, and conceptually represent the cognitive functioning of the exercise and sport participant. Only then can we begin to consider the appropriate intervention strategies that may be appropriate for particular cognitive deficits undergirding deviant, inappropriate, or ineffectual behavior.

There are many procedures that can help in the generation of questions and hypotheses (see Feltz, 1987), but it is not the purpose of this paper to enumerate them. Rather, my thesis is that sport psychologists need to spend more time considering hypothesis generation. It is my experience that sport scientists spend too little time considering the appropriate model for hypothesis generation. This fact is reflected in our graduate education. We spend more time teaching students how to collect and analyze data than how to generate appropriate questions and hypotheses. Both are important, but the creative phase is more important (McGuire, 1973). If our questions are inappropriate, or worse, trivial, then it is hardly worth collecting data in the first place. To paraphrase Hebb, if a question is not worth doing, it is not worth doing well.

The methodological procedures used by sport psychologists have also come under attack. The major criticism has been that laboratory studies are sterile and do not capture the essence of the real sporting world (Martens, 1979, 1987). A flight from laboratory to field studies has characterized research in sport psychology of late. Although the emphasis on field experiments and studies is welcome in many respects and parallels the emphasis on practical rather than theoretical hypotheses, it is a tactical evasion that fails to address the issue. The major issue is that our methodology is still locked into a parametric, linear processing model in which we test hypotheses in simplistic A-affects-B sequential designs (McGuire, 1973). We define and operationalize independent and dependent variables and spend most of our time debating the efficacy of our operational definitions, power, and behavioral variance accounted for.

We worry more about the psychometric properties of the variables than about their conceptual relevance. We study data, not people.

In the social and cognitive systems we are investigating, we need to be aware that effects are the outcome of multiple causes in complex interaction. Therefore, our measurement procedures must be sensitive to these multiple causes acting in a bidirectional manner. We need multivariate, time-series designs that recognize the obsolescence of the current methodologies. We must change our research practice to better cope with the dirty data of the real world, where variables do not meet the neat criteria we demand of them to use our parametric analyses. We need to be more sensitive to nonparametric procedures that are conceptually relevant to the questions we ask. In short, we need to develop a measurement technology consistent with our new emerging paradigm in sport psychology.

Conclusion

Sport psychology is going through a period of deep soul searching in terms of developing a conceptual paradigm to drive our research and practice, in terms of the measurement technology to use, and in terms of the appropriate model to use in our delivery of psychological services. It is the first two with which I have dealt in my paper. They take precedence in my mind. I have argued that we must be more creative in developing our questions, taking into account the complexities of the individual and social systems. Further, I argue that we need to develop a measurement technology sensitive to naturally oscillating variables. It is only when we have the inevitable confrontation of data with theory that the shape of the new paradigm will become evident. Only then will the true signal of advancement be discernible from the random noise of frenetic research activity. I share Landers's lament (1983). Too few of us are concerned with theory development, and, until more of us become active and thoughtful on this issue, progress, when it occurs, will be slow.

References

Andrews, G.R., & Debus, R.L. (1978). Persistence and the causal perception of failure: Modifying cognitive attributions. *Journal of Educational Psychology*, **70**, 154-166.

Bandura, A. (1977). *Social learning theory*. Englewood Cliffs, NJ: Prentice-Hall.

Bandura, A., & Simon, K.M. (1977). The role of proximal intentions in self-regulation of refrectory behavior. *Cognitive Therapy and Research*, **1**, 177-193.

Burton, D. (1983). *Evaluation of goal-setting training on selected cognitions and performance of collegiate swimmers*. Unpublished doctoral dissertation, University of Illinois.

Deci, E.L. (1975). *Intrinsic motivation*. New York: Plenum.

Dishman, R.K., & Gettman, L.R. (1980). Psychobiologic influences on exercise adherence. *Journal of Sport Psychology*, **2**, 295-310.

Duda, J.L. (1981). A cross-cultural analysis of achievement motivation in sport and the classroom. Unpublished doctoral dissertation, University of Illinois.

Dweck, C.S. (1975). The role of expectations and attributions in the alleviation of learned helplessness. *Journal of Personality and Social Psychology*, **31**, 674-685.

Dweck, C.S. (1980). Learned helplessness in sport. In C.H. Nadeau, W.R. Halliwell, K.M. Newell, & G.C. Roberts (Eds.), *Psychology of motor behavior and sport—1979* (pp. 1-11), Champaign, IL: Human Kinetics.

Ewing, M.E. (1981). *Achievement orientations and sport behavior of males and females*. Unpublished doctoral dissertation, University of Illinois.

Feather, N.T. (1966). Effects of prior success and failure on expectations of success and subsequent performance. *Journal of Personality and Social Psychology*, **3**, 287-298.

Feltz, D.L. (1987). Advancing knowledge in sport psychology: Strategies for expanding our conceptual frameworks. *Quest*, **39**, 243-254.

Hall, H.K. (1988). *A social cognitive approach to goal setting: The effects of achievement goals and perceived ability*. Unpublished doctoral dissertation, University of Illinois.

Halliwell, W.R. (1980). A reaction to Dweck's paper on learned helplessness in sport. In C.H. Nadeau, W.R. Halliwell, K.M. Newell, & G.C. Roberts (Eds.), *Psychology of motor behavior and sport—1979* (pp. 12-18), Champaign, IL: Human Kinetics.

Harter, S. (1981). The development of competence motivation in the mastery of cognitive and physical skills: Is there still a place for joy? In G.C. Roberts & D.M. Landers (Eds.), *Psychology of motor behavior and sport—1980* (pp. 3-29), Champaign, IL: Human Kinetics.

Hill, K. (1984). Debilitating motivation and testing: A major educational problem—Possible solutions and policy applications. In R. Ames & C. Ames (Eds.), *Research on motivation and education* (Vol. 1, pp. 245-272). New York: Academic.

Kuhn, T.S. (1970). *The structure of scientific revolutions* (2nd ed.). Chicago: University of Chicago Press.

Landers, D.M. (1983). Whatever happened to theory testing in sport psychology? *Journal of Sport Psychology*, **5**, 134-151.

Locke, E.A., & Latham, G.P. (1985). The application of goal setting to sports. *Journal of Sport Psychology*, **7**, 205-222.

Locke, E.A., Shaw, K.N., Saari, L.M., & Latham, G.P. (1981). Goal setting and task performance: 1969-1980. *Psychological Bulletin*, **90**, 125-152.

Maehr, J.L. & Nicholls, J.G. (1980). Culture and achievement motivation: A second look. In N. Warren (Ed.), *Studies in cross cultural psychology* (pp. 221-267). New York: Academic Press.

Martens, R. (1979). About smocks and jocks. *Journal of Sport Psychology*, **1**, 94-99.

Martens, R. (1987). Science, knowledge, and sport psychology. *The Sport Psychologist*, **1**, 29-55.

McGuire, M.J. (1973). The yin and yang of progress in social psychology: Seven Koan. *Journal of Personality and Social Psychology*, **26**, 446-456.

Morgan, W.P. (1980). Sport personology. The credulous-skeptical argument in perspective. In W.F. Straub (Ed.), *Sport psychology: An analysis of athlete behavior* (pp. 330-339). Ithaca, NY: Movement.

Pemberton, C. (1986). *Achievement goals and exercise adherence*. Unpublished doctoral dissertation, University of Illinois.

Roberts, G.C. (1982). Achievement motivation in sport. In R. Terjung (Ed.), *Exercise and sport science reviews* (Vol. 10, pp. 236-269). Philadelphia: Franklin Institute Press.

Roberts, G.C. (1984a). Achievement motivation in children's sport. In J.G. Nicholls (Ed.), *Advances in motivation and achievement* (Vol. 3, pp. 251-281). Greenwich, CT: JAI Press.

Roberts, G.C. (1984b). Toward a new theory of sport motivation. The role of perceived ability. In J.M. Silva & R.S. Weinberg (Eds.), *Psychological foundations of sport* (pp. 214-228). Champaign, IL: Human Kinetics.

Roberts, G.C., & Hall, H.K. (1988). Motivational goals and performance. In P. Kunath, S. Mueller, & H. Schellenberger (Eds.), *Proceedings of the VII Congress of the European Association of Sport Psychology* (pp. 700-708). Leipzig, D.R.: Deutsche Hochschule für Körperkultur.

Rushall, B.S. (1979). *Psyching in sports*. London: Pelham.

Rushall, B.S. (1982). *The content of competition thinking strategies*. Paper presented at the Annual Symposium of the Canadian Society for Psychomotor Learning and Sport Psychology, Edmonton, Canada.

Siedentop, D. (1976). *Developing teaching skills in physical education*. Boston: Houghton-Mifflin.

Storms, M.D., & McCaul, K.D. (1976). Attribution processes and emotional exacerbation of dysfunctional behavior. In J.H. Harvey, W.J. Ickes, & R.F. Kidd (Eds.), *New directions in attribution research* (Vol. 1, pp. 143-164). Hillsdale, NJ: Erlbaum.

Straub, W.F. (1978). *Sport psychology: An analysis of athlete behavior*. Ithaca, NY: Movement.

Weiner, B. (1972). *Theories of motivation: From mechanisms to cognitions*. Chicago: Rand McNally.

Weiner, B. (1974). *Achievement motivation and attribution theory*. Morristown, NJ: General Learning Press.

Weiner, B. (1979). A theory of motivation for some classroom experiences. *Journal of Educational Psychology*, **71**, 3-25.

Exercise Research on Persons of Below-Average Health and Fitness: A Commentary

James S. Skinner

It is obvious from the papers presented that below-average health and fitness may be associated with certain problems; these can be biomechanical (injuries, orthopedic differences), physiological (obesity, inactivity), medical (chronic disease), or psychological (neuroses, depression). In addition, one type of problem may, and often does, lead to another (e.g., chronic inactivity may lead to obesity or coronary heart disease). Similarly, although exercise can be useful, it may cause biomechanical, physiological, or medical problems if done incorrectly. It may also be that increased exercise does not change the status or course of a problem or disease, but improves only the ability to adapt biomechanically, physiologically, and psychologically to any restrictions associated with a disorder.

Two types of people need careful and precise information in exercise (Skinner, 1987): those who are well above average in fitness (athletes) and those who are well below average in health and fitness (the elderly and patients with such diseases as coronary heart disease and emphysema that may adversely affect their ability to exercise).

Although health, fun, and fitness may result from intense training, improved performance is the primary goal of most athletes. Exercise scientists should work with the coach and athlete to (a) determine the specific characteristics of the activity; (b) decide on the relative importance of biomechanical, physiological, and psychological factors; and then (c) design detailed programs to specifically train those factors so that the particular athlete can perform as close to his or her genetic potential as possible.

At the other end of the continuum, disease-limited persons are probably more interested in improving their health. Fun and fitness are generally secondary, and performance per se is less important. These people need more precise and controlled guidance on how to improve their functional capacity and possibly to counteract further degeneration. Because of their status, the amount and rate of improvement may also be less.

Persons of below-average health and fitness not only need precise prescriptions to know the types of exercises to emphasize and to avoid, but also may have to exercise under varying degrees of supervision. Exercise scientists should work with health-care professionals to help these people.

Between the two extremes are the average people. Although performance, health, and appearance may be important, they usually exercise for fun and fitness. Generally speaking, precise information on exercise is not needed for someone to be active. Only when average people migrate toward either end of the continuum do they need more assistance. In other words, the more risk factors these apparently healthy people have, the longer and more they have been sedentary, or the more they wish to compete, the more important is their need for precise information.

It appears that those who need exercise most are often the ones who (a) do less, (b) are less motivated to exercise, (c) have more problems and limitations if they do, (d) need more guidance, and (e) have been studied less. Thus, a multidisciplinary approach to the prevention and treatment of problems associated with below-average health and fitness is warranted and will probably be most effective. What sort of research should be done? The following are just a few examples for those working in various areas of exercise science to consider.

Probably the most difficult period for many is that associated with the initiation of an exercise program. Can sport psychology help those who feel that they have no control over events in their lives? How can these people be helped to overcome the inertia associated with sedentary living? Do attitudes toward oneself and toward life change with exercise? Dishman (1984) suggests that people who remain active after 3 to 6 months have psychological and biological skills that neutralize or minimize situational barriers to exercise. Those who do not have these skills are prone to drop out and should be identified early so that modifications can be made to maximize the support that they need.

During the early stages of increased activity, signs of incomplete adaptation (fatigue, soreness, and pain) and injuries are more common. Can biomechanical research aid the below-average person to prevent injuries, improve performance, and increase enjoyment? Given that these people start at such low levels, we need to know the minimal combinations of frequency, duration, and intensity that will produce improvement. For example, there is a suggestion that the training threshold for the elderly may be about 40% $\dot{V}O_2$max (deVries, 1977), whereas it is generally considered to be 50% to 60% $\dot{V}O_2$max in younger adults.

How much improvement can be expected once an exercise program is begun? Why are there different responses to the same exercise program? Bouchard (1986) suggests that a major part can be explained by genetics, in that studies done in his laboratory find that some people are high responders (they have large increases in $\dot{V}O_2$max) and some are low responders (they have small increases) to the same 8-week training program. As well, there are early and late responders who have variable patterns and rates of improvement over the 8 weeks. Bouchard (1986) concludes that high-performance athletes are those who are genetically endowed and high responders. Although not mentioned, it may also be that many below-average persons are low responders. It is not known if they also tend to be late responders. If they are, then it is easier to understand why some less-endowed people become easily discouraged when they begin so low and improve so slowly.

Skinner and Riddell (1983) compared never-active men with formerly active men aged 30 to 39 years who had been inactive for at least 10 years. Although there were no differences in lifestyle, fitness, or attitude toward physical activity, formerly active men were more trainable in the rate and amount of improvement in $\dot{V}O_2$max after 4 and 8 weeks of identical training. These findings also suggest that people react differently to the same exercise program.

However, there may be a question about the training stimulus in these studies, because both used the commonly accepted intensity expressed as a percentage of $\dot{V}O_2$max. There may be another method for estimating intensity and for possibly equating the exercise stimulus among people with different levels of fitness, namely, using the concept of the lactate threshold (i.e., the power output where ventilation and blood lactate levels rise markedly; this generally occurs from 70% to 90% $\dot{V}O_2$max). If one assumes that the power output associated with this threshold represents a similar stimulus for change in cellular homeostasis, then exercise requiring a given $\dot{V}O_2$max may produce a wide range of stimulation in people with similar $\dot{V}O_2$max values but different thresholds (McLellan & Skinner, 1985). The whole area of what constitutes adequate and equal stimulation needs more research.

The problem of adherence to exercise programs is one that needs more multidisciplinary research. Oldridge (1986) reported on his earlier research findings that dropouts from an exercise program were generally blue-collar workers who smoked. This suggests that there are socioeconomic differences between those who continue to exercise and those who do not. It is not clear whether psychological, physiological, and biomechanical differences are also present.

People often understand the need to exercise to relieve a chronic problem (e.g., low back pain). Once relief is obtained, however, they revert to a sedentary lifestyle, only to have the problem come back. How can they be motivated to continue and to make these exercises a part of their regular routine?

Nearly 80% of all elderly persons have some chronic disability (arthritis, hypertension, coronary heart disease, obesity, emphysema, etc.) that limits or affects their participation in exercise and their enjoyment of life. What can exercise science do to prevent, postpone, or ameliorate these problems, thereby improving the quality of life and decreasing these chronic disabilities, with their associated medical and personal costs? What is the critical amount of exercise and what types should be done to increase the functional ability and independence of this ever-increasing population?

Our society gives a great deal of attention and positive feedback to the gifted (i.e., to those who probably need it the least). Because of the complexities, limitations, and multifaceted issues involved, those who are below average in health and fitness present a special challenge that is probably best handled in a multidisciplinary manner. Exercise scientists, especially those who collaborate with scientists from other disciplines, are in a unique position to increase the theoretical understanding of exercise and its practical application to this population.

References

Bouchard, C. (1986). Genetics of aerobic power and capacity. In R.M. Malina & C. Bouchard (Eds.), *Sport and human genetics* (pp. 59-88). Champaign, IL: Human Kinetics.

deVries, H.A. (1977). Physiology of physical conditioning for the elderly. In R. Harris & L.J. Frankel (Eds.), *Guide to fitness after fifty* (pp. 47-52). New York: Plenum Press.

Dishman, R.K. (1984). Motivation and exercise adherence. In J.M. Silva & R.S. Weinberg (Eds.), *Psychological foundations of sport* (pp. 420-434). Champaign, IL: Human Kinetics.

McLellan, T.M., & Skinner, J.S. (1985). Submaximal endurance performance related to the ventilatory thresholds. *Canadian Journal of Applied Sport Sciences*, **10**, 81-87.

Oldridge, N.B. (1986). Compliance and exercise prescription. In M.L. Pollock & D. Schmidt (Eds.), *Heart disease and rehabilitation* (pp. 629-646). New York: Wiley.

Skinner, J.S. (1987). General principles of exercise prescription. In J.S. Skinner (Ed.), *Exercise testing and exercise prescription for special cases* (pp. 21-30). Philadelphia: Lea & Febiger.

Skinner, J.S., & Riddell, J. (1983). Trainability of formerly active (10 years or more before) vs. never-active males aged 30-39 years. *Medicine and Science in Sports and Exercise*, **15**, 133.

SECTION C:
PERSONS OF ABOVE-AVERAGE HEALTH AND FITNESS

Improving Elite Performance Through Precise Biomechanical Analysis

Charles J. Dillman

For the purpose of this paper, future directions in biomechanics research will be focused upon the study of high-performance athletes (persons of above-average health and fitness). When dealing with this population, we must first ask the question, Why do elite athletes warrant individual attention as a research topic? Perhaps there are several differences in the biomechanics field whereby research with top athletes varies from investigations with persons of *average* health and fitness.

The direction of biomechanics research with elite athletes is more applied and is primarily focused upon improving performance. Investigations are designed as case studies, in which the objective is to improve the performance of a few highly select individuals. In addition, analyses of performance generally isolate relatively small differences that tend to be very significant at this high level of international competition. For example, in cross-country skiing, Dillman, India, and Martin (1980) determined that if *average* performers assume a more flexed body position (hip and knee flexion), they can improve their performance because they are placed in a more effective position to generate force and receive energy while skiing. However, the differences in elite athletes' performance are more detailed. Based upon research, Dillman and Martin (1980) determined that if elite cross-country skiers could increase their stride length by a relatively small amount (13 cm), they could significantly improve their performance (22 s) while skiing up a 500-m hill. Accomplishing this at the elite level requires attention to detailed changes in technique, consisting of holding the body weight back on the ski during the glide phase and creating a poling motion that keeps the ski gliding while poling.

The needs of the elite athlete are also different in terms of presentation of results. To keep these athletes interested in research, investigations have to be structured such that athletes can get feedback immediately on their individual problems. In addition, more frequent evaluations are necessary if progress is going to be made in improving the small details of performance.

All of these differences (i.e., case study approach, attention to small details of performance, immediate feedback, and consistent follow-up) have influenced current approaches to the study of elite athletes. Certainly, there will be even more dramatic changes in the future study of high-performance athletes and these advances will certainly have an impact on the entire field of biomechanics.

Current Status of Sports Biomechanics

Typically, an experimental approach has been used in conducting biomechanical studies to enhance the performances of elite athletes. To study a sports skill from a mechanical perspective, the researcher must obtain a scientific record of the performance. Traditionally, the standard methodology for acquiring these performance records has been high-speed cinematography. With special high-speed 16-mm cameras with precision frame-rate control, performances in any event can be filmed in two or three dimensions.

Once the films are developed, they are projected onto an electronic grid, which is used by an operator to convert frame-by-frame body positions manually into digital numbers that can be processed by a computer. This methodology provides reliable and valid data that describe the movement patterns (*kinematic analysis*), and, in limited cases, calculations can be made of the interaction of forces that were responsible for producing the motion (*kinetic analysis*). The main disadvantage of the cinematographical method is that it is very labor intensive (taking films, developing films, and doing manual digitization) and, therefore, does not provide an immediate presentation of results. However, high-speed cinematography is currently the only reliable technique for studying performance under competitive conditions such as the Olympic Games in Los Angeles.

In structured experimental situations (training sessions, laboratory testing, etc.), recent trends have indicated a move away from film to electronic methods to automate the data-collection process. Several of the more frequently used instruments are the following:

1. Force platform—measurement of ground reaction forces and stability analysis
2. Electrodynogram—portable system for measurement of pressure points under the feet
3. Selspot system—optical-electronic motion measurement system
4. Electromyography—measurement of the electrical activity produced by contracting muscles
5. Electronic transducers—electronic measurement of selected motion and force parameters

These computerized systems are employed in the field and in laboratories to collect data and, in some cases, provide immediate feedback to athletes and coaches.

Once the data have been collected through the manual digitization of films or the automatic computerized electronic devices, the analysis of performance is initiated. Analysis of performance usually focuses on the mechanical factors (stride length, the speed of a body part, the horizontal breaking force, etc.) that have been judged to have a significant influence upon the objective of the skill.

Evaluation of the performance data is usually based on (a) comparative reference data collected on the best athletes in the world, (b) application of the laws of mechanics, and (c) in limited cases, computer simulation and optimization of performance.

Based upon these comparative or computer evaluations, recommendations are made for improving the technical aspects of performance. In some cases, related training improvements are also recommended based upon the biomechanical observation of the performance. Repeated analyses/evaluations are now being conducted for the first time within the Olympic program to determine if the observed problems in performance are being corrected.

It is difficult to determine the exact impact that biomechanics research/service has had upon elite athletes. However, feedback from coaches and athletes has been very positive, and, in general, they state that biomechanics has assisted them in their quest to be the best that they can be, with respect to their own capabilities.

Future Directions

Future developments and directions in sports biomechanics research as it relates to elite athletes will probably focus upon improvements in three areas: (a) techniques of data collection, (b) evaluation schemes, and (c) presentation of results.

Rapid advances are already being made in the development of new technologies to automate the process of motion analysis. Two systems, Vicon[1] and ExpertVision Motion Analysis[2], are video based for rapid analysis of performance. These systems track and digitize the brightest or most contrasting points in the field. Usually, reflective markers are placed on the athletes, and these points are tracked by a video processor. Motion data can be calculated a few minutes after a performance and immediately analyzed for review by the scientists and coach. Another system, CODA 3,[3] is optically based and has the potential of providing real-time motion data.

All three of these automated-motion-analysis systems have distinct advantages and disadvantages for various applications in sport, but they collectively represent the new directions within biomechanics. Within the foreseeable future, video will replace film in a majority of applications as the major technology for recording motion. In a similar fashion, the

---

[1]VICON, Oxford Metrics Inc., 11526 53rd St. North, Clearwater, FL.

[2]ExpertVision Motion Analysis System, Motion Analysis Corporation, 1211 North Dutton Ave., Suite E, Santa Rosa, CA.

[3]CODA 3, Movement Techniques Limited, Unit 5, The Technology Centre, Epinal Way, Loughborough, England.

collection of movement data will be completely automated by these video and/or optical scanning devices. Limited applications will still require manual digitization of motion, which will be completed on video-based systems rather than the current techniques of film analysis. Thus, in the near future, a scientist or teacher will be able to take a video of an event, place the video into a computer, and have a performance analysis completed automatically in several minutes.

Future developments in the electronic recording of motion will probably produce the greatest advancement in methodology. Athletes will wear smaller and more portable computerized systems in data collection sessions to measure various factors of performance. These wearable microprocessors will be linked to portable field computers for immediate analysis of the data. These devices will also be used in training to monitor performance variables and provide feedback to the athlete about his or her performance. The electrodynogram and the Adidas computerized shoe are the first examples of how electronic devices will be used in the future to monitor and improve performance.

Tremendous improvements in the biomechanical evaluation of performance will occur in the future through the use of computer modeling that optimizes performance. For example, the performance evaluation scheme of the future will include the following:

1. Immediate analysis of performance using video or electronic systems
2. Computerized displays of performance at training sites that simulate corrections relative to recent performance
3. Capability of the computer to optimize performance with respect to various limits and make recommendations for improvement
4. Reanalysis of repeated trials to follow and evaluate specific progress toward achieving optimal performance

Thus evaluation of performance will be significantly improved by such devices, which will enable coaches to make precise recommendations for each individual. Scientific systems not only will be used to study performance, but also will become part of the athlete's training equipment.

If the biomechanics field is to advance in the practical application of knowledge, new methods of data presentation will have to be developed. Although written materials aid the researcher and document results, the results of biomechanics research in the future will be presented to coaches and athletes using computer graphics, video, and laser disc summaries of scientific investigations. Results of studies and individual analyses will be available via a worldwide computer network for rapid and effective transmission of information. Thus future directions of sports biomechanics research will include automated systems for rapid analysis of performance; effective schemes of individual analysis that precisely determine the limiting factors of performance; simpler and more effective presentation of results; and a worldwide communication network for the storage, analysis, and transmission of biomechanical information.

Although rapid advances will be made in biomechanics and other individual areas of sports science, it will be the integration of these various fields that will produce the greatest gains in the future. If the goal of this aspect of research is to improve performance of elite athletes, then future progress can be effectively realized only through the study of sports skills from a multidisciplinary viewpoint. The high-performance athlete needs to be viewed as a total person with complex performance problems. Thus, in the future, more interdisciplinary studies will be conducted with elite athletes to determine the true causes of various performance problems. This interdisciplinary approach (e.g., psychology and biomechanics) will result in tremendous advances in the field of sports science.

As improvements are made in the analysis and evaluation of sports performance, there is no doubt that sports scientists will play an even greater role in the preparation of top athletes for international and Olympic competitions. The future will be an exciting time in which to be conducting research in the relatively new and developing discipline of sports science.

References

Dillman, C.J., India, D., & Martin, P.E. (1980). Biomechanical determinants of effective cross-country skiing techniques. In E. Hixon (Ed.), *Sports medicine for the cross-country skier*. Englewood Cliffs, NJ: Prentice-Hall.

Dillman, C.J., & Martin, P.E. (1980). Biomechanics of cross-country skiing. *Journal of Contemporary Orthopaedics*, **2**, 259-262.

Sport Psychology in Its Own Context: A Recommendation for the Future

William P. Morgan

There is an inherent danger in talking about future directions in sport psychology research, or the research literature of any of the subdisciplines within the exercise and sport sciences for that matter, and the danger stems from the potential problem of perpetuating the *disciplinary isolationism* that has characterized the history of this young field. The symposium organizers, however, have asked that I present a general overview of the state of the art in sport psychology research, and then focus on future trends I foresee, as well as those I would like to see. Even though it is unjustifiable from a scientific perspective to focus on sport psychology research and hence perpetuate the status quo (i.e., isolationism), such an approach can be justified on the grounds that most of the research in sport psychology has been carried out in an isolated context.

The organizers of the symposium have also instructed speakers to devote about 65% of their talks to a general overview of the state of the art in a given area, and the remaining 35% is supposed to focus on the future (i.e., up to about the year 2000). There is, in my view, far more to say about the future of research in sport psychology, and this, along with the limited research in this field, calls for an essential reversal of the prescribed formula. Actually, a ratio of 20:80 would be far more appropriate than one of 65:35.

Because this paper deals with sport psychology research for persons of above-average health and fitness, several guidelines or operating rules will be established. First, an individual with average health and fitness would receive a T-score of 50 ($\pm$10) on health and fitness measures. Second, an individual with a T-score of 60 on the same measure(s) would be above average, and those with T-scores of 70 would be well above average. Most college athletes, for example, would probably score at least one standard deviation above the general college population on fitness measures related to their particular sport, and those falling 2.5 or 3.0 standard deviations above the population mean could probably be classified as *elite*. It is merely caprice, however, that permits us to talk of persons being above average in fitness, and such a classification does not exceed an ordinal level on the measurement hierarchy. Although this issue could be a very significant problem in biomechanics, medicine, or physiology, the absence of an established research base in sport psychology renders the matter academic.

The State of the Art

A total of 1,203 articles appeared in the *Journal of Sport Psychology, Medicine and Science in Sports and Exercise, The Physician and Sportsmedicine,* and the *Research Quarterly for Exercise and Sport* during the 5-year period from 1980 to 1984. It is estimated that only 21 (1.8%) dealt with sport psychology research involving persons of above-average health and fitness. A summary of this analysis[1] appears in Table 1. There are many possible reasons for this statistic, but as with any area, it is much easier to describe than it is to explain; that is, the statistic is merely descriptive. Nevertheless, the statistic is important because one cannot devote much attention to any topic that has not been seriously researched.

Table 1 Frequency of Sport Psychology Articles Involving Persons of Above-Average Health and Fitness Appearing in Selected Exercise and Sport Science Journals During the Period 1980 to 1984

Journal	Total articles	Sport psychology research papers
Journal of Sport Psychology	132	10
Medicine and Science in Sports and Exercise	345	1
Research Quarterly for Exercise and Sport	294	4
The Physician and Sportsmedicine	432	6
Total	1,203	21

The 1984 Olympic Scientific Congress held in Eugene, Oregon, tells part of the story. Many papers and symposia involving sport psychology focused on the delivery of services or clinical applications as opposed to basic or applied research. Not only has there been very little sport psychology research dealing with persons of above-average health and fitness, but the limited research has been characterized by serious statistical and design inelegancies.

[1]Appreciation is expressed to John S. Raglin, project assistant, Sport Psychology Laboratory, University of Wisconsin-Madison for his assistance in this analysis.

It is also noteworthy from a historical perspective that the North American Society for the Psychology of Sport and Physical Activity (NASPSPA) was founded in 1966, and most sport psychologists were concerned with research issues of an applied or basic nature during the subsequent decade. Indeed, I recall two meetings of NASPSPA during the 1960s in which competent, well-intentioned clinicians were openly scorned because they had the audacity to present clinical case material at a ''scientific meeting.'' The pendulum has swung, of course, and the contemporary *zeitgeist* calls for application, and there is seldom, if ever, a question even raised as to whether or not these applications *work*. The test of any model, needless to say, is simply, Does it work? At any rate, future research in sport psychology will be impaired if the applied movement continues to gain momentum.

There are many other problems surrounding the research in this field, and Dishman (1982) has previously classified this research as being applied, descriptive, or predictive. He has also indicated that most of the clinical research has been applied, the social psychological research has been descriptive, and the psychobiologic research has been predictive. Very little of this research has had an explanatory focus, and as a result few mechanisms have been identified. Also, most of this research, irrespective of how it is classified, has been atheoretical. Furthermore, the limited theoretical research has relied on borrowed theory (e.g., psychoanalytic, drive, factor, attribution, self-efficacy, and/or cognitive), rather than models or theories grounded in sport psychology.

The absence of models and theories in this area should be viewed as a symptom rather than a problem. Another important symptom is the absence of systematic inquiry resulting in the development of technology. Although it is possible to theorize and build models in many areas without an existing technology, the interdependence of science and technology is the usual case. Discussion as to the relative merits of science and technology will continue, as will the debate over the importance of scientists versus technologists. In most cases, however, science and technology should be viewed in a symbiotic context. I am not arguing here that we have theory for the sake of theory, or science for the sake of science. Indeed, there is nothing as bad as a bad theory (Bass, 1974), and science for the sake of science is scientism, not science.

Many years ago, White (1938), in a rather provocative essay, argued that psychology is not ''the study of the mind,'' but rather, ''psychology is what psychologists do'' (p. 370). White also pointed out that ''science is not merely a collection of facts and formulas. It is preeminently a way of dealing with experience'' (p. 369). White concluded this important essay by stating that ''science is sciencing.'' If one were to employ White's logic, sport psychology could be defined as what sport psychologists do. Although psychology is best defined as what psychologists do, science sometimes translates to scientism, and sport psychology in particular often translates to folklore (or less).

If a model or theory is so narrow, myopic, or inflexible that serendipitous results are not permitted to surface, there can be little hope for the inquiry underway. A problem in this regard has been that sport psychology researchers have employed theoretical approaches from the field of general psychology in an effort to support or refute the underlying theory, rather than attempting to describe, explain, and predict behavior in exercise and sport settings. In other words, the research foci has tended to be on improving our understanding of psychological theory (e.g., attribution theory), rather than our understanding of exercise and sport. Furthermore, this research has usually been of a descriptive, rather than a predictive or explanatory, nature (e.g., Lau & Russell, 1980).

There is a new field of study known as *garbology* and garbologists maintain that one can make valid inferences about individuals by examining their garbage. There is a sport psychology "trash heap," and it contains discarded theories such as Freudian psychoanalytic theory, Hullian drive theory, Cattellian personality theory, locus of control theory, and attribution theory. Careful inspection of this garbage dump reveals extensions and operationalizations of these theories scattered about. The "rusting tin cans" on this dump, for example, are the TAT, TMAS, 16-PF, and so on. Also, if one waits a little while, a dump truck will surely back up with cognitive psychology scattered throughout its hold, along with numerous self-efficacy and self-appraisal measures. This prediction is based upon Averill's (1983) analysis of historical trends in psychology during the 20th century, and these trends are summarized in Figure 1. Averill points out that cognitive psychology, the current thrust in sport psychology, peaked in general psychology about 15 years ago (i.e., 1970). Many sport psychologists, especially those who rely exclusively on cognitive psychology, seem to believe that the head does not have a body—similar dualistic problems exist in physiology because many exercise physiologists seem to believe that the body doesn't have a head. In other words, sport psychologists are not alone in their penchant for dualistic conceptualization. Theory, however, has been adopted by sport

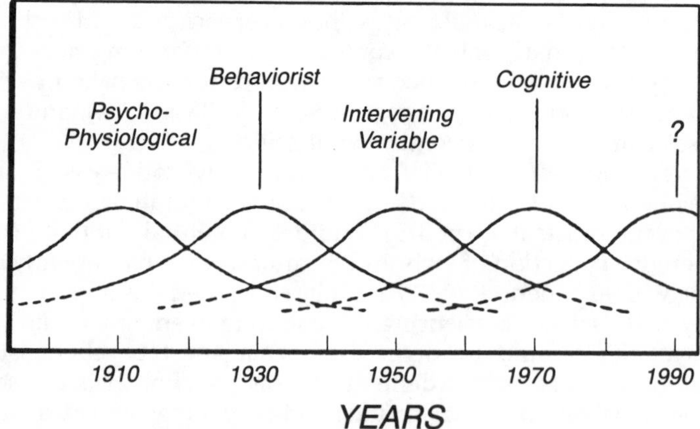

Figure 1. Historical Trends in Theories of Emotion During the 20th Century. From "Studies on Anger and Aggression: Implications for Theories on Emotion" by J.R. Averill, 1983, *American Psychologist*, **38**, p. 1145. Copyright 1983 by *American Psychologist*. Reprinted by permission.

psychologists, used (and misused), and finally discarded in anger or dissatisfaction because it did not do what it was not supposed to do (i.e., "work" in sport psychology). An excellent illustration of this point appears in a seminal piece by Spence (1971) titled "What Can You Say About a Twenty-Year-Old Theory That Won't Die?" Sport psychologists must give up their "ready, shoot, aim" paradigms in favor of theoretical, conceptually relevant, and systematic approaches. This does not mean, however, that prevailing theories should be borrowed from academic psychology. Indeed, progress will not occur in sport psychology until theoretical formulations are developed within the context of exercise and sport.

There are several problems associated with presenting state-of-the-art summaries of the status of research and practice in a given field. First, the knowledge broker may intentionally or unintentionally present an inaccurate characterization of the field. Second, there is always a good chance that significant exceptions to the generalization exist. I would like to briefly address this latter issue before proceeding, that is, I would like to qualify the generalization. First of all, there are sport psychologists such as Suinn (1985), who would not agree with much of the overview presented in the first portion of this paper. In a recent paper, Suinn (1985) concluded that "within a decade, sport psychology has developed substantially as a discipline with its own identity, technology, and research base" (p. 328). In point of fact, however, at least here in the United States, sport psychology lacks an identity. Rather than saying that the field has its own identity, I think it might be more appropriate to talk in terms of its notoriety, because most sport psychologists lack training in sport science and psychology. Seabourne, Weinberg, Jackson, and Suinn (1985) have recently attempted to create a technology in support of the performance enhancement intervention known as visuo-motor behavior rehearsal (VMBR) (Suinn, 1984), but this represents the exception, not the rule, in sport psychology. Finally, there is not a research base in the usual scientific sense. Most of the applications that are performed are based upon research conducted in general psychology, not sport psychology. Also where research has been carried out in sport settings, there has been a striking absence of external validity (i.e., generalizability). In other words, you cannot necessarily generalize from one sport group to another, nor can you generalize with confidence within a given sport (e.g., from the average to the above average on to the elite). If one is interested in evaluating whether or not a given psychological intervention will enhance the performance of elite speed skaters, for example, he or she must conduct investigations with athletes from the target group. This has generally not been the case in sport psychology up to this point.

Other exceptions to the generalization presented in this overview would be the writings and research of Dishman (1982, 1983), who has operated largely at a theoretical level. Although his contributions have been significant from a scientific and technological perspective, most of this research has dealt with individuals who possess average or below-average health and fitness. This is certainly not intended to be a criticism, and it is likely that a far greater impact potential exists for sport psychology research in the population sector he has elected to study. It is also important to recognize that some sport psychologists such as Heyman (1982) and Landers (1981) have argued for, and employed, empirical-theoretical models in their research and applications.

One of the most significant developments in sport psychology during the past 20 years has been the theory of arousal and performance advanced by Hanin (1978). This theory maintains that each athlete has a zone of optimal functioning (ZOF), and this is determined empirically for each individual. Hanin's research has clearly demonstrated that (a) performance is not correlated with anxiety, (b) female and male athletes do not differ in state anxiety precompetitively, and (c) anxiety is not governed by the task. Hanin has also demonstrated that athletes possess the ability to predict the level of state anxiety that they will experience prior to a forthcoming competition (prospective analyses), and they are also able to accurately recall how they felt prior to a previous competition (retrospective recall). Furthermore, in Hanin's research, some athletes consistently have their best performances when they are quite relaxed, whereas others perform their best when highly aroused. Others seem to perform their best when moderately aroused. Hence, any effort to enhance the performance of a team by means of psyching or relaxation procedures would be doomed to failure because such procedures would be inappropriate for a substantial number of individuals. In other words, Hanin's research has clearly demonstrated that interventions designed to manipulate the level of arousal in an effort to enhance performance must take the individual's (not the team's) previously determined ZOF into account.

It should also be pointed out that some of the best known clinical sport psychologists (Suinn, 1984, 1985) have provided services that are based upon established psychological principles and theory. Unfortunately, these theoretical-empirical models are probably outnumbered by 25 or 50 to 1. In other words, there is very little systematic sport psychology research currently underway with persons of above-average health and fitness, and a principal reason for this unfortunate state of affairs is that delivery of psychological services has become the primary focus of many workers in this area. This development is unfortunate because there is not an adequate research base for much of the application that is taking place. Also, the consumer (e.g., athlete or coach) is usually unaware that the provider (e.g., sport psychologist) does not have evidence to support the services he or she is providing. It is also likely that the provider is probably unaware that the services do not work either. The next section of this paper will deal with the future of sport psychology research for persons with above-average health and fitness.

Future Directions

Ethical Considerations

It is imperative that sport psychologists adhere to *Ethical Principles in the Conduct of Research with Human Participants* developed by the APA

Committee on Ethical Standards in Psychological Research, and *Principles for the Care and Use of Animals* developed by the APA Committee on Animal Research and Experimentation when conducting research with humans or animals. Although NASPSPA has developed its own ethical code, this code has not been enforced in the past. Also, there has never been a compelling argument presented concerning the reason why sport psychologists need an ethical code that is greater, or less, than the APA code. Second, the reports of some sport psychologists at the 1984 Olympic Scientific Congress suggest that certain investigators do not adhere to the APA or the NASPSPA code.

A lesson can be learned from our colleagues in exercise physiology because they did not reject the Nuremberg Code or Declaration of Helsinki, nor did they feel it was necessary to establish a separate ethical code for use in conducting sport research. Exercise physiologists tend to view themselves as physiologists, and they make every effort to conform to national and international guidelines in conducting animal and human research. Why shouldn't sport psychologists adhere to the ethical codes established for psychologists in general? It is inconceivable that rational men and women would argue that teaching, service, and research is governed by different ethical principles as one moves across campus, that is, from the psychology department to the physical education department.

It is necessary that major changes be made in the traditional approach to sport psychology research, and, regardless of the theoretical approaches or objectives of the research, it is recommended that future research in sport psychology with persons of above-average health and fitness, as well as research with animals, be conducted in compliance with established APA codes.

Health and Performance

There has been a tendency for sport psychologists to be concerned with the influence of psychological variables, such as anxiety, on performance. An equally important issue concerns the extent to which involvement in sport, or noncompetitive recreational activities (e.g., jogging), influences psychological variables such as anxiety, depression, self-esteem, and so on. For a paradigm shift to occur, it will be necessary for sport psychologists to begin to approach the questions they ask in a fundamentally different way. Rather than examining antecedent or stimulus variables, they must address consequent or response variables. This will require that parameterization be carried out within the context of health rather than performance.

There has been very little research involving the consequence of involvement in sport, acute or chronic, on pandemic health-related constructs such as anxiety and depression. Although there is evidence suggesting that acute physical activity is associated with reductions in anxiety, and although chronic physical activity is associated with reduction in depression in persons of below-average and average health and fitness, there is an absence of comparable research with individuals scoring above average in fitness. There is limited evidence, however, suggesting that intense training actually results in elevated anxiety and depression in athletes (Morgan, 1985b). It is thought that excessive training (i.e., overtraining) is responsible for the increased mood disturbance often seen in athletes. Whether one is concerned with the mental health benefits of regular exercise in persons of average or below-average health and fitness, or mood disturbance associated with overtraining in persons of above-average health and fitness, the mechanisms involved in the mediation of such changes must be elucidated.

The most compelling hypothesis at the present time suggests that alterations in brain monoamines are responsible for both positive and negative alterations in mood following chronic exercise. Another popular hypothesis, but one that is not supported by empirical evidence, maintains that alterations in brain peptides such as the beta endorphins bring about the observed changes. Neither hypothesis, however, can be directly tested with a human model. Confirmation or refutation of these hypotheses will require the use of animal models, and this will be discussed in the next section. It is recommended that future research in sport psychology with persons of above-average health and fitness focus on the consequences of involvement in sport and exercise.

Animal Models

It is somewhat surprising that animal models have seldom been employed in sport psychology research, because the theoretical basis for much of the research in this area is derived from animal models. Hullian drive theory, for example, was used extensively by sport psychologists during the period 1965 to 1975, and this theory was based largely upon animal experimentation (i.e., rat models). Much of the theory involving reinforcement and goal setting has been derived from rat and pigeon models, whereas concepts such as *learned helplessness* have been based upon dog models, and these theoretical views have been employed in sport psychology. In other words, sport psychologists have not hesitated to adopt theories and models based upon animal research, but they have not elected to employ animal models in their own work.

The absence of animal models in sport psychology is due to many factors, but certainly the training of sport psychologists, and the kinds of questions they have historically asked (i.e., nonmechanistic), probably represent the primary reasons. There are important and legitimate questions that remain to be asked and answered in sport psychology, but it will not be ethically possible to employ human models in this research.

One of the most significant areas of research in sport psychology at the present time involves the influence of exercise on mental health, and this applies to persons with below-average and average levels of health and fitness, as well as those scoring above average (Morgan & Goldston, 1987). Some investigators have demonstrated that it is possible to reduce depression in persons with mild to moderate depression (Greist, 1987), as well as those with more severe depression (Martinsen, 1987). Paradoxically, it has also been shown that overtraining is associated with the development of depression in previously healthy young men and women (Morgan, 1985b). However, the mechanisms underlying these affective changes remain obscure.

Overtraining is known to result in depression and staleness (Morgan, 1985b), but it would not be ethical for an investigator to produce psychopathology intentionally in humans for the purpose of studying this disease process. This problem could be addressed with an animal model because training, sacrifice, and direct assay of brain tissue would be possible. Although many psychologists are reluctant to employ animal models, Suomi (1982) has argued that it is not possible to employ human models to study human psychopathology. Furthermore, Suomi (1982) points out that an investigator would be ethically obligated to intervene and treat psychopathology if it were to be produced in previously healthy, experimental subjects. Therefore, it would not be possible to overtrain humans intentionally with the goal of producing depression. If this were to occur in a naturalistic setting, it would be unethical to withhold treatment. Also the direct study of brain metabolism would currently not be possible with a human model.

It is difficult to say whether there has been opposition to reductionism in sport psychology research, or whether investigators in this young field simply do not think in reductionistic terms. The latter is probably the case, because there have not been any antireductionistic papers in the sport psychology literature. At any rate, it is widely recognized that some of the most significant advances in psychiatry and clinical psychology have resulted from animal research (Suomi, 1982).

There have been several examples of animal research in the field of sport psychology. It is noteworthy that the father of American sport psychology, Coleman Roberts Griffith, maintained a rat colony in his Athletic Research Laboratory at the University of Illinois during the period 1925 to 1932 (Kroll & Lewis, 1970). There was an absence of reference to animal research in sport psychology until 1968 when Hutton (1970) reported on the use of a water maze for learning research with small animals. In a study of the influence of chronic exercise on emotionality in rats, Weber and Lee (1968) observed that forced exercise (e.g., swimming) was associated with lower levels of emotionality than voluntary exercise or a sedentary condition. These findings were subsequently replicated by Tharp and Carson (1975). It is also known that exercise alters brain levels of selected neurotransmitters (e.g., norepinephrine and serotonin), and there is limited evidence that brain levels of beta-endorphin increase when rats are forced to exercise (Morgan, 1985a; Ransford, 1982). It has also been reported by Olson and Morgan (1982) that brain levels of norepinephrine differ in rats classified as "stable" or "emotional." A rat model of psychopathology for use in exercise science has been developed, and it is possible to quantify stability and emotionality in rats before and following acute and chronic exercise (Morgan, Olson, & Pedersen, 1982). The existing correlational research suggests that chronic physical activity alters behavior and brain neurochemistry in rats, but this has not been demonstrated longitudinally.

The animal research of Brown and Van Huss (1973), Tharp and Carson (1975), Morgan, Olson and Pedersen (1982), Olson and Morgan (1982), and Weber and Lee (1968) opens the way for the study of exercise and emotionality, from the perspective of both eustress and stress. This work also posits that central monaminergic mechanisms mediate alterations in affect. As mentioned earlier, it is not ethically possible to induce depression, anxiety state, hypertension, or other stress responses in humans for the purpose of studying a given disease process. Furthermore, it is not possible to directly study central mechanisms even where such pathology occurs nonexperimentally as a consequence of being involved in exercise or sport. Therefore, it is recommended that future research in sport psychology employ animal models in the study of mental health and sports medicine problems such as depression and staleness.

Multidisciplinary Models

It is not possible for a given individual, operating from the perspective of a given discipline (e.g., psychology or physiology) or subdiscipline (e.g., sport psychology or exercise physiology), even to raise the right questions much less to answer the right questions. It is possible for the unique individual to become a true hybrid (e.g., bioengineer, exercise physiologist, engineering psychologist, or sport psychologist), but it is much more efficient for competent, well-trained individuals from two or more disciplines to join forces as an interdisciplinary or multidisciplinary team. That is why, at the outset of this paper, I voiced my concern about even talking about research in sport psychology. In other words, I believe we need to become problem-oriented in our applied research, and where the problem has been identified (e.g., staleness, exercise addiction, motivation, goal setting, depression, or arousal), the question to be asked should be developed by a multidisciplinary team in most cases. Also, once the question has been framed, the attempted solution should be based upon a multidisciplinary attack. Structuring the research team may be possible within a given department or institute, but, more likely, it will be necessary to draw upon disciplines and subdisciplines outside of a given research unit.

Consider a problem, for example, such as efficiency of movement. It is not surprising that biomechanists, physiologists, psychologists, and engineers have historically approached the study of efficiency from different vantage points because they possess different disciplinary perspectives. Furthermore, very few university departments or research institutes here in the United States possess multidisciplinary research groups. An alternative approach is to develop a research consortium for the purpose of studying a single problem. An example of this approach would be the multidisciplinary research team brought together by Michael L. Pollock at the Institute for Aerobics Research in 1974 for the purpose of attempting to understand the factors governing performance in elite male distance runners. The results of this research effort were summarized in a special issue of the *Annals of the New York Academy of Science* (Milvy, 1977). A very similar approach was recently carried out with elite female distance runners at the Georgia Institute of Technology. Although this consortium was organized by exercise physiologists (Phillip Sparling and Russell Pate), the research team also included specialists in biochemistry, cardiology, psychology, anthropometry, biomechanics, pulmonary function, nutrition, and internal medicine.

Research consortiums represent an excellent solution to the disciplinary and subdisciplinary isolationism that has characterized exercise and sport science in general, and sport psychology in particular. An alternative approach, and one that I hope will become common in the future, would be the development of multidisciplinary teams of exercise and sport scientists within our departments. It would be naive to think, however, that such an assemblage of scientists (with their own ids, egos, and superegos) could work effectively together on a day-to-day basis—especially if they have not been trained in this tradition. Nevertheless, multidisciplinary research teams could, and should, become a reality at our major research institutions. Otherwise, we will continue to live, learn, love, procreate, and work in the isolated, sterile, meaningless (but safe), dusty, pedestrian, disciplinary fortresses where most of us have spent the greatest portion of our careers.

Another approach that is not nearly as difficult is to organize a multidisciplinary symposium for the purpose of addressing a specific issue. An example of this approach would be the Symposium on Efficiency of Movement organized by Peter Cavanagh and recently published in *Medicine and Science in Sports and Exercise* (Cavanagh & Kram, 1985). Symposia of this nature are very important for a number of reasons. First, investigators from various disciplines and subdisciplines present state-of-the-art summaries of research in their respective areas that bear on the topic. Second, the audience, as well as the speakers, develops an appreciation for the potential role of each discipline in the subsequent framing of significant "what next" questions. Third, and perhaps most important, the futility and inappropriateness of single-discipline approaches to complex, multidisciplinary problems becomes apparent. This overall matter was placed in perspective by Killian (1985) during the 32nd Annual Meeting of the American College of Sports Medicine. He presented a colloquium dealing with alternative psychophysical strategies for use in the study of effort sense, and he commented that there are two types of people in this world: those with "methods who are looking for questions to answer," and those with "questions looking for methods to answer them." The disciplinary isolate, of course, falls in the former category, and there is very little research in the field of sport psychology that falls in the latter. This criticism, of course, could be leveled at other subdisciplines within the exercise and sport sciences, but investigators in sport psychology, in my view, are the most isolated of the isolates. It is recommended that future research in sport psychology should be carried out within a multidisciplinary context.

Training of Sport Psychologists

Many of the problems identified in this paper would not exist if all sport psychologists were actually trained in sport psychology. It is estimated that less than 10% of the sport psychologists in the United States, as opposed to 100% in Czechoslovakia, Germany, and Russia, are actually psychologists. Also, sport psychologists from Eastern Europe are usually trained in sport science, and most of these individuals have had personal experience in the sports with which they are assigned to work. The usual case in North America is for the sport psychologist to be trained in physical education *or* psychology. It is important to realize that possession of a degree in psychology will not ensure competence in sport psychology, and it is imperative that the psychologist, especially the applied or clinical sport psychologist, possess training in sport science. Otherwise, the psychologist may not be able to distinguish between oxygen debt and national debt! Unfortunately, psychologists have usually not been trained in sport science, and physical educators and kinesiologists have typically not been trained in psychology. For the future of research in sport psychology to improve, it will be necessary for new training models to be developed, and it is recommended that sport psychologists receive advanced training in both exercise and sport science *and* psychology.

Conclusion

There has been very little sport psychology research carried out with persons of above-average health and fitness. It is estimated that less than 2% of the published literature in the exercise and sport sciences would be so classified, and the limited research in this particular area has been characterized by a number of problems. First, it has often been atheoretical, and the few theoretical undertakings have relied upon theory borrowed from other areas. The former approach has led to the generation of a descriptive literature, and the latter has consistently resulted in rejection of the borrowed theory. There have been very few attempts to predict behavior, and even fewer efforts to explain phenomena. This fixation on descriptive approaches has also been associated with a failure to search for underlying mechanisms. It is proposed that future research in sport psychology with persons of above-average health and fitness (a) comply with established APA ethical codes, (b) focus on health or consequent issues as well as antecedent and performance issues, (c) consider animal models where the underlying question prevents the use of human models, and (d) rely on multidisciplinary approaches where appropriate. There is little likelihood that any of these recommendations will be adopted, or even considered, unless sport psychologists in the future are trained in both psychology and sport science. The training of future sport psychologists probably represents the single greatest challenge of all.

References

Averill, J.R. (1983). Studies on anger and aggression: Implications for theories of emotion. *American Psychologist*, **38**, 1145-1160.

Bass, B.M. (1974). The substance and the shadow. *American Psychologist*, **29**, 870-886.

Brown, B.S., & Van Huss, W.D. (1973). Exercise and rat brain catecholamines. *Journal of Applied Physiology*, **34**, 664-669.

Cavanagh, P.R., & Kram, R. (1985). The efficiency of human movement—A statement of the problem. *Medicine and Science in Sports and Exercise*, **17**, 304-308.

Dishman, R.K. (1982). Contemporary sport psychology. In R. Terjung (Ed.), *Exercise and sport sciences reviews* (Vol. 10, pp. 120-156). Philadelphia: Franklin Institute Press.

Dishman, R.K. (1983). Identity crises in North American sport psychology: Academics in professional issues. *Journal of Sport Psychology*, **5**, 123-134.

Greist, J.H. (1987). Exercise intervention with depressed outpatients. In W.P. Morgan & S.E. Goldston (Eds.), *Exercise and mental health* (pp. 117-122). New York: Hemisphere.

Hanin, Y.L. (1978). A study of anxiety in sports. In W.F. Straub (Ed.), *Sport psychology: An analysis of athlete behavior* (2nd ed., pp. 236-249). Ithaca, NY: Mouvement.

Heyman, S.R. (1982). A reaction to Danish and Hale: A minority report. *Journal of Sport Psychology*, **4**, 7-9.

Hutton, R.S. (1970). A water maze for small animal research. In G.S. Kenyon (Ed.), *Contemporary psychology of sport* (pp. 809-813). Chicago: Athletic Institute.

Killian, K. (1985, May). *Quantification of symptoms during exercise*. Colloquium presented at the 32nd Annual Meeting of the American College of Sports Medicine, Nashville, TN.

Kroll, W., & Lewis, G.L. (1970). America's first sport psychologists. *Quest*, **13**, 1-4.

Landers, D.M. (1981). Reflections on sport psychology and the Olympic athlete. In J. Segrave & D. Chu (Eds.), *Olympism* (pp. 189-200). Champaign, IL: Human Kinetics.

Lau, R.R., & Russell, D. (1980). Attributions in the sports pages. *Journal of Personality and Social Psychology*, **39**, 29-38.

Martinsen, E. (1987). Interaction of exercise and medication in the psychiatric patient. In W.P. Morgan & S.E. Goldston (Eds.), *Exercise and mental health* (pp. 85-95). New York: Hemisphere.

Milvy, P. (Ed.) (1977). The marathon: Physiological, medical, epidemiological, and psychological studies. *Annals of the New York Academy of Sciences*, **301**.

Morgan, W.P. (1985a). Affective beneficence of vigorous physical activity. *Medicine and Science in Sports and Exercise*, **17**, 94-100.

Morgan, W.P. (1985b). Selected psychological factors limiting performance: A mental health model. In D.H. Clarke & H.M. Eckert (Eds.), *Limits of human performance* (pp. 70-80). Champaign, IL: Human Kinetics.

Morgan, W.P., & Goldston, S.E. (Eds.). (1987). *Exercise and mental health*. New York: Hemisphere.

Morgan, W.P., Olson, E.B., Jr., & Pedersen, N.P. (1982). A rat model of psychopathology for use in exercise science. *Medicine and Science in Sports and Exercise*, **14**, 91-100.

Olson, E.B., Jr., & Morgan, W.P. (1982). Rat brain monoamine levels related to behavioral assessment. *Life Sciences*, **30**, 2095-2100.

Ransford, C.P. (1982). A role for amines in the antidepressant effect of exercise. A review. *Medicine and Science in Sports and Exercise*, **14**, 1-10.

Seabourne, T.G., Weinberg, R.S., Jackson, A., & Suinn, R.M. (1985). Effect of individualized, nonindividualized, and package intervention strategies on karate performance. *Journal of Sport Psychology*, **7**, 40-50.

Spence, J.T. (1971). What can you say about a twenty-year-old theory that won't die? *Journal of Motor Behavior*, **3**, 193-203.

Suinn, R.M. (1984). Visual motor behavior rehearsal. The basic technique. *Scandinavian Journal of Behavior Therapy*, **13**, 131-142.

Suinn, R.M. (1985). The 1984 Olympics and sport psychology. *Journal of Sport Psychology*, **7**, 321-329.

Suomi, S.J. (1982). Relevance of animal models for clinical psychology. In P.C. Kendall & J.N. Butcher (Eds.), *Handbook of research methods in clinical psychology* (pp. 249-270). New York: Wiley.

Tharp, G.D., & Carson, W.H. (1975). Emotionality changes in rats following chronic exercise. *Medicine and Science in Sports and Exercise*, **7**, 123-126.

Weber, J.C., & Lee, R.A. (1968). Effects of differing prepuberty exercise programs on the emotionality of male albino rats. *Research Quarterly*, **39**, 748-751.

White, L.A. (1938). Science is *sciencing*. *Philosophy of Science*, **5**, 369-389.

PART II
Future Directions for the Subdisciplines

SECTION A:
BIOMECHANICS

Future Directions in Biomechanics Research: Neuromuscular Performance

Paavo V. Komi

Biomechanics can be seen as either a more narrowly defined area (Hatze, 1974) or a flexible discipline that has projections to and common interests with other scientific fields (Komi, 1984; Zernicke, 1983). If the study of movement and mechanisms of motion deals with the structure and function of the neuromuscular system, then the integrative use of mechanics, muscle mechanics, muscle physiology, and neurophysiology is very useful (Komi, 1984).

Neuromuscular performance can also be examined from a variety of viewpoints, ranging from the detailed characteristics of single motor units (e.g., Burke, 1981) to activation patterns of leg extensor muscle under varying impact load conditions (Komi, Gollhofer, Schmidtbleicher, & Frick, 1987). Regardless of the approach of an individual researcher, the information available from studies on isolated muscle fiber, motor unit, or muscle preparation serves two purposes in studying neuromuscular performance during human locomotion: (a) it helps to explain some of the mechanisms of movement, and (b) it produces new hypotheses to be tested in natural movement conditions. Relying too heavily on the research of these isolated preparations may, however, hinder innovations of new testing methods for normal locomotion, which in many respects is far from the strict conditions used with isolated preparations. In the following discussion, the attempt is made to compare results obtained with isolated preparations with measurements made on human subjects. The major focus of the discussion is, however, on future problems and measurement approaches.

Neuromuscular Structure and Mechanical Performance

A bulk of information is available to demonstrate the performance of the fast- or slow-type motor units, muscle fibers, or muscles. In human skeletal muscle the fiber composition varies considerably, and several efforts have been made to examine the relationship between the muscle fiber composition and biomechanical performance. Great variations in muscle fiber composition among athletic populations (Costill et al., 1976; Forsberg, Tesch, Sjödin, Thorstensson, & Karlsson, 1978) and strong genetic influence on the variance in muscle fiber composition (Komi et al., 1977) have led to the assumption that the structural differences in muscle between individuals also determine their physical performance capacity. This assumption has proven to be more relevant to endurance capacity, reflecting the importance of the metabolic functions of the muscle fibers for maintained or repeated activities. Strong interrelationship has been established between muscle fiber composition and maintenance time of either 50% (Komi, Karlsson, Tesch, Suominen, & Häkkinen, 1982) or 60% (Viitasalo & Komi, 1978b) isometric tension level.

Unfortunately, the measurements of the force-time and force-velocity curve with human populations have not been encouraging because they have not revealed a strong relationship between muscle structure and performance. In the case of isometric force production, the existence of the significant relationship has been observed in some studies (Viitasalo & Komi, 1978a; Viitasalo, Häkkinen, & Komi, 1982), whereas in the others no statistically significant relationship has been found (Viitasalo & Komi, 1981). This would imply the existence of a strong environmental (e.g., training) influence on the force-time curve. Evidence has been presented to show the sensitivity of the force-time curve specifically to both heavy resistance and explosive-type strength/power training (Häkkinen & Komi, 1985a, 1985b). The suggestion has been made, however, that the effects of training are probably of greater importance to the force-time characteristics than the muscle structure itself (Viitasalo et al., 1982). A large sex difference in force-time characteristics (Komi et al., 1977) and electromechanical delays (Bell & Jacobs, 1986) imposes an additional problem in this regard. However, it is also quite possible that the available (bio)mechanical measure is not appropriate for the purpose of identifying the interdependence of structure and function in a similar way as in isolated muscle preparations.

The preceding hypotheses about structure and function should not be construed as meaning that, if some basic mechanisms have been obtained using isolated models in a closed system, similar observations should apply to human locomotion as well. One must be alert to the problem of the feasibility of the methods in human experiments. The question becomes more relevant if one examines the available methods for recording force-velocity relationships, as for the arm and leg muscles. With the exception of the Tihanyi, Apor, and Fekete (1982) study, the demonstration of interdependence between muscle fiber composition and the force-velocity curve has proven to be much less than would have been expected from animal experiments. The primary reason for the small amount of valid research in this area is probably the lack of available dynamometers that can load the muscles through the entire physiological range of contraction speeds. The maximum speed of most of the commercially available instruments can cover only 20 to 30% of the respective physiological maximum. As Goldspink (1978) has demonstrated, the peak efficiencies of the isolated fast-twitch (FT) and slow-twitch (ST) fibers occur at completely different contraction speeds. Therefore, it is possible that in measurements of the force-velocity curve, when the maximum angular velocity reaches the value of 3-4 rad $\times$ s^{-1}, only the efficient contraction speed of ST fibers will be reached. The peak power of FT muscle fibers may occur at angular velocities 3 times greater than our present measurement systems allow (Tihanyi et al., 1982).

The purpose of biomechanical research in neuromuscular performance should not be to find a relationship between selected traits. The problem presented in the above discussion should therefore be understood differently: A challenge for future research is to identify the mechanisms of movement under natural conditions, covering a greater functional range. The problem is equally relevant to research situations in which a stretch-shortening cycle of muscle function (Komi, 1984) is also examined.

Motor Unit Recruitment and Normal Muscle Activity

The speed of movement is not just a concern in the measurement of mechanical parameters. It is my belief that the recruitment order of motor units is known only for situations that use isometric or very slow concentric contractions. The original-size principle (Henneman, Somjen, & Carpenter, 1965) has not been greatly challenged in these situations, but they are far from the normal velocity conditions of human movement and exercise. It would be unwise to speculate on the recruitment order for fast contraction speeds, especially in situations where stretch-shortening cycles are used. The challenge to researchers in neuromuscular performance is to study these and other mechanisms in natural and variable situations. Encouraging attempts in formulating other possibilities for motor unit recruitment have been made (Figure 1).

Stretch-Shortening Cycle Exercises

Research in muscle mechanics and training has focused primarily on examining isolated contraction types (i.e., isometric, concentric, or eccentric). However, these contraction types seldom occur alone in normal human movements. The body segments are periodically subjected to impact forces (e.g., in running and jumping), or some external force lengthens the muscle. In these phases the muscle is contracting first eccentrically and then concentrically. This combination forms a natural muscle function called the *stretch-shortening cycle* (Komi, 1984; Norman & Komi, 1979). Figure 2 characterizes the nature of the stretch-shortening cycle (SSC) in connection with the impact load condition of walking or running.

The purpose of the SSC is to make the final action (concentric contraction) more powerful than the condition in which the movement is initiated by concentric contraction alone. It is unclear how the mechanical (and also metabolic) performance of the skeletal muscle is modified in a concentric contraction during an SSC. Researchers have sought the answer

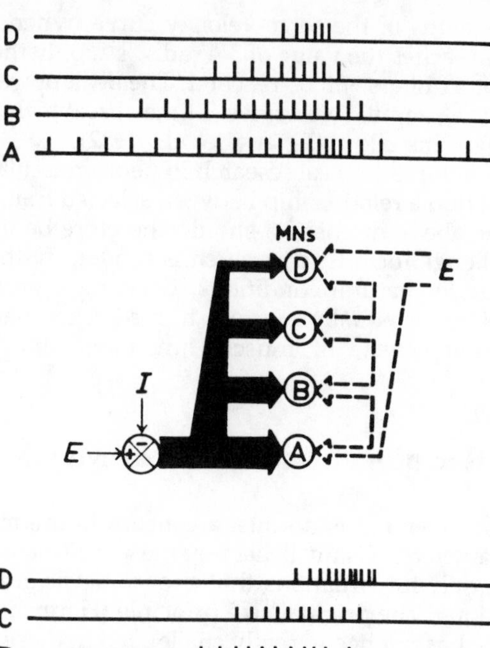

Figure 1. Two models for motor unit recruitment. The solid arrows demonstrate the recruitment and derecruitment sequence according to the upper set of spike diagrams. The dashed arrows and the lower set of spikes represent an additional input that could reverse the situations. *Note*. From "Motor Units: Anatomy, Physiology, and Functional Organization" by R.E. Burke. In *Handbook of Physiology*, 1981, Bethesda, MD: American Physiological Society. Copyright 1981 by the American Physiological Society. Adapted by permission.

to this question by performing experiments on both isolated muscle preparations and humans. Edman, Elzinga, and Noble (1978) demonstrated that, especially at higher sarcomere lengths, the sarcomere force-velocity curve shifts to the right when the shortening follows an active stretch. Cavagna, Saibene, and Margaria's (1965) experiments with isolated frog sartorius muscle can, however, be used to demonstrate how the performance of muscle in concentric action is potentiated when this contraction is preceded by an active stretch. Komi's (1983) experiments have demonstrated similar phenomena in human leg extensor muscles. In both cases, the potentiation occurred when the coupling between stretch and shortening phases was as short as possible.

Enhancement of performance through prestretching can be seen both in force-length and force-velocity curves (Cavagna, Dusman, & Margaria, 1968). When the force-velocity (F-V) curve is measured during a complex movement involving several joints (e.g., vertical jumps), a preparatory countermovement shifts the F-V curve to the right and thus causes the

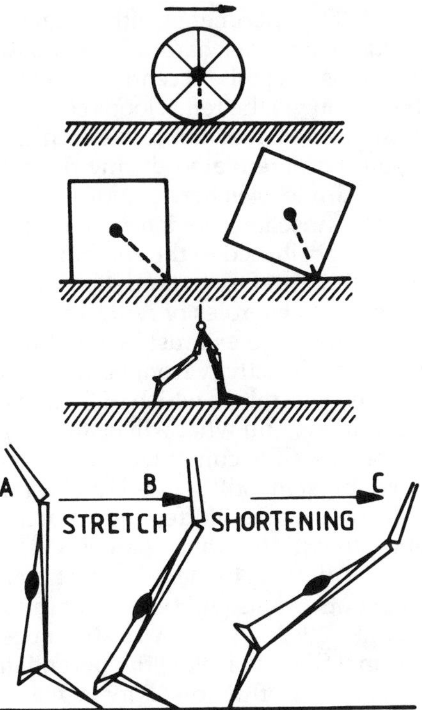

Figure 2. Human walking and running do not resemble the movement of a rotating wheel, in which the center of gravity is always directly above the point of contact and perpendicular to the line of progression. Instead, they resemble the action of a rolling cubic box and have considerable impact loads when contact takes place with the ground. Before contact the muscles are preactivated (A) and ready to resist the impact, during which they are stretched (B). The stretch phase is followed by a shortening (concentric) contraction (C). *Note.* From "Physiological and Biomechanical Correlates of Muscle Function: Effects of Muscle Structure and Stretch-Shortening Cycle on Force and Speed" by P.V. Komi. In R.L. Terjung (Ed.), *Exercise and Sport Sciences Reviews* (Vol. 12, p. 102), 1984, Lexington, MA: Collamore. Copyright 1984 by Collamore. Reprinted by permission.

leg extensor muscles to exert much higher forces at any knee angular velocity of the concentric phase (Bosco & Komi, 1979). Similarly, the power-angular velocity curve is also displaced so that a greater power output can be recorded at certain knee angular velocities in countermovement jumps as compared to pure squatting jumps.

Results such as these raise the question as to the cause of performance potentiation in stretch-shortening cycle exercises. Cavagna et al.'s (1965) original study was performed with isolated frog sartorius muscle, and thus it is likely that the performance potentiation in the SSC was due solely to the effects of elastic potentiation. Later, Cavagna et al. (1968) obtained similar results with intact human elbow flexor muscles. Edman,

Elzinga, and Noble's (1982) experiments with isolated fibrils also support the idea of pure elastic (chemomechanical) potentiation. However, because the stretching of muscles in the eccentric phase must activate muscle spindles, some potentiation via the reflex loops could be expected as well. Other research has suggested that the myoelectrical activity of the leg extensor muscles could be potentiated during the contact phase of the running cycle (Dietz, Schmidtbleicher, & Noth, 1979). Thus it is likely that, when the nervous connections are intact, the enhancement of performance in the SSC can be attributed to the combined effects of restitution of elastic energy and stretch-reflex potentiation of muscle.

In a discussion of the possible roles of reflex influence in performance potentiation, three additional notes must be mentioned. First, when an active muscle is stretched, the activity from both the muscle spindles and the Golgi tendon organs determines which of these reflexes—facilitatory or inhibitory—will dominate, and what will be the magnitude of potentiation. Second, it has been well documented (e.g., Hoffer & Andreassen, 1981) that with reflexes present, stiffness is larger for the same operating force than in an areflexive muscle. Hoffer and Andreassen calculated the net reflex contribution to stiffness during an eccentric contraction. This kind of estimation is more difficult to make in intact human skeletal muscle and especially in SSC contractions, although attempts in this regard have been made (Bosco et al., 1982). Another related question is whether it is possible, in the normal SSC, to isolate the potentiation effects of pure elasticity from those of reflex influences. Any increase in reflex potentiation should lead to enhancement of elastic influences. In addition, all the possible components that contribute to enhanced performance in SSC are adaptive, and their relative roles can change depending on the training/detraining status of the various parts of the neuromuscular system. And third, Denoth (1985) has introduced the concept of *resonance phenomenon* to explain the performance potentiation in the SSC. This approach, which is based primarily on muscle momentum, adds an interesting feature to the complexity of the SSC. Additional problems for future studies may derive from studies of the behavior of the multijoint movement in which the various cycles occur in sequence and in which the transfer of energy from segment to segment is also expected to occur.

Mechanical Efficiency

Calculations and/or estimates of mechanical efficiency (ME) should interest both physiologists and biomechanists. In fact, the definition of *mechanical efficiency*, "the ratio of produced mechanical work to the energy expenditure above that of the resting condition," calls for methodological solutions that take into consideration measurements of both chemical energy expenditure (biochemistry) and mechanical work (mechanics). The methodological problems in calculating the denominator may be smaller than those for the numerator. The problem becomes even greater when one examines the mechanical efficiency of SSC exercises. The following is a discussion of a new and more valid method of estimating mechanical efficiency. It is my hope that this will stimulate other and even better methodological improvements.

Prestretching an active muscle during SSC exercise is also expected to influence the mechanical efficiency of the positive work phase (concentric contraction) of the cycle. Both the eccentric and the concentric phases of the SSC can be performed differently and thus produce different net mechanical efficiencies. Some of the recent studies on isolated eccentric and concentric exercises have provided results that differ from those presented earlier, which indicated that negative work has a constant ME value of −1.2 (120%) (Davies & Barnes, 1972; Margaria, 1938), and that positive work has a constant value of 18 to 23% (Gaesser & Brooks, 1975).

To examine the ME values of isolated eccentric or concentric exercises or their combination, the sledge apparatus (Figure 3) was constructed. The apparatus consists of: (a) a sledge (m = 33 kg) on which the subject sits; (b) a slide on which the sledge runs along the slow-friction aluminum track; and (c) the force plate, which is perpendicular to the sliding surface.

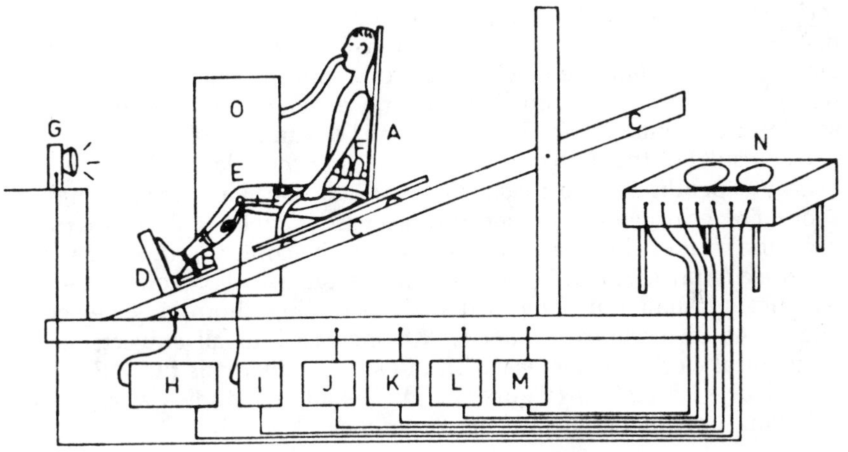

A. "Sledge"
B. Ankle support
C. Aluminic slide-bars
D. Force-plate
E. Electric goniometer
F. EMG-Telemetry transmitters
G. Audio signal
H. Amplifier, force
I. Amplifier, "Elgon"
J-M. EMG-Telemetry receiving units
N. FM-recorder RACAL 7 DS
O. OXYCON-4 analyser

Figure 3. The experimental procedure used in the study. *Note.* From "Effects of Prestretch Intensity on Mechanical Efficiency of Positive Work in Natural Locomotion" by O. Aura and P.V. Komi, 1986, *International Journal of Sports Medicine*, 7(3), p. 318. Copyright 1986 by *International Journal of Sports Medicine*. Reprinted by permisison.

Measurement of Mechanical Efficiencies of Isolated Concentric and Eccentric Exercises

To investigate the mechanical efficiencies of isolated concentric or eccentric exercises, several submaximal exercises can be selected. In concentric exercise the subject extends his or her legs so that the sledge slides uphill to a distance that corresponds to the specified submaximal energy level. When the sledge starts its movement downward, two assistants retard its motion with a rope that is attached to the sledge. The sledge is then returned to the starting position (e.g., 90° knee angle) so that no allowance is made for resistive muscular movement when the foot contact with the force plate is resumed. A sufficient number of concentric contractions (e.g., 80) can be performed with constant intercontraction intervals. No countermovement is allowed at the initiation of each contraction. Isolated eccentric contractions can be performed so that the sledge is released from a certain distance corresponding to the specific energy level. During contact with the force plate, the subject resists the downward movement. A rope is attached to the end of the sledge and fixed so that the movement of the sledge stops when a 90° knee angle is reached. Two assistants then pull the sledge back to the specific release distance for the next eccentric contraction. The force plate reaction forces are used to calculate the mechanical work, and the collected expired air during exercise is used to obtain the energy expenditure values (for details see Aura & Komi, 1986b; Kaneko, Komi, & Aura, 1984).

The results of this procedure indicated that the relationship between energy expenditure and mechanical work is linear in a small range of shortening velocities of the concentric exercise (Kaneko et al., 1984). However, the relationship was not linear when the contraction velocity was increased (Aura & Komi, 1986b). For this reason, ME of concentric exercise was not constant but decreased with increasing shortening velocities (Figure 4). In eccentric exercise, ME increased in all subjects when mechanical work was increased and in some individuals the ME values exceeded −1.5 (150%) (Figure 4). The results of studies suggest the following possibilities for further experimentation:

1. Mechanical efficiency of eccentric exercise is very high, but not constant.
2. This high efficiency can be increased by increasing stretch velocity.
3. Efficiencies above 100% can be obtained with low motor unit activation in eccentric exercise.
4. In concentric exercise EMG, energy expenditure, and mechanical work show parallel changes in slow contractions, but increases in shortening velocities will modify these relationships.

Measurement of Mechanical Efficiencies in SSC Exercise

The evaluation of ME becomes more difficult when this method is applied to the study of the potentiation of mechanical performance of the muscle in the SSC. Research has indicated that negative work does not

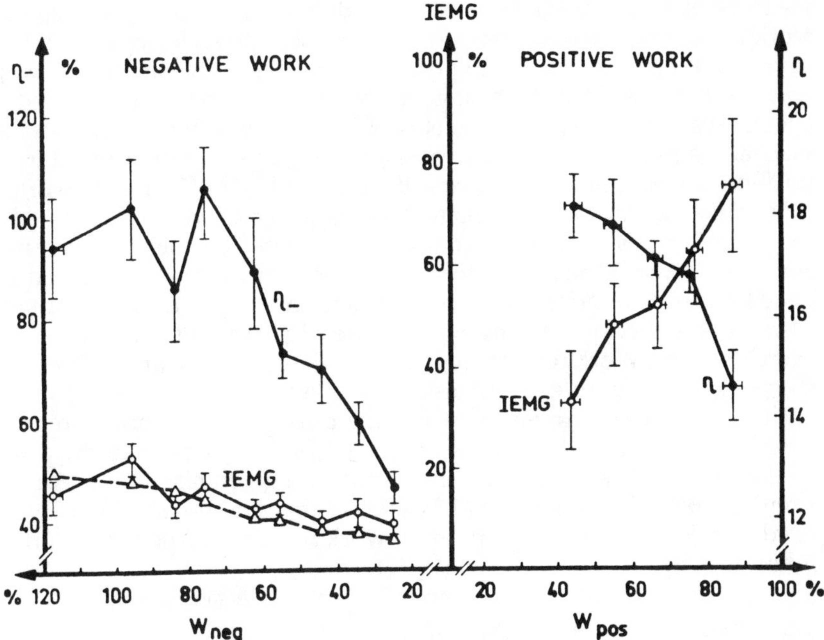

Figure 4. The relative IEMG (open circles) related to the work intensity (relWpos, right, and relWneg, left). Corresponding efficiency values are marked by dots. In the left figure, the relative IEMG during a 100-ms preactivation phase are marked by open triangles. The IEMG values are averages of the three muscles studied (vastus lateralis, vastus medialis, and gastrocnemius). *Note*. From "Mechanical Efficiency of Pure Positive and Pure Negative Work With Special Reference to the Work Intensity" by O. Aura and P.V. Komi, 1986, *International Journal of Sports Medicine*, 7, p. 47. Copyright 1986 by *International Journal of Sports Medicine*. Reprinted by permission.

have a constant efficiency value. Therefore, an investigation of the ME of SSC exercise must begin by defining the ME of pure eccentric exercise at exactly the same stretching velocity and amplitude as the one to be used in SSC exercise. We applied this method in recent experiments (Aura & Komi, 1986a) using the sledge apparatus. We used an additional measurement, maximum concentric exercise (Wmax), which was the energy level that the subject was able to exert in one pure concentric contraction. In actual SSC conditions, the positive work intensity of 60% of Wmax was kept constant for each subject, and the preceding eccentric contraction was varied from day to day. SSC contractions were repeated in each situation 80 times at a rate of once every 3 s.

At the beginning of each exercise cycle, the sledge was released from a certain distance corresponding to the specific energy level. The height of dropping varies the potential energy of the sledge-subject system and subsequently varies the negative (kinetic) work done during the breakdown. Within each exercise the dropping height was constant, but among exercises it varied between 20% to 120% of Wmax. During contact with the force plate, the subjects resisted the downward movement (negative work), and, immediately after stopping the sledge (knee angle 90°), they extended their legs to perform positive work. The effort in positive work was controlled so that the change in the potential energy of the sledge-subject system corresponded to 60% of the Wmax. When the sledge had reached its highest position, two assistants made sure that the starting position corresponded to the specific energy level of negative work.

Special care was taken to ensure that the subjects were accustomed to the exercise types. Additional control was achieved by using a small ankle support on which the feet rested during movement. This eliminated the need for muscular effort to support the legs in any position of the movement. The effect of learning was avoided by random selection of the exercise order. Work rate (frequency) was controlled by an auditory signal presented before each release (negative phase).

The MEs of the pure negative and the pure positive work were measured individually for all of the subjects 1 or 2 days prior to the actual SSC exercises. Exact methods and results are given elsewhere (Aura & Komi, 1986a). The individual ME values of the pure negative work were used to calculate the ME of positive work in negative/positive work as follows:

$$n_+ = \frac{\text{Wpos}}{\Delta\text{En.exp.} - \dfrac{\text{Wneg}}{n_-}} \times 100\%$$

where Wpos = the positive work/one contraction, Wneg = the negative work/one contraction, ΔEn.exp. = energy expenditure above the resting

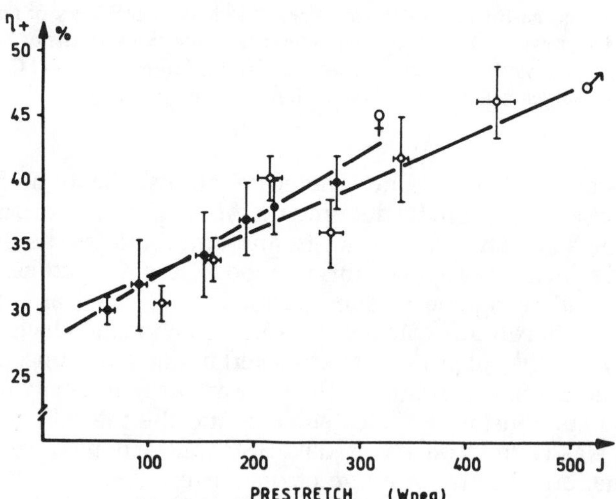

Figure 5. The mechanical efficiency of the positive work (n^+) in stretch-shortening cycle exercise—related to the prestretch intensity (Wneg) in both sexes. *Note.* From "The Mechanical Efficiency of Locomotion in Men and Women With Special Emphasis on Stretch-Shortening Cycle Exercises" by O. Aura and P.V. Komi, 1986, *European Journal of Applied Physiology*, **55**(1), p. 41. Copyright 1986 by *European Journal of Applied Physiology*. Reprinted by permission.

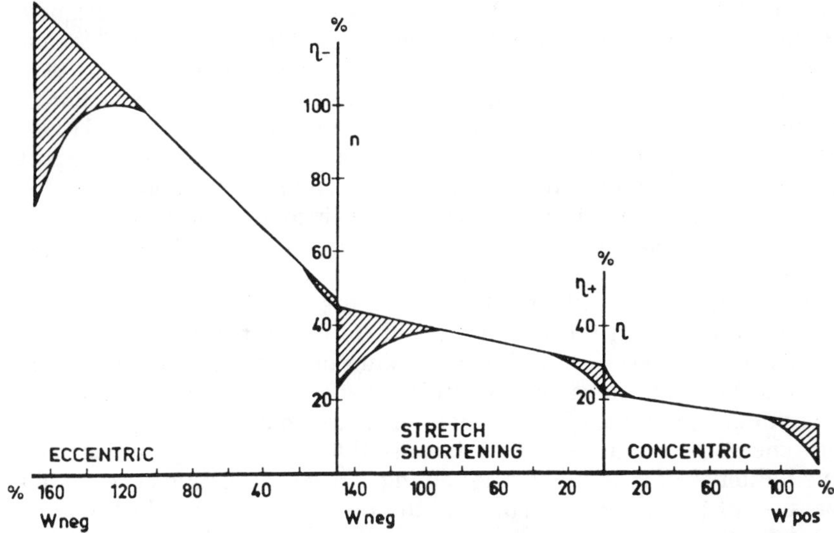

Figure 6. Net mechanical efficiencies of pure eccentric (left), pure concentric (right), and stretch-shortening cycle (middle) exercises. The dashed sections represent areas that need more exact experimentation and in which the adaptational response may vary greatly. Data combined from studies of Aura and Komi, 1986a and 1986c.

level (sitting posture)/one contraction, and n_- = the mechanical efficiency of the negative work, individually measured values. The prerequisite for the use of the equation is that n_- must be individually determined in advance in pure eccentric contractions, and these contractions should correspond to those eccentric phases used in the final SSC measurements.

Figure 5 shows how the efficiency of the positive work increases in SSC exercise when the prestretch load (negative work) is increased. The results suggest that the efficiency of the constant concentric exercise can be changed considerably by modifying the preceding eccentric stretch load. Figure 6 summarizes the results by showing the efficiency values for the isolated eccentric (left) and concentric (right) contractions and also for the SSC (middle) exercise. The lined areas represent those parts of the curves that need more exact experimentation. Although the use of the sledge apparatus was aimed at relatively normal SSC exercises, these are still far from the maximum conditions. The current method of measuring energy expenditure may not be applicable to an examination of the problem at higher SSC loads.

Stiffness Regulation and Its Relevance to Normal Movements

In many activities—especially in sports—generation of force by the skeletal muscle must take place quickly. More importantly, there is a high rate of force, which implies that the muscle is very stiff, especially in the eccentric phase of the SSC. One of the purposes of training could be to improve the ability of muscles to become stiff in the shortest possible time. Traditionally, biomechanics research has not typically examined the influence of training on neuromuscular performance, but biomechanical methods can be used to investigate these effects. For example, Houk's (1974) component analysis of a stretch reflex (Figure 7) identifies the parts of the system where training could occur. The length-feedback component, which originates from muscle spindles, increases stiffness. The force-feedback component, which comes from the Golgi tendon organ, decreases stiffness. The final result is the line segment a — b, the slope of which defines the stiffness. If the increase in stiffness is a desirable phenomenon, then the training could influence not only the length-feedback and force-feedback components but also the muscular component. Figure 8 shows the hypothetical effects of training on the three components, emphasizing that not only is the muscle an adaptive organ as a chemomechanical structure, but also that its nervous control is under the influence of training and detraining. These adaptations are possible because of the complex circuitry of the nervous system, which will not be detailed in this paper. Stiffness regulation is very important in SSC exercises (Komi, 1984). Figure 9 demonstrates that training has considerable influence on stiffness regulation, enabling muscle to sustain high-impact loads and subsequently maintain good recoil characteristics.

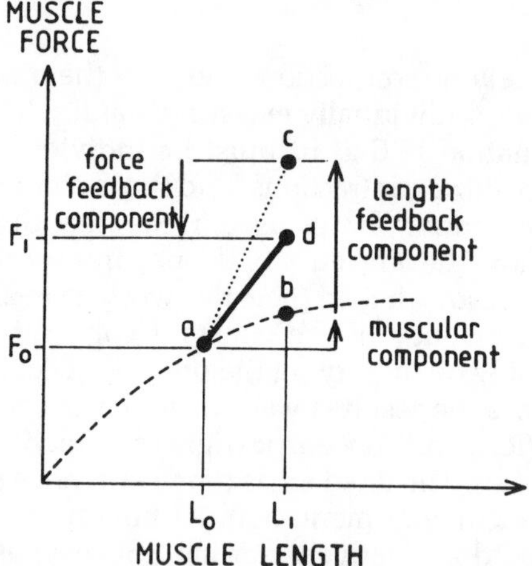

Figure 7. Houk's component analysis of hypothetical stretch reflex. Stretch from L_0 and L_1 causes force to increase from F_0 to F_1. This change can be attributed to three functional components: (1) a muscular component, expressing the basic length-tension characteristics of the muscle, (2) a length-feedback component originating from the facilitatory spindle discharge, and (3) a force-feedback component, which arises from inhibitory Golgi tendon organ discharge. The stiffness is defined by the slope of the force increase, and the length-feedback and force-feedback components, respectively, either increase or decrease stiffness. *Note*. From "Feedback Control of Muscle: A Synthesis of the Peripheral Mechanism" by J.C. Houk. In *Medical Physiology* by W.B. Mountcastle (Ed.), 1974, St. Louis: Mosby. Copyright by Mosby. Reprinted by permission.

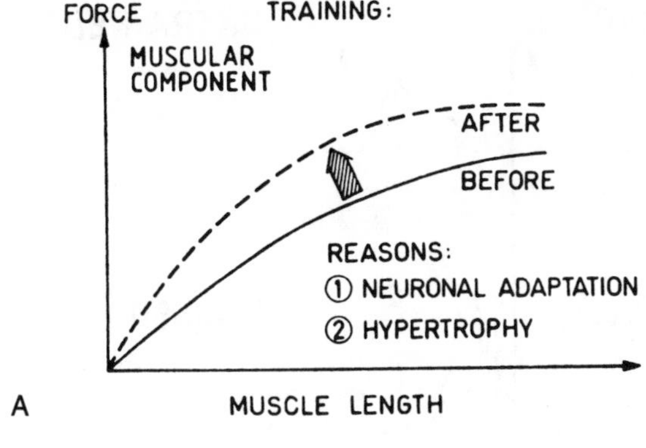

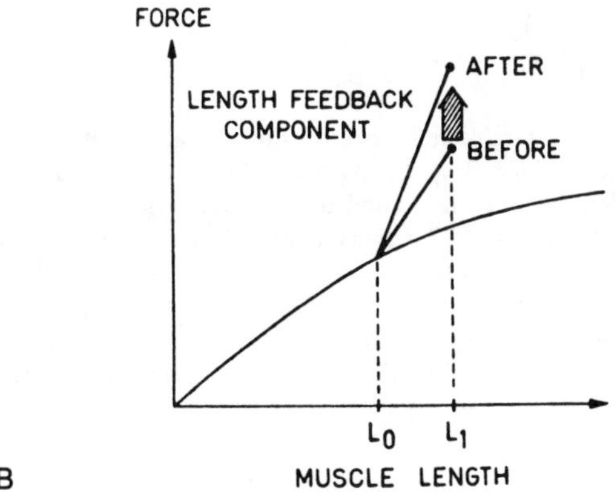

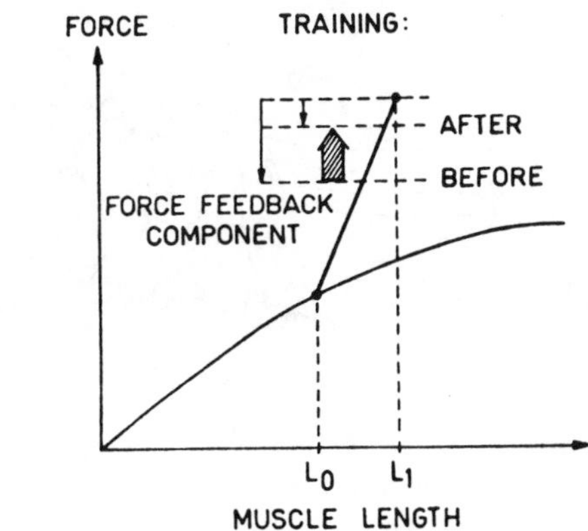

Figure 8. Three possible objectives of strength/power training on the force-length relationship of human skeletal muscle. A: Muscular component can be trained by increased motor unit activation and hypertrophy. The resulting influence is the shift to the left in the force-length curve. B: The influence of length-feedback component increases if training causes increases in muscle spindle discharge for the same stretch load. C: Inhibitory effect (decrease in stiffness) from Golgi tendon.

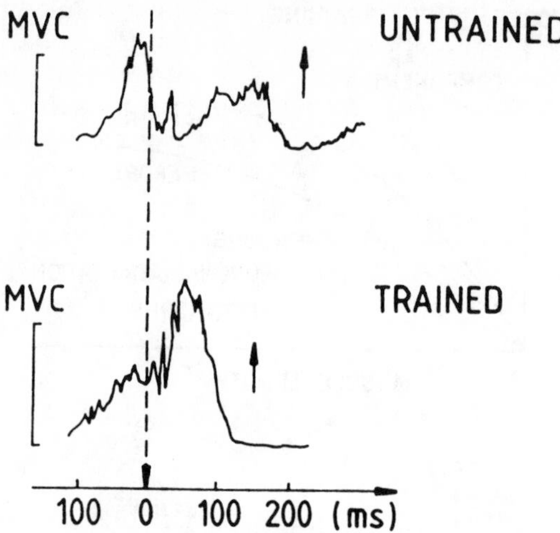

Figure 9. Training has considerable influence on the activation pattern of the gastrocnemius muscle measured during drop jumps from a height of 1.10 m. The trained subject (high jumper) demonstrates facilitated reflex potentiation during early impact, whereas in the untrained subject EMG activity is inhibited during the same instant. MVC denotes the values of the maximum isometric leg extension strength of the subjects. *Note.* From "Neuromuskuläre Untersuchungen zur Bestimmung Individueller Belastungsgrössen für ein Tiefsprungtraining" by D. Schmidtbleicher and A. Gollhofer, 1982, *Leistungssport*, **12**. Copyright 1982 by *Leistungssport*. Reprinted by permission.

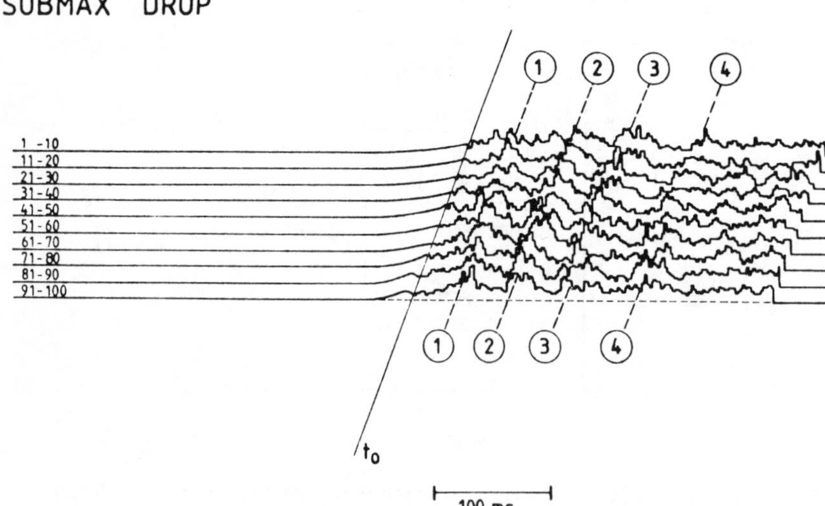

Figure 10. Examples of the use of averaging EMG technique in a fatigue experiment. The successive records show the rectified EMG pattern of m. triceps brachii during 100 successive stretch-shortening cycle contractions. The line (t_0) indicates the onset of touchdown of the right hand to the force plate. The circled numbers (1-4) count the wave numbers seen in the EMG pattern.

The discussion of the modification of stiffness regulation by training may remain hypothetical for two reasons. First, the concept of stiffness regulation is still problematic and not yet agreed upon by researchers (Stein, 1982). Second, identifying the adaptive responses in reflexes (i.e., facilitatory and inhibitory) under normal movement conditions and especially during fatigue is a very difficult task that may require considerable improvement in measurement techniques. Currently, an averaging technique is used to identify several reflex components from rectified EMG patterns (see Figure 10), and a similar approach may form a basis for future training and fatigue studies that employ human subjects and high-level muscle activation.

Impact Loads and Achilles Tendon Forces in Humans

If measurements on isolated muscle preparations and laboratory tests on humans don't provide correct predictions of the mechanical behavior of skeletal muscle under normal locomotion, then how can we identify this behavior? The human Achilles tendon may prove useful in this regard for the purpose of examining the impact load characteristics of the neuromuscular apparatus. There are two possible methods for evaluating the mechanical response of the human Achilles tendon (AT) during locomotion: (a) Force levels can be estimated mathematically with the help of force platform and film analysis and (b) forces can be recorded directly by applying suitable transducers around the tendon. The first method is useful especially in static loading situations, but its use for fast, dynamic-type movements is sometimes problematic. In vivo recording has been applied successfully to animal experiments and has produced considerable information on the mechanical behavior of AT (e.g., in cat locomotion; Walmsley, Hodgson, & Burke, 1978). The following is a short description of this technique, which directly records forces on human AT with a transducer that has been implanted around the AT under local anesthesia. Two major papers have been published (Komi, Salonen, Järvinen, & Kokko, 1987; Gregor, Komi, & Järvinen, 1987) and several others are in final preparation.

The in vivo technique uses either an E-form or a buckle-type transducer, the latter of which has proven to be more convenient. The transducer is implanted under local anesthesia around the AT of adult male volunteers. A critical problem is the calibration of the transducer. This was solved by constructing a special calibration table on which the subject was placed in a prone position. His operated leg had a special shoe, which was fastened to a freely moving lever arm that had its axis of rotation at the ankle joint. A pulley system with known weights was used to dorsiflex the foot. The direction of the pull was parallel to the AT. The strain-gauge system attached to the cable indicated the exact force of the passive dorsiflexion. Taking into consideration the geometrical arrangements of the tendon transducer, the axis of rotation, and the pulley system, we calculated the exact values of AT forces. The dynamic response of the AT transducer was calibrated by adding the spring system between the strain gauge and the weight of the dorsiflexing cable.

After the calibration the subjects performed normal activities including walking, running at different speeds, hopping, jumping, and bicycling. In some cases even maximal efforts were performed without any discomfort. All movements were performed either on a long force platform (Komi, 1985) or on a bicycle that had special force transducers on the pedals. EMG activities were recorded from the major leg muscles. AT forces and EMGs were telemetered, and all the signals were stored on magnetic tape (Racal-7 or Racal-14). All activities were also filmed at 100 frames•s^{-1}. The entire measurement lasted 2 to 3 hr, after which the transducer was removed.

In the present report only examples of the Achilles tendon forces are given. Figure 11 shows the basic AT force response during heel and ball running. As can be seen from the figure, the tendon force demonstrates a sudden release upon heel contact after which the rate of rise of force is quite high. A similar phenomenon did not occur in ball running.

The analysis of the AT measurements can include the following parameters: peak to peak forces, rate of force development, appearance of slack upon heel contact on the ground, interaction of the AT force

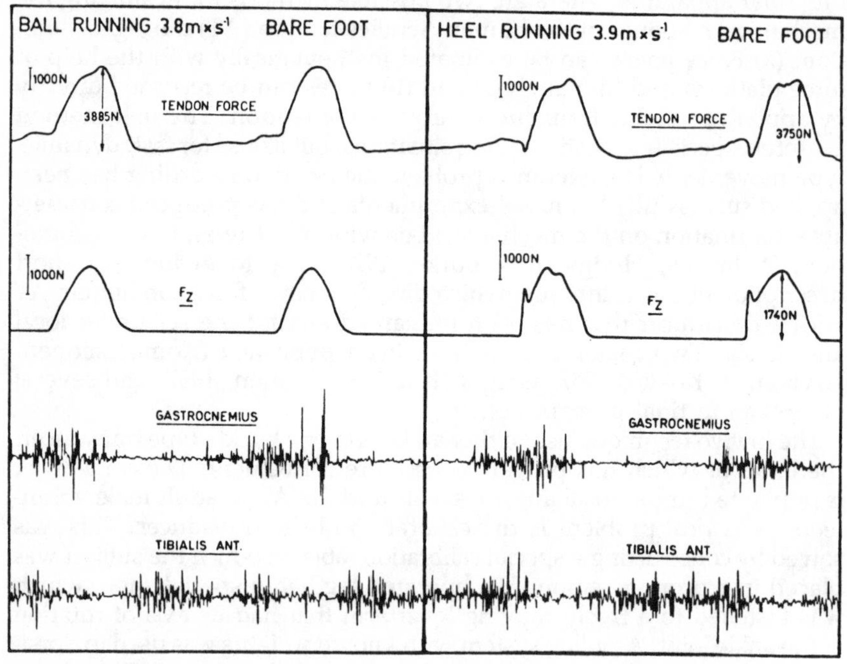

Figure 11. Direct in vivo measurements of tendon forces demonstrate that under normal movement conditions, the muscle develops force very rapidly over a short change in muscle length. In the example, the Achilles tendon force was recorded while the subject was running at a speed of 5 m × s^{-1} over the long force plate floor. EMG activity of the recorded muscles takes place primarily during the impact phase, which corresponds to the rising phase of the Achilles tendon force.

response with EMG activation of the leg extensor muscles, interaction of AT response and ground reaction forces, and force-length and force-velocity curves of the triceps surae muscle during different activities. These last parameters are perhaps the most informative with regard to muscle function during normal locomotion, and they require the use of appropriate methods (e.g., Grieve, Pheasant, & Cavanagh, 1978) to estimate the length changes of the respective muscles.

Human-Shoe-Surface Interaction

Running and walking have received considerable attention in biomechanics research. In most of these studies the focus has been the examination of the reaction forces of force plate signals (e.g., Nigg, 1983) or the description of kinematic movement patterns, obtained by film analysis (e.g., Mero & Komi, 1985). Less attention has been given to combining these two methodological approaches to relate different postures during gait or running cycles to the dynamics of ground reaction force components. In addition, little research has been done on the combination of muscle activation patterns, kinematic features, and ground reaction forces (e.g., Mero & Komi, 1986). Research has provided information on *basic* walking and running patterns in man, but little information exists about the *changes* in biomechanical and physiological behavior when the circumstances in which running takes place are systematically changed. For these reasons, the following comments may be useful for future research on this topic (for details, see Komi & Gollhofer, 1986).

Traditionally, one or two force plates have been used to measure the ground reaction forces. This measurement requires that the subjects must touch the plates with a normal running pattern without lengthening or shortening the step, especially at higher running velocities. This is one of the difficulties when using only one or two short force plates: one contact sample may not be representative. Therefore, a longer force platform should be used to record several ground contacts (Komi & Gollhofer, 1986).

With respect to the neurophysiological phenomenon, it is known that the innervation pattern of leg extensor muscles of one stance phase consists of a *pre-innervation* phase before the ground contact; an *activation* phase during the eccentric phase in which reflex-induced activation is also expected; and an *innervation* phase, which is attributable to the concentric phase of the movement (Dietz et al., 1979; Gollhofer, Schmidtbleicher, & Dietz, 1984). These durations are muscle specific when the ground contact is used as a reference. The literature also lacks information that describes the influence of running on the innervation patterns of the leg extensor muscles when the subjects use different types of shoes with various hardness characteristics. An averaging technique for EMG may be applied for these functional phases.

Examination of the qualities of running must therefore take into account the entire human-shoe-surface system. All three components have their own physical resonance characteristics, but when they act together, the human must respond physiologically to make the best of this combination. Only a positive opposition of all three components will lead to effective and efficient running.

The research strategy should be based on the assumption that it is the interaction of the three components that ultimately generates and controls running activity. It is further assumed that this interaction is so strong that it must be considered, especially in research that attempts to identify an optimal running shoe.

The results presented in our recent report (Komi & Gollhofer, 1986) have suggested that not only do the ground reaction forces change with differing shoe or surface characteristics, but also that the neuronal activation of the major leg extensor muscles change their activation pattern. Not only must we identify the magnitudes of the changes, but we must also examine which component of the human-shoe-surface interaction demonstrates the greatest sensitivity. It can be speculated that EMG activity of the selected muscle groups has an important role in identifying the interference components in the entire interaction. Further speculation should be given to the cause-and-effect relationship so that one can identify the regulatory mechanism in this interaction.

References

Aura, O., & Komi, P.V. (1986a). Effects of prestretch intensity on mechanical efficiency of positive work in natural locomotion. *International Journal of Sports Medicine,* **7**(3), 137-143.

Aura, O., & Komi, P.V. (1986b). Mechanical efficiency of pure positive and pure negative work with special reference to the work intensity. *International Journal of Sports Medicine,* **7**, 44-49.

Aura, O., & Komi, P.V. (1986c). The mechanical efficiency of locomotion in men and women with special emphasis on stretch-shortening cycle exercises. *European Journal of Applied Physiology,* **55**, 37-43.

Bell, D.G., & Jacobs, I. (1986). Electromechanical response times and rate of force development in males and females. *Medicine and Science in Sports and Exercise,* **18**(10), 31-36.

Bosco, C., Ito, A., Komi, P.V., Luhtanen, P., Rahkila, P., Rusko, H., & Viitasalo, J.T. (1982). Neuromuscular function and mechanical efficiency of human leg extensor muscles during jumping exercise. *Acta Physiologica Scandinavica,* **114**, 543-550.

Bosco, C., & Komi, P.V. (1979). Mechanical characteristics and fiber composition of human leg extensor muscles. *European Journal of Applied Physiology,* **41**, 275-284.

Burke, R.E. (1981). Motor units: Anatomy, physiology, and functional organization. In *Handbook of physiology; Section 1. The nervous system: Vol. II. Motor control: Part I* (pp. 345-422). Bethesda, MD: American Physiological Society.

Cavagna, G.A., Dusman, B., & Margaria, R. (1968). Positive work done by the previously stretched muscle. *Journal of Applied Physiology,* **24**, 21-32.

Cavagna, G.A., Saibene, F.P., & Margaria, R. (1965). Effect of negative work on the amount of positive work performed by an isolated muscle. *Journal of Applied Physiology*, **20**, 157-158.

Costill, D.L., Daniels, J., Evans, W., Fink, W., Krahenbuhl, G., & Saltin, B. (1976). Skeletal muscle enzymes and fiber composition in male and female track athletes. *Journal of Applied Physiology*, **40**, 149-154.

Davies, C.T.M., & Barnes, C. (1972). Negative (eccentric) work: 2. Physiological responses to walking uphill and downhill on a motor-driven treadmill. *Ergonomics*, **15**(2), 121-131.

Denoth, J. (1985). Storage and utilization of elastic energy in musculature. In D.A. Winter, R.W. Norman, R.P. Wells, K.C. Hayes, & A.E. Patla (Eds.), *Biomechanics IX-A* (pp. 65-70). Champaign, IL: Human Kinetics.

Dietz, V., Schmidtbleicher, D., & Noth, J. (1979). Neuronal mechanisms of human locomotion. *Journal of Neurophysiology*, **42**, 1212-1222.

Edman, K.A.P., Elzinga, G., & Noble, M.I.M. (1978). Enhancement of mechanical performance by stretch during tetanic contractions of vertebrate skeletal muscle fibres. *Journal of Physiology*, **281**, 139-155.

Edman, K.A.P., Elzinga, G., & Noble, M.I.M. (1982). Residual force enhancement after stretch of contracting frog single muscle fibers. *Journal of General Physiology*, **80**, 769-784.

Forsberg, A., Tesch, P., Sjödin, B., Thorstensson, A., & Karlsson, J. (1978). Skeletal muscle fibers and athletic performance. In P.V. Komi (Ed.), *Biomechanics V-A* (pp. 27-39). Baltimore: University Park Press.

Gaesser, G.A., & Brooks, G.A. (1975). Muscular efficiency during steady-rate exercise: Effects of speed and work rate. *Journal of Applied Physiology*, **38**(6), 1132-1139.

Goldspink, G. (1978). Energy turnover during contraction of different types of muscles. In E. Asmussen & K. Jϕrgensen (Eds.), *Biomechanics VI-A* (pp. 27-39). Baltimore: University Park Press.

Gollhofer, A., Schmidtbleicher, D., & Dietz, V. (1984). Regulation of muscle stiffness of human locomotion. *International Journal of Sports Medicine*, **1**, 19-23.

Gregor, R.J., Komi, P.V., & Järvinen, M. (1987). Achilles tendon forces during cycling. *International Journal of Sports Medicine*, **8** (Suppl.), 9-14.

Grieve, D.W., Pheasant, S., & Cavanagh, P.R. (1978). Prediction of gastrocnemius length from knee and ankle joint posture. In E. Asmussen & K. Jϕrgensen (Eds.), *Biomechanics VI-A* (pp. 405-412). Baltimore: University Park Press.

Häkkinen, K., & Komi, P.V. (1985a). Changes in electrical and mechanical behavior of leg extensor muscles during heavy resistance strength training. *Scandinavian Journal of Sports Sciences*, **7**(2), 55-64.

Häkkinen, K., & Komi, P.V. (1985b). Effect of explosive type strength training on electromyographic and force production characteristics of leg extensor muscles during concentric and various stretch-shortening cycle exercises. *Scandinavian Journal of Sports Sciences*, **7**(2), 65-76.

Hatze, H. (1974). The meaning of the term "biomechanics." *Journal of Biomechanics*, **7**, 189-190.

Henneman, E., Somjen, G., & Carpenter, D.O. (1965). Functional significance of cell size in spinal motor neurons. *Journal of Neurophysiology*, **28**, 560-580.

Hoffer, J.A., & Andreassen, S. (1981). Regulation of soleus muscle stiffness in premammillary cats: Intrinsic and reflex components. *Journal of Neurophysiology*, **45**(2), 267-285.

Houk, J.C. (1974). Feedback control of muscle: A synthesis of the peripheral mechanism. In W.B. Mountcastle (Ed.), *Medical physiology* (13th ed., pp. 668-677). St. Louis: Mosby.

Kaneko, M., Komi, P.V., & Aura, O. (1984). Mechanical efficiency of concentric and eccentric exercises performed with medium to fast contraction rates. *Scandinavian Journal of Sports Sciences*, **6**(1), 15-20.

Komi, P.V. (1983). Elastic potentiation of muscles and its influence on sport performance. In W. Baumann (Ed.), *Biomechanik und sportliche leistung* (pp. 59-70). Schorndorf, West Germany: Verlag Karl Hofmann.

Komi, P.V. (1984). Physiological and biomechanical correlates of muscle function: Effects of muscle structure and stretch-shortening cycle on force and speed. In R.L. Terjung (Ed.), *Exercise and sport sciences reviews, Vol. 12* (pp. 81-121). Lexington, MA: Collamore Press.

Komi, P.V. (1985). Ground reaction forces in cross-country skiing. In D.A. Winter, R.W. Norman, R.P. Wells, K.C. Hayes, & A.E. Patla (Eds.), *Biomechanics IX-B* (pp. 185-190). Champaign, IL: Human Kinetics.

Komi, P.V., & Gollhofer, A. (1986). Biomechanical approach to study man-shoe-surface interaction. In M. Kvist (Ed.), *Nordic Congress on Sports Traumatology* (pp. 135-156). Turku, Finland: Kupittaan Pikapaino Ltd.

Komi, P.V., Gollhofer, A., Schmidtbleicher, D., & Frick, U. (1987). Interaction between man and shoe in running: Considerations for a more comprehensive measurement approach. *International Journal of Sports Medicine*, **8**(3), 196-202.

Komi, P.V., Karlsson, J., Tesch, P., Suominen, H., & Häkkinen, E. (1982). Effects of heavy resistance and explosive type strength training methods on mechanical, functional and metabolic aspects of performance. In P.V. Komi (Ed.), *Exercise and sport biology* (pp. 90-102). Champaign, IL: Human Kinetics.

Komi, P.V., Salonen, M., Järvinen, M., & Kokko, O. (1987). In-vivo registration of Achilles tendon forces in man: I. Methodological development. *International Journal of Sports Medicine*, **8** (Suppl.), 3-8.

Komi, P.V., Viitasalo, J.H.T., Havu, M., Thorstensson, B., Sjödin, B., & Karlsson, J. (1977). Skeletal muscle fibers and muscle enzyme activities in monozygous and dizygous twins of both sexes. *Acta Physiologica Scandinavica*, **100**, 335-391.

Margaria, R. (1938). Sulla fisiologia e specialmente il consumo energetico della marcia e della corsa a varia velocita ed inclinazione del terrano. *Atti R Acc Naz Lincei (Rendiconti)*, **7**, 299-368.

Mero, A., & Komi, P.V. (1985). Effects of supramaximal velocity on biomechanical variables in sprinting. *International Journal of Sport Biomechanics*, **1**, 240-252.

Mero, A., & Komi, P.V. (1986). *Electromyographic activity in sprinting at different speeds ranging from submaximal to supramaximal*. Manuscript submitted for publication.

Nigg, B.M. (1983). External force measurements with sport shoes and playing surfaces. In B.M. Nigg & B.A. Kerr (Eds.), *Biomechanical aspects of sport shoes and playing surfaces* (pp. 11-23). Calgary, Alberta: University Printing.

Norman, R.W., & Komi, P.V. (1979). Electromechanical delay in skeletal muscle under normal movement conditions. *Acta Physiologica Scandinavica*, **106**, 241-248.

Schmidtbleicher, D., & Gollhofer, A. (1982). Neuromuskuläre Untersuchungen zur Bestimmung Individueller Belastungsgrössen für ein Tiefsprungtraining. *Leistungssport*, **12**, 298-307.

Stein, R.B. (1982). What muscle variable(s) does the nervous system control in limb movements? *The Behavioral and Brain Sciences*, **5**, 535-577.

Tihanyi, J., Apor, P., & Fekete, G. (1982). Force-velocity-power characteristics and fiber composition in human leg extensor muscles. *European Journal of Applied Physiology*, **48**, 331-343.

Viitasalo, J.T., Häkkinen, K., & Komi, P.V. (1982). Isometric and dynamic force production and muscle fibre composition in man. *Journal of Human Movement Studies*, **7**, 199-209.

Viitasalo, J., & Komi, P.V. (1978a). Force-time characteristics and fiber composition in human leg extensor muscles. *European Journal of Applied Physiology*, **40**, 7-15.

Viitasalo, J., & Komi, P.V. (1978b). Isometric endurance, EMG power spectrum, and fiber composition in human quadriceps muscle. In E. Asmussen & K. Jφrgensen (Eds.), *Biomechanics VI-A* (pp. 244-250). Baltimore: University Park Press.

Viitasalo, J., & Komi, P.V. (1981). Interrelationships between electromyographic, mechanical, muscle structure and reflex time measurements in man. *Acta Physiologica Scandinavica*, **111**, 97-103.

Walmsley, B., Hodgson, J.A., & Burke, R.E. (1978). Forces produced by medial gastrocnemius and soleus muscles during locomotion in freely moving cats. *Journal of Neurophysiology*, **41**, 1203-1216.

Zernicke, R.F. (1983). Biomechanical and biochemical synthesis. *Medicine and Science in Sports and Exercise*, **15**, 6-8.

Movement Dynamics and Connective Tissue Adaptations to Exercise

Ronald F. Zernicke

Two of the important questions that will focus future research in the biomechanics of exercise and sport sciences are (a) what are the biomechanical mechanisms that generate and control movement, and (b) what are the internal responses of the body to movement? The former question emphasizes the dynamics of the movement process, whereas the latter question emphasizes the specific adaptations of the body's tissues in response to exercise and physical activity. During movement, external contact forces, intersegmental inertial forces, and gravity can affect limb trajectories, passive and active muscle forces can modulate or generate limb motions, and these external and internal forces can directly influence the structure and function of the load-transmitting connective tissues (Zernicke, 1981). The resistance and transmission of forces by bone, tendon, ligament, and cartilage constitute the fundamental structural framework for movement, exercise, and sport activities. Further, acute or chronic injuries to these connective tissues pose significant threats to the physical well-being of exercise and sports participants of all ages and abilities (Emans, 1984; Mayer, 1984).

To begin to answer these two important research questions, an integrative and multidisciplinary approach is advocated strongly by several biomechanists (Bober, 1985; Hatze, 1984; Komi, 1984; Norman, 1985; Zernicke, 1983). Previously, I proposed that the methods of biochemistry and biomechanics be synthesized to explain more fully the structure and function of connective tissues, and that with an integrated approach there is an increased likelihood of results that explain *mechanisms* underlying connective tissue adaptations. In the present paper, I extend that earlier call for integrative research in two directions: (a) movement dynamics and (b) molecular biophysics. To some extent, these directions are related diametrically; on a more macroscopic level, movement dynamics involves the quantification of limb trajectories and kinetics, whereas on a more microscopic level, molecular biophysics involves the characterizations of the physical properties of the macromolecules that are associated with connective tissues.

Scope

In the following paragraphs, necessarily brief comments are given as background to the area of movement dynamics and to the area of molecular biophysics. Examples are then given of an integrated approach for examining bone and meniscus. Space limitations preclude a more extensive treatment of the adaptative responses of bones and menisci, but selected examples will serve to emphasize both the macroscopic and microscopic levels of integrative research in these tissues. Tendon and ligament responses to loading are not addressed in this paper, but several reviews are available that comprehensively discuss the present state of knowledge about fibrous tissue responses to mechanical loading (Akeson, Frank, Amiel, & Woo, 1985; Butler, Grood, Noyes, & Zernicke, 1978; Tipton, Matthes, Maynard, & Carey, 1976). Recent evidence shows that these fibrous connective tissues also possess substantial microstructural nonuniformities that affect their mechanical responses to loading (Butler, Grood, Noyes, Zernicke, & Brackett, 1984; Noyes, Butler, Grood, Zernicke, & Hefzy, 1984; Zernicke, Butler, Grood, & Hefzy, 1984), but the functional implications of such heterogeneity remains to be determined.

Methodologies

Movement Dynamics

Forces generated by and transmitted through load-bearing connective tissues have been quantified using modeling and direct measurements. Both approaches have their advantages and limitations, but to investigate how mechanical stresses will influence the functional and structural adaptations in connective tissues, valid estimates of tissue load-time histories are essential.

Musculoskeletal modeling. Hatze (1984) and King (1984) provide surveys of biomechanical models of the musculoskeletal system, and both of these biomechanists conclude that, although elegant theoretical models have been developed, the practical utility of most of the models remains problematical. Although the creation of a theoretical model may be stimulating and challenging in and of itself, the proving of a model should be its ability to accurately predict forces in muscles, tendons, ligaments, joints, and bones. This aspect of human motion research is still in its infancy, however, and only recently have signs of the maturation process begun to emerge (Hatze, 1984).

The inverse dynamics approach for modeling multilinked, musculoskeletal systems has been implemented for estimating joint forces and moments in a wide variety of movements in both humans (Aleshinsky & Zatsiorsky, 1978; Bresler & Frankel, 1950; Crowninshield, Johnston, Andrews, & Brand, 1978; Huang, Roberts, & Youm, 1982; Huston & Zernicke, 1982; Morrison, 1968, 1970; Paul, 1967; Röhrle, Scholten,

Sigolotto, & Sollbach, 1984; Winter, 1983; Zernicke, Garhammer, & Jobe, 1977; Zernicke & Roberts, 1978) and animals (Alexander, 1974; Alexander & Vernon, 1975; Biewener, Alexander, & Heglund, 1981; Biewener, Thomason, Goodship, & Lanyon, 1983; Hoy & Zernicke, 1985, 1986). In addition, optimization techniques (Hatze, 1981; Seireg & Arvikar, 1975; Zajac, Wicke, & Levine, 1984) may hold promise for future analyses of limb dynamics, but to date one of the major problems with this approach is in the choice of an "objective function" (King, 1984) or "performance criterion" (Hatze, 1984) for motion optimization. Extant physiological and anatomical data frequently do not map directly into formulated models, although advances are being made (Brand et al., 1982).

Nevertheless, results from an inverse dynamics approach using cine film coupled with force plates provide encouraging first steps in quantifying force distributions in limbs. In particular, the work on dogs, kangaroos, kangaroo rats, and horses by Alexander, Lanyon, Biewener, and associates (Alexander, 1974; Alexander & Vernon, 1975; Biewener et al., 1981, 1983) has led the way for further studies that may provide the estimates of joint forces, muscle forces, and tendon and bone stresses needed to explain the responses of connective tissues to motion. Here, too, advancements in model detail and complexity need to be made for this approach to prove consistently valid and reliable.

Direct measurement. Another approach for determining the loads transmitted through connective tissues is with the use of in vivo transducers. Primarily forces in tendons (Barnes & Pinder, 1974; Kear & Smith, 1975; Komi, 1985; Sherif, Gregor, Liu, Roy, & Hager, 1983; Walmsley, Hodgson, & Burke, 1978) and bones (Biewener et al., 1983; Brown, Burstein, & Frankel, 1982; Carter, Vasu, Spengler, & Dueland, 1981; Lanyon, Hampson, Goodship, & Shah, 1975; Rydell, 1966) have been analyzed with direct measurement techniques. The accurate extrapolation of local tissue strains sensed by a transducer to whole tissue loading, however, involves multiple assumptions and simplifications about a tissue's material and structural properties (Biewener et al., 1983). Direct comparisons between modeling methods and direct measurement methods are rare. One such comparison by Biewener and colleagues (1983) produced mixed but promising data on the longitudinal stresses acting in the cortices of the radius and metacarpus in the horse. Although the measurement of in vivo forces is technically difficult, there is an urgent need to develop experimental techniques to verify results from analytical models (King, 1984).

Molecular Biophysics

Although this research area appears to be far removed from limb dynamics, how connective tissues behave during load-bearing is inextricably linked to the tissue's microstructural composition. Bone, tendon, ligament, and cartilage all contain macromolecules that play vital roles in determining each tissue's mechanical properties. For example, in meniscal fibrocartilage, the extracellular matrix is composed of a network of collagen fibers and proteoglycans that interact with each other and with interstitial fluid to produce the tissue's material characteristics (Zernicke et al., 1986). These highly interactive features of the fibrocartilage extracellular matrix are generally consistent with the biophysical characteristics of polymer networks. Tanaka (1981) states that the mechanical integrity of a polymer network is related to polymer-polymer affinity, elasticity of individual polymer strands, and the pressure due to the solute hydrogen ion concentration. To a certain extent like hyaline cartilage (Mow, Holmes, & Lai, 1984), the mechanical behavior of meniscal fibrocartilage is a consequence of the osmotic swelling pressure of the extracellular matrix, anionic repulsion of glycosaminoglycans, ionic concentration, and steric and electrostatic interactions between glycosaminoglycans and collagen fibrils (Zernicke et al., 1986).

The nature of the physiochemical organization of load-bearing connective tissues requires much additional research to elaborate the structural correlates of tissue adaptations. But this basic research must be done so that exercise and sport scientists will be able to determine how the mechanical properties and ultrastructure of these connective tissues are changed by alterations in stress states, such as exercise or immobilization.

Integrating Movement Dynamics and Connective Tissue Adaptations

Bone

Limb bones, in particular, are highly responsive to altered loading states (Wolff, 1892). With exercise or increased physical activity, appendicular bones increase in size (Jones, Priest, Hayes, Tichenor, & Nagel, 1977), increase in mineralization (Smith, Reddan, & Smith, 1981; Steinberg & Trueta, 1981), and undergo substantial cortical remodeling (Cowin, Hart, Balser, & Kohn, 1985; Lanyon, 1980, 1984; Lanyon & Baggot, 1976; Lanyon & Bourn, 1979; Lanyon, Goodship, Pye, & McFie, 1982; Lanyon, Magee, & Baggot, 1979; Lanyon & Rubin, 1984; Rubin, 1984; Rubin & Lanyon, 1984; Woo et al., 1981). Conversely, with mechanical stress deprivation significant cortical remodeling and resorption may occur in bone (Geiser & Trueta, 1958; Globus, Bikle, Morey-Holton, 1984; LeBlanc et al., 1985; Morey, 1979; Morey & Baylink, 1978; Rambaut, Leach, & Whedon, 1979; Shaw et al., 1987; Uhthoff & Jaworski, 1978; Wronski & Morey, 1982, 1983a, 1983b).

That bone is sensitive to mechanical loads is clear, but what is not clear are the specific mechanisms to control the remodeling process. In summarizing the state of knowledge on the functional adaptations in bone tissue, Cowin, Lanyon, and Rodan (1984, p. S5) posed several unanswered questions, including (a) What is the nature of the mechanical change that affects remodeling? (b) What is the identity and manner of response of the cells initially receptive to that change? (c) What is the ability of the mechanically derived stimulus to compete with systemic stimuli? (d) What are the specific structural objectives of the bone remodeling process? Answers to questions (a) and (d) are intimately related to the accurate quantification of the stress distributions and limb loading histories during exercise or disuse.

In recent studies in our laboratory (Matsuda et al., 1986; Shaw et al., 1987) the influences of reduced mechanical loading or strenuous exercise on limb bones were investigated. The study by Shaw et al., in particular, reveals how information about limb dynamics helps to explain the selective cortical remodeling and mechanical alterations that occur in weight-bearing bones that have been shifted from their "normal physiologic band of activity" (Carter, 1984). For weight-bearing limbs, posture and locomotion provide the principal mechanical loading for long bones, and depriving the limb bones of weight-bearing forces or augmenting loading on the limb bones through exercise should have predictable consequences. Shaw et al. (1987) examined the influences of weight-bearing forces on the structural remodeling, matrix biochemistry, and mechanical characteristics of the rat femur and tibia by means of a hind limb suspension protocol coupled with highly intensive treadmill running. Female, young-adult rats were assigned randomly to either normal control, sedentary-suspended, or exercise-suspended groups. For a period of 28 days, sedentary-suspended rats were deprived of hind limb ground reaction forces and were able to ambulate only with their forelimbs, which still maintained contact with the ground (Morey-Holton & Wronski, 1981). The exercise-suspended rats were also suspended for 28 days, but once a day experienced hind limb ground reaction forces during intensive treadmill training sessions.

The unweighting of the hind limbs during suspension eliminates the limb-to-ground contact forces that normally must be resisted by antigravity muscles during standing and during the support phase of locomotion. Electromyographical data (Nicolopoulos-Strournaras & Iles, 1984) reveals that during rat locomotion, hind limb extensors and adductors are active just before and throughout stance during a wide range of speeds, and that flexor muscle activity occurs just prior to and during the swing phase of locomotion. Thus one can hypothesize that eliminating ground reaction forces during suspension should have negligible consequences for flexor muscle mechanical loading, because during the swing phase of locomotion the flexor muscles only have to counteract inertial and gravitational forces. For antigravity muscles, however, the lack of ground reaction forces produced a significant alteration in loading environment. The suspension produced generalized atrophy of hind limb skeletal muscles, with greater atrophy occurring in predominantly slow-twitch extensor and adductors, as compared with the mixed fiber-type extensor and flexors. If bone cortices respond to pressure locally applied to the periosteum from attaching muscle groups (Lanyon, 1980), the differential atrophy of various antigravity muscle groups may help to explain limb bone regional remodeling. For example, regional adaptations in mid-diaphyseal cortical thicknesses of the tibiae of sedentary suspended rats were consistent with both muscle recruitment patterns and muscle mass alterations. During suspension, the average daily electromyographical activity of tibialis anterior increases 89% (Alford, Roy, Chiang, & Edgerton, 1985) and remains elevated throughout a full 28 days of suspension. Concomitantly, the tibial anterior cortical thickness increased 69% in the sedentary-suspended rats. In contrast, the thickness of the posterior tibial cortex decreased (29%) in the sedentary-suspended rats, and that thickness decrease was correlated with a significant decrease (64%) in soleus muscle mass. Medial cortex of the rat tibia has essentially no muscle attachment sites, and no differences were found between the medial cortical thicknesses of the sedentary-suspended and control tibiae.

The lateral thickness of the tibia decreased by 11%, and although this may have been due in part to muscle force alterations, a more probable cause of the decreased lateral cortical thickness during suspension could be the decrease in bending-related compressive strains. It has been shown that cyclic bending strains account for most of the total strain in limb bones during locomotion (Lanyon & Baggot, 1976; Lanyon & Bourn, 1979; Lanyon et al., 1979; Rubin, 1984), and thus "bone strain" may be a mechanism to account for selective bone remodeling (Lanyon, 1980). Of the two principal strains that occur during bending, cyclic compressive strain is the more potent stimulus for bone remodeling (Carter, 1984; Chamay & Tschanz, 1972; Lanyon & Baggot, 1976; Lanyon & Bourn, 1979; Matsuda et al., 1986; Woo et al., 1981). Carter suggests that the accumulated fatigue microdamage is a possible explanation of the differential remodeling effects of tensile and compressive bone strain (Carter, 1984; Carter & Hayes, 1977).

There are data to indicate that during the stance phase of rat locomotion, the rat knee experiences significant valgus loading. Vailas, Zernicke, Matsuda, Curwin, and Durivage (1986) report that the posterior horn of the rat's lateral knee meniscus becomes significantly thicker as a result of the compressive loading during running. The posterior horn of the medial meniscus, however, is unaffected by the endurance training. This unequal response of these mechanically (Zernicke et al., 1986), morphologically, and biochemically (Vailas, Zernicke, Matsuda, & Peller, 1985) identical meniscal horns is consistent with the unequal tibial condyle compressive loads that occur during genu valgus. The ground reaction forces occurring during the stance phase of locomotion with the genu valgus will have a tendency to cause tibial bending strains about a cranial-caudal axis. The lateral surface of the tibia, therefore, will experience compression strains during normal locomotion, and the removal of the normal weight-bearing loads on the tibia may have stimulated the resorption of the tibia's lateral cortex in the suspended rats.

Shaw et al. (1987) indicated that the strenuous exercise that was superimposed on some of the suspension animals counteracted muscular atrophy during the suspension, to a moderate extent. This sparing effect was most pronounced in slow-twitch antigravity muscles. The exercise, however, did not mitigate the deterioration in bone mechanical properties and cross-sectional morphologies. Although exercise and training may enhance the mechanical properties and structural dimensions of bones (Booth & Gould, 1975; Goodship, Lanyon, & McFie, 1979; Jones et al., 1977; Rubin & Lanyon, 1984; Steinberg & Trueta, 1981), exercise intensity appears to be an important factor in determining the specific effects of exercise on bone remodeling. Booth and Gould (1975) hypothesize that low- and moderate-intensity training may stimulate bone growth and remodeling, whereas high-intensity training may inhibit bone formation. Both Kiiskinen (1977) and Matsuda et al. (1986) support that hypothesis. For example, Matsuda et al. show that with daily exercise at 70 to 80% of maximum oxygen capacity, a weight-bearing limb bone in the growing rooster experiences significant suppression of bone remodeling and significant reduction in bending stiffness, energy to yield, and energy to failure.

During rat hind limb suspension, without bone strains that normally occur during postural weight support and locomotion, the biological repair of accumulated fatigue microdamage (Carter, 1984) that may have occurred during the daily bouts of strenuous exercise may have been retarded, or the mechanical stimulus for bone adaptive remodeling may have been counteracted by another exercise-induced stimulus. Humoral concentrations that may be altered during intensive exercise can also influence bone growth and remodeling. For example, cyclic nucleotides (Rodan, Bourret, Harvey, & Mensi, 1975), osteocalcin, parathyroid hormone (Mohan, Linkhart, Farley, & Baylink, 1984), and prostaglandins (Yeh & Rodan, 1984) can affect bone remodeling; however, the influence that intensive exercise has on the localized concentrations of these humoral factors is still unknown.

Meniscus

Meniscal fibrocartilage is an important transmitter of loads across the knee joint and also enhances tibiofemoral congruity (Vailas et al., 1985; Vailas et al., 1986; Zernicke et al., 1986). Recently, several investigators reported morphologically and biochemically heterogeneous regions in menisci from various animals and human sources (Adams & Muir, 1981; Eyre & Wu, 1983; McNicol & Roughley, 1980; Pedrini-Mille, Maynard, Pedrini, & Vailas, 1985). None of these menisci, however, displays the marked contrast in matrix composition of the anterior and posterior regions as do rat knee menisci. The anterior region contains three times the calcium concentration of the posterior horn, and the posterior horn has significantly greater concentrations of collagen and glycosaminoglycans and greater cell density than the anterior horn (Vailas et al., 1985). These ultrastructural differences, however, are in harmony with functional demands placed on the tissue during normal use.

The primary load-bearing function for rat knee menisci will occur during locomotion. Gruner, Altman, and Spivak (1980), in a kinematic and electromyographic study, report that knee joint angles during each step cycle in rat locomotion remain at angles less than 1.87 rad (107°). Thus, the rat knee is typically in a flexed position, and the comparatively thicker and stiffer anterior horn of the meniscus is well adapted to enhance tibiofemoral congruity and to act as a retro-patellar spacer (Zernicke et al., 1986). In contrast, the posterior horn may be more important in shock absorption and load-bearing as a result of the orientation and contact areas of the femur and tibia during locomotion, and the recent study by Vailas et al. (1986) substantiates that only the posterior horn of the rat knee meniscus adapts to increased loading during exercise.

The differences in the anterior and posterior horns of the rat menisci provide a useful tissue model in which to study molecular biophysics. Characteristically, in fibrocartilage the collagen and proteoglycans interactions are primary (Comper & Laurent, 1978; Hardingham, 1981), but our data (Zernicke et al., 1986) demonstrate the substantial effect that calcium can have in modifying the mechanical response of fibrocartilage. Collagen resists tension, and Egner (1982) has described a three-dimensional, netlike framework of longitudinal fibers that is bound together by transverse and diagonal fibers. This fibrous network acts to maintain the morphological integrity of the menisci and to restrain the hydrophilic, highly charged glycosaminoglycans (Hardingham, 1981). Additionally, cross-linking of collagen is a fundamental prerequisite for the collagen fibers to withstand the physical stresses to which they are exposed (Akeson et al., 1977; Allain, LeLous, Bazin, Bailey, & DeLaunay, 1978). The physiochemical stability of collagen in menisci is most likely influenced by the presence of glycosaminoglycans (Snowden, 1982). With thermomechanical stress analyses, Zernicke et al. (1986) also show that in the calcium-stiffened anterior horn of the rat meniscus the collagen network is more stable than in the posterior horn. In the anterior horn, the smaller amounts of negatively charged glycosaminoglycans may not be able to expand significantly with increased temperature. Additionally, the large number of positively charged calcium ions in the anterior horn of the meniscus may diminish the electrostatic repulsion effects of glycosaminoglycans.

Summary

For the exercise or sport scientist in connective tissue mechanics and physiology, the directions of importance are to accurately model or measure the dynamics of the movement process and to elaborate the mechanisms of connective tissue adaptation to mechanical loading state. Significant progress is essential in each of these areas before a fully unified and integrated systems approach is realized. Innovative technical advancements and rigorous analytical methods must become the standard so that a multidisciplinary, integrative approach will yield answers about mechanisms rather than remaining at comparative and descriptive levels of analysis.

References

Adams, M.E., & Muir, H. (1981). The glycosaminoglycans of canine menisci. *Biochemistry Journal*, **197**, 385-389.

Akeson, W.H., Amiel, D., Mechanic, G.L., Woo, S.L.-Y., Harwood, F.L., & Hamer, M.L. (1977). Collagen crosslinking alterations in joint contractures: Changes in the reducible crosslinks in periarticular connective tissue collagen after nine weeks of immobilization. *Connective Tissue Research*, **5**, 15-19.

Akeson, W.H., Frank, C.B., Amiel, D., & Woo, S.L.-Y. (1985). Ligament biology and biomechanics. In G. Finerman (Ed.), *American Academy of Orthopaedic Surgeons symposium on sports medicine: The knee* (pp. 111-151). St. Louis: Mosby.

Aleshinsky, S.Y., & Zatsiorsky, V.M. (1978). Human locomotion in space analyzed biomechanically through a multi-link chain model. *Journal of Biomechanics*, **11**, 101-108.

Alexander, R.McN. (1974). The mechanics of jumping by a dog (*Canis familiaris*). *Journal of Zoological Research*, **173**, 549-573.

Alexander, R.McN, & Vernon, A. (1975). The mechanics of hopping by kangaroos (Macropodidae). *Journal of Zoological Research*, **177**, 265-303.

Alford, E.K., Roy, R.R., Chiang, P.C., & Edgerton, V.R. (1985). Hindlimb suspension effects on integrated electromyographic activity in selected rat hindlimb muscles. *The Physiologist*, **28**, 315.

Allain, J.C., LeLous, A., Bazin, S., Bailey, A.J., & DeLaunay, A. (1978). Isometric tension developed during heating collagenous tissues: Relationships with collagen cross-linking. *Biochimica Biophysica Acta*, **533**, 147-155.

Barnes, G.R.G., & Pinder, D.N. (1974). *In vivo* tendon tension and bone strain measurement and correlation. *Journal of Biomechanics*, **7**, 35-42.

Biewener, A.A., Alexander, R.McN., & Heglund, N.C. (1981). Elastic energy storage in the hopping of kangaroo rats (*Dipodomys spectabilis*). *Journal of Zoological Research*, **195**, 369-383.

Biewener, A.A., Thomason, J., Goodship, A., & Lanyon, L.E. (1983). Bone stress in the horse forelimb during locomotion at different gaits: A comparison of two experimental methods. *Journal of Biomechanics*, **16**, 565-576.

Bober, T. (1985). Comments on "Biomechanics: Are there substantive issues?" *International Society of Biomechanics Newsletter*, **20**, 6.

Booth, F.W., & Gould, E.W. (1975). Effects of training and disuse on connective tissue. *Exercise and Sport Sciences Reviews*, **3**, 83-112.

Brand, R.A., Crowninshield, R.D., Wittstock, C.E., Pedersen, D.R., Clark, C.R., & van Krieken, F.M. (1982). A model of lower extremity muscular anatomy. *Journal of Biomechanical Engineering*, **104**, 304-310.

Bresler, B., & Frankel, J.P. (1950). The forces and moments in the leg during level walking. *Transactions of the American Society of Mechanical Engineers*, **72**, 27-36.

Brown, R.H., Burstein, A.H., & Frankel, V.H. (1982). Telemetering *in vivo* loads from nail plate implants. *Journal of Biomechanics*, **15**, 815-824.

Butler, D.L., Grood, E.S., Noyes, F.R., & Zernicke, R.F. (1978). Biomechanics of tendons and ligaments. *Exercise and Sport Sciences Reviews*, **6**, 125-181.

Butler, D.L., Grood, E.S., Noyes, F.R., Zernicke, R.F., & Brackett, K. (1984). Effects of structure and strain measurement technique on the material properties of young human tendons and fascia. *Journal of Biomechanics*, **17**, 579-596.

Carter, D.R. (1984). Mechanical loading histories and cortical bone remodeling. *Calcified Tissue International*, **36**, S19-S24.

Carter, D.R., & Hayes, W.C. (1977). Compact bone fatigue damage. I. Residual strength and stiffness. *Journal of Biomechanics*, **10**, 325-338.

Carter, D.R., Vasu, R., Spengler, D.M., & Dueland, R.T. (1981). Stress fields in the unplated and plated canine femur calculated from *in vivo* strain measurements. *Journal of Biomechanics*, **14**, 63-70.

Chamay, A., & Tschanz, P. (1972). Mechanical influences in bone remodeling: Experimental research on Wolff's Law. *Journal of Biomechanics*, **5**, 173-180.

Comper, W.D., & Laurent, T.C. (1978). Physiological function of connective tissue polysaccharides. *Physiological Reviews*, **58**, 255-303.

Cowin, S.C., Hart, R.T., Balser, J.R., & Kohn, D.H. (1985). Functional adaptation in long bones: Establishing *in vivo* values for surface remodeling rate coefficients. *Journal of Biomechanics*, **18**, 665-684.

Cowin, S.C., Lanyon, L.E., & Rodan, G. (1984). The Kroc Foundation Conference on functional adaptation in bone tissue. *Calcified Tissue International*, **36**, S1-S6.

Crowinshield, R.D., Johnston, R.C., Andrews, J.G., & Brand, R.A. (1978). A biomechanical investigation of the human hip. *Journal of Biomechanics*, **11**, 75-85.

Egner, E. (1982). Knee joint meniscal degeneration as it relates to tissue fiber structure and mechanical resistance. *Pathology Research Practicum*, **173**, 310-324.

Emans, J.B. (1984). Upper extremity injuries in sports. In L.J. Micheli (Ed.), *Pediatric and adolescent sports medicine* (pp. 49-79). Boston: Little, Brown & Co.

Eyre, D.R., & Wu, J.J. (1983). Collagen of fibrocartilage: A distinctive molecular phenotype in bovine meniscus. *Federation of European Biochemistry Societies*, **158**, 265-270.

Geiser, M., & Trueta, J. (1958). Muscle action, bone rarefaction, and bone formation. *Journal of Bone and Joint Surgery*, **40B**, 282-311.

Globus, R.K., Bikle, D.D., & Morey-Holton, E. (1984). Effects of simulated weightlessness on bone mineral metabolism. *Endocrinology*, **114**, 2264-2270.

Goodship, A.E., Lanyon, L.E., & McFie, H. (1979). Functional adaptation of bone to increased stress. *Journal of Bone and Joint Surgery*, **61A**, 539-546.

Gruner, J.A., Altman, J., & Spivack, N. (1980). Effects of arrested cerebellar development on locomotion in the rat. *Experimental Brain Research*, **40**, 361-373.

Hardingham, T. (1981). Proteoglycans: Their structure, interactions and molecular organization in cartilage. *Biochemistry Society Transactions*, **9**, 489-497.

Hatze, H. (1981). A comprehensive model for human motion simulation and its application to the take-off phase of the long jump. *Journal of Biomechanics*, **14**, 135-142.

Hatze, H. (1984). Quantitative analysis, synthesis, and simulation of human motion. *Human Movement Science*, **3**, 5-25.

Hoy, M.G., & Zernicke, R.F. (1985). Modulation of limb dynamics in the swing phase of locomotion. *Journal of Biomechanics*, **18**, 49-60.

Hoy, M.G., & Zernicke, R.F. (1986). The role of intersegmental dynamics during rapid limb oscillations. *Journal of Biomechanics*, **19**, 867-877.

Huang, T.C., Roberts, E.M., & Youm, Y. (1982). Biomechanics of kicking. In D.N. Ghista (Ed.), *Human body dynamics—impact, occupational, and athletic aspects* (pp. 409-443). Oxford: Clarendon Press.

Huston, R.L. & Zernicke, R.F. (1982). Computerized simulation of whole body dynamics: Aspects of human movement modeling. *Proceedings of the Society of Photo-optical and Instrumentation Engineering*, **291**, 180-186.

Jones, H.H., Priest, J.D., Hayes, W.C., Tichenor, C.C., & Nagel, A. (1977). Humeral hypertrophy in response to exercise. *Journal of Bone and Joint Surgery*, **59A**, 204-208.

Kear, M., & Smith, R.N. (1975). A method of recording tendon strain in sheep during locomotion. *Acta Orthopaedica Scandinavica*, **46**, 896-905.

Kiiskinen, A. (1977). Physical training and connective tissue in young mice—physical properties of Achilles tendon and long bone growth. *Growth*, **41**, 123-127.

King, A.I. (1984). A review of biomechanical models. *Journal of Biomechanical Engineering*, **106**, 97-104.

Komi, P.V. (1984). Biomechanics and neuromuscular performance. *Medicine and Science in Sports and Exercise*, **16**, 26-28.

Komi, P.V. (1985). Measurement of *in vivo* Achilles tendon forces in man and their calibration. *Medicine and Science in Sports and Exercise*, **17**, 263.

Lanyon, L.E. (1980). The influence of function on the development of bone curvature. *Journal of Zoology* (London), **192**, 457-466.

Lanyon, L.E. (1984). Functional strains as a determinant for bone remodeling. *Calcified Tissue International*, **36**, S31-S38.

Lanyon, L.E., & Baggot, D.G. (1976). Mechanical function as an influence on the structure and form of bone. *Journal of Bone and Joint Surgery*, **58B**, 436-443.

Lanyon, L.E., & Bourn, S. (1979). The influence of mechanical function on the development and remodelling of the tibia. *Journal of Bone and Joint Surgery*, **61A**, 263-273.

Lanyon, L.E., Goodship, A.E., Pye, C.J., & McFie, J.H. (1982). Mechanically adaptive bone remodelling. *Journal of Biomechanics*, **15**, 141-154.

Lanyon, L.E., Hampson, W.G., Goodship, A.E., & Shah, J.S. (1975). Bone deformation *in vivo* from strain gauges attached to the human tibial shaft. *Acta Orthopaedica Scandinavica*, **46**, 256-268.

Lanyon, L.E., Magee, P.T., & Baggot, D.G. (1979). The relationship of functional stress and strain to the processes of bone remodelling. An experimental study of the sheep radius. *Journal of Biomechanics*, **12**, 593-600.

Lanyon, L.E., & Rubin, C.T. (1984). Static vs dynamic loads as an influence on bone remodelling. *Journal of Biomechanics*, **17**, 897-905.

LeBlanc, A., Marsh, C., Evans, H., Johnson, P., Schneider, V., & Jhingran, S. (1985). Bone and muscle atrophy with suspension of the rat. *Journal of Applied Physiology: Respiratory, Environmental, and Exercise Physiology*, **58**, 1669-1675.

Matsuda, J.J., Zernicke, R.F., Vailas, A.C., Pedrini, V.A., Pedrini-Mille, A., & Maynard, J.A. (1986). Structural and mechanical adaptation of immature bone to strenuous exercise. *Journal of Applied Physiology: Respiratory, Environmental, and Exercise Physiology*, **60**, 2028-2034.

Mayer, P.J. (1984). Lower limb injuries in childhood and adolescence. In L.J. Micheli (Ed.), *Pediatric and adolescent sports medicine* (pp.80-106). Boston: Little, Brown & Co.

McNicol, D., & Roughley, P.J. (1980). Extraction and characterization of proteoglycans from human meniscus. *Biochemistry Journal*, **185**, 713-715.

Meade, J.B., Cowin, S.C., Klawitter, J.J., Van Buskirk, W.C., & Skinner, H.B. (1984). Bone remodeling to continuously applied loads. *Calcified Tissue International*, **36**, S25-S30.

Mohan, S., Linkhart, T., Farley, J., & Baylink, D.J. (1984). Bone derived factors active on bone cells. *Calcified Tissue International*, **36**, S119-S145.

Morey, E.R. (1979). Spaceflight and bone turnover: Correlation with a new rat model of weightlessness. *BioScience*, **29**, 168-172.

Morey, E.R., & Baylink, D.J. (1978). Inhibition of bone formation during spaceflight. *Science*, **201**, 1138-1141.

Morey-Holton, E.R., & Wronski, T.J. (1981). Animal models for simulating weightlessness. *The Physiologist*, **24**, S45-S48.

Morrison, J.B. (1968). Bioengineering analysis of force actions transmitted by the knee joint. *Biomedical Engineering*, **3**, 164-170.

Morrison, J.B. (1970). The mechanics of muscle function in locomotion. *Journal of Biomechanics*, **3**, 431-451.

Mow, V.C., Holmes, M.H., & Lai, W.M. (1984). Fluid transport and mechanical properties of articular cartilage: A review. *Journal of Biomechanics*, **17**, 377-394.

Nicolopoulos-Stournaras, S., & Iles, J.F. (1984). Hindlimb muscle activity during locomotion in the rat (*Rattus norvegicus*) (Rodentia: Muridae). *Journal of Zoology* (London), **203**, 427-440.

Norman, R.W. (1985). Biomechanics: Are there substantive issues? *International Society of Biomechanics Newsletter*, **18**, 2-3.

Noyes, F.R., Butler, D.L., Grood, E.S., Zernicke, R.F., & Hefzy, M.S. (1984). Biomechanical analysis of human ligament grafts used in knee-ligament repairs and reconstructions. *Journal of Bone and Joint Surgery*, **66A**, 344-352.

Paul, J.P. (1967). Forces transmitted by joints in the human body. *Proceedings of the Institute of Mechanical Engineers*, **181** (Part 3J), Paper 8.

Pedrini-Mille, A., Maynard, J.A., Pedrini, V., & Vailas, A.C. (1985). Effect of strenuous exercise on menisci of growing animals. *Transactions of the Orthopaedic Research Society*, **10**, 59.

Rambaut, P.C., Leach, C.S., & Whedon, G.D. (1979). A study of metabolic balance in crewmembers of Skylab IV. *Acta Astronautica*, **6**, 1313-1322.

Rodan, G.A., Bourret, L.A., Harvey, A., & Mensi, T. (1975). Cyclic AMP and cyclic GMP: Mediators of the mechanical effects on bone remodeling. *Science*, **189**, 467-469.

Röhrle, H., Scholten, R., Sigolotto, C., & Sollbach, W. (1984). Joint forces in the human pelvis-leg skeleton during walking. *Journal of Biomechanics*, **17**, 409-424.

Rubin, C.T. (1984). Skeletal strain and the functional significance of bone architecture. *Calcified Tissue International*, **36**, S11-S18.

Rubin, C.T., & Lanyon, L.E. (1984). Regulation of bone formation by applied dynamic loads. *Journal of Bone and Joint Surgery*, **66A**, 397-402.

Rydell, N.W. (1966). Forces acting on the femoral head prosthesis. *Acta Orthopaedica Scandinavica*, Suppl. 88, 1-132.

Seireg, A., & Arvikar, R.J. (1975). The prediction of muscular load sharing and joint forces in the lower extremities during walking. *Journal of Biomechanics*, **8**, 89-102.

Shaw, S.R., Zernicke, R.F., Vailas, A.C., DeLuna, D., Thomason, D.B., & Baldwin, K.M. (1987). Mechanical, morphological, and biochemical adaptations of bone and muscle to hindlimb suspension and exercise. *Journal of Biomechanics*, **20**, 225-234

Sherif, M.H., Gregor, R.J., Liu, L.M., Roy, R.R., & Hager, C.L. (1983). Correlation of myoelectric activity and muscle force during selected cat treadmill locomotion. *Journal of Biomechanics*, **16**, 691-703.

Smith, E.L., Reddan, W., & Smith, P.E. (1981). Physical activity and calcium modalities for bone mineral in aged women. *Medicine and Science in Sports and Exercise*, **13**, 60-64.

Snowden, J.M. (1982). The stabilization of *in vivo* assembled collagen fibrils by proteoglycans/glycosaminoglycans. *Biochimica Biophysica Acta*, **703**, 21-25.

Steinberg, M.E., & Trueta, J. (1981). Effects of activity on bone growth and development in the rat. *Clinical Orthopaedics and Related Research*, **156**, 52-60.

Tanaka, T. (1981). Gels. *Scientific American*, **244**, 124-138.

Tipton, C.M., Matthes, R.D., Maynard, J.A., & Carey, R.A. (1976). The influence of physical activity on ligaments and tendons. *Medicine and Science in Sports and Exercise*, **7**, 165-175.

Uhthoff, H.K., & Jaworski, Z.F.G. (1978). Bone loss in response to long-term immobilization. *Journal of Bone and Joint Surgery*, **60B**, 420-429.

Vailas, A.C., Zernicke, R.F., Matsuda, J.J., Curwin, S., & Durivage, J. (1986). Adaptation of rat knee meniscus to prolonged exercise. *Journal of Applied Physiology: Respiratory, Environmental, and Exercise Physiology*, **60**, 1031-1034.

Vailas, A.C., Zernicke, R.F., Matsuda, J., & Peller, D. (1985). Regional biochemical and morphological characteristics of rat knee meniscus. *Comparative Biochemistry and Physiology*, **82B**, 283-285.

Walmsley, B., Hodgson, J.E., & Burke, R.E. (1978). Forces produced by medial gastrocnemius in moving cats. *Journal of Neurophysiology*, **41**, 1203-1215.

Winter, D.A. (1983). Moments of force and mechanical power in jogging. *Journal of Biomechanics*, **16**, 91-98.

Wronski, T.J., & Morey, E.R. (1982). Skeletal abnormalities in rats induced by simulated weightlessness. *Metabolism, Bone Diseases and Related Research*, **4**, 69-75.

Wronski, T.J., & Morey, E.R. (1983a). Alterations in calcium homeostasis and bone during actual and simulated space flight. *Medicine and Science in Sports and Exercise*, **15**, 410-414.

Wronski, T.J., & Morey, E.R. (1983b). Effect of spaceflight on periosteal bone formation in rats. *American Journal of Physiology: Regulatory, Integrative, and Comparative Physiology*, **244**, R305-R309.

Wolff, J. (1892). *Das Gesetz der Transformation der Knochen*. Berlin: A. Hirschwold.

Woo, S.L-Y., Kuei, S.C., Amiel, D., Gomez, M.A., Hayes, W.C., White, F.C., & Akeson, W.H. (1981). The effect of prolonged physical training on the properties of long bone: A study of Wolff's Law. *Journal of Bone and Joint Surgery*, **63A**, 780-787.

Yeh, C-K., & Rodan, G.A. (1984). Tensile forces enhance prostaglandin E synthesis in osteoblastic cells grown on collagen ribbons. *Calcified Tissue International*, **36**, S67-S71.

Zajac, F.E., Wicke, R.W., & Levine, W.S. (1984). Dependence of jumping performance on muscle properties when humans use only calf muscles for propulsion. *Journal of Biomechanics*, **17**, 513-524.

Zernicke, R.F. (1981). The emergence of human biomechanics. In G.A. Brooks (Ed.), *Perspectives on the academic discipline of physical education* (pp. 124-136). Champaign, IL: Human Kinetics.

Zernicke, R.F. (1983). Biomechanical and biochemical synthesis. *Medicine and Science in Sports and Exercise*, **15**, 6-8.

Zernicke, R.F., Butler, D.L., Grood, E.S., & Hefzy, M.S. (1984). Strain topography of human tendon and fascia. *Journal of Biomechanical Engineering*, **106**, 177-180.

Zernicke, R.F., Garhammer, J.J., & Jobe, F.W. (1977). Human patellar tendon rupture: A kinetic analysis. *Journal of Bone and Joint Surgery*, **59A**, 179-183.

Zernicke, R.F., & Roberts, E.M. (1978). Lower extremity forces and torques during systematic variation of non-weightbearing motion. *Medicine and Science in Sports and Exercise*, **10**, 21-26.

Zernicke, R.F., Vailas, A.C., Shaw, S.R, Bogey, R.A., Hart, T., & Matsuda, J. (1986). Heterogeneous mechanical response of rat menisci to thermomechanical stress. *American Journal of Physiology: Regulatory, Integrative, and Comparative Physiology*, **250**, R65-R70.

A Barrier to Understanding Human Motion Mechanisms: A Commentary

Robert W. Norman

Before embarking upon a journey into speculation about the directions of future biomechanics research on human movement, the ultimate objectives of that research should be outlined. Biomechanics has been criticized from time to time by scientists of other disciplines as being only descriptive, completely atheoretical, and preoccupied with methodology. I believe that the criticism is justified to some extent, although the situation is changing. With a few notable exceptions, the biomechanics literature of the 1950s, 1960s, and even the 1970s has been dominated by descriptive kinematic and EMG analyses of numerous sports movements and walking. In the 1970s there were increasing numbers of mechanical work, power output, and body joint moment of force papers that, by their kinetic nature, dealt with mechanical causes of motion. But even most of these papers simply presented joint moment or body energy time histories and made little attempt to interpret them. As late as 1983, Cappozzo stated that we (biomechanists) must go beyond our usual descriptions of human motion patterns and devote more time to interpreting the patterns with an eye to determining, through generalizations, the laws that govern them.

Although I agree with Cappozzo, I would argue that the research paradigm of the biomechanist is solidly based on well-substantiated laws and theories of Newtonian, Hamiltonian, and Lagrangian mechanics. The social and, to a large extent, the strictly biological sciences do not have the advantage of anchoring their research on such well-established laws. Moreover, a number of hypotheses have been proposed by biomechanists regarding control mechanisms of human motion, albeit usually by inference and often not central to the purpose of the particular study. These have appeared as "objective functions" in optimization models (e.g., Hatze, 1976; Nubar & Contini, 1961; Pedotti, Krishnan, & Stark, 1978; Yeo, 1976). The problem with the direction of much past biomechanics research has been an apparent lack of long-term objectives.

I have argued (Norman, 1985) that the long-term objective of basic biomechanics research should be the enhancement of understanding of *mechanisms*, not merely sophisticated documentation of patterns of human kinematic or kinetic variables. Without this understanding, progress in solving applied problems will, at best, be slow. Both Zernicke and Komi, in these proceedings and previously (1983 and 1984, respectively), referred to this same objective. Zernicke stated specifically that two important research questions in biomechanics of sport and exercise are (a) what are the biomechanical mechanisms that generate and control movements and (b) what are the internal responses of the body to movement? Of course, it is acknowledged that members of other disciplines lay claim to the same objective. The difference is in perspective.

Yet Another Definition of Biomechanics!

The research directions of a discipline are, to some extent, guided by the definition of the discipline. Indeed, Hatze (1974) has stated that for biomechanics to claim to be a science of its own it must have a clearly defined subject of study. There has been little agreement over the years as to an appropriate definition of biomechanics, perhaps the sign of a still emerging discipline (cf. Contini & Drillis, 1966; Hatze, 1974; Winter, 1979b). Furthermore, definitions can sometimes be unnecessarily constraining, and it is well known that boundaries between disciplines are becoming less and less sharp. But it may be that the definitions of biomechanics proposed in the past, undoubtedly a reflection of the perspective of the scientifically accomplished people who proposed them, have been, in part, responsible for our descriptive research.

Contini and Drillis (1966), for example, define biomechanics as "the science which investigates the effects of internal and external forces on human and animal bodies in movement and rest" (p. 163). This is an appealing definition because it is simply the modification of a widely accepted definition of engineering mechanics applied to the animal world. It has two shortcomings, however, because of implied constraints. It does not accommodate the important study of plant biomechanics and it excludes, perhaps purposely, the important area of control of forces, the neuromuscular aspect of human motion vital to the understanding of movement mechanisms. Zernicke (this volume) referred to the control of movement in one of his research questions, Komi's (this volume) entire presentation addressed the area of motor control, and the neural control of movement has been an identified topic of research presentation at all International Society of Biomechanics Congresses since 1976.

At the risk of generating yet another contentious definition of biomechanics, I will propose one that corrects what to me are deficiencies in that of Contini and Drillis (1966) and clearly defines the subject of study: Biomechanics is the study of the effects and control of forces that act on and are produced by living bodies. This definition includes all living bodies, animal or vegetable; emphasizes the special perspective of the biomechanist, that of forces and their effects, a prerequisite of the field of mechanics; and includes the concern for control of forces, a control that may be neurological or, in some cases, exclusively mechanical, via tissue elasticity and damping, for example. Moreover, the control component of the definition, rather than being limiting and exclusive, provides common ground with the interests of people working in many other disciplines. They include neurophysiologists, muscle physiologists, psychomotor behaviorists, neuropsychologists, and a host of people interested in particular aspects of applied research such as rehabilitation medicine, orthopedics, ergonomics, robotics, sport, and exercise.

The definition proposed is what biomechanics has become. The evidence appears in both Zernicke's and Komi's integrative papers in these proceedings, in the increasing common interests of psychomotor behaviorists and biomechanists in neural control of movement issues, and, to a lesser extent, in the interaction of biomechanists and physiologists on issues of efficiency of human movement, positive and negative work, and muscular strength. An escalation of this integration will undoubtedly be seen in the future with a concomitant influence on experimental designs and research focus.

More important than the mere escalation of interaction among biomechanists and members of other disciplines is a recognition of the growing need for that interaction. Indeed, interdisciplinary research cannot survive unless it is motivated first by mutual need. Artificially assembled research interest groups, or research interactions forced by administrative expediency or by future but not currently perceived needs, do not work. I believe that the interdisciplinary glue is found in what, in my estimation, is the most pressing problem facing researchers in the biomechanics of human movement today. The problem is pressing because it is blocking progress in understanding human movement mechanisms by scientists in several fields, not just biomechanics. Moreover, advances in the solution of a wide range of both basic and applied questions depend on a breakthrough in the solution of this problem.

A Barrier to Understanding Human Motion Mechanisms

In my opinion, the single most important problem in the study of human motion is the development of accurate, noninvasive methods of calculating individual muscle and ligament force-time histories during normal human movements. The issues and fields affected by our inability to deal with this problem in a general way include (a) the understanding of the mechanisms of the control of bone remodeling induced by changes in mechanical loading (such as those produced by exercise, immobilization, and space travel), of interest to tissue biomechanists, macromolecular biophysicists, and biochemists (Zernicke, this volume); (b) the study of neural control of human motion, investigated by psychomotor behaviorists, neuropsychologists, and neurophysiologists; (c) the identification and implementation of appropriate objective functions in optimization models of human motion, of interest to many biomechanists and biomathematicians and also of relevance to the neural control areas; (d) the understanding of the efficiency of human movement, and of positive and negative muscular work, of interest to some physiologists and biomechanists, notwithstanding the controversy involving the utility of the word *efficiency*; (e) the understanding of the mechanisms of acute and overuse injury to the lower back and to other body joints in the workplace and in athletic environments, of interest to ergonomists, sports medicine people, therapists, and physicians; (f) the development and evaluation of products for human use such as some prosthetics, orthotics, and protective equipment such as training shoes; and (g) the rationalization and assessment of the effects of some treatment modalities used by therapists. Elaboration on the relevance of the knowledge of individual muscle and ligament force-time histories to some of the above-mentioned fields is in order. I have selected a few.

Tissue Biomechanics

Zernicke (this volume) addressed the well-known phenomenon of bone and cartilage remodeling that results from gravitational and impact loading during physical activity and bone resorption that occurs with prolonged reductions in gravitational load. He noted, however, that little is known about the specific mechanisms or structural objectives that control bone (or connective tissue) remodeling. Understanding of these mechanisms requires quantified knowledge of tissue stress distribution and limb loading histories during exercise and disuse. Muscular and ligamentous forces are capable of elevating bone-on-bone forces to levels several times those induced by ground reactions or other external loads. This is particularly so when co-contractions of antagonistic muscles, observed in many movements, are present. For example, direct measures made by Hirsch and Rydell (1965) via a strain-gauged hip prosthesis in a patient who walked following recovery, indicated peak forces of about 1,800 N, more than two times the ground reaction force. Procter and Paul (1982) have shown ankle (talocrural) joint forces as high as 4 times body weight during walking, as estimated from a musculoskeletal model. Some work from our own laboratory (Galea & Norman, 1985) indicated that the bone-on-bone forces on the metatarsal-phalangeal and talocrural joints could be as high as 10 times body weight and more than 6 times the peak ground reaction force during a ballet movement of rising quickly to the tips of the toes with no appreciable impact. These evaluations were also model outputs, generated from a combination of EMG, cine, and force plate inputs to a linked segment dynamic model. Force plates by themselves measure only ground reaction, not bone-on-bone forces. Even relatively sophisticated dynamic joint moment calculations from combinations of force plate and cine (or opto-electronic) kinematic data cannot take into account muscle co-contractions and, although useful, are resultant moments only.

Komi has reported in these proceedings the successful use of a force transducer, mounted surgically on human Achilles tendons, which permitted direct measurement of force-time histories of these tendons during normal and vigorous movements such as running and jumping. This type of direct measurement on humans is a very exciting development and, as Komi himself declared, will become more versatile and applicable to other tendons and body joints as the technology of transducer development improves. However, the technique is invasive and is unlikely to evolve to the point where direct recordings of all model tendon and ligament forces are feasible. Problems with this approach are likely to be encountered in anatomically complex regions of the body such as the lumbar spine, where accurate estimates of disc compression and shear and facet joint loading are desired. This is not to minimize the importance of Komi's work with the tendon transducer in the solution of some important problems, but only to anticipate some limitations.

Zernicke (this volume) and King (1984) have reviewed a number of techniques that have been used in the past to obtain estimates of tissue loading. Their reviews included inverse dynamics models, direct transducer measurements in vitro and in vivo, finite element models, and direct dynamics models that usually involve optimization and, therefore, the selection of objective functions (i.e., the variable[s] that must be minimized or maximized) for the optimization. All of the available techniques have problems ranging from scaling and extrapolation from direct tendon force measures, to lack of validation of the objective functions or model output in general. Although Zernicke emphasized the need for the development of accurate models to measure the dynamics of movement processes and to shed light on tissue remodeling mechanisms, King urged the development of experimental techniques to verify results from models. Komi's work (this volume) is a step in this latter direction.

Motor Control and Human Movement Objective Functions

Much of the human motor control research has been done by people in the area of psychomotor behavior. The orientation of this work has been toward proposals of various mechanisms that are hypothesized to account for control of observed movement phenomena. Hasan, Enoka, and Stuart (1985) have divided these hypotheses into those with postural emphases, those with kinetic emphases, and those with combined emphases. Among the former is the *stiffness regulation* concept introduced by Nichols and Houk (1976). Rack (1970) had observed that muscle mechanical properties were capable of very quickly altering the force needed to regain equilibrium in response to a perturbance in the absence of reflexes. Nichols and Houk (1976) reasoned that, because it is physically impossible to maintain both muscle length and force constant when external loads varied, the net regulatory action conveyed by skeletal motor output should depend upon some relationship between muscle force and length change. The relationship was the ratio of force to length change with this stiffness being regulated via spindle and Golgi tendon organ feedback.

Although Nichols and Houk's (1976) hypothesis was studied using a posture perturbation paradigm, Komi (this volume) observed, using direct measures of muscle force on the human Achilles tendon and trigonometric estimations of muscle length change, that even in dynamic activities such as running there was only a relatively small muscle length change. He suggested that stiffness regulation may thus be relevant not only to quasistatic perturbations but also to a wide class of dynamic activities.

This may well be, but it should be noted that there are many other motor control hypotheses, each with its advocates. This is not the forum to present and critique each, but a partial list is useful. Details can be found in the original papers and in the review by Hasan et al. (1985), referred to earlier.

Bizzi, Polit, and Morasso (1976) have proposed an equilibrium point hypothesis relevant to the generation of movement rather than to response to perturbation. The central nervous system is postulated to specify the final equilibrium point between external forces and length-dependent tensions on an agonist/antagonist muscle set and to control trajectories of movement by varying the equilibrium point over time. There is also the generalized motor program idea, conceptualized as an abstract memory structure comprised of invariant and variant characteristics (e.g., Schmidt, 1975). Invariant characteristics appear to be the relative timing of various segments of a general movement pattern such as signing your name, regardless of which muscles or even body segments are used (e.g., fingers on a page vs. whole arm on a blackboard). Variant characteristics include force exerted, muscle selection, and amplitude and speed of movement.

Kelso (1981) and others have noted that there are some movement phenomena that do not fit the motor program notion and have proposed that these incongruities can be overcome using the concept of *homeokinetics*. Homeokinetics characterizes biological systems as ensembles of nonlinear limit-cycle oscillators coupled, mutually entrained and not dependent for control on reference levels, comparators, or error-detecting mechanisms. A similar concept calling on the use of neuronal central pattern generators (CPG) has been proposed as a regulator of locomotor patterns (e.g., Patla, Calvert, & Stein, 1985). CPGs are thought to be autonomous structures at the spinal level that produce muscle activity patterns in response to a tonic input and are independent of peripheral feedback, although feedback can shape the motor patterns.

Optimization Models

At the same time as numerous hypotheses of neural control and/or motor pattern generation and regulation have been emerging in the psychomotor behavior literature, a number of human motion optimization models have emerged in the bioengineering literature with little or no mutual cross-reference. The hallmark of nearly all of the optimization models is that assumptions were made about what objective function was optimized or numerous, seemingly logical, possibilities were tried. Examples of such studies include that of the wrist by Penrod, Davy, and Singh (1974), with muscles selected such that the sum of muscle forces was minimized; that of Seireg and Arvikar (1975), who studied lower extremity function in walking and squatting and selected muscles and/or ligaments to minimize the sum of muscle forces and ligament moments; Pedotti et al. (1978), who minimized muscle stress, among other objective functions presumed to be invoked during walking; Gracovetsky, Farfan,and Lamy (1981), who minimized joint stress in lifting studies; and Nelson (1983), who proposed the possibilities of minimization of time, force, impulse, energy, and jerk.

The fact is that no systematic assessment of what the body optimizes in various movements has been attempted. One reason, as noted earlier, is that direct methods of validating the models are lacking and qualitative comparison of raw EMG patterns, sometimes selected from the literature and not from the subjects tested in the models, has been the sole validation criterion. It seems entirely plausible that the objective function in human movement changes, not only in response obviously to the objective of the entire movement (e.g., sprint speed vs. minimum metabolic cost in distance events), but also in response to the current status of the person at the time (e.g., in pain or not). It is also possible that the objective function changes during different phases of a given movement cycle (e.g., minimum joint loading or joint stress during ground support in running but maximum joint torque during the relatively unloaded swing phase).

The point of this entire section is that neither the hypotheses of the neural control researchers nor the implicit hypotheses (via selection of objective function) of the optimization models can be ultimately tested until there are acceptable direct or indirect methods of measuring individual muscle and ligament force-time histories. The optimization models have often been quite detailed anatomically, but redundancy in muscle force generation and the ensuing mathematical indeterminacy had to be overcome via elimination of supposedly uninvolved muscles and ligaments. This usually meant excluding the possibility of antagonistic muscle co-contractions in spite of the common observation of their presence in many movements. On the other hand, most of the motor control hypotheses have sought to reduce muscle, joint, and even limb degrees of freedom in the search for neurological parsimony. In the few instances where there was some effort to generate a neuromuscular mechanical model to test or define neural control mechanisms, the models have been single muscle equivalents at one or more joints (e.g., Houk, 1979; Nashner & McCollum, 1985; Patla et al., 1985). This approach highly oversimplifies the structure, to say nothing of the function, of the system and brings into question the generalizability of the conclusions drawn from the models or experimental data.

Metabolic and Mechanical Efficiency

The question of relationships between metabolic and mechanical work rates has not been adequately resolved. Associated with this broad issue are unanswered questions of mechanisms of eccentric contractions, efficiency of negative and positive work, utilization and site of passive and active elastic energy storage, and a definitive explanation of energy exchanges within and between body segments during various forms of locomotion. Although there is not a lot of agreement by physiologists as to what metabolic rate (gross, net, delta) should be used in the denominator of the efficiency ratio (cf. Gaesser & Brooks, 1975; Morton, 1985), there is even less agreement among biomechanists as to how the mechanical work rate, needed for the numerator, should be calculated.

Point mass models (e.g., Cavagna, Saibene, & Margaria, 1964) have been criticized on the grounds that the energy cost of reciprocal limb movements is not accounted for and linked-segment approaches have been advocated (Pierrynowski, Norman, & Winter, 1981; Winter, 1979a). In their turn, the equations used by these authors have been criticized by Williams and Cavanagh (1983) on the grounds of implicit and questionable assumptions made about energy transfers between nonadjacent body segments. They also proposed a linked-segment approach, but one that attempted to produce a metabolic and mechanical power *balance* rather than the mechanical and physiologically justifiable estimate of mechanical power *output* attempted by previous authors. A somewhat more direct approach to mechanical power estimations than any of the above is the calculation based on the integral of the joint moments and segment angular velocities (e.g., Robertson & Winter, 1980). This method requires the direct measurement of ground reaction forces and is thus limited in the types of movements that can be studied. It also suffers from the same problem as all of the other methods in that only resultant moments are considered, in the absence of knowledge of the effects of co-contracting antagonistic muscles.

Definitive resolution of muscular-efficiency-related debates will have to await the ability to calculate mechanical work and power output from force/length and force/velocity relationships on a muscle-by-muscle basis. Once again, reliable and valid methods of calculating individual muscle force-time histories are the key.

Basic, Applied, and Integrated Research

The issues just discussed are all basic research issues in biomechanics. However, the rate of progress in applied research and the solution of applied problems, in domains that depend on the ability to exploit knowledge about the effects and control of forces that act on and are produced by the human body, cannot exceed that of the basic issues. The applied domains that have, as central concerns, problems related to tissue overload, muscle fatigue, motor control, skill acquisition, and performance efficiency certainly include ergonomics, rehabilitation medicine, orthopedics, sport, and physical activity.

It may be pedantic, but perhaps worthy of the risk, to state that neither biomechanics nor any other discipline can contribute substantially to the solution of applied problems without strong basic research aimed at understanding movement mechanisms and devoted to theory development. Caught in the same spiral, applied problems often generate questions that focus basic research. Mutual exclusion and/or dichotomization of basic and applied research by practitioners in the applied fields or by sport and other research funding agencies is short-sighted, illogical, and ultimately will retard progress.

Further, all of the research areas noted earlier require input, not only from biomechanists, but from physiologists, psychomotor behaviorists neurophysiologists, and others. Zernicke and Komi, here and in other forums, have urged this integration. It appears to me that increasing integration is already observable on some fronts and much more is inevitable. The administrative challenges of the immediate future will be determining how to maximize the research productivity of interdisciplinary groups, identifying the minimum common knowledge base required to foster effective communication, and encouraging scientists from diverse fields to acquire that base.

References

Bizzi, E., Polit, A., & Morasso, P. (1976). Mechanisms underlying achievement of final head position. *Journal of Neurophyisology*, **39**, 435-444.

Cappozzo, A. (1983). Considerations on clinical gait evaluation. *Journal of Biomechanics*, **16**(4), 302.

Cavagna, G., Saibene, F.P., & Margaria, R. (1964). Mechanical work in running. *Journal of Applied Physiology*, **19**, 249-256.

Contini, R., & Drillis, R. (1966). Biomechanics. In H.N. Abramson (Ed.), *Applied mechanics surveys* (pp. 161-172). New York: Spartan.

Gaesser, G.A., & Brooks, G.A. (1975). Muscular efficiency during steady-rate exercise: Effects of speed and work rate. *Journal of Applied Physiology*, **38**(6), 1132-1139.

Galea, V., & Norman, R.W. (1985). Bone-on-bone forces at the ankle joint during a rapid dynamic movement. In D.A. Winter, R.W., Norman, R.P. Wells, K.C. Hayes, & A.E. Patla, (Eds.), *Biomechanics IX-A* (pp. 71-76). Champaign, IL: Human Kinetics.

Gracovetsky, S., Farfan, H.F., & Lamy, C. (1981). The mechanism of the lumbar spine. *Spine*, **6**(3), 249-262.

Hasan, Z., Enoka, R.M., & Stuart, D. (1985). The interface between biomechanics and neurophysiology in the study of movement: Some recent approaches. In R. Terjung (Ed.), *Exercise and sport sciences reviews* (pp. 169-234). Philadelphia: Franklin Institute Press.

Hatze, H. (1974). The meaning of the term "biomechanics." *Journal of Biomechanics*, **7**(2), 189-190.

Hatze, H. (1976). The complete optimization of a human motion. *Mathematical Biosciences*, **28**, 99-135.

Hirsch, C., & Rydell, N. (1965). Forces in the hip joint. In R.M. Kenedi (Ed.), *Biomechanics and related bio-engineering topics* (pp. 341-357). London: Pergamon Press.

Houk, J.C. (1979). Regulation of stiffness by skeletomotor reflexes. *Annual Review of Physiology*, **41**, 99-114.

Kelso, J.A.S. (1981). Contrasting perspectives on order and regulation in movement. In J. Long & A. Baddeley (Eds.), *Attention and performance IX*. Hillsdale, NJ: Lawrence Erlbann.

King, A.I. (1984). A review of biomechanical models. *Journal of Biomechanical Engineering*, **106**, 97-104.

Komi, P.V. (1984). Biomechanics and neuromuscular performance. *Medicine and Science in Sports and Exercise*, **16**(1), 26-28.

Morton, R.H. (1985). Comment on "A model for the calculation of mechanical power during distance running." *Journal of Biomechanics*, **18**(2), 161-162.

Nashner, L.M., & McCollum, G. (1985). The organization of human postural movements: A formal basis and experimental synthesis. *The Behavioral and Brain Sciences*, **8**, 135-172.

Nelson, W.L. (1983). Physical principles for economics of skilled movements. *Biological Cybernetics*, **46**, 135-147.

Nichols, T.R., & Houk, J.C. (1976). The improvement in linearity and the regulation of stiffness that results from the actions of the stretch reflex. *Journal of Neurophysiology*, **39**, 119-142.

Norman, R.W. (1985). Biomechanics: Are there substantive issues? *International Society of Biomechanics Newsletter*, **18**, 2-4.

Nubar, Y., & Contini, R. (1961). A minimum principle in biomechanics. *Bulletin of Mathematical Biophysics*, **23**, 377-391.

Patla, A.E., Calvert, T.W., & Stein, R.B. (1985). Model of a pattern generator for locomotion in mammals. *American Journal of Physiology*, **248**, 484-494.

Pedotti, A., Krishnan, V.V., & Stark, L. (1978). Optimization of muscle force sequencing in human locomotion. *Mathematical Biosciences*, **38**, 59-76.

Penrod, D.D., Davy, D.T., & Singh, P.P. (1974). An optimization approach to tendon force analysis. *Journal of Biomechanics*, **7**, 123-129.

Pierrynowski, M.R., Norman, R.W., & Winter, D.A. (1981). Mechanical energy analyses of the human during load carriage on a treadmill. *Ergonomics*, **24**(1), 1-14.

Procter, P., & Paul, J.P. (1982). Ankle joint biomechanics. *Journal of Biomechanics*, **15**(9), 627-634.

Rack, P.M.H. (1970). The significance of mechanical properties of muscle in the reflex control of posture. In P. Andersen & J. Jansen (Eds.), *International Meeting of Neurobiology: 5. Excitatory synaptic mechanisms* (pp. 317-321). Oslo: Universitesforlaget.

Robertson, D.G.E., & Winter, D.A. (1980). Mechanical energy generation, absorption and transfer amongst segments during walking. *Journal of Biomechanics*, **13**, 845-854.

Schmidt, R.A. (1975). A schema theory of discrete motor skill learning. *Psychological Reviews*, **82**, 225-260.

Seireg, A., & Arvikar, R.J. (1975). The prediction of muscular load sharing and joint forces in the lower extremities during walking. *Journal of Biomechanics*, **8**, 89-102.

Williams, K.R., & Cavanagh, P.R. (1983). A model for the calculation of mechanical power during distance running. *Journal of Biomechanics*, **16**(2), 115-128.

Winter, D.A. (1979a). A new definition of mechanical work done in human movement. *Journal of Applied Physiology*, **46**(1), 79-83.

Winter, D.A. (1979b). *Biomechanics of human movement*. Toronto: John Wiley & Sons.

Yeo, B.P. (1976). Investigations concerning the principle of minimal total muscular force. *Journal of Biomechanics*, **9**, 413-416.

Zernicke, R.F. (1983). Biomechanical and biochemical synthesis. *Medicine and Science in Sports and Exercise*, **15**(1), 6-7.

Biomechanical Studies of Elite Distance Runners: Directions for Future Research

Peter R. Cavanagh

Running long distances is an activity that has been practiced as a sport and a profession since at least the beginning of recorded human history. The messenger from the Battle of Marathon (490 B.C.) probably made a living from his lungs in much the same way that today's marathon runners make a much more comfortable living from theirs. Throughout this long history of distance running, the elite runner has been identified using a fairly similar definition. An elite distance runner is one who can cover the fixed distance in the shortest period of time. This definition is repeated here, despite the risk of seeming banal, because it is a salutary beginning to a discussion of the biomechanics of distance running.

To date, no running contest that we know of has been judged by the stylistic beauty with which the athletes move around the track. This is in contrast to sports such as gymnastics, ice-skating, and diving, in which the quality of performance is all important. And this is just as well, because a number of the notable former champions exhibited running styles that were, subjectively at least, unpleasant to watch. The description of Emil Zatopek (Figure 1) by a contemporary reporter as "[running] like

Figure 1. Emil Zatopek (left), with his characteristically ugly style, leads Belgium's Gaston Reiff in Prague during a rematch of the 1948 Olympic 5,000-m final (Reiff won on both occasions).

a man with a noose about his neck'' is adequate proof of this. I shall present the hypothesis that, in contrast to a definition that a physiologist or psychologist might generate, elite performers may not always be elite in terms of the mechanical aspects of their running.

It must be made clear at the outset that, compared to knowledge in the area of the physiology of elite endurance performance, our knowledge in the area of biomechanics is minimal. Few elite runners have been comprehensively studied from a biomechanical perspective. This situation has both its positive and its negative aspects. On the positive side, there is an abundance of uncharted territory for researchers in biomechanics to explore. This makes it an exciting field and one that easily attracts good young researchers. It also makes the writing of a paper such as this a fairly pleasant task in which suggestions for future research flow easily. The negative aspect is that I have to go out on a limb concerning implications of present knowledge and make statements, some of which future researchers—and not too distant future researchers, at that—will probably show to be naive and incorrect. It is here that I must take refuge in a statement by the famous English physician William Harvey (1578–1657) that knowledge presents itself to us firmly grounded upon some pre-existing knowledge which we possessed.

Because of the paucity of data on the mechanics of elite runners, this paper will dwell principally on the needs for the future. The view of present and future given here is an entirely personal landscape that has been painted, somewhat impressionistically, to emphasize issues thought to be worthy of discussion. In many respects it represents my thinking aloud with the expectation and hope that it may stimulate others to respond with contrary points of view.

The Present Status

The Definition of an Elite Distance Runner

The opening remarks concerning the non-elite nature of elite running mechanics obviously need some substantiation. Let me begin by stating my position somewhat more firmly: A runner may be in the elite class *because* of his or her physiological and psychological equipment and *in spite of* the biomechanical aspects of his or her running style. I realize that this is a controversial statement and one that actually ignores evidence in the literature from physiological studies. For example, Pollock (1977) found a significant difference in submaximal economy (as determined by gross $\dot{V}O_2$ measurement) between elite and good distance runners at 4.47 m/s and between subgroups of elite middle-distance runners versus elite marathon runners both at 4.47 and 5.36 m/s (elite marathon > elite middle-distance > good). These differences may, of course, be physiological, in which case they would not deny the hypothesis.

It is also hard not to believe that self-optimization of a movement pattern occurs over the many hundreds of thousands of strides that the trained runner has performed. The near-optimal stride lengths of a group of middle-distance runners found by Cavanagh and Williams (1982) would appear to support this concept. Nevertheless, there were examples of both nonoptimal and uneconomical patterns within the groups formed, and these runners may provide the most interesting experimental subjects. Once we start to delve quantitatively into the mechanics of running, we begin to see that each athlete has a running style that represents a unique solution to the problems posed by individual development, training and injury histories, physiological characteristics, and the runner's image of what constitutes an effective running style. Those who expect the elite runner to be a model of symmetry and economy are likely to be disappointed. As evidence of this, Figures 2a-c represent a collection of individual patterns from elite athletes, all of whom have held American

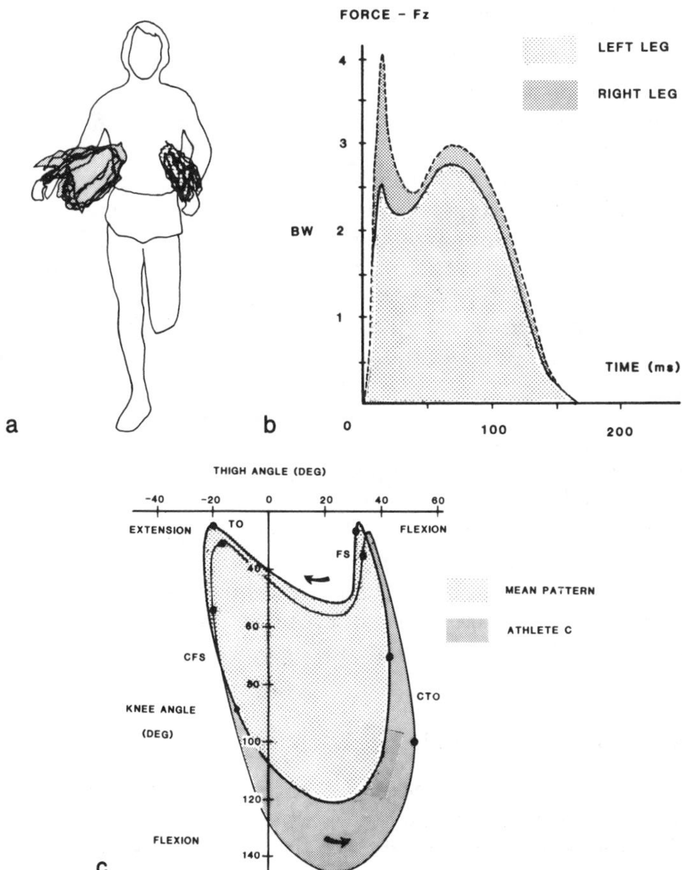

Figure 2. Measurements from three different elite athletes, all of whom have held the American 10,000-m record on the road or track. Note that each athlete has an asymmetry between the left and right sides or has an unusual feature that distinguishes him from a mean pattern. (a) An asymmetrical arm action; (b) a large difference between the peaks of the vertical component of the ground reaction force on the left and right sides; and (c) a pattern of knee flexion during the swing phase that is much greater than the mean pattern of a group of elite runners at a similar speed.

records at 10,000 m on road or track. The asymmetric arm action of Figure 2a is almost a trademark of this athlete and probably represents a compensation for asymmetric action in the lower extremity. The vertical components of ground reaction force of the three-time Olympian shown in Figure 2b reveal that there is approximately 700 N more force transmitted to the right leg than to the left. Figure 2c represents a thigh-knee diagram from the third champion athlete compared to the mean pattern of a group of elite distance runners (Cavanagh, Pollock, & Landa, 1977). It is apparent that this athlete had a tremendously high leg recovery compared to his peers.

Economy Is Not Exclusive to Elite Performers

To develop the point made above a little further, it is interesting to envisage a long-distance running competition whose rules might be defined by a committee of sport scientists rather than by the International Amateur Athletic Federation (IAAF). Such a competition would require each contestant to breathe exclusively from an enormous motorized Douglas bag containing 7W liters of oxygen (where W equals each athlete's body mass in kilograms). The winner would be the athlete who ran the farthest regardless of the elapsed time. Entrants could be any class of athlete who had previously finished a marathon, and this would presumably span the range of times from 4 hr to a world-record pace. The race would be reduced to a contest of economy, and predicting the winner would be uncertain.

The point here is to emphasize a further contrast between the physiological and the biomechanical determinants of a distance runner. There are unlikely to be many individuals not known for outstanding performance who have higher maximal oxygen uptakes than current champion marathoners. It is, however, very likely that there are average runners who, for whatever reason, are considerably more economical. Although these individuals would not win races, they almost certainly would repay study because of their superiority in economy over some elite runners. At present we do not fully understand the reasons for these differences.

Small Number of Elite Studies in Literature

The most important fact about the current status of biomechanical studies of elite distance running is that they are in their infancy. I have been able to locate in the literature only the seven studies shown in Table 1. The combined number of elite subjects that were measured in all these studies totals only 55. (Because the mean marathon time of the women in the study by Buckalew, Barlow, Fischer, & Richards, [1985], was 2:37:48, only half of their subjects were considered to be elite.) Many studies of average or varsity runners have been published (see Williams, 1985, for a complete review), and although these provide an essential background to the study of the elite runner, we really have no idea how generalizable their results are.

Table 1 Existing Biomechanical Studies[a] of Elite Distance Runners

Authors	Date	# of Elite runners	Measurements taken
Sykes	1975	1	1
Cavanagh et al.	1977	14	1, 2
Payne	1983	9 (approx)	3
Gregor & Kirkendall	1978	3	1, 8, F
Mann	1980	6	1, 4
Cavanagh et al.	1985	2	1, 2, 3, 4, 5, 6, 7, 8
Buckalew et al.	1985	20 (approx)	1, 2, F

Key to measurements made:

1 - Kinematics
2 - Stride variables
3 - Ground reaction forces
4 - EMG
5 - Pressure measurement
6 - Anthropometry
7 - Structural measurement
8 - Metabolic
F - Females (all other studies males only)

[a]Studies that were exclusively anthropometric in nature (e.g., Bale, Rowell, & Colley, 1985) have been excluded.

Asymmetry Is the Norm

One of the striking features of studying locomotor patterns in general is the frequent lack of symmetry between the left and right sides of the body. As was well demonstrated by the patterns in Figures 2a-2c, the elite athlete is quite likely to show left/right differences. In studies of locomotor mechanics, assuming that asymmetry is the norm may be a more realistic position than assuming symmetry.

There are a number of reasons why we would expect to find left/right differences in such measures as ground reaction forces and limb kinematics. The developmental histories of the two extremities may be different (injuries during growth, etc.), there may be actual limb length discrepancies, and limb dominance in nonrunning activities will probably have caused differences in muscle strength and girth between the two sides. The excessive training distances that most elite runners endure usually result in a variety of injuries that are not always entirely resolved, and this may lead to a favoring of one limb that could be reflected in the biomechanical measurements.

Major Structural Problems Are Unusual in Elite Runners

Having cast suspicion on the external mechanics of movement of elite distance runners, I should point out that, at least in our own experience, it is rare to encounter extreme lower extremity structural problems in the elite distance runner. For example, there are no quantitative or anecdotal reports that identify a pattern of extreme subtalar joint pronation during support in an elite distance runner. The generally held concept that overuse injury is, at least partly, a result of repeated stressing of a limb that is not well aligned has probably worked as a self-selection mechanism. Those runners who had the physiological equipment but not the structural framework have probably fallen by the wayside.

We Have Not Yet Tried to Modify Movement Patterns

Although coaches are routinely required to make suggestions regarding changes in form, there is no experimental evidence in the literature that demonstrates successful (or indeed, unsuccessful) changes in the running pattern of an elite athlete. Only two experiments were found in which changes were made to non-elite groups. These studies and their results will be discussed in a later section. This lack of data on what, to the layperson, is the province of biomechanical analysis, is further evidence of how far our discipline still has to go before we can claim to have been useful in this regard.

General Observations on Elite Athlete Studies

In concluding this section on current status, I think there are a number of general comments that may be relevant to the way experiments on elite athletes, not only in biomechanics, have been conducted to date. One is soon confronted with the fact that elite athletes are rarely more than a week away from an all-out effort in training or racing. This problem is compounded by the large number of distance runners who make their living from racing and who therefore see their earnings as directly related to their ability to produce a maximum effort often and on demand. This has several implications for the scientist. First, athletes may not be willing to provide an all-out performance in the laboratory at any time during the racing season. Second, even when they are willing, the nature of the effort will be directly related to their immediate previous history of maximum efforts. It has been our experience that most elite athletes will not run on the treadmill for more than about 30% of their known endurance times at race pace. This is certainly closely allied with the psychology of the elite runner and the absence of a competitive stimulus. However, for the biomechanist studying the changes in running mechanics during fatigue, it means that the results must be interpreted in the context of the known longer performance time during a race.

Many elite distance runners are, as mentioned earlier, constantly on the edge of some minor injury and may therefore participate in an experimental study with a nondisabling but nevertheless important injury. The present and past injury status of the athlete may not only cause asymmetries but may also influence running style in more subtle ways. For example, an athlete with pain from a heel spur may modify his or her footstrike by using a more anterior strike pattern on the shoe. The particular pattern observed on a given day must therefore be interpreted in light of known injury status.

Future Directions

Some specific goals for the future of studies in the biomechanics of running were proposed by Miller (1978). In the 10 years since her article was published, several of her important suggestions remain to be implemented. Nevertheless, I shall extend the list yet further.

The Ideal Concept Needs Revision

Clearly, in view of the earlier discussion, it is my opinion that we must abandon the view that the locomotor mechanics of an elite runner represent the ideal style to which runners of lesser ability must aspire. This offers a stark contrast to a physiological profile of an elite distance runner where certain characteristics that place the individual in the upper few percentiles of the normal distribution are invariably present. We must not be surprised to find dynamic asymmetries, skeletal differences, and movement patterns that deviate from the means of a group of performers at a similar level. Most areas of biomechanics have now left behind the concept of defining a template from the movement of a champion. Indeed, even the implication that the physiological profile of an elite performer can be predefined is an oversimplification. Fink, Costill, and Pollock (1977) have pointed out that elite middle-distance runners may display anywhere from 50% to 98% of slow-twitch fibers in the lateral gastrocnemius. This view does not preclude the establishment of certain criteria that should be either present in an elite runner or encouraged by training.

The Need to Establish Statistically Valid Estimates

An impartial observer could be forgiven for the impression that biomechanists are sometimes prisoners of their own instrumentation. This has been particularly true in the past of the cinematographic techniques for measuring the motion of body segments where it is possible in the course of 1 day to collect more data than can reasonably be analyzed in 3 months.

One consequence of this slow process of data reduction is that many of our statements have been based on an entirely inadequate sample of the process under study. Take, for example, the movements of the lower extremity during marathon running. A typical competitor may take over 12,000 strides in the entire race, yet our knowledge of the process is often inferred from measurements of a single stride (Cavanagh, Pollock, & Landa, 1977). Obviously a race of such distance needs to be split further into phases based on terrain, pace, tactical considerations, and fatigue. But even within these phases, the question of what constitutes a valid sample will not be easily answered. In the collection of ground reaction force information where data acquisition is more automated, Bates, James, and Osternig (1980) have suggested that a minimum of eight trials be taken to represent a specific locomotor condition. This approach has some merit but the sample still represents one observation from each of eight separate runs. It seems unlikely that we will be able, in the near future, to measure ground reaction forces from 10 successive strides. At present levels of cost, such a project would require an investment of at least $200,000 in multiple force platforms.

On the question of variability in movement patterns there is a somewhat brighter picture. Recent developments of new opto-electronic and video-based data acquisition systems offer the possibility of gaining insight into the magnitude of stride-to-stride differences. Even the 10 consecutive cycles of thigh-knee motion presented in Figure 3 provide more information than is, at the time of writing, available in the literature. Notice that even though the basic kinematic patterns themselves are fairly similar, the two athletes are very different in their variability. This may offer another important criterion in assessing an elite runner.

The data shown in Figure 3 were collected using the ''ExpertVision System'' from Motion Analysis, Inc., and the processed data were available within about 5 min of completion of the run. This represents a

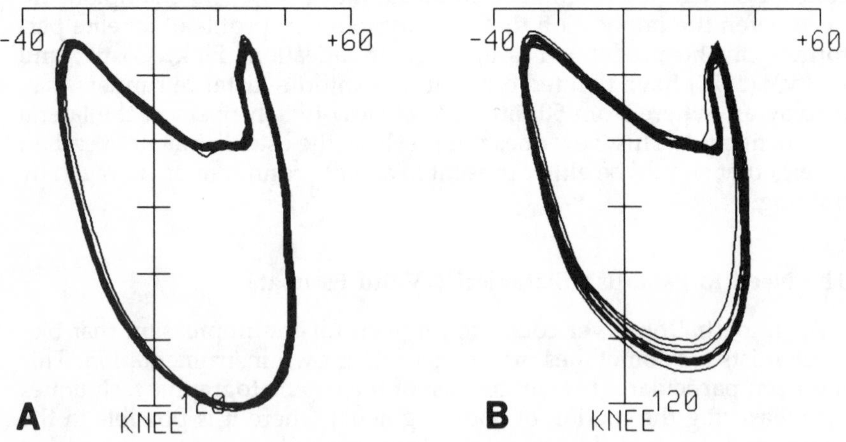

Figure 3. Thigh-knee diagrams from 10 consecutive cycles of running at 4.22 m/s. Runner A has a very consistent pattern, whereas Runner B shows a large amount of variability, particularly in knee flexion during swing. Both athletes are non-elite runners.

speeding up of almost 40 times compared to conventional film analysis. Such progress obviously opens many new possibilities, and a major direction in the future must be to take advantage of these possibilities.

Present Theoretical Models Need Refining

In many respects, locomotor biomechanics at the elite level has yet to emerge from a descriptive phase and progress to an analytical one. Part of the problem, as discussed in the preceding section, is that there is so much to describe. Much of our collective initial energy has been devoted to answering the question, How are these athletes built and how do they run? Such is a necessary beginning, but we must recall that description is only the first step toward understanding a phenomenon and not an end in itself.

The need for a theoretical base becomes most apparent when the experimental results are to be used to suggest changes in technique to an individual athlete. Suppose that preliminary observations have determined that the particular athlete has a vigorous arm action, a vertical oscillation that is 1 standard deviation above the mean, and a high peak in the vertical component of the ground reaction force immediately after landing. The coach hovers over the data, pronounces it interesting, but demands to know what recommendations, if any, should be made to the runner. Such a series of interrelated observations cannot be treated at the descriptive level. The alternative to the template approach discussed earlier must be a predictive or correlational model that will cope with the many factors that may be important determinants of running performance.

Our choice of models at the present time is severely limited. Most of the progress that has been made is in the area of energy analysis (Winter, 1979), which has been extended to provide a link with metabolic energy cost by Williams (1980). Hinrichs (1983) has also modeled the arm action in running from angular momentum considerations. These models represent a promising beginning, but there is much to be done before the kinds of subtle changes in running style that one would like to examine can be evaluated on a "what if" basis in front of a computer terminal.

Economy Remains the Key Problem That Must Be Solved

Success in distance running can be promised to those with a high aerobic capacity and the ability to use that capacity economically. Calculations of the effects of small improvements in economy upon race time yield dramatic results. One percent of the current world-best time for the marathon (2 hr 6 min 50 s) is 1 min and 16 s. One percent of the world record for 10 km is about 16 s. These differences can be put in perspective by an examination of the 1985 world rankings for the marathon shown in Table 2. A 1% improvement would move the 5th best performer into 1st place and the 13th best performer up to 6th.

Table 2 1985 Top 15 World Marathon Performers

Rank	Name	Time		
1	Carlos Lopes (Portugal)	2:07:12	-------------	0
2	Steve Jones (Great Britain)	2:07:13		
3	Djama Robleh (Djibouti)	2:08:08		
4	Ahmed Saleh (Djibouti)	2:08:09		
5	Takeyuki Nakayama (Japan)	2:08:15	-------------	+1[a]
6	Charles Spedding (Great Britain)	2:08:34		
7	Rob De Costella (Australia)	2:08:48		
8	Mark Plaatjies (S. Africa)	2:08:58		
9	Michael Heilmann (E. Germany)	2:09:03		
10	Abebe Mekonen (Ethiopia)	2:09:05		
11	Alistair Hutton (Great Britain)	2:09:16		
12	Christoph Herle (W. Germany)	2:09:23		
13	Henrik Jorgensen (Denmark)	2:09:43		
			-------------	+2[a]
14	Masanari Shintaku (Japan)	2:09:51		
15	Giovanni Boli (Italy)	2:09:57		

[a]Times 1% and 2% slower than the world-best 5 and 13 runners, respectively.

What is important about the 1% change used here as an example is that it is well within the effects that we know to be caused by changes in stride length (Cavanagh & Williams, 1982) and by different footwear (Frederick, 1983). Frederick (1983) has pointed out that, although the accuracy of measurement of submaximal oxygen uptake is generally accepted to be about 3%, this does not mean that smaller treatment effects cannot be identified statistically.

A recent study by Daniels, Scardina, and Foley (1984) presented evidence that, just because athletes are economical runners, they are not necessarily economical at other activities such as cycling, walking, or arm cranking. By demonstrating that economy is not a trait over all activities, this experiment seems to offer the indirect promise that at least part of the key to running economy may lie in the mechanical aspects.

The most comprehensive study of running economy to date is that by Williams (1980). His study, although of non-elite distance runners, included individuals with a range of net $\dot{V}O_2$submax measurements from 35.0 to 43.0 ml/kg/min—a range of almost 20%. He reported a number of biomechanical factors that were significantly related to submaximal oxygen uptake. These included certain ground reaction force and kinematic variables and measures of the energy transfer between segments of the body. Although these measurements were not strongly related to performance time, the importance of this experiment cannot be underestimated. Williams has shown for the first time what has long been assumed—elements of running style seen in the normal population measurably affect running economy. These initial findings must be expanded until a much better understanding of the relationship between the external mechanics and energy cost has been achieved.

More Perturbation Experiments Are Needed

A major experimental method in many fields for the elucidation of underlying mechanisms is to perturbate the system and study the response. Examples of this method include using different culture mediums or temperatures in cell biology and unexpectedly removing the support from a standing subject in postural studies. To date, only limited use has been made of this technique in biomechanical studies of locomotion. Examples include adding mass to the feet (Catlin & Dressendorfer, 1979) or forcing the individual into a different stride frequency (Cavanagh & Williams, 1982) or a different stride width (Williams & Ziff, 1984). Among other perturbations that might be tried in the future are changes in arm action, changes in the type of footstrike (rearfoot strike vs. midfoot strike, etc.), variations in the motion of the leg during the swing phase, and changes in the post-impact cushioning behavior. In each case the criterion measure would be the economy of running.

Two points are worth making in connection with this approach. First, as Hay (1983) has pointed out, differences in the amount of practice given to new tasks and differences in the complexity of different tasks cause problems in the interpretation of results. Task complexity is unlikely to be a major issue with small perturbations in running style, but practice certainly could be. Subjects will be unlikely to ever accumulate as much practice with a new technique as they had with their old technique. Fortunately, this biases the results toward what a statistician would call a Type II error—the new technique was actually better but we failed to detect it. I say "fortunately" because this leads us to conservative conclusions, and any perturbation that results in an improvement in economy can be celebrated as an important finding. The second point is that the magnitude of the perturbations that are made do not have to be within the bounds of reality to produce useful experimental results. Large modifications in each direction can result in points from which interpolation into the realistic region can be made.

What Are the Best Strategies for Changing Movement Patterns?

Once we have identified the changes in movement patterns that we believe to be desirable, the crucial and largely unexplored question becomes, What are the most effective learning strategies for the modification of the movement pattern? This is obviously an area in which the biomechanist, as a neophyte, has much to learn from colleagues in the area of motor learning. The issue of interdisciplinary research is discussed in more detail below. Cognitive modification of running style following specific instructions on the biomechanics of running has, to my knowledge, been attempted on a significant scale only once (Petray & Krahenbuhl, 1985). In this experiment children were encouraged to focus on "reducing unnecessary vertical displacement, awareness of stride rate and length and general suggestions regarding posture and relaxation" (p. 252). No significant differences were found in either running economy or technique after an 11-week training period.

There are many enhancements that could be made to the process of relearning. The most obvious are the identification of individualized criteria for the particular biomechanical aspects that are to be modified and the provision of feedback during learning. Sanderson (1986) has shown the efficacy of visual feedback for the modification of patterns of pedaling in naive cyclists. There have been no experiments in running to determine the most effective form of feedback, the best schedule of presentation and withdrawal of feedback, and indeed the movement characteristics that can be most easily modified. This is obviously an area of great promise for the future.

Techniques Should Be Perfected on Non-Elite Runners

It is my strong belief that any new techniques for the modification of movement patterns should be developed on non-elite athletes. This point is both an ethical issue and a methodological one. Ethically, there is no basis for subjecting an elite athlete to a procedure of unknown validity. There is simply too much at stake when the years of investment in their running careers are considered. Methodologically, we may learn more by studying runners who are much less practiced and are, by a process of careful screening and selection, particularly uneconomical. One would hope that the lessons learned at this level could be of benefit to elite runners.

The Range of Locomotor Conditions Studied Must Be Extended

The vast majority of biomechanical studies in the literature have examined straight-ahead, constant-speed running under nonfatigued conditions on a smooth surface. Although there are some notable exceptions to this statement (Greene, 1985; Nelson & Osterhoudt, 1971), it is important in the future that we extend our observations to other conditions. In particular, the mechanical changes that accompany fatigue in running are almost unknown (Cavanagh et al., 1985).

This is a case in which, initially at least, simple description may be of practical value. If athletes can be provided with a profile of the way in which their style deteriorates during fatigue, they may be able to develop cognitive strategies to maintain good form. Later, a more detailed study of fatigue running should be able to confirm or deny the popular notion that runners become less economical, at least that they do more mechanical work, when they are fatigued. The notion that injuries are more likely to occur during fatigued running also should be studied.

Grade running also deserves a more detailed examination. Runners know that there are good and bad hill runners and that something about the mechanics of a particular running style causes some runners to excel in uphill or downhill runs. The implication here is that some are more economical than others when grade is a factor. Recent studies by Breiner (1985) showed a good correlation between uphill and downhill economy in a group of well-trained runners, tending to deny this popular proposition.

More Information Is Needed on Women Runners

As is apparent from Table 1, to date only 22 elite women distance runners have been subjected to biomechanical scrutiny, and the only technique used in these studies was field cinematography. Gregor, Rozenek, Brown, and Garhammer (1979) studied 42 elite women distance runners, but a report of the study is only available in abstract form. Perhaps the recent Atlanta study, a multidisciplinary laboratory study of elite U.S. women runners, is the beginning of a trend toward more attention in this direction.

In any discussion of gender comparisons in the mechanics of distance running, almost regardless of the question, the answer given is always the same: Women have a wider pelvis. I am not only out of patience with such an explanation by cliché but also extremely skeptical that it is true for elite runners. Bale, Rowell, and Colley (1985) have shown from anthropometric studies of elite women marathoners that a slim physique high in ectomorphy offers the best potential for success. Although injuries to the general population of women distance runners may be related to pelvic dimensions, I believe that future research may show elite female distance runners to have pelvic dimensions that differ little from their male counterparts.

The Term *Custom Shoe* Needs Redefining

Most shoe companies now have extensive biomechanics laboratories available to them through either in-house facilities or the facilities of their consultants. I have been engaged recently in a war of subversion to persuade elite athletes to make more demands of the shoe companies who are their sponsors. Contrary to popular belief, few top athletes receive custom shoes. Those who do are generally individuals with unusual foot structures. It is axiomatic that the shoe should fit well, but we now have the knowledge to construct a shoe that fits the functional characteristics of the individual athlete and possibly allows the athlete to be more economical. The term *custom shoes* needs redefinition in an era where both craftsmanship and technology combine in the production of a shoe.

An obvious example of adaptation to function follows up on the theme of asymmetry mentioned earlier. If an athlete has a radically different strike pattern on the left and right sides, then he or she is clearly making different demands on similar regions of the left and right shoes. The shoes should be built differently to cater to this asymmetry. The techniques of force and pressure measurement during running can provide important help to custom shoe designers, and it is likely that biomechanists will play an important role in the design and testing of such footwear in the future.

In-shoe orthoses are common among runners of all categories and have proved remarkably successful in the conservative management of lower extremity pain. It is my belief that elite runners should not use these devices in the long term. Any device in the shoe represents just one more potential source of trouble and also, in general, adds weight to the shoe. Once the appropriate correction for the athlete has been determined by the use of an in-shoe device for a sufficiently long period of time, the correction should be built directly as part of a custom shoe.

How Do the Mechanics of Running Vary With Training Status?

Although the physiological changes due to training and detraining are well known, few experiments have considered how the mechanics of running may change as a function of training. This is likely to be a complex problem influenced by not only cardiovascular status but also by changes in flexibility, soreness, injury status, and exercise history. Nelson and Gregor (1976) have shown changes in stride length at a given speed of running over the 4 years of a collegiate running career. It is likely that there are major changes in running style over a much shorter time span. These must be identified both to help characterize the variance in measurements that are made and to further understand how the changes observed relate to running economy.

Injury Etiology and Prophylaxis Need More Scientific Study

The types of injuries experienced by distance runners have fostered a major trend toward conservative treatment in sports medicine. It has been realized that subtle forms of intervention and treatment can, at times, produce major improvements in the patient's status. Such factors as excessive pronation, shoe characteristics, and changes in training patterns have all been implicated in a variety of major running injuries (James, Bates, & Osternig, 1978). For the epidemiologist, this situation is particularly challenging because there are frequently no major traumatic events to which the injury can be related. The consequence is that clinicians must often use extended trial and error to determine the true cause of a running injury.

It is encouraging to see a trend toward a more detailed study of the etiology of running injuries (Blair & Casperson, 1985). There is a great need for the application of more rigorous methods in the study of both etiology and prophylaxis of running injuries. Elite athletes will benefit greatly from such studies because they are members of the group that is most at risk due to high mileage and has the most to gain.

Experimental Protocols Must Be Agreed Upon

Because of the relative infancy of the discipline, there is still no widespread agreement on such issues as experimental protocols, terminology, and conventions. This makes comparison of experiments by different investigators difficult and slows progress toward the mutual goals of different groups. There are moves underway (Winter, 1985, personal communication) to rectify this situation, and such effort should be encouraged and supported. Again it is hard to resist a comparison with physiology, where agreed upon protocols for a variety of procedures have existed for some time.

Conclusion

It should be apparent from the above remarks that much remains to be done in understanding the mechanics of elite distance running. It should also be clear that the biomechanist in isolation is not likely to make major advances in unlocking all of the secrets because the problem is so patently broad. Success will come from interdisciplinary research groups that are studying running in the broadest possible sense. Progress should be fairly rapid both because of renewed interest in funding studies of elite athletes and because the many studies of non-elite performers are beginning to shed light beyond their confines. As a final point, I would like to suggest that we should offer the elite athlete and his or her coach and physician an honest appraisal of the current status of our art and our ability to provide insight into running mechanics. If we promise too much, when the scientific base does not exist, there can only be disillusionment. If we are realistic, the resulting cooperation will lead to an extension of the bounds of current knowledge.

Acknowledgments

I would like to acknowledge the work of many present and former colleagues whose insights and energies have contributed to the ideas expressed here. I am indebted to Rodger Kram for mentioning the issue of the relationship between mechanics and training status.

References

Bale, P., Rowell, S., & Colley, E. (1985). Anthropometric and training characteristics of female marathon runners as determinants of distance running performance. *Journal of Sport Sciences*, **3**(2), 115-126.

Bates, B.T., James, S.L., & Osternig, L.R. (1980). Evaluation of within runner variability and subject-condition interaction when evaluating running shoes [abstract]. *Medicine and Science in Sports and Exercise,* **12**(2), 92.

Blair, S.N., & Casperson, C.J. (1985). Running injuries: Rates, risk factors, and prevention [abstract]. *Medicine and Science in Sports and Exercise,* **17**(2), 181.

Briener, T. (1985). *A comparison of running economy on level, uphill and downhill grades*. Unpublished master's thesis, Pennsylvania State University, University Park, PA.

Buckalew, D.P., Barlow, D.A., Fischer, J.W., & Richards, J.G. (1985). Biomechanical profile of elite women marathoners. *The International Journal of Sports Biomechanics,* **1**(4), 330-347.

Catlin, M.E., Dressendorfer, R.H. (1979). Effect of shoe weight on the energy cost of running [abstract]. *Medicine and Science in Sports and Exercise,* **11**(4), 80.

Cavanagh, P.R., Andrew, G.C., Kram, R., Rodgers, M.M., Sanderson, D.J., & Hennig, E.M. (1985). An approach to biomechanical profiling of distance runners. *The International Journal of Sports Biomechanics,* **1**(1), 36-62.

Cavanagh, P.R., Pollock, M.L., & Landa, J. (1977). Biomechanical comparison of elite and good distance runners. In P. Milvy (Ed.), *The marathon: Physiological, medical, epidemiological, and psychological studies* (pp. 328-345). New York: New York Academy of Sciences.

Cavanagh, P.R., & Williams, K.R. (1982). The effect of stride length variations on O_2 uptake during distance running. *Medicine and Science in Sport and Exercise,* **14**(1), 30-35.

Daniels, J., Scardina, N., & Foley, P. (1984). $\dot{V}O_2$submax during five modes of exercise. In N. Bachl, L. Prokop & R. Suckert (Eds.), *Proceedings of the World Congress on Sports Medicine,* Vienna, 1982 (pp. 604-615). Vienna: Urban and Schwartsenberg.

Fink, W.J., Costill, D.L., & Pollock, M.L. (1977). Submaximal and maximal working capacity of elite distance runners. Part II: Muscle fiber composition and enzyme activities. In P. Milvy (Ed.), *The marathon: Physiological, medical, epidemiological, and psychological studies* (pp. 323-327). New York: New York Academy of Sciences.

Frederick, E.C. (1983). Measuring the effects of shoes and surfaces on the economy of locomotion. In B. Nigg & B. Kerr (Eds.), *Biomechanical aspects of sport shoes and playing surfaces* (pp. 93-106). Calgary, Canada: University Printing.

Greene, P.R. (1985). Circle running: Experiments, theory and applications. *ASME Journal of Biomechanical Engineering,* **107**, 96-103.

Gregor, R.J., Rozenek, R., Brown, C.H., & Garhammer, J. (1979). Variations in running stride mechanics as a function of velocity in elite distance runners [abstract]. *Medicine and Science in Sports and Exercise,* **11**(1), 85.

Hay, J.G. (1983). Biomechanics of sport: An overview. In G.A. Wood (Ed.), *Collected papers on sports biomechanics* (pp. 1-23). Australia: University of Western Australia.

Hinrichs, R.N. (1983). Upper extremity function in running. (Doctoral dissertation, Pennsylvania State University, 1982). *Dissertation Abstracts International*, **43**, 3536A.

James, S.L., Bates, B.T., and Osternig, L.R. (1978). Injuries to runners. *American Journal of Sports Medicine*, **6**(2), 40-50.

Miller, D.A. (1978). Biomechanics of running—What should the future hold? *Canadian Journal of Applied Sport Science*, **3**(4), 229-236.

Nelson, R.C., & Gregor, R.J. (1976). Biomechanics of distance runnning: A longitudinal study. *Research Quarterly*, **47**(3), 417-428.

Nelson, R.C., & Osterhoudt, R.G. (1971). Effects of altered slope and speed on the biomechanics of running. In J. Vredenbregt & J. Wartenweiler (Eds.), *Medicine and Science in sport: Vol. 6. Biomechanics II* (pp. 220-224). Basel: Karger.

Petray, C.K., & Krahenbuhl, G.S. (1985). Running training, instruction on running technique and running economy in 10-year-old males. *Research Quarterly for Exercise and Sport*, **56**(3), 251-255.

Pollock, M. (1977). Submaximal and maximal working capacity of elite distance runners: Part 1. Cardiorespiratory aspects. In P. Milvy (Ed.), *The marathon: Physiological, medical, epidemiological, and psychological studies* (pp. 310-323). New York: New York Academy of Sciences.

Sanderson, D. (1986). *The use of augmented feedback for the modification of the pedalling mechanics of inexperienced cyclists*. Unpublished doctoral dissertation, Pennsylvania State University, University Park, PA.

Williams, K.R. (1980). A biomechanical and physiological evaluation of running efficiency. (Doctoral dissertation, Pennsylvania State University, 1980). *Dissertation Abstracts International*, **41**, 4332A.

Williams, K.R. (1985). Biomechanics of running. In R.L. Terjung (Ed.), *Exercise and sport sciences reviews* (Vol. 13, pp. 389-445). New York: Macmillan.

Williams, K.R., & Ziff, J.L. (1984). Changes in rearfoot motion associated with systematic variations in running style [abstract]. *Program of the 8th Annual Meeting of the American Society of Biomechanics* (pp. 71-72). Tucson: University of Arizona.

Winter, D.A. (1979). Calculation and interpretation of mechanical energy of movement. In R.S. Hutton (Ed.), *Exercise and sport science reviews* (Vol. 6, pp. 183-202). Philadelphia: Franklin Institute.

Assessment of Load Effects in the Reduction and Treatment of Injuries

Benno M. Nigg

A subject walking, running, or jumping exerts a force on the ground, and the ground reacts with an equal but opposite force on the subject (ground reaction force). A subject kicking a football or spiking a volleyball exerts a force on the ball, and the ball exerts an equal but opposite force on the part of the body contacting the ball. Generally, in all human motion, forces are acting on and within the human body. *Load* on the human body or on parts of it can be defined as the forces acting on the human body or on parts of it (Nigg, 1985).

The purpose of this paper is (a) to give an overview of biomechanical research related to load on the human body and (b) to speculate about future research directions in load analysis. The discussion will be limited to research related to load analysis in the lower extremities and frequently will use examples from running because this topic was extensively studied in the last 10 to 20 years.

Overview

Influencing Factors

Contact forces produced during locomotion have a point of application, a magnitude, and a direction, all of which change with time. The force-time functions are mainly influenced by three factors (Nigg, 1986):

1. The *movement* of the segment that makes contact and the neighboring segments *before contact*
2. The *deceleration* and acceleration of the whole body but especially of the segment making contact with the environment *during contact*
3. The gross *movement* of the whole body *before and after contact*

The influence of the movement before contact (1) and the deceleration during contact (2) can easily be understood by studying a simple drop test of a shot onto a surface. The ground reaction force depends on the movement (velocity) of the shot immediately before contact, the material properties of the surface, and the material properties of the shot. In this example, using an iron shot, velocity at touchdown, the geometry of the shot, and the material properties of the surface are the variable factors determining the magnitude of the reaction force. Such considerations were used by several authors in an explicit or implicit form in connection with studies analyzing ground reaction forces in running (Andreasson & Olofsson, 1983; Bates, Osternig, Sawhill, & James, 1983; Bojsen-Moller, 1983; Cavanagh, 1980; Clarke, Frederick, & Cooper, 1983b; Nigg & Denoth, 1980; Rodano, 1983; Segesser, 1976).

The influence of the gross movement (3) can be understood by studying the ground reaction forces. It is known that typical vertical ground reaction forces for running are different from the ones for walking (Cavanagh & Lafortune, 1980; Elftman, 1939).

Impact and Active Forces

The ground reaction force of a subject bobbing up and down on concrete is quite different from the ground reaction force of a subject sitting in a chair and pounding with a heel on the same surface. The main difference lies in the frequency content of the reaction forces. The main frequency components of the first movement, which is solely dependent upon muscle action, are smaller than 5 Hz, whereas the main frequency components of the second example (pounding heel), which is not solely dependent upon muscle action, are greater than 5 Hz (depending on heelpad, etc.). The reaction forces in the first example are called *active forces* (or propulsive or low frequency) and are frequently discussed in load assessment (Bates et al., 1983; Cavanagh et al., 1985; Cavanagh & Lafortune, 1980; Clarke, Frederick, & Cooper, 1983a, 1983b; Miller, Scheirman, & Fugelvand, 1984). The reaction forces in the second movement are called *impact forces* (or initial, high-frequency or passive forces) and are frequently discussed in the context of shoe and surface assessments (Cavanagh & Lafortune, 1980; Cavanagh, Williams, & Clarke, 1981; Clarke et al., 1983a, 1983b; Frederick, Clarke, Larsen, & Cooper, 1983; Nigg, 1986; Nigg & Luethi, 1980). They obviously have a high-frequency aspect.

In human locomotion, active and impact forces are often contained in the same movement. A ground reaction force curve of running, for instance, has an initial impact peak at about 10 to 30 ms followed by an active peak at about 100 to 200 ms, depending on various factors such as running speed, surface stiffness, and foot/shoe geometry. In running, the impact forces are mainly dependent on the mass and the deceleration of the body segment that first makes contact with the ground and its neighboring segments. (In heel landing, the contacting part is the heel, and the neighboring segments are the forefoot and the lower leg. In toe landing, the contacting part is the forefoot, and the neighboring segment is the rear part of the foot. The mass of the contacting and neighboring segments is much smaller for the landing. This explains why the impact forces in toe landing are smaller than in heel landing.) Impact forces can be influenced by equipment such as helmets (Norman, Bishop, Pierrynowski, & Pezzack, 1979), shoes (Cavanagh, 1980; Frederick, Clarke, & Hamill, 1984; Nigg, 1986), and also by surfaces (Nigg & Denoth, 1980). The active force peaks in running depend mainly on the gross movement. Increased vertical body displacement, for instance, is connected with increased active force peaks in the vertical ground reaction forces. Active force peaks are only slightly affected by equipment (e.g., running shoes). Periodic jumping on a trampoline or on concrete shows different active force peaks acting on the human body. However, running on asphalt, a synthetic surface, or even grass doesn't show relevant differences in the magnitude of the active force peaks.

Effects of Load

The title of this chapter suggests an association with pain and sport injuries. However, such an association may not always be correct. The biological system needs stimuli in the form of forces. If they are missing, the human body responds with negative reactions such as muscular or bone atrophy. However, excessive forces may produce an overload of specific structures of the locomotor system and so produce negative effects on these structures. Between these two extreme situations there is an optimal range in which forces acting on the locomotor system have a positive effect. This optimal range is different for each part of the locomotor system. An Achilles tendon, for instance, may have a different optimal range from a patellar tendon. The optimal range depends on the magnitude of the force and the loading rate, and it is different from subject to subject. These restrictions make it difficult to give a general assessment of the effect of forces acting on the locomotor system. However, in many sport activities the number of injuries is substantial. It is speculated that two out of three runners are afflicted with running injuries during 1 year (Cavanagh, 1980). It is reported that about 50% of all tennis players have a tennis injury per season (Nigg & Denoth, 1980), and that about 76% of instructors and about 43% of participants in aerobics have sport injuries each year (Francis, Francis, & Welshons-Smith, 1985; Richie, Kelso, & Bellucci, 1985). Further information about specific injuries can be found in various publications (Clement, Taunton, Smart, & McNicol, 1981; Hess & Hort, 1973; Hort, 1976; James, Bates, & Osternig, 1978; Segesser, 1970). These reports suggest that in many sport activities the human body *is* overloaded and that research in the direction of analyzing load on the human body with the purpose of reducing the number of injuries is a relevant goal in biomechanical research.

Possibilities for Determining Load On and In the Locomotor System

General Comments

Attempts to quantify forces acting on and within the human body are relatively new. Marey (1873), as one of the pioneers, tried to measure the pressure underneath the foot during human locomotion. Further attempts were made by Elftman (1939) and Bresler and Frankel (1950). At present a number of load assessment instruments, such as force platforms, are standard equipment in most biomechanics laboratories. The initial attempts to quantify load on the human body concentrated on walking, and only recently have measurements using force platforms and high-speed film been available to assess external and/or internal forces in various sport activities.

There are three approaches used in load assessment: (a) the experimental *measurement of external forces* such as ground reaction forces, (b) the theoretical *estimation of internal forces* with the help of a mathematical model using external measurements commonly as input into the model, and (c) the experimental *measurement of internal forces*. The following sections will concentrate on the first two methods and will discuss the most important aspects of them but will not discuss the third approach because experimental measurements of internal forces are only rarely performed.

Experimental Methods

Experimental methods have been frequently used to assess load on the locomotor system during sport activities. Various measuring devices are now available and are commonly used in load assessment.

Force platform measurements. Force platforms are commercially available and measure forces acting on the human body during various activities. They can be used to assess the ground reaction forces during activities such as running (Cavanagh & Lafortune, 1980; Frederick, Clarke, & Hamill, 1984; Miller et al., 1984) or jumping on different surfaces (Nigg & Denoth, 1980), or to quantify frictional forces on the ground for various shoe-surface combinations (Schlaepfer, Unold, & Nigg, 1983; Stucke, Baudzus, & Baumann, 1984). Usually force platforms provide (a) vertical, anterior-posterior, and mediolateral components of the resultant force; (b) the point of application of the force vector; and (c) the moment of force around the vertical axis through the point of application. The vertical forces have been studied most frequently, probably because they are usually the largest in magnitude.

Acceleration measurements. Accelerometers are commercially available and can be mounted on the human subject (for instance, at the tibia). They allow measurements of accelerations during different movements such as walking and running (MacLellan, 1984; Unold, 1974; Voloshin & Wosk, 1982) or in other activities such as skiing or gymnastics (Nigg, Neukomm, & Unold, 1974). Acceleration measurements provide axial or three-dimensional information about acceleration of one body segment and are usually measured in a body coordinate system. The most critical aspect of acceleration measurements is the mounting of the accelerometer. Depending on the mounting, the measured acceleration can vary drastically, and large errors may be introduced. A second critical aspect of accelerometer measurements is the fact that the locally measured acceleration is not proportional to the measured ground reaction force or to forces in joints close to the location where the acceleration is measured because the mass involved in the deceleration process (the efective mass) is not constant (Denoth, 1985). The effective mass depends on a number of factors, and there are difficulties in interpreting the results.

Pressure Distribution. Several devices have been developed in the last two decades to quantify the pressure distribution beneath the foot or the shoe during sport activities. They are based on capacitor constructions (Nicol & Hennig, 1976), optical methods (Cavanagh & Michiyoshi, 1980), or piezo-ceramic transducers (Cavanagh, Hennig, Bunch, & MacMillan, 1983; Hennig, Cavanagh, & MacMillan, 1983). They provide impressive pictures of the pressure distribution beneath the foot and are helpful in assessing local loading of the foot during locomotion. Compared to the force platforms, the pressure distribution devices are technically much more sophisticated and used only in a few laboratories in the world.

Kinematic analysis. Kinematic analysis (e.g., film analysis) has been frequently applied in load analysis of lower extremities (Bahlsen & Nigg, 1983; Cavanagh, 1980; Clarke, Frederick, & Hamill, 1984; Kaelin, Denoth, Stacoff, & Stuessi, 1985; Nigg, Eberle, Frey, & Segesser, 1977; Stacoff & Kaelin, 1983). It usually assesses ranges of motion and compares different footwear or different surfaces with respect to their effects on movements. In running, for instance, excessive pronation is reported by many authors and is considered to be an indicator of excessive loading of the ankle and the knee joints.

Electromyography. Currently, several attempts are being made to include electromyography (EMG) measurements in load analysis (Komi, 1983; Tiegermann, 1983). EMG measurements are used to assess the effect of changing boundary conditions such as equipment or contact surface on the EMG activity. Effects of surfaces, for instance, were studied by Tiegermann (1983) in a tennis movement. The muscle activities measured were clearly different for the same gross movement for clay and carpet surfaces.

These are the most frequently used experimental measurement techniques to assess load on the human body during sport activities. There are two critical points to be mentioned in this context. First, some of these methods are not well established with respect to load quantification. Probably the most critical method is the use of accelerometers. Errors can be introduced by inappropriate accelerometer mounting as well as by incorrect interpretation. This suggests that extreme caution must be taken in drawing conclusions from accelerometer data. Second, all of these measurements quantify external loads as seen by an external measuring device. However, the real variables of interest in analyzing loads on the human body are the internal loads (e.g., loads acting on tendons, ligaments, and bones, and the forces exerted by muscles).

Modeling

The human locomotor system has more muscles than needed to produce rotation with respect to each joint. There are, therefore, a number of possible strategies that the motor control system could use to produce a specific movement. In a mathematical sense, this means an indeterminate system of equations in a system that has more unknowns than equations. In a simple example, illustrated by Crowninshield and Brand (1981) for three muscles crossing one joint (no antagonist), the solutions for the muscle forces lie in a three-dimensional muscle force space where the three muscle forces can theoretically have an infinite number of combinations.

There are different possibilities to deal with this indeterminacy problem, and these can be categorized in the following manner:

(a) to reduce information (*reduction*)
(b) to add information (*addition*)
  (1) physiological
  (2) neurophysiological
  (3) additional criteria (e.g., optimization)
(c) to discuss various solution spaces (*discussion*)

Reduction. The reduction method solves the problem of having an indeterminate system of equations by replacing the various muscles crossing a joint by one muscle group with one origin, one insertion, and one line of action describing the common function of these muscles. Examples are the work of Paul (1965) for the hip joint, Morrison (1970) for the knee joint, Procter (1980) for the ankle joint (all for walking), and Baumann and Stucke (1980) for the ankle joint, medial triceps surae, Achilles tendon, and the knee joint in some sport activities. In certain cases the reduction is executed to the point where no muscles are introduced, which seems to be appropriate for a limited aspect of load in the locomotor system (Denoth, 1980). The reduction method provides a unique solution for the problem, estimating the forces in joints and muscle groups.

Addition. The models using additional information contain more muscles than minimally needed for a movement. Additional information is frequently used to increase the number of equations. These additional constraints may be based on physiological principles and/or mathematical techniques such as optimization methods (Crowninshield & Brand, 1981; Herzog, 1985; Pedotti, Krishnan, & Starke, 1978; Seireg & Arvikar, 1973). Some of these models are mainly mathematically oriented (b3), whereas others seem to have more physiological background (b1). The models with more physiological content seem at first glance to be more reasonable. The constraints imposed by physiological models, however, are reason for many discussions because one has to assume some governing rules for the additional constraints.

In the neurophysiological (control system) approach (b2), which is mainly represented by Hatze (1981), Pierrynowski (1982), and Denoth (1985), the function of the control system is used to a certain extent to provide additional information and additional equations for the indeterminate mathematical problem. Hatze (1981) uses additional physiological constraints as well as a control system. Pierrynowski (1982) uses pattern generators, which, as a matter of fact, are additional constraints imposed by the geometry of the muscle moment arms and therefore not a true neurophysiological approach. Denoth (1985) uses the latent period of muscles to solve the indeterminacy problem for impact forces. The control system approach seems to be the most realistic from the point of view of including the physiological and the neurological factors influencing movement. From the point of view of the actual solution of the problem, however, the control system approach usually results in a complicated mathematical system. As a result, only a few researchers in the field of biomechanics have gained a solution with this approach.

Discussion. Usually one of the previously mentioned approaches is selected to find a unique solution for the indeterminacy problem in modeling the human locomotor system. However, there is another possibility as suggested by Denoth (1985) for a not-too-complex model. Instead of solving the indeterminacy problem mathematically, he proposes to discuss the solution space. In a specific case one could ''check what forces would act if only one muscle would work and may get a more comprehensive understanding of the problem'' (p. 69). Denoth suggests that this may be of special importance in the analysis of sport injuries.

A review of the existing approaches for modeling the human body reveals that each shows advantages and disadvantages. It is evident that the results of a model are heavily dependent on the assumptions and the additional constraints that are put into the model. However, this general comment is valid for every modeling approach.

Modeling has not been used very extensively for load analysis in sport activities. With the exception of recent work (Denoth, 1985), the control system and the discussion approaches have not been used at all for load analysis in sports activities. A few models have been developed that have applied the reduction technique to sport-related questions (Baumann & Stucke, 1980; Denoth, 1980; Luethi, 1983). Generally, most of the locomotion models have been applied to slow movements such as walking, and many of these have been applied only in clinical situations. Little research has been done with respect to the modeling of highly dynamic movements such as jumping, landing, running, and sprinting.

Problems of Load Determination

Initial attempts to determine loads on the human body were partially directed toward material tests. It was assumed that a shot dropping down from a certain height with a velocity in the same range as the velocity of the contacting structure would produce impact forces similar to a human subject on the same surface or in the same shoe. However, recent research in the field of load analysis in sports activities (Denoth, Gruber, Keepler, & Ruder, 1985; Kaelin et al., 1985; Luethi, Nigg, & Bahlsen, 1984; Nigg, Luethi, Denoth, & Stacoff, 1983; Nigg, 1985) showed that a change of the boundary conditions (shoe or surface) may produce a change in the movement pattern of a subject during a specific movement (adaptation effect). Pronation velocity, for instance, may change due to a change of midsole hardness in a running shoe (Nigg, 1985), which illustrates the problematic aspect of using material tests in order to assess load on the locomotor system. Furthermore, it is evident from the comments made earlier that it is difficult to determine absolute forces or even the stress distribution in a structure (e.g., tendon, cartilage) of the human body. Results as illustrated by Cavanagh et al. (1985), however, suggest that huge internal force differences due to extreme asymmetries in the ground reaction forces and the center of pressure patterns for high-performance athletes can exist. This underlines the importance of assessing these internal forces. To overcome the difficulty of determining the internal forces with reasonable accuracy, one may be tempted to try to assess differences between two conditions with relatively simple mathematical models of internal structures of the locomotor system, an approach that is not widely used at the present time.

Even assuming that the above-mentioned problems could be solved, we are still confronted with the question about the relevance of certain variables. It is not clear whether the maximum force, the maximum gradient of the force (maximum loading rate), or some other variables are relevant in a biological sense. Furthermore, it may be relatively simple to estimate a force responsible for an acute injury, whereas it may be much more difficult to estimate the origin of the development of a chronic injury because one has to deal with repeated forces as well as with the reacting biological tissue. The comments made in this context show clearly that the determination of load on the human body during various sport activities is still an unsolved problem.

Future Development

The description of the current situation of load analysis for the locomotor system during various sport activities illustrates that the development of techniques measuring external variables is fairly advanced and allows a researcher to quantify many variables of interest in connection with load analysis. It may be that some of the existing techniques (e.g., acceleration measurements, EMG) will be developed further for applications in highly dynamic movements. It doesn't seem to be likely, however, that new experimental techniques for external variables will emerge in the next two decades. If new experimental techniques are developed, then they most likely will be used for assessing internal forces. An example of this possible development is the measurement of forces in the Achilles tendon by Komi, Salonen, Järvinen, & Kokko (1987) and by Gregor, Komi, & Järvinen (1987). Ethical considerations, however, will limit this development.

The comments about the state of the art in modeling of the human body in order to determine internal forces suggest that significant development may be expected in this field. It is speculated that the modeling techniques will improve so that load analysis in the applied sense can be done by using modular type of internal force estimating programs in which the area of interest is described with a relatively complex model and the rest of the body with a relatively simple model. The ideal scenario in about

20 years may be that an athlete with an injury may come to a physician who is associated with a biomechanical load analysis laboratory. The laboratory could, for instance, assess whether a shoe insole given to an athlete as a treatment reduces the forces in the ilio-tibial band where the athlete has pain. The mathematical modeling of the runner system would give a comparison between two situations, with and without insole, and assess the effect of a chosen mechanical treatment.

The influence of load on various structures in the locomotor system will also be investigated over the next two decades. It is speculated that studies analyzing athletes over a long time span will answer questions about the origin of various short-term and long-term problems. This approach may provide an answer to the question of the biological relevance of specific forces acting on the human locomotor system. This question is especially important because most of the explanations of cause and effect are currently based on speculations.

A third area in which development is expected is in the understanding of adaptation effects. As mentioned before, athletes do adapt to various external conditions. The neuromotor control pattern that governs these adaptation processes is not well understood, and it is speculated that work in this area may improve our understanding of the influence of load on the locomotor system.

In summary, there are three fields where future development is expected to be significant: the modeling of the locomotor system for high-dynamic movement, the biological relevance of loading, and the adaptation effects due to load.

Acknowledgments

Work in connection with research in this field was supported by the Natural Sciences and Engineering Research Council and the Alberta Heritage Foundation for Medical Research.

References

Andreasson, G., & Olofsson, B. (1983). Surface and shoe deformation in sport activities and injuries. In B.M. Nigg & B.A. Kerr (Eds.), *Biomechanical aspects of sport shoes and playing surfaces* (pp. 51-61). Calgary: University Printing.

Bahlsen, H.A., & Nigg, B.M. (1983). Selection of a lateral test movement for tennis shoes. In B.M. Nigg & B.A. Kerr (Eds.), *Biomechanical aspects of sport shoes and playing surfaces* (pp. 169-176). Calgary: University Printing.

Bates, B.T., Osternig, L.B., Sawhill, H.A., & James, S.W. (1983). An assessment of subject variability, subject-shoe interaction and the evaluation of running shoes using ground reaction force data. *Journal of Biomechanics*, **16**, 181-192.

Baumann, W., & Stucke, H. (1980). Sportspezifische Belastungen aus der Sicht der Biomechanik (Sport-specific load from a biomechanical point of view). In H. Cotta, H. Krahl, & K. Steinbrueck (Eds.), *Die Belastungstoleranz des Bewegungsapparates* (pp. 55-64). Stuttgart: Thieme.

Bojsen-Moller, F. (1983). Biomechanical effects of shock absorbing heels in walking. In B.M. Nigg & B.A. Kerr (Eds.), *Biomechanical aspects of sport shoes and playing surfaces* (pp. 73-76). Calgary: University Printing.

Bresler, B., & Frankel, J.P. (1950). Forces and moments in the leg during level walking, *Transactions of the American Society of Mechanical Engineers* (ASME), 27-36.

Cavanagh, P.R. (1980). *The running shoe book*. Mountain View, CA: Anderson World.

Cavanagh, P.R., Andrew, G.C., Kram, R., Rodger, M.M., Sanderson, D.J., & Hennig, E.M. (1985). An approach to biomechanical profiling of elite distance runners. *International Journal of Sport Biomechanics*, **1**, 36-62.

Cavanagh, P.R., Hennig, E.M., Bunch, R.P., & MacMillan, N.H. (1983). A new device for the measurement of pressure distribution inside the shoe. In H. Matsui & K. Kobayashi (Eds.), *Biomechanics VIII-B* (pp. 1089-1096). Champaign, IL: Human Kinetics.

Cavanagh, P.R., & Lafortune, M.A. (1980). Ground reaction forces in distance running. *Journal of Biomechanics*, **13**, 397-406.

Cavanagh, P.R., & Michiyoshi, A.E. (1980). A technique for the display of pressure distribution beneath the foot. *Journal of Biomechanics*, **13**, 69-75.

Cavanagh, P.R., Williams, K.R., & Clarke, T.E. (1981). A comparison of ground reaction forces during walking barefoot and in shoes. In A. Morecki, K. Fidelus, K. Kedzior, & A. Wit (Eds.), *Biomechanics VII-B* (pp. 151-156). Baltimore: University Park Press.

Clarke, T.E., Frederick, E.C., & Cooper, L.B. (1983a). Biomechanical measurement of running shoe cushioning properties. In B.M. Nigg & B.A. Kerr (Eds.), *Biomechanical aspects of sport shoes and playing surfaces* (pp. 25-33). Calgary: University Printing.

Clarke, T.E., Frederick, E.C., & Cooper, L.B. (1983b). Effects of shoe cushioning upon ground reaction forces in running. *International Journal of Sports Medicine*, **4**, 247-251.

Clarke, T.E., Frederick, E.C., & Hamill, C. (1984). The study of rearfoot movement in running. In E.C. Frederick (Ed.), *Sport shoes and playing surfaces* (pp. 166-189). Champaign, IL: Human Kinetics.

Clement, D.B., Taunton, J.E., Smart, G.W., & McNicol, K.L. (1981). A survey of overuse running injuries. *The Physician and Sports Medicine*, **9**, 47-58.

Crowninshield, R.D., & Brand, R.A. (1981). A physiologically based criterion of muscle force prediction in locomotion. *Journal of Biomechanics*, **14**, 793-801.

Denoth, J. (1980). Methoden zur Bestimmung von Belastungen (Methods to determine load). In B.M. Nigg & J. Denoth (Eds.), *Sportplatzbelaege* (Playing surfaces) (pp. 41-55). Zurich: Juris Verlag.

Denoth, J. (1985). Load on the locomotor system in modelling. In B.M. Nigg (Ed.), *Biomechanics of running shoes* (pp. 63-116). Champaign, IL: Human Kinetics.

Denoth, J., Gruber, K., Keepler, M., & Ruder, H. (1985). Forces and torques during sport activities with high accelerations. In S. Perren (Ed.), *Biomechanics: Principles and applications* (Vol. 2, pp. 663-668). Boston: Martinus Nijhoff.

Elftman, H. (1939). Forces and energy changes in the legs during walking. *American Journal of Phyisology*, **125**, 339-356.

Francis, L.L., Francis, P.R., & Welshons-Smith, K. (1985). Aerobic dance injuries: A survey of instructors. *The Physician and Sports Medicine*, **13**(2), 105-111.

Frederick, E.C., Clarke, T.E., Larsen, J.L., & Cooper, L.B. (1983). The effects of shoe cushioning on the oxygen demands of running. In B.M. Nigg & B.A. Kerr (Eds.), *Biomechanical aspects of sport shoes and playing surfaces* (pp. 107-114). Calgary: University Printing.

Frederick, E.C., Clarke, T.E., & Hamill, C.L. (1984). The effect of running shoe design on shock attenuation. In E.C. Frederick (Ed.), *Sport shoes and playing surfaces* (pp. 190-198). Champaign, IL: Human Kinetics.

Gregor, R.J., Komi, P.V., Järvinen, N. (1987). Achilles tendon forces during cycling. *International Journal of Sports Medicine*, **8**, 9-14.

Hatze, H. (1981). *Myocybernetic control models of skeletal muscle*. Pretoria: University of South Africa.

Hennig, E.M., Cavanagh, P.R., & MacMillan, N.H. (1983). Pressure distribution measurements by high precision piezoelectric ceramic force transducers. In H. Matsui & K. Kobayashi (Eds.), *Biomechanics VII-B* (pp. 1081-1088). Champaign, IL: Human Kinetics.

Herzog, W. (1985). *Individual muscle force prediction in athletic movement*. Unpublished doctoral dissertation, University of Iowa, Iowa City.

Hess, H., & Hort, W. (1973). Erhoehte Verletzungsgefahr beim Leichtathletiktraining auf Kunststoffboeden (Increased danger of injuries on artificial surfaces during training in track and field). *Sportarzt und Sportmedizin*, **12**, 282-285.

Hort, W. (1976). Ursachen, Klinik, Therapie und Prophylaxe der Schaeden auf Leichtathletik-kunststoffbahnen (Origin, clinical treatment, therapy and prevention of injuries on artificial track and field surfaces). *Leistungssport*, **1**, 48-52.

James, S., Bates, B., & Osternig, L. (1978). Injuries in runners. *American Journal of Sports Medicine*, **6**, 40-50.

Kaelin, X., Denoth, J., Stacoff, A., & Stuessi, E. (1985). Cushioning during running—material tests contra subject tests. In S. Perren & E. Schneider (Eds.), *Biomechanics: Principles and applications* (Vol. 2, pp. 651-656). Boston: Martinus Nijhoff.

Komi, P.V. (1983). Biomechanical features of running with special emphasis on load characteristics and mechanical efficiency. In B.M. Nigg & B.A. Kerr (Eds.), *Biomechanical aspects of sport shoes and playing surfaces* (pp. 123-134). Calgary: University Printing.

Komi, P.V., Salonen, M., Järvinen, N., & Kokko, O. (1987). In vivo registration of Achilles tendon forces in man: Methodological development, *International Journal of Sports Medicine*, **8**, 3-9.

Luethi, S.M. (1983). *Biomechanical analysis of short-term pain and injuries in tennis*. Unpublished doctoral dissertation, University of Calgary, Canada.

Luethi, S.M., Nigg, B.M., & Bahlsen, H.A. (1984). The influence of varying shoe sole stiffness on impact forces in running. *Proceedings of the Annual Conference of the Canadian Society of Biomechanics, Human Locomotion III*, 65-66.

MacLellan, G.E. (1984). Skeletal heel strike transients, measurement, implications, and modification by footwear. In E.C. Frederick (Ed.), *Sport shoes and playing surfaces* (pp. 76-86). Champaign, IL: Human Kinetics.

Marey, E.J. (1873). *La machine animale, locomotion terrestre et aerienne*. Paris: Centre Georges Pompidou Musée National d'Arte Moderne.

Miller, D.I., Scheirman, G.L., & Fugelvand, A.J. (1984). Ground reaction patterns related to running speed [abstract]. *Medicine and Science in Sports and Exercise*, **16**, 185.

Morrison, J.B. (1970). The mechanics of the knee joint in relation to normal walking. *Journal of Biomechanics*, **3**, 51-61.

Nicol, K., & Hennig, E.M. (1976). Time dependent method for measuring force distribution using a flexible mat as a capacitor. In P.V. Komi (Ed.), *Biomechanics V-B* (pp. 433-440). Baltimore: University Park Press.

Nigg, B.M. (1986). *Biomechanics of running shoes*. Champaign, IL: Human Kinetics.

Nigg, B.M. (1985). Loads in selected sport activities—an overview. In D.A. Winter, R.W. Norman, R.P. Wells, K.C. Hayes, & A.E. Patla (Eds.), *Biomechanics IX-B* (pp. 91-96). Champaign, IL: Human Kinetics.

Nigg, B.M., & Denoth, J. (1980). Sportplatzbelaege (Playing surfaces). Zurich: Juris Verlag.

Nigg, B.M., Eberle, G., Frey, D., & Segesser, B. (1977). Biomechanische Analyse von Fussinsuffizienzen (Biomechanical analysis of foot insufficiencies). *Medizinisch-Orthopaedische Technik*, **97**, 178-180.

Nigg, B.M., & Luethi, S.M. (1980). Bewegungsanalysen beim Laufschuh (Movement analysis for running shoes). *Sportwissenschaft*, **3**, 309-320.

Nigg, B.M., Luethi, S., Denoth, J., & Stacoff, A. (1983). Methodological aspects of sport shoe and sport surface analysis. In H. Matsui & K. Kobayashi (Eds.), *Biomechanics VII-B* (pp. 1041-1052). Champaign, IL: Human Kinetics.

Nigg, B.M., Neukomm, P.A., & Unold, E. (1974). Biomechanik und Sport (Biomechanics and sport). *Orthopaede*, **3**, 140-147.

Norman, R.W., Bishop, P.J., Pierrynowski, M.R., & Pezzack, J.C. (1979). Aircrew helmet protection against potential cerebral concussion in low magnitude impacts. *Aviation, Space and Medicine*, **50**, 553-561.

Paul, J.P. (1965). Bioengineering studies of the forces transmitted by joints. In R.M. Kennedy (Ed.), *Engineering analysis, biomechanics and related bioengineering topics* (pp. 369-380). Oxford: Pergamon Press.

Pedotti, A., Krishnan, V.V., & Starke, L. (1978). Optimization of muscle-force sequencing in human locomotion. *Mathematic Biosciences*, **38**, 57-76.

Pierrynowski, M.R. (1982). *A physiological model for the solution of individual muscle force during normal human walking*. Unpublished doctoral dissertation, Simon Fraser University, Vancouver, British Columbia.

Procter, P. (1980). *Ankle joint biomechanics*. Unpublished doctoral dissertation, University of Strathclyde, Glasgow.

Richie, D.H., Kelso, S.F., & Bellucci, P.A. (1985). Aerobic dance injuries: A retrospective study of instructors and participants. *The Physician and Sports Medicine*, **13**(2), 130-140.

Rodano, R. (1983). Analysis of the impact in running shoes. In B.M. Nigg & B.A. Kerr (Eds.), *Biomechanical aspects of sport shoes and playing surfaces* (pp. 35-42). Calgary: University Printing.

Schlaepfer, F., Unold, E., & Nigg, B. (1983). The frictional characteristics of tennis shoes. In B.M. Nigg & B.A. Kerr (Eds.), *Biomechanical aspects of sport shoes and playing surfaces* (pp. 153-160). Calgary: University Printing.

Segesser, B. (1970). Sportschaeden durch ungeeignete Boeden in Sportanlagen (Sport injuries as a consequence of unsuitable surfaces). *Arztdienst*, ETS Magglingen.

Segesser, B. (1976). Die Belastung des Bewegungsappartes auf Kunststoffboeden (Loading of the musculoskeletal system on artificial surfaces). *Sportstaettenbau und Baederanlagen*, **4**, 1183-1194.

Seireg, A., & Arvikar, R.J. (1973). A mathematical model for evaluation of forces in lower extremities of the musculoskeletal system. *Journal of Biomechanics*, **6**, 313-326.

Stacoff, A., & Kaelin, X. (1983). Pronation and sport shoe design. In B.M. Nigg & B.A. Kerr (Eds.), *Biomechanical aspects of sport shoes and playing surfaces* (pp. 143-151). Calgary: University Printing.

Stucke, H., Baudzus, W., & Baumann, W. (1984). On friction characteristics of playing surfaces. In E.C. Frederick (Ed.), *Sport shoes and playing surfaces* (pp. 87-97). Champaign, IL: Human Kinetics.

Tiegerman, V. (1983). Reaction forces and EMG activity in fast sideward movements. In B.M. Nigg & B.A. Kerr (Eds.), *Biomechanical aspects of sport shoes and playing surfaces* (pp. 83-90). Calgary: University Printing.

Unold, E. (1974). Erschuetterungsmessungen beim Gehen und Laufen auf verschiedenen Unterlagen mit verschiedenem Schuhwerk (Acceleration measurements during walking and running on various surfaces with different shoes). *Jugend und Sport*, **8**, 289-292.

Voloshin, A., & Wosk, J. (1982). An in vivo study of low back pain and shock absorption in the human locomotor system. *Journal of Biomechanics*, **15**, 21-27.

Locomotion: A Commentary

Robert J. Gregor

Locomotion, whether walking or running, is unquestionably the oldest form of transportation known to man. In a very real sense, however, gait analysis as an area of study has existed only since the late 19th century. Physiologists traditionally use gait to stress the body and investigate metabolic and cardiorespiratory responses. Neuroscientists have used locomotion to better understand the role played by the nervous system in controlling the movement, whereas biomechanists use gait to study the loads imposed on the musculoskeletal system. Although major advances in technology (e.g., high-speed cinematography and force measurement systems) form the basis for improved biomechanical studies, much of the data, thus far, are only descriptive in nature. This holds true across a range of applications from the clinical setting to the analysis of elite athletes.

Much of the research on locomotion has been carried out independently within each of the scientific disciplines mentioned above. An encouraging trend, however, and a challenge in the future, is the collaboration of physiologists, neuroscientists, and biomechanists in a more holistic approach to the study of human performance, specifically locomotion. For example, neural control scientists should be aware of the varying kinetic demands placed on the body in attempts to understand what the nervous system must deal with during each step cycle. Similarly, the physiologist should be aware of environmental loads (e.g., ground reaction forces) to better interpret metabolic and cardiorespiratory responses, whereas the biomechanist should be aware of connective tissue properties when investigating external loads imposed on the musculoskeletal system. Gait can no longer be studied by separate analysis of EMG, oxygen consumption, or net joint torques. Modern technology permits us to observe several variables simultaneously during the same testing session. The challenge, then, is to continue the trend toward collaboration among scientists from many disciplines during the design, data collection, and interpretation phases of the investigation.

The two papers presented in this session focused on the mechanics of locomotion. Dr. Cavanagh explored some interesting aspects of elite distance running, whereas Dr. Nigg presented a more general view of human locomotion with an emphasis on loads imposed on the body during a variety of activities. Both authors discussed correlating external mechanics with other variables such as the dynamic properties of connective tissue, muscle activation (EMG), and cardiorespiratory output. Additionally, each focused on future research directions.

Upon completing the paper by Cavanagh, one is left with distinct impressions regarding the role played by biomechanists in evaluating elite distance runners. Because a paucity of data exists on the biomechanics of elite distance runners, Cavanagh suggested research in several future directions. He made it clear, however, and there appeared to be consensus of those in attendance, that biomechanists should not work in isolation. He states that "success will come from interdisciplinary research groups who are studying running in the broadest possible sense." I personally agree with this position and think that each research question (e.g., identification of cause and treatment of stress fractures) will require that specific parameters be measured and this will then dictate the composition of the research group. The group may have different members depending on the questions being asked. If issues are broad and a great deal of screening information is needed, then a large, varied group of scientists would be needed to accumulate a wide range of information. Once this is digested, more specific questions may be addressed by a smaller, more focused group. The role of the biomechanist would be to interact and supply information regarding movement mechanics whenever that type of information became necessary.

A second topic of discussion focused on experimental protocols. There was consensus that they should be as consistent as possible, but questions were raised as to what variables should be measured and whether individual or group data would be more important. For example, Dr. Norman of the University of Waterloo noted that a wide variety of variables could be quantified but questioned what kinematic and kinetic variables would be most critical. Because distance running was the specific focus of the question, Dr. Cavanagh responded by indicating that we are currently in the early stages and specific variables are difficult to isolate. In dealing with elite athletes, however, Cavanagh would provide the following items to all runners who came to his lab: (a) a visualization of their running pattern, (b) some insight into factors that may explain some of their past injuries and information that might possibly help prevent future injuries (e.g., ground reaction force [GRF] information), and (c) some measurements that should help in designing appropriate footwear for safer and better performance.

Further discussion focused on whether individual analyses or group data would be more appropriate in identifying critical variables. Dr. Cavanagh suggested that both individual and group studies could contribute important information. Large amounts of group data are needed for a data base, but case studies are also important, especially at the elite level. In addition, to make some general statements about an individual athlete's running pattern, averaging of repeated trials may be needed. However, because this averaging process would mask certain important events, a case study may be more appropriate. The objective of the given project should help identify the correct approach.

Once the data are collected, whether it be from one individual during one step cycle, the same subject averaged across several step cycles, or data from a large group of subjects, the next major consideration is application of the results. Can one take information from one subject and apply it to another? Can one take group data and apply it to individuals? Specifically, regarding data obtained on elite athletes, Dr. Cavanagh believes that the "ideal" concept needs revision. What we find in elite performers does not necessarily apply nor should we attempt to apply it to other elite or non-elite athletes. Many in attendance agreed that each athlete, whether elite or not, has his or her own signature, and, depending on the objectives of the project, comparison of individual data may be appropriate (i.e., within athlete over a season of training), or group trends obtained through data averaging may be the important objective.

Continuing this line of thinking, I questioned whether we could apply what is learned from one runner (what has been identified as a case study) to the analysis of other performers? Cavanagh referred to studies by Williams, which have shown that there are some underlying features that may apply across a group of runners. For example, economical distance runners tend to transfer more energy from limbs to the trunk than do less economical runners. It is dangerous, however, to go beyond general statements. If you want to make changes in an individual's performance, it becomes a case study. Averaging the data of many runners may submerge important facts about their running patterns, and therefore results may be applied incorrectly to individual cases. Additionally, an elite performer may vary from day to day. There may be little value then in using biomechanics to characterize the performance of an athlete on an outstanding day and then use that profile for comparative purposes for those less than outstanding days in order to keep an athlete near his or her peak.

Dr. Cavanagh suggested that there was a need to study athelets on a more longitudinal basis—possibly twice a week, immediately after competition, or right after an exhaustive training session. For example, an athlete is usually very stiff after a marathon. What mechanical changes accompany this condition, and what changes occur with recovery? What day-to-day variations in mechanics are displayed by runners, and are such variations associated with changes in performance? These questions have not yet been considered. One should keep in mind, however, that these are very complex issues and ones that certainly require an interdisciplinary approach.

The second presentation by Dr. Nigg focused on the more general issue of loads imposed on the human body during a variety of sport activities. His major objective in measuring loads on the body was to reduce the incidence of injury. Nigg spent some time discussing why the biomechanist today must be aware of both internal and external loads experienced by the human body during movement. In close parallel to ideas presented by Ron Zernicke in a previous session, Nigg believes that these loads must be interpreted in light of current information on connective tissue mechanics. The theme, again, was to maximize performance and minimize injury.

To open the discussion at the conclusion of Nigg's presentation, David Winter questioned how shoe design could help protect the human body from injury. In Dr. Nigg's analysis of internal versus external forces, injury data suggest that internal forces are more responsible for many injuries (perhaps 60 to 80% of injuries) rather than external forces (e.g., impact). If this is so, how can shoe design help protect the system from injury? Is impact the major source of injury?

Dr. Nigg did not think that impact was the only cause of injury. A study should be designed in which the characteristics of a large number of healthy runners are measured. Investigators would then wait until the runners were injured so that they could remeasure them and gain some insight into injury mechanisms. With respect to shoes, they can have a large effect on the impact forces but a limited effect on what Dr. Nigg defined as *active* forces. The shoe does more to modify the initial contact phase than subsequent phases of stance. In addition, a shoe's geometry can be manipulated to change the nature of the active forces by changing the point of application of the ground reaction force. Dr. Andriacchi followed the same line of reasoning and stated that geometric changes in a shoe due to normal wear could also result in changes in gait. Nigg originally thought that changes in shoe materials were the key to modifying footwear but now thinks the key lies in changing the geometry of footwear. Dr. Cavanagh responded to this series of statements by pointing out that changes in material usually result in geometry changes as well and the two should not be considered independently.

Discussion at this point shifted to the methods employed in studying internal and external loads on the human body. Bob Norman suggested that these types of analyses only permit speculation about internal forces because of the method employed. Methods of direct measurement of internal forces should be developed. Nigg responded by saying there are essentially two ways we can proceed: (a) We can develop new methods for direct measurements as suggested, and/or (b) we can use relatively simple models in a comparative analysis of different conditions (e.g., with insole vs. no insole). The model may produce systematic errors in the analysis, but the comparison should still be valid. Dr. Norman's reply was that a simple model does not allow one to identify, convincingly, the source of the differences. In reality, minor differences in mechanics may result in different muscular responses (cocontractions, etc.). A simple model may not be sensitive to this. We therefore need more direct measurement techniques.

To complete this session, I posed a final question to each of the four speakers, two from each session (Zernicke, Komi, Cavanagh, and Nigg): "With an eye to the future, what dissertation topic would you recommend to your newest student that, if completed, would have a significant impact on the field of biomechanics?" In other words, what area of study or unit of analysis is most important at the present time? For example, should we focus on selected limb dynamics using inverse dynamics, refinement of modeling techniques, or more accurate direct measurement techniques?

Komi answered that internal direct measurement of muscle forces is what should be focused on at the present time, whereas Zernicke believed that establishing a good question was the most important and immediate demand. The subsequent analysis could be at any level (i.e., muscle or whole limb), and one could use a variety of analysis tools. Dr. Cavanagh's answer was that there should be further study on load sharing between muscles with an emphasis on animal studies and, on the more global level, that a student should gain expertise in cardiorespiratory function as well as the biomechanics of external factors in human locomotion. He would then propose they combine the two areas in the analysis of human movement. Dr. Nigg emphasized the interdisciplinary approach. One should consider the factors that control the load distribution in muscles (e.g., frequency content, velocity) and use simple models (e.g., Hatze's models are much too complicated for most applications) for sensitivity analyses. These statements represent a broad range of ideas that need to be considered in future biomechanics research.

In summary, it appears that most biomechanists believe that the interdisciplinary approach is the key to future success. Whether in student preparation, individual research projects, or larger, more extensively funded projects, the biomechanists must interact with scientists from other fields in a more holistic approach to the study of human movement. Each must contribute his or her own expertise and yet be ready to discuss a variety of approaches. Realization of objectives will then be enhanced and progress will be more efficient and effective.

Future Directions in Biomechanics Research of Human Movement

David A. Winter

In biomechanics research we can become immersed in the day-to-day problems of measurement, data processing, and modeling. All these efforts are aimed at improved accuracy, reduced noise, more valid predictions, or statistically significant results. But what is the end use of all these efforts? In the study of movement pathologies, we aim for more accurate and more valid diagnoses. In studies of normal movement, we may be motivated by nothing more than curiosity and a desire to find out how the human biological system works. However, there is almost always some direct spinoff as to how the research will help us improve human performance. For the sport scientist there are direct efforts to improve specific athletic performances. With these widely ranging approaches I would suggest that the operational word for both pathological and athletic assessments is *diagnosis*. We are trying to diagnose abnormal or inefficient motor patterns. This implies that we know what is normal or efficent and also assumes that those motor patterns have the potential of being improved.

A major conceptional viewpoint needs emphasis if we hope to improve motor patterns via exercise or training. We must recognize that the motor patterns that we look at (moments of force, muscle tension, joint powers) are really neurological patterns. In our laboratory we focus on that fact when we refer to the joint moments of force as the *final common mechanical pathway*. Only at the joint level do we see the algebraic summation of all muscle forces and therefore are able to identify the final desired pattern of the central nervous system. Many of us are active in documenting EMG patterns in a wide variety of movements, and we would have no difficulty in convincing neurophysiologists that these patterns are involved at the neural level. However, we would encounter some problem in convincing these same neurophysiologists if we presented them with curves plotted in Newtons, Watts, or Joules.

Probably the major future for biomechanics is through interaction with motor control and neurological researchers or with muscle physiologists. This interaction in the past has probably been hampered by our preoccupation with methodological and pragmatic problems and by a lack of aggressiveness on our part. However, we are also hampered by ignorance of or indifference to the neurologists and physiologists regarding the potential of biomechanics in answering major aspects of questions they are posing. Most neurophysiologists ignore the musculoskeletal system as being an inherent part of the very system they are studying; neural control ends at the motor end point and starts again with the receptors. Grillner (1973), for example, reports stance and swing times of the hind limbs of spinalized kittens as they walked with their hind limbs on a treadmill. The stance time varied inversely with the treadmill speed and the swing time decreased very slightly with treadmill speed. He attributed the timings to the motor programs but did not consider that the results he reported were explainable biomechanically. The timings were exactly what would be seen if a totally passive lower limb was pulled backward by the treadmill and was allowed to swing forward under control of passive series elasticity of the stretched anterior muscles. The fact that spinalized cats generate no active forward push was later shown by Forssberg, Grillner, and Halbertsma (1980). Thus the stance and swing times as reported earlier by Grillner (1973) were not neurological in origin but merely passive biomechanical phenomena. Most muscle physiologists interested in metabolic efficiency are quite ignorant of what should go into the numerator of their efficiency equations. Many different definitions of efficiency have been introduced (Donovan & Brooks, 1977; Gaesser & Brooks, 1975; Lloyd & Zacks, 1972; Whipp & Wasserman, 1969) and virtually all of them have incorrectly defined measures of mechanical work. Thus the results of their efficiency estimates are often meaningless in spite of the many corrections they make to the denominator of their efficiency equations.

Roadblocks to the Ideal Situation

In all research disciplines at any point in time there are major and fundamental limitations to progress. These roadblocks should be recognized and should be the focus of much of our research effort.

Logistics

Although we can speculate about the ideal world, we are faced with measurement limitations. Most systems, no matter how expensive, result in some encumbrance and are limited to the number of variables measured. All have some measurement errors. In spite of major improvements made over the past two decades, these limitations pose severe problems that hinder a meaningful analysis of most athletic movements.

Modeling

To make any analytical progress, we have simplified our biomechanical models, and in doing so we have compromised the validity of our analyses. We assume rigid segments with constant lengths, masses and inertias, hinge joints, simplified muscle models, and so on. Our forward solution models are particularly simplified, especially in the allowable degrees of freedom at joints such as the hips, shoulders, and vertebrae. Some researchers (Frank, 1970; Townsend & Seireg, 1972), for example, have simplified their model of human walking to include massless rigid limbs! Also, other researchers (Beckett & Chang, 1968; Ramey & Yang, 1981) forced predefined trajectories on their model, thus violating the first principle of any forward solution: The model must be allowed to assume any trajectory as dictated by its initial conditions and input kinetics. Not until we achieve valid models can we ask the question, "what would happen if," and thereby make any real progress toward optimization.

Indeterminacy and Coupling

Because the neuromuscular system is a converging system, it is virtually impossible at present to arrive at unique solutions at the muscle level. As is indicated in Figure 1, the joint moments of force are algebraic summations of the net effect of many muscle forces. Also, as indicated in this figure, the knee joint during weight bearing is under the control of moments at all three joints of the lower limb. Thus we can achieve the same kinematics with an infinite number of different muscle force patterns. Because of biarticulate muscles and tight neural coupling between adjacent joints, the net effect of moments of force at one joint on adjacent

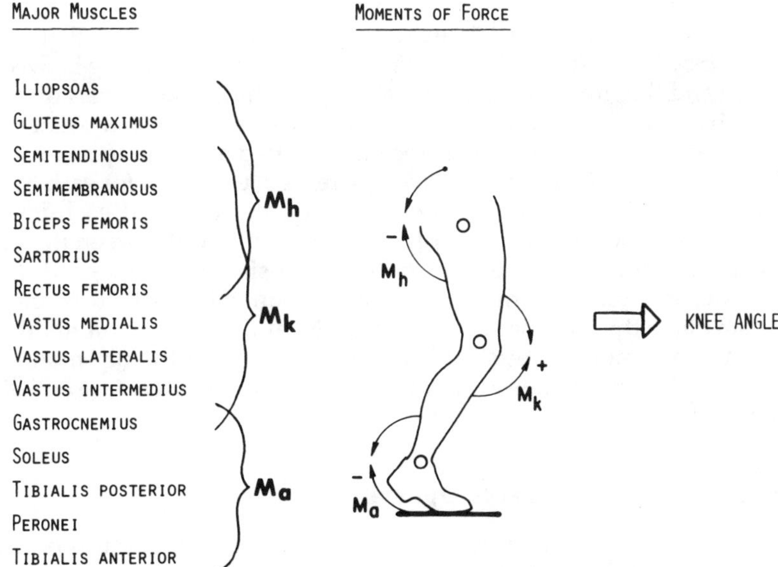

Figure 1. Major muscles that contribute to the moments of force at the ankle, knee, and hip, which in turn result in control of kinematics such as knee angle. Major indeterminacy results at the muscle level, and also an infinite number of combinations of muscle forces can result in the same kinematics.

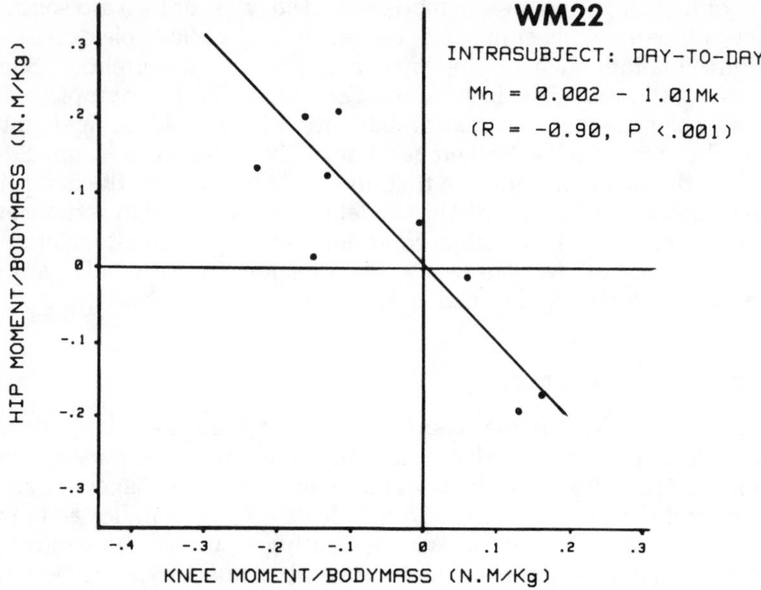

Figure 2. Mean hip moment versus mean knee moment during stance of repeat walking trials on the same subject whose joint kinematics were extremely consistent. Trial-to-trial changes demonstrate the indeterminacy predicted in Figure 1 but also show an almost one-for-one trade-off of moments between these joints.

and more remote segments is extremely difficult to predict. Figure 2 (Winter, 1984) illustrates both the indeterminacy and the coupling between the knee and the hip joints during walking. For nine repeat trials on the same subject (whose lower limb kinematics were extremely consistent), the mean knee moment during stance was plotted against the mean hip moment. There were different moment patterns at each joint for each trial, but there was close coupling between the changes seen at each joint. Evidence for a one-for-one trade-off of moment of force between the hip and knee is indicated by the slope of the regression curve = −1.01. On one stride, for example, the average knee moment was 0.16 N•m/kg (extensor) and the hip moment was 0.17 N•m/kg (flexor); on another stride the knee moment was 0.15 N•m/kg (flexor) and the hip moment was 0.13 N•m/kg (extensor), yet the kinematics were essentially unchanged.

What Is Normal and What Is Optimal?

It has taken researchers many years and hundreds of thousands of dollars to describe what is normal in even the more common stereotyped movements such as level walking. We are normalizing for height, weight, and cadence to some extent but what about age, sex, and body type? There are scores of other common movements for which the documentation is small or nonexistent. What are the normal moment of force patterns in uphill, downstairs, and backward walking or for sprinting and marathon running?

Many researchers have tried to define an optimal movement, and several attempts have been made in gait research to predict muscle forces using some form of optimal criterion. However, the results of those predictions have been quite unsuccessful in spite of contrary comments by the authors (Hardt, 1978; Seireg & Arvikar, 1975). Thus it is unlikely that we are now in a position to define optimal motor patterns for a wide variety of athletic movements.

Inherent Strengths and Progress in Biomechanics Research

In spite of the somewhat pessimistic statements made above, there are many inherent strengths to biomechanics research that must be recognized and exploited. Also, we are making some reasonable progress by chipping away at the body of knowledge regarding motor patterns in different movements.

Measurement and Analysis of Many Variables

In spite of the fact that we cannot measure or calculate every variable that we wish, we do have a handle on many input/output variables. We can predict moments of force, rates of energy generation and absorption and transfers by muscles, energy changes of segments, plus a host of kinematic and temporal variables. We have a good idea about how to predict muscle tension from a suitably calibrated EMG. Because we are dealing with variables that are governed by the laws of physics, we are not in the dark as to cause and effect. We are therefore capable of diagnosing abnormal motor patterns of first order importance in many movements. Compared with our colleagues in muscle metabolism who are stuck with global metabolic measures, we are much more at the diagnostic level. The motor patterns we analyze reflect not only the effect of metabolic conditioning, but also the net result of training on the neural control system.

Integration of Motor Patterns

Compared with the neurophysiologists, the biomechanist has a handle on the net motor pattern that the CNS is trying to achieve. We are analyzing the intact system, rather than an individual motor unit, sensor, or neural network. Therefore, we see the woods, not the trees, and are in a position to exploit the information content of those integrative biomechanical signals. We can now identify the presence of motor synergies in some complex integrative movements such as gait. Our challenge is to devise innovative experiments and control models to extract information as to how the control strategies are organized and possibly optimized. These deterministic models enable us to predict the entire response rather than statistical models that relate to single measures taken from those responses (e.g., time to peak, delay, peak amplitude).

Evolution of Normal Patterns to Serve as a Baseline

We are now starting to accumulate a wide variety of kinematic and kinetic patterns in some common movements such as gait. These patterns can now be used in the full diagnostic sense to pinpoint motor pathologies. In our laboratory we now have profiles on about 50 different kinematic and kinetic variables for the adult population: EMG patterns, moments of force at three walking speeds, powers at three walking speeds, joint angles, and foot trajectories at three walking speeds. The generation of these intersubject averages requires considerable effort but with the increased automation of data collection systems this should not be as formidable a task in the future.

Summary

The biomechanics researcher has a major role to play in answering many questions now posed by neurophysiologists and muscle metabolism physiologists. Biomechanics has many inherent characteristics that greatly enhance its potential role. These strengths should be exploited. The days of measurement, description, and data smoothing are over. We must roll up our sleeves, formulate difficult questions regarding motor performance, and be able to diagnose the cause of inefficient or pathological movement. This role will occur only through interaction with motor control and muscle metabolism researchers or with the research-oriented practitioner.

References

Beckett, R., & Chang, K. (1968). An evaluation of the kinematics of gait by minimum energy. *Journal of Biomechanics*, **1**, 147-159.

Donovan, C.M., & Brooks, G.A. (1977). Muscular efficiency during steady-rate exercise: 2. Effects of walking speed and work rate. *Journal of Applied Physiology*, **43**, 431-439.

Forssberg, H., Grillner, S., & Halbertsma, J. (1980). Locomotion of the low spinal cat: Part I. Coordination within the hind limb. *Acta Physiology Scandinavica*, **108**, 269-281.

Frank, A.A. (1970). An approach to the dynamic analysis and synthesis of bipedal locomotion machines. *Medical and Biological Engineering*, **8**, 465-476.

Gaesser, G.A., & Brooks, G.A. (1975). Muscular efficiency during steady-rate exercise: Effects of speed and work rate. *Journal of Applied Physiology*, **38**, 1132-1139.

Grillner, S. (1973). Locomotion in the spinal cat. In R.B. Stein, K.G. Pearson, R.S. Smith, and J.B. Redford (Eds.), *Control of posture and locomotion* (pp. 515-535). New York: Plenum Press.

Hardt, D.E. (1978). Determining muscle forces in the leg during normal human walking, an application and evaluation of optimization methods. *Transactions of the ASME, Journal of Biomechanical Engineering*, **100**, 72-78.

Lloyd, B.B., & Zacks, R.M. (1972). The mechanical efficiency of treadmill running against a horizontal impeding force. *Journal of Physiology*, **223**, 355-363.

Ramey, M.R., & Yang, A.T. (1981). A simulation procedure for human motion studies. *Journal of Biomechanics*, **14**, 203-213.

Seireg, A., & Arvikar, R.J. (1975). The prediction of muscular load sharing the joint forces in the lower extremities during walking. *Journal of Biomechanics*, **8**, 89-102.

Townsend, M.A., & Seireg, A. (1972). Synthesis of bipedal locomotion. *Journal of Biomechanics*, **5**, 71-83.

Whipp, B.J., & Wasserman, K. (1969). Efficiency of muscular work. *Journal of Applied Physiology*, **26**, 644-647.

Winter, D.A. (1984). Kinematic and kinetic patterns in human gait: Variability and compensating effects. *Human Movement Science*, **3**, 51-76.

Microcomputers in Biomechanics Research and Applied Settings

Doris I. Miller

Unlike many aspects of biomechanics, it is not necessary to return to Muybridge and Marey to review the history and development of micros. Dramatic improvements have been made in the last 1 to 2 years alone, and the exciting (and also somewhat frightening) realization from the standpoint of biomechanics is that the micro revolution is far from over—it may just be beginning. Advances in force transducers and photo, video, and imaging techniques, as impressive as they have been, fade into insignificance beside the strides made in microcomputer technology. And, in fact, the potential of instrumentation designed to collect kinematic and kinetic data will only be fully realized when linked with sophisticated state-of-the-art microcomputers.

Not long ago, a mainframe was characterized as a large, fast, and powerful machine with a 32- or 64-bit central processing unit (CPU) capable of simultaneously servicing multi-users. A minicomputer was substantially smaller physically and had a 16-bit CPU whereas a micro had an 8-bit CPU (Murtha & Waite, 1980). Today, some micros have 32-bit CPUs! The old sharp and simplistic distinctions among these computers have all but disappeared. Although minis and mainframes still retain some advantages in speed and storage capacity, the gap is rapidly closing.

There is no need to sell the efficacy of microcomputers in biomechanics. Combined with the considerable amount of sophisticated software now available on micros, their low cost, convenience, direct access, and portability permit a wide variety of applications while at the same time allowing them to be dedicated to a single use from short to extended periods. Nor do we have to worry about setting aside a temperature-controlled room in which to house microcomputer hardware. Gone are the exorbitant monthly maintenance contract bills associated with the minis and the run-, connect-, and storage-time charges of the mainframes.

In considering the micro revolution in biomechanics, I find it difficult to separate the present from the future. The state of the art today is beyond what most of our dreams and expectations were only 2 or 3 years ago. Certainly few technological advances have made such a direct, widespread, and deeply felt impact in as short a period of time. Microcomputer systems have already revolutionized virtually all aspects of biomechanics from administration and instruction to research. In the future, they will be used increasingly outside laboratory and academic environments. Permanent field installations will become more common, placing micros directly into the hands of the practitioner and allowing the motor performance of the individuals to be monitored on a more continuous and systematic basis than has been possible in the past.

System Considerations

In terms of basic microcomputer hardware needed for general purpose biomechanics applications, the following are essential: the microcomputer itself, a monitor, dual floppy disk drives, and dot matrix printer to accommodate hard copy graphics while providing near letter-quality printing. It is also useful to have a system saver, which serves as a central control for computer, monitor, and printer and provides some protection against overheating, static electricity, and current surges.

But what are the considerations in selecting a particular microcomputer system? Although cost always seems to be the first to come to mind, the potential buyer must be aware that just because a system offers what appear to be significant savings in the initial purchase, it may not be as cost-effective as others in the long run. In addition to operating speed and performance reliability, the following are four important questions that have to be addressed:

1. For what is the system going to be used? Possible uses include word processing, student instruction, on-line data collection, and data reduction/analysis. This becomes an important consideration when determining whether a sealed system will meet your needs or whether expandability is an important feature.
2. Who will be using the system? Possible users include technicians, faculty members, research assistants, and students. What is their level of computer literacy? Even experts appreciate a user-friendly system with good documentation.
3. Will the system be compatible with system(s) in: the home, the department, the institution, and/or other biomechanics labs? It is important to have this kind of compatibility to maximize efforts related to software development and to provide an informal network in which problems can be discussed and ideas shared.
4. What is the level of software and peripheral support, that is, whether it be custom or commercial, and what is the nature and extent of the support? The most powerful hardware will simply collect dust without adequate software to capitalize on its capabilities. Software development represents a major hidden cost in any computer system.

Micros in most biomechanics labs are employed for a variety of purposes and are operated by a number of different users. With this situation in

Table 1 Comparison of the Apple IIe and IBM/PC

Features	Apple IIe	IBM/PC
Microprocessor	6502 (8 bit)	8088 (16 bit)
Can address	64K bytes	1 megabyte
Operating systems	DOS 3.3 and ProDos	CP/M[a] and MS-DOS
Word processing	Appleworks	Wordstar[a]
Spreadsheets	Multiplan	Lotus 1-2-3
Statistics	AppStat	SPSS/PC
Expansion slots	Yes	Yes
Cost		2–3 × IIe

[a]Can be run on an Apple IIe with a Z80 card.

mind, and given the need for expandability essential for research/data collection applications, the two systems that immediately come to mind are the Apple IIe and IBM PC (Table 1). Others of course are also available (over 200, in fact), and some may be as good as, if not better than, these two for specific applications. It seems logical, however, to select a system that is compatible with the IIe and/or PC because most third-party development of software and peripherals is aimed at their markets and more and more toward the PC.

Because of the extensive number of IIes in use and the recent popularity of the IBM PC, significant efforts have been made to permit the Apple IIe to run software originally written for the PC. This can generally be accomplished by installing a Z80 card in one of the Apple expansion slots. The Z80 has its own 64K random access memory (RAM) and uses the Apple only as an I/O processor. If a lab has both PCs and IIes equipped with serial ports and a crossover cable, files can be sent from one to the other (Jones, 1984).

When multiple units are purchased, it is a major advantage to have them of the same type. This means that software is transferable, interface cards can be interchanged, substitutions can be made if necessary, and the intricacies of only one as opposed to several systems have to be mastered. If different systems are purchased, it is important that they be compatible if at all possible.

Administration

Although the administrative applications of micros are no different from those in many other areas of sport science, it is important to highlight their role in this context because it underlies and supports much of what is done in instruction and research. Aspects of administration that were formerly delegated to central office staff or that were unrealistic to computerize because of the limited access and availability of minis and mainframes for such computing are now being done in the biomechanics lab. This eliminates one or two intervening stages of information transmission, saves time, and, in the long run, usually results in a more efficient system.

Undoubtedly the first major administrative application that comes to mind is word processing. Many powerful and user-friendly word processing packages are now available (e.g., Wordstar for IBM/PC and Appleworks for Apple IIe). These packages have tutorial programs that walk the user through their capabilities step by step. Built-in help functions answer specific questions and provide information at the press of a key so there is often no need to try to locate a manual to solve problems when you are in the middle of preparing a document. And, for those whose typing skills leave something to be desired, there are even typing tutor packages! Spelling checker programs are also available including those with dictionaries of scientific and medical terms. You can also develop your own dictionary containing unusual terms or abbreviations specific to your application.

In addition to its mundane use for personalized form letters, mailing labels, course outlines, class handouts, and committee reports, word processing is a boon to the preparation of manuscripts, technical reports, and grant applications. Co-authors with equivalent micro systems and word processors exchange disks as each makes his or her contributions to the article. Multiple drafts can be written quickly and easily. Extensive minor polishing can be accomplished painlessly. Software furnishing special fonts can be used to prepare non-English abstracts. The turnaround from finished product to final hardcopy is virtually instantaneous—a definite advantage for those pushing abstract and grant application deadlines! More and more publishers are now accepting and, in fact, encouraging authors to submit book manuscripts on computer disks or via modem over the telephone lines (i.e., telecomputing).

Not unrelated to word processing are the spreadsheet applications. Not only do the micros serve well for budgeting and equipment inventories, but they are invaluable for student records. Insertion of the appropriate formula will average individual lab results, add the midterm and the final to produce a mark out of 100 along with the appropriate letter grade. And, the list can be ordered in just about any way desired: alphabetically, by student number, by final grade, and so forth. Lotus 1-2-3 and Multiplan are widely acclaimed for these capabilities.

The on-line literature search has also moved into the lab, this time from the library. For this and other telecomputing applications a modem is necessary (Gabel, 1984; Schwaderer, 1984) to link the micro with any of the rapidly escalating number of data bases. Three factors have helped to reduce the price of these services (Lisanti, 1984). First, special rates are available from some information systems on weekends and in the evenings (e.g., Knowledge Index and BRS/After Dark). Second, micro packages such as In-Search and Sci-Mate, called front-end search software, allow search terms to be entered off-line, thereby restricting connect-time charges to the search itself. Sci-Mate allows access to the Institute for

Scientific Information (ISI) and the National Library of Medicine (NLM) data bases among others. And finally, gateway systems such as EasyNet, with the approval of a credit card number, permit menu-driven access to a number of different data bases, no experience necessary (Friedman, 1984; Glossbrenner, 1984).

Also within the context of telecomputing are electronic bulletin board systems (BBS)—the computer equivalent of the CB radio. For the price of a phone call in most cases, a person can link his or her micro with any one of a number of BBS run by individuals or special interest groups. Messages can be left, answers received, information read, and programs contributed (uploaded) or copied (downloaded) (McGrath, 1985). A considerable amount of public domain software is available on BBS including programs to run BBS, one of the most popular for the IBM PC being RBBS-PC (remote bulletin board system for the PC) (Stone, 1985). Although no BBS yet exists for the biomechanics user group for sport (BUGS!), it is easy to see potential applications in the domain of software sharing, registration of users with their system specifications so that individuals having questions on a given peripheral or micro could get expert advice, and conferencing on joint biomechanics research projects or research questions. The future will probably hold a BBS for BUGS. Perhaps the U.S. Olympic Training Center (USOTC) in Colorado Springs might consider operating such a BBS.

There is little doubt that biomechanics budgets in the years to come should include increased telephone costs to reflect telecomputing applications.

Instruction

Computers have been used for several years to teach basic concepts in various disciplines. This application is known as computer-aided or computer-assisted instruction (CAI). The PLATO system available on mainframes is an example. The development of sophisticated instructional programs complemented by quality graphics is a major undertaking usually involving professional programming expertise. In addition, this type of application requires multiple terminals to accommodate large numbers of students. Adequate supervision and security measures must also be provided. With these factors in mind, the efficacy of using micros to teach basic mechanics concepts when these often can be more effectively presented in textbook and lecture formats or, if available, on mainframes is brought into question.

A more appropriate application of micros in biomechanics instruction from the standpoint of undergraduates is to introduce them to the research process and provide them with some hands-on experience in data collection and analysis. This can effectively be done through a series of laboratory experiences in which mechanical concepts and instrumentation gradually increase in complexity and sophistication (Miller, Le, & Scheirman, 1984; Nichol & Liebscher, 1983). Certain topics and concepts lend themselves more readily to microcomputer applications than others (e.g., CG determination; data smoothing and differentiation; segment position-, velocity- and acceleration-time histories; angle diagrams; projectile problems; and on-line data collection from a force platform).

In the case of the Apple IIe, a graphics tablet attached to each micro can provide the capability for basic digitizing operations. When students use a graphics tablet for data input, it is strongly recommended that they first acquire a composite tracing or other hard copy of the information to be digitized rather than projecting a film frame directly onto the digitizing surface. This process saves a great deal of time and frustration in the long run and also exposes students to an intermediate step in the analysis.

Students can view their results in graphic form on the monitor and then dump the desired graphics from the monitor to the printer for hardcopy. Provision for this is easily programmed on the Apple IIe if a Grappler or Fingerprint interface is used to control the printer.

In using micros, or any other technology for that matter, it is easy to succumb to the danger of becoming overawed by the technology and fail to impart the basic mechanical concepts and understandings (i.e., the black box syndrome). It is important that students not lose track of the basic principles. Consequently, frequent hand calculations and logical checks must be incorporated at various points in the laboratory exercise. Monitoring signals with an oscilloscope when appropriate is a useful technique.

It must be recognized, however, that incorporating this kind of experience in data collection and analysis for undergraduate students is often labor intensive. There are two major reasons for this situation. The first is that seldom is there an adequate number of micros for laboratory groups of 12 to 15 students. This necessitates scheduling multiple lab sessions with smaller numbers. The availability of centralized microcomputer labs in the library or computer center would help to alleviate this problem because the analysis would not have to be completed in the biomechanics lab. The second reason this approach is so costly in terms of instructor time is that most of the programs used are not as user-friendly as those developed commercially. To reduce the number of trivial questions regarding the running of the programs, software designed for students needs to be extremely explicit, especially with regard to the instructions provided on the monitor. The following are more specific suggestions:

1. Menu-driven programs are highly recommended. When a disk is booted, a list of program options should greet the student. The appropriate option can then be selected by letter or number and that program automatically loaded.
2. If the program is compiled allowing it to run faster (particularly where graphics are concerned), the loading process sometimes takes several seconds to complete, and it is helpful to have a flashing "loading" message on the screen so that students know that something is happening within the machine.
3. Numerous checking routines should be incorporated to ensure that incorrect responses do not hang up or otherwise abort program execution. Thus, if the response is supposed to be a 1, 2, or 3 and

the keyboard input is not one of these options, the question is repeated and a revised input is accepted (and again checked).

4. The type of response requested for questions posed should be consistent. For example, the student should get used to always pressing the Return key after supplying the appropriate input rather than one time pressing the space bar, another time hitting any key, and, in yet another instance, having the program execute automatically as soon as the response is entered.
5. If the program involves storing data files, specific instructions need to be provided on the screen as to how the file should be named. If the file name input is already on the catalog, the student should get another chance to name the file. Once the file name is entered and accepted, the accompanying file should be locked automatically by instructions within the program.
6. When reading data files into programs, if the specified file cannot be found on the catalog, the student should be prompted with the contents of the catalog and given another chance to enter the correct file name.
7. Whenever feasible, instructions that would usually be included on the lab handout should be displayed on the monitor in abbreviated form. This will reduce the number of instructor-student interactions to address minor procedural questions.
8. Because storage capacity is at a premium on micros, programs adapted from mainframes or minicomputers should be broken into a series of smaller functional programs or modules. One module should involve setting up a data file by either entering numbers from a keyboard or digitizing from a graphics tablet. These files should be written in the same format so that they can be entered as data into a number of different analysis programs.

In the contemporary situation, most faculty and university students are in a period of transition. Just as we struggle to catch up and keep up, we are now dealing with undergraduate students who, by and large, have had little exposure to micros in an educational setting. This will not be true of the next generation of students. As their level of computer literacy increases, we will need to devote less time to the technology, leaving more time for instruction in concepts and analysis skills. In addition, as students acquire their own micros just as they all now have sophisticated pocket calculators, the amount of lab time spent on data analysis should be eased as work can be completed at home or in a centralized micro lab. Students will purchase floppy disks much as they now invest in lab manuals. In the future, we may see electronic bulletin board systems being used for class purposes. Students will be able to phone in to get updates on lecture information and laboratory instructions, leave questions and messages, upload their laboratory results, have them graded, and receive marks and comments within a matter of moments.

It must be appreciated that the use of micros in undergraduate instruction is not divorced from the research focus. Rather, it provides one of the important initial steps in the process of encouraging individuals to pursue research in biomechanics.

Laboratory Research

In the laboratory research application, micros are used for data collection, data analysis, and simulation studies. It is particularly important, therefore, to be able to expand the system to accommodate additional peripherals such as an A/D converter, hardware clock, hard disk, and serial interface. Thus, for research, the micro must be the type that has expansion slots. It is here, too, where the differences between 8- and 16-bit machines are more acutely felt, with the 16-bit microprocessors (generally more costly) having advantages in terms of speed and amount of directly addressable RAM. As with the instructional application, it is helpful to have multiple micro systems of the same type in the lab so that failure of one component or unit does not bring all computer-related activities to a standstill.

It is also a distinct advantage to have software that is directly interchangeable among machines. And one major consideration in the development of software is the continuing proliferation of program languages (e.g., C, FORTH, Ada, LISP, PROLOG, etc.). There are now more than 200! Some have longevity whereas others seem to be destined to become defunct members of the "language-of-the-month club" (Elfring, 1985). The situation is a far cry from a decade ago when almost everyone was using FORTRAN on mainframes (Cole, 1983; Woliner, 1984). From the standpoint of biomechanics research, in addition to having portability from one micro to another, the selection of programming language is influenced by its speed of execution as well as programmer preference and expertise. If the main program is to be updated and modified by a number of nonprofessional programmers (as is often the situation in the educational setting), then the language selected must be one that is easily learned by its users. Because it satisfies this requirement, BASIC has served as the workhorse of micros (Kelly, 1983; Rayfield, 1982; Vaughan, 1985). BASIC's lack of inherent structure, however, often results in difficulty tracing the logic of a long program, making debugging more of a challenge than is the case with a structured language such as PASCAL. Generous commenting can help alleviate this problem. The slowness with which BASIC instructions are executed can be overcome by compiling the program (e.g., the Einstein compiler for Applesoft BASIC; Callamaras, 1984). In most on-line applications, when collecting data from force transducers or monitoring biological signals (Hallgren, 1984a, 1984b), however, a programmer has to write the sampling subroutine in assembly language to ensure sufficiently high sampling rates (Holt, 1985). Once written, a versatile assembly language routine can be used in numerous application programs.

Routine housekeeping tasks associated with the programming of micros are also important. These include regular backing up of programs and essential data, incorporating the latest revision date within the program code and on the data output, complete (yes, even excessive) documentation, and a consistent naming system for data files. Although most of the programming principles for minis and mainframes are also applicable to micros, storage space in the latter is at a premium, requiring more attention to be paid to streamlining the code and reducing the number and size of data arrays.

Many data collection applications in biomechanics involve sampling an analog voltage from a particular sensor such as a force transducer (e.g., Dickinson, Cook, & Leinhardt, 1985) and converting the sampled voltage to digital form. In the process of A/D conversion, data are subject to distortion due to nonlinearities in the system, limitations on sampling rate, insufficient resolution, and the influence of noise in the lab (Clune, 1985; Englemann & Abraham, 1984; Ford, 1985; Wyss, 1984). To minimize these problems, care must be taken in selecting hardware to meet application requirements. Two types of A/D converters are available. The integrating type (e.g., ADALAB) is appropriate where noise (especially 60 Hz) is significant and where high sampling rates are not important. The nonintegrating or successive approximation type (e.g., the 12-bit AI13) provides higher sampling rates but suffers in the noise rejection area. The latter, however, may be handled effectively with software filters in subsequent processing. For most research applications, a minimum 12-bit converter is necessary to achieve 4,096 (2^{12}) divisions of the measurement range (i.e., for a $\pm$ 5 volt range, each volt would equal 409.6 A/D units). In addition to these hardware considerations, software routines must be verified to ensure that they are actually providing the sampling rates assumed and not losing data in the process of running timing or voltage level checks. The latter can be a problem when a negative time feature is incorporated, as in the case of storing force platform values only after force in the vertical direction exceeds some preset value (e.g., 5 N).

Increasingly, manufacturers of force-sensing instrumentation are supplying microcomputer analysis systems and software with their products. With its force platform, for example, AMTI markets a North Star Horizon computer with 64K RAM and a 12-bit A/D converter. Programs are written in BASIC and in Z80A machine code. Kistler will provide a Data General Eclipse S/20 micro, which has a 16-bit high-speed processor and 128K to 2 megabytes RAM, a 12-bit A/D converter, and hard disk. Some manufacturers (e.g., Cybex) provide a sealed box to process the output signals from their instrumentation. The program code in these systems is often inaccessible to the user, and the output cannot be modified to meet changing needs. Consequently, such units are virtually dedicated to one piece of instrumentation and are more appropriate for clinical use in which there is heavy demand for a single application than for research in a laboratory environment that requires greater flexibility.

A second major research application in biomechanics involves photo and video analysis of motion. Mainframes and minicomputers have been used with film digitizers for a number of years, but now micros are also being recruited for this task. The digitizer is usually attached to the micro via an RS-232 connector and serial interface. The switches on both digitizer and interface card must be set for the same BAUD rate (often 9,600), number of stop bits (1 or 2), parity (odd, even, or none) and character length (usually 7 or 8 bits in a byte). Because of the amount of data to be stored in this application, a hard disk is almost essential. Electronic digitizing of video images is also moving in the same direction (Ferrigno & Pedotti, 1985). At present, some systems require minicomputers to run their software, but it seems logical to assume that, to remain competitive, most manufacturers of high-speed video (HSV) equipment will have to provide analysis packages for the popular micros. Some, in fact, already do. The ExpertVision system, for example, uses a Sun 2/130 microcomputer in its collection and processing of data from video images. This machine, built around the Motorola 68000 chip, has 2 to 8 megabytes RAM and is a 32-bit machine with 16-bit capability.

Once data are obtained, subsequent reduction, processing, and analysis can also be accomplished on the microcomputer, eliminating errors inevitably associated with data transfer. Sophisticated statistical packages such as AppStat, Statpro, and SPSS/PC have been developed for micros. Most such packages incorporate a data base for storing data, a statistical analysis program, and a graphics module for display purposes (Stahr, 1984). Having a hard disk is a distinct advantage when running analysis programs because of the number and size of the files involved. Some statistics packages such as SPSS/PC actually require a hard disk on the system (Vanderbok, 1985).

The convenience and economy of micros along with their increasingly elaborate graphics packages make them logical tools for simulation studies. One can virtually sit at the screen all day working on a simulation. Feedback is immediate and there are no connect- or run-time charges. Vaughan (1985), for example, has indicated how nonlinear optimization procedures can be readily implemented on microcomputers. The next few years will undoubtedly witness more of this type of activity.

There are two additional areas in the research domain that will depend upon improved execution speed and storage capacity of the currently emerging 32-bit microprocessors. These are artificial intelligence (the development of expert systems and voice recognition) (Buckler, 1985; Rothfeder, 1986) and real-time data analysis (Isaak, 1984).

Field Research and Applications

Formerly, field research often necessitated the storing of data on magnetic tape, which was then transported back to the lab for analysis. Because of their relatively low cost and portability, micros now permit on-site data collection and analysis in a way that was not previously possible. In a recent project conducted with elite shooters by Gary Scheirman of the USOTC, a light-emitting diode was attached to a rifle and the output fed to a micro, permitting motion analysis to be accomplished on the spot. In another USOTC application, the release characteristics of javelin performances determined through digitizing films using a micro were transmitted to the mainframe at the University of California-Davis where Mont Hubbard input them to his javelin simulation program and provided information on performance optimization to the athletes. Microprocessors have also been carried by downhill skiers to record the moments of force on the ski boots during various maneuvers (MacGregor & Hull, 1985; MacGregor, Hull, & Dorius, 1985).

In the near future, micro systems presently used by sport clubs and training centers to handle budgeting, correspondence, and meet scoring (Haggerty, 1985) will be adapted to collect biomechanical data during the training of athletes. Miller and Munro (1985) suggested, for example, that strain gauges permanently mounted on the end of a springboard could give temporal and force information on takeoffs that could be used to assess an athlete's readiness to proceed to higher degree of difficulty dives. In addition to the analysis of data from force transducers, the use of micros for high-speed video analysis will provide rapid knowledge of results needed in training situations. There is no doubt that the technology is currently available, but its widespread application in the field has yet to be realized. The permanent field installation of microcomputers permitting long-term tracking of the performance of individuals will be an important contribution to be made in the next few years.

Summary

What will be the outcome of this revolution in which we are currently engaged? How can we help ensure this potentially productive future for micros in biomechanics in the administrative, instructional, research, and field applications? It would seem that our principal challenge in the coming decade will be to capitalize on micro hardware, firmware, and software developed by researchers in other disciplines, on what is available in the public domain, and on the progress and experience of our colleagues in biomechanics. Steps toward accomplishing the latter could be taken by establishing a section in a publication such as the *International Journal of Sports Biomechanics* for the exchange of software, firmware and hardware product information based on firsthand experience, and generally useful comments or hints on microcomputer applications. Only through efforts such as this will we avoid wasting unnecessary time and effort in ''reinventing the chip'' (Gates, 1984) and instead be able to use these important resources in productive research to better understand and to improve motor performance of individuals at various states of health.

Acknowledgments

Input from the following individuals is gratefully acknowledged: Betty Atwater, Chuck Dillman, Andy Fuglevand, Terry Haggerty, Beth Kerr, Marc Pizzimenti, and Gary Scheirman.

References

Buckler, G. (1985). Artificial intelligence today. *InfoAge*, **4**(6), 43-44.
Callamaras, P. (1984). The Einstein compiler. *Byte*, **9**(1), 349-351.
Clune, T.R. (1985). Interfacing for data acquisition. *Byte*, **10**(2), 269-282.

Cole, B. (1983). The family tree of computer languages. *Popular Computing*, **2**(11), 82-83.

Dickinson, J.A., Cook, S.D., & Leinhardt, T.M. (1985). The measurement of shock waves following heel strike in running. *Journal of Biomechanics*, **18**, 415-422.

Elfring, G. (1985). Choosing a programming language. *Byte*, **10**(6), 235-240.

Englemann, B., & Abraham, M. (1984). Personal computer signal processing. *Byte*, **9**(4), 94-110.

Ferrigno, G., & Pedotti, A. (1985). ELITE: A digital dedicated hardware system for movement analysis via real-time TV signal processing. *IEEE Transactions on Biomedical Engineering*, **32**, 943-949.

Ford, L.E. (1985). Laboratory interfacing. *Byte*, **10**(2), 263-266.

Friedman, B. (1984). A 22-hour library card. *PC Magazine*, **3**(24), 375-377.

Gabel, D. (1984). Modem mistakes you don't have to make. *Personal Computing*, **8**(6), 120-134.

Gates, S.C. (1984). Laboratory data collection with an IBM PC. *Byte*, **9**(5), 366-378.

Glossbrenner, A. (1984). Tricks of the on-line trade. *PC Magazine*, **3**(20), 177-192.

Haggerty, T.R. (1985). *Developing microcomputer literacy: A guide for sport, physical education and recreation managers*. Champaign, IL: Stipes.

Hallgren, R.C. (1984a). Putting the Apple II work: Part 1. The hardware. *Byte*, **9**(4), 152-164.

Hallgren, R.C. (1984b). Putting the Apple II work: Part 2. The software. *Byte*, **9**(5), 382-396.

Holt, J.R. (1985). 6502 tricks and traps. *Byte*, **10**(6), 295-302.

Isaak, J. (1984). Designing systems for real-time applications. *Byte*, **9**(1), 127-132.

Jones, R. (1984). IBM/Apple communication. *Byte*, **9**(2), 331-339.

Kelly, M.G. (1983). BASIC. *Popular Computing*, **2**(11), 121-126.

Lisanti, S. (1984). The on-line search. *Byte*, **9**(13), 215-230.

MacGregor, D., & Hull, M.L. (1985). A microcomputer controlled snow ski binding system: 2. Release decision theories. *Journal of Biomechanics*, **18**, 267-275.

MacGregor, D., Hull, M.L., & Dorius, L.K. (1985). A microcomputer controlled snow ski binding system: 1. Instrumentation and field evaluation. *Journal of Biomechanics*, **18**, 255-265.

McGrath, L. (1985). Software on a shoe string. *A+ Magazine*, **3**(1), 71-78.

Miller, D.I., Le, T., & Scheirman, G.L. (1984). Teaching data smoothing and differentiation using microcomputers. In R. Shapiro & J.R. Marett (Eds.), *National Symposium on Teaching Kinesiology and Biomechanics in Sports* (pp. 137-140). DeKalb, IL: R. Shapiro.

Miller, D.I., & Munro, C.F. (1985). Greg Louganis' Springboard takeoff: 1. Temporal and joint position analysis. *International Journal of Sport Biomechanics*, **1**, 209-220.

Murtha, S.M., & Waite, M. (1980). *CP/M Primer*. Indianapolis: Howard W. Sams.

Nichol, K., & Liebscher, F.F. (1983). An integrated system for biomechanics designed for small working groups and for teaching. *Journal of Human Movement Studies*, **9**, 135-144.

Rayfield, F. (1982). Experimental control and data acquisition with BASIC in the Apple computer. *Behavior Research Methods and Instrumentation*, **14**, 409-411.

Rothfeder, J. (1986). Is there intelligent life in the PC? *PC Magazine*, **5**(1), 139-148.

Schwaderer, D. (1984). Modems demystified. *Tech Journal*, **2**(1), 73-85.

Stahr, L.B. (1984). Working with statistical analysis. *Personal Computing*, **8**(10), 73-83.

Stone, M.D. (1985). E-mail for the well connected office. *PC Magazine*, **4**(18), 137-150.

Vanderbok, W.G. (1985). SPSS arrives on the PC. *PC Magazine*, **4**(5), 191-195.

Vaughan, C.L. (1985). A BASIC program for nonlinear optimization studies in sport biomechanics. *International Journal of Sport Biomechanics*, **1**, 63-72.

Woliner, S.R. (1984). Picking a programming language. *A+ Magazine*, **2**(5), 145-148.

Wyss, C.R. (1984). Planning a computerized measurement system. *Byte*, **9**(4), 114-123.

Mechanical Descriptors of Movement and Microcomputer Applications: A Commentary

James G. Hay

Dave Winter's paper, with its emphasis on the interpretation of the data generated in a biomechanical analysis, was a stimulating and provocative one. For my own part, I would like to comment on some of the issues raised by Winter and to raise some of my own.

Winter mentioned the collection and analysis of normative data on human gait at several points in his presentation. The collection of descriptive data on motor skills has frequently been advocated as a necessary preliminary to further work in biomechanics. Hinson (1982, p. 28), for example, has stated that "our development, I think, should be and, I believe, will be formulated along the lines of every other area of expertise, that is, the building of a data bank—a data bank which must inevitably begin with observations of one, then two, then four, then ten, then a thousand, and so on."

Such comments raise the obvious issue of what use should be made of the data in the data bank. Consider, for example, a case in which the gait profile of a person falls outside normal limits and suppose that this person is capable of modifying the gait to eliminate the apparent faults. Should such modification be prescribed? Perhaps this person has physical characteristics that have not been taken into account by normalization—characteristics that place him or her in a subpopulation for whom the normal limits are quite different. Your question as to whether age, sex, and body type should be normalized—in addition to height, weight, and cadence—effectively raises the same issue. If the answer to the question, Should such modifications be prescribed, is no, what functions do the data base and the established norms serve? Couldn't it be argued that an extensive data base merely permits deviations from the norm to be identified in an objective fashion and leaves untouched the question of whether these deviations are artifacts of the sampling procedures used or differences of real clinical significance? Couldn't it also be argued that trained clinicians can identify all or most of these deviations subjectively with a mere fraction of the time, effort, and expense necessary to establish an acceptable data base? Finally, couldn't it be argued that identifying what is normal (or average) is at best an interim goal for biomechanists—a goal that is of interest only until such time as we can identify the optimum movement pattern (or technique) for a given individual? Furthermore, it is a goal that is of practical significance only to those people, that half of the population, who are below average in the performance of the motor skill of interest. Athletes and others who are already well above normal in the performance of a motor skill should surely have little interest in the techniques of those who are average.

Several people spoke to one or more of these issues during the discussion session that followed. Andriacchi expressed his view that we should be careful about attempting to make changes in the gait of a person in whom we have observed a deviation from normal. Such a deviation is not necessarily bad and may even be optimal for the individual concerned. He contended, however, that it is useful to know what is normal and what deviations from the normal pattern are associated with a disease process or injury. Winter agreed wholeheartedly with these comments and cited cases from his own experience in which orthopedic surgeons had insisted that knee-replacement patients not walk with a stiff leg, in spite of the likelihood that such a deviation from normal was optimal for them. Miller stated that she had found a data base invaluable in her studies of amputee gait and, in particular, in monitoring changes that took place as a result of an intervention program. She said that changes that took the subjects further away from the norm than they were at the outset would be cause for concern and careful reevaluation.

At several points in his presentation Winter made reference to various methodological issues, including the early emphasis on methodology, logistic problems that remain unresolved, and some problems of validity in mathematical modeling. Among the logistic problems that were not mentioned, and one that seems deserving of some comment because it is so frequently overlooked, is what our colleagues in motor behavior and control have called *ecological validity*. In the biomechanics context, this is the notion that the generalizing of research findings requires that a skill analyzed under controlled (or laboratory) conditions be a faithful replica of the skill performed in its natural habitat. It is now fairly well recognized that the techniques used when walking or running on a treadmill, and when swimming while tethered to the edge of the pool, are not identical to those used under normal conditions. However, if one can judge from what appears in the literature, the doubtful validity of (a) using a short approach to the test area in studies of running, (b) adjusting (or targetting) the stride to place the foot in a designated area, and (c) performing skills requiring maximal effort under nonstandard (and, in particular, noncompetitive) conditions is either not as well recognized or conveniently ignored.

Finally, I'd like to make a few observations concerning future developments in sport biomechanics. Some 20 years ago, I compiled *An Annotated Bibliography of Biomechanics Literature*. In the course of this work, I observed that most of the research in sport biomechanics up to that time had been done by people who conducted no more than one or two studies in the area, before moving on to other things. Furthermore, those few people who had done more seemed almost invariably to have dealt with a wide range of unrelated topics. This practice continued until the early to mid-1970s. Most of you who were active in the field at that time will remember publishing papers on a wide range of topics. As one might expect with a rapidly maturing field, things have changed substantially over the past 10 years. Today, most of the more active researchers in the field have narrowed their focus to just one or two research topics. This narrow focus—a characteristic of any well-developed field of inquiry—has had some predictable, but not always well-recognized, effects.

On the positive side, it has greatly advanced our knowledge of the topics upon which our focus has been directed, improved our ability to obtain external funds to support research, and has established (or confirmed) the legitimacy of sport biomechanics as a field of inquiry. On the negative side, it has narrowed the options of those entering the field as graduate students and, in so doing, highlighted the need for more American graduates with PhD degrees in biomechanics.

The slow growth in the number of American graduates with training in biomechanics—and thus in the number of options available to prospective graduate students—has been due in large part to the limited number of qualified American applicants and the relative abundance of foreign applicants for admission to our graduate programs. The increased status that sport biomechanics now enjoys in the U.S.—thanks in large measure to the visibility the field enjoyed through associations with the Los Angeles Olympic Games—has led to a pronounced increase in the number of Americans applying for admission to our graduate programs. This will, I believe, have a noticeable impact on the future of sport biomechanics both here and abroad.

The paper by Doris Miller is an excellent summary of the present status of microcomputers in biomechanics and has provided us with some insight as to what we might expect in the next few years. The prospects for the future are, as Miller said, both exciting and frightening—exciting for what the microcomputer might make possible; frightening for what it may demand of us all to keep abreast of developments. Microcomputers are frightening, too, because they are a particularly attractive, some might even say a seductive, form of technology, and there is a real possibility of becoming so enamored of the means that the end is forgotten—a point to which Winter alluded in his presentation.

Miller mentioned numerous ways in which microcomputers are being used in biomechanics and how they might be used in the near future. I'd like to elaborate on just two of these.

Microcomputers are frequently used in gait labs for on-line evaluative and rehabilitative purposes. However, with the notable exceptions that Miller has mentioned, relatively few applications of this nature appear to have been made in sport biomechanics. This is certainly not due to any lack of appropriate opportunity.

Many devices have been developed over the years to measure the temporal, kinematic, and kinetic characteristics of the techniques used by athletes in the practical coaching situation. The Soviets have been especially active in this regard, and their biomechanics and coaching publications bristle with often fascinating examples.

For the most part, the output from devices of this kind is relatively modest. In addition, their use is normally limited to national training centers or an occasional university with a well-established program in sport biomechanics. There are few, if any, such devices in regular use at all levels from school to club to national and international.

Microcomputers have greatly increased the potential for training devices of this type, and their steadily decreasing price has brought them within reasonably easy reach. Although we certainly have a long way to go before such things become common, it seems likely that we will shortly see systems developed that combine the capabilities of our standard measuring devices (e.g., timing devices, electrogoniometers, strain gauges, etc.) with those of the microcomputer to provide immediate and readily usable information to athlete and coach. I visualize systems that not only will record characteristics of an athlete's technique on a given day and keep records over days and months to show progress, but also will guide the athlete's training.

Many investigators have developed devices for the purpose of recording characteristics of the starting techniques used by sprinters in athletics. These devices have yielded useful research data but have not been widely used for training purposes, probably because they have been costly, labor intensive, and perhaps even user-hostile. They need not remain so, however. In the near future, we might well see a microbased system that, once booted, displays a menu and asks the athlete

---

What would you like to do?

1. Determine how many starts you should take as part of your pre-race warm-up?
2. Determine the optimum spacing of your hands and feet?
3. Determine the optimum amount of weight to place on your hands in the set position?
4. Identify ways in which to improve your present starting technique?

The athlete is then led through a well-established protocol that makes use of the temporal, displacement, and force data provided by the system to arrive at the required result. At their present stage of development of microcomputers, the starting commands would probably be best given by an assistant coach or teammate. It will surely not be long, however, before such commands can be given by a standard microcomputer—a computer, incidentally, that could simultaneously monitor the consistency of the forces exerted in the set position to ensure that the athlete does not beat the gun. It is easy to visualize the development of many such systems for use in sport and athletics, and the future will surely see growth in this general area.

Miller made passing reference to the field of artificial intelligence (AI). AI research is divided into four areas (Shurkin, 1985, p. 290). These are

1. *robotics,* "the study of machines that simulate human physical activity";
2. *expert systems,* which consist of "computer programming that attempts to solve problems and make decisions at the level of a human expert in a particular field";
3. *natural language,* "which includes such things as translating from one language to another, or attempting to get computers to understand vernacular language"; and
4. *epistemology,* which involves "using computers to understand human thought at its most philosophical—almost metaphysical—level."

Not all of these offer much that is likely to be of professional interest to sport biomechanists. Expert systems, however, seem to me to offer some intriguing possibilities.

Expert systems have been developed for a wide variety of purposes. They have been used, for example, in the diagnosis of medical conditions, for geological exploration, for the customizing of insurance policies, and for troubleshooting telephone cable networks. As far as I know, no attempt has yet been made to develop an expert system that can provide athletes and coaches with advice on problems of technique. With the procedures already developed in other fields, there seems little reason to doubt that such expert systems are entirely feasible. This is certainly not a simple matter, but possible nonetheless.

As with other expert systems, the data base would consist of (a) whatever *quantitative* information is available (e.g., data on the physical characteristics of the athlete and biomechanical measures of his or her technique), (b) *qualitative* information on the athlete's technique (e.g., such information as may be obtained from simple visual observation), and (c) various rules and probabilities that emerge from an analysis of how experts on the technique diagnose faults in the athlete's performance.

Once developed, such systems could have a profound effect on practices in sport and athletics. For example, "a [coach] in a remote area, confronted by a situation he or she does not fully comprehend, might be able to discuss the problem with an 'expert' any time, from any place. And the 'expert' would be the machine" (Shurkin, 1985, p. 296). I look forward to the day when that dream becomes a reality.

References

Hinson, M. M. (1982). Applications. In H.M. Eckert (Ed.), *The Academy papers*. Reston, VA: The American Academy of Physical Education.

Shurkin, J. (1985). *Engines of the mind*. New York: Washington Square Press.

SECTION B:
EXERCISE PHYSIOLOGY

Children: Lower Anaerobic Power, Testing, Puberty, and Carryover to Adulthood

Oded Bar-Or

The same physiologic principles govern the responses to exercise in children, adolescents, and adults. There are, however, growth- and maturation-related differences in such responses. The purposes of this article are to highlight some of these differences and to suggest challenges for future research. The topics selected for discussion reflect my interest and bias: No attempt has been made to comprehensively cover the field of pediatric exercise physiology.

Development of Anaerobic Characteristics

Children's ability to produce high mechanical power and to contract their muscles at a fast speed and against intense resistance is lower than in adolescents and adults. Low muscle endurance has been shown for a variety of physical fitness items. In the recently completed National Children and Youth Fitness Study (1985), for example, the 50th percentile for knee-bent sit-ups during 60 s was 34 in the 10-year-old boys and 43 in the 17-year-olds. The respective values among the girls were 31 and 36.

Until recently, laboratory data for age-related development of supramaximal power were limited to the Margaria step-running test (Margaria, Aghemo, & Rovelli, 1966). Four studies have shown that peak mechanical power is distinctively lower in children than in adolescents or adults (Davies, Barnes, & Godfrey, 1972; di Prampero & Cerretelli, 1969; Kurowski, 1977; Margaria et al., 1966). An example is the study by Margaria et al. (1966) in which peak power, corrected for body mass, of 10-year-old boys was 34 $kcal \cdot kg^{-1} \cdot hr^{-1}$, compared with 43 and 50 $kcal \cdot kg^{-1} \cdot hr^{-1}$ at ages 15 and 20, respectively.

One report is available on age-related changes in both peak mechanical power and muscle endurance (Inbar & Bar-Or, 1986). These anaerobic characteristics were reported for 306 8- to 45-year-old nonathletic Israeli males, who performed the Wingate anaerobic test. The two performance indices in this 30-s cycling or arm cranking test are peak mechanical power at any 5-s interval and mean power throughout the 30-s period. Results

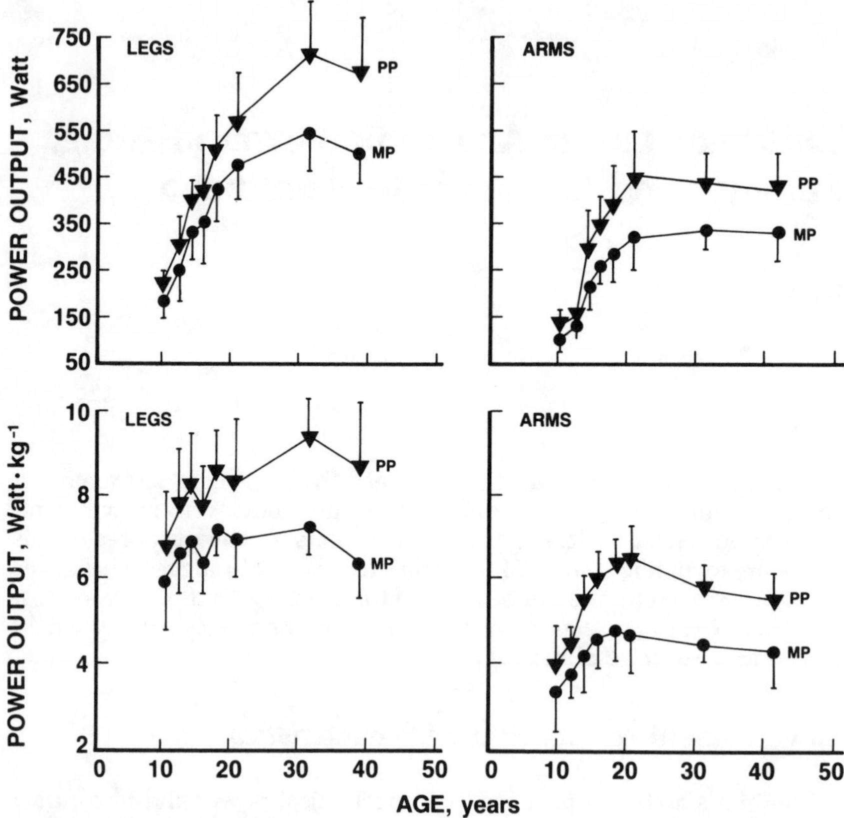

Figure 1. Anaerobic performance in children, adolescents, and adults. Cross-sectional data on 306 Israeli males who performed the Wingate Anaerobic Test with their legs or arms. Vertical lines denote 1 *SD*. PP = peak power; MP = mean power. From "Anaerobic Characteristics in Male Children and Adolescents" by O. Inbar and O. Bar-Or, 1986. *Medicine and Science in Sports and Exercise,* **18**(3), p. 266. Copyright 1986 by *Medicine and Science in Sports and Exercise.* Reprinted by permission.

for the legs and the arms are summarized in Figure 1. Scores for the children were markedly lower than for the adolescents and the young adults, even when calculated per kg body mass. Based on this study, anaerobic power seems to peak at age 20 for the arms and at age 30 for the legs.

Table 1 describes the anaerobic performance of children and adolescents as a percentage of scores by young adults. Data, calculated per kg body mass, are taken from the literature for both the Margaria and the Wingate tests. Peak and mean power in the 10-year-old boys and girls ranged from 67% to 86% of the adult values. One exception was the African (Bantu and Nilo-Hamitic) girls, whose score at age 10 was 104% of the young women's values. At age 15 scores ranged from 85% to 102% of the adults' values.

Table 1 Anaerobic Performance of Non-Athletic Children and Adolescents, Expressed as Percentage of the Performance of Young Adults. Calculations Are Based on Per kg Body Mass Values.

Author (year)	Population	Sex	Test	Limb	Performance index[a]	Performance at age 10 (%)	Performance at age 15 (%)
Margaria et al. (1966)	Italian	M	Margaria	Legs	PP	72	86
	Italian	F	Margaria	Legs	PP	74	86
di Prampero & Ceretelli (1969)	African	M	Margaria	Legs	PP	72	95
	African	F	Margaria	Legs	PP	104	102
Kurowski (1977)	USA	M	Margaria	Legs	PP	86	98
	USA	F	Margaria	Legs	PP	85	102
Inbar & Bar-Or (1986)	Israeli	M	Wingate	Legs	PP	75	85
	Israeli	M	Wingate	Legs	MP	82	90
	Israeli	M	Wingate	Arms	PP	67	92
	Israeli	M	Wingate	Arms	MP	75	96

[a]PP = peak mechanical power. MP = mean mechanical power.

The above pattern differs markedly from that found for maximal *aerobic* power. Corrected for body mass, maximal O_2 uptake of males varies only little from childhood to adulthood. (For a recent review see Krahenbuhl, Skinner, & Kohrt, 1985.) Among females, maximal aerobic power per kg mass is *higher* in the prepubescents than in the adolescents and even higher in the young women (e.g., Åstrand, 1952).

An index was recently described that takes into account both the aerobic and the anaerobic performance of an individual (Bar-Or, 1986). Preliminary work in my laboratory suggests that the ratio of peak anaerobic power to peak aerobic power increases during prepuberty in both sex groups and levels off during adolescence (Blimkie, Roche, & Bar-Or, 1986). The applicability of this ratio to such special groups as athletes or disabled children has yet to be evaluated.

The reason for the relatively low anaerobic power of children is not clear. One possibility is their lower muscle mass. Lean limb volume indeed explained a greater variance of the performance in the Wingate test than did total body mass among adolescents (Blimkie, Roche, Hay, & Bar-Or, 1985) and young adults (Murphy, Patton, & Frederick, 1984). However, even when calculated per fat-free mass, peak power of preadolescent girls and boys was distinctly lower than in adolescents and young adults (di Prampero & Cerretelli, 1969).

Another possible cause for the low anaerobic performance of children is *qualitative* characteristics of their muscles. One piece of supportive evidence is the low activity of phosphofructokinase in children's skeletal muscle (Eriksson, Karlsson, & Saltin, 1971; Fournier et al., 1982). This may explain the lower rate of glycolysis in children's muscles, as reflected by lower maximal concentration of blood (for a recent review see Bar-Or, 1983) and, especially, muscle lactate.

It is also possible that children's lower muscle power and endurance result from differences in neural control (e.g., rate of recruitment of fast-twitch motor units), and not only in metabolism. This possibility has yet to be studied.

An intriguing question is whether children's low glycolytic capacity is compensated for by a *lesser need* for anaerobic energy turnover. It has been suggested that children incur lower O_2 deficit at the onset of exercise and reach a steady-state faster than do adults at equivalent submaximal exercise intensities (Mácek & Vávra, 1980; Robinson, 1938). Faster metabolic transients in prepubertal boys have also been shown for supramaximal power intensities (Sady, 1981). In contrast, preliminary results of a breath-by-breath study (Cooper, 1985) suggest that the time constant (i.e., the time required to reach 63% of the difference between resting and steady-state metabolism) for O_2 uptake is not different between children and adolescents. The discrepancy between these findings might result from the difficulty of equating power loads among individuals who vary in body size and maturity.

An additional finding that might suggest the lesser reliance of children on anaerobic metabolism is that the running velocity at lactate threshold (defined as the blood lactate concentration just under $2 mmol \cdot l^{-1}$) is higher in prepubertal and pubertal boys than in young adults (Tanaka & Shindo, 1985). This is shown in Figure 2.

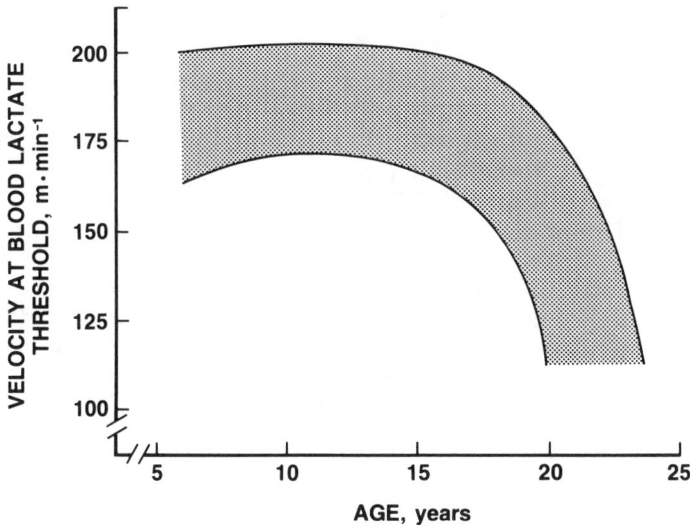

Figure 2. Relationship between running velocity at blood lactate threshold (VLT) and chronological age. Sixty-six untrained boys and 19 untrained young men performed 4-min runs on a track, at various velocities. Shaded area represents range of individual data. From "Running Velocity at Blood Lactate Threshold of Boys Aged 6-15 Years Compared With Untrained and Trained Young Males" by H. Tanaka and M. Shindo, 1985, *International Journal of Sports Medicine*, **6**. Copyright 1985 by *International Journal of Sports Medicine*. Adapted by permission.

Challenges for Future Research on the Development of Anaerobic Characteristics

Possible topics for future research on the anaerobic characteristics of children and adolescents include the following:

- The effect of circulating androgens in circumpubertal boys on their anaerobic exercise performance and glycolytic capacity.
- Anaerobic performance of females during childhood, adolescence, and young adulthood.
- Effects of growth on the relationship between neural control and muscle power, muscle endurance, and fatigability.
- Growth-related changes in the ratio of anaerobic to aerobic performance.
- Trainability of anaerobic exercise performance during various stages of growth.
- The carryover effect of anaerobic training during childhood on morphologic and functional muscle characteristics in later years.
- The use of anaerobic exercise testing in the assessment of therapy (or functional deterioration) in children with neuromuscular disease. Specific conditions, to which this approach can be applied, include muscular dystrophy, cerebral palsy, advanced anorexia nervosa, and other nutrition deficiencies with muscle wasting.

O_2 Cost of Locomotion

It has long been shown (Robinson, 1938), and repeatedly confirmed (Åstrand, 1952; Daniels, Oldridge, Nagle, & White, 1978; Girandola, Wiswell, Frisch, & Wood, 1981; Krahenbuhl, Pangrasi, & Chomokos, 1979; MacDougall, Roche, Bar-Or, & Moroz, 1983; Piacentini & Bollettino, 1942; Silverman & Anderson, 1972; Skinner et al., 1971; Waters, Hislop, Thomas, & Campbell, 1983), that the O_2 cost of running and walking, when calculated per kg body mass, is higher in children than in adults. The implication is that, at any given velocity, children operate at a higher percentage of their maximal aerobic power and may fatigue easier (Bar-Or, 1983). Furthermore, as summarized in Figure 3, adolescents' middle-distance running performance is inferior to that of adults, even when their maximal aerobic power per kg mass is the same (Davies, 1980).

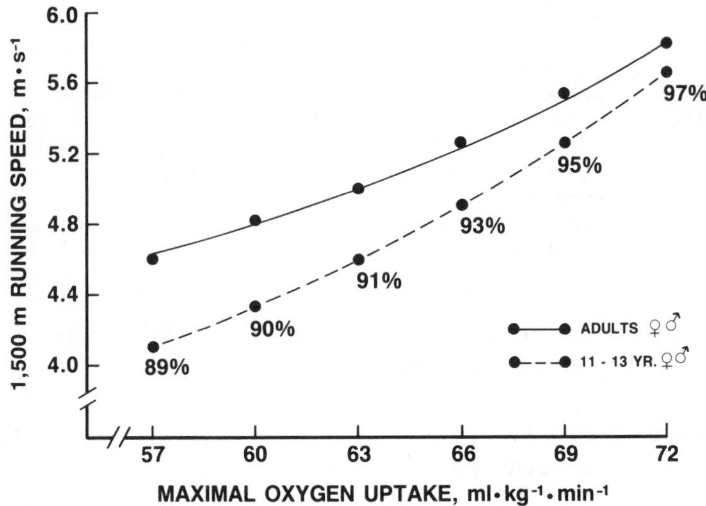

Figure 3. Relationship between running performance during a 1,500 m race and maximal O_2 uptake in children and adults. Mean values of 11–13 year-old trained girls and boys are compared with those of young adult female and male long-distance runners. Running performance of the children is also expressed as a percentage of adults' performance at equivalent maximal aerobic power. From "Metabolic Cost of Exercise and Physical Performance in Children With Some Observation on External Loading" by C.T.M. Davies, 1980, *European Journal of Applied Physiology*, **45**. Copyright 1980 by *European Journal of Applied Physiology*. Adapted by permission.

The cause for the high O_2 cost of locomotion among children is not clear. It does not seem to reflect low biomechanical-to-mechanical turnover efficiency, as is evident from data on cycling. Various authors, comparing children, adolescents, and adults, found no age-related differences in O_2 uptake at any given cycling power (Bal, Thompson, McIntosh,

Taylor, & McLeod, 1953; Bengtsson, 1956; Godfrey, Davies, Wozniak, & Barnes, 1971; Taylor, Bal, Lamb, & McLeod, 1950; Wilmore & Sigerseth, 1967).

Åstrand (1952) hypothesized that the low economy of the running child may be due to the high frequency and shortness of the child's stride. However, neither stride length nor frequency could explain the differences in O_2 cost of running among preadolescent and adolescent trained runners (Davies, 1980), nor could short body stature per se explain the high O_2 cost of running among untrained boys (MacDougall et al., 1983). Davies, in the above study, added 5% to the body mass of his subjects by having them wear a weight jacket. The O_2 uptake per kg (combined body and jacket mass) was lower than without the added mass. This difference was particularly apparent at high running speeds (13 to 16 km•hr^{-1}). The author concluded that, based upon force-velocity principles, children's body mass (and, thus, the force needed to move it) is too low for achieving an optimal mechanical power at high speeds. This experiment cannot explain the age-related differences in the O_2 cost during walking or low-speed running. Whether adding weights would yield similar results with younger or untrained children has yet to be shown.

Another approach to understanding differences in metabolic cost of locomotion is biomechanical gait analysis. It is possible, for example, that children have an exaggerated vertical shift of their center of mass, greater tilting and other movement in their pelvis, or wasteful limb motion. Mechanical work during locomotion should be analyzed in terms of movement of the body's center of mass (i.e., external work) and the movements of the limbs relative to the center of mass.

Using a strain-gauge platform, Cavagna, Franzetti, and Fuchimoto (1983) calculated the mechanical energy changes of the center of mass in children and adults who were walking at various speeds. The children were 1–12 years old. For each individual, a walking speed was identified at which the work to move the center of mass was lowest. This optimal speed increased with age, being 2.8 km•hr^{-1} in the 2-year-old children and 5 km•hr^{-1} at age 12. At speeds above this optimum, the transfer of energy between kinetic and potential was least efficient in the youngest children, implying a great need for mechanical energy production by their muscles. As shown in Figure 4, at 4.5 km•hr^{-1} the muscle power (per kg mass) needed to move the center of mass was 2.3 times higher in the 1–2 year-old children than in adults. At the same walking speed this ratio was 1.2 in the 3–4 year-old group and 1.1 at age 5–6.

From the above, it might be deduced that the higher O_2 cost in children occurs only when they walk at speeds higher than their optimal speed. Waters et al. (1983) have shown, however, that, even when children walk at their most comfortable speed, their O_2 uptake per kg is higher than in adolescents and adults.

The study by Cavagna et al. (1983) did not provide data on the mechanical energy needed to accelerate the limbs relative to the center of mass. This approach requires cinematography. However, assuming geometric similarity across ages, the authors predicted that, at 5.5 km•hr^{-1},

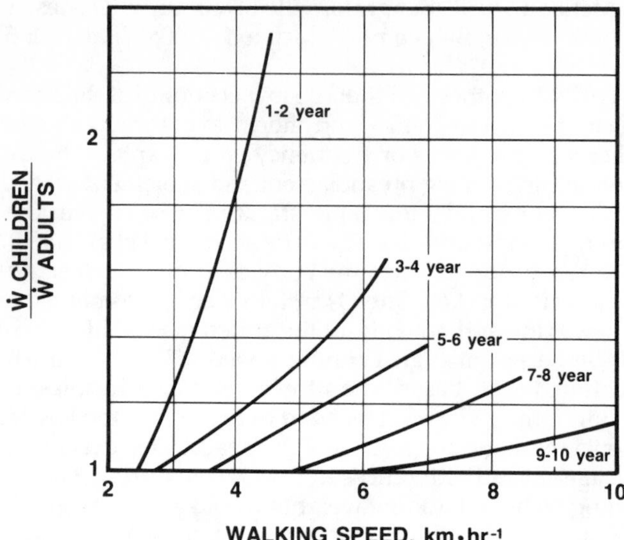

Figure 4. The ratio between children's and adults' mechanical power (W) that is needed to move their center of mass at various walking speeds. Analysis based on force platform data. From "The Mechanics of Walking in Children" by G.A. Cavagna et al., 1983, *Journal of Physiology*, **343**. Copyright 1983 by *Journal of Physiology*. Reprinted by permission.

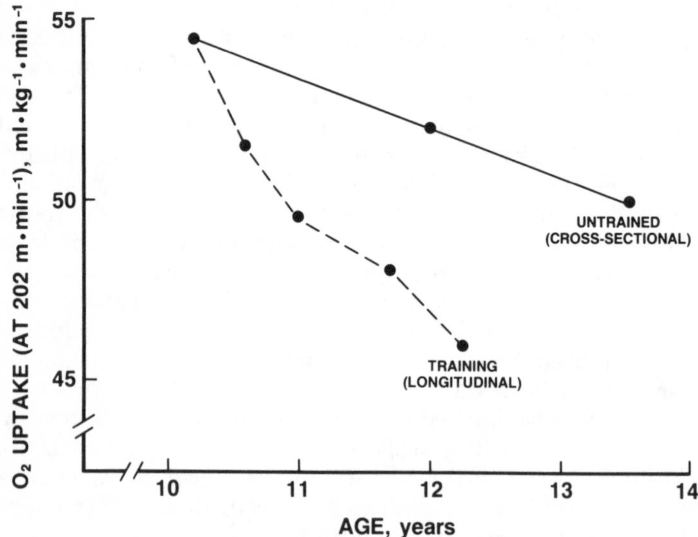

Figure 5. The effects of growth and aerobic training on the O_2 cost of running in boys. Data for the effect of growth are based on a cross-sectional comparison among untrained boys. The training data represent a 2.1-year longitudinal observation. From "Differences and Changes in $\dot{V}O_2$ Among Young Runners 10 to 18 Years of Age" by J. Daniels, N. Oldridge, F. Nagle, and B. White, 1978, *Medicine and Science in Sports*, **10**. Copyright 1978 by *Medicine and Science in Sports*. Adapted by permission.

the mass-specific power for accelerating the limbs would be 33% higher at age 3–4 than in adults. At age 11–12 this power would still be 15% higher than in adults.

Various authors have suggested that aerobic training of prepubescents may not increase their maximal O_2 uptake, in spite of an improvement in their running performance (Bar-Or & Zwiren, 1973; Daniels et al., 1978; Gilliam & Freedson, 1980; Mocellin & Wasmund, 1973; Schmücker, & Hollmann, 1974; Stewart & Gutin, 1976; Yoshida, Ishiko, & Muraoka, 1980). A possible explanation for this apparent discrepancy is that running performance may be improved by a more economical running style and, thus, a lower O_2 cost. This possibility has been confirmed for teenaged boys by Daniels et al. (1978), as shown in Figure 5. In this mixed longitudinal, cross-sectional study, the lowering effect of aerobic training (details of the training program were not described) on the submaximal O_2 cost of running was greater than that caused by mere growth. It is tempting to speculate that a training program that focuses on the running *style* of children might improve their running performance, even when the regimen does not include aerobic components.

Challenges for Future Research on the O_2 Cost of Locomotion During Growth

The following approaches are suggested for studies meant to expand our understanding of the energetics of locomotion in children:

- Observations, by a combined metabolic-kinematic analysis, to determine whether children's high O_2 cost can be explained by wasteful limb and trunk movements during the gait cycle.
- This technique can also be used to understand the training-induced reduction in metabolic cost.
- A combined metabolic-kinematic approach will also be useful for gait analysis of children with neuromuscular disease. For example, the effects of physiotherapy, leg prosthesis or brace, and orthopedic surgery can be assessed, as can the natural history of such diseases as Duchenne muscle dystrophy.
- The separate effects of growth and training on the O_2 cost of locomotion should be identified throughout childhood and adolescence. A mixed longitudinal, cross-sectional design can be used, as shown by Daniels et al. (1978).
- A training regimen can be instituted that is directed exclusively toward improvement of running style, with no aerobic components. This will help us understand the effect of running style on the metabolic economy of children.

Future Directions in Pediatric Exercise Physiology Research

I will close with some thoughts on general topics in pediatric exercise physiology that merit priority for future research.

Methodology of Exercise Testing

Study of children's response to exercise will keep lagging behind research on young adults, unless methods for testing are improved. For example, novel ergometers are needed for toddlers, other preschoolers, and children with marked mental retardation. These could be modified toys that, while played with, register the mechanical work produced by the child. The need for noninvasive, nondamaging, socially acceptable protocols cannot be overemphasized. Imaging, scanning, and other technologies will, I hope, be perfected for this purpose.

Methodology of Training and Trainability Studies

Because of the fast morphologic and functional changes that occur in the growing individual, much attention must be given to the optimal design of training studies. Particular care is needed to partial out such variables as growth, maturation, secular changes, habituation, and preselection. To compare trainability across ages, one must equate the training stimulus given to all age groups.

Puberty and the Response to Exercise

Some physiologic characteristics change gradually from childhood to adulthood. Others, such as sweating capacity, strength, rate of glycolysis, aerobic trainability, and gender-related differences, change primarily during or around puberty. Much research is still needed to understand puberty from the exercise perspective.

Carryover Effects of Activity, Fitness, and Training

A question of immense importance to the public health practitioner, educator, coach, and theoretician is whether habitual activity patterns and innate and acquired fitness track from childhood to adulthood. Animal models may be useful for preliminary information, but long-term longitudinal studies of humans are needed for definitive answers.

References

Åstrand, P.O. (1952). *Experimental studies of physical working capacity in relation to sex and age*. Copenhagen: Munksgaard.

Bal, M.E.R., Thomson, E.M., McIntosh, E.H., Taylor, C.H., & McLeod, G. (1953). Mechanical efficiency in cycling of girls six to fourteen years of age. *Journal of Applied Physiology*, **6**, 185-188.

Bar-Or, O. (1983). *Pediatric sports medicine for the practitioner: From physiologic principles to clinical applications*. New York: Springer Verlag.

Bar-Or, O. (1986). Pathophysiological factors which limit the exercise capacity of the sick child. *Medicine and Science in Sports and Exercise*, **18**(3), 276-282.

Bar-Or, O., & Zwiren, L. (1973). Physiological effects of increased frequency of physical education classes and of endurance conditioning on 9- to 10-year-old girls and boys. In O. Bar-Or (Ed.), *Pediatric work physiology* (pp. 183-198). Natanya: Wingate Institute.

Bengtsson, E. (1956). The working capacity in normal children, evaluted by submaximal exercise on the bicycle ergometer and compared with adults. *Acta Medica Scandinavica*, **154**, 91-109.

Blimkie, C.J.R., Roche, P.D., Hay, J.T., & Bar-Or, O. (1985). Development of arm anaerobic power during childhood and adolescence: Relationship to lean tissue. Paper presented at the 12th International Symposium on Pediatric Work Physiology, Hardehausen, West Germany.

Blimkie, C.J.R., Roche, P.D., & Bar-Or, O. (1986). The anaerobic-to-aerobic power ratio in adolescent boys and girls. In J. Rutenfranz, R. Mocellin, & F. Klimt (Eds.), *Children and Exercise XII* (pp. 31-37). Champaign, IL: Human Kinetics.

Cavagna, G.A., Franzetti, P., & Fuchimoto, T. (1983). The mechanics of walking in children. *Journal of Physiology*, **343**, 323-339.

Cooper, D.M. (1985). Gas exchange kinetics at the onset of exercise during growth in children. *Scandinavian Journal of Sports Sciences*, **7**, 3-9.

Daniels, J., Oldridge, N., Nagle, F., & White, B. (1978). Differences and changes in VO_2 among young runners 10 to 18 years of age. *Medicine and Science in Sports*, **10**, 200-203.

Davies, C.T.M. (1980). Metabolic cost of exercise and physical performance in children with some observation on external loading. *European Journal of Applied Physiology*, **45**, 95-102.

Davies, C.T.M., Barnes, C., & Godfrey, S. (1972). Body composition and maximal exercise performance in children. *Human Biology*, **44**, 195-214.

di Prampero, P.E., & Cerretelli, P. (1969). Maximal muscular power (aerobic and anaerobic) in African natives. *Ergonomics*, **12**, 51-59.

Eriksson, B.O., Karlsson, J., & Saltin, B. (1971). Muscle metabolites during exercise in pubertal boys. *Acta Paediatrica Scandinavica*, **217** (Suppl.), 154-157.

Fournier, M., Ricci, J., Taylor, A.W., Ferguson, R.J., Monpetit, R.R., & Chaitman, B.R. (1982). Skeletal muscle adaptation in adolescent boys: Sprint and endurance training and detraining. *Medicine and Science in Sports and Exercise*, **14**, 453-456.

Gilliam, T.B., & Freedson, P.S. (1980). Effects of a 12-week school physical fitness program on peak VO_2, body composition and blood lipids in 7- to 9-year-old children. *International Journal of Sports Medicine*, **1**, 73-78.

Girandola, R.N., Wiswell, R.A., Frisch, F., & Wood, K. (1981). Metabolic differences during exercise in pre- and post-pubescent girls (Abstract). *Medicine and Science in Sports and Exercise*, **113**, 110.

Godfrey, S., Davies, C.T.M., Wozniak, E., & Barnes, C.A. (1971). Cardiorespiratory response to exercise in normal children. *Clinical Sciences*, **40**, 419-431.

Inbar, O., & Bar-Or, O. (1986). Anaerobic characteristics in male children and adolescents. *Medicine and Science in Sports and Exercise*, **18**(3), 264-269.

Krahenbuhl, G.S., Pangrasi, R.P., & Chomokos, E.A. (1979). Aerobic response of young boys to submaximal running. *Research Quarterly*, **50**, 413-421.

Krahenbuhl, G.S., & Skinner, J.S. (1985). Developmental aspects of maximal aerobic power in children. *Exercise and Sports Sciences Reviews*, **13**, 503-538.

Kurowski, T.T. (1977). *Anaerobic power of children from age 9 through 15 years*. Unpublished masters thesis, Florida State University.

MacDougall, J.D., Roche, P.D., Bar-Or, O., & Moroz, J.R. (1983). Maximal aerobic power of Canadian schoolchildren: Prediction based on age-related oxygen cost of running. *International Journal of Sports Medicine*, **4**, 194-198.

Mácek, M., & Vávra, J. (1980). The adjustment of oxygen uptake at the onset of exercise: A comparison between prepubertal boys and young adults. *International Journal of Sports Medicine*, **1**, 75-77.

Margaria, R., Aghemo, P., & Rovelli, E. (1966). Measurement of muscular power (anaerobic) in man. *Journal of Applied Physiology*, **21**, 1662-1664.

Mocellin, R., & Wasmund, U. (1973). Investigation on the influence of a running-training programme on the cardiovascular and motor performance capacity in 53 boys and girls of a second and third primary school class. In O. Bar-Or (Ed.), *Pediatric work physiology* (pp. 279-285). Natanya: Wingate Institute.

Murphy, M.M., Patton, J.F., & Frederick, F.A. (1984). A comparison of anaerobic power capacity in males and females accounting for differences in thigh volume, body weight and lean body mass (Abstract). *Medicine and Science in Sports and Exercise*, **16**, 108.

National Children and Youth Fitness Study (1985). Summary of findings. *Journal of Physical Education, Recreation and Dance*, **56**, 44-90.

Piacentini, V., & Bollettino, A. (1942). Il metabolismo respiratorio dei bambini duranto l'esercizio muscolare. *Arbeitphysiologie*, **12**, 272-285.

Robinson, S. (1938). Experimental studies of physical fitness in relation to age. *Arbeitphysiologie*, **10**, 251-323.

Sady, S.P. (1981). Transient oxygen uptake and heart rate responses at the onset of relative endurance exercise in prepubertal boys and adult men. *International Journal of Sports Medicine*, **2**, 240-244.

Schmücker, B., & Hollmann, W. (1974). The aerobic capacity of training athletes from 6 to 7 years of age on. *Acta Paediatrica Belgica*, **28** (Suppl.), 92-101.

Silverman, M., & Anderson, S.D. (1972). Metabolic cost of treadmill exercise in children. *Journal of Applied Physiology*, **33**, 696-698.

Skinner, J.S., Bar-Or, O., Bergsteinová, V., Bell, C.W., Royer, D., & Buskirk, E.R. (1971). Comparison of continuous and intermittent tests for determining maximal oxygen uptake in children. *Acta Paediatrica Scandinavica*, **217** (Suppl.), 24-28.

Stewart, K.J., Gutin, B. (1976). Effects of physical training on cardiorespiratory fitness in children. *Research Quarterly*, **47**, 110-120.

Tanaka, H., & Shindo, M. (1985). Running velocity at blood lactate threshold of boys aged 6-15 years compared with untrained and trained young males. *International Journal of Sports Medicine*, **6**, 90-94.

Taylor, C.H., Bal, M.E.R., Lamb, M.W., & McLeod, G. (1950). Mechanical efficiency in cycling of boys seven to fifteen years of age. *Journal of Applied Physiology*, **2**, 563-570.

Waters, R.L., Hislop, H.J., Thomas, L., & Campbell, J. (1983). Energy cost of walking in normal children and teenagers. *Developmental Medicine and Child Neurology*, **25**, 184-188.

Wilmore, J.H., & Sigerseth, P.O. (1967). Physical work capacity of girls 7-13 years of age. *Journal of Applied Physiology*, **22**, 923-928.

Yoshida, T., Ishiko, I., & Muraoka, I. (1980). Effect of endurance training on cardiorespiratory functions of 5-year-old children. *International Journal of Sportsmedicine*, **1**, 91-94.

Women: Menstrual Dysfunction, Premature Bone Loss, and Pregnancy

Barbara L. Drinkwater

One of the lessons to be learned from the many studies of women's response to exercise that have appeared in the last 15 years is that if one wants to know the physical potential of a particular group of individuals one does not select sedentary members of that group as subjects. The difficulty of assessing women's capacity for endurance activities in the years prior to 1970 were evident in Shephard's (1966) paper. Although there were data from around the world describing the aerobic power ($\dot{V}O_2max$) of trained and untrained males, there were no data for active or athletic women. At that time there were so few female endurance athletes that there were no data describing their response to a maximal exercise test. Even for untrained women, there were no $\dot{V}O_2max$ values for those over the age of 30 in the United States.

In retrospect, it is apparent that rules and regulations prohibiting women from participating in many endurance sports were based on physiological data obtained from untrained women. With the advent of Title IX of the Education Amendments, athletic opportunities for young women increased dramatically, and scientists at last had active, well-trained women to study. The results of those studies have forced us to reassess our opinions regarding the female response to vigorous physical activity.

Training Versus Gender

By far the largest body of data describing women's response to exercise is the descriptive statistics characterizing the response of trained and untrained women to a maximal exercise stress test. In activities as diverse as golf and mountaineering, ballet and speed skating, swimming and volleyball, one fact is immediately obvious: The body responds to the physical demands placed upon it regardless of whether it is a female body or male body.

Training, not the sex of the athlete, is the primary factor in determining aerobic power. When male and female athletes in the same sport are tested in the same laboratory and ranked by $\dot{V}O_2max$, the order in which the sports appear is almost identical for each sex (Table 1). The average difference in $\dot{V}O_2max$ between male and female athletes in the same sport is about 11 ml. Within each sex the difference across sports can be as much as 20 to 30 ml. Nevertheless, it is readily apparent that in any given sport male athletes have higher values of aerobic power. For these 11 groups of athletes the difference averages 16.6%. In many sports this difference in $\dot{V}O_2max$ translates into a difference in performance.

The physiological consequences of an aerobic conditioning program appear to be both qualitatively and relatively the same for men and women, an increase in those variables associated with endurance capacity as well as an improved submaximal exercise performance. Although women were seldom included in those training studies designed to determine the relative role of frequency, duration, and intensity of exercise in improving cardiovascular fitness, the similarity in the percent improve-

Table 1 Aerobic Power ($ml\ O_2 \cdot kg^{-1} \cdot min^{-1}$) of Male and Female Athletes Matched for Age and Sport

	Female		Male		
Sport	Aerobic power	n	Aerobic power	n	Reference
Nordic skiing	68.2	5	78.3	17	Rusko, Havu, & Karvinen, 1978
Running (mid. dist.)	68.0	4	76.0	7	Ready, 1984
Nordic skiing	61.5	10	73.0	10	Haymes & Dickinson, 1980
Marathon	58.2	9	72.5	13	Davies & Thompson, 1979
Swimming	55.3	11	68.6	12	Holmer, Lundin, & Eriksson, 1974
Alpine skiing	52.7	13	66.6	12	Haymes & Dickinson, 1980
Cycling	50.2	7	62.1	22	Burke, Cerny, Costill, & Fink, 1977
Orienteering	46.1	5	61.6	13	Knowlton, Ackerman, Fitzgerald, Wilde, & Tahamont, 1980
Volleyball	50.6	14	56.1	8	Puhl & Case, 1982
Speed skating	46.1	13	56.1	10	Maksud, Wiley, Hamilton, & Lockhart, 1970
Tennis	44.2	25	50.2	25	Vodak, Savin, Haskell, & Wood, 1980

Table 2 Percent Improvement in Selected Maximal and Submaximal Performance Variables for Men and Women

Variable	Percent improvement Men	Percent improvement Women	Reference
$\dot{V}O_2max$, ml•kg^{-1}•min^{-1}	15.0%	14.2%	Eddy, Sparks, & Adelizi, 1977
$\dot{V}_Emax$, L•min^{-1}	11.7%	11.0%	Daniels, Kowal, Vogel, & Stauffer, 1979
Heart volume, ml	1.3%	1.5%	Holmgren, Mossfeldt, Sjostrand, & Strom, 1960
Blood volume, L	6.4%	4.9%	Holmgren et al., 1960
Strength, lb[a]	20.0%	23.0%	Wilmore, 1974
Resting heart rate, bpm	5.9%	7.9%	Holmgren et al., 1960
Submaximal heart rate, bmp	7.4%	10.1%	Eddy et al., 1977

[a]Average for curl, leg press, and bench press.

ment (Table 2) between the sexes suggests that recommendations for effective conditioning programs for males apply to females as well.

Although the magnitude of aerobic power is of interest to athletes and coaches concerned with the performance of the female athlete, there is a more basic reason why exercise scientists are interested in the quantitative differences in $\dot{V}O_2max$ between men and women. Are there inherent biological factors that limit the ability of women to transport and utilize oxygen, or does the difference represent some factor amenable to training? This question has a practical implication for those physiological studies in which the physical fitness of the research subjects can be a confounding factor. What is the most appropriate method to match male and female subjects on the fitness factor to ensure that the functional status of the oxygen delivery and utilization systems are similar?

There are a number of ways the sex difference in aerobic power can be expressed, and the magnitude of the difference varies accordingly. If men and women must perform the same absolute work, the appropriate comparison is in liters (L) of O_2•min^{-1}. In weight-bearing activities where the workload is the athlete's body weight, aerobic power as ml O_2•kg^{-1}•min^{-1} is a more useful comparison. For the physiologist who must control the effect of cardiorespiratory fitness on some other physiological variable of interest, normalizing differences on lean body mass (ml O_2•kg LBM^{-1}•min^{-1}) is the final step in removing the effect of body size and composition on the magnitude of $\dot{V}O_2max$. Are men and women matched numerically on $\dot{V}O_2max$ relative to LBM now equated on physical fitness? Current evidence suggests they are not.

Table 3 Effect of Body Size and Composition on the Difference in Aerobic Power ($\dot{V}O_2max$) Between Men and Women

	Percentage differences	
$\dot{V}O_2max$ Measures	Sparling, 1980	Drinkwater, 1984b
$L \bullet min^{-1}$	56%	51.5%
$ml \bullet kg^{-1} \bullet min^{-1}$	28%	18.6%
$ml \bullet kg\ LBM^{-1} \bullet min^{-1}$	15%	9.0%

A meta-analysis by Sparling (1980) using 13 studies of trained and untrained subjects attempted to identify the contribution of body size and composition to sex differences in aerobic power (Table 3). The residual difference of 15% was slightly larger than the 9% found between male and female athletes training for the same sport, at the same level of competition, and tested in the same laboratory (Drinkwater, 1984b). Current theory suggests that this residual difference is biological in origin and represents the lower hemoglobin levels and maximal cardiac output of women. If so, an experimental design that matches men and women on aerobic power relative to LBM would bias the results by selecting women who had overcome this biological disadvantage by training harder than the men.

Cureton (1981) recommends that a 5% biological correction factor be applied when matching male and female subjects on $\dot{V}O_2max$, in $ml \bullet kg\ LBM^{-1} \bullet min^{-1}$, and that the groups be matched on activity histories as well. Further research is needed to confirm the applicability of this recommendation. Until this question is resolved, we can expect conflicting results from studies that use different standards for matching men and women on cardiovascular fitness. Obvious examples of this can already be seen in the thermoregulation literature (Drinkwater, 1986a).

Gynecological Aspects of Exercise

Menstrual Dysfunction

One of the reasons women were discouraged from participating in strenuous physical activity for so many years was the belief that prolonged vigorous exercise would adversely affect future reproductive function. This belief was challenged in the 1960s by a number of survey studies that reported active women had less dysmenorrhea, easier labor, and suffered no damage to either the uterus or breast as a result of their athletic activities (Gendel, 1967; Zaharieva, 1965). As access to the athletic world opened up for young female athletes in the early 1970s, so did the intensity of their training and their choice of events. Women were free to participate in most of the physically demanding sports open to men, and many chose to take advantage of that opportunity. By the mid-1970s it was becoming evident that there was an increasing incidence of menstrual dysfunction among female athletes.

Research in this area has progressed from the survey approach, which attempted to pinpoint traits characteristic of women reporting menstrual irregularities, to sophisticated endocrine studies, which are trying to identify the relationship between exercise and specific hormones that may be disrupting the complex relationships of the hypothalamic-pituitary-ovarian axis. The lack of a clear definition of terms has been a serious problem for investigators. Until standard definitions of *amenorrhea* (absence of menses) and *oligomenorrhea* (infrequent menses) are adopted, there will continue to be conflicting reports in the literature relative to the incidence, cause, and effects of the dysfunction.

The etiology of the amenorrhea/oligomenorrhea associated with exercise is as yet unknown. The body fat hypothesis proposed by Frisch and colleagues (Frisch & McArthur, 1974; Frisch, Wyshak, & Vincent, 1980) is no longer accepted as a valid explanation. The technique they used to predict percent body fat has been strongly criticized by Trussell (1978) and Reeves (1979), and a number of other investigators have failed to find a significant difference in body weight or percent fat between amenorrheic and eumenorrheic athletes (Baker, Mathur, Kirk, & Williamson, 1981; Calabrese, et al., 1983; Feicht, Johnson, Martin, Speakes, & Wagner, 1978; Wakat, Sweeny, & Rogol, 1982). Low body fat may be one factor in a complex interrelationship of factors that disrupt the regularity of the menstrual cycle. It is unlikely to be the sole explanation.

Other proposed mechanisms are related to the physical stress or energy drain of the activity, psychological factors, diet, and personal characteristics of the individual athlete, such as age, menstrual history, parity, and so forth. A number of studies have addressed the issue of how each of these factors might influence the hormonal events that regulate the menstrual cycle or alter the concentration of hormones and/or neurotransmitters that affect the cycle indirectly via the hypothalamus. Unfortunately, conflicting results from many of these studies have only added to the confusion surrounding the amenorrhea issue. An excellent critical review of the literature in this area has been compiled by Loucks and Horvath (1985).

There are a number of steps that could be taken to expedite the identification of the mechanism(s) underlying the amenorrhea associated with exercise. The first step is agreement on a definition of eumenorrhea, oligomenorrhea, and amenorrhea. Loucks and Horvath (1985) suggest that the term *amenorrhea* be reserved for cycle intervals in excess of 90 days to coincide with the definition used in several large population studies of amenorrhea. They would reserve the term *eumenorrhea* for cycle intervals of 25 to 38 days and *oligomenorrhea* for intervals of 39 to 90 days. If these definitions were adopted, it would not preclude some investigators stipulating that their subjects must have been amenorrheic for a longer period of time in order to observe the effect on a specific variable. In bone density studies, for example, it is unlikely that one could detect a significant change in bone mineral content in 3 months. The magnitude of the measurement error plus the relatively slow turnover rate of bone might dictate a requirement that the women identified as amenorrheic by the standard definition remain amenorrheic for a minimum of 12 months.

Research into the etiology of athletic amenorrhea has begun to move away from the purely descriptive study and delve more deeply into the endocrine basis of the proposed mechanisms. Although a number of studies evaluating the acute and chronic effects of exercise on hormonal concentrations have been published, the data are often conflicting and difficult to interpret (Drinkwater, 1984a). If this avenue is to be productive, greater attention must be paid to experimental design, appropriate methodology, and proper statistical techniques. The complexity of the problem demands an interdisciplinary approach. Gynecologists and endocrinologists lack the expertise to design exercise studies; many physicians are not familiar with the finer points of experimental design; exercise physiologists may be unaware of some of the methodological problems in endocrine research; and none may have the statistical knowledge to evaluate the data properly.

A number of avenues need to be explored. The basal gonadotropin and ovarian hormone profile of the amenorrheic athlete must be identified. In spite of the wide interest in identifying the etiology of athletic amenorrhea, no one has yet characterized the hormonal patterns of these young women for a period of time equivalent to a normal menstrual cycle. No one can state with confidence that there are no cyclic fluctuations of these hormones across time.

In addition to measuring the concentration of these and other hormones, the researcher must give thought to how they are to be interpreted. For example, a change in concentration may represent a change in clearance, a change in secretion, a failure to account for plasma volume shifts following exercise, or some other extraneous factor. Even when these factors are accounted for, there is no assurance that peripheral concentrations reflect biological activity at any target organ. A related problem is defining threshold levels for physiological effect. Some women have had significantly higher levels of testosterone following exercise (Fahey, Rolph, Moungmee, Nagel, & Mortara, 1976; Shangold, Gatz, & Thysen, 1981; Sutton, Coleman, Casey, & Lazarus, 1973). However, the concentrations were still within normal limits for females and well below male values. How much meaning does one attach to ''significant'' changes that are unlikely to have a physiological effect?

More longitudinal studies are needed in which training is carefully quantified, prescribed, and intensified while basal hormonal patterns are monitored on a daily basis. The selection of hormones to be measured should go beyond the gonadotropins and ovarian hormones and include those that may affect the cycle by acting directly on the hypothalamus and/or pituitary. Potential candidates can be found among the adrenal and thyroid hormones, the endogenous opiates, and the neurotransmitters.

The endocrine response to acute exercise needs to be quantified for amenorrheic and eumenorrheic athletes and eumenorrheic non-athletes.

Tests should be conducted at low-, moderate-, and high-intensity exercise and at different phases of the cycle for the eumenorrheic athletes. It would also be useful to know how long concentrations remain elevated post-exercise. Although the physiological effect of changes in hormonal concentrations are debatable at present, the eventual answer will depend not only on the concentration of hormones but the length of time the levels remain above (or below) a yet undetermined threshold.

The original concern over the menstrual irregularities associated with exercise focused on the reproductive aspects. Would these young women be able to conceive and bear children? In time it became evident that a decrease in training intensity, usually accompanied by an increase in weight, resulted in resumption of normal menses. Anecdotal evidence accumulated about former amenorrheic athletes completing successful pregnancies and the anxiety evaporated. Many young athletes actually welcomed the absence of the monthly cycle, because they were able to train and compete free of the menstrual discomfort many of them had experienced. Within the past 3 years that complacency has been challenged by new evidence linking hypoestrogenic amenorrhea to a decrease in bone mass (see "Health Related Issues"). The potential consequences of this bone loss emphasize the importance of identifying the mechanisms underlying athletic amenorrhea.

Pregnancy

At the opposite end of the continuum from the amenorrheic athlete is the pregnant athlete and her concerns. The basic question for these women is how to modify their normal activity programs to ensure the health and safety of both mother and fetus. At the present time there is very little definitive information for these women. The American College of Obstetricians and Gynecologists (1985) has published guidelines for exercise during pregnancy and the postpartum period appropriate for the average woman, but they do not address the concerns of the highly trained, competitive athlete. An obvious problem in determining the safe limits of exercise for these women is an ethical one, and it is unlikely that the safety threshold will ever be investigated using human subjects.

Animal studies have addressed two of the basic issues related to exercise: a reduction in uterine blood flow as blood is shunted to the active muscles and the rise in core temperature as metabolic heat production increases. Results have been equivocal. Strenuous exercise has resulted in fetal growth retardation in some species, whereas moderate exercise has had no marked effect on fetal outcome (Lotgering, Gilbert, & Longo, 1985). Under mild or moderate physiologic stress, a number of effective mechanisms appear to maintain fetal homeostasis.

Human studies have been limited in scope; no investigator will propose a protocol that may adversely affect the fetus or the mother. The result is a lack of data to answer the important question of how much exercise is too much. Although physicians may feel comfortable urging moderation, there are athletes who are more likely to base their decisions on anecdotal reports of other athletes continuing to train and compete throughout most of their pregnancy. Additional research is needed to provide a scientific basis for the guidelines offered the female athlete.

Because it is not feasible or ethical to assign pregnant women randomly to exercise protocols in which the outcome is unknown, prospective epidemiological studies of self-selected exercising groups offer a viable alternative. The study must be prospective in order to quantify the exercise program and monitor the course and outcome of the pregnancy. Subgroups of the larger sample could be studied more intensively in both laboratory and field settings.

The potential teratogenic effect of fetal hyperthermia during the first trimester is of particular concern to those women who train at high intensities for extended periods of time. Under what conditions is the fetal environment compromised? Is it possible to determine a prescriptive zone for the pregnant athlete based on her fitness level, the intensity and duration of exercise, and the environmental conditions?

Animal studies have suggested that a reduction in uterine blood flow is compensated by an increase in maternal hemoglobin concentration during exercise. The result is a relatively unchanged uteroplacental oxygen delivery (Lotgering et al., 1985). Lack of a noninvasive technique to measure these variables has made it impossible to confirm a similar adjustment in humans. Because invasive procedures not dictated by the medical needs of the fetus or the mother are unlikely to be approved by any Human Subjects Review Board, other methods of monitoring the physiological consequences of maternal exercise are urgently needed.

Health-Related Issues

Amenorrhea and Premature Bone Loss

Since the first report of a decrease in vertebral bone density associated with athletic amenorrhea appeared (Cann, Martin, Genant, & Jaffer, 1984), three other independent studies (Drinkwater et al., 1984; Lindberg et al., 1984; Marcus et al., 1985) have verified that finding. The decrease in bone density has been most apparent in those areas that have a high proportion of trabecular bone such as the spine. This does not mean that cortical bone is immune to the effect of the decreased estrogen level. The higher turnover rate of trabecular bone may simply reflect the hypoestrogenic effect on bone metabolism more quickly. Concern for the athlete centers around the potential for increased traumatic or stress fractures now and a greater risk for osteoporosis in the future.

Because this is a relatively new area of investigation, there are many directions research might take. Perhaps the most important question is whether or not bone loss can be halted or even reversed in these amenorrheic athletes. What are the most effective treatment modalities? Is the answer hormone replacement therapy? If so, what is the effective dose and the best treatment regimen? Can increasing calcium intake offset the decrease in calcium absorption and increase in calcium excretion associated with low estrogen levels? Can women who have lost bone mass regain normal levels? Does the length of time a woman has been amenorrheic determine the extent of recovery? How does age affect the amount of bone mass that can be regained?

Most of the athletes studied to date have been runners. Does the sport affect the pattern or extent of bone loss? Can some activities protect athletes against any decrease in density? Other skeletal areas should be examined, particularly those that are subjected to gravitational force and mechanical stress during specific activities, such as the tibia or femur during running.

At the present time the bone loss associated with athletic amenorrhea is the black cloud overshadowing women's athletics. It is the only adverse consequence of strenuous conditioning programs unique to women. Already there are suggestions that women limit their training to avoid menstrual irregularity (Heath, 1985; Marcus et al., 1985). Whereas this suggestion may be acceptable to women who exercise for fun and fitness, it is not likely to be welcomed by the competitive athlete.

There is an urgent need for research in this area, but it is equally important that investigators plan their experimental design carefully, matching experimental and control groups on those factors that influence bone density, confirming menstrual status through biochemical analysis of ovarian and/or gonadotropin hormones, selecting appropriate measurement sites, assuring that the amenorrhea is indeed related to activity, and using appropriate statistical techniques.

Menopause, Exercise, and Bone Health

Several recent studies (Aloia, Cohn, Ostuni, Cane, & Ellis, 1978; Krolner, Toft, Nielsen, & Tondevold, 1983; Smith, Reddan, & Smith, 1981) have suggested that physical activity programs can halt or even reverse bone loss in postmenopausal women. Female athletes, particularly Masters athletes, have been intrigued by the notion that an active lifestyle will protect them from osteoporosis without recourse to hormone replacement therapy in their postmenopausal years. Is this true?

There is no doubt that inactivity, weightlessness, or immobilization of a limb, will result in bone loss or that bone is regained when normal activity is resumed (Krolner & Toft, 1983). It is also evident that athletes and other active men and women have a higher bone mineral density than less active individuals (Jones, Priest, Hayes, Tichenor, & Nagel, 1977; Nilsson & Westlin, 1971). However, the basic question remains unanswered: Can exercise, with or without additional calcium, offset the deleterious effect of decreased endogenous estrogen levels on bone? If young amenorrheic athletes, training more intensely than most postmenopausal women would tolerate, are losing bone mass, why should we expect exercise to protect less active older women?

A number of questions have been raised that must be addressed before the interaction of exercise, calcium, and estrogen can be understood (Drinkwater, 1986b). One would feel more confident in prescribing exercise as a prophylaxis for osteoporosis if the mechanism underlying the exercise effect on bone were thoroughly understood. Is it a purely local effect as a result of mechanical stress on the bone, a centrally-mediated effect related to hormonal changes associated with exercise, an interaction of the two, or some yet unrecognized route of action?

Some women are more at risk than others for osteoporosis. Among the risk factors are a family history of osteoporosis, a northern European background, and some personal and lifestyle characteristics. Is physical activity effective for these high-risk women?

How much exercise is required to obtain a positive effect on bone mass? Can exercise for bone health be prescribed in the same way as exercise for cardiovascular fitness? Does the effective threshold vary with age, calcium intake, or estrogen level? What happens when a woman stops activity? Does she lose all benefit of her prior exercise program as the skeletal system adapts to the decreased demands placed upon it?

How much increase in bone density can be expected from an activity program? Is there an upper limit? What determines the amount of improvement that can be anticipated from an exercise program: age, initial status, genetic potential, nutritional factors, type of exercise?

These are only a few of the issues that must be addressed. Physical activity plays a vital role in maintaining bone health in the postmenopausal years. However, it is premature to assume that exercise alone will protect women against osteoporosis.

References

Aloia, J.F., Cohn, S.H., Ostuni, J.A., Cane, R., & Ellis, K. (1978). Prevention of involutional bone loss by exercise. *Annals of Internal Medicine*, **89**, 356-358.

American College of Obstetricians and Gynecologists. (1985). *Exercise during pregnancy and the postnatal period* (ACOG Home Exercise Programs). Washington, DC: Author.

Baker, E., Mathur, R.S., Kirk, R.F., & Williamson, H.O. (1981). Female runners and secondary amenorrhea: Correlation with age, parity, mileage, and plasma hormonal and sex-hormone-binding globulin concentrations. *Fertility and Sterility*, **36**, 183-187.

Burke, E.R., Cerny, F., Costill, D., & Fink, W. (1977). Characteristics of skeletal muscle in competetive cyclists. *Medicine and Science in Sports*, **9**, 109-112.

Calabrese, L.H., Kirkendall, D.T., Floyd, M., Rapoport, S., Williams, G.W., Weiker, C.G., & Bergfeld, J.A. (1983). Menstrual abnormalities, nutritional patterns, and body composition in female classical ballet dancers. *The Physician and Sportsmedicine*, **11**(2), 86-98.

Cann, C.E., Martin, M.C., Genant, H.K., & Jaffe, R.B. (1984). Decreased spinal mineral content in amenorrheic women. *Journal of the American Medical Association*, **251**, 626-629.

Cureton, K.J. (1981). Matching male and female subjects using $\dot{V}O_2max$. *Research Quarterly for Exercise and Sport*, **52**, 264-268.

Daniels, W.L., Kowal, D.M., Vogel, J.A., & Stauffer, R.M. (1979). Physiological effects of a military training program on male and female cadets. *Aviation, Space, and Environmental Medicine*, **50**, 562-566.

Davies, C.T.M., & Thompson, M.W. (1979). Aerobic performance of female marathon and male ultramarathon athletes. *European Journal of Applied Physiology*, **41**, 233-245.

Drinkwater, B.L. (1984a). Athletic amenorrhea: A review. *Exercise and Health* (pp. 120-131). Champaign, IL: Human Kinetics.

Drinkwater, B.L. (1984b). Women and exercise: Physiological aspects. *Exercise and Sport Sciences Reviews*, **12**, 21-51.

Drinkwater, B.L. (1986a). Gender differences in heat tolerance: Fact or fiction? In B.L. Drinkwater (Ed.), *The female endurance athlete*. Champaign, IL: Human Kinetics.

Drinkwater, B.L. (1986b). Osteoporosis and the female masters athlete. In J.R. Sutton & R.M. Brock (Eds.), *Sports medicine for the mature athlete* (pp. 353-359). Indianapolis, IN: Benchmark Press.

Drinkwater, B.L., Nilson, K., Chesnut, C.H., III, Bremner, W.J., Shainholtz, S., & Southworth, M.B. (1984). Bone mineral content of amenorrheic and eumenorrheic athletes. *New England Journal of Medicine*, **311**, 277-281.

Eddy, D.O., Sparks, K.L., & Adelizi, D.A. (1977). The effects of continuous and interval training in women and men. *European Journal of Applied Physiology*, **37**, 83-92.

Fahey, T.D., Rolph, R., Moungmee, P., Nagel, J., & Mortara, S. (1976). Serum testosterone, body composition, and strength of young adults. *Medicine and Science in Sports*, **8**, 31-34.

Feicht, C.B., Johnson, T.S., Martin, B.J., Speakes, K.E., & Wagner, W.W. (1978). Secondary amenorrhea in athletes. *Lancet*, **2**, 1145-1146.

Frisch, R.E., & McArthur, J.W. (1974). Menstrual cycles: Fatness as a determinant of minimum weight for height necessary for maintenance or onset. *Science*, **185**, 949-951.

Frisch, R.E., Wyshak, G., & Vincent, L. (1980). Delayed menarche and amenorrhea in ballet dancers. *New England Journal of Medicine*, **303**, 17-19.

Gendel, E.S. (1967). Pregnancy, fitness, and sports. *Journal of the American Medical Association*, **201**(10), 125-128.

Haymes, E., & Dickinson, A.L. (1980). Characteristics of elite male and female ski racers. *Medicine and Science in Sports and Exercise*, **12**, 153-158.

Heath, H., III. (1985). Athletic women, amenorrhea, and skeletal integrity. *Annals of Internal Medicine*, **102**, 258-260.

Holmer, I., Lundin, A., & Ericksson, B.O. (1974). Maximum oxygen uptake during swimming and running by elite swimmers. *Journal of Applied Physiology*, **36**, 711-714.

Holmgren, A., Mossfeldt, F., Sjostrand, T., & Strom, G. (1960). Effect of training on work capacity, total hemoglobin, blood volume, heart volume, and pulse rate in recumbent and upright positions. *Acta Physiologica Scandinavica*, **50**, 72-83.

Jones, H.H., Priest, J.D., Hayes, W.C., Tichenor, C.C., & Nagel, D.A. (1977). Humeral hypertrophy in response to exercise. *Journal of Bone and Joint Surgery*, **59A**, 204-208.

Knowlton, R.G., Ackerman, K.J., Fitzgerald, P.I., Wilde, S.W., & Tahamont, M.V. (1980). Physiological and performance characteristics of United States championship class orienteers. *Medicine and Science in Sports and Exercise,* **12**, 164-169.

Krolner, B., & Toft, S.P. (1983). Vertebral bone loss: An unheeded side effect of therapeutic bed rest. *Clinical Science,* **64**, 537-540.

Krolner, B., Toft, B., Nielsen, S.P., & Tondevold, E. (1983). Physical exercise as prophylaxis against involutional bone loss: A controlled trial. *Clinical Science,* **64**, 541-546.

Lindberg, J.S., Fears, W.B., Hunt, M.M., Powell, M.R., Boll, D., & Wade, C.E. (1984). Exercise-induced amenorrhea and bone density. *Annals of Internal Medicine,* **101**, 647-648.

Lotgering, Gilbert, R.D., & Longo, L.D. (1985). Maternal and fetal responses to exercise during pregnancy. *Physiological Reviews,* **65**, 1-22.

Loucks, A.B. & Horvath, S.M. (1985). Athletic amenorrhea: A review. *Medicine and Science in Sports and Exercise,* **17**, 56-72.

Marcus, R., Cann, C., Madvig, P., Minkoff, J., Goddard, M., Bayer, M., Martin, M., Gaudiani, L., Haskell, W., & Genant, H. (1985). Menstrual function and bone mass in elite women distance runners. *Annals of Internal Medicine,* **102**, 158-163.

Maksud, M.G., Wiley, R.L., Hamilton, L.H., & Lockhart, B. (1970). Maximal VO_2, ventilation, and heart rate of Olympic speed skating candidates. *Journal of Applied Physiology,* **29**, 186-190.

Nilsson, B.E., & Westlin, N.E. (1971). Bone density in athletes. *Clinical Orthopaedics,* **77**, 179-182.

Puhl, J.L., & Case, S. (1982). Physical and physiological characteristics of elite volleyball players. *Research Quarterly for Exercise and Sport,* **53**, 257-262.

Ready, A.E. (1984). Physiological characteristics of male and female distance runners. *Canadian Journal of Applied Sports Sciences,* **9**, 70-77.

Reeves, J. (1979). Estimating fatness. *Science,* **204**, 881.

Rusko, H., Havu, M., & Karvinen, E. (1978). Aerobic performance capacity in athletes. *European Journal of Applied Physiology,* **38**, 151-159.

Shangold, M.M., Gatz, M.L., & Thysen, B. (1981). Acute effects of exercise on plasma concentrations of prolactin and testosterone in recreational women runners. *Fertility and Sterility,* **35**, 699-702.

Shephard, R.J. (1966). World standards of cardiorespiratory performance. *Archives of Environmental Health,* **13**, 664-672.

Smith, E.L., Reddan, W., & Smith, P.E. (1981). Physical activity and calcium modalities for bone mineral increase in aged women. *Medicine and Science in Sports and Exercise,* **13**, 60-64.

Sparling, P.B. (1980). A meta-analysis of studies comparing maximal oxygen uptake in men and women. *Research Quarterly,* **51**, 542-552.

Sutton, J.R., Coleman, N.J., Casey, J., & Lazarus, L. (1973). Androgen responses during physical exercise. *British Medical Journal,* **1**, 520-522.

Trussell, J. (1978). Menarche and fatness: Reexamination of the critical body composition hypothesis. *Science,* **200**, 1506-1509.

Vodak, P.A., Savin, W.M., Haskell, W.L., & Wood, P.D. (1980). Physiological profile of middle-aged male and female tennis players. *Medicine and Science in Sports and Exercise*, **12**, 159-163.

Wakat, D.K., Sweeny, K.A., & Rogol, A.D. (1982). Reproductive system function in women cross-country runners. *Medicine and Science in Sports and Exercise*, **14**, 263-269.

Wilmore, J.H. (1974). Alterations in strength, body composition, and anthropometric measurements consequent to a 10-week weight training program. *Medicine and Science in Sports*, **6**, 133-138.

Zaharieva, E. (1965). Survey of sportswomen at the Tokyo Olympics. *Journal of Sports Medicine and Physical Fitness*, **5**, 215-219.

Exercise in the Elderly to Prolong and Improve the Quality of Life

Everett L. Smith

People have tried to understand the cause of aging for centuries. Historically, aging was considered a specific disease that could be cured or prevented if the right potion could be found. Scientists no longer think of aging as a disease process or caused by a single entity, but rather as a result of genetically controlled decrements of cellular function. Most gerontologists think that human aging is a complex interaction among biological processes, personality, behavior, and social and environmental forces (Shock et al., 1984). Multidisciplinary longitudinal studies are necessary to more clearly understand this complex process. This does not, however, preclude necessary short-term research on specific mechanisms of the aging process. Our current understanding of aging is based on studies of animals and multiple cross-sectional studies, some time lag studies, and very few longitudinal studies on humans. Directions for future research are tied both to knowledge gained in the past and to present technological breakthroughs that make more sophisticated studies feasible. Researchers are now looking at the complex interactions between the genetic (nature) and the environmental (nurture) components of aging.

An ethical consideration that arises in studying older adults is possible risk to the participants, particularly at high levels of stress. Conversely, exploring the functional physiologic limits is important both to researchers and to older adults themselves. For example, a 73-year-old marathoner complained that he could only get his heart rate up to 145 bpm when exercising hard. When told this approximates the maximum for the average person of his age, he was not satisfied and asked how to raise his maximum heart rate. He wanted to know what the limiting factor was. It is not clear why healthy humans age or what factors permit some to resist aging better than others.

The major purpose of research on the biological aging process should be to determine how to prolong life and to enhance the quality of life. One goal is to prevent premature decay through disuse or unnecessary environmental insults, such as falls. Older adults fall and are injured more often than any other segment of our population. Falls may be partly due to declines in freedom of movement related to sensory, nerve, muscle, bone, and joint function. In our sedentary society, all of these functions peak, on the average, between the ages of 30 and 35 and then decline. The loss of visual acuity and depth perception with age limit mobility. Through physical activity and education many falls could be prevented in the older adult thus enhancing the quality of life.

Work capacity, cardiac output, maximal heart rate, total body water, renal function, liver function, adaptability to heat and cold, nerve conduction velocity, flexibility, and bone decline, whereas systolic and diastolic blood pressure increase with age (Table 1). Physical activity can reduce, prevent, or even reverse many of these trends in the cardiovascular, muscular, and skeletal systems.

Table 1 Biological Functional Changes Between the Ages of 30 and 70

Biological function	Change
Work capacity (%)	↓25–30
Cardiac output (%)	↓30
Maximum heart rate (bpm)	↓24
Blood pressure (mmHg)	
Systolic	↑10–40
Diastolic	↑ 5–10
Respiration (%)	
Vital capacity	↓40–50
Residual volume	↑30–50
Basal metabolic rate (%)	↓ 8–12
Musculature (%)	
Muscle mass	↓25–30
Hand grip strength	↓25–30
Nerve conduction velocity (%)	↓10–15
Flexibility (%)	↓20–30
Bone (%)	
Women	↓25–30
Men	↓15-20
Renal function (%)	↓30–50

Note. From "Physical Activity Prescription for the Older Adult" by E.L. Smith and C. Gilligan, 1983, *The Physician and Sportsmedicine*, **11**(8), p. 92. Copyright 1983 by *The Physician and Sportsmedicine*. Reprinted by permission.

Declines in flexibility with age may be attributed to histological and morphological changes in cartilage, ligament, and tendon (Adrian, 1981). Aging per se might cause the decline, but there is no evidence that tendon stiffening, joint capsule changes, or muscle changes limit flexibility. In

Table 2 Change in the Range of Joint Motion Following a 12-Week Exercise and Dance Program

Joints	Percent change Experimental group	Control group
Neck (flexion/extension)	↑27.8%	↓3.6%
Shoulder (abduction/adduction)	↑ 8.3%	↓5.1%
Wrist (flexion/extension)	↑12.8%	↓2.3%
Hip/back (flexion/extension)	↑26.9%	↓3.7%
Knee (flexion/extension)	↑11.6%	↓2.7%
Ankle (flexion/extension)	↑48.3%	↓5.1%

Note. From "Effects of Exercise on the Range of Joint Motion in Elderly Subjects" by K. Munns. In *Exercise and Aging: The Scientific Basis* (p. 175) by E.L. Smith and R.C. Serfass (Eds.), 1981, Hillside, NJ: Enslow. Copyright 1981 by Enslow. Reprinted by permission.

a study of 40 senior citizens, flexibility improved significantly with a 3-month exercise program (Table 2). For example, ankle flexibility improved 48%, which would facilitate walking and help prevent falls (Munns, 1981).

With age the immune system and thymus function decline (Makinodan, 1976). Very little research has been done on the relationship of immune function to exercise. Colacino (1973) found that animals exercised 27 to 32 weeks had fewer and smaller tumors than control animals exposed to the same carcinogens. The carcinogens 7, 12-dimethylbenzothiazine (DMBA) and B-propiolactone (BPL) were used in Experiments 1 and 2, respectively. In Experiment 1, control animals (n = 20) had an average of 16.3 tumors and no animals were tumor-free, whereas pretrained interval-exercised animals (n = 20) had 10.3 tumors and 32% were tumor free. In Experiment 2, the control group (n = 25) had 10.5 tumors (5% tumor-free), the pretrained continuous exercise group (n = 20) had 8.6 tumors (11% tumor-free), the pretrained interval exercise group (n = 20) had 3.6 tumors (42% tumor-free), and the nonpretrained interval exercise group (n = 15) had 6.1 tumors (8% tumor-free).

This research indicates that physical activity may play a significant role in reducing susceptibility to neoplasms. Further research is needed to determine whether exercise can help to prevent neoplasms in humans, which would enhance the quality of life.

Recent research on the satellite cell provides insight into muscle growth and maintenance. The satellite cell, the mitogen of muscle tissue, rests between the sarcolemma and the basal lamina in muscle fibers. During growth, the satellite cell is a myoblast that divides outside the muscle fiber. One of the daughter cells fuses with the sarcolemma and forms new muscle, while the other remains outside the sarcolemma. The ability of muscle to regenerate depends on the satellite cell. Schultz and Lipton (1982) cultured satellite cells from 6-day-, 15-day-, 3-month-, 12-month-, 24-month-, and 30-month-old rats and counted cell numbers after 3, 4, 5, 6, and 7 days. Cells from older animals produced significantly smaller colonies, or failed to replicate at all. This supports the concept that the satellite cell follows Hayflick's limit.

Gibson and Schultz (1983), using the same culture model, compared satellite cells cultured from the extensor digitorum longus (EDL, fast-twitch) and the soleus (slow-twitch). In young animals, damaged soleus and EDL replicated itself four times and three times, respectively. In aged animals (24 months), replication was significantly reduced to 70% in the soleus and 30% in the EDL. Although replication was significantly decreased, the older muscle still had a relatively large reserve capacity. Moritani (1981) hypothesized that humans could not increase muscle mass after about age 60. If the satellite cell research holds true in vivo, muscle hypertrophy should be possible even in old age. Older adults, however, would take longer for the same amount of hypertrophy, and would have a lower limit on maximum hypertrophy than young adults.

Schultz and Jaryszak (1985) injected chemicals into muscle that destroy muscle fiber but leave satellite cells intact. They showed that satellite cells regenerate destroyed muscle fibers. Replication of satellite cells in culture, however, decreased with repeated injuries. Thus, it seems that the fewer insults to the muscle the greater the reserve of the satellite cell.

The above research indicates that even in advanced age muscle can be maintained. Muscle atrophy might then be preventable or reversible depending on the individual genetics and environmental history. Increasing muscle mass and strength through physical activity would significantly reduce falls in the older adult. Atrophy of the quadriceps muscle, which begins early in life, particularly contributes to the likelihood of falling.

Increased reaction time in older adults may also contribute to falls. Changes in the neuromuscular junction account for part of this increase. Both the nerve and muscle segments of the neuromuscular junction change with age. The distance between the nerve and muscle increases and the junctional folds are fewer, which decreases surface area and thus, receptors for acetylcholine (ACh).

Muscles and motor end plates most frequently stimulated atrophy the least. For example, the diaphragm (a continuously contracting non-voluntary muscle) does not atrophy significantly with age, whereas the EDL (noncontinuous voluntary muscle) does (Rosenheimer & Smith, 1985). Disuse may be responsible for the differential. Rosenheimer and Smith (1985) demonstrated that ACh of the EDL declines significantly with age, whereas it declines minimally in the diaphragm. In the diaphragm, proliferation of motor end plates, or arborization, increases the overall surface area and partially compensates for this decline. Another adaptation in the end plate is changes in hydrolyzation of ACh. Acetylcholinesterase (AChase), which hydrolyzes ACh, appears in two forms. The globular form is found at the postsynaptic membrane and the globular-plus-collagen form is found in the cleft. With age, a greater portion of the globular form appears, allowing more nonhydrolyzed ACh to pass to the muscle surface (Jedrzejczyk, Silman, Lai, & Barnard, 1984).

Although the animal model research on the diaphragm indicates that frequent stimulation significantly retards neuromuscular decline, extrapolation to the whole organism may not be defensible. In support of the effects of frequent stimulation, Spirduso (1975) found reaction time increases with age in the habitually inactive, whereas chronically active older adults have reaction times similar to those of younger people. She studied young (aged 20–30) and old (aged 50–70) handball, racquetball, and squash players and sedentary men. Court players of either age group had faster reactions than either young or old sedentary men, whereas young men had faster reactions than the older men within the same activity category. This study may be confounded in that active older adults may have had a special genetic endowment. To determine the effects of physical activity alone, Spirduso and Farrar (1981) studied reaction time in genetically matched rats. Prior to a 6-month training program, young and old rats had similar response times to an electric shock (unconditioned stimulus, UCS). The young trained group maintained their reaction time over the 6 months, whereas all other groups were slower. The rats were also trained to respond to the conditioned stimulus (CS) of a buzzer. In this task, young and old trained rats were significantly faster than their untrained cohorts at 300 and 200 ms CS-UCS intervals. This research supports the importance of chronic stimulation of nerve and muscle to prevent declines in reaction time.

Declines in the skeletal system parallel those in muscle and nerve. The skeletal system is dynamic and responds to both systemic hormones and local stress and strain. Individual bones vary from one another in their integrity. An individual may have an osteoporotic femur and normal spine, or an osteoporotic spine and normal femur. Early researchers believed that hand-wrist X-rays could be used to predict changes in the rest of the skeleton, but current research has shown this to be unsatisfactory. Each segment of the skeleton must be considered. Like other parts of the body, bone has a genotype determining its general structure. Other factors acting on bone mass include endocrines, nutrition, and mechanical stress and strain. Endocrines and nutrition are important in maintaining serum calcium. The skeletal system as a whole acts as a calcium reservoir and responds to hormonal stimulation to replete serum calcium when nutritional calcium is inadequate. With years of negative calcium balance, eventually the skeleton can no longer support the body. Consequently, osteoporosis develops.

Mechanical stress and strain act on bone. At one time, we assumed that exercise of a general nature would maintain the skeleton, but the effect appears to be localized. Thus, each individual bone must be stressed to build its mass. In addition, each bone has a specific threshold for the amount of stress necessary to produce hypertrophy. Stress to the humerus must be at a greater level than that to the radius or ulna to get a response. Because they are weight bearing, the femur and spine have even greater thresholds. Although each bone responds locally to mechanical stress, the skeletal system as a whole responds to calcium stress. If specific bones are stressed and dietary calcium is inadequate, calcium will be mobilized from skeletal segments under less stress. For example, Krolner, Toft, Nielsen, and Tondevold (1983) observed that calcium was mobilized from the non-weight-bearing arms to meet the demands of the lower extremities.

Bone responds to stress by producing electrical charges. When bone is bent, a negative charge forms on the compressed segment, stimulating bone formation (Basset, 1971). Microfractures may also occur, stimulating osteoclastic and osteoblastic activity (Carter, 1984). Osteoclastic activity releases a skeletal growth factor that stimulates osteoblastic activity and thus, bone formation (Mohan, Linkhart, Farley, & Baylink, 1984).

Our research has shown that bone responds to stress at any age. Smith, Smith, Ensign, and Shea (1984) studied women aged 36 to 65, 86 who participated in an exercise program and 62 controls. Exercise subjects participated in an exercise class 45 min/session, 3 days/week. The radius, ulna, and humerus bone mineral content and bone mineral content over width of the control group declined significantly over the 4-year study. The rate of decline in the exercise group was significantly less than that of the control group in 12 of the 18 bone variables measured.

We also studied elderly women in a nursing home (mean age 82). Twelve subjects who participated in a mild physical activity program increased radius bone mineral by 2.29% and 18 control subjects lost 3.29% (Smith, Reddan, & Smith, 1981).

References

Adrian, M.J. (1981). Flexibility in the aging adult. In E.L. Smith & R.C. Serfass (Eds.), *Exercise and aging: The scientific basis* (pp. 45-57). Hillside, NJ: Enslow.

Bassett, C.A. (1971). Biophysical principles affecting bone structure. In G.H. Bourne (Ed.), *The biochemistry and physiology of bone* (2nd ed., Vol. III, pp. 1-76). New York: Academic Press.

Carter, D.R. (1984). Mechanical loading histories and cortical bone remodeling. *Calcified Tissue International*, **36** (Suppl.), 19-24.

Colacino, D.L. (1973). *The effects of continuous and interval endurance training upon reduction of chemically induced skin papillomas in female mice.* Unpublished doctoral dissertation, University of Wisconsin, Madison.

Gibson, M.C., & Schultz, E. (1983) . Age-related differences in the absolute number of satellite cells in rat soleus and extensor digitorum longus muscles. *Muscle and Nerve*, **6**, 574-580.

Jedrzejczyk, J., Silman, I., Lai, J., & Barnard, E.A. (1984). Molecular forms of acetylcholinesterase in synaptic and extrasynaptic regions of avian tonic muscle. *Neuroscience Letters*, **46**, 283-289.

Krolner, B., Toft, B., Nielsen, S.P., & Tondevold, E. (1983). Physical exercise as prophylaxis against involutional vertebral bone loss: A controlled trial. *Clinical Science*, **64**, 541-546.

Makinodan, T. (1976). Immunobiology of aging. *Journal of the American Geriatrics Society*, **24**(6), 249-252.

Mohan, S., Linkhart, T., Farley, J., & Baylink, D. (1984). Bone-derived factors active on bone cells. *Calcified Tissue International,* **36** (Suppl.), 139-145.

Moritani, T. (1981). Training adaptations in the muscles of older men. In E.L. Smith & R.C. Serfass (Eds.), *Exercise and aging: The scientific basis* (pp. 149-166). Hillside, NJ: Enslow.

Munns, K. (1981). Effects of exercise on the range of joint motion in elderly subjects. In E.L. Smith & R.C. Serfass (Eds.), *Exercise and aging: The scientific basis* (pp. 167-178). Hillside, NJ: Enslow.

Rosenheimer, J.L., & Smith, D.O. (1985). Differential changes in the end-plate architecture of functionally diverse muscles during aging. *Journal of Neurophysiology,* **53**(6), 1583-1597.

Schultz, E., & Jaryszak, D.L. (1985). Effects of skeletal muscle regeneration on the proliferation potential of satellite cells. *Mechanisms of Aging and Development,* **30**, 63-72.

Schultz, E., & Lipton, B.H. (1982). Skeletal muscle satellite cells: Changes in proliferation potential as a function of age. *Mechanicsms of Aging and Development,* **20**, 377-383.

Shock, N.W., Greulich, R.C., Costa, P.T., Andres, R., Lakatta, E.G., Arenberg, D., & Tobin, J.D. (1984). *Normal human aging: The Baltimore longitudinal study of aging* (NIH Publication No. 84-2450). Washington, DC: U.S. Government Printing Office.

Smith, E.L., Reddan, W., & Smith, P.E. (1981). Physical activity and calcium modalities for bone mineral increase in aged women. *Medicine and Science in Sports and Exercise,* **13**(1), 60-64.

Smith, E.L., Smith, P.E., Ensign, C.J., & Shea, M.M. (1984). Bone involution decrease in exercising middle-aged women. *Calcified Tissue International,* **36**, S129-S138.

Spirduso, W.W. (1975). Reaction and movement time as a function of age and physical activity level. *Journal of Gerontology,* **30**, 435-440.

Spirduso, W.W., & Farrar, R.P. (1981). Effects of aerobic training on reactive capacity: An animal model. *Journal of Gerontology,* **36**, 654-662.

Age and Gender Effects on Exercise Physiology: A Commentary

Christine L. Wells

I have long held that one of the principal reasons for studying biological differences between the sexes is that it tells us much about the range of human potential as well as individual limitations. Such study also forces us to be more critical about some of the answers we often glibly provide coaches, teachers, and parents about performance differences. The same, I think, could be said for the study of aging and its effects on human performance. If we are to fully understand the effects of exercise—whether it be purely recreational, for improved health, or at high levels of competition—it is important for us to realize that not all humans are alike. Physiologically, we develop (grow), mature, and decline in functional responses. Physical training alters this progression, in some instances by speeding it up and in others, by slowing it down. Training forces us to higher, more optimal levels of homeostasis. Not all humans of the same age are alike either. Although there is an extremely wide range of similar responses among people of all ages, sexual bimorphism often creates quantitative differences that are important for us to understand at each major age classification.

Interdisciplinary Research

The three preceding papers (Bar-Or, Drinkwater, & Smith) have outlined some of what we know about children, women, and the elderly. Their topic assignments were narrowly defined, and each carefully stayed away from the assignment of the others to avoid overlap of material. They have provided us a survey of known facts (limited by time and space allotments), suggested some areas for future study, and provided much food for integrated thought about where to go from here. Their papers and known expertise speak to the concept that an individual can not know all there is to know about our species, and so we develop more limited expert knowledge about segments of our species, in the instances here, children, women, and the elderly. Of course, as exercise scientists we all specialize to some extent, and in fact, as serious academics we are usually very suspicious of anyone who claims to have the fuller picture, the more universal view, the global perspective. No one can know all there is to know about exercise, growth and development, sexual morphology, and aging. Our way out of this dilemma is usually to welcome other experts to participate in our meetings, and to be consultants on our grant propsals. We call this interdisciplinary study. It is our noble attempt to more fully understand the problems that confront us as we study that segment of the human population we work most closely with, and to integrate the work of other scientists and physicians (e.g., pediatricians, gynecologists, geriatricians, and endocrinologists) as it relates to our work.

Although this is very well and good, I would suggest that sometimes this process has a rather limited outcome because we *too* carefully narrow the scope of the questions we ask. Perhaps I can develop an improved model for interdisciplinary research by elaborating on the example of exercise-associated amenorrhea, while reemphasizing some of the points made by Drinkwater.

There is an increased incidence of secondary amenorrhea among highly trained female athletes. Although this has been extensively documented, the etiology of this menstrual dysfunction remains unknown. Careful review of the athletic amenorrhea literature reveals considerable confusion (Loucks & Horvath, 1985), but we are now at the stage where conceptual models should be developed and methodically tested. A number of steps in the process of determining a cause have been outlined (Loucks & Horvath, 1985; Wells, 1985):

1. Agreement on a standardized definition of the phenomenon
2. Determination of the basal gonadotropin and ovarian hormone profile of the amenorrheic athlete
3. Determination of hormone dynamics during exercise (including such complicated problems as hormone clearance, hormone turnover, biological activity, the function of sex-hormone-binding globulins, and threshold levels for physiological effect)
4. Determination of the role of other hormones (particularly the adrenal and thyroid hormones, and testosterone)
5. Determination of the role of factors affecting the CNS-hypothalamus interaction (particularly the endogenous opiates and various neurotransmitters)
6. Determination of the acute effects of exercise upon endocrine hormones (with careful attention to the quantification of exercise intensity, menstrual phase, interrelationships of changes observed, recovery to control levels, and plasma volume shifts)
7. Determination of the role of body fat and lean body mass (particularly muscle mass) in the peripheral feedback process

Although I do not suggest that the above items are unworthy of massive research attention, perhaps there is another approach. We have a fairly complete understanding of the underlying feedback mechanisms of the normal menstrual cycle, but we have yet to understand the endocrinology of puberty and menarche. Nor do we understand the mechanism of ovarian failure occurring at menopause. I suspect there is much to be learned in regard to the delay in menarche and secondary amenorrhea in athletic girls and women, and in the study of the commencement and decline of regular menstrual function.

I believe that the usual sort of interdisciplinary research in which we commonly engage is insufficient. I suggest that a think-tank or coalition approach be undertaken with massive cooperation between outstanding research groups of biochemists, endocrinologists, gynecologists, and exercise physiologists. Obviously, large numbers of athletic and sedentary subjects ranging from prepubertal to postmenopausal ages must be studied with such an approach. Unfortunately, such an enormous undertaking would require considerable financial support, but the scientific and medical spinoffs would also be considerable. In my opinion, with the most influential voices speaking with imagination, such support is not inconceivable from national funding sources, pharmaceutical companies, and industry.

Health-Related Issues

Osteoporosis

Health-related issues were discussed by both Drinkwater and Smith. From their different perspectives, it became quite clear that much needs to be learned regarding the dynamics of bone growth, the deposition and resorption of bone mineral, the effects of endogenous as well as pharmaceutical hormones, the role of calcium and vitamin D, and the role of exercise in bone health. It was previously thought that serious loss of bone mineral was limited to advanced age, menopause, or specific disease states. We now know that it also occurs with conditions such as anorexia nervosa and athletic amenorrhea characterized by a hypoestrogenic state. In short, serious bone mineral loss is seen today in groups previously thought to be protected by virtue of their young age and physical activity level. Again, many questions remain to be answered:

1. What is the exact interrelationship between estrogen and bone dynamics?
2. Can bone loss be reversed in amenorrheic athletes?
3. What levels of calcium intake are appropriate at various age groups and bone densities?
4. How can dietary calcium absorption be enhanced?
5. Does the loss of bone density with amenorrhea differ from the loss of bone density with menopause?
6. What other factors (besides diet, estrogen, and exercise) are involved?
7. Is there such a thing as too much exercise in terms of bone mineral loss? (Drinkwater asks, Why should we expect exercise to protect hypoestrogenic menopausal women from bone loss if hypoestrogenic amenorrheic athletes are not protected? Smith, working

at less than athletic levels of exercise, says that bone hypertrophies in response to stress at any age.)

8. If each bone has a specific threshold for the amount of stress necessary to produce hypertrophy (Smith), how can appropriate levels of exercise be prescribed to attain those levels (Drinkwater)? Should exercise be prescribed for all areas of the body? Or is there also a general effect?
9. What mechanisms are in effect in high-risk women (Caucasian, northern European background, smokers, caffeine and alcohol consumers) that they have earlier bone mineral losses than other women? Is it possible that exercise is particularly effective for them?

If the prevention of osteoporosis truly begins in childhood (Loucks, 1985), then these questions are of direct interest to those who study and work with children as well as those who deal with amenorrheic athletes and menopausal women. It appears that dietary and other lifestyle habits learned from a very early age become increasingly important in later life.

Obesity

Another age/gender issue for which this last statement is pertinent (and not discussed in the earlier papers) is the problem of obesity. At least 30% (many say 40%) of the adults in this country are obese. The U.S. Public Health Service reports that as many as 10 million teenagers are overweight—that's about 20% of the teenage population in this country. Recent physical fitness surveys of our children reveal that they are fatter today than in the 1960s (Ross & Gilbert, 1985). Obesity is linked with so many illnesses and health risks—hypertension, coronary heart disease, thrombophlebitis, diabetes mellitus, respiratory problems, liver and gall bladder disorders, difficulties with pregnancy, osteoarthritis, increased surgical risk, premature death—that it is a major problem in the industrialized world.

Although the health-related issues involved with obesity should be of considerable interest to us as exercise physiologists, there are also issues of economics, fraudulent practices, and human happiness at stake. Many people are faced with body weight and composition problems nearly all their lives despite much effort (and expense) on their part to solve the problem. All too often we smugly ignore them with such statements as, "If they'd only stop eating and start exercising, they wouldn't be so fat." More carefully coordinated interdisciplinary research with nutritionists, psychologists (behavior modification?), and endocrinologists, among others, is essential. This is a massive problem that transcends age and gender barriers. Much yet needs to be learned about basal metabolic rate, fat cell hyperplasia (both brown and white), hormones, satiety and appetite, and the interrelationships of diet and exercise. We have not been very successful putting together what we know about exercise and hyperlipidemia/hypercholesterolemia into practice for the obese. Perhaps the current set-point concept will provide the impetus necessary to stimulate the sort of basic and applied research so sorely needed by millions.

Pregnancy

Pregnant women often gain weight that is never lost again. Many assume an almost totally sedentary lifestyle while pregnant out of fear that physical activity, especially strenuous physical activity, is detrimental to the health of the fetus they carry. Others do so because they find physical activity uncomfortable. A recent study (Clapp & Dickstein, 1984) reported that relatively few women continued physical activity beyond the 28th week of gestation despite their original intention to do so.

Drinkwater points out that, although the physician usually urges moderation in activity while pregnant, the athlete doesn't want to hear that, and often will continue to train at high exercise intensities or for long durations (e.g., run marathons). Such practice, she states, provides an excellent opportunity for prospective epidemiological studies that could do much toward answering the questions we seek and find impossible to get at with the typical research approach. In reality, of course, such study would take considerable time and effort because one rarely has a sufficient number of highly trained pregnant athletes available at any one time. Nevertheless, such an opportunity offers a unique approach.

Some basic questions that remain unanswered in regard to exercise during pregnancy are as follows:

1. What is the fetal temperature in relation to the elevation of maternal temperature in response to various levels of exercise? What are safe and unsafe levels? Are there differences at different gestation periods?
2. Is there a reduction in uterine blood flow during strenuous exercise in the human? What is the physiological significance of altered uterine blood flow to the fetus? Is the fetus hypoxic with strenuous maternal exercise? There are conflicting data regarding exercise and training during pregnancy in human and animal models. More information is needed on responses to high levels of exercise in the human (Gorski, 1985).
3. Do maternal or fetal responses to exercise differ if the mother exercises in the upright, weight-bearing position as opposed to a sitting or semi-reclining weight-supported position?
4. What are the effects of relaxin on joint stability in relation to weight-bearing exercise? To jarring movements like aerobic dance? To weight lifting?
5. What are the effects of maternal hypohydration on the fetal blood supply and oxygen delivery?
6. How can commonly seen maternal hypoglycemic responses to exercise be avoided? What are the dangers to the fetus?
7. How can we best prescribe exercise for the pregnant woman, and how can she and the fetus be adequately monitored throughout the duration of a pregnancy?
8. How can the prospective mother best monitor herself while exercising?

Sport-Related Issues

Sport-related issues are those more related to performance than to health. Bar-Or, Drinkwater, and Smith all referred to such issues—most notably differences in oxygen uptake ($\dot{V}O_2$). Bar-Or elaborated on anaerobic power and the differences in the oxygen cost of locomotion in children. Drinkwater focused on the problem of appropriately matching male and female subjects to ensure that "the functional status of the oxygen delivery and utilization systems are similar" for comparative studies. Smith referred to the deterioration of biological function with advanced age. Obviously there is a continuum here. The young child's cardiorespiratory system is developing. How best can that be enhanced? There are sexual differences due to body size, body composition, and, perhaps, cultural expectations. Are these important? In our elderly citizens, Smith indicates that there are "decrements of cellular function dependent on genetic controls." Can this be slowed?

It has been well established that training programs directed toward improving aerobic power demonstrate beneficial effects in both sexes at *all* adult ages—teenaged through elderly. The capacity of prepubescent children to improve in aerobic fitness, however, has been controversial, with conflicting data. Rowland's (1985) analysis of these data revealed that exercise programs employing adult criteria of exercise intensity, duration, and frequency resulted in improved $\dot{V}O_2max$ in prepubescent children similar to that observed in adults. This interpretation may need additional confirmation, but I believe we can safely state that aerobic training programs yield many performance-based and health-based benefits to all ages.

With the increasing prevalence of obesity, and the shift to an older median age due to increasing life expectancy, we need to be more vocal about what we know about the benefits of regular aerobic exercise. There is considerable need for a massive public education program specifically directed toward middle-aged women, blue-collar workers, lower socioeconomic classes, and the elderly.

Exercise physiology is a field that often deals with athletic performance. We study it, pick it apart to find underlying mechanisms, and develop innovative training concepts to enhance it. To justify ourselves to the nonsport community (and perhaps to make ourselves more respectable in the academic community as well), we have commonly dealt with exercise-related health issues. In both instances, in my opinion, we have limited ourselves too extensively to the young adult male (often an athlete) and the middle-aged male (the potential heart attack victim). With renewed interest in general health and physical fitness among many citizens of the world, the time is right for expanding our view, and for developing more comprehensive research ventures that integrate age- and gender-related issues for the benefit of all humankind.

References

Clapp, J.F., III., & Dickstein, S. (1984). Endurance exercise and pregnancy outcome. *Medicine and Science in Sports and Exercise*, **16**, 556-562.

Gorski, J. (1985). Exercise during pregnancy: Maternal and fetal responses. A brief review. *Medicine and Science in Sports and Exercise*, **17**, 407-416.

Loucks, A.B. (1988). Osteoporosis prevention begins in childhood. In E.W. Brown & C.F. Branta (Eds.), *Competitive sports for children and youth* (pp. 213-223). Champaign,IL: Human Kinetics.

Loucks, A.B., & Horvath, S.M. (1985). Athletic amenorrhea: A review. *Medicine and Science in Sports and Exercise*, **17**, 56-72.

Ross, J.G., & Gilbert, G.G. (1985). A summary of findings: The national children and youth fitness study. *Journal of Physical Education, Recreation and Dance*, **56**(1), 45-50.

Rowland, T.W. (1985). Aerobic responses to endurance training in prepubescent children: A critical analysis. *Medicine and Science in Sports and Exercise*, **17**, 493-497.

Wells, C.L. (1985). *Women, sport and performance: A physiological perspective*. Champaign, IL: Human Kinetics.

Skeletal Muscle Morphology: Adaptation to Altered Demands

Philip D. Gollnick

The charge given to the speakers of this symposium was to look into the future. Thus we are to be soothsayers. The charge given to me was the area of exercise physiology as related to muscle. As always, a look to the future first requires a review of the past. Thus, a brief review of some of the topics that are covered will be given. This review is not intended to bring one to the point of embarking upon research in any of the areas discussed. Rather, key references are given to support the general concepts.

Due to space limitations the only topics related to skeletal muscle discussed in this paper are (a) muscle morphology, (b) metabolic potential, (c) metabolic control, and (d) muscle damage. This does not imply that these are the only areas in need of future effort, but rather it reflects the space limitation and the areas in which I am most knowledgeable. These topics are addressed from the standpoint of (a) what is generally known, (b) why changes occur with exercise and training, and (c) how changes occur. As will become clear, some of these are multiple questions.

Muscle Morphology

What Is Known About Exercise and Training and Muscle Morphology?

Muscles are conglomerates of fibers, assembled into discrete functional units, motor units, controlled by a single motor nerve. The individual fibers are formed by the fusion of myoblasts progressively joined into units of long, multinucleated cells, the myotubes. Once united into myotubes, the myoblasts lose their capacity for future division. Under most normal conditions, the total number of fibers appears to be established prior to birth. Subsequently, normal muscular growth occurs by longitudinal and circumferential enlargement of the fibers existing within the muscle. This maturational growth has been examined in some detail from either prior to or immediately after birth to full maturity in several animals, including man (Aherne, Ayyar, Clarke, & Walton, 1971; Colling-Saltin, 1980; Mera, 1947). Such studies are by their very nature cross-sectional, and the magnitude of the absolute changes in the size of the fibers within a single muscle of a person or animal varies considerably. However, the general pattern of growth can be accepted with confidence.

Overloading of muscle induces an enlargement in the cross-sectional area (hypertrophy) of the fibers beyond that which exists in normal man and animals (for references see Saltin & Gollnick, 1983). In man, the cross-sectional area of fibers in overloaded muscle has been determined in both biopsy samples and whole muscle of deceased persons who had performed heavy labor, whereas in animals it has been done primarily on entire muscles. The differences in the area of the fibers of muscles is sufficient to account for the large bulk of weight-lifters and bodybuilders (Tesch, Thorsson, & Kaiser, 1984) and in the muscle enlargement that occurs in animals with overloads (Gollnick, Parsons, Riedy, & Moore, 1983; Riedy, Moore, & Gollnick, 1985). Although there have been suggestions that there is an addition of new fibers, produced by a division of preexisting fibers, in muscle during work-induced enlargement, the experiments in which this has been reported are fraught with technical difficulties that render the results equivocal.

Another area of interest in muscle morphology is the mutability of fibers in response to different physiological loads. There is good evidence that the percentage composition of fibers in the muscle varies considerably among individuals. Evidence for the mutability of muscle fibers comes from studies of hormonal modification (Ianuzzo, Patel, Chen, O'Brien, & Williams, 1977), chronic electrical stimulation, and cross-reinnervation (Pette, 1984). The observation that there can be a high percentage of Type I fibers in the muscles of highly trained endurance athletes has led to speculation that an interconversion of fiber types occurs with endurance training and with inactivity. Some evidence from studies with rats seems to confirm this suggestion (Green et al., 1984); however, only a few animals were examined in these studies and the magnitude of the changes were rather small in spite of a training program whose strenuousness probably exceeded that in which most athletes engage.

Why Do Changes in Muscle Morphology Occur With Growth and With Overloading?

The question of why muscle fibers increase in length and cross-sectional area is easy to answer. First, the length of the muscle corresponds closely to the length of the skeletal attachments and the longitudinal growth of muscle must keep pace with that of skeletal growth. This is true even in muscles where the fibers do not lie parallel to the long axis of the muscle and do not traverse the entire muscle length. The second part of this question is, Why do the fibers get larger in cross-sectional area? This is due to the fact that the force-generating capacity of a muscle is a function of its physiological cross-sectional area, that is, the sum of the cross-sections of all fibers. As animals grow, the requirement for force development increases due to the locomotor requirements and those of work and/or sport activities. The growth of existing fibers, rather than the addition of new ones, is a logical method for increasing muscle bulk because it avoids problems associated with either the expansion of existing motor units or the addition of more motor units. The expansion of motor units would require a constant retraining of the nervous system to handle differences in expected force development, and the expansion of the total motor unit pool would entail the growth of entire motor units. A major problem with the generation of new motor units lies not only in producing new motoneurons, but also in the fact that fibers of a motor unit lie at considerable distance from each other. It would represent a difficult task to generate the new fibers and to have the new motoneuron find and innervate them over a wide area of the muscle.

The reason for a conversion of fiber types has been suggested as being related to different contractile properties and efficiency in the conversion of ATP to contractile force. Such arguments are not overly convincing.

How Do the Changes in Muscle Morphology Occur?

As in most areas there are clearly two aspects of the "how." The first "how" is, How do these changes occur? A lengthening of the fibers occurs by an addition of sarcomeres to the ends of the muscle fibers. One could imagine that this would be more simply done by the fusion of more myoblasts to the fibers. However, because the fibers are attached on each end to either the origin or insertion of the muscles, the addition of new myoblasts would cause considerable disruption in the fiber. Moreover, there is no evidence that myoblasts exist in muscle after birth. In some muscles, the fibers lie parallel to the long axis of the muscle. In some of these muscles, the muscle fibers may traverse the entire distance from the origin to the insertion of the muscle, and in such muscles the fiber length corresponds closely to total muscle length. However, in most muscles, particularly those with a pennate fiber arrangement, the length of the fibers is far less than the total muscle length. Here the muscle length is due to a combination of the fiber length and diameter. Of some interest and importance in the overall growth (and atrophy) of muscle fibers is that DNA concentration per unit of protein remains surprisingly constant. This appears to be due to an incorporation of satellite cells into the fibers during growth and the destruction of the nuclei with atrophy. The satellite cells also appear to be important in the repair of damaged fibers. With fiber growth there is an expansion of support systems such as the sarcoplasmic reticulum, sarcoplasm, and so forth, which also remain relatively constant per unit of protein. An exception to be discussed below is that of mitochondrial concentration per unit protein during rapid growth.

The second "how" is a more interesting and difficult question and one on which future research will probably be focused. This question is, What is (are) the stimulus (stimuli) for producing the changes that occur with normal growth and with overload? The stimulus for this addition of new contractile units that ultimately results in an elongation of the fibers may be a stretching of the fibers. It is currently unknown how such a stretch is converted into a chemical signal that is sensed by the genes in the cell to initiate the synthesis of new proteins at the ends of the fibers. It is known that when a mature muscle is fixed in a shortened position there is a decease in sarcomere number per fiber, resulting in a shortening of the fiber and muscle. The factors that regulate sarcomere number and total muscle length have been discussed by Herring, Grimm, and Grimm (1984).

With prolonged immobilization there is a disruption of the contractile elements of muscle, with loss of fibrillar material, and if allowed to proceed long enough, fibers appear to undergo death. There are questions concerning the manner in which new contractile elements are added within the fibers to produce increases in diameter. Here the stimulus appears to be one of total tension development. It can also be envisaged as being a stretch-induced effect. However, in this instance there is an increase in the size and number of myofibrils per fiber such that there is a fiber enlargement. The major problems to be solved in this area are (a) what are the inducers for longitudinal and circumferential growth, (b) what are the differences between the induction of protein synthesis with normal growth and that which accompanies functional overloading, and (c) how is protein synthesis and degradation controlled? These vexing questions will require the application of techniques in molecular biochemistry that are currently being developed. Their application to the complex problems associated with mammalian growth will require carefully designed and skillfully executed experiments but should yield new and exciting findings in this rather old area of interest.

Another area in which continued effort is needed is that of identifying fibers within muscle and their mutability in response to a number of perturbations. Thus, although skeletal muscles are generally recognized as being composed of different types of fibers, there is a lack of unanimity as to what constitutes a fiber type and what criteria must be met for a fiber conversion to have taken place. Part of this problem relates to the existence and use of diverse systems for identifying fiber types in skeletal muscle (Gollnick & Hodgson, 1986). The number of fiber types that can be identified in muscle varies considerably depending upon the method used for fiber-typing. Some of the methods for establishing fiber types depend upon the supposed existence of specific iso-forms of key proteins within the fibers. The uncertainty of how many fiber types exist can be atrributed to the uncertainty that exists with regard to what should establish the base characteristic for a fiber type and whether this characteristic is due to the presence of single iso-form of one or several proteins. Moreover, there is uncertainty as to what produces the intermediate properties of some fibers, particularly those where staining intensities are produced with histochemical methods. The question, therefore, is, Are the different fibers the result of the existence of different iso-forms of key proteins or are they due to a co-mingling of the iso-forms of key proteins within single fibers? It is unknown whether regional differences in the proteins exist within single muscle fibers. It will be necessary to answer some of these questions when considering the overall question of the extent to which muscle fibers change in response to alternative patterns of activity, including endurance training, high-resistance training, and inactivity.

Metabolic Potential

What Is Known About the Metabolic Potential of Muscle and the Effects of Training Upon It?

The metabolic character of skeletal muscle is influenced by its chronic participation in physical activity. Examples of this in nature are the differences in oxidative potential of muscles of birds that fly extensively as compared to those that fly very little. This is evident from both the color of the muscle (e.g., the white breast muscle of the domesticated chicken and turkey as compared to the dark red of the same muscle of wild pigeons, ducks, hummingbirds, etc.) and the approximately sevenfold difference in citrate synthase activity of the pectoralis muscle of the pigeon compared to the pheasant. Armstrong, Ianuzzo, and Kunz (1977) also observed that the succinate dehydrogenase activity of bat pectoralis muscle was greater in summer when the animals were active as compared to that in winter when the animals were inactive.

Longitudinal and cross-sectional studies with animals and man have demonstrated that dramatic changes can occur in skeletal muscles in response to endurance training (see Saltin & Gollnick, 1983). These studies have demonstrated that large (several-fold) increases in the concentration of mitochondrial protein can occur in skeletal muscles exposed to chronic endurance exercise training. This increases the capacity of the citric acid cycle, β-oxidation, and electron transport chain for terminal oxidation of the muscle. The magnitude of the adaptations to training vary as a function of the duration and intensity of the exercise program.

There is relatively little change in the capacity of the Embden-Meyerhof pathway in response to endurance-type training, sprint training, or heavy resistance training. If anything, there is a slight decline in the total capacity of this system with endurance training. With heavy resistance training, by which there is an increase in the size of the muscle and muscle fibers, there is a decline in oxidative capacity per unit of muscle. Thus, with such growth there is a preferential accumulation of contractile material and enzymes associated with the Embden-Meyerhof pathway, which results in a dilution of mitochondrial protein concentration. The ability of the Embden-Meyerhof pathway to keep pace with this growth may be due to the fact that these enzymes appear to be associated with components of the contractile and other support systems (Pette, 1975).

Why Does Oxidative Potential Increase With Endurance Training?

Two hypotheses exist to explain why the oxidative potential of muscle increases with endurance training. One is that the total oxidative potential of muscle limits total body oxygen uptake ($\dot{V}O_2max$). Those espousing the concept that an increase in the concentration of mitochondrial protein is needed for the increase in total $\dot{V}O_2max$ cite the fact that there can be an increase in the a-$\bar{v}O_2$ difference with training and that this is produced by the increase in mitochondrial protein (Hoppeler et al., 1985). However, the following points can be used to support the concept that the increase in $\dot{V}O_2max$ is not related to the change in the oxidative potential of the skeletal muscles but rather in the capacity to deliver oxygen to the muscles.

1. The increase in the concentration of mitochondrial protein that occurs with endurance training greatly exceeds that of the increase in total body $\dot{V}O_2max$ (Saltin & Gollnick, 1983).
2. When reasonably well-trained individuals continue to train for a prolonged period of time, there is a greater increase in cardiac output than in the total body $\dot{V}O_2max$ (Ekblom, 1969).
3. There is an increase in the $\dot{V}O_2max$ that can be generated in the nontrained limb of individuals who have trained the other limb (Clausen, 1977; Klausen, Secher, Clausen, Hartling, & Trap-Jensen, 1982; Saltin et al., 1976).
4. The increase in $\dot{V}O_2max$ in middle-aged and older individuals with training is almost completely due to increases in the cardiac output (Hartley et al., 1969; Saltin, Hartley, Kilbom, & Åstrand, 1969).
5. There is a greater percentage increase in the $\dot{V}O_2max$ when one limb is exercised following training than when both limbs are exercised (Davies & Sargent, 1975).
6. Some animals, such as the dog, have very high $\dot{V}O_2max$ per kg body weight, yet their muscles have only average oxidative potential (Musch, Haidet, Ordway, Longhurst, & Mitchell, 1985) and when trained they can experience an increase in the $\dot{V}O_2max$ without a change in mitochondrial concentration (Parsons, Musch, Moore, Haidet, & Ordway, 1985).
7. With inactivity there is a sharper decline in the concentration of mitochondrial protein than in the $\dot{V}O_2max$ (Henriksson & Reitman, 1977).

The second hypothesis is that the increase in oxidative capacity is important for metabolic regulation and the effective control of substrate flux and maintenance of the intracellular milieu. The evidence for the concept that the increase in oxidative potential is primarily for controlling substrate flux and for enhancing endurance capacity is as follows:

1. The time to exhaustion during a standard exercise test at a constant power output or when the power production is adjusted to the $\dot{V}O_2max$ is increased far more after endurance training than is the $\dot{V}O_2max$.
2. There are larger decrements in the ATP and creatine phosphate (CrP) (Karlsson, Nordesjö, Jorfeldt, & Saltin, 1972) and glycogen use is less and fat use greater (Karlsson, Nordesjö, & Saltin, 1974)

at the same absolute work load after as compared to before endurance training.

3. The intensity of exercise in which lactate (Saltin, Hartley, Kilbom, & Åstrand, 1969) and inosine monophosphate (IMP) (Dudley & Terjung, 1985) accumulates in muscle and blood is greater after as compared to before training.

Thus, it can be concluded that the increase in the concentration of mitochondrial protein that occurs in muscle is important for enhancing work capacity and not for increasing $\dot{V}O_2$max.

How Are Increases in Oxidative Potential Produced?

Once again there are two answers to this question. The first answer is that the increase in mitochondrial protein is produced by an increase in both the number and the size of the mitochondria (Gollnick & King, 1969), with the essential nature of the mitochondria being retained. An exception to this generalization is that the activity of mitochondrial α-glycerophosphate dehydrogenase does not keep pace with other mitochondrial components (Holloszy & Oscai, 1969).

The second aspect of how the increase in mitochondria is produced remains largely unknown. This is not to imply that there is no information available regarding the question of how and where mitochondrial components are synthesized and assembled within cells, but rather that there is little information as to what are the specific inducers of the process as they occur in response to the chronic exposure of muscle to high and prolonged rates of substrate flux.

Metabolic Control

What Is Known About Metabolic Control?

With muscular exercise, ATP turnover in contracting muscle fibers can be several hundred times that of rest. In spite of this tremendous use of ATP, the energy generating systems of the cell replenish ATP at a rate whereby little or no decline in its concentration occurs until very high-intensity exercise, when it may fall to 60% of the rest value (Karlsson & Saltin, 1971). This ability of skeletal muscle to increase its energy consumption without a major fall in ATP until very high work rates testifies to the exquisite control systems for mating the consumption and production of energy. Space is not available for a description of the control of individual reactions or flux through systems. Therefore only a short overview of the area is given, which considers only some aspects of control of glycogenolysis and mitochondrial oxidation.

A rapid acceleration in the flux of glucose units through the Embden-Meyerhof pathway occurs at the onset of exercise. This occurs before there is a major fall in CrP (Jacobs, Tesch, Bar-Or, Karlsson, & Dotan, 1983;

Saltin, Gollnick, Eriksson, & Piehl, 1976) within the muscle and well before a decline in ATP can be detected either with biochemical analysis of rapidly frozen muscle samples or P^{31} nuclear magnetic resonance (P^{31} NMR). With the acclerated substrate flux, there can be an increase in the glucose-6-phosphate, glucose-1-phosphate, lactate, and glucose concentrations in the muscles (Saltin & Gollnick, 1983). The result of this enhanced rate of substrate flux through the Embden-Meyerhof pathway is an increased ATP production, the delivery of pyruvate to the mitochondria for oxidation, an increased lactate production, and a decrease in muscle glycogen.

The muscle has directed considerable attention toward the control of the enzymes involved in Embden-Meyerhof pathway. The control of this process will be discussed only in terms of activation of glycogenolysis by phosphorylase (PHOS). This will illustrate only some aspects of control and it should be realized that other steps in the system, particularly that of phosphofructokinase, also are tightly controlled by a number of factors (Tornheim & Lowenstein, 1976).

Some insight into the importance that muscle cells have placed upon PHOS in the metabolic regulation can be gleaned from the fact that in some fibers between 1% and 5% of the soluble protein is either PHOS or proteins involved in its regulation (Fischer, Heilmeyer, & Haschke, 1971). This is a surprisingly large investment in cellular protein for the control of a single enzyme. PHOS is one of the most extensively studied of all enzymes, and it is known that several factors can produce increases in its phosphorolysis of glycogen in response to muscular activity. The first is its conversion from the *b* to the *a* form, which is important because PHOS *a* is active in the absence of AMP whereas PHOS *b* is not. At least two mechanisms exist for producing the *b* to *a* conversion. One is activation of phosphorylase *b* kinase by an elevation of free Ca^{2+} within the cytosol, which links glycogen degradation directly to the contractile process. A second method for the PHOS *b* to the PHOS *a* conversion is via the catecholamine activation of the adenylate cyclase system, which increases the cytosolic concentration of 3′, 5′-cyclic AMP. 3′, 5′-cyclic AMP activates phosphorylase *b* kinase to catalyze the PHOS *b* to PHOS *a* conversion. This method for PHOS activation is not essential for the initial burst of glycogenolysis at the onset of exercise (Drummond, Harwood, & Powell, 1969) but may be a method for sustaining glycogenolysis during prolonged exercise. The third method for activation of phosphorolysis is a direct activation of PHOS *b* in response to an elevated intracellular 5′-AMP. Additional control of phosphorolysis of glycogen may come from an elevation in the concentration of inorganic phosphate (Pi) in muscle during contraction, which can be more than 20-fold (from about 1 μmol/g to over 22 μmol/g; Kusmerick, 1985).

An important control of the metabolism during exercise centers on how the oxygen uptake is mated to energy consumption. Several suggestions have been proposed as to what controls the respiratory rate of muscle, including changes in some of the compounds involved in the process of total energy transduction within the muscle cell, such as ATP, ADP, AMP,

CrP, Cr, and Pi. Changes in the concentrations of these compounds, or perhaps the ratios of their concentrations within the cells, may be important. A number of these ratios have been proposed as being the factor that controls cellular respiration. Included are the energy charge ([ATP] + 1/2[ADP] / [ATP] + [ADP] + [AMP]), the phosphate potential ([ATP] / [ADP] × [Pi]), and simply the [ATP] / [ADP] ratio. The ratio of CrP to Cr has also been used to assess cellular energetics. In each of these, expression of the energy status of the muscle cell is based on a monitoring of the total adenine nucleotide pool, with it being crucial that the [ATP] be maintained at or near the rest value. The important concentrations in these expressions of the energy status of the cell are the free ($_f$) and not total concentrations. Thus, any compound bound to cellular components, such as actin-bound ADP, does not participate in the control of metabolism. In terms of absolute concentration, $[ATP]_f$ is many-fold higher (∿ 7 mmol 1^{-1}) than that of the other components, for example $[ADP]_f$ (∿ 1–10 μmol^{-1}) and Pi (∿ 1 μmol 1^{-1}). The importance of this disparity in the concentration of the principal components of the energy compounds in muscle is that it allows for a large change in any of the ratios without a major decline in the [ATP]. For example, a 10-fold change in the $[ADP]_f$ can be produced by increasing $[ADP]_f$ from 10 to 100 μmol/1^{-1}, whereas $[ATP]_f$ would be reduced only a very small amount (from 7 to 6.91 mmol 1^{-1} or less). This increase in $[ADP]_f$ would result in a concentration that is two or three times that of the Km for mitochondrial respiration. Thus, the existence of the adenine nucleotides in the ratio that they exist within muscle cells at rest results in a very sensitive system for a rapid transition from a low metabolic rate to that required for maximal activity.

ADP does produce a rapid increase in the respiratory rate of isolated mitochondria and, as indicated above, its free concentration with the muscle cell could change within the right order of magnitude to be an effective metabolic regulator. However, it is currently being debated as to whether it is $[ADP]_f$ that is transported into the mitochondria to initiate respiration or whether it is the delivery of Cr to the outer surface of the inner mitochondrial membrane. The Cr is then phosphorylated to replenish CrP, the ADP produced in the process is then cycled back into the mitochondria to stimulate respiration, and the CrP is used to rephosphorylate ADP to ATP in the cytosol. This latter scheme, referred to as the creatine shuttle, was originally proposed by Bessman and has been the subject of recent reviews (Bessman & Carpenter, 1985; Jacobus, 1985). The fact that mitochondria are much more sensitive to changes in the concentration of Cr than to ADP gives strong support to the idea that this shuttle is important in the control of cellular respiration (Jacobus, 1985).

There appear to be some changes in metabolic control as a result of training, particulary endurance training and the resulting enhancement of the total mitochondrial protein concentration of muscles. Of prime importance are (a) a delay in the accumulation of lactate in muscle and blood, (b) a decreased utilization of muscle glycogen, and (c) an increased use of fat as a fuel during exercise intensities below that which elicits $\dot{V}O_2max$.

Why Is It Necessary to Have Precise Control of Metabolism?

The answer to this question is simple and self-evident. As stated above there must be a rapid replenishment of the ATP of muscle for contractile activity to continue. Thus the processes by which this is accomplished must be controlled to mate ATP use with its production. Without precise control this system could not function as smoothly as it does. It is also important to conserve the energy stores of the muscle as much as possible. Thus, with training there appear to be some changes in the control of metabolism.

How Is Metabolic Control Altered by Exercise and Training?

At the onset of exercise there is a rapid activation of glycogenolysis catalyzed by the PHOS *b* to *a* interconversion. With continued muscular activity there is a decline in glycogenolysis that is accompanied by a fall in PHOS *a* (Cartier & Gollnick, 1985; Conlee, McLane, Rennie, Winder, & Holloszy, 1979). This fall in PHOS *a* concentration occurs in the face of a continued cycling of free calcium in the cytosol and an elevation of the catecholamines in the blood. There is no information as to how this change in control of glycogenolysis occurs during exercise; this is an area in which additional research is needed.

With training there is a shift to a greater use of fats during submaximal exercise. This produces a decline in glycogen use and a lowered accumulation of lactate in muscle and blood at the lower exercise intensities. The exact mechanisms that produce these shifts in metabolism are not completely known. The concentration of enzymes in a system appears to be one mode by which the control of reactions can be changed. This effect of concentration on the regulation of enzyme activities and on mitochondrial respiration has been discussed in some detail elsewhere (Gollnick, Riedy, Quintinskie, & Bertocci, 1985). Although a rationale for the shift in the pattern of substrate use during exercise can be developed based on kinetic considerations of the effect of a change in enzyme or mitochondrial concentration, more information is needed to firmly establish how the shift in metabolism occurs. One of the primary effects of regulating the relative use of fat and carbohydrate has been suggested as being due to a tighter control of $[ADP]_f$ and $[AMP]_f$ as a result of a greater mitochondrial sink. Considerable effort may be required to fully elucidate the effects of training on metabolic control.

The reason for the effect of variations in the availability of substrates on metabolism—why there is a shift to a greater use of fat during exercise when carbohydrates stores are low (e.g., during two-legged exercise when one leg has a reduced glycogen concentration)—is completely unknown.

For the entire problem of metabolic control it will be important to perform studies in which changes in muscle enzyme concentrations and the regulation of substrate flux after training and detraining are examined under normal, in vivo conditions.

Muscle Damage

What Is Known About Muscle Damage With Exercise?

The development of soreness in muscle following exercise is a common occurrence. It can be assumed that this soreness is a reflection of damage to some component within the muscle. In recent years, there has been an acceleration in the amount of effort devoted to understanding this process, with the general topic having been recently reviewed by Armstrong (1984). In this review, Armstrong discussed three hypotheses that have been proposed to explain the development of muscle soreness following exercise. These were (a) structural damage in the contractile and/or elastic tissues due to high tension, (b) cell membrane damage leading to a disruption of calcium homeostasis in the injured fibers that produces a cellular necrosis, and (c) stimulation of free nerve endings of Group IV sensory neurons due to accumulation in the interstitium of intracellular contents and products of macrophage activity.

There is evidence that damage may occur in different components of the muscle fibers themselves. Here it should be borne in mind that there are no nerve endings for pain within the fibers, and the sensation of pain in muscle cannot be considered as evidence for the existence of damage to the fibers. There were a number of reports some years ago, using electron microscopy, that exercise could produce a focal damage and disruption of mitochondria in the heart and skeletal muscle of the dog and rat (Gollnick & King, 1969; King & Gollnick, 1970). Gollnick and King also observed myofibrillar disruption and T-tubular swelling in response to exhaustive exercise. Similar changes were observed in the myocardium after experimentally-induced ischemia (Jennings, Baum, & Herdson, 1965). Shortly after publication of these papers, it was demonstrated (Gale, 1974; Tomanek & Banister, 1972) that, by using a different fixation method, these changes could not be observed, and the findings were dismissed as being fixation artifacts. However, it could be aruged that, although the magnitude of the disruption of tissue may not have been that depicted in the published micrographs, the tissues from the exercised and nonexercised muscles were treated similarly and the findings were indicative of an exercise-induced change in tissues. Changes in the ultrastructure of mitochondria, almost identical to those observed early in the rat, have recently been reported (Nimmo & Snow, 1982) in horse muscle after short heavy exercise and in marathon runners after competition (Warhol, Siegel, Evans, & Silverman, 1985). There are also reports of structural damage in muscle such as Z-line streaming, structural knots, and sarcolemmal disruption after exercise (Sjöström & Fridén, 1984). Thus, it appears that the early observations made it possible to identify the fact that exercise can cause damage to some components in the muscle fibers. Studies with light microscopy also indicate the existence of damage to some components of muscle.

There have also been reports of an impaired function of mitochondria prepared from the skeletal and heart muscle and livers of exhausted rats

(Dohm, Barakat, Stephenson, Pennington, & Tapscott, 1975; Dohm, Huston, Askew, & Weiser, 1972) and liver (Radeva-Domustcheiva & Russanov, 1976). Such findings were disputed for both heart and skeletal muscle (Maher et al., 1972; Terjung, Baldwin, Molé, Klinkerfuss, & Holloszy, 1972; Terjung, Klinkerfuss, Baldwin, Winder, & Holloszy, 1973). Currently it is difficult to verify either claim. The finding of no change in mitochondrial function after exercise may be an artifact of the isolation procedure. This statement is based on the fact that during the process of isolation there is a considerable mitochondrial loss due to breakage resulting from the mechanical homogenization of the tissue. As a result those mitochondria that have been damaged as a result of the exercise may be the most fragile and be preferentially lost during isolation, whereas those that remain are in fact normal. This may give the biased impression that no damage had occurred as a result of the exercise.

It is also a consistent observation that the isozymes of some enzymes that are normally found in muscle appear in the blood after strenuous exercise. Elevations in the activities of lactate dehydrogenase and creatine kinase (CK) in blood have been used as indicators of damage to skeletal muscle in response to heavy exercise. This has been interpreted as being evidence that there was sufficient damage to the muscle fibers to allow leakage of these enzymes into the blood. With severe damage to muscle, myoglobin may appear in the blood and be excreted in the urine. This condition is identified clinically as rhabdomyolysis and is indicative of severe muscle degeneration. Tidus and Ianuzzo (1983) found an early rise in serum CK activity that paralleled the subjective sensation of soreness in muscle following exercise. However, others (e.g. Newham, Jones, & Edwards, 1983) have found that, rather than a similar relationship, there was a large delay in the serum enzymes that was not as closely allied to the soreness.

Why Does Damage Occur in Muscle Tissue in Response to Exercise?

Damage to muscle appears to be the result of excessive use. It cannot be considered to be beneficial.

How Is the Damage in Muscle Produced by Exercise?

Although there is no definitive evidence that there is a single cause for the damage that occurs in muscle after exercise, several candidates exist. These are (a) a tearing of the tissue due to forces within the muscle; (b) exposure to prolonged heat; (c) a decline in muscle pH; (d) the accumulation of metabolites such as lactate, independent of the pH effect; and (e) the production and accumulation of superoxide anion radicals and hydrogen peroxide.

Evidence for a physical tearing of muscle due to mechanical forces comes from the fact that there is a greater development of pain during eccentric than concentric contractions and evidence of physical damage to the fibers that are forcefully stretched during contraction (McCully & Faulkner,

1985). This is similar to the soreness that occurs during the eccentric contractions as reported by Asmussen (1956). This has been interpreted as being due to the fewer number of motor units being engaged, with the result that there is a greater possibility for their being ruptured.

Brooks, Hittelman, Faulkner, and Beyer (1971) observed a sharp rise in state 3 oxygen consumption of mitochondria when incubations were performed between 30 °C and 45 °C. Under these conditions there was also more than a 50% decline in the respiratory control index and about a 20% decline in the ADP:O_2 ratio. These investigators also observed a muscle temperature of above 44 °C in the skeletal muscle of rats after a run to exhaustion. The temperature of human skeletal muscle has been observed to exceed 39 °C with short-term, heavy exercise (Saltin & Hermansen, 1966), whereas that of the horse has been reported to exceed 43 °C following repeated bouts of exercise (Lindholm & Saltin, 1974). Such temperatures could produce mitochondrial damage within the muscles.

The suspicion that a fall in the pH of muscle causes muscle soreness is an old one. There is ample evidence that the pH of skeletal muscle may be as low as 6.0 or lower depending upon the type and duration of exercise. However, it is difficult at this time to relate this to the structural damage that occurs in muscle following exercise. This is due in part to such empirical evidence as (a) muscle soreness can occur following relatively mild exercise in which there would probably be little or no lactate formed and no reduction in muscle pH; (b) soreness does not always exist when the exercise has been intense enough to produce lactate and when pH may be reduced; (c) following a period of training the lactate level can be higher during maximal efforts, the drop in pH greater, whereas little or no muscle soreness may develop in the muscle; and (d) the onset of soreness is often delayed, occurring and intensifying many hours (24–48) after the exercise, when the lactate would have long been cleared from the muscle and pH would have long since returned to normal.

There is, however, evidence that a reduction in pH can have adverse effects on the contractile and metabolic properties of muscle. Thus, it could be involved with the onset of fatigue during very intense exercise.

An accumulation of metabolites in skeletal muscle cannot be dismissed as a cause for muscle damage. Of the metabolites, lactate is the most likely candidate for producing such an effect. The incubation of myocardial sections in 33 μmoles lactate/g at neutral pH has been shown to produce mitochondrial damage similar to that observed following ischemia (Arminger, Gavin, & Herdson, 1974). The studies of Neely and Grotyohann (1984) also suggest that lactate and/or other metabolic intermediates may cause damage to the myocardium and to ATP-producing capacity.

The production of superoxide free radicals is known to produce tissue damage (Bulkley, 1983; McCord, 1983), and there is evidence that exhaustive exercise can result in an excessive production of superoxide anion radicals (O_2^-) and hydrogen peroxide (H_2O_2) (Davies, Quintanilha, Brooks, & Packer, 1982). Damage to tissues produced by the superoxide free radicals includes changes in tissues such as lipid peroxidation, inactivation of enzymes, membrane lysis, and alterations in DNA.

The use of changes in the activities of selected enzymes in the blood may be a method for identifying that some damage has occurred in skeletal muscle. However, there is currently inadequate information to quantitatively establish the extent of the damage in skeletal muscle from the changes in the activities of enzymes in the blood.

All of the proposed causes for muscle damage are without firm experimental support. This is an area in which considerable research is needed to identify the extent of the damage that occurs, what is causing it, and how it can be treated or prevented.

Summary

The response of skeletal muscle to altered demands is perhaps the oldest stimulus-response adaptation known to man. In spite of the long history of interest in strength, speed, and endurance and how these functions are altered by different types of training and the extensive knowledge that has accumulated over the years, major questions are unanswered as to the mechanism for the adaptation and the specific inducers of the changes. The importance of studying muscle comes from several standpoints. First, muscle disease and dysfunction are important medical problems whose solutions are being actively sought. Second, athletic performance, in humans at all levels and for some animals such as the horse, occupies an important social and economic position in the world. Finally, muscle has the greatest capacity of any tissue to increase its metabolic rate and to alter its mass in response to altered functional demands. Thus, it is an ideal tissue to use for studying systems in the process of change. It is during the process of change that mechanisms for the control of such processes are most likely to be elucidated. The current revolution in methods to study control mechanisms for protein synthesis and degradation will undoubtedly open doors for the further understanding of how cellular metabolism is regulated and how it can be altered with training. It is clear that this will be an important avenue of investigation in the next decade.

References

Aherne, W., Ayyar, D.R., Clarke, P.A., & Walton, J.N. (1971). Muscle fiber size in normal infants, children and adolescents. *Journal of the Neurological Sciences*, **14**, 171-182.

Arminger, L.C., Gavin, J.B., & Herdson, P.B. (1974). Mitochondrial changes in dog myocardium induced by neutral lactate *in vitro*. *Laboratory Investigation*, **31**, 29-33.

Armstrong, R.B. (1984). Mechanisms of exercise-induced delayed onset muscular soreness: A brief review. *Medicine and Science in Sports and Exercise*, **16**, 529-538.

Armstrong, R.B., Ianuzzo, C.D., & Kunz, T.H. (1977). Histochemical and biochemical properties of flight muscles of the little brown bat, *Myotis lucifugus*. *Journal of Comparative Physiology*, **119**, 141-154.

Asmussen, E. (1956). Observations on experimental muscular soreness. *Acta Rheumatoidia Scandinavica*, **2**, 109-116.

Bessman, S.P., & Carpenter, C.L. (1985). The creatine-creatine phosphate energy shuttle. *Annual Review of Biochemistry*, **54**, 831-862.

Bulkley, G.B. (1983). The role of oxygen free radicals in human disease process. *Surgery*, **94**, 407-411.

Brooks, G.A., Hittelman, K.J., Faulkner, J.A., & Beyer, R.E. (1971). Temperature, skeletal muscle mitochondrial functions, and oxygen debt. *American Journal of Physiology*, **220**, 1053-1059.

Cartier, L.-J. , & Gollnick, P.D. (1985). Sympathoadrenal system and activation of glycogenolysis during muscular activity. *Journal of Applied Physiology*, **58**, 1122-1127.

Clausen, J.P. (1977). Effect of physical training on cardiovascular adjustments to exercise in man. *Physiological Review*, **57**, 779-815.

Conlee, R.K., McLane, J.A., Rennie, M.J., Winder, W.W., & Holloszy, J.O. (1979). Reversal of phosphorylase activation in muscle despite continued contractile activity. *American Journal of Physiology*, **237**, R291-R296.

Colling-Saltin, A-S. (1980). Skeletal muscle development in the human fetus and during childhood. In K. Berg & B. Eriksson (Eds.), *Children and exercise IX* (pp. 193-207). Baltimore: University Park.

Davies, K.J.A., Quintanilha, A.T., Brooks, G.A., & Packer, L. (1982). Free radicals and tissue damage produced by exercise. *Biochemical Biophysical Research Communication*, **107**, 1198-1205.

Davies, C.T.M, & Sargent, A.J. (1975). Effects of training on the physiological response to one- and two-leg work. *Journal of Applied Physiology*, **38**, 377-381.

Dohm, G.L., Barakat, H., Stephenson, T.P., Pennington, S.N., & Tapscott, E.B. (1975). Changes in muscle mitochondrial lipid composition resulting from training and exhaustive exercise. *Life Science*, **117**, 1075-1080.

Dohm, G.L., Huston, R.L., Askew, E.W., & Weiser, P. (1972). Effects of exercise on activity of heart and muscle mitochondria. *American Journal of Physiology*, **223**, 783-787.

Dudley, G.A., & Terjung, R.L. (1985). Influence of aerobic metabolism on IMP accumulation in fast-twitch muscle. *American Journal of Physiology*, **248**, C37-C42.

Drummond, G.I., Harwood, J.P., & Powell, C.A. (1969). Studies on the activation of phosphorylase in skeletal muscle by contraction and by epinephrine. *The Journal of Biological Chemistry*, **244**, 4235-4240.

Ekblom, B. (1969). Effect of physical training on oxygen transport system in man. *Acta Physiologica Scandinavica*, (Suppl. 328), 5045.

Fischer, E.H., Heilmeyer, L.M.G., Haschke, R.H. (1971). Phosphorylase and the control of glycogen degradation. *Current Topics Cellular Regulation*, **4**, 211-251.

Gale, J.B. (1974). Mitochondrial swelling associated with exercise and method of fixation. *Medicine and Science in Sports*, **6**, 182-187.

Gollnick, P.D., & Hodgson, D.R. (1986). The identification of fiber types in skeletal muscle: A continual dilemma. *Exercise and Sport Sciences Reviews*, **14**, 81-104.

Gollnick, P.D., & King, D.W. (1969). Effect of exercise and training on mitochondria of rat skeletal muscle. *American Journal of Physiology*, **216**, 1502-1509.

Gollnick, P.D., Parsons, D., Riedy, M., & Moore, R.L. (1983). Fiber number and size in overloaded chicken anterior latissimus dorsi muscle. *Journal of Applied Physiology*, **54**, 1292-1297.

Gollnick, P.D., Riedy, R., Quintinskie, J.J., & Bertocci, L.A. (1985). Differences in metabolic potential of skeletal muscle fibers and their significance for metabolic control. *The Journal of Experimental Biology*, **115**, 191-199.

Hartley, L.H., Grimby, G., Kilbom, Å., Nilsson, N.J., Åstrand, I., Bjure, J., Ekblom, B., & Saltin, B. (1969). Physical training in sedentary middle-age and older men. III. Cardiac output and gas exchange at submaximal and maximal exercise. *Scandinavian Journal of Clinical and Laboratory Investigation*, **24**, 335-344.

Henriksson, J., & Reitman, J.S. (1977). Time course of changes in human skeletal muscle succinate dehydrogenase and cytochrome oxidase activities and maximal oxygen uptake with physical activity and inactivity. *Acta Physiologica Scandinavica*, **99**, 91-97.

Herring, S.W., Grimm, A.F., & Grimm, B.R. (1984). Regulation of sarcomere number in skeletal muscle: A comparison of hypotheses. *Muscle and Nerve*, **7**, 161-173.

Holloszy, J.O., Oscai, L.B. (1969). Effect of exercise on α-glycerophosphate dehydrogenase activity in skeletal muscle. *Archives of Biochemistry and Biophysics*, **130**, 653-656.

Hoppeler, H., Howald, H., Conley, K., Lindstedt, S.L., Claassen, H., Vock, P., & Weibel, E.R. (1985). Endurance training in humans: Aerobic capacity and structure of skeletal muscle. *Journal of Applied Physiology*, **59**, 320-327.

Ianuzzo, C.D., Patel, P., Chen, V., O'Brien, P., & Williams, C. (1977). Thyroidal tropic influence on skeletal muscle myosin. *Nature*, **270**, 74-76.

Jacobs, I., Tesch, P.A., Bar-Or, O., Karlsson, J., & Dotan, R. (1983). Lactate in human skeletal muscle after 10 and 30 s of supramaximal exercise. *Journal of Applied Physiology*, **55**, 365-367.

Jacobus, W.E. (1985). Respiratory control and the integration of heart high-energy phosphate metabolism by mitochondrial creatine kinase. *Annual Review of Physiology*, **47**, 707-725.

Jennings, R.G.,, Baum, J.H., & Herdson, P.B. (1965). Fine structure change in myocardial ischemic injury. *Archives of Pathology*, **79**, 135-143.

Karlsson, J., Nordesjö, L.-O., Jorfeldt, L., & Saltin, B. (1972). Muscle lactate, ATP, and CP levels during exercise after physical training in man. *Journal of Applied Physiology*, **33**, 199-203.

Karlsson, J., Nordesjö, L.-O., & Saltin, B. (1974). Muscle glycogen utilization during exercise after physical training. *Acta Physiologica Scandinavica*, **90**, 210-217.

Karlsson, J., & Saltin, B. (1971). Oxygen deficit and muscle metabolites in intermittent exercise. *Acta Physiologica Scandinavica*, **82**, 115-122.

King, D.W., & Gollnick, P.D. (1970). Ultrastructure of rat heart and liver after exhaustive exercise. *American Journal of Physiology*, **218**, 1150-1155.

Klausen, K., Secher, N.H., Clausen, J.P., Hartling, O., & Trap-Jensen, J. (1982). Central and regional circulatory adaptations to one-leg training. *Journal of Applied Physiology*, **52**, 976-983.

Kusmerick, M.J. (1985). Patterns in mammalian muscle energetics. *The Journal of Experimental Biology*, **115**, 165-177.

Lindholm, A., & Saltin, B. (1974). The physiological and biochemical response of standardbred horses to exercise of varying speed and duration. *Acta Veterinaria Scandinavica*, **15**, 1-15.

Maher, J.T., Goodman, A.L., Francesconi, R., Bowers, W.D., Hartley, L.H., & Angelakos, E.T. (1972). Responses of rat myocardium to exhaustive exercise. *American Journal of Physiology*, **222**, 207-212.

McCord, J.M. (1983). The superoxide free radical: Its biochemistry and pathophysiology. *Surgery*, **94**, 412-414.

McCully, K.K., & Faulkner, J.A. (1985). Injury to skeletal muscle fibers of mice following lengthening contractions. *Journal of Applied Physiology*, **59**, 119-126.

Mera, P.J. (1947). Post-natal growth and development of muscle, as exemplified by the gastrocnemius and psoas muscles of the rabbit. *Onderstepoort Journal of Veterinary Science and Animal Industry*, **21**, 329-482.

Musch, T.I., Haidet, G.C., Ordway, G.A., Longhurst, J.C., & Mitchell, J.H. (1985). Dynamic exercise training in foxhounds: 1. Oxygen consumption and hemodynamic response. *Journal of Applied Physiology*, **59**, 183-189.

Neely, J.B., & Grotyohann, L.W. (1984). Roll of glycolytic products in damage to ischemic myocardium. *Circulation Research*, **55**, 816-824.

Newham, D.J., Jones, D.A., Edwards, R.H.T. (1983). Large delayed plasma creatine kinase changes after stepping exercise. *Muscle and Nerve*, **6**, 380-385.

Nimmo, M.A., & Snow, D.H. (1982). Time course of ultrastructural changes in skeletal muscle after two types of exercise. *Journal of Applied Physiology*, **52**, 910-913.

Parsons, D., Musch, T.I., Moore, R.L., Haidet, G.C., & Ordway, G.A. (1985). Dynamic exercise training in foxhounds: 2. Analysis of skeletal muscle. *Journal of Applied Physiology*, **59**, 190-197.

Pette, D. (1975). Some aspects of supramolecular organization of glycogenolysis and glycolytic enzymes in muscle. *Acta Histochemica*, (Suppl. 15), 47-68.

Pette, D. (1984). Activity-induced fast to slow transitions in mammalian muscle. *Medicine and Science in Sports and Exercise*, **16**, 517-528.

Radeva-Domustcheiva, D., & Russanov, E. (1976). Effect of exhaustive swimming on the oxidative phosphorylation and the activity of some enzymes in rat liver mitochondria. *Acta Physiologica Pharmacologica Bulgaria*, **2**, 72-77.

Riedy, M., Moore, R.L., & Gollnick, P.D. (1985). Adaptive response of hypertrophied skeletal muscle to endurance training. *Journal of Applied Physiology*, **59**, 127-131.

Saltin, B., & Gollnick, P.D. (1983). Skeletal muscle adaptability: Significance for metabolism and performance. In L.D. Peach, R.H. Adrian, & S.R. Geiger (Eds.), *Handbook of physiology: Skeletal muscle* (pp. 555-631). Baltimore: Williams & Wilkins.

Saltin, B., Gollnick, P.D., Eriksson, B.O., & Piehl, K. (1976). Metabolic and circulatory adjustments at onset of maximal work. In A. Gilbert & P. Guille (Eds.), *Onset of exercise* (pp. 63-76). Toulouse, France: University of Toulouse Press.

Saltin, B., Hartley, L.H., Kilbom, Å., & Åstrand, I. (1969). Physical training in sedentary middle-age and older men: 2. Oxygen uptake, heart rate, and blood lactate concentration at submaximal and maximal exercise. *Scandinavian Journal of Clinical and Laboratory Investigation*, **24**, 323-334.

Saltin, B., & Hermansen, L. (1966). Esophageal, rectal, and muscle temperature during exercise. *Journal of Applied Physiology*, **21**, 1757-1762.

Saltin, B., Nazar, K., Costill, D.L., Stein, E., Jansson, E., Essén, B., & Gollnick, P.D. (1976). The nature of the training response: Peripheral and central adaptations to one-legged exercise. *Acta Physiologica Scandinavica*, **96**, 289-305.

Sjöström, M., & Fridén, J. (1984). Muscle soreness and muscle structure. In P. Marconnet, J. Poortmans, & L. Hermansen (Eds.), *Physiological chemistry of training and detraining* (pp. 169-186). Basel: Karger.

Terjung, R.L., Baldwin, K.M., Molé, P.A., Klinkerfuss, G.H., & Holloszy, J.O. (1972). Effect of running to exhaustion on skeletal muscle mitochondria: A biochemical study. *American Journal of Physiology*, **223**, 549-554.

Terjung, R.L., Klinkerfuss, G.H., Baldwin, K.M., Winder, W.W., & Holloszy, J.O. (1973). Effect of exhausting exercise on rat heart mitochondria. *American Journal of Physiology*, **225**, 300-305.

Tesch, P.A., Thorsson, A., & Kaiser, P. (1984). Muscle capillary supply and fiber type characteristics in weight and power lifters. *Journal of Applied Physiology*, **56**, 35-38.

Tidus, P.M., & Ianuzzo, C.D. (1983). Effects of soreness and serum enzyme activities. *Medicine and Science in Sports and Exercise*, **15**, 461-465.

Tomanek, R.J., & Banister, E.W. (1972). Myocardial ultrastructure after acute exercise stress with special reference to transverse tubules and intercalated discs. *Cardiovascular Research*, **6**, 671-679.

Tornheim, K., & Lowenstein, J.M. (1976). Control of phosphofructokinase from rat skeletal muscle. *The Journal of Biological Chemistry*, **251**, 7322-7328.

Warhol, J.M., Siegel, A.J., Evans, W.L., & Silverman, L.M. (1985). Skeletal muscle injury and repair in marathon runner after competition. *The American Journal of Pathology*, **118**, 331-339.

Temperature Regulation During Exercise: Sites, Circuits, and Neurochemistry

Carl V. Gisolfi and Ian C. Bruce

A review of the field of environmental physiology is beyond the scope of this paper and our expertise. Within the broad area, we have selected the regulation of body temperature during exercise as the focus of our report. Recent reviews in this field have dealt with circulatory adjustments to exercise and heat stress (Brengelmann, 1983), heat intolerance (Kenney, 1985), the role of aspirin in exercise-induced hyperthermia (Johnson & Ruhling, 1985), the effects of exercise and thermal stress on blood volume and fluid shifts (Harrison, 1985; Senay & Pivarnik, 1985), and the role of temperature regulation in sports performance and training (Fortney & Vroman, 1985). Although it is difficult not to overlap some of these areas, this report will focus on central mechanisms of control.

Robinson (1949) was the first investigator to examine the relationships between thermoregulatory effector responses (R) and core body temperature (T_c) and how these relationships were modified by changes in mean skin temperature (T_{sk}). This approach to the study of temperature regulation has only recently been adopted (Brengelmann, 1977; Nadel, 1977). Figure 1 shows the idealized effector response to a change in the weighted

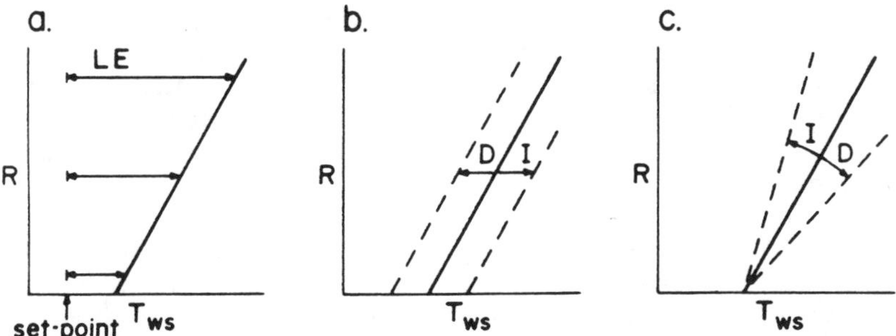

Figure 1. Schematic diagram illustrating the idealized effector response (R) to increasing T_{ws}. **(a)** Set point and threshold T_{ws} that elicits an effector response, R. R changes linearly with the load error (LE), or the difference between the set-point and T_{ws}. **(b)** Idealized (parallel shift) increase (I) or decrease (D) in threshold. **(c)** Idealized increase or decrease in gain.

sum (T_{ws}) of afferent thermal information from the core and skin (Gisolfi & Wenger, 1984). The more familiar depiction of this approach is to plot the R-T_c relation at a constant T_{sk}. T_c exerts nine times the influence of T_{sk} over R, where R is sweating or forearm blood flow (Nadel, Bullard, & Stolwijk, 1971; Wenger, Roberts, Stolwijk, & Nadel, 1975). A perturbation of the system shifts T_{ws} away from the set-point and, at some threshold, will initiate an effector response. This stress imposes a load on the system and the T_{set}-T_{ws} product is called the *load error*. Different effectors have different thresholds, but if all effector thresholds are shifted in the same direction by an intervention, the set-point of the controller is considered to have shifted in that direction. If the slope of the R-T_{ws} relation is changed, the gain or sensitivity of the response is said to have changed. Thus, by studying the effect of different interventions on the sensitivity and threshold of the different effector mechanisms, we learn much about the characteristics of the controller.

Sweating Response

In humans, 2 to 5 million eccrine sweat glands distributed over the general body surface are responsible for thermal sweating. These glands respond to both adrenergic and cholinergic stimulation, but quantitatively adrenergic-induced sweating is only 10% of cholinergic-induced sweating (Sato, 1973a). Compared with skin blood flow, the sweating response is less complicated to study because it is readily quantified and relatively independent of cardiovascular control (Solack, Brengelmann, & Freund, 1985). Moreover, eccrine glands can be isolated from biopsy specimens, and their morphology, physiology, and pharmacology can be studied in vitro (Sato, 1973b).

Exercise per se provides a nonthermal input to the thermoregulatory controller and can augment an existing sweating response (Gisolfi & Robinson, 1970; Van Beaumont & Bullard, 1963); however, the SR-T_c relationship is not altered by exercise (Johnson & Park, 1981). On the other hand, compared with an untrained and unacclimated subject, physical training in a cool environment not only decreases the T_c threshold for the onset of sweating, but also increases the sensitivity of the SR-T_c relation (Baum, Bruck, & Schwennicke, 1976; Nadel, Pandolf, Roberts, & Stolwijk, 1974). Heat acclimation produces a similar response (Nadel et al., 1974), although the shift in sweating threshold depends on the level of training of the subject.

In addition to exercise per se, other nonthermal inputs influence the SR-T_c relation. For example, hypohydration reduces its sensitivity without markedly changing its threshold (Fortney, Nadel, Wenger, & Bove, 1981), whereas increasing plasma osmolality increases the T_c threshold for the onset of sweating without markedly changing its sensitivity (Fortney, Wenger, Bove, & Nadel, 1984). For a more detailed discussion see Gisolfi and Wenger (1984).

Myers (1981) recently reviewed the neurochemistry of thermoregulation, but the control of sweating was not mentioned. The reason is the lack of an appropriate animal model to study this response. In humans, intracerebroventricular injections of cholinergic compounds elicit mild to profuse sweating together with other reactions (coughing, retching, vomiting) that are blocked by atropine sulfate similarly administered (see Crawshaw, 1979). Other likely candidates to participate in sweating control that have been shown to reduce T_c in primates are norepinephrine (Myers, 1981), dopamine (Gisolfi, Mora, & Wall, 1980), and met-enkephalin (Owen, Gisolfi, Reynolds, & Gurll, 1984).

Although indirect studies indicate that a direct effect of ADH on the sweat gland is unlikely (Jacobsson & Kjellmer, 1964; Pearcy, Robinson, Miller, Thomas, & DeBrota, 1956; Ratner & Dobson, 1964; Senay & Van Beaumont, 1969), Senay (1979) and Fortney et al. (1981) have suggested that ADH could influence sweating via a direct effect on neuronal processes within the CNS. Cooling the Preoptic Anterior Hypothalamus (POAH) of pigs exposed to hot ambient temperatures reduced plasma ADH levels (Forsling, Ingram, & Stanier, 1976; Szczepanska-Sadowska, 1974), whereas warming rats increased the hypothalamic concentration of ADH threefold above controls (Epstein, Horowitz, Bosin, Shapiro, & Glick, 1984). Intracerebroventricular injections produce hypothermia in rats (Kasting, Veale, & Cooper, 1980) and hyperthermia in rabbits (Lipton & Glyn, 1980).

Skin Blood Flow

Skin blood flow (SBF) varies primarily with changes in T_c and T_{sk}. It ranges from 200 to 500 ml/min under normal resting conditions and from 7 to 8 L/min during prolonged direct heating of the entire body (see Rowell, 1974). Total SBF can not be measured directly. Our understanding of what controls this regional vascular bed is inferred from measures of limb blood flow, assuming that underlying muscle blood flow is constant (Edholm, Fox, & MacPherson, 1956; Roddie, Shepherd, & Whelan, 1956).

During exercise, SBF does not reach maximal values observed at rest with whole body heating. The SBF:T_c relationship is shifted to the right (Johnson & Park, 1981), but this shift is not proportional to exercise intensity (Johnson, 1979; Nadel, Cafarelli, Roberts, & Wenger, 1979; Wenger et al., 1975). Other nonthermal inputs such as upright posture, hypovolemia, hyperosmolality, and positive pressure breathing also shift the SBF:T_c relationship to the right or reduce its slope (for a review, see Brengelmann, 1977; Fortney & Vroman, 1985). Training and heat-acclimation shift the relation to the left (Roberts, Wenger, Stolwijk, & Nadel, 1977). However, these shifts by themselves do not necessarily indicate a set-point shift (Gisolfi & Wenger, 1984).

Unlike the sweating response, control of SBF is influenced by both thermoregulatory and cardiovascular systems (Nadel, 1980; Rowell, 1977). During exercise, these two systems compete, and SBF is the result of opposing drives from exercise-induced vasoconstriction and heat-induced vasodilation. The result of this competition is an increase in SBF, which is produced by an initial decline in constrictor tone in veins and resistance vessels (Fox, Goldsmith, Kidd, & Lewis, 1963; Wenger & Roberts, 1980) followed by active vasodilation (AVD) (Blair, Glover, & Roddie, 1960). The latter process requires an intact sympathetic nervous system, but the precise mechanism underlying the response is unknown (Fox & Edholm, 1963; Greenfield, 1963; Rowell, 1981). It has been linked to sudorific activity, but increments in sweating and SBF do not always parallel each other (Senay, Prokop, Cronau, & Hertzman, 1963; Wyss, Brengelmann, Johnson, Rowell, & Silverstein, 1975). Bradykinin has been implicated in the process (Fox & Hilton, 1958), but supporting evidence is weak (Rowell, 1981).

More recent studies from the Seattle group have provided renewed support for a link between sweating and AVD. In a patient with a healed skin graft in which no sweat glands survived, AVD did not occur after elevating internal temperature 1 °C to 1.5 °C (Freund, Brengelmann, Rowell, Engrav, & Heimbach, 1981). Moreover, in patients with anhidrotic ectodermal dysplasia (congenital absence of sweat glands), elevations in oral temperature by 1.4 °C to 1.7 °C, as a result of whole body heating, failed to produce measurable sweating or a significant rise in SBF (Brengelmann, Freund, Rowell, Olerud, & Kraning, 1981). In a case study of a patient with acquired anhidrosis, however, an exercise-induced rise in T_c provoked a normal vasodilation even though there was no measurable sweating on the same forearm (B. Wenger, personal communication, January, 1986).

Future Directions

Primate Models

Research investigating the central control of sweating and SBF has been limited by the availability of appropriate animal models. Few animals possess functional sweat glands, and no animal has been shown to possess a cutaneous vascular bed with an active vasodilatory system. Thermal balance studies in rhesus (Johnson & Elizondo, 1983), patas (Kolka & Elizondo, 1983; Mahoney, 1980), squirrel (Stitt & Hardy, 1971), and Japanese monkeys (Nakayama, Hori, Nagasaka, Tokura, & Takadi, 1971) indicate that these animals regulate their body temperature in a manner similar to humans; but in the latter two species, evaporative cooling is limited and these animals rely primarily on behavioral adjustments and vasomotor control to regulate body temperature. In rhesus monkeys, eccrine sweat gland histology, histochemistry, distribution, innervation, and pharmacology are similar to those in humans (Johnson & Elizondo, 1974); however, heat loss by evaporative cooling does not exceed their resting metabolic rate (Johnson & Elizondo, 1983). In contrast, patas monkeys sweat considerably more than rhesus monkeys and can maintain thermal balance at ambient temperatures in excess of 40 °C (Kolka & Elizondo, 1983; Mahoney, 1980). In a case study, Mahoney (1980) found that a 6-kg patas monkey dissipated 80% of its heat load by evaporative cooling while running 16 km•hr^{-1} (eight times resting metabolic rate) at an ambient temperature of 53 °C. If evaporation is prevented by covering the skin of these animals with polyethylene they become hyperthermic when exposed to heat (Sugiyama & Tokura, 1974).

The patas monkey possesses cholinergic eccrine sweat glands over the general body surface that can be activated by heating the hypothalamus with water-perfused thermodes (Gisolfi, Owen, Wall, & Kregel, 1988; Gisolfi, Sato, Wall, & Sato, 1982). The SR-T_{HYPO} relation is similar to the SR-T_c relation in humans and shows similar shifts with changes in T_{sk}. These animals can also be conditioned to exercise (Gisolfi, Mora, Natterman, & Myers, 1978), and their sweat glands can be biopsied and studied in vitro (Gisolfi et al., 1982). Thus, an animal model has been developed that allows us to study central mechanisms of temperature regulation as well as the isolated sweat gland.

Central Mechanisms

Thus far we have described how the R-T_c relationships are modified by different perturbations and how at least the sweating response can be simulated in an animal model. However, the sites of action, neuronal circuits, and neurochemical correlates associated with these responses are unknown. Thermosensitive neurons are located not only in the preoptic anterior hypothalamus (Boulant & Hardy, 1974; Eisenman & Jackson, 1967; Hardy, Hellon, & Sutherland, 1964; Hellon, 1967; Nakayama, Eisenman, & Hardy, 1961; Nakayama, Hammel, Hardy, & Eisenman, 1963), but also in the midbrain reticular formation (Nakayama & Hardy, 1969), medulla (Cronin & Baker, 1976); Hori & Harada, 1976; Inoue & Murakami, 1976), posterior hypothalamus (Edinger & Eisenman, 1970), and spinal cord (Simon, 1974; Thauer, 1970). Moreover, they are sensitive not only to changes in their own local temperature, but also to other brain temperatures, spinal temperature, and/or skin temperature (Hellon, 1970, 1972; Nakayama, Ishikawa, & Tsurutani, 1979; Nutik, 1973). Some are also sensitive to osmotic pressure, metabolites, and endocrines (Silva & Boulant, 1984).

Development of the in vitro perfused tissue slice technique has provided a tool to study how individual neurons respond to endogenous factors (Kelso, Nelson, Silva, & Boulant, 1983). By perfusing these tissue slices with nutrient media containing synaptic blocking agents (high [Mg^{2+}] or low [Ca^{2+}]), it has been shown that POAH cold sensitive neurons depend on chemically mediated synaptic input whereas warm-sensitivity is an independent property of certain POAH neurons (Kelso & Boulant, 1982). A disadvantage of this technique is that the tissue slice is devoid of normal afferent input. Furthermore, electrotonic junctions have been found in the inferior olive (Llinas, 1981), and in slice preparations of the hippocampus (MacVicar & Dudek, 1981), and magnocellular regions of the hypothalamus (Cobbett & Hatton, 1984). Thus, the possibility remains that synaptic interactions continue in the presence of high Mg^{2+}/low Ca^{2+}.

In contrast to the rather pessimistic view of the future usefulness of single unit recording expressed by Hellon (1981), we propose that the new technologies that have revolutionized our understanding of the central control of movement will be equally powerful in the area of temperature regulation, especially in the context of exercise. Temperature regulation can be thought of as a special case of motor control, the inputs being thermal feedback and central commands, the outputs comprising a wide spectrum of autonomic and skeletal effector systems. In addition to the capability for recording in the awake, behaving brain uncontaminated by anesthetics (e.g., Gerber, Kussman, & Heller, 1984), the combination of axonal tracing techniques with microstimulation and averaging methods are likely to prove essential to defining the structural and functional characteristics of the neuronal circuits that control temperature.

For a variety of reasons (whose consideration lies outside the scope of this article), it appears that many of the new techniques developed over the past two decades have been successfully applied in some areas, for example, in revealing functional mechanisms underlying the control of movement, but have not rapidly diffused into other fields of study. The following section is an attempt to argue the case for adapting some of the most potentially useful methods to the study of temperature regulation. In brief, these techniques provide essential information of the following kinds:

1. Single unit recording (see Lemon, 1984, for a detailed review of methods). As an initial step, it is crucial to ascertain whether neurons in a given region are directly involved in processing thermal information as opposed to, for example, the pain pathways on the afferent side, or the numerous homeostatic mechanisms regulated from the hypothalamus on the efferent side. As noted above, single unit recordings have revealed a number of regions containing temperature-sensitive neurons, and Boulant and others have demonstrated that temperature sensitivity provides strong, if not unequivocal, identification of a given neuron as being directly involved in thermoregulation (see Boulant, 1980). However, once the identification has been made, single unit recording must be combined with other approaches.
2. Axonal tracing techniques. Retrograde and anterograde tracing methods provide anatomical information concerning the distributions of neurons projecting to the injected structure (retrograde, e.g., horseradish peroxidase), and of the terminals of neurons projecting from the injected structure (anterograde, e.g., tritiated amino acids) (see Saint Cyr, 1983). The advantages of such methods, especially in the POAH, where tracts and nuclei are intermingled, are that the tracers are not readily taken up by axons, and that they do not readily cross synaptic clefts. Consequently, careful application of such tracers to those nuclei containing temperature-sensitive neurons identified for single unit studies provides candidate structures for their inputs and outputs. Nevertheless, as before, we cannot assume that the candidate structures are specifically involved in temperature regulation.

3. Microstimulation. First developed in studies of the motor cortex (Stoney, Thompson, & Asanuma, 1968), this method uses small (3 to 10 μA) currents delivered through microelectrodes to activate limited numbers of neurons in the vicinity of the electrode tip. The major advantages of this method are that single unit recordings can be made through the same electrode, and known volumes of tissue can be activated. In the application considered here, two microelectrodes are required. A number of configurations are possible, of which one could be a recording electrode in a region containing temperature-sensitive neurons (for ease of description, let this be Area A) and a second in one of its afferent projections previously identified by retrograde tracing (Area B). Microstimulation in Area B then provides a means of determining the functional effects of afferent activity on Area A neurons identified as temperature-sensitive. The necessary data are extracted by averaging.
4. Stimulus-triggered averaging (see Cheney & Fetz, 1985). The unpredictable levels of spontaneous activity in POAH neurons have posed problems in the interpretation of changes of activity in response to environmental perturbations (discussed by Boulant, 1980). The contribution of a small population of afferents would almost certainly be obscured by this background noise in examination of the raw data. However, by taking advantage of computer averaging, we can reveal and quantify the response(s). Simply put, the response is time-locked to the stimulus, whereas spontaneous activity occurs randomly with respect to the stimulus. So, by averaging the events following the stimulus, we average out the spontaneous activity, whereas the stimulus-locked activity remains (see Kirkwood & Sears, 1980, for a detailed discussion). Such averaged records provide the latency of the input, and the nature of its effect (excitation and/or inhibition, or no effect).

The following conclusions could be drawn from such a thought experiment: (a) At least some of the neurons in Area A are temperature-sensitive (determined by single unit recording). (b) Neurons in Area A receive afferent projections from Areas B, C, D, and themselves project to Areas I, II, III. (c) At least some of the neurons in Area B are/are not temperature-sensitive (determined by single unit recording). (d) The latency of the pathway from Area B to temperature-sensitive neurons in Area A is n ms (determined by microstimulation and averaging). This value reflects the diameters of axons and the number of synapses in the pathway. (e) Temperature-sensitive neurons in Area A are excited and/or inhibited or unaffected by neural activity in Area B (determined by microstimulation and averaging).

Therefore, by combining the above approach with the experimental armamentarium readily available in laboratories devoted to the study of temperature regulation, we can evaluate and improve existing models, designing them to account for the directly observed interactions between neurons in defined thermoregulatory pathways.

Although axonal tracing methods combined with catecholamine fluorescence and immunohistochemical techniques identify the locations and transmitter biochemistry of neurons of interest, they provide no information as to whether a given pathway is directly involved in temperature control (as opposed to, for example, nociception or osmoregulation), whether connections are excitatory or inhibitory, and how the afferent/efferent signals are modulated along a given pathway. For example, axonal tracing techniques have revealed direct inputs to the POAH from brain stem structures associated with pain and temperature (nucleus of the solitary tract), with cardiac and intestinal control (vagus nucleus), and with a plethora of autonomic and skeletomotor functions (reticular nuclei) (Conrad & Pfaff, 1976; Day, Blessing, & Willoughby, 1980; Sakumoto et al., 1978; Sofroniev & Schrell, 1980). Combining single unit recording in the POAH (to identify neurons as temperature-sensitive) with microstimulation in the projection nuclei (to establish excitatory or inhibitory linkages) would provide data essential to understanding the participation of these pathways in temperature control.

Let us consider how these methods might be applied to an existing model for temperature control. Of the various schemes discussed by Hardy (1972) we will, for simplicity of description, use the chemical model proposed by Myers (1970). The model first requires input from peripheral thermoreceptors to the POAH along presently unknown pathways. Dickenson (1977) used single unit recordings to demonstrate that neurons of the nucleus raphe magnus receive input from cutaneous thermoreceptors. However, transport of tracer between the POAH and the raphe has not, to our knowledge, been reported. Is the nucleus raphe magnus a relay with a polysynaptic projection to the POAH, as postulated by Hellon (1981)? A detailed analysis of neurons filled from anterograde tracer injections into the raphe and retrograde tracers into the POAH would provide likely targets, whereas single unit recording combined with averaging could begin to define the functional impact of raphe activity (if any) upon the activity of thermosensitive POAH neurons.

Similar considerations apply to the polysynaptic connection from the POAH to the posterior hypothalamus proposed in the model. Tracer studies may be used in defining intrahypothalamic pathways, as for example, they have revealed a projection from the POAH to the paraventricular nucleus (Tribollet & Dreifuss, 1981).

Finally, the Myers (1981) model places the posterior hypothalamus at the effector end of the circuit, with projections to heat loss/gain structures in the mesencephalon and lower regions. As noted above, the posterior hypothalamus projects to a number of potential effector circuits. Again, the methods of microstimulation, single unit recording, and averaging at sites selected on the basis of detailed anatomical information could do much to elucidate the underlying mechanisms. Of particular interest in the context of exercise is the application of such techniques to exploring interactions between known temperature control regions and the subthalamic, mesencephalic, and pontine locomotor regions (see review by Grillner, 1981).

Acknowledgments

The authors thank Ms. Joan Seye for preparation of the manuscript. Supported by NIH Grants HL38959 and HL32731.

References

Baum, K., Bruck, K., & Schwennicke, J.P. (1976). Adaptive modifications in the thermoregulatory system of long-distance runners. *Journal of Applied Physiology*, **40**, 404-410.

Blair, D.A., Glover, W.E., & Roddie, I.C. (1960). Vasomotor fibers to skin in the upper arm, calf, and thigh. *Journal of Physiology* (London), **153**, 232-238.

Boulant, J.A. (1980). Hypothalamic control of thermoregulation: Neurophysiological basis. In J.P. Morgane & J. Panskepp (Eds.), *Handbook of the hypothalamus: Vol. 3. PTA* (pp. 1-82) New York: Marcel Dekker.

Boulant, J.A., & Hardy, J.D. (1974). The effect of spinal and skin temperatures on the firing rate and thermosensitivity of preoptic neurones. *Journal of Physiology* (London), **240**, 639-660.

Brengelmann, G.L. (1977). Control of sweating and skin blood flow during exercise. In E.R. Nadel (Ed.), *Problems with temperature regulation during exercise* (pp. 27-48). New York: Academic Press.

Brengelmann, G.L. (1983). Circulatory adjustments to exercise and heat stress. *Annual Review of Physiology*, **45**, 191-212.

Brengelmann, G.L., Freund, P.R., Rowell, L.B., Olerud, J.E., & Kraning, K.K. (1981). Absence of active cutaneous vasodilation associated with congenital absence of sweat glands in humans. *American Journal of Physiology*, **240**, H571-H575.

Cheney, P.D., & Fetz, E.E. (1985). Comparable patterns of muscle facilitation evoked by individual corticomotoneuronal (CM) cells and by single intracortical microstimuli in primates: Evidence for functional groups of CM cells. *Journal of Neurophysiology*, **53**, 786-804.

Cobbett, P., & Hatton, G.I. (1984). Dye coupling in hypothalamic slices: Dependence on in vivo hydration state and osmolality of incubation medium. *Journal of Neuroscience*, **4**, 3034-3038.

Conrad, L.C.A., & Pfaff, D.W. (1976). Efferents from medial basal forebrain and hypothalamus in the rat: 2. An autoradiographic study of the anterior hypothalamus. *Journal of Comparative Neurology*, **169**, 221-262.

Crawshaw, L.I. (1979). Acetylcholine. In P. Lomax & E. Schonbaum (Eds.), *Body temperature: Regulation, drug effects, and therapeutic implications* (pp. 305-335). New York: Dekker.

Cronin, M.J., & Baker, M.A. (1976). Heat-sensitive midbrain raphe neurons in the anesthetized cat. *Brain Research*, **110**, 175-181.

Day, T.A., Blessing, W., & Willoughby, J.O. (1980). Noradrenergic and dopaminergic projections to the medial preoptic area of the rat. A combined horseradish peroxidase/catecholamine fluorescence study. *Brain Research*, **193**, 543-548.

Dickenson, A.H. (1977). Specific responses of rat raphe neurones to skin temperature. *Journal of Physiology* (London), **273**, 277-293.

Edholm, O.G., Fox, R.H., & MacPherson, R.K. (1956). The effect of body heating on the circulation in skin and muscle. *Journal of Physiology* (London), **134**, 610-612.

Edinger, H.M., & Eisenman, J.S. (1970). Thermosensitive neurons in tuberal and posterior hypothalamus of cats. *American Journal of Physiology*, **219**, 1098-1103.

Eisenman, J.S., & Jackson, D.C. (1967). Thermal response patterns of septal and preoptic neurons in cats. *Experimental Neurology*, **19**, 33-45.

Epstein, Y., Horowitz, M., Bosin, E., Shapiro, Y., & Glick, S.M. (1984). Changes in vasopressin distribution in brain of heat-stressed and heat-acclimated rats. In J.R.S. Hales (Ed.), *Thermal physiology* (pp. 137-140). New York: Raven Press.

Forsling, M.L., Ingram, D.L., & Stanier, M.W. (1976). Effects of various ambient temperatures and of heating and cooling the hypothalamus and cervical spinal cord on antidiuretic hormone secretion and urinary osmolality in pigs. *Journal of Physiology*, **257**, 673-686.

Fortney, S.M., Nadel, E.R., Wenger, C.B., & Bove, J.R. (1981). Effect of blood volume on sweating rate and body fluids in exercising humans. *Journal of Applied Physiology*, **51**, 1594-1600.

Fortney, S.M., Wenger, C.B., Bove, J.R., & Nadel, E.R. (1984). Effect of hyperosmolality on control of blood flow and sweating. *Journal of Applied Physiology*, **57**, 1688-1695.

Fortney, S.M., & Vroman, N.B. (1985). Exercise, performance and temperature control: Temperature regulation during exercise and implications for sports performance and training. *Sports Medicine*, **2**, 8-20.

Fox, R.H., & Edholm, O.G. (1963). Nervous control of the cutaneous circulation. *British Medical Bulletin*, **19**, 110-114.

Fox, R.H., Goldsmith, R., Kidd, D.J., & Lewis, H.E. (1963). Blood flow and other thermoregulatory changes with acclimatization to heat. *Journal of Physiology* (London), **166**, 548-562.

Fox, R.H., & Hilton, S.M. (1958). Bradykinin formation in human skin as a factor in heat vasodilation. *Journal of Physiology* (London), **142**, 219-232.

Freund, P.R., Brengelmann, G.L., Rowell, L.B., Engrav, L., & Heimbach, D.M. (1981). Vasomotor control in healed grafted skin in man. *Journal of Applied Physiology*, **51**, 168-171.

Gerber, R.L., Kussman, F.W., & Heller, H.C. (1984). Preoptic/anterior hypothalamic neuron responses to thermal stimulation of the hypothalamus and spinal cord in unanesthetized, unrestrained rabbits. In J.R.S. Hales (Ed.), *Thermal physiology* (pp. 83-86). New York: Raven Press.

Gisolfi, C., Mora, F., Nattermann, R., & Myers, R.D. (1978). New apparatus for exercising a monkey seated in a primate chair. *Journal of Applied Physiology*, **44**, 129-132.

Gisolfi, C.V., Mora, F., & Wall, P.T. (1980). Dopamine and temperature regulation in the primate: Effects of apomorphine and pimozide. *Brain Research Bulletin*, **5**, 349-352.

Gisolfi, C.V., Owen, M.D., Wall, P.T., & Kregel, K.C. (1988). Effects of changing hypothalamic temperature on eccrine sweating in the patas monkey. *Brain Research Bulletin*, **20**, 179-182.

Gisolfi, C., & Robinson, S. (1970). Central and peripheral stimuli regulating sweating during intermittent work in man. *Journal of Applied Physiology*, **29**, 761-768.

Gisolfi, C.V., Sato, K., Wall, P.T., & Sato, F. (1982). In vivo and in vitro characteristics of eccrine sweating in patas and rhesus monkeys. *Journal of Applied Physiology*, **53**, 425-431.

Gisolfi, C.V., & Wenger, C.B. (1984). Temperature regulation during exercise: Old concepts, new ideas. In R.L. Terjung (Ed.), *Exercise and sport science reviews: Vol. 12* (pp. 338-372). Lexington, MA: D.C. Heath.

Greenfield, A.D.M. (1963). The circulation through the skin. In *Handbook of physiology: Circulation* (pp. 1325-1351). Washington, DC: American Physiological Society.

Grillner, S. (1981). Control of locomotion in bipeds, tetrapods and fish. In J.M. Brookhart & V.B. Mountcastle (Eds.), *Handbook of physiology: Sec. 1. Vol. II. Part 2* (pp. 1179-1236). Bethesda: American Physiological Society.

Hardy, J.D. (1972). Models of temperature regulation—A review. In J. Bligh & R. Moore (Eds.), *Essays on temperature regulation* (pp. 163-186) Amsterdam: North-Holland.

Hardy, J.D., Hellon, R.F., & Sutherland, K. (1964). Temperature-sensitive neurones in the dog's hypothalamus. *Journal of Physiology* (London), **175**, 242-253.

Harrison, M.H. (1985). Effects of thermal stress and exercise on blood volume in humans. *Physiological Reviews*, **65**, 149-209.

Hellon, R.F. (1967). Thermal stimulation of hypothalamic neurones in unanesthetized rabbits. *Journal of Physiology* (London), **193**, 381-395.

Hellon, R.F. (1970). The stimulation of hypothalamic neurones by changes in ambient temperature. *Pflüegers Archiv*, **321**, 56-66.

Hellon, R.F. (1972). Temperature-sensitive neurones in the brain stem: Their responses to brain temperature at different ambient temperatures. *Pflüegers Archiv*, **335**, 323-334.

Hellon, R.F. (1981). Neurophysiology of temperature regulation: Problems and perspectives. *Federation Proceedings*, **40**, 2804-2807.

Hori, T., & Harada, Y. (1976). Responses of midbrain raphe neurons to local temperature. *Pflüegers Archiv*, **364**, 205-207.

Inoue, S., & Murakami, N. (1976). Unit responses in the medulla oblongata of rabbit to changes in local and cutaneous temperatures. *Journal of Physiology* (London), **259**, 339-356.

Jacobsson, S., & Kjellmer, I. (1964). Accumulation of fluid in exercising skeletal muscle. *Acta Physiological Scandinavica*, **60**, 286-292.

Johnson, J.M. (1979). Responses of forearm blood flow to graded leg exercise in man. *Journal of Applied Physiology*, **46**, 457-462.

Johnson, G.S., & Elizondo, R.S. (1974). Eccrine sweat gland in Macaca mulatta: Physiology, histochemistry, and distribution. *Journal of Applied Physiology*, **37**, 814-820.

Johnson, G.S., & Elizondo, R.S. (1983). Thermoregulation in Macaca mulatta: A thermal balance study. *Journal of Applied Physiology*, **46**, 268-277.

Johnson, J.M., & Park, M.K. (1981). Effect of upright exercise on threshold for cutaneous vasodilation and sweating. *Journal of Applied Physiology*, **50**, 814-818.

Johnson, S.C., & Ruhling, R.O. (1985). Aspirin in exercise-induced hyperthermia: Evidence for and against its role. *Sports Medicine*, **2**, 1-7.

Kasting, N.W., Veale, W.L., & Cooper, K.E. (1980). Convulsive and hypothermic effects of vasopressin in the brain of the rat. *Canadian Journal of Physiology and Pharmacology*, **58**, 316-319.

Kelso, S.R., & Boulant, J.A. (1982). Effect on synaptic blockade on thermosensitive neurons in hypothalamic tissue slices. *American Journal of Physiology*, **243**, R480-R490.

Kelso, S.R., Nelson, D.O., Silva, N.L., & Boulant, J.A. (1983). A slice chamber for intracellular and extracellular recording during continuous perfusion. *Brain Research Bulletin*, **10**, 853-857.

Kenney, W.L. (1985). Physiological correlates of heat intolerance. *Sports Medicine*, **2**, 279-286.

Kirkwood, P.A., & Sears, T.A. (1980). The measurement of synaptic connections in the mammalian central nervous system by means of spike triggered averaging. *Progress in Clinical Neurophysiology*, **8**, 44-71.

Kolka, M.A., & Elizondo, G.S. (1983). Thermoregulation in Erythrocebus patas: A thermal balance study. *Journal of Applied Physiology*, **55**, 1603-1608.

Lemon, R. (1984). *Methods for neuronal recording in conscious animals*. Chichester: Wiley.

Lipton, J.M., & Glyn, J.R. (1980). Central administration of peptides alters thermoregulation in the rabbit. *Peptides*, **1**, 15-18.

Llinas, R.R. (1981). Electrophysiology of cerebellar networks. In J.M. Brookhart & V.B. Mountcastle (Eds.), *Handbook of physiology: Sec. 1. Vol. 2. Part 2* (pp. 831-876). Bethesda: American Physiological Society.

MacVicar, B.A., & Dudek, F.E. (1981). Electrotonic coupling between pyramidal cells: A direct demonstration in rat hippocampal slices. *Science*, **213**, 782-785.

Mahoney, S.A. (1980). Cost of locomotion and heat balance during rest and running from 0 to 55 °C in patas monkey. *Journal of Applied Physiology*, **49**, 789-800.

Myers, R.D. (1970). Hypothalamic mechanisms of pyrogen action in the cat and monkey. In Joan Birch (Ed.), *Ciba Symposium on "Pyrogens and Fever"* (pp. 131-153). London: Churchill.

Myers, R.D. (1981). Hypothalamic control of thermoregulation: Neurochemical mechanisms. In P. Morgane & J. Panksepp (Eds.), *Handbook of the hypothalamus: Vol. 3. Part A. Behavioral studies of the hypothalamus* (pp. 83-210). New York: Marcel Dekker.

Nadel, E.R. (1980). Circulatory and thermal regulation during exercise. *Federation Proceedings*, **39**, 1491-1497.

Nadel, E.R. (Ed.). (1977). *Problems with temperature regulation during exercise*. New York: Academic Press.

Nadel, E.R., Bullard, R.W., & Stolwijk, J.A.J. (1971). Importance of skin temperature in the regulation of sweating. *Journal of Applied Physiology*, **31**, 80-87.

Nadel, E.R., Cafarelli, E., Roberts, M.F., & Wenger, C.B. (1979). Circulatory regulation during exercise in different ambient temperatures. *Journal of Applied Physiology*, **46**, 430-437.

Nadel, E.R., Pandolf, K.B., Roberts, M.F., & Stolwijk, J.A.J. (1974). Mechanisms of thermal acclimation to exercise and heat. *Journal of Applied Physiology*, **37**, 515-520.

Nakayama, T., Eisenman, J.S., & Hardy, J.D. (1961). Single unit activity of anterior hypothalamus during local heating. *The Sciences*, **134**, 560-561.

Nakayama, T., Hammel, H.T., Hardy, J.D., & Eisenman, J.S. (1963). Thermal stimulation of electrical activity of single units in the preoptic region. *American Journal of Physiology*, **204**, 1122-1126.

Nakayama, T., & Hardy, J.D. (1969). Unit responses in the rabbit's brain stem to changes in brain and cutaneous temperature. *Journal of Applied Physiology*, **27**, 848-857.

Nakayama, T., Hori, T., Nagasaka, T., Tokura, H., & Takadi, E. (1971). Thermal and metabolic responses in the Japanese monkey at temperatures of 5–38 °C. *Journal of Applied Physiology*, **31**, 332-337.

Nakayama, T., Ishikawa, Y., & Tsurutani, T. (1979). Projection of scrotal thermal afferents to the preoptic and hypothalamic neurons in rats. *Pflüegers Archives*, **380**, 59-64.

Nutik, S.L. (1973). Posterior hypothalamic neurons responsive to preoptic region thermal stimulation. *Journal of Neurophysiology*, **36**, 238-249.

Owen, M.D., Gisolfi, C.V., Reynolds, D.G., & Gurll, N.J. (1984). Effects of central injections of D-ala^2-met-enkephalinamide (DAME) in the monkey. *Peptides*, **5**, 737-742.

Pearcy, M., Robinson, S., Miller, D.I., Thomas, J.T., & DeBrota, J. (1956). Effects of dehydration, salt depletion and pitressin on sweat rate and urine flow. *Journal of Applied Physiology*, **8**, 621-626.

Ratner, A.C., & Dobson, R.L. (1964). The effect of antidiuretic hormone on sweating. *Journal of Investigative Dermatology*, **43**, 379-381.

Roberts, M.F., Wenger, C.B., Stolwijk, J.A.J., & Nadel, E.R. (1977). Skin blood flow and sweating changes following exercise training and heat acclimation. *Journal of Applied Physiology*, **43**, 133-137.

Robinson, S. (1949). Physiological adjustments to heat. In L.H. Newburg (Ed.), *Physiology of heat regulation and the science of clothing* (pp. 193-231). Philadelphia: Saunders.

Roddie, I.C., Shepherd, J.T., & Whelan, R.F. (1956). Evidence from venous oxygen saturation measurements that the increase in forearm blood flow during body heating is confined to the skin. *Journal of Physiology* (London), **134**, 444-450.

Rowell, L.B. (1974). The cutaneous circulation. In T.C. Ruch & H.D. Patton (Eds.), *Physiology and biophysics: Vol. 2* (pp. 185-199). Philadelphia: Saunders.

Rowell, L.B. (1977). Competition between skin and muscle for blood flow during exercise. In E.R. Nadel (Ed.), *Problems with temperature regulation during exercise* (pp. 49-76). New York: Academic Press.

Rowell, L.B. (1981). Active neurogenic vasodilation in man. In P.M. Van Houtte & I. Leusen (Eds.), *Vasodilation* (pp. 1-17). New York: Raven Press.

Saint Cyr, J.A. (1983). The projection from the motor cortex to the inferior olive in the cat: An experimental study using axonal transport techniques. *Neuroscience*, **10**, 667-684.

Sakumoto, T., Toyhama, M., Satoh, K., Kimoto, V., Kinugasa, T., Tanizawa, O., Kurachi, K., & Shimizu, N. (1978). Afferent fibre connections from lower brain stem to hypothalamus studied by the horseradish peroxidase method with special reference to noradrenaline innervation. *Experimental Brain Research*, **31**, 81-94.

Sato, K. (1973a). Stimulation of pentase cycle in the eccrine sweat gland by adrenergic drugs. *American Journal of Physiology*, **224**, 1149-1154.

Sato, K. (1973b). Sweat induction from an isolated eccrine sweat gland. *American Journal of Physiology*, **225**, 1147-1152.

Senay, L.C., Jr. (1979). Temperature regulation and hypohydration: A singular view. *Journal of Applied Physiology*, **47**, 1-7.

Senay, L.C., & Pivarnik, J.M. (1985). Fluid shifts during exercise. In R.T. Terjung (Ed.), *Exercise and sport sciences reviews: Vol. 13* (pp. 335-387). Lexington, MA: D.C. Heath.

Senay, L.C., Jr., Prokop, L.D., Cronau, L., & Hertzman, A.B. (1963). Relation of local skin temperature and local sweating to cutaneous blood flow. *Journal of Applied Physiology*, **18**, 781-785.

Senay, L.C., Jr., & Van Beaumont, W. (1969). Antidiuretic hormone and evaporative weight loss during the heat stress. *Pflüegers Archiv*, **312**, 82-90.

Silva, N.L., & Boulant, J.A. (1984). Effects of osmotic pressure, glucose, and temperature on neurons in preoptic tissue slices. *American Journal of Physiology*, **247**, R335-R345.

Simon, E. (1974). Temperature regulation: The spinal cord as a site of extrahypothalamic thermoregulatory functions. *Review of Physiology, Biochemistry, and Pharmacology*, **71**, 1-76.

Sofroniev, M.V., & Schrell, U. (1980). Hypothalamic neurons projecting to the rat caudal medulla oblongata, examined by immunoperoxidase staining of retrogradely transported horseradish peroxidase. *Neuroscience Letters*, **19**, 257-263.

Solack, S.D., Brengelmann, G.L., & Freund, P.R. (1985). Sweat rate vs. forearm blood flow during lower body negative pressure. *Journal of Applied Physiology*, **58**, 1546-1552.

Stoney, S.D., Thompson, W.D., & Asanuma, H. (1968). Excitation of pyramidal tract cells by intracortical microstimulation: Effective extent of stimulating current. *Journal of Physiology*, **31**, 659-669.

Stitt, J.T., & Hardy, J.D. (1971). Thermoregulation in the squirrel monkey (Saimiri sciureus). *Journal of Applied Physiology*, **31**, 48-54.

Sugiyama, K., & Tokura, H. (1974). Sweating in the patas monkey (Erythrocebus patas) exposed to a hot ambient temperature. In S. Kondo, M. Kawai, & A. Ehara (Eds.), *Contemporary primatology* (pp. 189-192). Basel: Kargel.

Szczepanska-Sadowska, E. (1974). Plasma ADH increase and thirst suppression elicited by preoptic heating in the dog. *American Journal of Physiology*, **226**, 155-161.

Thauer, R. (1970). Thermosensitivity of the spinal cord. In J.D. Hardy, A.P. Gagge, & J.A.J. Stolwijk (Eds.), *Physiology and behavioral temperature regulation* (pp. 472-492). Springfield, IL: Thomas.

Triobollet, E., & Dreifuss, J.J. (1981). Localization of neurones projecting to the hypothalamic paraventricular nucleus area of the rat: A horseradish peroxidase study. *Neuroscience*, **6**, 1315-1328.

Van Beaumont, W., & Bullard, R.W. (1963). Sweating: Its rapid response to work. *Science*, **141**, 643-646.

Wenger, C.B., & Roberts, M.F. (1980). Control of forearm venous volume during exercise and body heating. *Journal of Applied Physiology*, **48**, 114-119.

Wenger, C.B., Roberts, M.F., Stolwijk, J.A.J., & Nadel, E.R. (1975). Forearm blood flow during body temperature transients produced by leg exercise. *Journal of Applied Physiology*, **38**, 58-63.

Wyss, C.R., Brengelmann, G.L., Johnson, J.M., Rowell, L.B., & Silverstein, D. (1975). Altered control of skin blood flow at high skin and core temperatures. *Journal of Applied Physiology*, **38**, 839-845.

Muscle Morphology and Environmental Physiology: A Commentary

Charles M. Tipton

This symposium is the second (Borer, Eddington, & White, 1983) in recent years to address the future. Therefore, readers are encouraged to become familiar with its contents as well as select review papers by the presenters (Gisolfi & Wenger, 1984; Saltin & Gollnick, 1983) when they reflect on what the future should become. According to the second edition of Webster's New World Dictionary (Guralnik, 1984), the word *future* is from the Latin term *futurus*, which means "about to be," whereas the word *direction* is derived from the Latin term *directo*, which means "to lay straight." We should recognize that scientific investigations will occur with or without direction; hence, the theme of what should be done and why it needs to be done is an important reference concept to keep in mind throughout this symposium.

The focus of this particular session is muscle. Because energy transformation occurs in muscle that seldom results in mechanical efficiency higher than 30% (Andersen, Adams, Sjøgaard, Thorboe, & Saltin, 1985; Brooks & Fahey, 1984), the dissipation of the heat produced in muscle tissue becomes a major physiological issue during exercise. Because the speakers, especially Gollnick (Saltin's presentation was not available), did not have the time to address the future in subtopics such as forces being developed, motor unit recruitment, fatigue, force-velocity changes, gene expression, or muscular diseases and their effects on performance, the reader must refer to other sources (Gisolfi & Wenger, 1984; Saltin & Gollnick, 1983) for such information. This is especially true for the area of muscle diseases because it is my belief that this aspect (Florence & Hagberg, 1984; Haller & Lewis, 1984; Lewis, Haller, & Blomquist, 1984) should be of prime concern for exercise physiologists interested in muscle. Although it is my bias that exercise training will do little to prevent the gene expression of disease, I believe training can significantly delay, modify, or blunt the disease process and its manifestations.

It would appear that a key area investigators of the future should pursue is the existence and functioning of metabolic receptors in muscle. Numerous advances have been made with the use of receptor inhibitors in cardiovascular physiology, and the same thrust is needed in muscle physiology. Because of the large number of Type III and IV afferent fibers in muscle whose functions are unknown, the distinction between local and central regulation of metabolic functions could be associated with the characterization of these receptors. Implicit in the area of regulation and the role of metabolic regulation is the contribution(s) of circulating hormones. Although both Gollnick and Saltin agree on the use of animal models for future research, they favor more in-depth investigations with humans before seeking suitable animal models or being concerned with the extrapolations to humans from animal results. Saltin's human muscle (Andersen et al., 1985; Andersen & Saltin, 1985) does provide an effective invasive method to address many of the problems of the future and to secure results that can be better quantified. Because the model appears to be one in which a specific muscle mass has uncompromised blood flow and oxygen delivery systems, one must consider experiments that impose constraints on these parameters so that the results can be used to explain whole body responses and mechanisms during maximal exercise conditions by normal and abnormal individuals.

It is conceivable that the greatest advances in temperature regulation will occur with the aid of the animal models described by Gisolfi. Unlike the muscle investigators, it would appear that the future in temperature regulation during exercise will necessitate a clearer focus on the characterization and identification of the numerous transmitters that have been identified. It would appear prudent for exercise scientists concerned with temperature regulation to resolve the confusing issue of whether the set-point is changed with training with or without heat acclimatization. The time has arrived for neurophysiologists, neuroanatomists, and exercise physiologists to combine their talents to better understand and to explain the CNS role in the adjustments associated with acute and chronic exercise in the heat. Equally important in future temperature regulation studies is the investigation of the influences of maturation, aging, and disease. States such as Arizona, Florida, and Texas should take the lead in temperature regulation just because of these aspects. All areas of exercise physiology need to improve on their modeling of the mechanisms associated with a system's response to exercise, and the temperature regulation system is an ideal one to model.

The investigators of tomorrow are the students of today; consequently, they must be more critical and better educated, motivated, technically oriented, and informed than their current teachers. This means a strong science background with more instruction and laboratory experience with aspects pertaining to molecular biology, computer science, receptor and transmitter characterization, gene expression, and statistical evaluation. However, exercise physiologists must never forget that the functioning of the whole organism can never be adequately explained by adding up the sum of the parts or by studies that are concerned only with the molecular biology of cells. In essence, we must retain the integration components of the various organ systems as we encourage future investigators to probe deeply into the functioning of cells and their molecular composition and contributions.

References

Andersen, P., Adams, R.P., Sjφgaard, G., Thorboe, A., & Saltin, B. (1985). Dynamic knee extension as model for study of isolated exercising muscle in humans. *Journal of Applied Physiology*, **59**, 1647-1653.

Andersen, P., & Saltin, B. (1985). Maximum perfusion of skeletal muscle in man. *Journal of Physiology* (London), **366**, 233-249.

Borer, K.T., Edington, D.W., & White, T.P. (1983). *Frontiers of exercise biology*. Champaign, IL: Human Kinetics.

Brooks, G.A., & Fahey, T.D. (1984). *Exercise physiology: Human bioenergetics and its applications*. New York: John Wiley & Sons.

Florence, J.M., & Hagberg, J.M. (1984). Effect of training on the exercise responses of neuromuscular disease patients. *Medicine and Science in Sports and Exercise*, **16**, 460-465.

Gisolfi, C.V., & Wenger, C.B. (1984). Temperature regulation during exercise: Old concepts, new ideas. *Exercise and Sport Science Reviews*, **13**, 338-372.

Guralnik, D.B. (1984). *Webster's New World Dictionary* (2nd ed.). New York: Simon and Schuster.

Haller, R.G., & Lewis, S.F. (1984). Pathophysiology of exercise performance in muscle disease. *Medicine and Science in Sports and Exercise*, **16**, 456-459.

Lewis, S.F., Haller, R.G., & Blomquist, C.G. (1984). Neuromuscular diseases as models of cardiovascular regulation during exercise. *Medicine and Science in Sports and Exercise*, **16**, 466-471.

Saltin, B., & Gollnick, P.D. (1983). Skeletal muscle adaptability: Significance for metabolism and performance. In L.D. Peachy, R.H. Adrian, & S.R. Geiger (Eds.), *Handbook of physiology: Skeletal muscle* (pp. 555-631). Baltimore: Williams & Wilkins.

Pulmonary Physiology: Feedback and Feed-Forward Mechanisms

Jerome A. Dempsey, Kathe G. Henke, and Elizabeth A. Aaron

Our approach to this very broad topic is not all inclusive. Rather, we will examine in some detail one currently controversial and unresolved problem concerning ventilatory control during heavy exercise and then provide an overview of what we believe to be some of the key problems in pulmonary physiology deserving future investigation. Recent reviews provide a broader overview of the general topic of the pulmonary response to exercise (Dempsey, Vidruk, & Mitchell, 1985; Whipp, 1981).

The Dilemma of Ventilatory Control During Heavy Exercise

According to conventional thinking, this question is really not a dilemma at all. It is presumed that the mechanical limits of the ventilatory pump—lung and chest wall—far exceed that required to produce the demanded hyperventilatory response to heavy exercise. It is also presumed that the ventilatory response is mediated by the metabolic acidosis of heavy exercise acting at the carotid body chemoreceptors (Whipp, 1981). Thus, as presented in Figure 1, stimulus:response is presumed to proceed smoothly and uninhibited, one for one from metabolic acidosis *to* chemo-reflex receptor stimulation *to* augmented respiratory motor output from the brainstem integrating neurons *to* the generation of inspiratory muscle pressure *to* the appropriate amount of tracheal airflow.

We propose that this schema is markedly oversimplifed and misleading. For starters, consider the magnitude of the so-called compensatory hyperventilatory response in heavy exercise shown by contrasting the three conditions for trained or moderately trained subjects in Figure 2. Note that, in terms of compensatory effects on arterial [H^+], the normal hyperventilatory response is clearly better than no hyperventilation but is substantially less than perfect. Why is this? There is obviously plenty of chemical stimulus to hyperventilate under these conditions in terms of one obvious feedback stimulus acting at an established receptor site (i.e.,

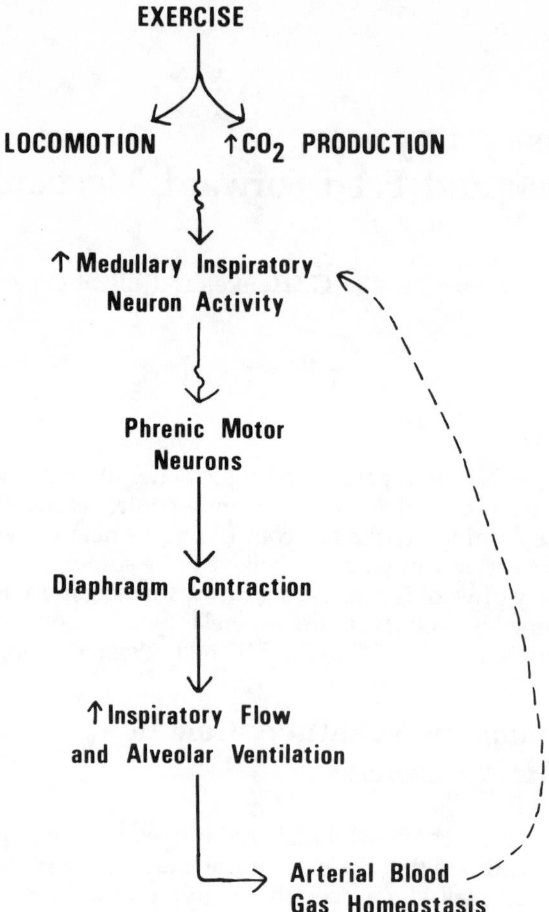

Figure 1. Generally accepted schema for control of exercise hyperpnea. Primary exercise stimuli might include a humoral component (CO_2 flow to the lung), an ascending neural component (from working skeletal muscle), and/or a descending feed-forward neural component (from higher locomotor areas of the CNS). The important error-detector feedback mechanism shown here is chemoreceptor (carotid and medullary chemoreceptors).

arterial [H^+]). Recent data also point to additional available stimuli because acid [H^+], per se, was not *required* to produce the hyperventilatory response in either normal subjects who were glycogen depleted or McArdle syndrome patients who did not produce a metabolic acidosis in heavy exercise (Dempsey et al., 1985; Hagberg et al., 1982; Heigenhauser, Sutton, & Jones, 1983). Other unexplained neural and/or humoral stimuli deserve study here. We believe that circulating norepinephrine is particularly appealing as a potential humoral mediator (Dempsey et al., 1977; Heistad, Wheeler, Mork, Schmid, & Abbord, 1972). On the neurogenic side, it is not unreasonable to suspect that the postulated

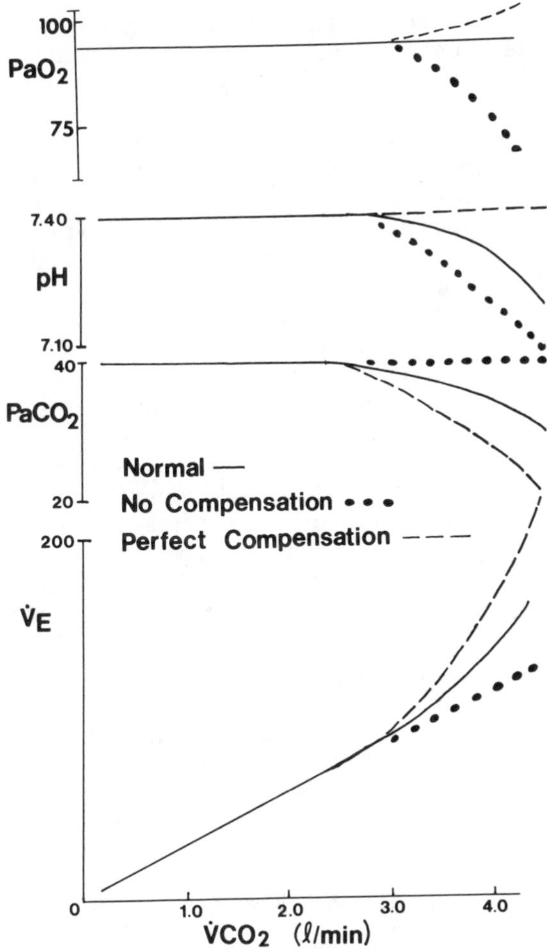

Figure 2. Three potential ventilatory responses to heavy work. Note the proportional ventilatory response to increasing $\dot{V}CO_2$ during moderate exercise. As the metabolic acidosis of heavy exercise occurs (arterial $[HCO_3^-]$ falls to 10 to 15 meq/L at $\dot{V}O_2max$) and arterial pH falls, three types of accompanying ventilatory responses are shown: (a) the usual normal response of a partial compensatory hyperventilation; (b) the completely uncompensated response where $\dot{V}_A$ continues to increase in direct proportion to $\dot{V}CO_2$—thus $PaCO_2$ stays constant, pH falls precipitously, and we would generally predict that arterial hypoxemia also occurs; and (c) a perfect compensatory hyperventilation in which the fall in $[HCO_3^-]$ is completely compensated by the hypocapnia, because of a marked hyperventilation. (We are not aware of option (c) ever actually occurring at maximal exercise in health.)

descending locomotor stimulus to hyperpnea (at moderate work loads) might acquire a curvilinear response (vs. $\dot{V}CO_2$ or work load) as locomotor muscles begin to fatigue—perhaps feedback ascending neurogenic influences might be added to the total drive in these heavy exercise situations (Dempsey et al., 1985).

So it seems reasonable to suggest that if the appropriate stimuli were permitted to exert their effect without impediment from the receptor site source to the final production of airflow from the effector organ, then ventilation in excess of 200 $L \bullet min^{-1}$ would be readily achieved and a perfect compensation of arterial $[H^+]$ would occur. Obviously, the ventilatory control system must pay attention to other requirements so that the criteria for our optimal ventilatory response must consider at least two types of mechanical considerations, in addition to the usual problems of chemical homeostasis. The ventilatory response must be at least within the maximal mechanical and metabolic limits of the lung and chest wall. From a regulatory viewpoint, the response also must be achieved with minimal work done by the respiratory muscles.

The ventilatory control system must have additional key components concerned with the physiologic cost of individual breaths, arranged with such considerations in mind as those shown in Figures 3a and 3b. The feed-forward and feedback stimuli and pathways shown here must be concerned with several factors that would minimize respiratory muscle energy expenditure. The principal factors that regulate muscle energy expenditure and thus endurance time are as follows:

$$\text{Endurance Time} = \frac{\text{Energy stores (a)} \times \text{Efficiency (E)}}{\begin{array}{l}\text{Magnitude of} \\ \text{muscle force (W)}\end{array} - \begin{array}{l}\text{Rate of} \\ \text{energy supply } (\beta)\end{array} \times \text{Efficiency (E)}}$$

Thus, muscle fatigue may occur in cases of reduced efficiency of muscle contraction, reduced energy supply, or increased power development beyond some critical requirement. For the respiratory muscles, power development is determined by the magnitude, time, and rate of pressure development:

$$[\text{Pressure developed} \times V_t/Ti \times Ti/T_{tot}]$$

where V_t = tidal volume, Ti = inspiratory time and T_{tot} = total breath time. Thus the *relative magnitude of the pressure development* (P_{di}/P_{diMax}) by the major inspiratory muscle, the diaphragm—which can be sustained almost indefinitely—was estimated to be about 40–50% (Roussos & Moxham, 1986). These critical values vary widely among healthy subjects according to a number of factors:

1. The *velocity of muscle shortening*, as indicated indirectly by the mean inspiratory flow (V_t/Ti).
2. The *length of the muscle* relative to its optimal length is an important determinant of force and pressure development at any level of shortening velocity. The Functional Residual Capacity (FRC) volume provides an indirect estimate of respiratory muscle length in humans.
3. The *breath duty cycle* (Ti/T_{tot}) or time of contraction. Diaphragmatic flow is reduced during contraction, and sufficient time during relax-

ation must be provided so that net flow over the total cycle is not compromised.

4. *Frequency* of muscle contraction (f_b).

What evidence is there that the ventilatory response to exercise and especially to heavy exercise behaves in a manner consistent with the principle of optimizing the work of the chest wall musculature? Some traditional considerations, plus more recent evidence, strongly suggest that both feed-forward and feedback stimuli are operative during exercise to determine the magnitude, time, and rate of power development by the respiratory muscles and the efficiency of this power development. Even the patterns of recruitment of respiratory muscles seem to be designed and regulated to serve this goal of minimization of respiratory muscle energy expenditure. We now present three types of evidence that support the application of the regulatory schemes shown in Figure 3 to the exercising state.

Load compensation (feedback pathways shown in Figure 3a). A certain amount of mechanical impedance to airflow and to lung volume expansion does exist even in the healthy young pulmonary system. Mechanical impedance, which is determined primarily by the *time constant* (i.e., the resistance-compliance product) in addition to the breathing frequency and lung inertance, dictates that a temporal lag will occur between the pattern (rate and magnitude) of neural input to the respiratory muscles and airflow from the lung (Mead, 1979). Because this neural input-mechanical output relationship may be further dissociated as breathing frequency and airflow rates increase during exercise, it is important that inspiratory neural drive must also increase in a compensatory fashion. If neural drive increased *only* in proportion to the increasing $\dot{V}CO_2$ (Figure 1), the ventilatory response would be inadequate and arterial PCO_2, acid-base status, and oxygenation would not be closely regulated. That this compensation does occur is evidenced by the immediate effects of decreasing this normally occurring pulmonary lung impedance via administration of a few breaths of a low-density gas mixture (He:O_2). Within the first breath or two, the airway resistance fell as expected to 50–60% of the air-breathing value and the rate of rise and peak electromyographic activity of the diaphragm fell substantially as $\dot{V}_E$, tidal volume, and/or breathing frequency increased (Hussain, Pardy, & Dempsey, 1985). Thus, in the physiologic air-breathing state during even mild exercise, a significant portion of the inspiratory neural drive to breathe must be devoted to compensating for the normal mechanical load presented by the lung to the inspiratory muscles. The magnitude of this compensatory response increases with increasing work load (Dempsey, Hanson, & Henderson, 1984).

Proprioception of effort ensures efficiency in the involuntary control of breathing (feedback pathways shown in Figure 3a). An even simpler experiment demonstrates that the control system via mechanoreceptor feedback from the chest wall and/or lung is aware of and indeed usually prevents the development of any excessive or wasteful pressure development by the respiratory muscles for the purposes of flow generation. During a forced exhalation, flow increases linearly with the increase in muscular effort. As lung volume falls to less than ∿ 60% of vital capacity, the lung recoil pressure is reduced along with the tethering action of the lung parenchyma. All of these tend to hold the intrathoracic airways open. A critical volume is reached at which the advantage gained by increasing effort and therefore pleural pressure outside the airway is offset by airway compression. The healthy subject exercising heavily will produce very high flow rates, but the amount of effort exerted during exhalation never appears to reach the wasteful effort-independent portion of the flow:volume relationship. If, however, one chooses by strictly voluntary means (while at rest) to reproduce the identical high expiratory flow rate achieved during exercise, a major portion of every exhalation will now be conducted with the airways dynamically compressed, and the effort (and therefore work) generated by the expiratory muscles will be far in excess of that needed for the flow generated (Dempsey & Fregosi, 1985; Hesser, Linnarsson, & Fagraeus, 1981). Lessons from this simple comparison of voluntary versus involuntary regulation are twofold: (a) some type of feedback control (sensing perhaps either airway pressure or muscle tension) prevents excessive use of expiratory muscle effort during heavy exercise, and (b) this type of efficient control achieved with the involuntary regulation of breathing is overridden by the higher CNS voluntary control input. This contrast also emphasizes that it probably makes little sense, in terms of economy of muscular effort, to try to coach athletes to control their breathing during exercise.

The recruitment pattern of respiratory and accessory muscles is another important factor under the supervision of the ventilatory control system to ensure economy of effort in the hyperpnea of exercise and hyperventilation of heavy exercise (see feed-forward and feedback pathways in Figures 3a and 3b). Increased activation of phrenic motor neurons and of inspiratory muscles is accompanied almost simultaneously by activation of the upper (extra-thoracic) airway abductor muscles, so that the airway caliber at the laryngeal level is increased in diameter. Thus substantial increases in inspiratory (and expiratory) flow rates, even into the range of turbulent airflow, may occur without substantial increases in overall airway resistance (i.e., in the pressures required to produce a given flow rate). The diaphragm is spared as accessory (intercostal) inspiratory muscles are recruited for rib cage expansion. Expiratory (abdominal) muscles are also recruited even in moderate exercise to such an extent that end-expiratory lung volume falls significantly during exercise. This recruitment is crucial because it ensures not only that expiration is completed in the shortened time available during exercise, but also that the inspiratory muscles are placed at a longer length so that they may develop a greater tension (for any given neural input) upon the subsequent inspiration. Thus active expiration also generates stored energy in expiratory muscles that, upon release, may actually assist passively with the generation of negative intrapleural pressure during the subsequent inspiration.

A potential disadvantage to this active expiration and reduced FRC during exercise may be found in the reduced compliance of the lung and chest wall (i.e., a stiffer lung as lung volume is sufficiently reduced to

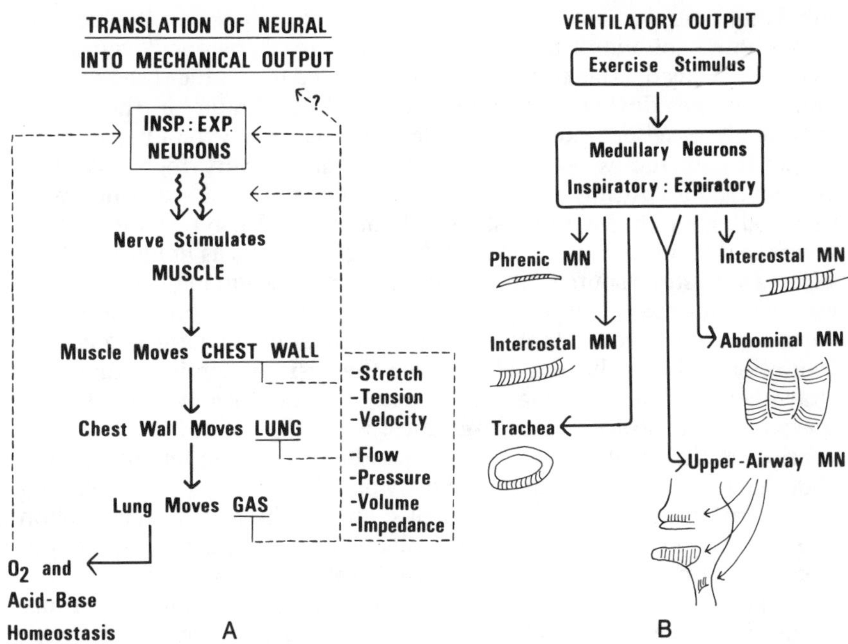

Figure 3. Proposed modifications to the control of exercise hyperpnea. (A) This schema emphasizes that the mechanoreceptor feedback from the chest wall and lung is critical to the control of breathing pattern and to the minimization of ventilatory work. (B) This schema shows that the motor control system is concerned with much more than just the innervation to and activation of the diaphragm. To the contrary, stimulation of brainstem neurons also controls activation of important accessory respiratory muscles that become especially important in such hyperpneic states as exercise. These include (a) muscles in the upper airway (e.g., genioglossus and posterior cricoayratenoid) to ensure a stable and maximal diameter upper airway to accept the augmented airflows; (b) inspiratory intercostal muscles; and (c) expiratory muscles of the rib cage and abdomen. Some modulating effect of brainstem inspiratory activity on bronchiolar smooth muscle might also be present.

the lower, alinear portion of the pressure:volume curve). Most evidence suggests that this does not occur even in maximal exercise. The control of expiratory muscle recruitment is probably primarily under vagal feedback control (Remmers & Bartlett, 1977) and sensitive to any change in the rate of change of lung volume (e.g., as occurs with a change in expiratory flow resistance). However, as with inspiratory muscles, expiratory muscles may also be activated via purely feed-forward stimuli and pathways, perhaps even by locomotor-linked stimuli from the central nervous system.

Capacity of the pulmonary system. In addition to these mechanoreceptor-type feedback regulators, we also emphasize the importance of the sheer magnitude of the pulmonary system's morphologic capacity in permitting an efficient ventilatory response to heavy work. For example, because of the abundant elastic recoil properties of healthy lung tissue, substantial intraluminal alveolar pressure is maintained in the airways throughout expiration, thereby maintaining airway patency even in the face of the considerable muscular effort required to produce the requisite high flow rates during active expiration. The diaphragm, as the body's only really essential skeletal muscle, also has many fatigue-resistant properties, including a dense vascularity and a very high oxidative capacity. Thus, during heavy exercise, blood flow to the diaphragm is very high. Even during exhaustive endurance exercise in rats, this muscle seems to depend primarily on such blood-borne fuels as lipids and even lactate as substrate sources. Increased lactate production in the diaphragm was not evident even at the point of exercise to exhaustion in the whole animal or prolonged tetanic electrical stimulation in vitro (Fregosi & Dempsey, 1986; Rochester, 1986). Even the basic anatomic location and attachments of the diaphragm seem designed for efficient generation of pressure: (a) contraction increases chest wall volume, both by lowering the floor of the chest cavity and by expanding the circumference; (b) the abdominal contents are used effectively as a fulcrum by the descending diaphragm in expanding the lower ribs; and (c) the increased activation of the intercostal muscles stiffens the rib cage, thereby permitting the contracting diaphragm to expand the chest wall more effectively.

The above examples emphasize the importance of feedback and those mechanical influences in the lung and chest wall that determine total work by the respiratory muscles. We do not imply that all of these influences are purely reflexively mediated via pathways and receptor sites that do not require cortical involvement. To the contrary, changes in peak pressure generation are very sensitively perceived, and because they minimize the intensity of muscular force generation (as well as its duration and frequency), they also minimize the sensory magnitude of the effort (Burdon, Killian, & Campbell, 1982; Jones, Killian, & Stubbing, 1986). During exercise, therefore, regulated factors such as breathing pattern, magnitude of pressure generation, active expiration and inspiratory drive, activation of upper airway musculature, and inhibition of antagonistic muscle activity may be behaviorally selected on the basis of sensory information.

Although effort perception must play a role in regulating some aspects of the ventilatory response to exercise and probably contributes to exercise limitations, we believe that reflex effects operating at the level of brainstem respiratory neurons and/or at segmental spinal cord alpha-motor neuron levels are primarily responsible for the optimization of parameters concerned with minimization of ventilatory work during exercise. This view is supported by the fact that many of these optimization mechanisms are operative at very low exercise levels with ventilatory work loads that are substantially below the perceptual level. Behavioral influences may operate more appropriately to override the more basic reflex mechanisms, but, as we observed with the comparisons of voluntary versus involuntary control, the purely conscious control of pressure development is not always the wisest or most efficient. Finally, we point out that consciousness, per se, clearly has a critical role in ventilatory compensation to mechanical loads, even though the actual perception of this load may not be crucial. For example, with both elastic and resistive loads, we observed that ventilatory compensation to these perturbations is completely lost during slow-wave sleep in normal humans (Iber, Berssenbrugge, Skatrud, & Dempsey, 1982; Wilson, Skatrud, & Dempsey, 1984). It is also of interest, however, that different kinds of loads may differ here, because a near-perfect compensation for length changes in the respiratory muscles occurred in both sleeping and waking states.

Evidence of mechanical constraint on exercise hyperventilation. At the outset of this paper, we suggested that the ventilatory response to exercise (and especially to heavy exercise) was not simply a matter of sufficient stimulation to produce the observed response (i.e., there might be a mechanical limit to this response). The experimental evidence for this limitation is recently available from a group of highly trained athletes capable of achieving very high $\dot{V}CO_2$ and $\dot{V}O_2$ ($\geqslant$5 L•min^{-1}) (Dempsey et al., 1984; Dempsey et al., 1985). In essence, they achieved ventilatory responses ($\dot{V}_E$) that often exceeded 150 L•min^{-1}. However, at these very high $\dot{V}CO_2$ levels, they needed even greater responses than those observed to obtain appropriate compensation. Thus, their arterial PCO_2 was 35–42 mmHg (rather than 25–32 mmHg in the untrained), alveolar PO_2 was less than 115 mmHg (vs. 115–130 mmHg in the untrained), arterial pH became quite acid, and arterial PO_2 was significantly reduced (−20 to −40 mmHg < resting values). If these subjects breathed helium:O_2 and reduced airway resistance by $\sim$ 40%, they showed substantial compensatory hyperventilation. While we attribute much of this hyperventilatory response to a mechanical "unloading" of the lung and chest wall, we also emphasize that the increased breathing frequency which accompanies helium inhalation might be attributable to stimulation of receptors in the upper airway.

We do not have the available measurements to determine whether respiratory muscle fatigue occurred in these subjects who failed to show compensatory hyperventilation in heavy short-term exercise, but some of these subjects were clearly well within their maximal flow:volume limits at maximal exercise. One possibility is that an inhibitory feedback effect on ventilatory drive and output may preserve the energy state of the respiratory muscles at the expense of arterial blood gas and acid-base homeostasis. Thus this preventive response might then be provoked by excessive tension or pressure developed by the chest wall musculature, so that the mechanical status of the ventilatory control system would in essence limit ventilatory response, even though the actual metabolic and mechanical limits of the chest wall to sustain minute ventilation have not actually been met or exceeded.

We emphasize that not all athletes engaging in short- or long-term heavy work at these high metabolic rates chose to compromise their compensatory ventilatory response (Dempsey et al., 1984). Indeed, even at $\dot{V}CO_2$ $\gtrsim$ 5–6 L•min^{-1}, some runners showed sufficient alveolar hyperventilation to reduce $PaCO_2$ to 28–32 mmHg, thereby avoiding extreme arterial hypoxemia. Perhaps fundamental intraindividual differences in mechanical capacity and/or efficiency of the lung-thorax system and their associated feedback control among athletes is a determinant of the ventilatory response to heavy work. We should emphasize (Figure 1) that some sort of mechanical limitation probably operates in all individuals (fit or unfit) in heavy work. Otherwise, full $[H^+]$ compensation would probably occur in all persons (Figure 1). The increased hyperventilation under reduced-load conditions while breathing helium during heavy work also occurs in all healthy persons studied to date and probably reflects a reduction of a mechanical constraint present in the normal (loaded) air-breathing state. Finally, in a recent study of long-term, heavy exercise in trained cyclists and rowers, we found that endurance time at > 80% $\dot{V}O_2max$ was significantly prolonged while breathing He:normoxia versus room air. Based on accompanying data in some of these subjects, we attributed this change in endurance performance primarily to the reduced effort sensation of extreme sustained hyperventilation during heavy exercise, rather than to the relief of any respiratory muscle fatigue, hypoxemia, or acidosis.

Future Directions

Some of the current and future problems in basic pulmonary physiology are listed in Table 1. The neurophysiologic basis of ventilatory regulation has received considerable attention in recent years and will continue to attract researchers as intracellular and extracellular techniques

Table 1 Some Key Problems in Respiratory Physiology: Basic Regulatory Mechanisms.

Pulmonary functions	Regulatory mechanisms
Regulation of breathing	Rhythm generation
	Higher CNS
	Chemoreception
	Neurochemistry
	Mechanoreceptor feedback
Ventilatory muscle regulation	Actions and coordination
	Recruitment patterns
	Efferent and afferent neural control
	Blood flow, energetics, basic morphology
Gas exchange	Lung water
	Vascular reactivity
	Bronchiolar reactivity
	$\dot{V}_A:\dot{Q}c$ (In*tra*regional)

for recording neuronal activity are further developed. Examples of fundamental topics that still remain include the site and mechanism of central rhythm generation and the mechanisms for terminating inspiration or regulating expiratory time. The neurochemistry of ventilatory control remains completely unknown. The broad problem of ventilatory muscle regulation is a relatively new one that continues to include such fundamental questions as the mechanical actions of various muscles on rib cage expansion and patterns of muscle recruitment with application of different types of drives to breathe. The upper airway muscles are now firmly recognized as important respiratory muscles, but their mode of activation and coordination with the chest wall muscles remains to be determined. Active regulation of the lung's tracheobronchial tree smooth muscle and that in the pulmonary vascular bed are hotly pursued problems. The regulation of extravascular lung water also continues to attract attention, but a serious obstacle in this research continues to be the problem of accurate, sensitive, quantification of changes in this fluid volume.

The adaptation to exercise continues to be one of the fascinating applications of basic pulmonary physiology (see Table 2). The primary mechanism for exercise hyperpnea (the most precise and greatest ventilatory response that occurs in any physiologic state) remains a major mystery and will probably continue to be elusive because of the apparent redundancy of mechanisms within biological control systems. The recent application of new neurophysiologic techniques to this question has raised the intriguing possibility of a very strong feed-forward stimulus linked with a central-command-type of locomotor control. Animal models for this study of hyperpnea remain a serious problem (Dempsey et al., 1985). Very little is known of even the very basics of respiratory muscle recruitment patterns and their mechanical effects during exercise. Whether ventilatory muscles are even severely taxed during heavy exercise remains unknown, because only generalized estimates have been made for this state of fatigue of the chest wall in humans during exercise (Bye, Esau, Walley, Macklem, & Pardy, 1984; Dempsey & Fregosi, 1985). We really have no idea of just what fraction of the total body metabolic rate is consumed by respiratory muscles or how much blood flow might be stolen from exercising muscles for ventilatory purposes during heavy exercise. Indeed, we remain almost totally ignorant of the exact nature of the basic perturbations within the lung and/or chest wall that give rise to the control of breathing pattern, ventilatory drive, and the perplexing sensation of dyspnea. As outlined in previous sections, the once apparently straightforward hyperventilatory response to heavy exercise is now also a dilemma, as neither the humoral nor the neural stimulus mediating the hyperventilatory response is known and the magnitude of the proposed mechanical inhibition to hyperventilation remains undefined.

Finally, we recognize that the ventilatory control system is a plastic one that changes radically during maturation in the animal. The effects of this plasticity in neuronal development has not yet been applied to the control of breathing at rest or especially in the exercising state.

The adaptability of the healthy pulmonary system in chronic and/or intermittent stress encountered in physical training or in various types

Table 2 Important Research Questions in Pulmonary-Exercise Physiology

Research areas	Specific topics for investigation
Basic problems	Hyperpnea mechanisms (link with locomotion)
	Hyperventilation mechanisms (heavy exercise)
	Dyspnea mechanisms
	Mechanical feedback
	Muscle recruitment and coordination
	Respiratory muscle fatigue ($\dot{V}O_2$ and $\dot{Q}$)
	Diffusion limit (lung water, transit times)
	Regulation of heat loss from the airway
Adaptability	Physical training (chest wall)
	Extremes—supramax —endurance work —heat, hypoxia, hyperbaria
	Pulmonary limitations to performance?
	The aging pulmonary system
Pathophysiology	Exercise training?
	and/or
	Intermittent resting of muscles?
	Patient population—COPD[a] —aged
	Pulmonary stress testing
	Regulation of exercise-induced bronchospasm

[a]COPD = chronic obstructive pulmonary disease.

of alien environments has received some attention to date, but few attempts have been made to thoroughly document morphologic and functional aspects of chest wall adaptation to various types of chronic exercise, both within and among species. Current dogma suggests that chronic physical training has no significant effect on lung structure or function and little if any effect on the metabolic capacity of respiratory muscles (Dempsey et al., 1985). Perhaps, then, the capacities of the more trainable (cardiovascular and muscle metabolic) organ-system links of O_2 transport may surpass that of the untrainable pulmonary system, resulting in hypoxemia and the absence of appropriate hyperventilatory compensation in some highly trained athletes (Dempsey, 1986). This hypothesis needs a more thorough testing, and appropriate animal models need to be developed to more thoroughly explore training effects on chest wall mechanics and metabolism. Whether chest wall skeletal muscles show some of the remarkable capacities of locomotor muscles in the elite (endurance-trained) athlete remains completely unexplored.

The effects of the aging process on the limitations of the lung and chest wall have received only cursory examination. What effects do the changing compliances of the lung and chest wall have on respiratory muscle function in the aged (e.g., coordination, endurance, and strength)? Problems of control in ventilatory pattern and stability are well known during sleep in the aged. Does this problem extend to the control and efficiency of ventilatory pattern and muscle recruitment during exercise?

Does chronic exercise training have any legitimate place in the rehabilitation of patients with lung disease, especially in view of the irreversible nature of the structural damage to the effector organ? On the one hand, the locomotor muscle conditioning that accompanies training assists in the ambulation and well-being of the chronically sedentary patient with chronic obstructive lung disease. However, exercise programs should not be applied indiscriminately! For example, patients with exercise hypoxemia and/or reduced dimensions of their pulmonary vascular bed will undergo substantial increases in pulmonary arterial pressure when pulmonary blood flow increases during even mild exercise. The effect of supplemental oxygen during the training process should be very helpful in this regard but has not been studied. Perhaps respiratory muscles are chronically fatigued in many of these patients and, instead of (or in addition to) a program of physical training, intermittent resting of the muscles may be desirable. These highly practical questions need to be addressed before any more mass application of exercise training programs is made to patients with pulmonary disease.

Acknowledgments

This work was supported by funds from the National Institute of Health (NHLBI) and the U.S. Army Research and Development Command. We are indebted to Ms. Pamela Bradford for her excellent preparation of the manuscript.

References

Burdon, J.G., Killian, K., & Campbell, E.J.M. (1982). Effect of ventilatory drive on the perceived magnitude of added loads to breathing. *Journal of Applied Physiology*, **53**, 901-907.

Bye, T., Esau, S.A., Walley, K.R., Macklem, P.T., & Pardy, R.L. (1984). Ventilatory muscles during exercise in air and oxygen in normal men. *Journal of Applied Physiology*, **56**, 464-471.

Dempsey, J.A. (1986). Is the lung built for exercise? *Medicine and Science in Exercise and Sports*, **18**, 143-155.

Dempsey, J.A., & Fregosi, R.F. (1985). Adaptability of the pulmonary system to changing metabolic requirements. *American Journal of Cardiology*, **55**, 59D-67D.

Dempsey, J.A., Gledhill, N., Reddan, W.G., Forster, H.V., Hanson, P.G., & Claremont, A.D. (1977). Pulmonary adaptation to exercise: Effects of exercise type and duration, chronic hypoxia, and physical training. *Annals of the New York Academy of Science*, **301**, 243.

Dempsey, J.A., Hanson, P., & Henderson, K. (1984). Exercise-induced arterial hypoxemia in healthy human subjects at sea-level. *Journal of Physiology* (London), **355**, 161-175.

Dempsey, J.A., Vidruk, E., & Mitchell, G. (1985). Regulation of pulmonary control systems during exercise: Update. *Federation Proceedings*, **44**, 2260-2270.

Fregosi, R.F., & Dempsey, J.A. (1986). The effects of exercise in normoxia and acute hypoxia on respiratory muscle metabolites. *Journal of Applied Physiology*, **60**, 1274-1283.

Hagberg, J., Coyle, E., Corall, J., McMillen, J., Martin, W., & Broule, J. (1982). Exercise hyperventilation in patients with McArdle's syndrome. *Journal of Applied Physiology*, **52**, 991-994.

Heigenhauser, G.J.T., Sutton, J.R., & Jones, N.L. (1983). Effect of glycogen depletion on the ventilatory response to exercise. *Journal of Applied Physiology*, **54**, 470-474.

Heistad, D., Wheeler, R., Mork, A., Schmid, P., & Abboud, R. (1972). Effects of adrenergic stimulation on ventilation in man. *Journal of Clinical Investigation*, **51**, 1469-1475.

Hesser, C.M., Linnarsson, D., & Fagraeus, L. (1981). Pulmonary mechanics and work of breathing at maximal ventilation and raised air pressure. *Journal of Applied Physiology*, **50**, 747-753.

Hussain, S.N.A., Pardy, R.L., & Dempsey, J.A. (1985). Mechanical impedance as determinant of inspiratory neural drive during exercise in humans. *Journal of Applied Physiology*, **59**(2), 365-375.

Iber, C., Berssenbrugge, A., Skatrud, J.B., & Dempsey, J.A. (1982). Ventilatory adaptations to resistive loading during wakefulness and non-REM sleep. *Journal of Applied Physiology*, **52**, 607-614.

Jones, N.L., Killian, K., & Stubbing, D. (1986). The thorax in exercise. In C. Roussos & P. Macklem (Eds.), *The thorax* (pp. 627-656). New York: Marcel Dekker.

Mead, J. (1979). Responses to loaded breathing. A critique and a synthesis. *Bulletin Europa of Physiopathology and Respiration*, **15**, 61-71.

Remmers, J., & Bartlett, D. (1977). Reflex control of expiratory airflow and duration. *Journal of Applied Physiology*, **42**, 80-87.

Rochester, D. (1986). Respiratory muscle blood flow and metabolism. In C. Roussos & P. Macklem (Eds.), *The thorax* (pp. 393-436). New York: Marcel Dekker.

Roussos, C., & Moxham, J. (1986). Respiratory muscle fatigue. In C. Roussos & P. Macklem (Eds.), *The thorax* (pp. 829-870). New York: Marcel Dekker.

Whipp, B. (1981). Control of exercise hyperpnea. In T.F. Hornbein (Ed.), *Regulation of breathing: Part II* (pp. 1069-1140). New York: Marcel Dekker.

Wilson, P., Skatrud, J.B., & Dempsey, J.A. (1984). Effects of slow-wave sleep on ventilatory compensation to inspiratory elastic loading in humans. *Respiratory Physiology*, **55**, 103-120.

Neurohormonal System

Henrik Galbo, Michael Kjaer, and Kari J. Mikines

The autonomic nerves and the endocrine glands—the peripheral neuroendocrine system—serve to coordinate the various functions of the body during the varying conditions of daily life. Exercise endocrinology deals with the study of the relationship between these control systems and physical activity. It is the newest field within exercise physiology and has only recently begun to appear in textbooks. The development of sensitive hormone assays has made physiological studies possible, and over the past few years, probably more new information has been gathered in this area than in any other area of exercise physiology. This paper begins with an exemplified outline of the discipline, after which we present our working hypothesis for the control of autonomic neurohormonal changes in exercise. Finally, we give directions for future research in exercise endocrinology. The reader is referred to Christensen and Galbo (1983) and Galbo (1983, 1985, 1986a, 1986b) for reviews of previous research.

Research Principles in Exercise Endocrinology

The first step in the study of the role of a given hormone in exercise is measurement of its concentration in plasma during exercise of various intensities and durations. Frequent discoveries of new putative hormones still make such simple experiments relevant. Figure 1 shows a recent experiment in which it was found that the plasma concentrations of the peptides substance P, PHI, VIP, and secretin increase during prolonged exercise, whereas those of neurotensin and GRP do not.

If exercise elicits a change in the concentration of a hormone in plasma, it should be clarified whether this reflects a change in secretion or elimination (clearance) of the hormone. Many hormones, including epinephrine, are eliminated in the liver and kidneys, and because blood flow to these organs is reduced during exercise, clearance of these hormones might decrease following exercise. However, epinephrine studies with continuous infusion of radiolabeled tracer have shown that its clearance decreases only 20% during heavy work, a change far too small to explain the simultaneous rise in its plasma concentration (Kjaer,

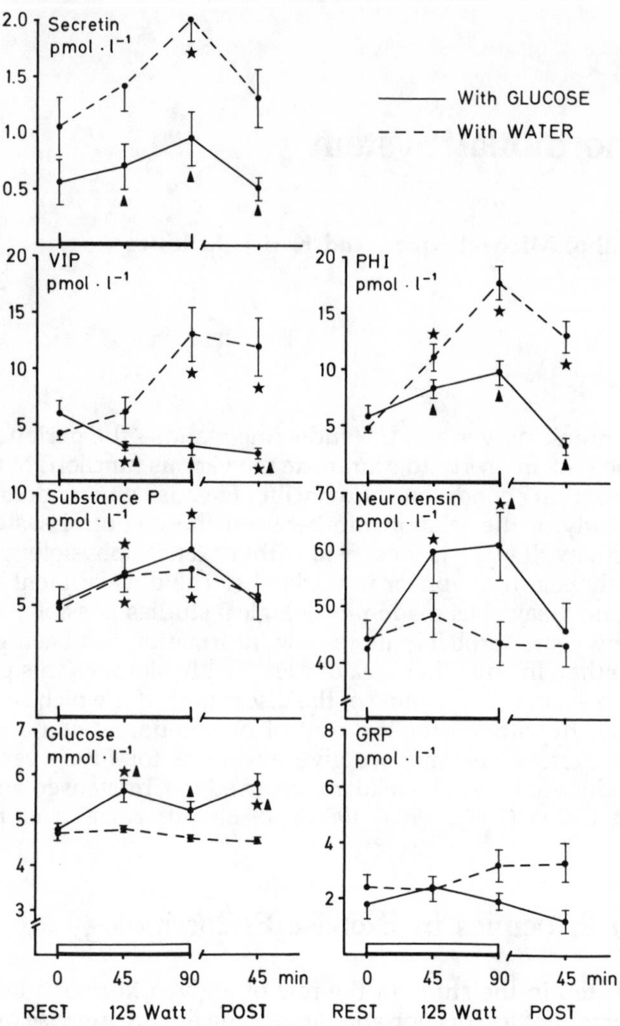

Figure 1. The effect of bicycle exercise on the plasma concentrations of some peptide hormones and neurotransmitters for which reliable radioimmunoassays have recently been developed. Ten subjects who had fasted overnight were studied. One day, they drank 250 ml of a 5% glucose solution every 15 min during exercise. Another day, they drank water. Values are means ± SE. VIP = vasoactive intestinal polypeptide, PHI = peptide histidine isoleucine, and GRP = gastrin-releasing peptide (bombesin). ★ designates difference ($p < .05$) from preexercise value, and ▲ designates difference ($p < .05$) between corresponding values in the two experiments. Subdivision of the group into five trained and five untrained subjects ($\dot{V}O_2max$ = 72 [69–75] and 45 [40–55] ml•min⁻¹•kg⁻¹, respectively, mean and range) did not reveal differences in responses. *Note*. From "The Effect of Training and Glucose Ingestions on Responses of Some GEP Hormones to Exercise" by H. Galbo et al., 1985, *Clinical Physiology*, **5**, Suppl. 4, p. A45. Copyright 1985 by *Clinical Physiology*. Adapted by permission.

Christensen, Sonne, Richter, & Galbo, 1985). In fact, only the increase in plasma concentration of gonad hormones seen in exercise has been found to be due primarily to a decrease in clearance. Nevertheless, clearance has been measured for only a few hormones during exercise.

If a change in secretion does take place, the origin of this should be clarified. Regarding the newly discovered peptides that respond to exercise, the origin of their release is unknown. Interestingly, such peptides may be cosecreted alone or with traditional hormones and neurotransmitters. For example, enkephalins may be secreted with epinephrine (Ganten, Lang, Archelos, & Unger, 1984), VIP with acetylcholine (Lundberg, Fahrenkrug, Larsson, & Änggard, 1984), and neuropeptide Y with norepinephrine (Ekblad et al., 1984; Ganten et al., 1984). VIP and PHI have been found in the same postganglionic parasympathetic, peptidergic nerve fibers (Lundberg et al., 1984), and there is a correlation between the responses of these substances during exercise, suggesting that they are cosecreted (Figure 2). The exact stimulus for a change in secretion is sought by experimental manipulations of the external and internal

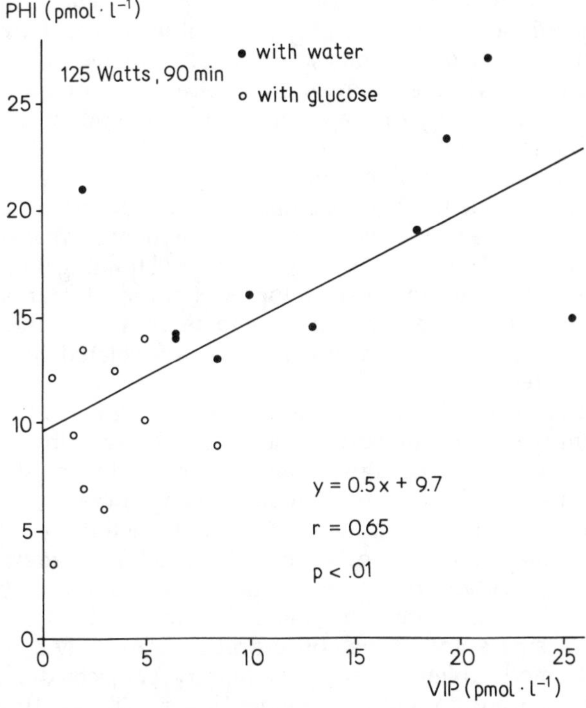

Figure 2. The relationship between plasma concentrations of PHI and VIP at the end of 90 min of cycling in 10 subjects studied twice. Linear regression analysis was carried out, and the regression equation and correlation coefficient are given. For further explanation, see Figure 1.

environment during exercise. Figure 1 shows that glucose administered orally in amounts that do not produce hyperglycemia inhibits the responses of VIP, PHI, and secretin to exercise, but not that of substance P.

When the regulation of the plasma level of a hormone in exercise is understood, one is then able to define the role of the hormone more precisely. It is important to emphasize that this cannot be inferred from studies carried out during resting conditions because the effects of the hormone depend upon the internal milieu, and this is not the same during rest and exercise. As an example, epinephrine in concentrations seen during severe exercise enhances glycogen breakdown in isolated muscle during contractions but not during rest (Richter, Ruderman, Gavras, Belur, & Galbo, 1982). In the elucidation, the actual hormone is eliminated by pharmacological means, disease, or surgical destruction. In contrast to the adrenomedullary hormones, experiments of the latter kind have recently and somewhat surprisingly shown that the sympathetic liver nerves are of no importance for the exercise-induced increase in hepatic glucose production in rats (Sonne, Mikines, Richter, Christensen, & Galbo, 1985). For an optimal evaluation of the role of a hormone, elimination experiments are carried out with and without substitution of the hormone by exogenous administration of physiological amounts. It appears that animal experiments may be of value, and such experiments are necessary when isolated muscle preparations have to be studied in the clarification of whether a given effect of a hormone on contracting muscle is exerted directly or via a change in some other variable that, in turn, influences muscle.

Physical exercise may induce adaptations within the neurohormonal system and within the target cells controlled by this system. Effects of a single bout of exercise have to be separated from more permanent changes induced by regularly repeated exercise or physical training (Figure 3). The mechanisms responsible for the development of the adaptations and the molecular nature of the adaptations have to be unraveled. It follows that exercise endocrinology also includes studies of isolated cells and subcellular structures.

New neurohormonal adaptations are being discovered, and our understanding of established adaptations is still increasing. Thus, after only 1 week of vigorous endurance training, a reduction in catecholamine response to a given absolute work load is seen. There is evidence that prolonged endurance training increases adrenal medullary secretory capacity (i.e., it may cause a sports adrenal medulla), an adaptation that makes it less unavoidable than hitherto thought to find lower epinephrine secretions at given absolute work loads in trained subjects. It has been found that plasma epinephrine concentrations are higher in top-level, endurance-trained athletes than in sedentary subjects during similar degrees of insulin-induced hypoglycemia (Kjaer et al., 1984); at comparable relative work loads (% $\dot{V}O_2max$), norepinephrine levels, and heart rates at the end of exhausting submaximal exercise (Kjaer et al., 1985); and after identical periods of supramaximal exercise (Galbo, Kjaer, Richter, Sonne, & Mikines, 1986).

In the postexercise period, insulin concentrations are low relative to glucose concentrations in plasma during oral glucose loading in man

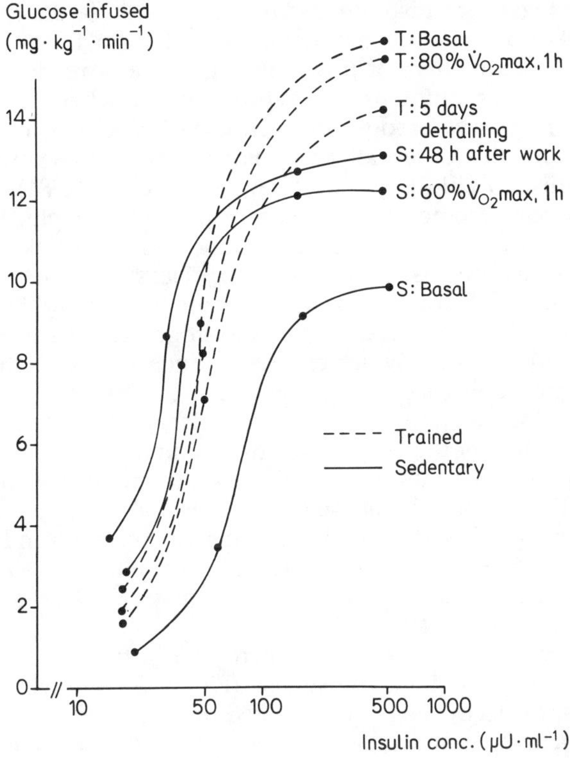

Figure 3. Example of a protocol to determine the extent to which an adaptation seen in the trained state reflects an effect of the last exercise bout per se. Whole-body insulin sensitivity was determined by graded insulin infusion in four sequential, 2-hr steps. The rate of glucose infusion necessary to maintain euglycemia is given on the ordinate. When studied in the basal state, the athlete had carried out his usual long-distance training the day before. In this state, 1 hr of heavy cycling did not influence the response to insulin. An effect of acute exercise was seen in the sedentary subject and the effect lasted 48 hr. It disappeared after 5 days (not shown), whereas after 5 days of detraining, the response of the athlete still differed from that of the sedentary subject. For a full account of the effect of physical activity, bed rest studies should also be carried out.

(Blom, Høstmark, Flaten, & Hermansen, 1985). This may be due to diminished glucose-induced secretion from the gut of gastric inhibitory polypeptide (GIP), which stimulates insulin secretion (Blom et al., 1985). In accordance with this view, the steady-state, dose-response relationship between plasma glucose levels and insulin secretion studied in man during intravenous glucose infusion is identical in studies with and without previous exercise (Mikines, Farrell, Sonne, & Galbo, 1985). In sedentary rats, a reduction in the sensitivity of insulin secretion to glucose per se may develop more readily in response to exercise, because lower plasma insulin concentrations after an intravenous glucose bolus have been found in the postexercise period than in the basal state (James,

Burleigh, Kraegen, & Chisholm, 1983). However, differences in distribution volume and clearance may have accounted for these findings.

In studies on the effect of physical training, a reduction in glucose-induced insulin secretion is more pronounced when glucose is administered orally compared to intravenously (Björntorp, 1981), and the reduced insulin and C-peptide responses to oral glucose are associated with a diminished GIP-response (Krotkiewski et al., 1984). In man, an effect of physical training on the insulin response to oral glucose has been demonstrated 4 days after the last training session (Krotkiewski et al., 1984), but the last exercise bout has nevertheless been found to account for a major part of the difference between the trained and the untrained state (Heath et al., 1983). Again indicating a difference between man and caged rats in the extent to which exercise influences the insulin-secreting cells, training diminishes the insulin response of caged rats to intravenous glucose, tolbutamide, and arginine loads (Richard & LeBlanc, 1983), and the effect lasts longer than that of a single bout of exercise (James et al., 1983). In fact, trained rats have a decreased sensitivity of the beta-cells to in vitro stimulation by glucose (Galbo, Hedeskov, Capito, & Vinten, 1981). At least in this species, this indicates that training-induced hypoinsulinemia is not due solely to alterations in hormonal or metabolic milieu or in neurogenic stimulation of the islets, but may reflect adaptations within the pancreatic beta-cells.

Whole-body insulin sensitivity is increased in trained and untrained subjects after a single bout of exercise (Figure 3). In vivo and in vitro experiments, respectively, have indicated that these effects can be partly ascribed to an increased glucose transport in skeletal muscle. Acute exercise does not influence glucose transport in fat cells, whereas this *is* increased by training. The latter effect has recently been shown to be due to an increase in the number of insulin-displaceable glucose transporters after training (Figure 4) (Vinten, Petersen, Sonne, & Galbo, 1985).

Control of Neurohormonal Changes in Exercise

The time course of hormonal changes during exercise and in the post-exercise period (at the start of which activity in the CNS motor centers and the flow of impulses from mechanoreceptors suddenly cease) indicates that the regulation of the autonomic neuroendocrine response to exercise has a *fast, nervous component* and a *slow, internal-milieu component*. The response may be regulated as follows. At the onset of exercise, impulses from motor centers in the brain (central command) and from working muscles elicit a work load-dependent increase in sympathoadrenal activity and the release of some pituitary hormones (GH, ACTH, Prolactin [PRL], and ADH); an increase in TSH has been disputed; (Rolandi et al., 1985). Thus these changes control the changes in secretion of subordinate endocrine cells. That is, sympathoadrenal activity depresses insulin secretion and stimulates the renin-angiotensin-ADH system and the secretion of pancreatic polypeptide (PP) (and of glucagon in some subhuman species), and possibly the secretion of parathyroid

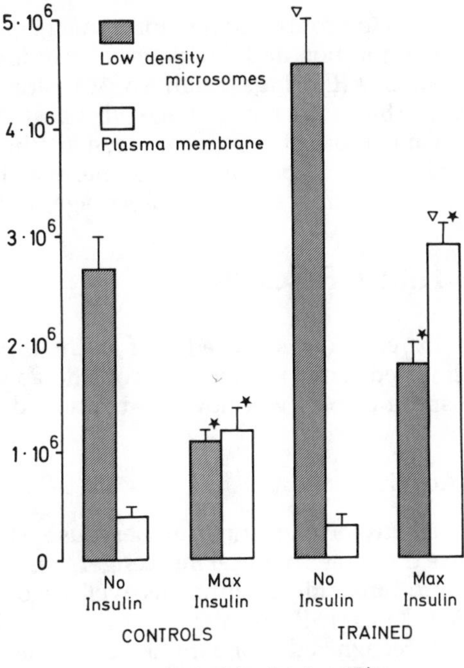

Figure 4. Effects of 11-week swim training on insulin-induced translocation of specific cytochalasin B binding sites. Trained rats were killed 43 hr after their last swim. Three pools of cells from trained rats and four pools from control rats were used. Each pool was prepared from 20-24 rats. Values are means ± SE. ▼ and ★ denote significant ($p < .05$) effect of training and insulin, respectively. *Note.* From "Effect of Physical Training on Glucose Transporters in Fat Cell Fractions" by J. Vinten, N. Petersen, B. Sonne, and H. Galbo, 1985, *Biochimica et Biophysica Acta*, **841**, pp. 223-227. Copyright 1985 by *Biochimica et Biophysica Acta*. Adapted by permission.

hormone (PTH) and gastrin. ACTH stimulates adrenal cortical secretion. In man, the secretion of the gonadotropins is not influenced by acute exercise, and increases in gonad hormone concentrations are due to decreased clearance.

The state of the organism prior to exercise is important for the magnitude of the hormonal response. Thus exercise capacity influences the response because this depends on the relative rather than on the absolute work intensity. Furthermore, the concentrations of other hormones are higher during exercise under several conditions in which insulin availability is lower than normal in the time preceding exercise. If exercise is continued, the hormonal changes may be gradually intensified due to feedback from metabolic error signals (among which a decrease in glucose availability probably is the most important), as well as from nonmetabolic error signals sensed by pressure, volume, osmolality, and temperature receptors.

In principle, the depicted control of the hormonal response to exercise is similar to that of respiration and circulation, including feed-forward and feedback components (Eldridge, Millhorn, & Waldrop, 1981; Stone, Dormer, Foreman, Thies, & Blair, 1985). Interestingly, hormonal responses very similar to those of exercise are seen in other kinds of stress (e.g., psychological stress, hyper- and hypothermia, hypoxia, hypoglycemia, trauma, burn injury, sepsis, hemorrhage, and surgery).

Directions for Future Research

Within the next 15 years, our knowledge of all the aspects of exercise endocrinology delineated above will increase considerably. Some general trends and more specific goals will now be mentioned.

Neuroendocrine Activity

A sharp distinction between endocrine and nervous systems is no longer appropriate because the same chemical messengers may act both as hormones and as neurotransmitters within as well as outside the CNS (Ganten et al., 1984; Krieger, Brownstein, & Martin, 1983). In addition to the about 10 well-recognized monoamines and amino acids, almost overnight nearly 40 small peptides have been discovered that are putative chemical messengers in the CNS (Ganten et al., 1984; Krieger et al., 1983). Exercise studies of the turnover of the new messengers in the periphery will be carried out, but turnover measurements in discrete brain areas that map the activity in various neuronal pathways will be of even greater interest. At least in animals, this should be possible (a) by measuring local pool sizes of the messengers and their metabolites (Smythe, Grunstein, Bradshaw, Nicholson, & Compton, 1984), (b) by following the pool size and local specific activity of the messengers after prelabeling with radioactive precursors, and (c) by quantitative histochemistry (Andersson, Fuxe, & Agnati, 1985) using fluorescent antibodies for peptides. Of special interest is the characterization of responses to exercise in CNS regions that potentially regulate endocrine and autonomic functions.

The distribution of peripheral sympathetic nervous activity during exercise will be studied in detail. It will be interesting to see if the present view that a threshold exercise intensity exists for recruitment of sympathetic activity is upheld. In man, regional sympathetic function will be estimated by infusion of radiolabeled norepinephrine, determination of local blood flow, arterial and venous concentrations of labeled and unlabeled norepinephrine, and calculation of organ-specific norepinephrine spillover rates (Galbo et al., 1985). In animals, direct recordings of electrical nervous activity can be made. Vagal activity should also be considered. Vagal activity to the heart is withdrawn during exercise but it cannot be ignored that its activity to other organs may increase (e.g., if hypoglycemia develops). In accordance with this assumption, the plasma concentrations of VIP and PHI, which may be derived from parasympathetic neurons (Lundberg et al., 1984), increase during prolonged exercise, as does the concentration of PP, which is known to be released by vagal activity in response to insulin-induced hypoglycemia (Kjaer et al., 1984).

Regulation

A more careful elucidation is needed of the involvement of central command in control of autonomic neurohormonal changes in exercise. Experiments in intact man can follow protocols used earlier in studies of central versus peripheral control of respiration and circulation in exercise (see Figure 5). In animals, it should be studied whether electrically stimulated or spontaneously developed episodes of sham locomotion are

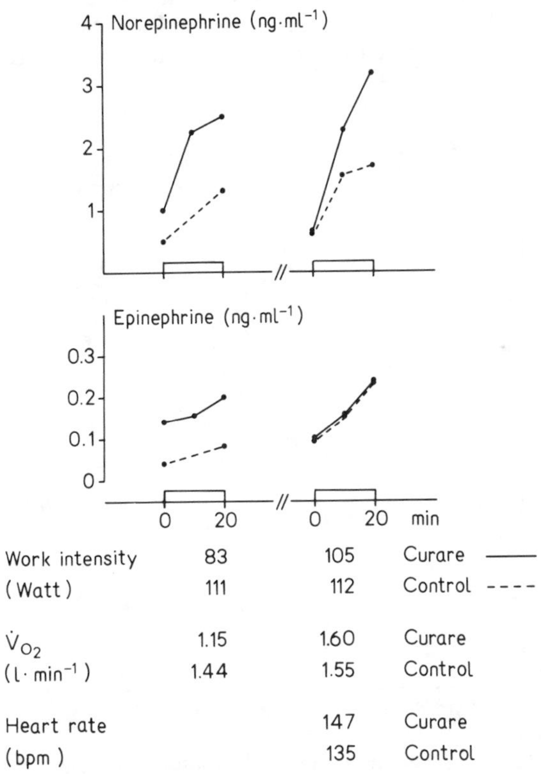

Figure 5. Catecholamine concentrations in plasma from an arterialized hand vein. On two different mornings, a subject performed supine cycling with and without partial neuromuscular blockade. Blockade increased the perceived exertion and probably the central command and was accompanied by high catecholamine and heart rate responses, relative to the absolute work intensity.

accompanied by neurohormonal changes (Eldridge et al., 1981). The central nervous pathways involved in the triggering of peripheral neuroendocrine changes in exercise should be further defined and their relative importance determined by application of specific lesions in the CNS (Stone et al., 1985) and by neurochemical techniques. The latter would include intracerebroventricular administration (Brown & Fisher, 1984) or more specific microinjection into brain nuclei (Iguchi, Matsunaga, Nomura, Gotoh, & Sakamoto, 1984) of putative chemical messengers and receptor-blocking agents. The influence of slowly developing feedback signals during exercise may be studied along the same lines and may include determination of the relationship between a given feedback signal and brain neuronal activity, as was shown in an experiment carried out at rest (Smythe et al., 1984).

Role

The role of the newer putative hormones in exercise should be elucidated following the principles outlined above. Progress in protein chemistry and molecular biology will reveal the structure of their receptors, and

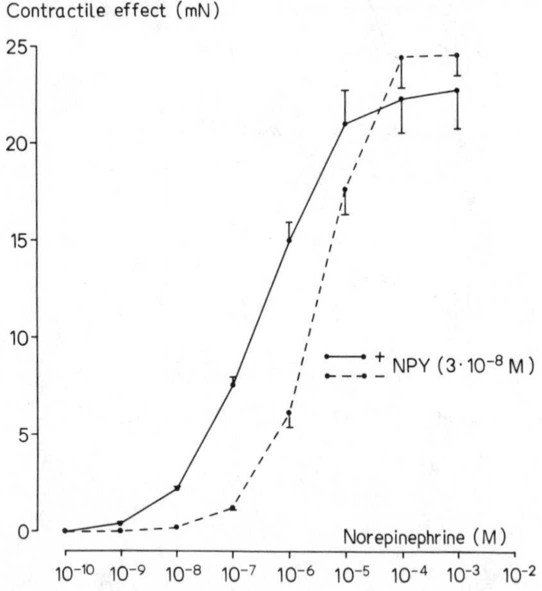

Figure 6. Concentration-response curves for the contractile effect of norepinephrine on smooth muscle (rabbit femoral artery) in the absence or presence of neuropeptide Y (NPY). Values are mean ± SE, n ⩾ 4. It can be seen that NPY markedly increased sensitivity to adrenergic stimulation. From "Neuropeptide Y Co-Exists and Co-operates With Noradrenaline in Perivascular Nerve Fibers" by E. Ekblad et al., 1984, *Regulatory Peptides*, **8**, pp. 225-235. Copyright 1984 by *Regulatory Peptides*. Adapted by permission.

specific receptor-blocking agents that are applicable in such studies will be developed. In the further elucidation of the role of neurohormonal changes in exercise, independent variation of several parameters is desirable and will be possible by computer-guided control of essential variables aided by more rapid chemical measurements than are used today. We know that during exercise, a delicate interplay exists between the well-recognized hormones, and an important interplay between these and the new putative messengers probably also occurs. An example of such an interplay demonstrated in vitro is shown in Figure 6. Interestingly, due to differences in local metabolism, the molar ratio between classical neurotransmitters and cosecreted peptides may change during prolonged nerve activation (Ganten et al., 1984).

Many of the newly discovered circulating peptides are released from the gut, with the secretion depending upon the gut content. Such peptides may be responsible for the newly discovered fact that an oral but not an intravenous glucose load influences the effect of insulin on fat cells (Bolinder, Östman, & Arner, 1985). Future research will probably confirm that the difference between work with and without food intake is not only a matter of substrate availability but also of activation (or lack of it) of a huge endocrine organ. Figure 1 shows that oral administration of glucose during exercise increases the plasma concentration of neurotensin, which may be derived from the small intestine.

The regulation of the mobilization of the various fuel stores is not equally well understood. Exercise-induced depletion of intramuscular triglyceride is difficult to measure precisely due to large biological variability in resting levels (Richter, Sonne, Mikines, Ploug, & Galbo, 1984; Spriet, Peters, Heigenhauser, & Jones, 1985), and its regulation is not clear. Intramuscular lipoprotein lipase may hydrolyze endogenous triglyceride in muscle of exercised rats (Oscai, Caruso, & Wergeles, 1982) and may be activated by beta-adrenergic mechanisms (see Spriet et al., 1985). A definitive characterization of the muscle lipase accounting for triglyceride breakdown in exercise and its regulation by extracellular and intracellular factors are important issues for future studies. Some investigators think that triglyceride stored in fat cells between the muscle fibers is more important than sarcoplasmic triglyceride as a local FFA source, but it is completely unclear how the former triglyceride store could be mobilized rather selectively during exercise. Muscle lipoprotein lipase activity may increase during exercise, especially in the fasting state (Budohoski et al., 1982), and increased blood flow and number of perfused capillaries containing lipoprotein lipase may also enhance uptake of triglycerides from plasma (Mackie, Dudley, Kaciuba-Uścilko, & Terjung, 1980). The hormonal regulation of the turnover of plasma triglycerides and protein has not been studied in detail during exercise, perhaps because neither substance is an important fuel in this condition. Finally, it has been pointed out that fuel mobilization enhanced by neurohormonal mechanisms may not be accurately adjusted to the energy needs of the working muscles during exercise (Galbo et al. 1986). The quantitative importance of such mismatching remains to be settled.

Adaptations

New adaptations to exercise within the neurohormonal system and the target cells influenced by this system have yet to be revealed. Recent examples include the discovery of a training-induced increase in the number of Na^+ and K^+ pumps in skeletal muscle and heart (Kjeldsen, Richter, Galbo, Lortie, & Clausen, 1986) and a decrease in the c'AMP response to epinephrine in liver. As indicated by the changed activity in the peripheral neuroendocrine system during exercise after a period of training, a search for adaptations within the CNS will be fruitful (Stone et al., 1985).

However, there is still much to be learned about the mechanisms responsible for the adaptations already known. Regarding the adaptation of pancreatic beta-cells mentioned above, the sensitivity of these cells to stimulation is directly related to the preceding plasma glucose level in normal subjects (Ward, Halter, Beard, & Porte, 1984). It is possible that a lower average glucose level in physically active individuals contributes to a diminished insulin response to physiological glucose concentrations. Another factor that might contribute is the high catecholamine levels in exercising individuals. In accordance with this hypothesis, rats' beta-cells develop an enhanced response to glucose during treatment with clonidine, which decreases sympathetic tone (Ishii, Yamamoto, & Kato, 1985).

Repeated sympathetic nervous stimulation may also cause increased adrenal medullary responsiveness (Kjaer et al., 1984), increased sensitivity of lipolysis in fat cells to adrenergic stimulation (Galbo, 1983) and an increased number of glucose transporters (Figure 4). The gene coding for the synthesis of the glucose transporter has recently been cloned, making possible studies at the levels of transcription and translation of the control of transporter concentration (Mueckler et al., 1985). A profound molecular characterization along such lines of all training-induced adaptations represents a huge and important problem, which will be intensively attacked during the next decades.

As suggested by the finding of increased adrenal medullary responsiveness in endurance-trained athletes who trained many years (Kjaer et al., 1984), differences in duration of training may explain discrepancies among previous studies of training-induced adaptations of endocrine and metabolic responses to exercise. The time courses of the adaptations should be clarified to establish whether major changes may take place after $\dot{V}O_2max$ has stopped increasing.

Attempts to further support the belief that exercise can be applied in the prevention and treatment of endocrine and metabolic diseases, and even aging, should be made by physiological and epidemiological investigations (Taylor, Ram, Zimmet, Raper, & Ringrose, 1984). Development of Type-II diabetes probably can be prevented in lean and hyperinsulinemic obese subjects by exercise-induced enhancement of insulin sensitivity (DeFronzo, 1982; Taylor et al., 1984; Unger & Grundy, 1985). It is also possible that beta-cells in overt hyperglycemic Type-II diabetics that are overloaded as a result of reduced average plasma glucose levels will adapt to training by an enhanced secretory responsiveness (Fujii et al., 1982; Garvey, Olefsky, Griffin, Hamman, & Kolterman, 1985; Reitman, Vasquez, Klimes, & Nagulesparan, 1984; Unger & Grundy, 1985).

Incorporation of exercise in slimming treatments may be helpful by increasing metabolic rate in the basal state (Lennon, Nagle, Stratman, Shrago, & Dennis, 1985) and possibly during food ingestion (Balon, Zorzano, Goodman, & Ruderman, 1984). This view is supported by the recent findings that insulin increases thermogenesis in muscle following exercise (Balon et al., 1984) and that training increases the basal epinephrine level (Kjaer et al., 1984), the number of Na^+ and K^+ pumps (Kjeldsen et al., 1986), and the stimulatory effect of epinephrine on oxygen consumption in muscle (Table 1). These observations relevant to treatment of obesity also indicate that studies of the interaction between exercise and drugs in the treatment of disease should be carried out.

Aging is accompanied by insulin resistance and decreased beta-cell function (Chen, Bergman, Pacini, & Porte, 1985). Nevertheless, identical insulin responses to glucose have been found in old and young athletes (Seals et al., 1984). Studies of young subjects indicate that the decreases in capacity to secrete epinephrine and in sensitivity of fat cells to beta-adrenergic stimulation can be counteracted by training. Future research will further clarify the extent to which training may interfere with changes in endocrinology and metabolism that are due to aging.

Finally, enhancement of training-induced adaptations by pharmacological means (i.e., doping) represents a depressing problem today (Alén, Häkkinen, & Komi, 1984). However, as this paper represents a look into the future, it should be pointed out that scientists someday will have to face even greater doping problems. Undoubtedly, the possibility

Table 1 The Effect of Epinephrine on Oxygen Uptake in Perfused Rat Hindquarter.

	Mean oxygen uptake (μmol/g muscle/hr) values (SEs in parentheses)		
Groups	No additions	Epinephrine 4 ng/ml	Epinephrine 9 ng/ml
Control rats	20 (1)	22 (2)	25 (1)*
Trained rats	20 (1)	24 (1)*	33 ± 1*,**

Note. 6–8 observations in each case. Data from "Endurance Training Augments the Stimulatory Effect of Epinephrine on Oxygen Consumption in Perfused Skeletal Muscle" by E.A. Richter, N.J. Christensen, T. Ploug, and H. Galbo, 1984, *Acta Physiologica Scandinavica*, **120**, p. 614. Copyright 1984 by *Acta Physiologica Scandinavica*. Adapted by permission.

* $p < .05$ compared to no addition.
** $p < .05$ compared to control rats.

will arise that exercise performance may be enhanced by administration of genes coding for desired properties to selected tissues in the prenatal state or in adult life.

Acknowledgments

The authors received support from The Danish Medical and Sports Research Councils, NOVO's Fund, The Danish Heart Foundation, and The P. Carl Petersen and Ib Henriksen Foundations.

References

Alén, M., Häkkinen, K., & Komi, P.V. (1984). Changes in neuromuscular performance and muscle fiber characteristics of elite power athletes self-administering androgenic and anabolic steroids. *Acta Physiologica Scandinavica*, **122**, 535-544.

Andersson, K., Fuxe, K., & Agnati, L.F. (1985). Determinations of catecholamine half-lives and turnover rates in discrete catecholamine nerve terminal systems of the hypothalamus, the preoptic region and the forebrain by quantitative histofluorimetry. *Acta Physiologica Scandinavica*, **123**, 411-426.

Balon, T.W., Zorzano, A., Goodman, M.N., & Ruderman, N.B. (1984). Insulin increases thermogenesis in rat skeletal muscle following exercise. *American Journal of Physiology*, **248**, E148-E151.

Björntorp, P. (1981). Effects of exercise on plasma insulin and glucose tolerance. In G. Enzi, G. Crepaldi, G. Pozza, & A.E. Renold (Eds.), *Obesity: Pathogenesis and treatment* (pp. 197-205). New York: Academic Press.

Blom, P.C.S., Høstmark, A.T., Flaten, O., & Hermansen, L. (1985). Modification by exercise of the plasma gastric inhibitory polypeptide response to glucose ingestion in young men. *Acta Physiologica Scandinavica*, **123**, 367-368.

Bolinder, J., Östman, J., & Arner, P. (1985). Effects of intravenous and oral glucose administration on insulin action in human fat cells. *Diabetes*, **34**, 884-890.

Brown, M.R., & Fisher, L.A. (1984). Brain peptide regulation of adrenal epinephrine secretion. *American Journal of Physiology*, **247**, E41-E46.

Budohoski, L., Kozlowski, S.T., Terjung, R.L., Kaciuba-Uśilko, H., Nazar, K., & Falecka-Wiezorek, I. (1982). Changes in muscle lipoprotein lipase activity during exercise in dogs fed on a mixed fat-rich meal. *Pflügers Archiv*, **394**, 191-193.

Chen, M., Bergman, R.N., Pacini, G., & Porte, D., Jr. (1985). Pathogenesis of age-related glucose intolerance in man: Insulin resistance and decreased beta-cell function. *Journal of Clinical Endocrinology and Metabolism*, **60**, 13-20.

Christensen, N.J., & Galbo, H. (1983). Sympathetic nervous activity during exercise. *Annual Review of Physiology*, **45**, 139-153.

DeFronzo, R.A. (1982). Insulin secretion, insulin resistance, and obesity. *International Journal of Obesity*, **6** (Suppl. 1), 73-82.

Ekblad, E., Edvinsson, L., Wahlestedt, C., Uddman, R., Håkanson, R., & Sundler, F. (1984). Neuropeptide Y co-exists and co-operates with noradrenaline in perivascular nerve fibers. *Regulatory Peptides*, **8**, 225-235.

Eldridge, F.L., Millhorn, D.E., & Waldrop, T.G. (1981). Exercise hyperpnea and locomotion: Parallel activation from the hypothalamus. *Science*, **211**, 844-846.

Fujii, S., Okuno, Y., Okada, K., Tanaka, S., Seki, J., & Wada, M. (1982). Effects of physical training on glucose tolerance and insulin response in diabetics. *Osaka City Medical Journal*, **28**, 1-8.

Galbo, H. (1983). *Hormonal and metabolic adaptation to exercise*. Stuttgart: Thieme-Stratton.

Galbo, H. (1985). The hormonal response to exercise. *Proceedings of the Nutrition Society*, **44**, 257-265.

Galbo, H. (1986a). Autonomic neuroendocrine responses to exercise. *Scandinavian Journal of Sports Science*, **8**, 3-17.

Galbo, H. (1986b). The hormonal response to exercise. *Diabetes/Metabolism Reviews*, **1**(4), 385-408.

Galbo, H., Hedeskov, C.J., Capito, K., & Vinten, J. (1981). The effect of physical training on insulin secretion of rat pancreatic islets. *Acta Physiologica Scandinavica*, **111**, 75-79.

Galbo, H., Hermansen, L., Fahrenkrug, J., Schaffalitzy de Muckadell, O.B., Holst, J., Holst Pedersen, J., & Hagen, C. (1985). The effect of training and glucose ingestion on responses of some GEP hormones to exercise. *Clinical Physiology*, **5** (Suppl. 4), A45.

Galbo, H., Kjaer, M., Richter, E.A., Sonne, B., & Mikines, K.J. (1986). The effect of exercise on norepinephrine and epinephrine responses with special reference to physical training and metabolism. *Proceedings of the Alfred Benzon Symposium 23: Adrenergic Physiology and Pathophysiology*. Copenhagen: Munksgaard International.

Galbo, H., Sonne, B., Vissing, J., Kjaer, M., Mikines, K., & Richter, E.A. (1986). Lack of accuracy of fuel mobilization in exercise. In G.L. Benzi, L. Packer, & N. Siliprandi (Eds.), *Biochemical Aspects of Physical Exercise* (pp. 221-234). Amsterdam: Elsevier Science.

Ganten, D., Lang, R.E., Archelos, J., & Unger, T. (1984). Peptidergic systems: Effects on blood vessels. *Journal of Cardiovascular Pharmacology*, **6**, S598-S607.

Garvey, W.T., Olefsky, J.M., Griffin, J., Hamman, R.F., & Kolterman, O.G. (1985). The effect of insulin treatment on insulin secretion and insulin action in Type II diabetes mellitus. *Diabetes*, **34**, 222-234.

Heath, G.W., Gavin, J.R., III, Hinderliter, J.M., Hagberg, J.M., Bloomfield, S.A., & Holloszy, J.O. (1983). Effects of exercise and lack of exercise on glucose tolerance and insulin sensitivity. *Journal of Applied Physiology*, **55**, 512-517.

Iguchi, A., Matsunaga, H., Nomura, T., Gotoh, M., & Sakamoto, N. (1984). Glucoregulatory effects of intrahypothalamic injections of bombesin and other peptides. *Endocrinology*, **114**, 2242-2246.

Ishii, K., Yamamoto, S., & Kato, R. (1985). Increase in insulin response to glucose in the rat chronically treated with clonidine. *Naunyn-Schmiedeberg's Archives of Pharmacology*, **328**, 253-257.

James, D.E., Burleigh, K.M., Kraegen, E.W., & Chisholm, D.J. (1983). Effect of acute exercise and prolonged training on insulin response to intravenous glucose in vivo in rat. *Journal of Applied Physiology*, **55**, 1660-1664.

Kjaer, M., Christensen, N.J., Sonne, B., Richter, E.A., & Galbo, H. (1985). The effect of exercise on epinephrine turnover in trained and untrained men. *Journal of Applied Physiology*, **59**, 1061-1067.

Kjaer, M., Mikines, K.J., Christensen, N.J., Tronier, B., Vinten, J., Sonne, B., Richter, E.A., & Galbo, H. (1984). Glucose turnover and hormonal changes during insulin-induced hypoglycemia in trained humans. *Journal of Applied Physiology*, **57**, 21-27.

Kjeldsen, K., Richter, E.A., Galbo, H., Lortie, G., & Clausen, T. (1986). Training increases the concentration of (3 H) oriabain = binding sites in rat skeletal muscle. *Biochimica et Biophysica Acta*, **860**, 708-712.

Krieger, D., Brownstein, M., & Martin, J. (Eds.). (1983). *Brain peptides*. New York: Wiley.

Krotkiewski, M., Björntorp, P., Holm, G., Marks, V., Morgan, L., Smith, U., & Feurle, G.E. (1984). Effects of physical training on insulin, connecting peptide (C-peptide), gastric inhibitory polypeptide (GIP) and pancreatic polypeptide (PP) levels in obese subjects. *International Journal of Obesity*, **8**, 193-199.

Lennon, D., Nagle, F., Stratman, F., Shrago, E., & Dennis, S. (1985). Diet and exercise training effects on resting metabolic rate. *International Journal of Obesity*, **9**, 39-47.

Lundberg, J.M., Fahrenkrug, J., Larsson, O., & Änggard, A. (1984). Corelease of vasoactive intestinal polypeptide and peptide histidine isoleucine in relation to atropine-resistant vasodilation in cat submandibular salivary gland. *Neuroscience Letters*, **52**, 37-42.

Mackie, B.G., Dudley, G.A., Kaciuba-Uśilko, H., & Terjung, R.L. (1980). Uptake of chylomicron triglycerides by contracting skeletal muscle in rats at rest. *Journal of Applied Physiology*, **49**, 851-855.

Mikines, K.J., Farrell, P.A., Sonne, B., & Galbo, H. (1985). Glucose dose response curve for plasma insulin after exercise in man. *Clinical Physiology*, **5** (Suppl. 4), A66.

Mueckler, M., Caruso, C., Baldwin, S.A., Panico, M., Blench, I., Morris, H.R., Allard, W.J., Lienhard, G.E., & Lodish, H.F. (1985). Sequence and structure of a human glucose transporter. *Science*, **229**, 941-945.

Oscai, L.B., Caruso, R.A., & Wergeles, A.C. (1982). Lipoprotein lipase hydrolyzes endogenous triacylglycerols in muscle of exercised rats. *Journal of Applied Physiology*, **52**, 1059-1063.

Reitman, J.S., Vasquez, B., Klimes, I., & Nagulesparan, M. (1984). Improvement of glucose homeostasis after exercise training in non-insulin-dependent diabetes. *Diabetic Care*, **7**, 434-441.

Richard, D., & LeBlanc, J. (1983). Pancreatic insulin response in relation to exercise training. *Canadian Journal of Physiology and Pharmacology*, **61**, 1194-1197.

Richter, E.A., Christensen, N.J., Ploug, T., & Galbo, H. (1984). Endurance training augments the stimulatory effect of epinephrine on oxygen consumption in perfused skeletal muscle. *Acta Physiologica Scandinavica*, **120**, 613-615.

Richter, E.A., Ruderman, N.B., Gavras, H., Belur, E.R., & Galbo, H. (1982). Muscle glycogenolysis during exercise: Dual control by epinephrine and contractions. *American Journal of Physiology*, **242**, E25-E32.

Richter, E.A., Sonne, B., Mikines, K.J., Ploug, T., & Galbo, H. (1984). Muscle and liver glycogen, protein, and triglyceride in the rat. Effect of exercise and of the sympatho-adrenal system. *European Journal of Applied Physiology*, **52**, 346-350.

Rolandi, E., Reggiani, E., Franceschini, R., Bavastro, G., Messina, V., Odaglia, G., & Barreca, T. (1985). Comparison of pituitary responses to physical exercise in athletes and sedentary subjects. *Hormone Research*, **21**, 209-213.

Seals, D.R., Hagberg, J.M., Allen, W.K., Hurley, B.F., Dalsky, G.P., Ehsani, A.A., & Holloszy, J.O. (1984). Glucose tolerance in young and older athletes and sedentary men. *Journal of Applied Physiology*, **56**, 1521-1525.

Smythe, G.A., Grunstein, H.S., Bradshaw, J.E., Nicholson, M.V., & Compton, P.J. (1984). Relationships between brain noradrenergic activity and blood glucose. *Nature*, **308**, 65-67.

Sonne, B., Mikines, K.J., Richter, E.A., Christensen, N.J., & Galbo, H. (1985). Role of liver nerves and adrenal medulla in glucose turnover in running rats. *Journal of Applied Physiology*, **59**, 1640-1646.

Spriet, L.L., Peters, S.J., Heigenhauser, G.J.F., & Jones, N.L. (1985). Rat skeletal muscle triacylglycerol utilization during exhaustive swimming. *Canadian Journal of Physiology and Pharmacology*, **63**, 614-618.

Stone, H.L., Dormer, K.J., Foreman, R.D., Thies, R., & Blair, R.W. (1985). Neural regulation of the cardiovascular system during exercise. *Federation Proceedings*, **44**, 2271-2278.

Taylor, R., Ram, P., Zimmet, P., Raper, L.R., & Ringrose, H. (1984). Physical activity and prevalence of diabetes in Melanesian and Indian men in Fiji. *Diabetologia*, **27**, 578-582.

Unger, R.H., & Grundy, S. (1985). Hyperglycaemia as an inducer as well as a consequence of impaired islet cell function and insulin resistance: Implications for the management of diabetes. *Diabetologia*, **28**, 119-121.

Vinten, J., Petersen, N., Sonne, B., & Galbo, H. (1985). Effect of physical training on glucose transporters in fat cell fractions. *Biochimica et Biophysica Acta*, **841**, 223-227.

Ward, W.K., Halter, J.B., Beard, J.C., & Porte, D., Jr. (1984). Adaptation of B and A cell function during prolonged glucose infusion in human subjects. *American Journal of Physiology*, **246**, E405-E411.

SECTION C:
MOTOR DEVELOPMENT

Naturalistic Research Can Drive Motor Development Theory

Jerry R. Thomas

Bronfenbrenner (1977) has defined contemporary developmental psychology as "the science of the strange behavior of children in strange situations with strange adults for the briefest possible periods of time" (p. 513). Unfortunately, that description fits motor development equally well. Although motor development is defined as the change in individuals' motor behavior across the lifespan, in practice we take such small cross-sectional snapshots of peoples' behavior that the results are nearly uninterpretable.

> In fact, we rarely take the time to keep our experimental hands off a behavior long enough to make systematic descriptive observations in naturalistic settings of the several dimensions and circumstances of the behavior we wish to study. Although we are intensely empirical about drawing cause and effect conclusions, we are quite nonempirical when it comes to selecting the behavior of interest, the particular measurement variable(s), the ecological context, the age of the subjects, and a host of other parameters. We apparently prefer to make all of these vital decisions a priori, rather than from a base of empirical descriptive information. As a consequence, much of our research represents a nearly blind run into a forest of behavior to study the growth of a single tree. (McCall, 1977, pp. 336-337)

These types of problems have resulted, at least to some extent, from the type of research paradigm motor development has adopted. Table 1 provides a contrast of some of the distinctions between the more frequently used (in recent years) motor development approach derived from experimental child psychology, and the less popular approach from child development (Reese & Lipsitt, 1970). In particular the methods of controlled laboratory settings versus observation in naturalist settings and the view of the child as reactive rather than self-active have been damaging to the generation of cohesive theories and rules of development and behavior. However, the important point in noting these distinctions is that if motor development is to make progress in developing theory that

Table 1 Differences in Approach for Experimental Child Psychology and Child Development

Experimental child psychology	Child development
	Purpose
Study of child as small adult	Study of behavioral change during childhood
Use of child as a convenient subject	Interest in the whole child as a developing person
	Methods
Manipulation of relevant variables in controlled laboratory settings	Observing children in naturalistic settings
	Theory
General behavioral or learning theories	Cognitive development or organismic theories
Child as reactive	Child as self-active
Emphasis on environmental effects	Emphasis on hereditary effects
Development is continuous	Development proceeds in stages
Explaining behavior	Describing behavior
	Philosophy
More basic in research	More applied in research

Note. From *Experimental Child Psychology* (p. 1-32) by H.W. Reese and L.P. Lipsitt, 1970, New York: Academic. Copyright 1970 by Academic. Adapted by permission.

ultimately finds use by practitioners, the merging of the benefits to be derived from both approaches must occur.

Developmental Methodology

Traditionally, developmental research (including motor development) has used either cross-sectional designs that evaluate age differences, or longitudinal designs that look at age changes. The two designs include three components (age, cohort, and time of measurement) that have proven difficult to separate in order to determine the source of differences and changes associated with development. *Age* refers to the chronological age of the subject; *cohort* refers to the experiences a certain age group of subjects have because of the generation into which they were born;

and *time of measurement* refers to the unique set of circumstances that surround a particular point at which measurements are made.

Cross-sectional designs have inherent confounding of age and cohort, that is, do 6- and 12-year-old subjects perform differently due to age effects or because the experiences of the current 6-year-olds differ from the experiences the 12-year-olds had when they were 6. Longitudinal designs cannot separate age effects from time of measurement, that is, do older subjects change from when they were younger because they become increasingly familiar with the test items on repeated testings. In addition, Botwinick (1973) has suggested that age and cultural effects may be confounded in longitudinal studies and that this problem may become more severe in the future due to the rapid rate of cultural change.

The design problems of age, cohort, and time of measurement appeared to have been solved by Schaie's (1965) proposal of the *general developmental model,* which allowed the evaluation of the relative contributions of age, cohort, and time of measurement to developmental trends. However, Schaie's approach was later questioned in an interesting series of articles in the *American Psychologist* (Baltes & Schaie, 1976; Horn & Donaldson, 1976, 1977); then a paper by Adam (1978) demonstrated the invalidity of the approach developed by Schaie. It appears that age, cohort, and time of measurement are certainly confounded and current methodology cannot separate them. However, this discussion is only meant to demonstrate the difficulty the motor developmentalist faces, not to indicate a reduced need for developmental research.

Purpose of This Paper

Motor development encompasses such a wide spectrum of areas and approaches that for any one paper to address the total field is impossible. For example, from a brief search I can identify ten general books that attempt an overview of motor development (Corbin, 1980; Cratty, 1970; Espenschade & Eckert, 1980; Gallahue, 1982; Keogh & Sugden, 1985; Rarick, 1973; Ridenour, 1978; Thomas, 1984; Williams, 1983; Zaichkowsky, Zaichkowsky, & Martinek, 1980), as well as five books that focus on some specific aspect of motor development (Connolly, 1970; Kelso & Clark, 1982; Roberton & Halverson, 1984; Roche & Malina, 1984; Wickstrom, 1983). Of course, innumerable books exist that devote one or more chapters to some aspect of motor development. In essence, motor development has encompassed topics such as how growth influences motor performance, physiological development and the differential influence of exercise across childhood and adolescence, developmental changes in the quantitative and qualitative aspects of movement patterns and motor performance, interaction of age with the learning and control of movements, and the influence of psychosocial variables on children's motor performance. Smoll (1982) has recommended the inclusion of this total field of study under the title *developmental kinesiology*.

Thus it is necessary for me to delimit this paper to a more circumscribed area—the study of developmental changes in motor performance and learning during childhood and adolescence. I will attempt to (a) trace the study of age changes in motor performance with particular attention to gender differences, (b) overview the theory development that has occurred in motor development, (c) briefly review some of the cognitive factors involved in the skill acquisition process, and finally (d) suggest some directions that research on children's skill acquisition should take. In particular, when suggesting the directions for future research, I will emphasize the need to study skill acquisition within real sport settings that demand an understanding of knowledge about the use of specific sport skills. I will suggest a paradigm within which that research might take place. Finally, I will spend a little time on whether motor development researchers can advance knowledge most effectively as a unified subdiscipline or as parts of other subdisciplines such as exercise physiology or motor learning and control.

Development and Skill Acquisition

Tracing the Study of Motor Performance in Children

Studies of children's motor performance have a 60-year history. Early studies in the 1920s and 1930s (Ames, 1937; Bayley, 1936; Burnside, 1927; Gutterige, 1939; McCaskill & Wellman, 1938; McGraw, 1935; Shirley, 1931; Wild, 1938) provided valid descriptions of the milestones of motor development as well as ages at which certain achievements in motor performance occurred. In addition, Wild (1938) provided a classic framework for evaluating the qualities of movement with her study of the development of overhand throwing patterns (much of which continues to be valid by today's standards, e.g., Roberton, 1982; Seefeldt & Haubenstricker, 1982). Various summaries of these early and subsequent age-related motor performance studies are available in the motor development textbooks previously cited. Most of these summaries focused on motor performance as it related to age and gender differences (e.g., Eckert, 1973), cultural and racial comparisons (e.g., Malina, 1973), and growth and physique (e.g., Malina, 1984; Malina & Rarick, 1973).

The most recent of these summaries is a meta-analysis by Thomas and French (1985) comparing gender differences across age in motor performance. Results of their analyses are based on 20 motor performance tasks using over 30,000 subjects. They reported 12 motor performance tasks in which gender differences were significantly related to age (Table 2), resulting in three distinct types of development curves (Figure 1). Curve *A* reflects what has been generally accepted as typical of gender differences in motor performance across age, but actually reflects only 5 of the 20 tasks reported. Thomas and French argue that gender differences represented by this type of curve are environmentally induced prior to puberty by parents treating boys and girls differently from birth. Teachers and coaches then accept these differences created by parents during preschool years as if they were biological and continue to expect and treat girls and boys as if they should perform motor tasks differently. Because

Table 2 Tasks for Which Gender Differences Were or Were Not Related to Age

Tasks in which gender differences were related to age	Tasks in which gender differences were not related to age
Balance	Agility
Catching	Anticipation timing
Dash	Arm hang
Grip strength	Fine eye-motor coordination[a]
Long jump	Flexibility[a]
Pursuit rotor tracking	Reaction time
Shuttle run	Throwing accuracy[b]
Sit-ups	Wall volley[b]
Tapping	
Throwing distance	
Throwing velocity	
Vertical jump	

Note. From "Gender Differences Across Age in Motor Performance: A Meta Analysis" by J.R. Thomas and K.E. French, 1985, *Psychological Bulletin*, **98**, p. 260-282. Copyright 1985 by *Psychological Bulletin*. Reprinted by permission.

[a]Girls performed better on these two tasks; boys performed better on all other tasks. [b]Gender differences in this category were relatively small except for these two tasks.

better performance on these 5 tasks is associated with increased size and strength, the differential effects of puberty on boys and girls produce increasingly larger differences in performance. However, the results are not all biological but represent the interaction between environment and biology. Our culture continues to influence adolescent males toward "masculine" behavior and adolescent females toward "feminine" behavior. Because many motor performance tasks are perceived as more appropriate for males, the motor performance differences due to biology are increased due to this attitude, which results in more practice and encouragement for males.

Curve *B* reflects two highly related tasks, throwing for distance or velocity. Thomas and French believe that, because these differences are so large (1.5 standard deviation units), occur so early in life (3–4 years of age), are present in cross-cultural studies, and are difficult to reduce by training, some biological basis exists for their presence prior to puberty. They identify several growth variables as possible contributors, including prepubescent boys having slightly more total lean body mass and less

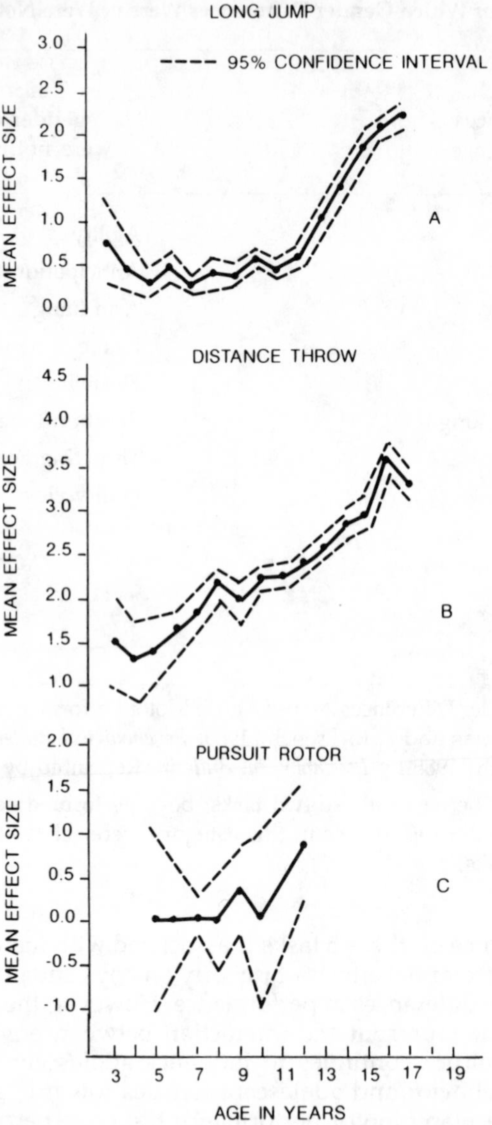

Figure 1. Three typical gender differences curves (expressed as effect sizes—standard deviation units) for motor performance across age. *Note*. From "Gender Differences Across Age in Motor Performance: A Meta-Analysis" by J.R. Thomas and K.E. French, 1985, *Psychological Bulletin*, **98**, p. 260-282. Copyright 1985 by *Psychological Bulletin*. Adapted by permission.

fat than girls, boys having a larger mesomorphic body-type component than girls, boys having more muscle tissue in the arm and shoulder than girls, boys having slightly longer forearms than girls, and boys having a greater biacromial/bicristal ratio than girls. But environment probably plays a greater role in the development of gender differences in throwing in our culture than in nearly any other task. Our society has developed a phrase that brings to mind an exact immature throwing pattern (i.e., "throws like a girl"). Thus, although some of the gender difference in throwing prior to puberty (and a larger portion after puberty) is due to biology, a considerably greater portion is due to the apparent lack of concern by parents, teachers, and coaches about the poor quality of girls' ability to throw.

Curve C reflects a situation in which gender differences are small or lacking until puberty, when boys' performance becomes substantially better than girls'. For tasks like tapping and pursuit rotor tracking, this postpuberty difference is probably environmentally induced by gender role identification. Attitudes like trying hard and persistence on these types of tasks are more likely to be encouraged in boys. Other tasks following this pattern such as balance, catching, and the vertical jump are more difficult to explain, but Thomas and French suggested that environmental factors were more likely for balance and catching, whereas biology played a larger role in the vertical jump.

For the eight tasks in which gender differences were not age related (see Table 2), only throwing accuracy and wall volley had large gender differences. These were generally attributed to environmental influences such as more encouragement and practice opportunities for males.

In summary, Thomas and French suggested that gender differences in all of the tasks except throwing for distance and throwing velocity were environmentally induced prior to puberty. However, beginning with adolescence, biology and environment interact to produce gender differences on tasks in which size, strength, and power are important. Throwing is the only task for which Thomas and French suggest that biology plays a role in the gender differences prior to puberty.

The implications from findings that synthesize this type of literature (Thomas & French, 1985) are consistent with theories regarding the development of sex roles. For example, cognitive-developmental (Kohlberg & Ullian, 1974) and transcendence (Hefner, Rebecca, & Oleshansky, 1975) approaches suggest that parents and peers have a major impact on the early development of children's sex roles. Teachers, parents, and peers become the most important influence on sex stereotyping when children enter elementary school. As adults, women and men choose the type of sex role that fits their nature. These same processes appear to be influential in the development of gender differences in motor performance.

Describing the Quality of Movement

Describing the developmental changes in the quality or form of movement has a long history. Beyond Wild's (1938) study of overhand throwing patterns, attention has been focused on many of the fundamental skills such as running, throwing, jumping, kicking, striking, and catching. Much of this work in recent years has been concentrated at the University of Wisconsin (for a review, see Roberton, 1982, 1984; Roberton & Halverson, 1984) and at Michigan State University (for a review, see

Seefeldt & Haubenstricker, 1982). Wickstrom (1983) provides a good overview of all this work.

The intent of these efforts is apparently to develop a standardized visual model of how children make these fundamental movements at various age levels. This information is then used with teachers in an attempt to change children's motor behavior toward a more mature pattern of performance.

Theories and Motor Development

As I have previously suggested, most of the research in motor development has been directed toward describing children's motor performance across age. These descriptions have resulted in information about the typical levels of performance at various ages (e.g., how fast children can run, how far children can throw) and visual models of how children's movements (e.g., running, throwing) look at various ages. In addition, there have been a few longitudinal studies reporting how children's movement outcome and form change (e.g., Halverson, Roberton, & Langendorfer, 1982; Roberton, 1978).

Very little theory building has occurred in motor development. Of course, unified theory building in an area with the scope of motor development is very difficult. But theories specific to areas of motor development (e.g., how fundamental skills develop, how children learn skills) have also been lacking. What has generally occurred (and maybe what is most appropriate) is the adaptation of theoretical constructs from other areas to important issues in motor development. The most common of these is whether the development of fundamental skills and the cognitive processes for the acquisition and control of these skills proceeds in *stages* or is *continuous*. A proposed basis for this approach has been presented by Wohlwill (1973) and summarized nicely by Roberton (1982):

1. discovery and synthesis of developmental dimensions—that is, determining what behavioral phenomena change regularly over time and how one might measure that change;
2. descriptive study of ages changes along the developmental dimension chosen;
3. study of the interpatterning of changes along two or more developmental dimensions;
4. study of the determinants of development;
5. study of individual differences in development. (p. 293)

One might note how nicely Wohlwill's framework corresponds to the major problems identified in the opening quote from McCall (1977), suggesting that we begin experimental work before ever discovering the developmental dimensions of interest, observing and accurately describing their development, and evaluating similar changes across more than one developmental dimension.

> Developmental psychologists should accord description the esteem other disciplines do because much has been learned at its hand: consider the theory of evolution, the plate theory of continental drift, and our knowledge of the early evolution of *Homo sapiens*. Paleontology, geology, and astronomy seem to be alive and well without manipulating fossils, continents, or heavenly bodies. (McCall, 1977, p. 337)

However, not everyone agrees with the need for exhaustive description prior to or in place of experimentation. Bronfenbrenner (1977) argues that those who advocate description prior to experimentation mistake the historical order of science for a causal one. Because naturalistic observation occurred prior to experimentation in the biological and physical sciences does not mean that is the natural order or the order of choice for the study of human behavior. He suggested that making this inference is simply a post hoc judgment of cause-effect. If the techniques and research strategies we use today had been available to earlier scientists, they could have made more rapid strides in formulating laws and principles than by using the techniques of exhaustive description. Bronfenbrenner (1977) then develops the following dictum: "If you wish to understand the relation between the developing person and some aspect of his or her environment, try to budge the one, and see what happens to the other" (p. 518).

Motor developmentalists appear to be divided into two groups, with each group being stuck at a different stage of work. One group observes and describes developmental behaviors of interest but does not continue to determine the causes of the changes in motor behavior. The other group jumps into determining causes before establishing clearly the developmental dimensions of the phenomenon they are studying. To some extent this is analogous to the models we have adopted from experimental child psychology and child development presented in Table 1. Unfortunately, neither group spends much time observing children's movements in naturalist settings, an important characteristic that Bronfenbrenner (1977), McCall (1977), and Wohlwill (1970) all believe to be essential to progress in all the areas that study human development. For example, children seldom throw balls with as much velocity as they can, especially with markings to identify various body segments (e.g., Roberton & Halverson, 1984); nor do they move linear slides and release reaction time switches (e.g., Thomas, 1980, 1984). I will suggest some solutions to these problems later in this paper.

There have been a few attempts at either theory building or theory testing in motor development. For example Roberton (1982) reports the procedures followed by her and her colleagues in attempting to test a stage theory model for overhand throwing. Keogh (1977), Newell and Barclay (1982), Thomas (1980), and Wade (1976) have reviewed the developmental nature of memory processes that influence motor skill development. Connolly (1970) attempted to integrate the area of developmental skill acquisition 15 years ago and Kelso and Clark (1982) have done so more recently.

Cognitive Factors in Children's Skill Acquisition

The study of children's skill acquisition has followed two approaches. One is to use models of memory derived from developmental psychology as a basis for understanding how children learn and perform. The models used most frequently have been adopted from general information processing (e.g., Kail & Hagen, 1977; Naus & Ornstein, 1983; Ornstein, 1978). Examples of tests of certain components related to motor development have been reported by Clark (1982), Newell and his colleagues (Barclay & Newell, 1980; Newell & Barclay, 1982; Newell & Kennedy, 1978), Thomas and his colleagues (Gallagher & Thomas, 1980, 1984; Thomas, 1980; Thomas, Gallagher, & Purvis, 1981; Thomas, Pierce, & Ridsdale, 1977; Thomas, Mitchell, & Solmon, 1979; Thomas, Thomas, Lee, Testerman, & Ashy, 1983; Winther & Thomas, 1981), Weiss (1983), and Wickens and Benel (1982). In general, these studies have suggested the following about children's movements: The speed with which information is moved through the memory system increases across childhood and adolescence, certain memory processes (e.g., encoding, rehearsal, response selection) are used less efficiently by younger children when compared to older children and adults, attention switching is less efficient in younger children, and knowledge-base deficits associated with younger age groups reduce the efficiency of memory function during movement (French & Thomas, 1987; McPherson & Thomas, in press). Some of these studies (Gallagher & Thomas, 1984; Thomas et al., 1983; Winther & Thomas, 1981) have indicated that younger children's motor performance becomes more similar to that of older children and adults when younger children are induced to use the more sophisticated memory strategies of the older age groups.

Stage models have also been used with studies of memory development and motor performance. The one most frequently used has been Pascual-Leone's (1976) *theory of constructive operators*. Pascual-Leone developed a neo-Piagetian theory that not only described the characteristics of stages but attempted to explain the transition rules that underlie a child's movement from one Piagetian stage to the next. Applications of this theory to children's motor performance have been undertaken by Thomas and his colleagues (Gerson & Thomas, 1977, 1978; Thomas & Bender, 1977) and Todor (1975, 1978, 1979). Although partial support for the usefulness of this theory for motor development was provided by these studies, stage theories in general have been questioned by Brainerd (1978), Piagetian and neo-Piagetian theory in particular by Chi (1976), and the application of neo-Piagetian theory to motor development by Thomas (1980). In general, stage theories have provided useful descriptions of developmental characteristics but have been unable to explain age-related changes in performance (Brainerd, 1978).

The second type of approach to explaining children's skill acquisition has been the adaptation of adult motor learning and control theories to developmental considerations. However, this approach has not been used consistently. What has occurred is that over several years certain learning and control investigators have found it useful for children to serve as subjects in their research. The results from this approach are summarized in a chapter by Shapiro and Schmidt (1982) regarding the developmental implications of *schema theory*. They suggest that the variability of practice hypothesis finds better support in studies using children because

> the differences appear to be larger and easier to demonstrate with children than with adults, perhaps suggesting that schemata are already developed in adults by the time the experimental tests are given; with children, it is possible that schema-rules are still being formed, and that the varied practice in the experiments provides substantial increases in schema strength. (p. 143)

A shortcoming of schema theory in particular and motor program theory in general is how the program is learned. The theorists sidestep this issue by assuming that the program is already in memory and thus concentrate on how it functions (Shapiro & Schmidt, 1982). However, the major questions of interest to a developmentalist are *how the program got there* and *how it changes with experience/practice*.

Further, none of the attempts at theory building in motor development consider how growth is taken into account as children are acquiring movement skills. How does increase in size (longer levers, changing points of balance) and change in proportion (e.g., decreasing proportion of total height made up by the head, increasing proportion of total height made up by the legs) influence the levels children go through in developing fundamental skills? How do motor programs account for growth, which sometimes occurs very rapidly, as they are being developed? Kugler, Kelso, and Turvey (1982) suggested that a motor programming approach (or a more general informational approach) is not a parsimonious way to explain the control of movement and particularly to account for growth. For example, changes in body scale require disproportionate changes in the force necessary to control movement. In a study of a 12-month growth period on the moments of inertia of children of varying ages, Jensen (1981) reported that the best predictor of the change was mass times height squared. These kinds of findings suggest that, although a movement may appear to remain the same from an external view during a period of growth, the quantities of forces and their timing must be changing—a view that is basically incompatible with motor programming theory. Additional support for this point of view using infants' early leg movements has been provided by Thelen (1983) and Thelen and Fisher (1983). For a different perspective, see Zelazo (1983). For a comprehensive look at an approach such as this using a basic postural response (balancing), read Shumway-Cook and Woollacott's (1985) paper on the growth of stability. Newell (1984) provides an interesting overview of the physical constraints that should be considered when theorizing about motor development.

Clearly, future research should consider growth in whatever theoretical model is to be used or developed. In particular, a means for motor programming theory to accommodate growth must be proposed and tested if that model is to be of any value for motor development. Maybe Kugler, Kelso, and Turvey (1982) offer a more useful direction, but tests of their proposals for naturally developing systems requiring little central control must be made. Thus there are numerous directions for future inquiry for researchers in motor development. Or, said more plainly, all the good research problems in motor development have not been used up; in fact, we have not even scratched the surface.

Directions for Future Research

The Need to Consider Experience

I believe that two deficiencies are present in the motor development literature that inhibit theory development and reduce the value of the findings to practitioners. To some extent the two deficiencies represent dimensions of the same issue. Motor developmentalists who have studied the development of fundamental skill patterns have failed to continue their descriptions of these patterns into the important sport skills of our culture. Thus we know essentially nothing about the relation of fundamental skills to specific sport skills; in fact, we have not even established whether fundamental skills are precursors to specific sport skills. The other deficiency is that researchers who have investigated children's motor skill acquisition have failed to study the use of sport skills and their most important component, previous experience. In fact, we have done just the opposite—trivial and novel skills have been used, which may have no relation to the acquisition of sport specific skills and certainly fail to consider the most important aspect of skilled performance, the knowledge base about the use of skills in sport settings. However, we are not alone. The same problem exists in developmental psychology where they have used nonsense tasks negating previous experience and controlled settings to attempt to study how memory and learning develop in children. Only recently have studies been conducted that attempt to examine learning in more ecologically valid situations where the evaluation of the child's previous knowledge may be used in assessing memory and task performance (e.g., Chi, 1978; Chi & Koeske, 1983; Lindberg, 1980; Ornstein & Naus, 1984).

Those of us who are interested in the development and acquisition of children's motor skills must change our focus to study the skills that are important in the movements and sports of our culture. I am not suggesting that we no longer study fundamental skills or the processes that underlie the acquisition of skilled behavior. But I am suggesting that we can no longer study these skills and processes in isolation from their major purpose—people's movement in sport and exercise settings.

I believe the logical conclusion of this line of thought is that we must study the developmental nature of skill acquisition in a sport-specific way. Doing so will allow us to develop a paradigm that can contribute to theory, yet have value for the persons who apply the knowledge—the mover and teacher of movement. The value of a sport-specific paradigm is that the important components of successful movement can be evaluated and their interaction studied (Thomas, French, & Humphries, 1986). Action, in the sense of sport performance, involves three components: knowledge about the game, the sport's skills, and their uses; the performer's ability to use the sport skills; and the interaction of knowledge and performance during game situations. For example, in a baseball game a runner is on first with one out. A ground ball of medium speed is hit to the shortstop. Several possibilities exist for action that depend on important aspects of cognitive and physical performance. Of course, the physical performance aspects are, can the shortstop field the ground ball and throw it successfully? But several cognitive actions are important:

- Has the shortstop developed a plan in advance that involves several if/then statements? If the ball is hit hard near me, then I will attempt a double play; if the ball is hit slowly to me, then I must charge it and throw to first base; if the ball is hit to the pitcher or the first or second basemen, then I must cover second base.
- Has the shortstop given the if/then statements differential probabilities depending on certain game circumstances? Is the batter a right- or left-handed hitter; what type of hitter is the batter based on previous experience?

Then, can the shortstop execute the cognitive plan while performing the correct motor action, depending on what the batter does?

From the previous description, the study of skilled performance can be divided into the performer's sport-specific knowledge base, the skills possessed by the performer, and the performer's ability to use the knowledge and skills during practices and games. A research paradigm is possible that includes the measurement of the knowledge and skill characteristics and a study of their interaction during practice and game situations. For example, using this approach, French and Thomas (1987) studied children's basketball performance by developing an inventory to measure specific knowledge about basketball, using tests to measure specific basketball skills, and then videotaping actual game situations and analyzing individual children's performances. These components were in two types of models. First, they looked at more skilled (expert) and less skilled (novice) players within two age levels. Then, they evaluated the interaction of knowledge and skill in game performance within this model. Second, they followed the younger age level (with a matched control group) through the course of the season to evaluate change in knowledge, skill, and their interaction in game performance.

French and Thomas's (1987) results were quite interesting, indicating that expert players at both age levels possessed more shooting skill and basketball knowledge than did novices, but the maximum discriminator between experts and novices was cognitive decision making during game performance. Basketball knowledge was related to decision-making skills, whereas dribbling and shooting skills were related to the motor components of game performance, control, and execution. In looking at changes over a basketball season, they noted that cognitive decision making during the game and basketball knowledge were the only components to improve. Only basketball knowledge was a significant predictor of decision making at the end of the season. Thus improvements in basketball performance during a season were basically cognitive in nature—players used their increased knowledge about basketball to make better decisions during the course of the game.

If a sport-specific approach is developed within a theoretical model of memory development and learning, I believe this approach offers considerable hope for contributing to theory as well as a meaningful advancement in the techniques for teaching and coaching of children in physical activity and sport. This approach is not unlike Costill's (1985) call for exercise physiologists to begin studying training methods and physiological responses within the sport and physical activity situations in which people exercise.

Should Motor Development Be a Separate Subdiscipline?

I want to end this paper with a question that causes me some consternation: Does it make sense for motor development to exist as a separate subdiscipline? I am not approaching this question from the standpoint of justifying a discipline or subdiscipline area (see Smoll, 1982). Rather, I want to consider how the greatest contribution can be made to knowledge about the development of children's movement. Before discussing this question, I think it is important to identify the alternative to motor development existing as a separate subdiscipline. The obvious alternative is for developmental researchers to function within other subdisciplines such as motor learning and control, exercise physiology, biomechanics, and sport psychology.

What are the advantages to having motor development exist separately? Clearly the major focus is our similar interest in the developing child. This allows us to provide intellectual and emotional support for each other. Another obvious advantage is that a body of knowledge is created from which teachers and coaches can more conveniently draw knowledge for use in such areas as elementary physical education, youth sports, and adapted physical education.

However, there are also some disadvantages. For example, motor developmentalists usually take an approach to their research that is closely associated with another subdiscipline. For example, what I do is closely associated with motor learning and control; what Roberton does is closely associated with biomechanics; Rarick's work is closely associated with growth factors in exercise. In fact, I would judge that our methodologies and paradigms are much more like these other subdisciplines than each other. A legitimate question might then be posed as to whether we might advance knowledge more rapidly by a closer association with the appropriate subdiscipline rather than with each other.

I am not sure of the best answer to this question, but I believe we may be asking the question from the wrong perspective. In my view the question is not whether we have a body of knowledge, a unique methodology, and a critical mass of scholars. The more important question is, How can we most rapidly advance knowledge about the important questions associated with children's movement, sport, and exercise?

References

Adam, J. (1978). Sequential strategies and the separation of age, cohort, and time-of-measurement contributions to developmental data. *Psychological Bulletin*, **85**, 1309-1316.

Ames, L. (1937). The sequential patterning of prone progression in the human infant. *Genetic Psychology Monographs*, **19**, 409-460.

Baltes, P.B., & Schaie, K.W. (1976). On the plasticity of intelligence in adulthood and old age: Where Horn and Donaldson fail. *American Psychologist*, **31**, 720-725.

Barclay, C.R., & Newell, K.M. (1980). Children's processing of information in motor skill acquisition. *Journal of Experimental Child Psychology*, **30**, 98-108.

Bayley, N. (1936). *The California infant scale of motor development*. Berkeley, CA: University of California Press.

Botwinick, J. (1973). *Aging and behavior*. New York: Springer.

Brainerd, C.J. (1978). The stage question in cognitive-developmental theory. *The Behavioral and Brain Sciences*, **2**, 173-213.

Bronfenbrenner, U. (1977). Toward an experimental ecology of human development. *American Psychologist*, **32**, 513-531.

Burnside, L. (1927). Coordination in the locomotion of infants. *Genetic Psychology Monographs*, **2**, 283-372.

Chi, M.T.H. (1976). Short-term memory limitations in children: Capacity or processing deficits? *Memory and Cognition*, **4**, 559-572.

Chi, M.T.H. (1978). Knowledge structures and memory development. In R. Siegler (Ed.), *Children's thinking: What develops?* (pp. 73-105). Hillsdale: Erlbaum.

Chi, M.T.H., & Koeske, R.D. (1983). Network representation of a child's dinosaur knowledge. *Developmental Psychology*, **19**, 29-39.

Clark, J.E. (1982). The role of response mechanisms in motor skill development. In J.A.S. Kelso & J.E. Clark (Eds.), *The development of movement control and co-ordination* (pp. 151-173). New York: Wiley.

Connolly, K. (Ed.) (1970). *Mechanisms of skill development*. New York: Academic Press.

Corbin, C. (Ed.) (1980). *A textbook of motor development* (2nd ed.). Dubuque, IA: Wm. C. Brown.

Costill, D. (1985). Practical problems in exercise physiology research. *Research Quarterly for Exercise and Sport*, **56**, 378-384.

Cratty, B.J. (1970). *Perceptual and motor development in infants and children*. New York: Macmillan.

Eckert, H.M. (1973). Age changes in motor skills. In G.L. Rarick (Ed.), *Physical activity: Human growth and development* (pp. 155-175). New York: Academic Press.

Espenschade, A.S., & Eckert, H.M. (1980). *Motor development* (2nd ed.). Columbus, OH: Charles E. Merrill.

French, K.E., & Thomas, J.R. (1987). The relation of knowledge development to children's basketball performance. *Journal of Sport Psychology*, **9**, 15-32.

Gallagher, J.E., & Thomas, J.R. (1980). Effects of varying post-KR intervals upon children's motor performance. *Journal of Motor Behavior*, **12**, 42-46.

Gallagher, J.D., & Thomas, J.R. (1984). Rehearsal strategy effects on developmental differences for recall of a movement series. *Research Quarterly for Exercise and Sport*, **55**, 123-128.

Gallahue, D.L. (1982). *Understanding motor development in children*. New York: Wiley.

Gerson, R.F., & Thomas, J.R. (1977). Schema theory and practice variabililty within a neo-Piagetian framework. *Journal of Motor Behavior*, **9**, 127-134.

Gerson, R.F., & Thomas, J.R. (1978). A neo-Piagetian investigation of the serial position effect in children's motor learning. *Journal of Motor Behavior*, **10**, 95-104.

Gutteridge, M. (1939). A study of motor achievements of young children. *Archives of Psychology*, No. 244.

Halverson, L.E., Roberton, M.A., & Langendorfer, S. (1982). Development of the overarm throw: Movement and ball velocity changes by seventh grade. *Research Quarterly for Exercise and Sport*, **53**, 198-205.

Hefner, R., Rebecca, M., & Oleshansky, B. (1975). Development of sex-role transcendence. *Human Development*, **18**, 143-158.

Horn, J.L., & Donaldson, G. (1976). On the myth of intellectual decline in adulthood. *American Psychologist*, **31**, 701-719.

Horn, J.L., & Donaldson, G. (1977). Faith is not enough: A response to Baltes-Schaie claim that intelligence does not wane. *American Psychologist*, **32**, 369-373.

Jensen, R.K. (1981). The effect of a 12-month growth period on the body moments of inertia of children. *Medicine and Science in Sports and Exercise*, **13**, 238-242.

Kail, R.V., & Hagen, J.W. (Eds.) (1977). *Perspectives on the development of memory and cognition*. Hillsdale: Erlbaum.

Kelso, J.A.S., & Clark, J.E. (Eds.) (1982). *The development of movement control and co-ordination*. New York: Wiley.

Keogh, J.F. (1977). The study of movement skill development. *Quest*, **28**, 76-88.

Keogh, J., & Sugden, D. (1985). *Movement skill development*. New York: Macmillan.

Kohlberg, L., & Ullian, D.Z. (1974). Stages in the development of psychosexual concepts and attitudes. In R.C. Friedman, R.M. Richart, & R.L. Vande Wiele (Eds.), *Sex differences in behavior* (pp. 209-222). New York: Wiley.

Kugler, P.N., Kelso, J.A.S., & Turvey, M.T. (1982). On the control and co-ordination of naturally developing systems. In J.A.S. Kelso & J.E. Clark (Eds.), *The development of movement control and coordination* (pp. 5-78). New York: Wiley.

Lindberg, M.A. (1980). Is the knowledge base development a necessary and sufficient condition for memory development? *Journal of Experimental Child Psychology*, **30**, 401-410.

Malina, R.M. (1973). Ethnic and cultural factors in the development of motor abilities and strength in American children. In G.L. Rarick (Ed.), *Physical activity: Human growth and development* (pp. 334-363). New York: Academic Press.

Malina, R.M. (1984). Physical growth and maturation. In J.R. Thomas (Ed.), *Motor development during childhood and adolescence* (pp. 2-26). Minneapolis, MN: Burgess.

Malina, R.M., & Rarick, G.L. (1973). Growth, physique, and motor performance. In G.L. Rarick (Ed.), *Physical activity: Human growth and development* (pp. 125-154). New York: Academic Press.

McCall, R.B. (1977). Challenges to a science of developmental psychology. *Child Development*, **48**, 333-344.

McCaskill, C.L., & Wellman, B. (1938). A study of common motor achievements at the preschool level. *Child Development*, **9**, 141-150.

McGraw, M.B. (1935). *Growth: A study of Johnny and Jimmy*. New York: Appleton-Century Co.

McPherson, S.L., & Thomas, J.R. (in press). Relation of knowledge structure and performance in boys' tennis: Age and expertise. *Journal of Experimental Child Psychology*.

Naus, M.J., & Ornstein, P.A. (1983). Development of memory strategies: Analysis,'questions, and issues. In M.T.H. Chi (Ed.), *Trends in memory development research: Vol. 9. Contributions to human development* (pp. 1-30). Basel: Karger.

Newell, K.M. (1984). Physical constraints to the development of motor skills. In J.R. Thomas (Ed.), *Motor development during childhood and adolescence* (pp. 105-120). Minneapolis, MN: Burgess.

Newell, K.M., & Barclay, C.R. (1982). Developing knowledge about action. In J.A.S. Kelso & J.E. Clark (Eds.), *The development of movement control and co-ordination* (pp. 175-212). New York: Wiley.

Newell, K.M., & Kennedy, J.A. (1978). Knowledge of results and children's motor learning. *Developmental Psychology*, **14**, 531-536.

Ornstein, P.A. (Ed.) (1978). *Memory development in children*. Hillsdale: Erlbaum.

Ornstein, P.A., & Naus, M.J. (1984). *Effects of knowledge base on children's processing*. Unpublished manuscript. University of North Carolina, Chapel Hill.

Pascual-Leone, J. (1976). Metasubjective problems of constructive cognition: Forms of knowing and their psychological mechanism. *Canadian Psychological Review*, **17**, 110-125.

Rarick, G.L. (Ed.) (1973). *Physical activity: Human growth and development*. New York: Academic Press.

Reese, H.W., & Lipsitt, L.P. (Eds.) (1970). *Experimental child psychology*. New York: Academic Press.

Ridenour, M.V. (Ed.) (1978). *Motor development: Issues and applications*. Princeton, NJ: Princeton Book Co.

Roberton, M.A. (1978). Longitudinal evidence for developmental stages in the forceful overarm throw. *Journal of Human Movement Studies*, **4**, 161-175.

Roberton, M.A. (1982). Describing "stages" within and across motor tasks. In J.A.S. Kelso & J.E. Clark (Eds.), *The development of movement control and co-ordination* (pp. 293-307). New York: Wiley.

Roberton, M.A. (1984). Changing motor patterns during childhood. In J.R. Thomas (Ed.), *Motor development during childhood and adolescence*. Minneapolis, MN: Burgess.

Roberton, M.A., & Halverson, L.E. (1984). *Developing children—their changing movement: A guide for teachers*. Philadelphia: Lea & Febiger.

Roche, A.F., & Malina, R.M. (Eds.) (1983). *Manual of physical status and performance in childhood* (Vol. 1). New York: Plenum.

Schaie, K.W. (1965). A general model for the study of developmental problems. *Psychological Bulletin*, **64**, 92-107.

Seefeldt, V., & Haubenstricker, J. (1982). Patterns, phases, or stages: An analytical model for the study of developmental movement. In J.A.S. Kelso & J.E. Clark (Eds.), *The development of movement control and co-ordination* (pp. 309-318). New York: Wiley.

Shapiro, D.C., & Schmidt, R.A. (1982). The schema theory: Recent evidence and developmental implications. In J.A.S. Kelso & J.E. Clark (Eds.), *The development of movement control and co-ordination* (pp. 113-150). New York: Wiley.

Shirley, M. (1931). *The first two years. A study of 25 babies: Postural and locomotor development* (Vol. 1). Minneapolis, MN: University of Minnesota Press.

Shumway-Cook, A., & Woollacott, M.H. (1985). The growth of stability: Postural control from a developmental perspective. *Journal of Motor Behavior*, **17**, 131-147.

Smoll, F.L. (1982). Developmental kinesiology: Toward a subdiscipline focusing on motor development. In J.A.S. Kelso & J.E. Clark (Eds.), *The development of movement control and co-ordination* (pp. 319-354). New York: Wiley.

Thelen, E. (1983). Learning to walk is still an "old" problem: A reply to Zelazo (1983). *Journal of Motor Behavior*, **15**, 139-161.

Thelen, E., & Fisher, D.M. (1983). The organization of spontaneous leg movements in newborn infants. *Journal of Motor Behavior*, **15**, 353-377.

Thomas, J.R. (1980). Acquisition of motor skills: Information processing differences between children and adults. *Research Quarterly for Exercise and Sport*, **51**, 158-175.

Thomas, J.R. (Ed.) (1984). *Motor development during childhood and adolescence*. Minneapolis, MN: Burgess.

Thomas, J.R., & Bender, P.R. (1977). A developmental explanation for children's motor behavior: A neo-Piagetian interpretation. *Journal of Motor Behavior*, **9**, 81-93.

Thomas, J.R., & French, K.E. (1985). Gender differences across age in motor performance: A meta-analysis. *Psychological Bulletin*, **98**, 260-282.

Thomas, J.R., French, K.E., & Humphries, C.A. (1986). Knowledge development and sport skill performance: Directions for motor behavior research. *Journal of Sport Psychology*, **8**, 259-272.

Thomas, J.R., Gallagher, J.D., & Purvis, G.J. (1981). Reaction time and anticipation time: Effects of development. *Research Quarterly for Exercise and Sport*, **52**, 359-367.

Thomas, J.R., Mitchell, B., & Solmon, M.A. (1979). Precision knowledge of results and motor performance: Relationship to age. *Research Quarterly*, **50**, 687-698.

Thomas, J.R., Pierce, C., & Ridsdale, S. (1977). Age differences in children's ability to model motor behavior. *Research Quarterly*, **48**, 592-597.

Thomas, J.R., Thomas, K.T., Lee, A.M., Testerman, E., & Ashy, M. (1983). Age differences in use of strategy for recall of movement in a large scale environment. *Research Quarterly for Exercise and Sport*, **54**, 264-272.

Todor, J.I. (1975). Age differences in integration of components of a motor task. *Perceptual and Motor Skills*, **41**, 211-215.

Todor, J.I. (1978). A neo-Piagetian theory of constructive operators: Application to perceptual-motor development and learning. In D.M. Landers & R.W. Christina (Eds.), *Psychology of motor behavior and sport* (pp. 507-521). Champaign, IL: Human Kinetics.

Todor, J.I. (1979). Developmental differences in motor task integration: A test of Pascual-Leone's theory of constructive operators. *Journal of Experimental Child Psychology*, **28**, 314-322.

Wade, M.G. (1976). Developmental motor learning. In J. Keogh & R.S. Hutton (Eds.), *Exercise and sport science reviews* (Vol. 4, pp. 375-394). Santa Barbara, CA: Journal Publishing Affiliates.

Weiss, M.R. (1983). Modeling and motor performance: A developmental perspective. *Research Quarterly for Exercise and Sport*, **54**, 190-197.

Wickens, C.D., & Benel, D.C.R. (1982). The development of time-sharing skills. In J.A.S. Kelso & J.E. Clark (Eds.), *The development of movement control and co-ordination* (pp. 253-272). New York: Wiley.

Wickstrom, R.L. (1983). *Fundamental motor patterns* (3rd ed.). Philadelphia: Lea & Febiger.

Wild, M.R. (1938). The behavior patterns of throwing and some observations concerning its course of development in children. *Research Quarterly*, **9**, 20-24.

Williams, H. (1983). *Perceptual and motor development*. Englewood Cliffs, NJ: Prentice-Hall.

Winther, K.T., & Thomas, J.R. (1981). Developmental differences in children's labeling of movement. *Journal of Motor Behavior*, **13**, 77-90.

Wohlwill, J. (1973). *The study of behavioral development*. New York: Academic Press.

Zaichkowsky, L.D., Zaichkowsky, L.B., & Martinek, T.J. (1980). *Growth and development*. St. Louis, MO: C.V. Mosby.

Zelazo, P.R. (1983). The development of walking: New findings and old assumptions. *Journal of Motor Behavior*, **15**, 99-137.

Developmental Sequence and Developmental Task Analysis

Mary Ann Roberton

Two aspects of motor development immediately come to mind when one thinks of application: (a) the use of developmental sequences by teachers and therapists, and (b) the use of developmental task analysis (Herkowitz, 1978) by teachers. I would like to discuss the present and future of research in these two areas. In so doing, I occasionally find myself straying from the topic of "applied" research. In retrospect, I believe this happens because current problems in the applied research of motor development reflect current problems in its theoretical research. Indeed, great gulfs have never existed between the theoretical and applied aspects of motor development. Perhaps this is due to the relative immaturity of the field, although I would prefer to think it due to the fact that most motor development researchers are actually interested in both topics! Certainly, many motor development scholars were originally stimulated to begin their research for clinical reasons. Basically, however, I suspect the lack of strong division between theoretical and applied motor development simply emphasizes that, like most dichotomies, applied versus theoretical research is a false dichotomy (Roberton, 1984). Rather than admitting that I can't stay on the topic, I will simply say that my paper will be journeying along a continuum formed by these two notions.

Developmental Task Analysis

The literature of motor development has always contained incidental reference to the effects that the immediate environment surrounding the performer or actor can have on that actor's movement; recent developmental studies by Barnett (1984) on jumping and Roberton (1987) on throwing in the face of moving environments reflect a new, systematic interest in this topic, stimulated primarily by J. Gibson's (1979) ecological approach to perception and E. Gibson's (1982) casting of that approach into a developmental framework. At the close of this paper, I will briefly address the theoretical importance of these ideas.

In terms of applied research, however, many physical educators point to Halverson's (1966) essay on motor pattern development in children as the seminal article in focusing contemporary thought on the applied aspects of the environmental question. Herkowitz (1978) subsequently cast the area into useful form for application when she proposed her *developmental task analysis*. As indicated in Table 1, developmental task analysis basically involves analyzing the environmental factors that affect performance on a given skill.[1] Each factor is then further analyzed in terms of levels of difficulty. Thus, in the striking example shown, it is presumed that under the factor, "length of handle," it would be easiest for a child to use an implement with no handle at all, then progress to a short handle and, gradually, to a longer handled implement. By looking across the top row of this particular task analysis, a teacher could easily formulate a beginning practice situation for striking: one that involved a large, motionless, lightweight ball having plenty of color contrast with the background (perhaps an 8 1/2 in. vinyl ball suspended or sitting on a tee). The child would strike this with his or her hand or with a glove-paddle, an enlarged surface fixed to the hand via an elastic strap. Successful performance in this practice situation would suggest to the teacher that the child was ready for added complexity. To do this, the teacher would simply move downward in one of the columns, changing the total practice difficulty by changing the level of complexity in one or more columns.

Developmental task analysis is appealing as a teaching tool for several reasons. It focuses on the individual child, showing in chart form how different children could be practicing at the same time, yet have the practice situation individualized for each of them. In addition to making individualized instruction seem manageable to teachers, developmental task analysis tells them exactly how to add complexity to the child's environment. At the same time, it allows for teacher creativity and decision making because teachers can design the specific environments that fulfill the descriptions in the task analysis. Moreover, they can choose which particular column to manipulate for a particular child.

For the creative teacher, developmental task analysis also can lead to equipment design, for certain cells in the analysis may suggest equipment that does not exist commercially. The chart gives a developmental rationale for equipment that far exceeds those rationales usually given in the equipment monographs now available for teachers. The equipment designed at Ohio State University under Herkowitz's guidance shows the fine degree to which creativity and developmental understanding can join to produce useful and stimulating (as opposed to "cute") equipment for children (Herkowitz, 1980).

Clearly, then, developmental task analysis could be one of motor development's most tangible contributions to physical education. Indeed, I would predict that its use will increase dramatically in the next 15 years as teachers become more aware of its possibilities. The problem, however, from the standpoint of applied research is that teachers must currently *guess* both the environmental factors to be included in the task analysis and the levels of difficulty within each column. Surprising as

Table 1 Developmental Task Analysis
Task: Striking With an Implement

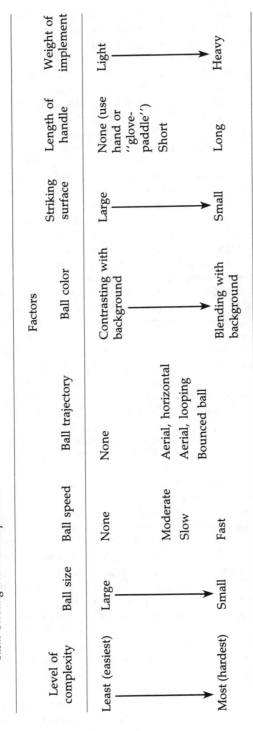

Level of complexity	Factors						
	Ball size	Ball speed	Ball trajectory	Ball color	Striking surface	Length of handle	Weight of implement
Least (easiest) ↓	Large ↓	None	None	Contrasting with background ↓	Large ↓	None (use hand or "glove-paddle")	Light ↓
						Short	
		Moderate	Aerial, horizontal				
		Slow	Aerial, looping				
			Bounced ball				
Most (hardest)	Small	Fast		Blending with background	Small	Long	Heavy

Note. From *Developing Children—Their Changing Movement: A Guide for Teachers* (p. 139) by M.A. Roberton and L. Halverson, 1984, Philadelphia: Lea & Febiger. Copyright 1984 by Lea & Febiger. Reprinted by permission.

it may seem, relatively little applied research exists to help fill a developmental task analysis table. Table 1, for instance, is simply a best guess taken from Roberton and Halverson (1984).

This is not to say that no research exists on the relative effects of the immediate environment on children's movement. Some published work has been done on factors such as ball/background colors (Morris, 1976), ball size (DuRandt, 1985; McCaskill & Wellman, 1938; Payne, 1985), ball velocity and/or trajectory (DuRandt, 1985; Ridenour, 1974; Williams, 1983), but almost all involve single studies with little followup. In addition, other work in this area exists (e.g., Bruce, 1967; Victors, 1961), but it is composed of unpublished master's and doctoral theses, or pilot work. Although the Herkowitz (1978) task analysis framework can easily be placed in an ANOVA or MANOVA design, no motor development researcher has yet done this. Current studies tend to be one-shot affairs, lacking the central focus that the Herkowitz (1978) framework could provide, or that a more generalized framework, such as that of Gentile, Higgins, Miller, and Rosen (1975), or an even more encompassing, theoretical framework, such as Gibson's (1979), could provide.

These comments are symptomatic of a key problem with motor development research as a whole, whether theoretical or applied. Unlike the area of motor control/learning (our alter ego), motor development has been unable to stimulate groups of people to work on a common issue, or individuals to do more than one study on a topic. The result is a literature formed of isolated studies that fail to build theory. One only needs to look at the powerful heuristic effects that Adams' (1971) closed-loop theory or Schmidt's (1975, 1976) generalized motor program theory have had on the development of research in motor control to know what a serious problem it is for motor development to be devoid of attempts at theory building.

It is apparent that few motor development researchers follow the ideal of "strong inference" research (Platt, 1964) in which a logical flowchart of studies is designed a priori to answer a research question. The result of each study determines which subsequent path of the flowchart (succeeding experiment) will be carried out. Moreover, each experiment is designed so that each finding rules out alternative hypotheses. Typically, motor development studies are just the opposite: They rarely are conceived ahead of time as a series of studies, and they almost always are *weak inference*, that is, countless alternative hypotheses exist for the findings presented due to insufficient logical or statistical controls.

One reason for the presence of one-shot, applied, environmental studies in motor development is that they have frequently been performed by people intending to be practitioners rather than researchers. These people have done their one study to get their degree and then have gone back to the real world. It seems to me that the only way long-term validation of a developmental task analysis is going to take place is for permanent researchers in motor development to take leadership in this area. Yet, this is currently a frustrating suggestion to make because so much work needs to be done. A generous estimate of the number of *active* (one or two publications yearly) American researchers in motor development is around 20. Membership in the Motor Development Academy (a group within the American Alliance for Health, Physical Education, Recreation, and Dance interested in sharing applied motor development information among practitioners) is close to 3,000. Thus, in just this one example, we would have 20 individuals trying to do the research needed to answer 3,000 requests.

In the future, I can envision teams of teachers collecting data within a developmental task analysis framework, under the leadership of a trained motor development researcher. What better way for applied research to take place? I have other predictions to make about the future place of environmental questions in motor development research, but I shall save these until I have discussed the current status of my second topic, developmental sequence research.

Describing Developmental Sequences

The question of developmental sequences in motor behavior has both applied and theoretical aspects, just as do questions about the role of the environment surrounding the mover. The existence of developmental sequences for specific motor skills seems well accepted in contemporary motor development literature, although the usefulness of describing such sequences for individual tasks has been questioned by some motor development theorists (e.g., Keogh & Sugden, 1985). These criticisms are well taken if description is done only for the sake of describing, but if the description is undertaken as part of a larger theoretical viewpoint, such as classical stage theory (Langendorfer, 1982; Roberton, 1982), then I believe the criticisms are unwarranted. Moreover, as Flavell (1982) argues about cognitive developmental sequences, "a careful analysis of sequences may give us hints about possible developmental mechanisms or processes that produce these sequential changes" (p. 22).

Yet, the so-called "process" literature of motor development is full of urgings to "go beyond" description, which usually has meant to abandon description. I would like to argue that going beyond description does not have to mean abandoning it; rather, it should mean using the descriptive information as a reality check on our theoretical constructs. As I have said for a number of years (Roberton, 1978), the descriptive information we now have should become the dependent variables in experimental studies of motor development. Only in this way will studies of the processes of development be directly tied to the outcomes of those processes. At present, we have process-oriented studies that minimize movement *or* we have movement-oriented studies that minimize process. Obviously, I would like to see studies that can directly relate process to a specific developmental function, such as a specific motor development sequence. To do that accurately, one would need to have both variables in the same study.

Examples of the kind of research I am talking about abound in the ethological literature, which is one reason, I suspect, that ethologists win Nobel prizes. Behaviors described in an animal's natural setting are subsequently reproduced in the laboratory where environmental events are simulated and manipulated in order to find which fostered the actions of interest or explained the reasons for those actions. A classic example is Tinbergen's (1951) studies of the stickleback fish. In the natural setting he had observed that the male stickleback stayed near the entrance to the nest when it contained fertilized eggs. In this location the male continuously produced a fanning-like movement of the pectoral fins and tail. The reason for this peculiar behavior was not readily discernible in field studies. Replicated in the laboratory, experiments were made on preventing the fanning, and on allowing it but covering the eggs with a glass dish. Tinbergen discovered that, in both cases, the eggs died. This led to the deduction that the fanning produced a current of aerated water that passed over the eggs in the nest, providing needed ventilation. A subsequent experiment showed that, in the absence of a male, the eggs did develop normally if a stream of aerated water was passed through the nest artificially.

Konrad Lorenz demonstrated that the direction of inquiry can also go from the laboratory to the field (cited in Tinbergen, 1970). He observed that his captive jackdaws often flew low over his head with repeated passes and wagged their tails just in front of him. In the laboratory the adaptive significance of such behavior was totally unclear, so he returned to the field to study wild jackdaws. He found that the behavior was the signal used by jackdaws to stimulate other flock members to join them in flight.

Thus the ethologist, who is a highly trained observer of the animal in its natural environment, has not been content to "just" describe; rather, he or she works back and forth between description in the natural setting and laboratory experimentation. In fact, Tinbergen also brought the laboratory to the field (Hinde, 1983). That is, many of his early experiments did not place the animal in a rigidly controlled laboratory situation; rather, they involved experimental control of one or more factors in the natural setting. I would like to point out that Jerry and Kathi Thomas have recently attempted studies of this type (Thomas, Thomas, Lee, Testerman, & Ashy, 1983), replicating in the field laboratory findings on memory for distance and location. Interestingly, the findings from jogging out of doors were the same as those from lever positioning in the laboratory!

My urging to adopt an ethological perspective does not condone what I see as present weaknesses in the descriptive literature on motor patterns. The clear difference in the descriptive work of motor development and the descriptive work of the ethologists is that the motor development literature has failed to describe the *environment* that was surrounding the documented motor changes (Roberton, 1984; 1987). Thus it is often more difficult to go directly into the laboratory with testable ideas from the descriptive research. Moreover, most of the descriptively oriented researchers in motor development have simply failed to take the next step of laboratory research.

I would argue, however, that description should not be considered the lowly, bottom rung in a hierarchy that is climbed in the desire for scientific respectability; rather, it should be continually used as a verification of laboratory results and as a suggestion for further, interesting independent variables. Moreover, I would predict that future researchers in motor development will be both movement- *and* process-oriented, much like the ethologists of today.

From an applied standpoint, however, the usefulness of developmental sequence description does not need to be defended. Knowledge of developmental sequences can help teachers know if their interventions are working in a positive or negative fashion (Roberton & Halverson, 1984); for instance, seeing whether a child's movement is progressing or regressing would be the key to knowing when a child was ready for further complexity or was needing simplification within a particular task. Also, teachers can use developmental sequences as formal or informal assessment instruments (Harper, 1979; Roberton & Halverson, 1984).

Indeed, almost every motor development textbook writer publishing since 1980 has felt a certain obligation to provide the reader with a listing of developmental sequences for at least some motor skills. Much of the credit for this state of affairs is due to Wickstrom's (1983) well-known book entitled *Fundamental Motor Patterns*. In this text he popularized for physical educators the notion that children's movement does not look like skilled, adult movement but that, over time, it undergoes predictable, successive transformations that eventuate in adult (or "mature") behavior. Prior to Wickstrom, McGraw (1935/1975; 1945/1969) and others had described developmental sequences for infant motor tasks. These have had particularly great influence on physical therapists, some of whom try to model therapeutic progressions for recovery on such sequences (e.g., Bobath, 1971). In addition to current textbooks, the popularity of motor development sequences can be seen in convention programs. National associations such as the American Alliance for Health, Physical Education, Recreation, and Dance and the American Physical Therapy Association devote many sessions of their conventions to providing such information to teachers and therapists. So, interest in the topic is currently very high.

The problem, again, from the applied research standpoint is that few developmental sequences have been validated for motor skills of interest to physical educators or physical therapists. Validation of a sequence ultimately requires longitudinal studies and studies of generalizability. Although shortcuts exist (Roberton, Langendorfer, & Williams, 1980), they can never substitute for longitudinal validation. Hence, a serious shortage of validated sequences exists.

Second, a misconception has occurred in the field between what is a *validated* developmental sequence and what is a developmental sequence that will be *useful* for practitioners (Roberton, 1977). Writers of texts oriented toward teachers/therapists have tended to do one of three things: (a) they have used the most valid sequences they can obtain verbatim from the theoretical literature, (b) they have modified the theoretical information into their best guess at what teachers may be able to see, or (c) they have simply made up their own sequences from, cursory at best, reviews of literature. Obviously, each of these procedures has self-evident problems.

The basic reason for these problems is that a key intermediate step between theory and application is missing. To make validated motor development sequences useful to teachers or therapists, applied researchers must take those movement descriptions into the field to see which parts of them can be seen by the practitioner under typical clinical conditions. A possible research design might involve the teacher and a second observer, and a videotaped record of the class. The second observer would allow interobserver reliability checks of live observation, whereas the videotape would allow both observers to recheck what really happened (i.e., their actual accuracy in identifying developmental levels as they appeared). Armed with precise information about what teachers can *see* out of what researchers *know* is a valid developmental sequence, we could then construct *accurate* and *useful* modified sequence information for clinicians.

What I am arguing for here is a clear sense of the difference between scientifically accurate data and data that are useful to teachers (Roberton, 1977). Once people understand that distinction more clearly, the future should bring a host of these intermediate, applied studies. Again, however, that cannot be done until more research is performed on the actual validity of more developmental sequences.

Coordination Within a Changing Environment

I would like to close this paper on applied aspects of motor development with a few comments about the future of the theoretical side of the two topics I've spoken about today: the environment and development sequences. I do this only briefly because theory was not my charge; however, as I said at the onset, applied research is necessarily tied to the theoretical. As such, it can be only as good as its theoretical base.

Turvey (Fitch & Turvey, 1978) has alerted those of us who study motor behavior to James Gibson's (1979) ecological theory of perception in which he stressed that the environment and the organism have co-evolved. As a result, each organism has an ecological niche, a place in the environment to which it is uniquely adapted. Because of this adaptation, Gibson argued that the perceptual pickup of the organism is very direct, with little need for mediating structures such as schemas or memory traces. From a developmental perspective, this possibility is demonstrated by Gibson and Walk's (1960) visual cliff experiments in which crawling babies refused to crawl to their mothers over a hard surface that looked like it did not afford support (see E. Gibson, 1982 for this interpretation). Schiff's (1965) looming experiments with various young animals, from chicks to fiddler crabs, demonstrated equally convincingly that a spot of light enlarging at a rapid rate on a screen in front of these animals caused them to flinch or duck as though an object were approaching at a rapid rate. The visual cliff, the looming object each provided action-oriented information to these organisms, information that was not mediated from past experience (i.e., a memory store), but was more likely inherent in the patterned texture of the surface, in the one case, and in the rapid magnification within the optic array, in the second case.

This view of perception as direct rather than indirect or mediated is an alternative proposal to current theories of information processing as they relate to action. It is not that human beings cannot process information in the ways that have been described (Stelmach, 1982; Thomas, 1980); the question is, rather, is this the way they relate perception and action normally? In daily movement interactions with their environments, might they operate more in terms of the affordances (Gibson, 1979) that they perceive in those environments: walking where it appears stepable; picking up only objects that appear graspable (Gibson, 1979)?

If Gibson's paradigm of perception and action takes hold, as I am predicting that it will, then motor development research on the actor within the environment will expand rapidly. We will be asking more specific questions about what the affordances for action are and, in particular, how we develop the perception of those affordances (Gibson, 1982), and how that relates to the changes in movement that occur with development.

Finally, I shall add a comment on some theory-related changes that are occurring in the description of motor skill development. I believe that future descriptions will attempt to go below the surface kinematics of the skill to explore the deeper structure of the movement. Gentile et al. (1975) attempted to do this in 1975. A more current example is the search for the complement of development, that is, invariance (Schmidt, 1985). Both the animal and the human motor control literature is replete with references to the notion that the control structures of movement, be they motor programs (Schmidt, 1985) or coordinative structures (Kugler, Kelso, & Turvey, 1980), may have some parameters that do not change over increases in speed, for instance. Such invariant parameters presumably represent an organizational given within the neuromotor system. I have suggested elsewhere (Roberton, 1986) that developmental study would provide the best search for the presence of invariance. Indeed, both Thelen (Thelen, Bradshaw, & Ward, 1981; Thelen & Fisher, 1982; Thelen, Ridley-Johnson, & Fisher, 1983) and Clark (Clark, Phillips, & Boyer, 1983; Clark, Phillips, & Whitall, 1984) have presented some interesting, developmental data suggesting that certain gait invariances appear quite early in development.

I (Roberton, 1986) have also recently discovered that relative timing invariances (time for an event divided by time for the total movement cycle) exist in the skill of hopping, some of which I have tracked longitudinally from their emergence at age 3 to age 18 in the same children. Although the children hopped farther, slower, and with longer flight times at age 18 than they did at age 3 (and had progressed through all the developmental levels of hopping), several timing actions in their hopping leg stayed relatively the same as when they were 3 years of age. These invariances may represent the way in which timing aspects of coordination are simplified for ease of control. Moreover, one of these, the time from landing to deepest knee flexion, also shows an invariant relationship across running and walking (Shapiro, Zernicke, Gregor, & Diestal, 1981). It would seem to represent a fundamental control characteristic or coordinative structure within foot locomotion (Roberton, 1986).

My point in mentioning these findings is that they represent a developmental approach, which uses the description of old but, then, attempts to look for the structure underlying that description. In this particular case, it is looking for variables that do not change in the face of other overt changes, such as those represented in developmental sequences. The lack of change over great periods of time seems to say that this is the way the nervous system is wired; in the face of body size changes, information-processing changes, and so forth, the relative timing of some aspects of the skill seems to be fixed. As Kugler, Kelso, and Turvey (1980, 1982) would say, a coordinative structure has been formed to simplify the control difficulties inherent in gait. Not all coordinative structures are formed so early, of course; my data show that the relative timing of the arms in the hop does not coalesce until age 14.

This type of research blends the descriptive tools of motor development and biomechanics, the questions of motor control, and the unique perspective of motor development into an exciting approach for answering fundamental questions on the development of coordination. Combined with an ecological or ethological perspective of the organism-environment singularity, as suggested by Kugler, Kelso, and Turvey (1982), this total approach has the possibility of giving renewed excitement to the study of motor development. The seeds for a rich, productive future for both theoretical and applied research are already in the literature of today.

References

Adams, J. (1971). A closed-loop theory of motor learning. *Journal of Motor Behavior*, **6**, 33-46.

Barnett, B. (1984). The use of potential visual cues in the organization of the jump by children and adults. *Dissertation Abstracts International*, **45**, 693B. (University Microfilms No. DA8411255)

Bobath, B. (1971). *Abnormal postural reflex activity caused by brain lesions* (2nd ed.). London: Heinemann.

Bruce, R. (1967). The effects of variations in ball trajectory upon the catching performance of elementary school children. (Doctoral dissertation, University of Wisconsin, Madison, 1966). *Dissertation Abstracts International*, **28**, 480A.

Clark, J., Phillips, S., & Boyer, J. (1983). Temporal characteristics of infant gait across speeds. *Psychology of motor behavior and sport-1983*. Abstracts of the Annual Convention of the North American Society for the Psychology of Motor Behavior and Sport, East Lansing, MI.

Clark, J., Phillips, S., & Whitall, J. (1984). The development of interlimb coordination in upright locomotion. *Abstracts of the 1984 Olympic Scientific Congress*, Eugene, OR.

DuRandt, R. (1985). Ball-catching proficiency among 4-, 6-, and 8-year-old girls. In J.E. Clark & J.H. Humphrey (Eds.), *Motor development: Current selected research* (Vol. 1, pp. 35-43). Princeton, NJ: Princeton Book Co.

Fitch, H., & Turvey, M. (1978). On the control of activity: Some remarks from an ecological point of view. *Psychology of motor behavior and sport—1977* (pp. 3-35). Champaign, IL: Human Kinetics.

Flavell, J. (1982). Structures, stages, and sequences in cognitive development. In W.A. Collins (Ed.), *The concept of development* (pp. 1-28). Hillsdale, NJ: Erlbaum.

Gentile, A., Higgins, J., Miller, E., & Rosen, B. (1975). The structure of motor tasks. In C. Bard (Ed.), *Mouvement* (pp. 11-28). Actes du 7 symposium en apprentissage psycho-moteur et psychologie du sport.

Gibson, E. (1982). The concept of affordances in development: The renascence of functionalism. In W.A. Collins (Ed.), *The concept of development* (pp. 55-81). Hillsdale, NJ: Erlbaum.

Gibson, E., & Walk, R. (1960). The visual cliff. *Scientific American*, **202**, 64-71.

Gibson, J. (1979). *The ecological approach to visual perception*. Boston: Houghton Mifflin.

Halverson, L. (1966). The development of motor patterns in young children. *Quest*, **6**, 44-53.

Harper, C. (1979). *Learning to observe children's motor development: Part 3. Observing children's motor development in the gymnasium*. Paper presented at the national convention of the American Alliance for Health, Physical Education, Recreation and Dance, New Orleans.

Herkowitz, J. (1978). Developmental task analysis: The design of movement experiences and evaluation of motor development status. In M. Ridenour (Ed.), *Motor development: Issues and applications* (pp. 139-164). Princeton, NJ: Princeton Book Co.

Herkowitz, J. (1980). Developmentally engineered equipment and playspaces for motor development and learning. In C. Nadeau, W. Halliwell, K. Newell, & G. Roberts (Eds.), *Psychology of motor behavior and sport—1979* (pp. 300-313). Champaign, IL: Human Kinetics.

Hinde, R. (1983). Ethology and child development. In P. Mussen (Ed.), *Handbook of child psychology* (Vol. 2, pp. 27-93). New York: Wiley.

Keogh, J., & Sugden, D. (1985). *Movement skill development*. New York: Macmillan.

Kugler, P., Kelso, J.A.S., & Turvey, M. (1980). On the concept of coordinative structures as dissipative structures: 1. Theoretical lines of convergence. In G. Stelmach & J. Requin (Eds.), *Tutorials in motor behavior* (pp. 3-47). New York: North-Holland.

Kugler, P., Kelso, J.A.S., & Turvey, M. (1982). On the control and coordination of naturally developing systems. In J.A.S. Kelso & J. Clark

(Eds.), *The development of movement control and coordination* (pp. 5-78). New York: Wiley.

Langendorfer, S. (1982). Horizontal structure in the development of motor skills. *Abstracts of Research—1982*. Reston, VA: American Alliance for Health, Physical Education, Recreation and Dance.

McCaskill, C.L., & Wellman, B. (1938). A study of common motor achievements at the preschool ages. *Child Development*, **9**, 141-150.

McGraw, M. (1969). *The neuromuscular maturation of the human infant*. New York: Hafner. (Original work published 1945)

McGraw, M. (1975). *Growth: A study of Johnny and Jimmy*. New York: Arno. (Original work published 1935)

Morris, G.S.D. (1976). Effects ball and background color have upon the catching performance of elementary school children. *Research Quarterly*, **47**, 409-416.

Payne, V.G. (1985). Effects of object size and experimental design on object reception by children in the first grade. *Journal of Human Movement Studies*, **11**, 1-9.

Platt, J. (1964). Strong inference. *Science*, **146**, 347-353.

Ridenour, M. (1974). Influence of object size, speed, and direction on the perception of a moving object. *Research Quarterly*, **45**, 293-301.

Roberton, M.A. (1977). Motor stages: Heuristic model for research and teaching. *Proceedings of the Annual Convention* (pp. 173-180). Orlando, FL: National Associations for Physical Education for College Men and Women.

Roberton, M.A. (1978). Stages in motor development. In M. Ridenour (Ed.), *Motor development: Issues and applications* (pp. 63-81). Princeton, NJ: Princeton Book Co.

Roberton, M.A. (1982). Describing 'stages' within and across motor tasks. In J.A.S. Kelso & J. Clark (Eds.), *The development of movement control and coordination* (pp. 293-307). New York: Wiley.

Roberton, M.A. (1984, May). *The weaver's loom: A developmental metaphor*. Paper presented to the R. Tait McKenzie Symposium, Motor behavior: An integrated perspective, University of Tennessee, Knoxville.

Roberton, M.A. (1986). Developmental changes in the relative timing of locomotion. In H.T.A. Whiting & M.G. Wade (Eds.), *Themes in motor development* (pp. 279-293). Dordrecht, The Netherlands: Martinus Nijhoff.

Roberton, M.A. (1987). Developmental level as a function of the immediate environment. *Advances in Motor Development Research*, **1**, 1-15.

Roberton, M.A., & Halverson, L. (1984). *Developing children—Their changing movement: A guide for teachers*. Philadelphia: Lea & Febiger.

Roberton, M.A., Langendorfer, S., & Williams, K. (1980). Pre-longitudinal screening of motor development sequences. *Research Quarterly for Exercise and Sport*, **51**, 724-731.

Schiff, W. (1965). Perception of impending collision. *Psychological Monographs*, **79**, No. 604.

Schmidt, R. (1975). A schema theory of discrete motor skill learning. *Psychological Review*, **82**, 225-260.

Schmidt, R. (1976). Control processes in motor skills. *Exercise and Sport Sciences Reviews*, **4**, 229-261.

Schmidt, R. (1985). The search for invariance in skilled movement behavior. *Research Quarterly for Exercise and Sport*, **56**, 188-200.

Shapiro, D., Zernicke, R., Gregor, R., & Diestal, J. (1981). Evidence for generalized motor programs using gait pattern analysis. *Journal of Motor Behavior*, **13**, 33-47.

Stelmach, G. (1982). Information-processing framework for understanding human motor behavior. In J.A.S. Kelso (Ed.), *Human motor behavior: An introduction* (pp. 63-91). Hillsdale, NJ: Erlbaum.

Thelen, E., Bradshaw, G., & Ward, J.A. (1981). Spontaneous kicking in month-old infants: Manifestation of a human central locomotor program. *Behavioral and Neural Biology*, **32**, 45-53.

Thelen, E., & Fisher, D. (1982). Newborn stepping: An explanation for a "disappearing reflex." *Developmental Psychology*, **18**, 760-775.

Thelen, E., Ridley-Johnson, & Fisher, D. (1983). Shifting patterns of bilateral coordination and lateral dominance in the leg movements of young infants. *Developmental Psychobiology*, **16**, 29-46.

Thomas, J.R. (1980). Acquisition of motor skills: Information processing differences between children and adults. *Research Quarterly for Exercise and Sport*, **51**, 158-173.

Thomas, J.R., Thomas, K., Lee, A., Testerman, E., & Ashy, M. (1983). Age differences in use of strategy for recall of movement in a large scale environment. *Research Quarterly for Exercise and Sport*, **54**, 264-272.

Tinbergen, N. (1951). *The study of instinct*. Oxford: Clarendon Press.

Tinbergen, N. (1970). Behavior and natural selection. In J. Moore (Ed.), *Ideas in evolution and behavior* (pp. 521-542). New York: The Natural History Press.

Victors, E. (1961). A cinematographical analysis of catching behavior of a selected group of seven and nine year old boys. (Doctoral dissertation, University of Wisconsin, Madison, 1961). *Dissertation Abstracts International*, **22**, 1903.

Wickstrom, R. (1983). *Fundamental motor patterns* (3rd ed.). Philadelphia: Lea & Febiger.

Williams, H. (1983). *Perceptual and motor development*. Englewood Cliffs, NJ: Prentice-Hall.

Note

1. Herkowitz (1978) actually included organismic factors as well as environmental ones in her developmental task analysis. Roberton and Halverson (1984) removed these to make the analysis procedure more clear.

Motor Development: A Commentary

G. Lawrence Rarick

Prior to commenting on the Thomas and Roberton papers, I want to remark on the meaning of motor development and the nature and problems of developmental research.

Biological development is the process of differentiation and evolution of living organisms by successive changes from a less perfect to a more highly organized state in structure and function. *Motor* as used here means movement as brought about by one's own neuromuscular system. Thus motor development is concerned with the changes or evolution of movement behavior that occurs with the passage of time. As an area of inquiry, it is dependent on the research methodologies of such fields of study as biomechanics, developmental anatomy, and developmental psychology.

Developmental research can be done on animals with relative ease, for their life spans are short, samples can be kept intact, genetic and environmental factors can be controlled, and experimental treatments can be introduced at will. This is difficult to do with humans. That is why most of the developmental research on humans has been done with infants and young children, essentially captive groups, where dropouts are minimal, reasonable controls can be applied, and the developmental changes are rapid and well defined.

The alternative to longitudinal research is the cross-sectional approach, one in which one-time measurements are taken on different age groups from which inferences can be made regarding developmental changes. Data from this source are useful in many ways, but such information may be misleading during periods of rapid growth. For example, the Harvard Growth Study (Shuttleworth, 1937, 1938, 1939) demonstrated that the timing and magnitude of the adolescent spurt in height and weight were essentially lost with the use of cross-sectional data due to the masking of age differences in sexual maturation and the effects of such differences on physical growth. Similarly, the impact of individual differences in rates of sexual maturation on the strength and motor performance of boys and girls was dramatically shown from the longitudinal data used in the California Adolescent Growth Study (Espenschade, 1940; Jones, 1949).

The above is not meant to imply that the cross-sectional method is of no value, for it serves a useful purpose not only in providing norms, but also, within limits, for predictive purposes.

As Thomas has pointed out, both longitudinal and cross-sectional methods are not without their problems. Yet, if the researcher is concerned with development per se, the factors affecting it, and the individuality of growth careers, the longitudinal method is the better approach. It is interesting that many of the papers in the present symposium have given considerable emphasis to individual differences and to how individuals of similar characteristics are affected differently by a given treatment or by a similar lifestyle.

Comments

Thomas poses the question, Why as children get older does their motor performance get better? This question would seem to have an obvious answer, namely that advancing age carries with it increases in body size, strength, and coordination, and an ever-increasing range of motor experiences. Although the foregoing is in a broad sense true, it is an oversimplified answer, for it gives no consideration to how these and other variables interact within a developmental framework.

The relative influence of biological and environmental factors lies at the heart of many developmental studies. Thomas elected to address the nature-nurture question by commenting on gender differences in motor performance in childhood and adolescence, using as a primary source the large-scale cross-sectional investigation by Thomas and French (1985). Although this investigation found age-related gender differences favoring boys on 12 of the 20 tasks, these investigators concluded that there is little to support a biological basis for this difference prior to puberty. On this there is general agreement, for boys are on the average only slightly larger and more muscular than girls prior to puberty. For example, at 9 years of age boys are only 8% heavier and 6% stronger than girls. After puberty, conditions are very different, for at 18 years of age boys are approximately 16% heavier and have 80% greater upper body strength than girls (Tuddenham & Snyder, 1954).

Few would disagree with the Thomas thesis that societal expectations are different for girls than for boys and that certain physical activities are viewed within our culture as being primarily either male or female appropriate.

The observation by Thomas that the immature throwing form of most girls is a product of our environment is generally accepted. Yet, the large and early-appearing gender differences in the performance of this skill led Thomas and French (1985) to conclude that this was the one activity for which such differences have a biological basis. Although it is true that research has shown that little is gained by attempts to improve the throwing performance of young girls, these studies were of limited duration (Glassow, Halverson, & Rarick, 1965; Halverson, Roberton, Safrit, & Roberts, 1977). In view of the slight sex difference in body size, body proportions, and muscular mass prior to puberty, it is difficult to believe that gender differences in this skill are biological.

By looking at sex differences in throwing performance of sexually mature champion athletes, a clearer picture of biological-cultural influences emerges, conditions under which training effects might be expected to be reasonably well balanced. For example, the Olympic record on the javelin throw for women was 40% less than for men in 1932 and only 24% less in 1984. This shows considerable catch-up on the part of women over this time frame. If one then compares these figures with the mean performance in the throw for boys and girls at 18 years of age, the performance of boys is almost twice that of girls (Espenschade, 1940). Furthermore, Plowman (1974) reports that gender performance comparisons of world records in most events show that female performance records are only 7 to 13% below those of males. Such differences are not great when one considers that male adults are on the average some 8% taller and 20% heavier than females. In view of these relatively small gender performance differences at a period in development when biological growth factors give a marked advantage to the male, the significance of cultural factors in accounting for sex differences in motor performance at younger ages becomes apparent.

The comment by Thomas that there have been few attempts at either theory building or theory testing in motor development is a fair statement. The principles of developmental morphology and developmental direction (Gesell, 1946) have provided a biological explanation for the sequential changes that occur in structure and behavior in early life, principles that are behaviorally less clearly defined in childhood and adolescence.

Psychologists over the years have likewise been faced with the problem of generating theories of intelligence that will stand the test of time. Recently, Sternberg (1985) proposed a three-faceted model of intelligence built around the individual's (a) internal world, (b) external world, and (c) the interface between the individual's internal and external worlds. Several methodologies have been used to get at the person's internal world such as factor analysis, information processing, schemata-mediated learning experiences, and real-world simulation. The external world of the individual, a major contributor to intelligence, cannot be understood solely by looking into the head, but rather by looking at the society in which the individual lives. The interface between the internal and external worlds as conceptualized by Piaget (1972) is oriented to the biological concept that survival is dependent on intelligent adaptation, in opposition to the developmental theory of Vygotsky (1978), who argues that intelligence has its origins in social processes. This triarchic theory will, Sternberg believes, result in research that will move us to a broad rather than a narrow conceptualization of intelligence.

If the above were used as a general model for the motor domain we have some of the ingredients for theory building. With respect to the individual's internal world, factor analysis has given us some insight into the structure of motor abilities of children by sex and age and across levels of intelligence (Rarick, 1980; Rarick, Dobbins, & Broadhead, 1976), and our understanding of the information-processing abilities across age levels for some motor tasks is increasing (Clark, 1982).

The influence of the external world on the child's motor development is self-evident. The role of significant others in the development of sport interests (Kenyon & McPherson, 1973) and the influence of our culture on gender differences in motor performance (Thomas & French, 1985) are illustrative.

The principle of similitude as proposed by Kugler, Kelso, and Turvey (1982) is a theoretical construct illustrative of the interaction between the child's internal and external worlds. This construct provides a logical association between the child's developing body and the motor programming mechanism that permits adaptations of a developing movement pattern to approximate the demands of the task.

Thomas proposes that future research direct attention to studying the learning of the sport skills of our culture within a normal sports setting. It is true that practically no research of this kind has been done. Over the years the tasks selected for research purposes have been laboratory bound and have for the most part had little relationship to sport skills. Those with a theoretical orientation would argue that the primary purpose of research is to generate new knowledge or basic information about human movement from which generalizations to sports activities can be made. It would seem safe to say that such research has had little if any impact on practice. The exception is in the area of biomechanics, where considerable applied research has been done on such individual sports as swimming, gymnastics, and track-and-field activities. This research, however, has usually not been developmental in nature.

The problem in researching team sports from a developmental perspective is the global nature of the problem, the many specific skills involved, and the complex nature of the decision-making processes. Coaches have for years used film analyses successfully to analyze individual and group performance under game conditions, but attempts to quantify such information from a research or developmental point of view have received scant attention.

Comments on Roberton

Roberton's paper on applied research in motor development has been directed primarily to two considerations, namely developmental task analysis and motor development sequences. The former, she holds, is a logical outgrowth of the latter.

The concept of developmental tasks is built upon the writings of Havighurst (1950), who proposed that throughout one's life span there are tasks common to our culture that, if successfully accomplished at the appropriate time, are not only psychologically satisfying but also the foundation for similar and more complex future tasks. When not successful, this experience leads to frustration and unfortunate consequences in the performance of future-related tasks. Basic to this concept is the need to select tasks appropriate to the developmental level of the individual. Roberton proposes to do this by selecting the proper task, modifying the implement, or simplifying the task condition. This general approach is not new, but Roberton has logically systematized the tasks in such a way that their effectiveness can be studied. This clearly is a fertile area for future research.

Roberton decries the small number of motor development specialists who are producers of research. This is in part a reflection on institutions of higher learning that have failed to impart to their students the value of combining applied research with their teaching, and on university researchers' failure to organize field research teams to test new ideas. Clearly, a major part of the future of motor development research rests on the collaboration of school systems in the conduct of long-term developmental studies.

A good case is built by Roberton for the use of descriptive research in investigating sequences in motor development, a method that has proved useful over the years (McGraw, 1946). She proposes that we now go beyond description by introducing descriptive information as dependent variables in experimental motor development studies as a check on our theoretical constructs. Thus the processes of development, she believes, can be associated directly with outcomes of these processes.

The general concept of attempting to verify the findings of field studies by controlled laboratory research is a widely accepted procedure and one that has merit, if the laboratory situation faithfully reflects the environment. In animal studies this can be done rather easily, but with humans, particularly if the investigation has a developmental orientation, it is difficult. It can be done if the researcher is willing to settle for short-term studies of a cross-sectional nature, but developmental inferences from such findings are suspect. Furthermore, manipulation of variables in a laboratory will tell us little about developmental processes per se, although the variables that affect developmental outcomes can in this way be identified, thus providing a reasonable basis for making inferences.

Basic information on neuromotor control mechanisms and their development must for the most part come from research on infra-humans or from humans with identifiable neuromotor disabilities. Neurophysiologists are cautious about making sweeping generalizations about motor control mechanisms and how they function. As Grillner (1985) points out, there is "now a variety of pieces of indirect evidence that is compatible with a unit central program generator hypothesis" (p. 148). Such unit pattern generators are housed in the spinal cord and lower brain centers and appear to be the mechanism for both automated and volitional control. How the interconnecting unit program generators function to carry out the multiple movements in such a simple task as walking is still not well understood. It would be hoped that in the future neurophysiologists and motor development researchers might join together in research of mutual interest.

Roberton presents some interesting comments on invariance in motor development, an area to which she and her colleagues have devoted considerable attention. The established role that nature plays in the sequential changes that occur in physical growth and early motor development is frequently given as an example of invariance. Behaviorally, invariance is a tendency to respond to a given situation in a particular way such that the accommodation processes result in structural or functional changes of a relatively permanent nature (Piaget, 1952). This invariance, according to Piaget (1971, 1976), in no small measure reflects our biological inheritance and is guided by relatively inflexible genetic programming systems. As applied to motor development, the basic question would seem to be, how invariant is the invariance and over what periods of time and for what kinds of movements does it apply?

Investigations by Roberton (1977, 1978) have led her to conclude that there is considerable within-year invariance in the pattern of movement in the humerus and forearm in young children executing the overarm throw, but when longitudinal observations of this movement were made on children over a period of 9 to 14 years (Roberton, 1978), the invariant model ranged from fair to excellent. This led her to propose a probability stage model, one that has the flexibility to account for individual exceptions.

The foregoing raises questions about invariance within stages and the transition of movement patterns from one stage to another. Some variance within stages would seem to be desirable, for it is difficult to believe that the transition would be abrupt, and such variance would presumably be in the direction of the next, more advanced sequence of the skill. Opponents of stage theory argue that transitions in behavior are gradual and occasionally coupled with some regression, although the general trend is in the direction of greater maturity.

The issue of invariance in motor development is clouded by the classic study on locomotion by Bernstein (1967), who concluded that the development of the structural elements of walking is in no sense direct, with some of the infantile characteristics surviving into adulthood and others disappearing in middle childhood only to make their appearance later. Improvements in this skill, as in others, are achieved by "utilizing all possible roundabout methods to reduce the number of degrees of freedom at the periphery to a minimum" (p. 107-108).

Stage theory raises the question of the importance of ensuring that children have the opportunity of moving through an ordered sequence of motor development. How does such a concept apply to particular skills? How flexible is nature in this regard? Clearly, the influence on motor behavior of central nervous system maturation and genetic programming lessens with advancing age, but how these factors function in sequencing motor behavior is an area of needed research.

Summary

Future research tends to evolve from ongoing research and from issues that are of concern to practitioners. The general discussion was largely directed to the latter, issues that can be best resolved by developmental investigations.

With the continuing increase in early sports specialization as seen in privately sponsored age group sports, some have questioned the long-term effects of such participation on the physical and psychological well-being of the participants. Investigations in this area have largely been one-time assessments, and hence little is known about long-term effects. Nor do we know the effects that early sport specialization may have on the development of a broad repertoire of motor skills or the impact that the time spent in such activities may have on academic achievement and the development of other worthwhile interests.

The question was raised regarding the impact of the women's movement on the motor development of school-age girls and the extent of their participation in school- and agency-sponsored individual and team sports. What are the attitudes of parents, medical personnel, and school authorities in this respect?

Concern was expressed for the possible long-term deleterious effects of physical activities that may place undue stress on the body's supportive structures. For example, can excessive daily jogging result in mild but progressive undetected trauma to the lower extremities? This is a future research need, as is the long-term effects of repeated strains and injuries to the musculoskeletal system of young athletes competing in contact sports.

Catch-up growth is a phenomenon characteristic of the physical growth of animals and humans. Is such a phenomenon characteristic of human motor development? How flexible or inflexible are developmental sequences in the acquisition of a particular motor skill? Do we have sufficient knowledge about motor development to apply this information effectively in helping the awkward child?

Present knowledge of the relative effects of hereditary and environmental factors in motor development is at best sparse (Kovar, 1981). This is a fruitful but difficult area of research, one that has practical significance for those involved in sports guidance for aspiring young athletes.

As the foregoing indicates, much research is needed in motor development. It is an area that is at present short of competent researchers. The question was asked if motor development as a special field of research should be retained. It is a specialty not unlike developmental anatomy, developmental psychology, and developmental physiology, each of which must call upon a parent discipline for its basic substance. If motor development as a speciality is not retained, who will study the developmental aspects of human movement?

References

Bernstein, N. (1967). *The coordination and regulation of movements.* New York: Pergamon.

Clark, J.E. (1982). Developmental differences in response processing. *Journal of Motor Behavior,* **14**, 247-254.

Espenschade, A. (1940). Motor performance in adolescence. *Monographs of Society for Research in Child Development,* **5**(1), 126-127.

Gesell, A. (1946). The ontogenesis of infant behavior. In L. Carmichael (Ed.), *Manual of child psychology* (pp. 295-331). New York: Wiley.

Glassow, R.B., Halverson, L.E., & Rarick, G.L. (1965). *Improvement of motor development and physical fitness of elementary school children* (Cooperative Research Project #696). Madison: University of Wisconsin.

Grillner, S. (1985). Neurobiological bases of rhythmic motor acts in vertebrates. *Science*, **228**, 143-149.

Halverson, L.E., Roberton, M.A., Safrit, M.J., & Roberts, T.W. (1977). Effect of guided practice on overhand-throw ball velocities of kindergarten children. *Research Quarterly*, **48**, 311-318.

Havighurst, R.J. (1950). *Developmental tasks and education*. New York: Longmans, Green.

Jones, H. (1949). *Motor performance and growth*. Berkeley: University of California.

Kenyon, G.S., & McPherson, B.D. (1973). Becoming involved in physical activity and sport: A process of socialization. In G.L. Rarick (Ed.), *Physical activity: Human growth and development*. New York: Academic Press.

Kovar, R. (1980). *Human variation in motor abilities and its genetic analysis*. Prague: Charles University.

Kugler, P.N., Kelso, J.A.S., & Turvey, M.T. (1982). On the control and coordination of naturally developing systems. In J.A.S. Kelso & J.E. Clarke (Eds.), *The development of movement control and coordination*. New York: Wiley.

McGraw, M.B. (1946). Maturation of behavior. In L. Carmichael (Ed.), *Manual of child psychology* (pp. 332-369). New York: Wiley.

Piaget, J. (1952). *The origins of intelligence in children*. New York: International Universities Press.

Piaget, J. (1971). *Biology and knowledge*. Chicago: University of Chicago Press.

Piaget, J. (1972). *The psychology of intelligence*. Totowa, N.J.: Littlefield Adams.

Piaget, J. (1976). The attainment of invariants and reversible operations in the development of thinking. In S. Campbell (Ed.), *Piaget sampler*. New York: Wiley.

Plowman, S. (1974). Physiological characteristics of female athletes. *Research Quarterly*, **45**, 349-362.

Rarick, G.L. (1980). The factor structure of the motor domain of mentally retarded children and adults. In M. Ostyn, G. Beunen, & J. Simons (Eds.), *Kinanthropometry II* (pp. 149-160). Baltimore: University Park Press.

Rarick, G.L., Dobbins, D.A., & Broadhead, G.D. (1976). *The motor domain and its correlates in educationally handicapped children*. Englewood Cliffs, NJ: Prentice-Hall.

Roberton, M.A. (1977). Stability of stage categorization across trials: Implications for the "stage theory" of overarm throw development. *Journal of Human Movement Studies*, **3**, 49-59.

Roberton, M.A. (1978). Longitudinal evidence for developmental stages in the forceful overarm throw. *Journal of Human Movement Studies*, **4**, 167-175.

Shuttleworth, F.K. (1937). Sexual maturation and the physical growth of girls six to nineteen. *Monographs of the Society for Research in Child Development*, **2**(5), 253.

Shuttleworth, F.K. (1938). Sexual maturation and the skeletal growth of girls age six to nineteen. *Monographs of the Society for Research in Child Development*, **3**(5), 56.

Shuttleworth, F.K. (1939). The physical and mental growth of girls and boys age six to nineteen in relation to age at maximum growth. *Monographs of the Society for Research in Child Development*, **4**(3), 291-292.

Sternberg, R.J. (1985). Human intelligence: The model is the message. *Science*, **230**, 1111-1118.

Thomas, J.R., & French, K.E. (1985). Gender differences across age in motor performance: A meta-analysis. *Psychological Bulletin*, **98**, 260-282.

Tuddenham, R.D., & Snyder, M.M. (1954). Physical growth of California boys and girls from birth to eighteen years. *University of California Publication in Child Development*, **1**, 183-364.

Vygotsky, L.S. (1978). *Mind in society: The development of higher psychological processes*. Cambridge: Harvard University Press.

SECTION D: MOTOR LEARNING

Toward a Better Understanding of the Acquisition of Skill: Theoretical and Practical Contributions of the Task Approach

Richard A. Schmidt

Understanding the acquisition of skill has been the focus of formal scientific interest for nearly a century, with a considerable increase in these activities in the 1960s. As beginning scientists at about this time, we were tremendously enthusiastic about the future of motor learning and its many relatives. Of course, for physical education one goal had always been the teaching of skills, and a vigorous approach to the scientific study of the motor learning seemed only natural. But more broadly, we were convinced that the acquisition of skill was a central concern for human functioning in general, being relevant to such diverse applications as job training and accident prevention in industry, artistic performance in music and dance, man-machine interactions in equipment and vehicle design, and the relearning of lost skill capabilities after traumatic injury or stroke. We believed that we could bring rigorous scientific procedures to bear on this largely understudied area and have a major impact on both theoretical understanding and practical application. Now, some 20 years later, I find it interesting to consider (a) what we have accomplished, (b) what forces have acted to direct our thinking and research, and (c) what we should do next in the study of these important general problems.

Motor Skills Acquisition—One View of Our Current Status

One of the major forces acting on researchers in motor behavior in the 1970s came from the idea, popularized by Pew (1970), that a task-oriented approach to motor behavior was not going to be sufficient for the future. At about this time in psychology, there was a shift toward a new cognitive tradition (Neisser, 1967), in which many underlying cognitive processes, stages, and mechanisms were being proposed and studied to account for observed behavior. This trend was paralleled by the call for process-oriented theories and research methods in movement behavior, in which analogous motor processes would be the focus of study rather than the overt movement behaviors of the earlier task-oriented tradition. This had a nice ring to it, as it seemed to allow researchers in movement behavior to develop and test theories concerned with the fundamental processes underlying movement control and learning. And this style seemed to carry with it much more status, which was (unfortunately) quite important at the time, following as it did the current thinking in cognitive science.

Process- and Task-Oriented Approaches

The paradigms associated with the older task-oriented approach usually tended to focus on the performance of rather global tasks such as the pursuit rotor, the Mashburn task, and the like, and asked about the effect of nearly countless variables that affected the nature of practice (e.g., massed vs. distributed practice, the nature of feedback, the effect of fatigue, etc.). These tasks were usually quite complex, involving many perceptual and motor processes simultaneously, and it was usually not possible to attribute performance changes to variations in a particular process (e.g., response programming). Also, although these tasks involved rather elaborate movement control, the measurement systems were usually quite gross, with a single score (time on target) summarizing perhaps 30 s of behavior.

Increased use of simple tasks. This new tradition demanded a change to simpler tasks. We began to see many more studies using reaction time to study the processes in motor programming, linear-positioning tasks to evaluate whether movements were based on displacement or distance cues, and ballistic-timing tasks to evaluate the role of error-detection processes. These tasks were well suited to the investigation of some questions, but were disappointing to those who wanted to understand how complex movement behaviors in everyday life were controlled and learned. The tasks involved performances that, for the most part, the learners could already perform (e.g., linear positioning); what was apparently learned in the laboratory was the fine-tuning associated with making the particular already learned action conform to the requirements of the experimental situation. Almost never were new coordinations learned, such as would be involved in learning a complex gymnastics stunt, and the movements were usually governed by a single degree of freedom. And, largely because of this, there seemed to be a systematic shift away from relevance and real-world motor behaviors. This shift is obvious when one examines the kinds of motor tasks that we were willing to label as "motor behavior."

Small amounts of practice. The study of learning gradually declined in popularity during this period, although there were exceptions. When learning was studied, it was usually done with these simple tasks, in which the improvements seemed to be extremely rapid; many learning experiments were done in which the practice phase was a few dozen trials, and seldom did practice periods exceed 100 trials. The use of relatively small amounts of practice seemed to remove us further from relevance to real-world problems, as it was difficult to argue convincingly that the 50 trials or so of a linear positioning task were in some way informative about the analogous processes leading to high-level skill in sport, industry, or music.

Simple tasks and motivation. These simple tasks had other problems as well. In our own research with various simple timing tasks, the learners tell us that the actions are overly simple. When lengthy practice is provided, the subjects often become quickly and visibly bored. With questionable subject motivation, we wonder whether we are meeting the basic assumptions for the meaningful study of learning. And, these difficulties meant that the problems of small levels of practice could not be solved simply by increasing the amount of practice. What seems to be needed is more interesting tasks for the learners that will sustain motivation through relatively advanced levels of practice, allowing the effects of various independent variables to be examined.

Assumptions of the Process-Oriented View

But the criticism that the process-orientation led to tasks that were overly simple, and to paradigms that were not particularly relevant to real-world behaviors, is perhaps too strong. Behind this research tradition are various assumptions that, if correct, would seem to argue that this approach will be most effective for understanding motor learning.

Principles of complex and simple tasks. One assumption is that the principles of movement learning will be the same for simple and complex motor tasks. That is, the effect of a particular independent variable (e.g., the nature of information feedback) will not *interact with* task complexity. If this assumption is correct, then it makes sense to study tasks that are simple, because measurement, control, and manipulation are far easier here than in tasks that are more complex. But, if this assumption is incorrect, it is possible that the principles of learning derived from the study of simple tasks will be largely irrelevant to real-world situations involving more complex movement behaviors. We need solid evidence about the viability of this assumption, as seldom have the same variables been examined in the same way for simple and complex movements.

The levels of practice. A second assumption (also present in the task approach) is that the principles of learning will be similar for various levels of practice. That is, the effect of some independent variable will not *interact with* the level of practice of the learners. Thus we are often tempted to talk about various laws of motor learning that are generated from tasks with very low levels of practice, thus assuming (or at least not seriously questioning) whether these principles will also apply for higher levels of practice so often seen in real-world situations. If this assumption is correct, much effort can be saved by examining simple tasks under relatively low levels of practice. But if, as many suspect, this assumption is not correct, then the low levels of practice that are typically used will have poor applicability to many real-world situations.

Technology has also played a role in these shifts, as response complexity usually implied measurement difficulties. Such problems were faced in the older task-oriented tradition by measurement of only the global response outcome (e.g., time-on-target for a 30-s trial), and ignoring the patterns of limb movement behavior completely. When the shift was made to the process-oriented approach, patterns of limb movement behavior were also ignored, but here by making the task so simple that the pattern of movement behavior was nearly trivial. Now, however, with the arrival of affordable laboratory computer methods for the recording of various simple dimensions of limb movement (e.g., the position-time record of a hand-held lever), measurement problems in more complex behaviors can be examined in a time-efficient manner and do not provide justification for avoiding complex movement behaviors in our research.

Consequences of the Process Orientation

My own view is that, although the process tradition has had a number of strong points and interesting findings, on the whole it has not been healthy. When I speak with my colleagues in other subfields of kinesiology, the sport sciences, or physical education, nearly all seem to agree that understanding the phenomena involved in the acquisition of skill is of central importance. But most politely hasten to add that our current field of motor learning does not address these questions very well. What, for example, can our field really tell, in some empirically based and non-intuitive way, about the teaching of Olympic athletes, the improvement of methodology in teaching, or the procedures used to train skilled workers in industry? Very little, I think (although there are a few bright spots that I will address in a later section). And, many university programs in physical education—even those focusing on the preparation of teachers—are increasingly discovering that they can do very well without courses in motor learning. Administrators apparently believe, with good justification, that course work in motor learning is simply not relevant to the problems involved in teaching.

I want to be clear that I am not simply calling for an applied focus. Some (e.g., Adams, 1972; Schmidt, 1988) argue that an applied focus too strongly emphasized can impede progress in a field because it prevents the establishment of more fundamental principles that lead to theory. The development of effective theory can, after some years of waiting for its refinement and testing, become enormously effective for guiding decisions about many practical matters. In this vein, Kerlinger (1973) argued that "there is nothing more practical than a good theory" (p. 10). When these fundamental problems have been worked out, application to teaching situations (by us or someone else) should be relatively easy.

But the theories we developed and tested in the past decade or so have not been very satisfactory in meeting this objective. Many were too global (e.g., schema theory) to be an effective source of guidance for particular situations. These views have contributed to our overall insights about motor learning, but there is not enough that is concrete on which to base intelligent changes in practical circumstances. But perhaps more serious is the fact that most of these theories were studied with the simplistic tasks that seemed to be demanded by the process-oriented approach. Thus, even if the theories seemed to account relatively well for the data in such situations, the question is raised about the relevance of these tasks—and the theory that explains them—to any important real-world situation.

In many ways, this argument is parallel to that used by the ecological psychologists, who argue, for example, that the many investigations of visual information processing with tachistoscopic displays and suddenly presented stimuli were fine for telling us about *these* situations, but produced results and principles that may be largely irrelevant to understanding how an animal uses visual information to orient itself in the world (e.g., Turvey, 1977). In this sense, the process-oriented tradition for motor behavior has led us to become extremely nonecological in our research. We design tasks that are perhaps well suited for uncovering or manipulating a certain hypothetical process, but at the same time these activities may take us systematically farther from the understanding of real movement behaviors because they are so contrived, stripped of intrinsic feedback, or otherwise made artificial[1]. It can be said that the brain (and motor system, it must be added) can do many wonderful things; but it can also perform many silly things that we ask of it in the laboratory. One must wonder whether the principles of learning the silly things discovered in the laboratory are going to tell us about the normal movement behavior phenomena that motivated most of us in the first place.

Overall, my most critical view is that the field of motor learning has, with considerable success during the past decade or so, worked extremely vigorously and systematically—through the development of theoretical thinking, new experimental paradigms, and simple motor tasks—to become as esoteric and as irrelevant as it can be to the solutions of real-world problems. Part of the problem is based on status, where it became much more acceptable to study abstract motor processes, with highly contrived and simple motor responses, than it was to examine problems that were more nearly representative of many real-world situations. Certain paradigms and tasks seemed to be used mainly because they were in fashion. And, part of the problem has been a relative lack of interesting problems to examine with the procedures associated with the older task-oriented approach, with the newer issues about underlying motor processes apparently being genuinely more interesting to some.

This last point leads to the second major section of this paper. After a decade or so of work associated with the process-oriented approach, a number of new ideas, methods, and empirical findings have surfaced that appear to provide justification for returning to the older task-oriented approach. These problems appear to have considerable potential for study in tasks with somewhat more complexity, and the principles that are emerging appear to be reasonably applicable to many real-world settings involving motor learning. These benefits have not come, as one might assume, at the expense of theory development; rather, many interesting theoretical ideas are being formed and tested in these situations, that should lead to a much better understanding of motor-learning processes in general.

Future Directions: Some Examples and Suggestions

The examples of these new directions for research in movement learning are numerous, but two major lines of work serve to illustrate this kind of direction. One of these directions involves some new thinking on various conditions of practice, and the other concerns the effects of various manipulations of feedback about goal achievement.

Research on the Conditions of Practice

After most researchers in the field of motor behavior had either abandoned the study of learning, or shifted to process-oriented studies of motor behavior, Shea and Morgan (1979) published a study that resides squarely in the task-oriented tradition. Their theoretical orientation stemmed from the late William Battig, who was interested in the idea that various aspects of a practice situation that initially cause difficulty for the subjects (keeping slightly different versions of the tasks separate), and that make performance in practice poor, seem to provide greater learning of the task(s) when they are later evaluated on a retention test (e.g., Battig, 1966, 1979). This *intratask interference*, also called *contextual interference*, had been studied to some extent in verbal tasks, but it had not really been generally recognized as an important factor for learning.

Shea and Morgan (1979) used a number of different versions of a relatively simple movement task, in which the learner had to begin with the hand on a "home" key, and then move to knock over three small barriers in a prescribed order before returning to the home position again; the task was to minimize movement time. Three different task versions involved placing the barriers in different positions, so that the movement directions and distances were different in the different tasks. Subjects practiced these three tasks in an acquisition session of 54 trials, where the order of practice was varied between groups. In one condition, practice was *blocked*, in that 18 trials of Version A were completed, then 18 trials of Version B, and 18 trials of Version C. In the *random* condition, the same number of trials of A, B, and C were completed, but the order was randomized, with no single version being present on two consecutive trials.

Figure 1 (left) shows the movement times for these two groups on the initial practice trials. The blocked condition produced much more effective performance than the random condition, with steeper improvements and faster movements at the end of practice. In Battig's terms, the mixing of the different versions of the tasks in the random condition produced

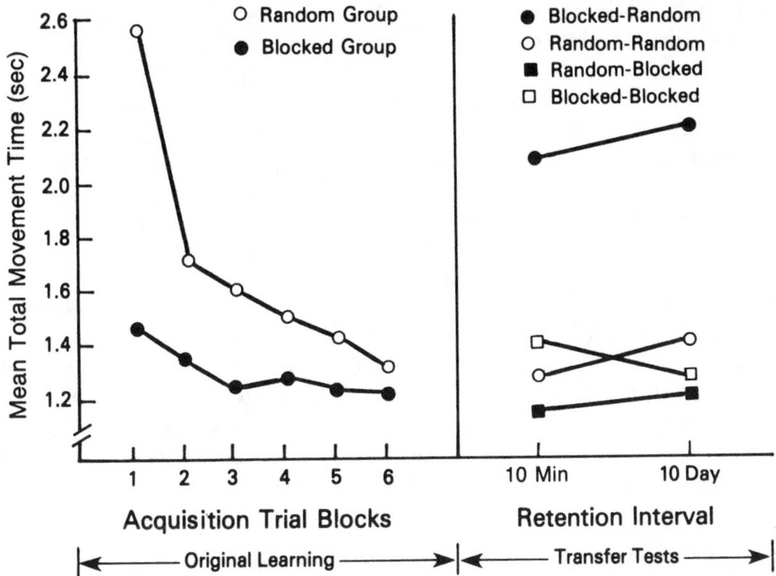

Figure 1. Mean movement time for a simple motor task during acquisition and retention phases for random and blocked conditions of practice. *Note.* From "Contextual Interference Effects on the Acquisition, Retention, and Transfer of Motor Skill" by J.B. Shea and R.L. Morgan, 1979, *Journal of Experimental Psychology*, **5**, p. 183. Copyright 1979 by *Journal of Experimental Psychology*. Reprinted by permission.

some sort of contextual interference, making the performance of each of the versions of the task less effective than if the learners had an opportunity to work on each of the versions repeatedly.

However, the interesting finding occurs on the retention tests. The procedures generated essentially two separate experiments, where the effect of blocked or random practice in the acquisition phase was evaluated on (a) the blocked retention tests or on (b) the random retention tests, with retention tests either 10 min or 10 days after acquisition. These results are shown in the right portion of Figure 1. Consider first the random retention tests, shown as the circles. Here the group with random practice in acquisition (open circles) was far faster than the group with blocked practice in acquisition (filled circles). Notice also that the blocked-random group performed better than the random-random group in the acquisition phase, but that this order was reversed in the retention phase. It could be argued that the blocked group in acquisition had to shift conditions to the random retention test, whereas the random group did not, and that this shift per se was in some way disrupting for the subjects.

But this concern is reduced if we examine the blocked retention tests, seen as the squares in Figure 1. Here, the random-blocked condition (filled squares) was faster than the blocked-blocked condition (open squares), and random practice in acquisition was again more effective for long-term retention than blocked, even though it was now the random subjects who were required to shift conditions for the retention test. In general, subjects who practiced under random conditions in the acquisition phase were more effective on the long-term retention tests, regardless of the conditions under which they were tested (blocked or random), but the effect was much larger for subjects tested on the random retention test.

These long-term retention tests, aside from providing evidence about the effectiveness of the conditions of practice in acquisition, have an important status of their own. In most real-world learning situations, we engage in practice to acquire the capability for responding that is to be demonstrated in the future. The dancer practices long hours during the week not so much because of effective performance in practice per se, but rather so that she can perform effectively in the concert next month. So this line of research on contextual interference tells us that, for maximization of the goal of effective long-term retention, excellent performance in the practice session per se is not necessarily the answer. It also suggests that we understand practice far less well than we are inclined to believe.

Theories of contextual interference. These effects, due in some way to the *context* in which a particular version of the task is practiced in acquisition, have been the subject of an interesting theoretical debate. Shea and Morgan (1979) and Shea and Zimny (1983) have argued that the effect is due to the fact that random practice causes the subjects to process information about the various versions more deeply and completely, leading to increased distinctiveness between the tasks, more elaborate associations being formed for the various versions, and hence better long-term retention. Shea and Zimny, using postpractice interview techniques, found that the subjects reported many more descriptions of the tasks that used extraexperimental associations (statements similar to ''That pattern looked like a Z'') and intraexperimental distinctions (''This figure was like that one''), which tend to support their views about the deeper and more elaborative processing as a basis for the better retention.

In contrast, Lee and Magill (1983) and Magill (1983) have argued that the effects are caused by forgetting the solution to the movement problem—the way in which it was programmed or the particular strategy used, analogous to the views presented by Cuddy and Jacoby (1982). Here, the presentation of a different version (e.g., B) of the task causes the subject to forget the solution to the movement problem that was just generated on the previous trial (e.g., with Version A), which then requires the learner to generate the solution for A again when it is next required. Subjects under blocked conditions do not have to regenerate the solution on the next trial, because it is very similar to that just used on the previous trial. In this view, the generation of solutions to the movement problem is an important factor in learning, and conditions that prevent or minimize this generation process (e.g., blocked practice) will be poor for learning and long-term retention as a result. These issues have generated considerable interest and attention, and a number of additional experiments.

Implications for future research directions. In addition to the interesting debate about the source(s) of these counterintuitive learning effects, implications for the problems raised in the first part of this paper are provided. First of all, the paradigms involve what most would classify as a task-oriented approach, in which the effects of some conditions of practice in the acquisition phase are evaluated on measures of learning (or retention). Second, such an approach is strongly theoretically motivated; the conditions of practice are designed specifically to test various hypotheses about the nature of the learning effects (e.g., Lee & Magill, 1983). Thus this style of work is not, as some have claimed about the task-oriented approach in general, just empirically motivated, an approach in which experimenters search without a theoretical direction for those conditions of practice that happen to be most effective for learning. The search identified here is a principled one, done for solid, fundamental, theoretical reasons.

These aspects also contribute a great deal to other goals of motor learning research discussed earlier. For example, although Shea and Morgan's (1979) research uses relatively simple and artificial motor tasks, the tasks are, by almost any criterion, considerably more complex than those used in the process-oriented approach. And, even more complex tasks *could* have been used, perhaps including elaborate measures of the subjects' movement patterns. The result is that such work has considerable relevance to many real-world situations.

This feature has an additional, related aspect, however, dealing with the applicability to teaching situations. The variable manipulated here—the nature of practice sequences—is one of critical importance for real-world teaching activities in physical education, music, and industry, where practice on various tasks has to be scheduled intelligently by instructors who wish to maximize learning efficiency. The findings that come from these laboratory experiments not only can be reasonably generalized to real-world settings, but they suggest experiments in naturalistic settings themselves. This latter aspect is particularly interesting for me, as I can imagine a new approach to the science of instruction (integrated with those concerned with teacher-learner interactions) based on paradigms of this general kind, and where the payoff is a theoretically oriented, empirically based, yet applicable study of practice phenomena. Viewed in these terms, the task-oriented approach appears to have much to contribute.

Feedback and Knowledge of Results

A second general research area relevant to the present problem deals with what most workers in the field consider a critically important variable for learning: the information feedback received after attempting a movement. This feedback is usually called knowledge of results (KR), and is defined as verbal (or verbalizable) information, over and above that usually received in the task via other sensory channels, which evaluates whether the movement has met the environmental goal. Early work has shown that, if the task is structured so that the learners cannot obtain information about the consequences of the actions by themselves, then essentially *no* learning is achieved from practice unless KR is provided to inform about errors (Bilodeau, Bilodeau, & Schumsky, 1959; Trowbridge & Cason, 1932; see Salmoni, Schmidt, & Walter, 1984, for a review). Such findings have led researchers in the area to believe that KR is the single most important variable for learning, except possibly for practice itself (Bilodeau, 1966).

Methodological concerns with KR research. Our review of these issues (Salmoni et al., 1984) has led us to question some of these strong interpretations for KR and learning. Most of the studies examining the experimental manipulations of KR have conclusions based on the performances measured during the time that the KR variable is being manipulated. The difficulty is that one cannot be sure with this procedure whether (a) the experimental manipulation of KR has affected some relatively permanent acquired capability for responding (i.e., it has influenced learning), or (b) it has simply influenced performance temporarily, in which case the beneficial effects of the KR manipulation would disappear when it is removed. There is ample reason to suspect that KR may have temporary performance effects, such as the well-known energizing (motivating) effects of KR, its guidance properties that tell the performer what to do next, and so on. The result is that what we thought were the principles of KR for learning may simply be principles of KR for temporary performance.

One solution to this problem is to examine performance on a retention test in which the KR has been withheld. When this is done, the temporary effects of the KR manipulations are largely removed, leaving behind the relatively permanent effects that are the products of the learning process. A few largely ignored studies in the KR literature have used this procedure. When it is used, the effects of the KR manipulations (measured on the retention test) are often quite different from those seen in the acquisition phase. These results are often quite counterintuitive, suggesting major revisions about the principles of KR and learning.

Summary KR. Lavery (1962) examined a method of giving feedback called *summary KR*, in which the experimenter drew a graph of the subject's performances over each of a series of trials (e.g., 20), but the subject was only allowed to see this graph after he or she completed the set. Other subjects received KR in the usual way (called *immediate KR*), whereas yet another group had both immediate and summary KR (*both*). The performances of these three groups over 6 days of practice are shown in the left portion of Figure 2. The groups with immediate KR (immediate and both) were far more effective in performance than the summary group, which performed relatively more poorly and improved at a slower rate. Thus, because the summary KR condition was very poor for performance, these and other findings have forced the view that summary KR and the trials delay technique that resembles it were devastating for learning (Bilodeau, 1956, 1966).

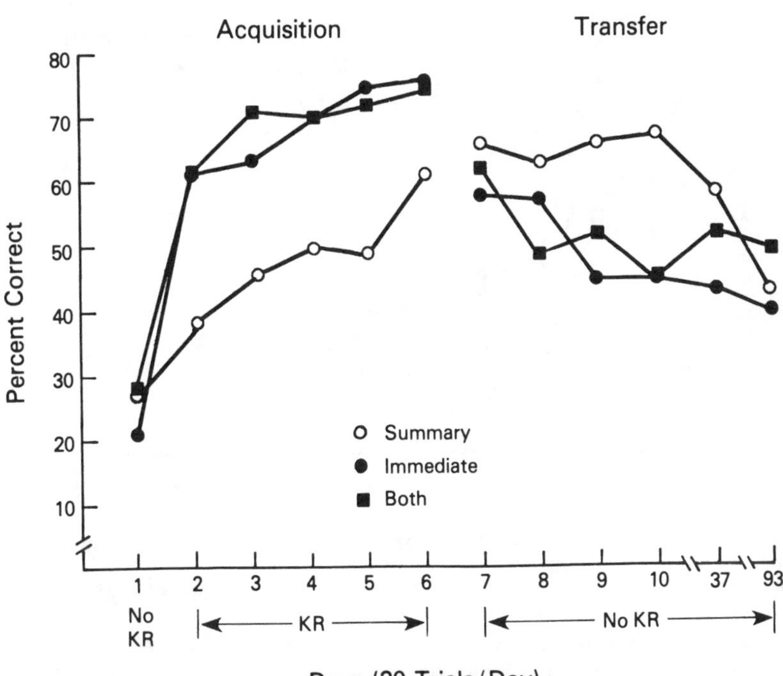

Figure 2. Mean percent correct responses in a simple movement task under three conditions of knowledge of results during an acquisition phase when KR is present, and during a retention phase where KR was withdrawn. *Note.* From "Retention of Simple Motor Skills as a Function of Type of Knowledge of Results" by J.J. Lavery, 1962, *Canadian Journal of Psychology*, **16**, p. 305. Copyright 1962 by *Canadian Journal of Psychology*. Reprinted by permission.

But notice the performance differences when the KR is removed on a retention test (Days 7–10, 37, and 93). Here, the performance of the group with summary KR in the acquisition phase is approximately the same as it was in acquisition, indicating very strong long-term retention; but the performances of the immediate and both conditions show large losses on Day 7, and continuing losses on subsequent days. If learning is measured, as I have suggested, via the performance on a no-KR retention test, then we are forced to conclude that summary KR was the most effective practice method for learning. This is a very nonintuitive finding, because it suggests that the most effective conditions for performance during practice (immediate and both) are the least effective for learning. Furthermore, it was not the case that the summary KR condition improved learning, because the both condition also had the summary information, and it performed most like the immediate condition in acquisition and retention phases. Rather, the conclusion seems to be that immediate KR *interferes* with learning of the task, perhaps by causing the subject to be

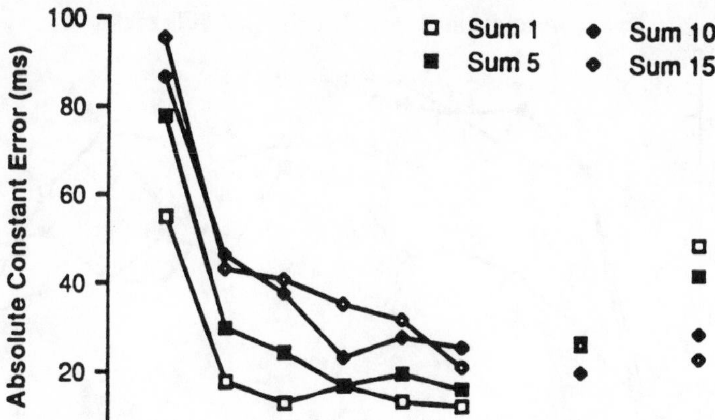

Figure 3. Mean absolute constant error during acquisition (left) and for immediate (10 min) and delayed (2 days) no-KR retention tests as a function of the summary KR length in acquisition. *Note.* From "Summary knowledge of results for skill acquisition: Support for the guidance hypothesis" by R.A. Schmidt, D.E. Young, D.C. Shapiro, and S. Swinnen, *Journal of Experimental Psychology: Learning, Memory, and Cognition* (in press). Reprinted by permission.

guided by it too heavily in the practice phase, as I have suggested elsewhere (Schmidt, 1988).

Following Lavery's lead, my colleagues and I at UCLA have been investigating these and other similar phenomena. In one study,we (Schmidt, Young, Shapiro, & Swinnen, in press) searched for an optimum number of trials for the summary report. With a relatively simple timing task, we used summaries of 1 (i.e., immediate KR), 5, 10, and 15 trials, with these KR reports spread over 100 practice trials. Our results are shown in Figure 3, for immediate (10 min) and delayed (2 days) retention tests without KR. At 10 min, there was essentially no effect of the various feedback treatments manipulated in the acquisition phase. But by 2 days later, the errors were ordered inversely with the length of the summaries, with the 15-trial summary condition showing essentially no loss over 2 days, and the 1-trial summary condition showing considerable decrement. Again, this is a very curious finding, because the groups with the most effective performance during acquisition (here, the 1-trial summary condition) were the poorest in terms of learning, measured on a long-term retention test. All of these results suggest that we do not understand the processes of feedback utilization very well.

Implications for future research directions. These results on manipulations of KR, like those on context effects discussed in the previous section, share strong common implications for future research directions. First, these findings are empirically oriented, in that they are concerned with the fundamental relationships between the variations of KR and subsequent learning and retention. The establishment of such empirical laws are absolutely essential for a field that claims to understand the processes in motor learning. However, these findings are also theoretically oriented, in that they ask about how KR works to produce learning. Various theoretical ideas (such as the guidance hypothesis mentioned above) are possible to explain these effects, and considerable effort is being directed at understanding these phenomena.

But what impresses me most about these results is their potential applicability. These experiments manipulate variables (the schedule of delivery of information about response errors) that are under the direct control of teachers in real-world settings. It seems a relatively small jump from these laboratory manipulations to applications in which summary KR procedures could be used. This kind of work seems to suggest studies that could actually be conducted in natural settings, which could perhaps reveal instances where these variables would be most effective for maximizing learning or uncovering limitations to generalizability. And finally, these results on KR utilization—like the context-effects research discussed above—represent an older task-oriented approach to motor learning, in which various conditions of practice are manipulated to determine the effects on task learning. This suggests an important use for this old paradigm in the future.

The Task Approach: Paradigm of the Future?

In asking about what kinds of empirical and theoretical directions we as a field of motor learning should take as we approach the end of this century, I have tried to assess the contributions of the various approaches that have been predominant (at least in my brief tenure) in relation to the kind of problems that we are to address as a field. Many see our field (as I do) as the study of the acquisition of motor skills, with a major emphasis on the (empirical) principles of learning, on how these principles lead to theories about the underlying processes of learning, but at the same time with considerable focus on where these fundamental principles might be applied in real-world learning situations. If so, then the process-oriented approach so prevalent in the past decade does not suit my purposes very well, because it has lacked two important features: (a) it seems to lack generality to real-world situations because of the emphasis on simple motor behaviors, and (b) it focuses on classes of fundamental problems that do not have obvious external validity. This situation is not necessarily related only to the task-orientation, but perhaps also to our underdeveloped thinking about fundamental principles of learning. But, for whatever the reasons, I have argued here that, primarily because of the focus we have adopted during the 1970s, we have made ourselves largely irrelevant to the understanding of what most of us would agree are interesting motor skills.

I believe that one solution is to readopt the task-oriented approach to the study of motor learning. In a discussion of these ideas with my long-time colleague and good friend George Stelmach (Stelmach, personal communication, 1984), he asked essentially, "How can you really justify taking such a large step backward to a tradition we all rejected years ago?" My response, which is the theme of this paper, is based on a number of factors. First, if our field has to do with the establishment of empirical relationships between conditions of practice and learning, then it is clear that we have a long way to go before that goal is realized. Many interesting and important phenomena have never been studied seriously. And new findings, such as the KR and contextual-interference effects described here, suggest that we do not understand very much about the nature of such fundamental things as feedback and practice. The task approach is beautifully suited to the examination of such questions.

Second, the process approach has taken us away from situations that have much potential for practical application. Simple tasks and the focus on rather esoteric, overly simple theoretical ideas have not, in cold retrospect, proven to be very useful either as explanations of motor learning, or as guidance for application. Perhaps it is too early to be so critical, as theories take considerable time to be developed and tested effectively, but the examples I have provided here suggest that use of the task orientation may be a more direct and effective way to understand problems relevant to our field. The problems here deal with effects of conditions of practice, an area of central interest to motor learning. The methods might (or might not) use more complex tasks that provide important increases in external validity. The ideas are strongly theoretical and have led to many interesting explanations of practice phenomena and to experiments designed to test them.

Many of these problems could actually be investigated in real-world situations, sacrificing nothing with respect to experimental rigor (provided that the measurement system for the tasks is adequate), while gaining a great deal in terms of generality. Along these lines, I think it is time for an increased collaboration between motor learning and the new field known as *teacher behavior*, whose primary concern is teacher-learner interactions in classroom stiuations, where often groups of learners with realistic tasks are involved. The new findings I have mentioned here, and numerous others, could form an attractive model for collaborative work between these two areas, as the findings have strong relevance to, and could actually be replicated and extended in, classroom settings.

For some, my recommendation to regress to an earlier, and supposedly discarded, research tradition will seem strange and perhaps unworkable. But such an approach seems reasonable in light of my admittedly personal biases about the nature of the practical and theoretical goals of our field. The research examples mentioned here, in which interesting theoretical and practical issues are studied simultaneously in the same experimental paradigm, represent excellent models for the nature of future work in this area, and seem to provide considerable justification for at least considering the task orientation as the paradigm of the future.

Acknowledgments

This manuscript and research reported here was supported in part by Contract No. MDA-903-85-K-0225 from the U.S. Army Research Institute for the Behavioral and Social Sciences (Basic Research) to R.A. Schmidt and D.C. Shapiro, UCLA.

Note

1. But, to be fair, Zelaznik (personal communication, 1985) has pointed out that many of our real-world situations are pretty silly and non-ecological, too, such as doing giant swings on the horizontal bar or flying a helicopter. It is just that these particular activities have, for various reasons, become popular and accepted as skills, whereas linear-positioning tasks and the like have not. And, perhaps *because* they are often nonecological and contrived, many accepted skills are difficult to perform, which makes them interesting as sports (e.g., pole vaulting), or important to study for societal reasons (e.g., helicopter safety).

References

Adams, J.A. (1972). Research and the future of engineering psychology. *American Psychologist*, **27**, 615-622.

Battig, W.F. (1966). Facilitation and interference. In E.A. Bilodeau (Ed.), *Acquisition of skill* (pp. 215-244). New York: Academic Press.

Battig, W.F. (1979). The flexibility of human memory. In L.S. Cermak & F.I.M. Craik (Eds.), *Levels of processing in human memory* (pp. 23-44). Hillsdale, NJ: Erlbaum.

Bilodeau, I.M. (1956). Accuracy of a simple positioning response with variation in the number of trials by which knowledge of results is delayed. *American Journal of Psychology*, **69**, 434-437.

Bilodeau, I.M. (1966). Information feedback. In E.A. Bilodeau (Ed.), *Acquisition of skill* (pp. 255-296). New York: Academic Press.

Bilodeau, E.A., Bilodeau, I.M., & Schumsky, D.A. (1959). Some effects of introducing and withdrawing knowledge of results early and late in practice. *Journal of Experimental Psychology*, **58**, 142-144.

Cuddy, L.J., & Jacoby, L.L. (1982). When forgetting helps memory. Analysis of repetition effects. *Journal of Verbal Learning and Verbal Behavior*, **21**, 451-467.

Kerlinger, F.N. (1973). *Foundations of behavioral research* (2nd ed.). New York: Holt, Rinehart, & Winston.

Lavery, J.J. (1962). Retention of simple motor skills as a function of type of knowledge of results. *Canadian Journal of Psychology*, **16**, 300-311.

Lee, T.D., & Magill, R.A. (1983). The locus of contextual interference in motor-skill acquisition. *Journal of Experimental Psychology: Learning, Memory, and Cognition*, **9**, 730-746.

Magill, R.A. (1983). Insights into memory and control in motor behavior through the study of context effects: A discussion of Mathews et al. and Shea and Zimny. In R.A. Magill (Ed.), *Memory and control of action* (pp. 367-376). Amsterdam: North-Holland.

Neisser, U. (1967). *Cognitive psychology*. New York: Appleton-Century-Crofts.

Pew, R.W. (1970). Toward a process-oriented theory of human skilled performance. *Journal of Motor Behavior*, **2**, 8-24.

Salmoni, A.W., Schmidt, R.A., & Walter, C.B. (1984). Knowledge of results and motor learning: A review and critical reappraisal. *Psychological Bulletin*, **95**, 355-386.

Schmidt, R.A. (1988). *Motor control and learning: A behavioral emphasis* (2nd ed.). Champaign, IL: Human Kinetics.

Schmidt, R.A., Young, D.E., Shapiro, D.C., & Swinnen, S. (in press). Summary knowledge of results for skill acquisition: Support for the guidance hypothesis. *Journal of Experimental Psychology: Learning, Memory, and Cognition*.

Shea, J.B., & Morgan, R.L. (1979). Contextual interference effects on the acquisition, retention, and transfer of a motor skill. *Journal of Experimental Psychology: Human Learning and Memory*, **5**, 179-187.

Shea, J.B., & Zimny, S.T. (1983). Context effects in memory and learning movement information. In R.A. Magill (Ed.), *Memory and control of action* (pp. 345-366). Amsterdam: North-Holland.

Trowbridge, M.H., & Cason, H. (1932). An experimental study of Thorndike's theory of learning. *Journal of General Psychology*, **7**, 245-260.

Turvey, M.T. (1977). Preliminaries to a theory of action with reference to vision. In R. Shaw & J. Bransford (Eds.), *Perceiving, acting, and knowing* (pp. 211-265). Hillsdale, NJ: Erlbaum.

Whatever Happened to Applied Research in Motor Learning?

Robert W. Christina

Lest this introduction be wasted on remarks of little value, let it be enough to say that this paper has three main purposes. The first is to assess the current status of our motor learning knowledge in relation to the potential it has for helping us to find immediate solutions to practical problems. The second is to discuss the view that has been the dominant force in guiding our research efforts in motor learning for approximately the past 15 years. The third is to argue that we need to change that view and increase our effort to conduct applied research that attempts to build a specialized body of knowledge directed toward understanding the learning of skills in sport and physical education settings.[1]

Motor Learning Knowledge: Its Current Status and Potential for Practical Application

How does the learning of different motor skills take place? What are the mechanisms underlying the learning of motor skills and how do they operate? What variables determine how rapidly we will learn motor skills? What variables determine how long we remember the motor skills we have learned? These are but a few of the kinds of questions to which basic research in motor learning has been seeking answers. This type of research is motivated by the need to secure scientific understanding of the processes and mechanisms underlying motor learning with no requirement to demonstrate practical value or current relevance. Ultimately, basic research seeks to develop a body of theory-based knowledge that will enable us to explain why the learning of motor skills occurs as it does; and if we can do that we will have the power to make predictions about motor learning phenomena. However, this need to secure scientific understanding is not the only reason for wanting to conduct research on motor learning. Quite often we also are driven by practical needs to conduct applied research on motor learning.

There are innumerable people who need to find immediate solutions to specific learning problems that occur in real-world settings such as those found in physical education and sport. I think immediately of (a) athletes and coaches searching for more effective ways to practice, (b) teachers and coaches seeking better methods of diagnosing performance errors and of determining appropriate corrections, and (c) teachers and coaches trying to find better ways of providing information feedback to their students and athletes. Essentially, they all are looking for the best ways and conditions of skill learning that make up their respective sports. But where do they look?

They might begin by searching through textbooks written on motor learning and by reviewing the available literature. They will not find a large body of practical knowledge produced by applied research that was conducted in sport settings in which the learning of sport skills was being studied. What they will find is a body of knowledge that was predominantly generated by basic research, conducted in controlled laboratory settings in which experimenter-designed motor tasks were being learned. They also will find that this scientific knowledge is far from being as comprehensive and formalized as that found in advanced physical sciences such as chemistry and physics. Without going into any great detail, I will present several of my general impressions of the current body of motor learning knowledge.

1. I see a considerable amount of empirical information in the form of observations and facts about the learning and performance of simple movements in laboratory settings. However, much of this information still needs to be theoretically organized.
2. I find a number of hypotheses, many of which were borrowed from the verbal learning and memory theories of psychology and tested within an information-processing framework to determine if they were appropriate for the motor learning of simple movements in laboratory settings.
3. I see a number of principles that are actually summaries of empirical relationships that appear to hold for simple, experimenter-designed motor tasks under controlled laboratory conditions. However, none of these principles are stated with sufficient precision to be considered laws except for Fitts' (1954) Law, which is a mathematical relationship of the speed-accuracy trade-off.
4. I am aware of only two theories of motor learning, Adams's (1971) closed-loop theory and Schmidt's (1975) schema theory, that were specifically designed for the motor domain to help us understand acquisition. Although these two theories have made a considerable contribution to our understanding, neither one can be considered to be as comprehensive and formalized as some of the theories of the advanced sciences such as the kinetic theory of matter.

It is clear that much needs to be done before the current body of motor learning knowledge can be considered as advanced as the fundamental knowledge of the physical sciences like physics or chemistry. My impression is that the present plan is to continue to develop our scientific knowledge about motor learning mainly through basic research and hope that eventually it will become advanced enough to take the lead in developing practice.

Because the current body of motor learning knowledge is far from becoming as comprehensive and formalized as that of some of the advanced physical sciences, it seems reasonable to ask if it can be of any value in helping practitioners find immediate solutions to specific skill learning problems in practical settings such as those typically observed in physical education and sport. The answer is that it can be of some value, but direct application of that scientific information to practice will not always work. It would be naive to think that it would and to expect that when a problem arises all teachers or coaches have to do is search through the motor learning literature to select the appropriate principle and apply it to their specific sport setting, and the problem will be solved. Indeed, direct application doesn't even work that way or that easily with the most exact scientific theories of the physical sciences, which are far more advanced than any theory we have in motor learning. If it did, there would be no need for the technological disciplines of engineering that have a formal disciplinary organization that parallels that of the physical sciences. You see, even with the most exact scientific theories, we find that engineers are needed who can use their creativity and training to apply the theory to the solution of practical problems. For most of us, the available theory-based knowledge in motor learning serves two main purposes. First, it provides us with a conceptual plan and a language for interpreting and understanding the motor skill learning that we see in practical settings. Second, and closely related to the first, this knowledge can serve to guide us toward noticing those variables that are critical in finding solutions to the skill learning problems that we often see in practical settings.

Thus, although the current motor learning knowledge does not provide us with solutions to our practical problems, it does increase our understanding, which in turn has the potential to help us find the solutions. In the process of searching for the specific solutions to our practical problems, we will discover that applied research quite often will be needed. This is so because the motor learning knowledge that currently exists frequently is not capable of predicting to the complex, uncontrolled conditions of the real world. Whatever precise predictions this knowledge is capable of making, more often than not they are applicable only to the learning of experimenter-designed motor tasks under controlled laboratory conditions.

To determine in a scientific manner if these precise laboratory-based predictions about motor learning actually hold in the real world, applied research that tests the appropriateness of these predictions in controlled practical settings will have to be conducted. You see, it simply is not possible in most instances to move from basic research predictions directly to practical application without at least one or more intervening steps of applied research. Yet, in spite of this critical role that applied research plays in determining the practical utility of fundamental knowledge generated by basic resarch, there has been a noticeable decline in our effort to conduct it over the past 15 years or so. Although there may be several reasons for this decline, my impression is that it was mainly due to the view of applied research in relation to basic research that prevailed during the past decade and a half and that currently prevails. Let's take a closer look at this view and how it could have led us to concentrate most of our efforts on basic research instead of applied research in motor learning.

The View Guiding Our Research Efforts in Motor Learning

One view has greatly influenced the direction of our research efforts in motor learning for roughly the past 15 years. This view holds that applied research is subordinate to and almost completely dependent on basic research and therefore is considered to be predominantly an extension of it. Resulting from this view is the argument that a major systematic effort to conduct applied research at the present time or in the future, before our fundamental knowledge from basic research on motor learning is sufficiently developed, is a highly questionable endeavor. Let's examine this view and two types of applied research it has suppressed.

Applied Research That Seeks Immediate Solutions

One type of applied research tries to find immediate solutions to specific motor learning problems that arise in practical settings. It bypasses the need to secure scientific understanding that is at the heart of basic research. The findings from such research rarely contribute to the development of motor learning theory that some day could form a body of fundamental knowledge that practitioners would find useful in helping them discover solutions to their practical problems. This type of applied research is mainly motivated by practitioners who cannot wait for basic research to develop the fundamental knowledge to overcome practical problems that students have in learning the sport skills.

We have been encouraged by eminent scholars and leaders in our subdiscipline of motor learning to concentrate most of our efforts on basic research rather than applied research, and we have done just that. Perhaps the article published by Jack Adams in 1971 had the greatest influence on directing many of us more toward basic rather than applied research in motor learning. In that article, Professor Adams (1971) quite forcefully advanced the following argument:

> The villain that has robbed ''skills'' of its precision is applied research that investigates an activity to solve a particular problem, like kicking a footall, flying an airplane, or operating a lathe. This accusation sounds more damaging than intended, because applied research is necessary when basic science lacks the answers.

> Nevertheless, the overall outcome of applied research is a collection of answers on specific problems, particularly important to someone at a particular moment, but not the steady building of scientific knowledge that can some day have power to answer all the problems. (p. 112)

Nine years later we see Adams's (1971) call for a strong basic research effort reinforced and perpetuated in a textbook on motor learning written by Robert Singer (1980). In that book Singer also gives us an update of the progress that has been made in answering Adams's call. Singer (1980) stated that "many research and conceptualization efforts in the 1970s show much promise to alleviate Adams's concerns" (p. 25).

Eleven years later in another book on motor control and learning written by Richard Schmidt (1982), once again we see Adams's (1971) position kept alive. Schmidt (1982) stated that

> perhaps, in the long run, answers to practical problems are found through basic research. The disadvantage is that practical applications must wait for sufficient knowledge to be accumulated. Hopefully, coming to an understanding of how the motor system operates through theories and principles will contribute more to application than will studying the areas of applicability directly. (p. 47)

Schmidt's use of the words *perhaps* and *hopefully* seem to suggest a hint of some doubt on his part. Nonetheless, his view and that of Adams of this type of applied research is quite clear. Essentially, they see applied research as nothing more than the application of fundamental knowledge derived from basic research to the solution of practical problems. Viewed in this way, applied research is unquestionably dependent upon basic research and hence, is considered to be an extension of it. However, because our present fundamental knowledge of motor learning is less than adequately developed in most instances to make such applications, increasing our effort to conduct applied research is viewed as a highly questionable venture at this time.

Applied Research That Develops a Specialized Knowledge

There is another type of applied research that was acknowledged by Henry (1978), but seems to have been overlooked by both Adams and Schmidt and many other scholars in motor learning, and I am not sure why. Henry (1978) classified this type of applied research "as a secondary level organization of fundamental knowledge directed toward specific and immediate practical needs. Thus, it affords a rational basis for a profession or technology" (p. 25). Unlike the type of applied research discussed earlier, this type tries to develop a specialized body of scientific knowledge that is derived from the fundamental knowledge of basic research. This is accomplished by determining the appropriateness of motor learning hypotheses, principles, and theories derived from basic research to learning in either a controlled sport setting or a laboratory that has the conditions of the actual sport setting of interest.

This type of applied research is a way of not only putting what we know about motor learning from basic research to practical use, but also improving it. Improvement may come from this research by either determining the boundary conditions for our motor learning hypotheses, principles, and theories, or uncovering new information that may then be used to revise them or even construct new ones. Let's look at a hypothetical example of how this could happen in motor learning.

Suppose a theory based on laboratory data, such as Schmidt's (1975) schema theory of discrete motor skill learning, is used to make predictions about a practical setting like movement education, and the predictions are not confirmed by applied research. This result indicates that the theory is not appropriate for that setting. However, the theory may still be of value for making predictions about motor learning in other practical settings. Of course, it is also possible that most of the theoretical predictions are confirmed by applied research, but a few of them are not. This result reveals that the theory is appropriate for that setting, but the predictions that were not confirmed need to be revised or even replaced with new ones. In fact, such applied research can uncover new information that may then be used in revising the old predictions or building new ones. This is indeed what happened when Fitts (1962) discovered how important cognitive activity was in the early stages of motor skill learning as a result of his applied research on airplane pilot training. This was a new finding at the time because cognitive activity was a feature commonly missing from traditional basic research on motor skill learning under controlled laboratory conditions. Furthermore, it was a new finding from applied research that changed some of our thinking about motor skill learning.

Incidentally, it is interesting to note that Schmidt (1977) did try to stimulate this type of applied research. Essentially, he proposed some future research directions that involved the testing of schema theory predictions in a movement education setting. Presumably, Schmidt had hoped that his schema theory would become useful to movement educators or practitioners in movement education by stimulating their own research. Unfortunately, that hope has not yet been realized, perhaps because most movement educators or practitioners realize that they lack the training necessary to conduct this type of research and, hence, do not attempt it.

Specialized knowledge generated by this type of applied research is generally applicable to a fewer number of situations than fundamental knowledge because it is constrained by the practical needs of the particular profession or technology it serves. Essentially, it could provide a logical foundation for a profession such as physical education or coaching, and, as Henry (1978) has pointed out, it is more dependable than the first type described in this paper because it's based on the fundamental knowledge from basic research.

Although this type of applied research would seem to be quite useful in helping practitioners find solutions to their practical problems, I found that very little of it has been conducted in our subdiscipline of motor learning in the last 15 years. Perhaps one reason for a lack of this type of applied research is that it, too, is viewed as an extension of basic research just as is the first type. Both types are seen as the application of fundamental knowledge derived from basic research to the solution of practical problems. The only difference is that the second type includes the intervening step of building a specialized body of knowledge from which practitioners might better be able to draw their application, whereas the first type does not. Nonetheless, because this specialized knowledge is derived from the fundamental knowledge of basic research, this second type of applied research also is considered an extension of basic research. Moreover, because our current fundamental knowledge of motor learning is not advanced enough to derive such a specialized knowledge, a concerted effort to conduct this type of applied research also is viewed as a questionable venture at this time.

Future Research Directions

I don't know for certain what the future research directions in motor learning will be, but I will share with you three trends that I'd very much like to see happen. Let's begin by referring to Table 1, which shows three levels from the most basic research on human motor learning to the most applied research divided according to their relevance for providing solutions to practical problems in sport.[2] For approximately the past decade and a half, most of our research has been conducted at Level 1. I strongly recommend that we continue this basic research effort to build a body of fundamental knowledge of motor learning. Such an effort is not only necessary if we are to increase our scientific understanding of the processes and mechanisms underlying motor learning, but also important to a profession such as physical education. As Henry (1978) has pointed out, "the fundamental knowledge derived from uninhibited basic research is the life blood of any respectable profession" (p. 25). I will not discuss the specific directions these basic research efforts should take because Professor Schmidt has already discussed them.

Now let's focus on the applied research at Level 3. This type of research is inevitable as long as there are researchers who are willing to come to the aid of people who need to have immediate solutions to practical problems. Perhaps this is why it is not too surprising to find that some of this type of research has been conducted during the past 15 years even though a strong basic research effort prevailed. Although there has not been as much of it relative to the amount of basic research that has been generated during those years, there may be more of an increase in applied research at Level 3 in the future. This increase is likely to occur if private corporations, the United States Olympic Committee, and more sport-governing bodies such as the United States Ski Coaches Association, United States Diving Association, and the National Rifle Association are able to provide funds to support it. This increase is desirable as long as it does not take too much time away from our basic research at Level 1 or our research at Level 2. If it does, the growth of our scientific understanding of the processes underlying motor learning would be seriously threatened as would the development of our subdiscipline of motor learning as a science.

Table 1 Levels of Relevance of Motor Learning Research for Finding Solutions to Practical Problems in Sport

Level 1 Least direct relevance Basic research	Level 2 Moderate direct relevance Applied research	Level 3 Most direct relevance Applied research
Ultimate goal Develop theory-based knowledge appropriate for understanding motor learning in general with no requirement to demonstrate its relevance for solving practical problems.	Ultimate goal Develop theory-based knowledge appropriate for understanding the learning of sport skills in sport settings with no requirement to find immediate solutions to learning problems in sport.	Ultimate goal Find immediate solutions to learning problems in sport with no requirement to demonstrate or develop theory-based knowledge at either Level 1 or Level 2.
Main approach Test hypotheses in a laboratory setting using experimenter-designed motor tasks.	Main approach Test hypotheses in a sport setting or in a laboratory setting similar to it using sport skills or motor tasks that have the properties of those skills.	Main approach Test solutions to specific learning problems in sport in the settings described under the applied research at Level 2.

We must never let this happen, and it will not happen if we concentrate most of our effort on research at Levels 1 and 2 rather than on applied research at Level 3.

What about our efforts to conduct applied research at Level 2? I found very little of this type of applied research in the past decade and a half. It has been either overlooked or suppressed by the current view that guides our research efforts. If we continue to allow this view to direct our research efforts, there will be no increase in the amount of this kind of applied research in the future. This would be unfortunate, because applied research at Level 2 is not a questionable venture at this time. It is desperately needed mainly for three reasons. First, it is needed because direct application of fundamental knowledge from basic research to practice frequently does not work without at least one if not more intervening steps of applied research. Second, applied research at Level 2 has a great potential for contributing to the development of fundamental knowledge and, hence, hastening the progress of motor learning's becoming further advanced as a basic science. And third, the specialized knowledge it produces could constitute a much needed rational basis for a profession such as teaching physical education or coaching. This relevance of our subdiscipline of motor learning to a profession would demonstrate the importance of our subdiscipline to colleagues, administrators, and practitioners, some of whom could be in a position one day to determine its future. Let's be realistic. As a science our subdiscipline is currently controlled by the availability of funds, the consensus of the scientific community, the university committees. Moreover, values intrinsic to basic science research on motor learning are being challenged more and more today by people who pay for it. It is clear that we are living in an age of increasing accountability largely because of the decreasing availability of funds, and I don't envision this situation improving any in the near future. In my opinion, a solid applied research effort at Level 2 would enrich our motor learning knowledge with relevance, and this could help us justify the existence of our subdiscipline during these difficult economic times in which university administrators are looking for programs to eliminate.

However, before we agree to making more of a concerted effort to conduct applied research at Level 2, we must change our view of it in relation to basic research. Rather than thinking of applied research at Level 2 as being an extension of basic research because its specialized knowledge must be derived from the fundamental knowledge of basic research, we should think of this type of applied research as being an independent, but cooperating, companion of basic research, because its specialized knowledge does not have to be derived from the fundamental knowledge of basic research. There is no reason why this specialized knowledge cannot be developed by applied research at Level 2 in places where the fundamental knowledge of basic research is inadequate.

Where there are no motor learning hypotheses available from basic research, we can create our own and test them in a controlled practical setting. If we are fortunate enough to develop a new hypothesis or discover some new information from our applied research at this level, its contribution to fundamental motor learning knowledge can be evaluated by subjecting it to the rigor of controlled laboratory testing of basic research at Level 1. In this way applied research can contribute to basic research. In places where fundamental knowledge from basic research is sufficiently developed, we can determine the appropriateness of applying that knowledge to practical settings through applied research at Level 2. There is no reason why we can't take existing motor learning hypotheses from basic research and design experiments to test their appropriateness for learning sports skills in a controlled sport setting or in a controlled laboratory setting that has the conditions of the sport setting of interest. This is one way that basic research can contribute to applied research.

It is clear that when we view basic and applied research as independent, but cooperating, endeavors, basic research at Level 1 has something to contribute to applied research at Level 2, and applied research at Level 2 has something to contribute to basic research at Level 1. Under our current view, however, this type of applied research is seen as being subordinate to basic research, almost completely dependent on it, and as having very little, if anything, to contribute to basic research. Allowing this kind of thinking to guide our research efforts these past 15 years, we have suppressed applied research at Level 2 and isolated it from basic research at Level 1. This is truly unfortunate because, by suppressing applied research at Level 2, we have not only ignored the great potential it has for helping practitioners find solutions to their practical problems, but left untapped the unique potential it has for assisting basic research in its attempt to build a body of fundamental knowledge. Moreover, isolating these two types of research from each other is quite unfortunate, because theory and research in the basic processes and mechanisms of motor learning are intimately related to the applied aspects of learning skills in practical settings such as those found in sport and physical education. Although basic research provides us with fundamental knowledge that leads to the basic understanding of motor learning, applied research at Level 2 determines the appropriateness of that knowledge to practical settings and also searches for new information that leads to an understanding specific to skill learning in practical settings, which, in turn, could contribute to our basic understanding of motor learning.

Clearly the time has come for us to change the view that has guided our research efforts. Instead of thinking of applied research at Level 2 predominantly as an extension of basic research, we should think of it as an independent, but cooperating, companion of basic research. Within the framework of this alternative view I strongly recommend that we work toward a two-track system in which applied research at Level 2 attempts to build a specialized body of practical knowledge that parallels the body of fundamental knowledge of basic research at Level 1. For applied research at Level 2, this specialized knowledge would focus on the scientific understanding of learning sport skills in sport settings, whereas the fundamental knowledge of basic research at Level 1 would continue to focus on the scientific understanding of motor learning with no regard to specific or immediate practical needs. Such a system is similar to that of the physical sciences in which applied disciplines such as chemical and electrical engineering have a specialized body of practical knowledge that parallels the body of fundamental knowledge of chemistry and physics.

Of course, it is also possible for us to conduct applied research that is a combination of Levels 2 and 3. I'd very much like to see us do more of this combined type of applied research in the future. The chance to conduct such research does not occur all that often, but when it does we should seize the opportunity. This type of applied research can be accomplished by devising experiments that have the power not only to provide immediate solutions to our practical problems, but also to determine the appropriateness of our theory-based knowledge from basic research to practical settings. Creating experiments that have this power is not an easy task, but it is well worth the effort because such experiments not only solve practical problems, but also contribute to our scientific understanding of learning sport skills in sport settings.

Summary and Conclusions

So, whatever happened to applied research in motor learning? It was suppressed by the view that has guided our research efforts for the past

15 years and it will continue to be suppressed in the future unless we change it. According to this view, basic research is the prerequisite for increasing our scientific understanding of motor learning, and applied research contributes very little to that understanding. This is true for applied research at Level 3, which seeks immediate solutions to practical learning problems in sport because it bypasses the need for scientific understanding. However, it is not true for applied research at Level 2, which attempts to build a body of specialized knowledge that is appropriate for understanding the learning of sport skills in sport settings. This type of applied research can contribute to our scientific understanding of motor learning (a) by creating new explanations for how the learning of sport skills takes place in sport settings when the fundamental knowledge of basic research lacks the answers, and (b) by uncovering new information that may be used to modify old ways of thinking about the processes and mechanisms of motor learning. Because this view currently guiding our research efforts does not hold for applied research at Level 2, I have argued that it needs to be changed to a view that encompasses this type of applied research. I propose that we work toward a two-track system in which (a) applied research at Level 2 attempts to develop specialized knowledge that parallels the fundamental knowledge of basic research, and (b) our effort to conduct each type of research is given more equal time.

Undoubtedly, there will be some of my colleagues who will not be too enthused about my recommendation that we change our current view to one that makes applied research at Level 2 less subordinate to basic research and that encourages us to increase our effort to conduct this type of applied research. These individuals are quite comfortable with the current view that guides our research efforts, and they are not concerned with applying what they know or even with the relevance of their motor learning research. They seem to continue to cling to the belief that motor learning research is more pure as a science and more significant the further removed it is from anything that is applied or even relevant. I respect their right to this belief, but I do not agree with it. I see this belief as an excuse to escape from the responsibility for application and relevance of their motor learning research. I am of the conviction that if we are not always concerned with application, we should at least be concerned with the relevance of our motor learning research. You see, I am of the conviction that a sound basic research prediction or theory of motor learning must at sometime in the future be validated by its influence on the arts of practice. If our techniques of learning sport skills in physical education and athletic settings cannot eventually be improved as a result of our motor learning research, then I think there is something wrong with that research.

References

Adams, J.A. (1971). A closed-loop theory of motor learning. *Journal of Motor Behavior*, **3**, 111-150.

Christina, R.W. (1987). Motor learning: Future battlefronts of research. In H. Eckert (Ed.), *The cutting edge in physical education and exercise science research. American Academy of Physical Education Papers* (No. 20, pp. 26-41). Champaign, IL: Human Kinetics.

Fitts, P.M. (1954). The information capacity of the human motor system in controlling the amplitude of movement. *Journal of Experimental Psychology*, **47**, 381-391.

Fitts, P.M. (1962). Factors in complex skill training. In R. Glaser (Ed.), *Training research and education* (pp. 177-197). Pittsburgh: University of Pittsburgh.

Henry, F.M. (1978). The academic discipline of physical education. *Quest*, **29**, 13-29.

Schmidt, R.A. (1975). A schema theory of discrete motor skill learning. *Psychological Review*, **82**, 225-260.

Schmidt, R.A. (1977). Schema theory: Implications for movement education. *Motor Skills: Theory into Practice*, **2**, 36-48.

Schmidt, R.A. (1982). *Motor control and learning*. Champaign, IL: Human Kinetics.

Singer, R.N. (1980). *Motor learning and human performance* (3rd ed.). New York: Macmillan.

Notes

1. Because the main focus of this symposium was on exercise and sport research, and my charge was to address applied aspects of motor learning, I placed special emphasis on the need for motor learning research applied to sport and physical education. However, I am in no way suggesting that applied motor learning research be limited only to sport and physical education. On the contrary, as I have argued elsewhere (Christina, 1987), we should make every attempt to extend our applied motor learning research beyond the boundaries of sport and physical education to other areas such as gerontology and health and physical rehabilitation as well as military and industrial settings.
2. Although Table 1 was designed specifically as a broad framework for guiding and coordinating motor learning research efforts with regard to sport and physical education, it also may be appropriate for other subdisciplines (e.g., exercise physiology, motor development, sport psychology) and practical settings other than sport and physical education.

The Importance of Process-Oriented Research: A Commentary

George E. Stelmach

> As people used to be wrong about the motion of the sun, so they are still wrong about the motion of the future. The future stands still; it is we who move in infinite space.
>
> Rainer Maria Rilke

When I was sitting in my hotel room this past week I began to read a complimentary issue of *Arizona Highways* and quickly noticed a feature article entitled "Arizona State University: Visions for Tomorrow" (Campbell, 1984). This article began with the foregoing quote by Rainer Maria Rilke. Because we are on the campus of Arizona State and this quote is so relevant for a conference that focuses on future directions, I thought it appropriate to include it here. Anyone who has seriously thought about the motor control and learning area quickly realizes that it also relates to a much larger research enterprise that deals with motor behaviors in industry, safety, music, and disorders of movement.

In 1974, I presented a paper at a joint conference of the NAPECW and the NCPEAM in Orlando (Stelmach, 1974). I advocated that motor learning research move toward a process-oriented perspective if we in motor behavior (motor control and learning) are to begin to understand learning and skilled performance. I believed then, as I still do, that the keys to understanding learning and performance lie in the complexities of the central nervous system. Without knowledge about the process mechanisms underlying movement control, little progress will be made in our quest to understand motor learning. Although the process-oriented perspective has been widely adopted and is still being pursued, its image is somewhat tarnished by the way in which process methods have been applied.

A few years later, I presented a paper entitled "The Psychological Perspective: Future Directions" at the American Academy of Physical Education meeting in New Orleans (Stelmach, 1979). I suggested, among other things, that motor skills research appears to be moving beyond reductionism. I speculated that we were entering a period in which there will be a demand that the scientific community address problems and concerns that are ecologically valid and that we in the motor behavior area must move beyond the study of artificially created laboratory situations that differ radically from the real world. It is apparent that this prediction has not been realized to any great extent—reductionism is still rampant. However, it is encouraging to see that we as a field have recognized this problem and are attempting to find ways to move beyond it (this conference is an example). It is my pleasure to be able to comment again on the future directions of the field by reacting to the papers of Schmidt and Christina, who forecast the future for the theoretical and applied dimensions of our field.

In this paper I will provide a historical sketch of the field of motor learning and control. Then, I will react to Schmidt's contention that the motor behavior area should abandon process-oriented research and readopt a task (product) orientation. Subsequently, I will explain why I think that the process orientation should remain the central focus of motor learning research for years to come. After commenting on Schmidt's concern, I will turn my thoughts to those of Christina, who suggests that motor learning's embrace of basic science (primarily process research) has relegated applied motor learning research to a secondary and insignificant status.

Christina's solution is to create a two-track system in which applied research attempts to build a specialized body of practical knowledge that parallels the body of fundamental knowledge of basic research in motor learning. He envisions a field in which each track would be given approximately equal time and effort. Although I strongly advocate that motor learning research retain its process orientation, I am sympathetic to Christina's recommendation. However, I advocate an approach that calls for the study of motor behaviors that are more molar and less artificial, and that typify real-life sport situations. Our field should have experts in developing training programs, solving skill acquisition problems, and using emerging technologies to assess skill development. It is apparent that if those in the motor learning and control area want to contribute in significant ways to exercise and sport science, they must begin to study complex skills that deal with real-life concerns.

A Historical Perspective

During the last 60 years some have claimed that the field of motor behavior has undergone some tremendous changes. Yet, despite these claims motor learning research is in some ways remarkably similar to what it was 75 years ago. The theoretical orientations of Thorndike (1911), Hull (1943), Adams (1971), and Schmidt (1975) have remarkable similarities. We have moved beyond behaviorism, but the driving aim that caused these scientists to advocate their theories was the belief that there could be a general theory of learning. In his book on animal intelligence, E.L. Thorndike (1911) wrote that "two laws explain all learning, the law of effect and the law of exercise" (p. 66). Since that writing, it has been commonly acknowledged that all forms of learning could be explained in terms of a set of general principles. The view that is central to these global theories is not only that there is a set of general principles applicable to all learning, but also that all instances of learning are manifestations of a general learning process.

After many years of study, those in the mainstream of the psychology of learning have openly acknowledged that the pursuit of global theories was, perhaps, too ambitious. Consequently, many subtheories of learning emerged that attempt to explain how learning may take place in some specific kind of skill or domain. However, in the motor research area very little has emerged to question the notion of general principles. The theoretical propositions advocated by Adams (1971), Gentile (1972), and Schmidt (1975), which are anchored in behaviorism, are still envoked and often quoted. However, there is the feeling (also expressed by Schmidt) that enthusiasm has dwindled and the global learning theory view may be finally feeling its age in the motor skills area. The vitality that characterized the arrival of Adams' closed-loop theory and Schmidt's schema theory is ebbing. More and more motor behavior theorists are realizing that a global theory orientation, which is an admirable goal, is probably not the best way to advance learning research. The implication of this realization is rather dramatic because it suggests that the basis of theory development (general principles) borrowed from the physical sciences may not be so appropriate for motor behavior. The general principles notion is still lurking about; however, it has been displaced by a move to study the processes that underlie skill acquisition.

The Move Toward Process

Although there are many issues involved, motor learning research took an abrupt turn in the 1970s to embrace a process orientation to motor skills research, despite the emergence of Adams' (1971) closed-loop theory of learning and Schmidt's (1975) schema theory, which advanced the view that motor learning could be explained by a few hypothetical constructs. The reasons for such a shift are many: (a) the emerging computer metaphor, (b) the realization that behavioral methods can help neurophysiology understand structure and function relationships, (c) the fascination with rigorous experimental methods, and (d) the acceptance of motor behavior research as a legitimate area of study. The overriding impetus, however, for the shift to process paradigms was the hope that if the processes and mechanisms that underlie skill learning could be discovered, our understanding of motor learning and performance would be enhanced (Stelmach & Diggles, 1982).

Researchers soon came to realize that the study of motor learning up to this point in time had contributed little to understanding behavior when so little was known about the control of movement. After all, motor learning was thought to be a change in motor control. With increasing frequency, researchers became aware that many of the keys to learning and performance lie in the complexities of the central nervous system, and, without knowledge about the mechanisms underlying performance, the likelihood of being able to explain learning would be small. Thus motor behavior investigators began turning toward motor control and associated processes to provide a better understanding of skilled behavior. They believed that knowing more about control would lead to better ideas about coordination, which would lead to better understanding of learning.

The shift to a process orientation led motor behavior research on a difficult and painful journey and in directions that perhaps some did not wish to go, or perhaps more profoundly in which they perceived they did not belong. As Schmidt says in his paper, "the process-oriented approach has taken us away from situations that have much potential for practical application." The first reality of the extensive use of process-oriented paradigms was that it splintered our field into many subgroups (e.g., those studying motor programming, short-term retention, feedback, context effects, etc.), and these groups rarely communicated. Students of each topic proceeded without much concern for what those in other areas were doing. This provincial outlook created fragmented, isolated, and competitive subdisciplines in which research ideas often became ends in themselves.

A second reality was that scholars in the area became obsessed with improving and refining experimental methodologies. Many experiments were conducted to refine a previous method, clarify a previous experimental flaw, or debate some hypothetical structure/function relationship. When real-world tasks were used (e.g., long jumping, typing, handwriting, playing a piano, etc.), they were seldom studied with the hope of improving performance. These tasks were usually studied because they were suitable to reduction methods or allowed examination of some hypothetical construct. This indulgence and concern for method—although giving the area some respect as a science—came at the expense of studying relevant, real-life motor problems. Gardner (1986) has made a similar indictment of experimental psychology.

The intoxication with methodological concerns also led to another anomalous trend that hampered our ability to accumulate knowledge. There is a noticeable pattern in the past 15 years of research. As soon as an exciting experiment or theory was published, almost immediately a considerable number of experiments were directed at the main finding (or theory). The primary aim of most of these reactionary studies appears to have been to determine whether there was some defect or flaw in the previously published paper (Gardner, 1986). Henceforth, all of our most interesting findings (also theories) were shot down and eventually discarded. It may be argued that some of this methodological refinement was necessary and useful, but it made the knowledge accumulation in our field pretty meager.

Should Process Research Be Abandoned?

In response to this drift away from motor learning research and into the study of fundamental processes that underlie skilled execution, Schmidt suggests that "the process-oriented approach needs to be abandoned" and offers the task-oriented approach as a more direct and effective way to understand the problems relevant to motor learning." I am sympathetic to Schmidt's concern and acknowledge that we have a growing problem of relevance. (This problem is also discussed by Christina from a slightly different perspective.) It is an indisputable fact that many process studies have used reaction time to study mental processes associated with motor programming, linear-positioning to examine the representation of movement codes, and a simple ballistic movement to evaluate error detection processes. I believe, however, that it is not the process-oriented paradigms that should be indicted as much as it is the way process-oriented research has been used in the motor behavior area. It was the pursuit of methodology and the zeal of reductionism that was implemented with bottom-up research (Stelmach & Hughes, 1983) that has caused parts of our field to lose direction.

I want to make it clear what I mean by process-oriented research. It is unfortunate, but some believe that process-oriented research deals only with how incoming information is processed, stored, and retrieved, and uses only reaction-time methods. To me this is a very narrow view and one that was dispensed with for the most part in the 1970s when motor behavior moved beyond the von Neuman serial processing analogies (see Neisser, 1976). Process-oriented research is concerned with all aspects of skilled movements: how skilled movements are controlled, how actions are planned, how movements are organized and executed, how feedback is used. Further, it also deals with the underlying neural events associated with skilled behavior. The main point of process research is that it goes beyond merely examining movement outcomes and attempts to understand the manner in which the performance outcomes are obtained. As stated by Kelso (1982), "the process approach not only involves an understanding of the functional capacities and interactions among receptor, central, and effector mechanisms, but also a careful analysis of the kinematics of the output" (p. 12). The process-oriented approach can be used to study real-world problems and in particular to investigate sport skills.

Few scientists in motor behavior have used process-oriented paradigms to understand complex motor skills or to improve performance as have scientists in some areas of ergonomics or human factors. Here experiments are performed that are similar to those in motor control and learning, but they are often employed in a manner designed to help improve performance, modify task design, and/or select better performers. It is time for motor learning and control research to forge its methodological sophistication to address problems that are more molar and less artificial and that typify real-life sport situations (see also Gardner, 1986).

It is much too early to abandon process-oriented research and to return to the task orientations of the past that stress procedural issues of learning. Such a move in my opinion would be a mistake. Motor behavior's journey from behaviorism to process-oriented issues that stress the cognitive as well as the motor aspects of skill acquisition is just beginning. There are many new research methods emerging that, if properly used, can make our contributions to exercise and sport science significant. What needs to happen in the motor learning and control area is for some (of course, learning research is not for all) to return to the problem of learning and performing complex behaviors and use current methods to advance our understanding.

The original goals of the process-oriented approach that attempt to describe the processes and mechanisms that underlie motor behavior are reasonable and offer considerable rewards. Although it is probably unrealistic to think that process paradigms can produce a complete theory of learning, I think it is still our best way to understand in fundamental ways skilled motor behavior and to promote improvement in skilled performance. There should be little debate that from such knowledge emerges ideas on how to improve performance, and that the knowledge obtained will also suggest how to change the task itself and select more successful participants.

Returning to Schmidt's concern about the type of experiments being performed and the way they are done using laboratory tasks, I acknowledge that he has identified an important problem. Heretofore, most experiments have selected a task primarily by its availability to reductionism, that is, whether a task can be manipulated to isolate some hypothetical process, with little concern for how performance can be improved. It is clear that if motor learning research is to have relevance to real-life sport concerns, research must be aimed at practical problems. Where I would differ from Schmidt is that I would advocate that, rather than study laboratory tasks only (i.e., even if complex) and hope that they generalize to real-world problems, we should also directly study the practical skills in which we are interested. Of course, there is nothing wrong with experiments conducted under artificial laboratory conditions per se, but there is something troublesome about extrapolating the findings to more complex movement patterns outside the laboratory. Up to now, researchers have studied real-world skills to learn about control processes and not to improve performance in those tasks. If we studied these tasks with the aim of improving performance in them, some of the concerns discussed in this paper, as well as in Schmidt's and Christina's, would probably disappear.

The motor control and learning area, with its sophisticated methodology, is suited to studying real-world tasks, isolating the problems athletes have, and showing how to improve performance in fundamental ways. Further, advances in methodology are allowing motor behavior scientists to study some of the oldest questions in motor learning from a new perspective. Neural investigations of learning and memory are progressing rapidly and taking scientists beyond the primitive notions of the past. It is becoming possible for scientists to explain how the brain stores, codes, and retrieves information. What remains is for these methods to be used to achieve an understanding of human performance in real-life situations. If process-oriented research is implemented properly, we should be in a position to suggest better ways to train people, optimize performance, and improve selection procedures.

Schmidt's Examples Call for a Processing Framework

Schmidt gives two examples of recent work that he believes are types of findings that could be used to forge a new beginning for motor learning research through the return to task-oriented paradigms. One of these findings involves some data on how various conditions of practice affect response initiation (random-blocked effect), and the other deals with the effect of various feedback manipulations about goal achievement (knowledge of results). Both of these findings are interesting for theoretical and practical reasons and should be vigorously pursued. However, it would be a mistake to use only product-oriented methods on these findings, because these paradigms are not well suited to unravel the processes or mechanisms that lie behind them. After all, if these findings are to have any practical relevance they must be understood. The only way to begin to understand them is to ask fundamental questions about their underlying causes and then set out to manipulate the relevant variables experimentally. I maintain that it is process-oriented research that can unravel the fundamental processes behind the Schmidt findings. I do not see how task-oriented paradigms can fully advance our understanding of why these phenomena occur.

There Is a Need for Applied Research

One of the results of the move to process-oriented research was the abandonment of applied research. This move was initiated by those who claimed that motor skills research had a limited theoretical perspective due to its rush to find solutions to practical problems (Adams, 1971). This criticism was taken seriously, and motor behavior research abandoned all concern for applied problems and vigorously pursued theoretical issues about fundamental motor processes. In the past 15 years there are few examples of quality motor learning research directed toward sport skills. So, I think Christina is right when he says that the adoption of a basic science point of view has relegated applied research to second-class citizenship.

Now, after more than a decade of pursuing fundamental issues, the scientific community's mood is changing again. The ivory-tower attitudes of the 1970s, during which the pursuit of knowledge, any knowledge, was for its own sake a sufficient end in itself, are gradually retreating. It is slowly becoming acceptable again to perform applied research, and the trite phrase, "those who do applied research are those who are not good enough to perform fundamental research," is hardly mentioned. One of the reasons for this change is that the anticipated success from the study of fundamental processes has not been as informative as expected. Scientists are returning to applied research because all scientists like to believe that they are doing something potentially useful and relevant. Of course, the fact that the National Institute of Health and the National Science Foundation are beginning to fund research that tackles real-life problems may have something to do with the change in attitude. When money is limited there is always the attraction of funding research that can yield practical benefits.

The search for general principles has divided the field into two camps: those who pursue fundamental issues surrounding motor behavior and attempt to develop our theories, and those who take these theories and apply them in practical settings. This is the old axiom that theory leads to practice, which assumes that the flow of information is typically in one direction. Basic scientists are supposed to work out a detailed theory of how a process like learning takes place, and the theory specifies the role of different variables governing this learning. After basic scientists have developed their theory, it is given to practitioners so they can apply it. This idea is borrowed from the physical sciences (Christina gives an account of this tradition), from which there are many examples of how basic science has developed theories that can be applied in a variety of settings.

I believe that it is a mistake to continue this type of relationship between the basic and applied aspects of motor learning research. It is hopeless at present to think that basic scientists will produce the kind of motor learning theory that would make the efforts of teachers and coaches routine. In the practical world, the problems performers encounter in acquiring skills in sport are usually quite specific. However, this does not mean that basic science is irrelevant to the job of application. Rather, basic science serves as a guide for the teachers and coaches to implement realistic training procedures. I am suggesting that basic science can provide cues for direction, a common language for communication, and the tools to understand more fully the abilities required to perform a skilled action.

If basic science cannot provide a complete theory of learning, it is apparent that we must move away from the view that applied research is completely dependent on basic sciences and a literal extension of it. This view is similar to that of Christina, who states "that rather than think of applied research as being almost completely dependent on basic research, we must think of both as being partially dependent on each other." He suggests that experiments be devised that not only can provide immediate solutions to practical problems, but also have the power to provide immediate improvements in theory-based knowledge. I see nothing wrong with the statement, in fact I applaud it. As I see it, the study of real-world problems can help our pursuit of fundamental motor behavior by drawing attention to interesting and important questions and by ensuring that our theories and concepts do not become too laboratory bound.

Just how to accomplish this is not an easy question to answer. Realizing that someone has to recommend how to proceed, I suggest we follow the lead of cognitive science, in which it has become acceptable to study real-life skills such as problem solving, composing, keyboarding, chess playing, and the like. These real-life skills have their counterparts in the many skills acquired in the sport world. However, good applied work is technically more difficult, and it is easy to end up with findings that are as trivial and frustrating as those obtained from routine laboratory research. Once we get a few examples of good, theoretically interesting experiments on skilled motor behavior, the appeal will be irresistible for some to follow.

Our aim should not be simply to apply our paradigms to practical problems but to attempt to understand the phenomenon of skill acquisition. This is initially more appealing to basic motor control scientists and is also a viable route into applied work. To accomplish this will require a willingness to step back from the paradigms with which we all tend to become obsessed and to use our theoretical concepts and methods to examine relevant sport and exercise problems outside the laboratory. I believe it is reasonable to expect some of us in the motor behavior community to become experts in the area of sport learning and skill development. This is a reasonable future direction that needs to be taken and can offer considerable rewards.

Conclusions

Finally, I believe the ultimate challenge for the motor control and learning area is to provide a coherent scientific account of how individuals achieve their most skilled actions: how we acquire gymnastic routines, how we acquire diving skills, and how we learn to control complex machines. Such an account will have to explain how individuals integrate complex information from a variety of sources such as how they memorially represent movement patterns, implement plans of action, and use feedback. Subsequently, as part of this challenge, it will also be necessary to relate our explanations to what is known about neural substrates. To accomplish this goal, scientists will have to work at several levels of analysis. As Arbib (1972) so aptly stated, "a scientist who works on any one level needs occasional forays both downward to find mechanisms for the functions studied and upward to understand what role the studied function can play in the overall scheme of things" (p. 13). Such a scientific enterprise cannot succeed, however, without having a process-oriented approach as its central focus. This type of research, coupled with a move to study skills that are more molar, less artificial, and more representative of the movement behaviors used in sport and industry should provide us with a sound and rewarding future.

Acknowledgments

The preparation of this manuscript was supported in part by research awards from the U.S. Public Health Service Nos. AGO5154 and NS17421, and NATO No. 227/82.

References

Adams, J.A. (1971). A closed-loop theory of motor learning. *Journal of Motor Behavior*, **3**, 111-150.
Arbib, M. (1972). *The metaphorical brain: An introduction to cybernetics as artificial intelligence and brain theory*. New York: Wiley.
Campbell, D.G. (1984, March). Arizona State University: Visions for tomorrow. *Arizona Highways*, **60**(3), 3-22.
Gardner, H. (1986). Cognitive science. *APA Monitor*, **17**, 9-12.
Gentile, A.M. (1972). A working model of skill acquisition with application to teaching. *Quest*, **17**, 3-23.
Hull, C.L. (1943). *Principles of behavior*. New York: Appleton-Century.
Kelso, J.A.S. (1982). The process approach to understanding human motor behavior: An introduction. In J.A. Scott Kelso (Ed.), *Human motor behavior: An introduction* (pp. 3-19). Hilldale, NJ: Erlbaum.
Neisser, V. (1976). *Cognition and reality*. San Francisco: W.H. Freeman.
Schmidt, R.A. (1975). A schema theory of discrete motor skill learning. *Psychological Review*, **82**, 25-260.
Stelmach, G.E. (1974). *Towards an information processing approach in motor behavior*. Paper presented at the Joint NAPECW-NCPEAM Conference, Orlando, FL.
Stelmach, G.E. (1979). The psychological perspective: Future directions. *The Academy Papers*, **13**, 33-41.
Stelmach, G.E., & Diggles, V.A. (1982). Control theories in motor behavior. *Acta Psychologica*, **50**, 63-92.
Stelmach, G.E., & Hughes, B.G. (1983). Cognitivism and a theory of action. In W. Prinz & A. Sanders (Eds.), *Cognition and motor process* (pp. 3-18). Heidelberg: Springer-Verlag.
Thorndike, E.L. (1911). *Animal intelligence*. New York: Hafner.

SECTION E:
SPORT PSYCHOLOGY

Theoretical Research in Sport Psychology: From Applied Psychology Toward Sport Science

Deborah L. Feltz

Those who have tracked the history of research in sport psychology agree that it has been only since the late 1960s that sport psychology has emerged as a recognizable subdiscipline within exercise and sport science (Alderman, 1984; Gill, 1981; Landers, 1983; Wiggins, 1984). Even with its short history as a recognizable subdiscipline, the research emphasis within sport psychology has changed considerably. An analysis of where the theoretical research in sport psychology is going rests somewhat on where it has been in the past and thus necessitates an overview of major research areas and state-of-the-art research.

An Overview of the Theoretical Research in Sport Psychology

In any area of science, the choice of topics to investigate, the methods employed, and the perspective one takes are often not freely and logically determined; rather, they are determined by the sociological forces both within and outside the discipline (Keller, 1985; Shadish, 1985). Sport psychology is no exception. Morgan (1980) has indicated that trends in sport psychology have tended to parallel those in general psychology. As Landers (1983) noted, the research during the 1950 to 1965 time period was characterized by empiricism, most of which were personality studies, at a time when the trait approach was in vogue in psychology. The next time period, from 1966 to 1976, was characterized by a social analysis approach. Research consisted of testing a single theory at a time from mainstream psychology in the area of sport and motor performance (Landers, 1983). Such topics as social facilitation, achievement motivation, social reinforcement, and arousal and motor performance were investigated. Much of this research was influenced by Martens's (1970) recommendation of a social analysis approach. The late 1970s to the present has also been influenced by leaders in psychology and sport psychology. Wankel (1975) advocated the application of cognitive approaches to sport psychology issues. These approaches included causal attributions, intrinsic motivation, and self-efficacy/self-confidence. Also, Martens (1980) emphasized the use of more field research to test these concepts, and Landers (1983) advocated a resurgence of theory testing using the method of strong inference. Many sport psychologists have incorporated these approaches into their research. In the sections that follow, a sample of these topics will be briefly reviewed.

Personality Research

The relationship of personality to participation in sport and physical activity has been one of the most popular research areas in sport psychology. Much of the early research took a trait approach to studying personality profiles in athletes or athletic groups and has been described by Ryan as being of the shotgun variety (cited in Martens, 1975). Researchers would gain access to a sample of athletes (from high school to Olympic caliber) and test them on the most convenient personality test without having any theoretical basis for their selection. Few conclusive answers resulted from the hundreds of studies conducted, which subsequently led to strong criticism of the area by a number of investigators who were leaders in sport psychology (e.g., Kroll, 1970; Martens, 1975). Most of the criticisms were based on theoretical and methodological shortcomings of the research. The use of univariate instead of multivariate statistics, questionable sampling techniques, and lack of specificity in the operationalization of variables have been some of the major criticisms lodged against sport personality research. In addition, the applicability of general personality assessment techniques for sport and physical activity that may not have a logical link to participation or performance has been questioned (Kroll, 1970).

In response to this growing skepticism, some investigators (Kane, 1978; Morgan, 1980) argued for (a) more scientifically rigorous investigations, (b) employment of personality inventories within the context of the personality theories, (c) sport-relevant theories, and (d) assessment of psychological states as well as traits of athletes to more fully account for their behavior. Most researchers currently employ this interactionist approach, and more scientifically rigorous investigations in sport personality are being conducted (Fisher & Zwart, 1982; Schurr, Ashley & Joy, 1977). In addition, assessment instruments specific and relevant to sport have been and are continuing to be developed (e.g., Martens, 1977; Tenenbaum, Furst, & Weingarten, 1984; Vealey, 1986).

For instance, Morgan (1980) has found a mental health model to be effective in predicting success in sport and to be more relevant to sport than other trait models. Martens (1977) has developed the Sport Competition Anxiety Test (SCAT), which measures competitive trait anxiety and is an example of a personality assessment instrument that is specific and relevant to sport. The SCAT has also been employed in many studies in combination with a state anxiety measure, following the recommended interactional approach. Only a few investigators have recently begun to combine personality, physiological, and motoric components in psychobiological models in an attempt to integrate multiple perspectives of behavior (e.g., Dishman, Ickes, & Morgan, 1980).

Although it appears that personality research in sport is making a comeback, Fisher's (1984) review of this literature indicated that sport personality studies have dwindled drastically since the late 1970s. Landers (1983) suggested that the criticism of the personality literature has led to an almost irrational overreaction against this area. Recall that this criticism was generated by leaders in the field who influenced what was considered socially acceptable research. Martens (1970, 1975) was one of the major critics of the sport personality research, and he had a major influence on the subsequent research direction taken by the field of sport psychology. When he advocated using a social analysis approach that combined empirical methods with theory and started testing psychological theories within a motor performance context, others followed. Most of this research was conducted in controlled laboratory settings.

Social Facilitation and the Arousal-Performance Relationship

Although many authors treat social facilitation and arousal-performance separately, they are treated together in this paper because the bulk of the research occurred around similar time periods, used similar methods, and was based on the same theories/hypotheses. The presence of others in social facilitation was considered to be a form of arousal.

Much of the research in social facilitation and arousal in sport psychology flourished after Zajonc's (1965) paper on social facilitation. Zajonc's hypothesis, based on drive theory, was that the presence of an audience creates arousal and thus enhances the emission of dominant responses. The dominant response in initial learning of a complex task is the incorrect response, but the dominant response is the correct response when the skill is mastered. Martens (1969) initiated a series of laboratory studies on social facilitation using motor skill tasks and supported Zajonc's theory. A number of other investigators also attempted to extend this research to motor tasks by varying the task, audience, and subject characteristics (e.g., Carron & Bennett, 1976; Haas & Roberts, 1975). Their findings varied depending on the variables studied. Reviewers of this research have generally concluded that the evidence for a drive theory explanation of social facilitation effects in motor performance has been mixed (Bond & Titus, 1983; Carron, 1980; Landers, 1980; Wankel, 1984). In addition, the size of social facilitation effects have been shown to be very small (Bond & Titus, 1983; Landers, Snyder-Bauer, & Feltz, 1978).

Another aspect of the social facilitation research that investigators found troublesome was the assessment of arousal. Regardless of the particular autonomic arousal measure employed, no clear pattern of results has been obtained. Some studies have demonstrated increased arousal with the presence of others and some have reported no effect. Some reviewers believe the problem lies in the nature and assessment of arousal because of its multidimensionality and individual specificity (Carron, 1980;

Landers, 1980; Wankel, 1984). Due to these measurement problems, mixed results, and the small percentage of variance accounted for by audience effects, many researchers abandoned the area of social facilitation in search of other psychological theories to apply to sport.

The most frequently cited alternative to drive theory for social facilitation and arousal-performance research has been the inverted-U hypothesis (Carron, 1980). This hypothesis predicts that there is a progressive enhancement in performance as a subject's arousal level increases up to some optimal point, beyond which further increases in arousal will progressively decrease performance efficiency. Much of the arousal-motor performance literature of the 1970s has also tested the inverted-U hypothesis (e.g., Klavora, 1978; Martens & Landers, 1970). However, just as in social facilitation research, the measurement of arousal has been problematic because it has not been assessed in terms of its multidimensional nature.

Self-report measures such as Spielberger's A-state scale (Spielberger, Gorsuch, & Luschene, 1970) and Martens's (1977) Competitive Short Form of the State Anxiety Inventory (CSAI) have been the most popular means of assessing arousal (or anxiety states). These questionnaires have been criticized, however, for failing to differentiate between relevant physiological, behavioral, and cognitive components of anxiety (Landers, 1980). Evidence from psychology has shown that individuals have different responses to stress depending on their learning histories and the type of situation (Borkovec, 1976). In addition, the CSAI may not be sensitive enough to detect subtle differences in anxiety states (Passer, 1981).

Landers (1980) has argued for the need for researchers in sport to redirect their unidimensional conceptualizations of sport-anxiety toward a model that (a) emphasizes the reciprocal relationships among cognitions, physiological responses, and behavior; (b) uses a multidimensional-multimethod approach; and (c) is not tied to a single assessment instrument. Some investigators have begun to do just that (Feltz, 1982; Feltz & Mugno, 1983; Martens, Burton, Vealey, Smith & Bump, 1982) Martens et al. (1982) recently developed the Competitive State Anxiety Inventory-2 (CSAI-2), which measures cognitive and perceived somatic anxiety and self-confidence components of competitive anxiety. This inventory may have promise in the future but research will need to include psychophysiological assessments and self-report assessment instruments other than the CSAI-2 to achieve more valid knowledge of competitive anxiety (Campbell & Fiske, 1959; Webb, Campbell, Schwartz, & Sechrest, 1966).

My research (Feltz, 1982, 1988; Feltz & Mugno, 1983) in this area has involved the comparison of a model based on the three-systems approach to anxiety (Borkovec, 1976) and a cognitive mediating model based on self-efficacy (Bandura, 1977) in high-avoidance motor behavior. The time series design employed permitted an analysis of the reciprocal-causal relationships among the measures of anxiety, self-efficacy, and behavior. Research efforts in these directions may further our understanding of an individual's anxiety response in a sport context.

Cognitive Approaches

Cognitive models in the social facilitation, arousal-performance, and other motivation areas have been proposed because of the dissatisfaction with the simplistic and mechanistic drive theory perspective for explaining complex human behavior (Landers, 1980; Wankel, 1975, 1984). Landers (1980) has advocated a cognitive arousal-attention model based on Easterbrook's cue utilization theory (1959). This model suggests that increased arousal leads to a narrowing of attentional focus and cue utilization, thus limiting performance. Similarly, an attention-distraction interpretation of audience effects proposes that the presence of others creates drive-like effects by serving as a source of attentional distraction (Baron, Moore, & Sanders, 1978; Sanders, 1981).

The concept of objective self-awareness (Duval & Wicklund, 1972) has also been used to interpret audience effects. This theory suggests that the presence of others leads to objective self-awareness (attention directed inward upon the self), which affects task motivation. Baumeister (1984) has suggested that audience-induced pressure increases conscious attention to the performer's own process of performance, which is disruptive to smooth execution.

Wankel (1975) has outlined how attribution theory may be used to explain motivation in the presence of an audience. Wankel (1984) also advocates a closer look at Borden's (1980) model, which acknowledges the performer as a proactive rather than a reactive individual who interprets information from the situation and makes predictions about the audience's reactions and alters the behavior accordingly.

Much of the attribution research in sport psychology was, again, borrowed from work in mainstream psychology. Weiner and his associates (Weiner, 1972) identified four standard causal attributions that individuals use to explain their behavior: ability, effort, luck, and task difficulty. They proposed a two-dimensional classification system that classifies these attributions as internal-external and stable-unstable. This theoretical framework, like previously mentioned cognitive theories, considers the person as an active perceiver rather than a passive responder to the environment. Individuals logically processed information based on the stability and locus of causality of outcomes, which in turn could affect future behavior.[1]

In sport psychology, most of the studies, especially the early ones, were conducted in the laboratory using novel tasks such as the motor maze and the stabilometer. The four standard attributions were typically imposed by investigators. Researchers generally found that individuals made internal attributions for success and external attributions for failure (e.g., Gill & Gross, 1979; Gill & Martens, 1977). These results were interpreted as support for a motivational or self-serving bias explanation rather than Weiner's cognitive information processing explanation.

One problem in laboratory experiments is that investigators could not safely assume a subject's ego involvement in the novel task. A subject may respond with self-serving attributions when ego-involved and logical cognitive attributions when the task is unimportant to self-esteem. Thus there was a move to field investigations in sport where athletes were assumed to be more ego-involved (e.g., Brawley, 1980). Results of field investigations have also been generally interpreted with a self-serving bias explanation; however, because most studies did not allow manipulations of independent variables (e.g., game outcome) only post hoc explanations could be offered (see Brawley, 1980, as an exception).

Rejeski and Brawley (1983) suggested that a number of factors in sport (e.g. social situation) may influence subjects' attributions to function in cognitive or motivational fashion or both, thus mingling both perspectives. In addition, they suggested that conceptual and measurement problems in the area of sport attributions need to be recognized. For instance, the four traditional attributions from social psychology may not be the most appropriate in sport based on work by Roberts and Pascuzzi (1979). In addition, objective outcome (win/loss) should not be considered synonymously with subjective perceptions of success/failure. Subjective and objective outcomes may evoke different causal ascriptions (Spink & Roberts, 1980).

Rejeski and Brawley (1983) have called for innovative approaches and broader conceptual views if this area is to help us understand motivation in sport. The cognitive concepts of perceived ability and self-efficacy (Bandura, 1977; Harter, 1978; Maehr & Nicholls, 1980) may play a key role in mediating motivation. These concepts are being incorporated into the sport psychology research in motivation (Ewing, 1981; Feltz, 1982; Roberts, Kleiber, & Duda, 1981; Weiss, Bredemeier, & Shewchuk, 1986).

Like much of the sport psychology research, these concepts have also been borrowed from mainstream psychology. Researchers in sport psychology who have not developed a systematic plan of research seem to have fallen into a pattern of (a) borrowing theories from psychology; (b) obtaining mixed results; (c) due to discouragement, leaving the area or searching for an explanation; and (d) modifying the methods, measures, or theories for sport. This describes much of the research that I have reviewed thus far. Borrowing from psychology, however, has not been all that harmful. As Alderman (1980) has noted, psychology has brought us a long way in increasing our body of knowledge. Being a relatively new area in the exercise and sport sciences, sport psychology will naturally be more dependent on knowledge in the parent discipline of psychology to help us understand behavior in sport. This knowledge outside or apart from sport, as Alderman suggests, however, can carry us only so far in understanding behavior in sport. Researchers have begun to advocate the development of our own theories within sport psychology to gain a better understanding of behavior as it occurs in sport (Alderman, 1980; Dishman, 1983; Martens, 1980).

The inadequacy of the laboratory-oriented social psychological paradigm for sport psychology research may be what discouraged many researchers and led them to abandon an area when mixed results were obtained. Some researchers skipped from one area of interest to another, conducting laboratory experiments without completely answering the question raised by the initial study. Martens (1980), however, advocated abandoning the paradigm rather than the topic. He suggested switching from laboratory settings to field settings, to exchange our "smocks for our jocks" (or sports bras) to observe and understand the real world of sport.

Current Trends in Research

Although Martens (1980) believed that field-based research need not be divorced from theory, much of the research community is currently giving scant attention to theory. Landers (1983) has not witnessed much theory testing as editor of the *Journal of Sport Psychology*. Only 13% of all submitted articles during his editorship have tested theory (Landers, Boutcher, & Wang, 1986). Researchers have gone to the field, as Martens suggested, and emphasized more applied topics such as mental practice, imagery, psych-up strategies, stress management and other intervention techniques, and coach/player relationships. Landers et al. (1986) found that, although 16% of the articles submitted to the journal were laboratory experiments, 67% were field experiments, field studies, or surveys. Some of these studies have used experimental designs, comparing a psychological skills technique to control and/or placebo conditions. Others have been descriptive studies in field settings, but not much theory testing or theory construction has been initiated.

For the most part, we have not been developing the new conceptual frameworks or models within sport that Alderman (1980) suggested we should. The few exceptions are attempts at concepts such as movement confidence (Griffin, Keogh, & Maybee, 1984), sport confidence (Vealey, 1986), and sport enjoyment (Scanlan & Lewthwaite, 1986). Even where theories already exist, Landers (1983) indicated researchers are rarely using them as a starting point from which to modify them for sport.

The current theoretical research that is being conducted, as previously mentioned, is more cognitively oriented. Theories such as self-efficacy (Bandura, 1977), attribution (Weiner, 1972), achievement orientation (Maehr & Nicholls, 1980), competence motivation (Harter, 1978), and intrinsic motivation (Deci, 1975) are examples of these. As Landers (1983) has noted, however, many of the research studies testing these theories have tested only one theory at a time. He has criticized sport psychology researchers for making premature commitments to a theory, which he believes leads to trying to prove (or "probabilify") rather than modify or disprove the theory. It is Landers' contention that this approach to theory testing has slowed the growth of our field and has resulted in the increasing frustration with theory testing.

Future Directions

Landers (1983) has suggested that future research in sport psychology incorporate the method of strong inference (Platt, 1964) where possible to advance our knowledge more rapidly. In this approach, based on

Popper's (1959) view that science can only advance by disproofs, alternative hypotheses are devised to explain phenomena in sport, experiments are devised with the potential to exclude or disprove one or more of these hypotheses, and further subtests or sequential hypotheses are developed and tested. Platt (1964) referred to this as a *conditional inductive tree* or *logical tree*. At the first fork, the choice is made to go to the right branch or the left, depending on the experimental outcome; at the next fork, to go left or right, and so on.

I reinforce Landers' (1983) suggestions that we should test multiple theories and/or hypotheses where possible in our research; however, I do not agree that using the strong inference approach, as described by Platt (1964), will advance valid knowledge in our field more rapidly. The basis of this approach, that science can only advance by disproofs and that a single disconfirmation can refute a theory is a faulty one. Although most modern philosophers of science would agree that scientific propositions cannot be verified conclusively, they would also agree that scientific propositions cannot be disproven conclusively either (Weimer, 1979). In addition, in sophisticated falsificationist theories, a single disconfirmation never refutes a theory; rather, the cautious appraisal of competing theories is emphasized (Lakatos, 1976; Laudan, 1977).

One may wonder how scientific theories can be assessed if they cannot be either proved (or probabilified) or disproved. In Popper's later paper (1963), he suggested that only a competing plurality of theories can be assessed (as does strong inference), but also that this assessment consists of the scrutiny of inconsistencies rather than in refutations. Laudan (1977) and Lakatos (1976) also advocate the cumulative criticism of research in the context of competing research programs rather than a single disconfirmation and believe this is what is most important to scientific progress. According to Lakatos (1976), the growth of science requires new theories even more than it requires falsifications. Rejection of theories or models must be a slow, reasonably reluctant process so that we do not abandon them prematurely. Corroborating evidence, especially novel corroborations, is, therefore, accorded a more salient role in scientific progress by recent philosophers of science, such as Lakatos. As Shadish (1985) has noted,

> the location of novel corroborations indicates the presence of a bias of omission, and suggests that the limits of a theory need to be extended. Disconfirming observations indicate biases of commission, and suggest that the boundaries that qualify the range of a theory need to be tightened. (p. 79)

The strong inference approach places too much emphasis on disproof and may lead an investigator to reject a hypothesis or theory prematurely. Rather than employing Platt's (1964) definition of a strong inference approach in our theory testing, I believe an approach that Shadish (1985) has labeled *planned critical multiplism* is needed for our future research. This approach involves the planned use of multiple heterogeneous options that each reflect different biases plus a commitment to seek and use criticism of the biases present in the options one chooses, which increases the opportunity for the scrutiny of inconsistencies. The remainder of this paper is devoted to explaining this approach and how this approach relates to interdisciplinary sport and exercise science research.

Planned Critical Multiplism

Planned critical multiplism incorporates the multiple theory and hypothesis testing of strong inference but includes other multiples as well in a planned systematic program of research. These approaches, suggested by Shadish (1985), include multiple operationalism, multimethod research, planned research programs based on multiple interconnected studies, multivariate causal models, the use of multiple stakeholders to formulate research questions, the use of multiple theoretical and value frameworks to interpret research questions and findings, the use of multiple analysts to examine important data sets, and the use of multitargeted research that seeks to probe many different types of issues within a single study. This approach is in accord with Landers's (1983) recommendation that we become more flexible in our research by giving up constraining commitments to theories, methods, apparatus, and research settings, and Dishman's (1982) request for integration of multiple paradigms at the empirical level. This approach goes further, however, to put this flexibility into a systematic plan.

The strategy of planned multiplism is not to use as many operations, methods, measures, and theories as possible, but rather that multiple heterogeneous options be implemented that have biases operating in different directions. Examples of these options include using physiological and self-report measures of anxiety, qualitative as well as quantitative methods for analyzing phenomena in sport, social psychological and psychobiological models in investigations, and qualitative and quantitative measures of sport and motor performance. Including a feminist perspective, which tends to focus on interaction, interdependence, and process, in addition to the more traditional separation, compartmentalization, and search for prime causes is another example of heterogeneous options (Lott, 1985). In these ways, investigators may quickly find important biases in their knowledge claims.

Shadish (1985) suggests that the feasibility of planned critical multiplism may increase if it is a scientist's research program rather than a single study that is made multiplistic. For example, one might start with a meta-analysis of the research area of interest. This is a technique for synthesizing the results of multiple independent studies, each having its own systematic and random biases. This procedure provides a characterization of the tendencies of the research and information about the magnitude of any differences between conditions among studies. Unfortunately, many scientists think that new research is better, or more insightful, or more powerful than existing research. They seldom consider investing time and resources to synthesize the information that already exists. As Landers (1980) noted, when disagreements among findings occur, sport psychology researchers have concluded that the research is hopelessly contradictory or that more research is needed. Light and Pillemer (1984) suggest, however, that such conflicts can teach us a lot. They offer an opportunity to examine and learn about divergent findings. A meta-analysis is one technique to help identify the source(s) for the contradictions and the biases that exist.

Landers (1980) recommended using a meta-analysis to reexamine the sport personality literature rather than abandoning the area. In addition, a critical multiplist analysis (Shadish, 1985) could also be conducted to identify the features of the sport personality literature that could be multiply operationalized. Houts, Cook, and Shadish (1986) conducted such an analysis of the person-situation debate in psychology and found that traits, situations, criterion behaviors, occasions, and data-analysis techniques could be multiply operationalized. These features had been homogeneously implemented in the literature when at least some evidence existed that the conclusions would vary if they had been more heterogeneous. For instance, they found most research used two or fewer traits, often chosen by convenience rather than according to any theory that might maximize trait heterogeneity.

Resource constraints can present a problem to implementing all the plausible options that could be multiply operationalized. Shadish (1985), therefore, has suggested some guidelines to follow in making choices among the options. One of these includes making the least expensive options, multiple measure assessment and multiple analyses on the same data, a routine part of any research study. I would like to see journal editors give preference to authors that incorporate these procedures into their studies.

The criticism component in planned critical multiplism pertains to a commitment to seeking and using criticism of the multiple options one chooses in a research program in order to compensate for one's own weaknesses in perceiving such things as confirming observations, competing hypotheses and theories, novel corroborations, and errors or gaps of logic (Shadish, 1985). This component is included because of evidence that suggests scientists, like all human beings, are biased in their interpretations of findings (Mahoney, 1976). Although the peer review process in journals is a step toward this type of criticism, it too can be biased (Mahoney, 1977, 1985; Shadish, 1985). Other critical multiplistic strategies that Shadish suggested include (a) soliciting consultants who have different perspectives on the problem to be involved during all stages of the research, (b) submitting drafts of final reports to diverse critics, (c) collaborating with other authors from different conceptual and methodological frameworks on a piece of research, (d) commissioning multiple investigators with different perspectives to conduct studies on a particular topic, and (e) submitting raw data from any single study to multiple analysts who might use differing assumptions and models. Criticism is probably the most problematic component of planned critical multiplism, but an important one. As Shadish notes,

> if planned multiplism is to work optimally, then scientists may have to seek criticism when it could be avoided, in hopes of identifying the major limitations in their work more rapidly than

> would be the case by relying on, for example, the occasional journal review. (p. 80)

Expanding one's conceptual and methodological horizons is part of the psychological commitment to using criticism in planned multiplism according to Shadish (1985). A number of researchers in sport psychology (Dishman, 1982; Landers, 1980; Rejeski & Brawley, 1983; Wankel, 1984) have also called for expanded conceptual views to help us gain a better understanding of behavior in sport. This may require a consideration of other domains, such as exercise physiology, sport biomechanics, motor learning/control, motor development, and sport sociology.

Interdisciplinary Research

As I have mentioned throughout this paper, much of our research in sport psychology has focused on applications of psychological theories and concepts in a sport setting. It was noted that this has not been detrimental to sport psychology; rather, it has provided us with a starting point from which we have been able to examine its applicability to sport and modify it accordingly. It was also noted, though, that psychological knowledge can carry us only so far in understanding behavior in sport and that the development of sport psychology models and theories are needed to understand further behavior as it occurs in sport. Sport psychology models, however, will also frequently be inadequate in understanding phenomena specific to sport according to Dishman (1983). The best models to answer sport-specific questions will undoubtedly include knowledge from other subdisciplines within sport and exercise science. Dishman has advocated combining our talents across subdisciplines within sport and exercise science to answer sport and exercise questions of practical impact: a recycled suggestion, he notes, that is more frequently ignored than followed.

For instance, in trying to explain why children drop out of youth sports, sport psychology researchers have previously looked entirely for psychological reasons (Ewing, 1981; Feltz & Petlichkoff, 1983; Gould, Feltz, Horn, & Weiss, 1982). Training and conditioning or maturational explanations for dropping out have often been overlooked. To examine these possibilities adequately, longitudinal, systematic, and interdisciplinary research programs, such as the young runners study being conducted by the Institute for the Study of Youth Sports (Seefeldt & Steig, 1986), are needed that focus on a number of interrelated questions rather than a single, isolated one. This study of young long-distance runners included a battery of tests and assessments in the following areas: anthropometry, blood sample (KDA profile and serum lipids), cinematographic recording of gaits, densitometry, hand-wrist X ray (biological maturity), history of illness and injuries, motor performance battery, muscular endurance, nutritional profile, psychological profile, review of activity and competitive history, and treadmill test of work capacity. These runners are being followed as some drop out and others continue in competitive long-distance running. Explanations for these runners' decisions may be only partially psychological (Feltz & Albrecht, 1986).

Another example of an interdisciplinary approach to examining sport-specific questions is Beuter and Duda's (1985) analysis of the arousal/motor performance relationship. They used movement kinematics (an assessment of the quality of performance) to examine the effect of arousal on motor performance. This approach allowed them to focus on the process by which arousal influences performance rather than to focus on just the outcome or end products of performance. These types of studies may uncover explanations that a study based solely on psychological models could not provide.

It seems apparent, therefore, that theoretical models that are being called for to be specifically built to answer sport and exercise questions (Alderman, 1980; Dishman, 1983; Martens, 1980) must come from an interdisciplinary sport and exercise knowledge base. To achieve this integrated body of knowledge in sport and exercise science, departments may have to change their reward structure so that researchers are rewarded to a greater degree for publishing within sport and exercise science than in their parent discipline (Hoffman, 1985) and so they are not penalized for doing collaborative research (Mahoney, 1985). In addition, graduate curricular programs would need to be modified to better prepare students for interdisciplinary research (Hoffman, 1985). Rather than taking the bulk of their course work in psychology, students should take the majority of their course work in sport science. An integrated knowledge of sport and exercise science does not eliminate intensive study in sport psychology; both will be necessary if students are to be successful in conducting state-of-the-art research.

Summary

It has been only since the late 1960s that sport psychology has emerged as a recognizable subdiscipline within exercise and sport science. Even with its short history as a recognizable subdiscipline, the research emphasis within sport psychology has changed considerably. Most research areas started with tests of psychological theories and concepts in a sport setting. Such topics as personality, social facilitation, achievement motivation, social reinforcement, and emotional arousal were popular. When researchers found that these general psychological theories were inadequate to explain sport behavior, some advocated abandoning the specific topic area, some advocated modifying the theories for sport, and others advocated focusing on more cognitively oriented theories that were being developed in general psychology. A few stressed the need for sport psychology to develop its own theories in the real world of sport rather than applying psychological theories in artificial, laboratory-type settings.

These recommendations have left sport psychology with some researchers doing field-based research, completely divorced from theory, others trying to modify measures and theories to fit sport, and a few trying to develop sport psychological theories. The growth in our understanding of sport behavior, however, has been slow. My recommendation for improving the growth of sport psychology is to use an approach to research that is based on the *planned* use of multiple ways to (a) formulate research questions, (b) measure constructs, (c) design the studies, (d) analyze the data, and (e) interpret the findings. In line with the recommended multiple approach, I have also advocated a move toward interdisciplinary research within sport and exercise science. If the best models to answer sport-specific questions include knowledge from all subdisciplines within sport and exercise science, this knowledge will be more rapidly obtained through expanded conceptual frameworks and a multiple approach toward investigation.

Acknowledgments

The author expresses appreciation to Brenda J. Bredemeier, Rod K. Dishman, Daniel M. Landers, and Michael J. Mahoney for their helpful comments during the development of this paper.

Note

1. Weiner (1979) has since added a third dimension, controllability, which has been largely ignored in sport psychology.

References

Alderman, R.B. (1980). Sport psychology: Past, present, and future dilemmas. In P. Klavora & K.A.W. Wipper (Eds.), *Psychological and sociological factors in sport* (pp. 3-19). Toronto: Publications Division, School of Physical and Health Education, University of Toronto.

Alderman, R.B. (1984). The future of sport psychology. In J.M. Silva & R.S. Weinberg (Eds.), *Psychological foundations of sport* (pp. 45-54). Champaign, IL: Human Kinetics.

Bandura, A. (1977). Self-efficacy: Toward a unifying theory of behavioral change. *Psychological Review*, **84**, 191-215.

Baron, R.S., Moore, D., & Sanders, G.S. (1978). Distraction as a source of drive in social facilitation research. *Journal of Personality and Social Psychology*, **36**, 816-824.

Baumeister, R.F. (1984). Choking under pressure: Self-consciousness and paradoxical effects of incentives on skillful performance. *Journal of Personality and Social Psychology*, **46**, 610-620.

Beuter, A., & Duda, J.L. (1985). Analysis of the arousal/motor performance relationship in children using movement kinematics. *Journal of Sport Psychology*, **7**, 229-243.

Bond, C.F., & Titus, L.J. (1983). Social facilitation: A meta-analysis of 241 studies. *Psychological Bulletin*, **94**, 265-292.

Borden, R.J. (1980). Audience influence. In P.B. Paulus (Ed.), *Psychology of group influence* (pp. 99-131). Hillsdale, NJ: Erlbaum.

Borkovec, T.D. (1976). Physiological and cognitive processes in the regulation of anxiety. In G.E. Schwartz and D. Shapiro (Eds.), *Consciousness and self-regulation: Advances in research* (Vol. 1, pp. 261-312). New York: Plenum.

Brawley, L.R. (1980). *Children's causal attributions in a competitive sport: A motivational interpretation*. Unpublished doctoral dissertation, Pennsylvania State University, University Park, PA.

Campbell, D.T., & Fiske, D.W. (1959). Convergent and discriminant validation by the multitrait-multimethod matrix. *Psychological Bulletin*, **56**, 81-105.

Carron, A.V. (1980). *Social psychology of sport*. Ithaca, NY: Mouvement.

Carron, A.V., & Bennett, B. (1976). The effects of initial habit strength differences upon performance in a coaction situation. *Journal of Motor Behavior*, **8**, 297-304.

Deci, E. (1975). *Intrinsic motivation*. New York: Plenum.

Dishman, R.K. (1982). Contemporary sport psychology. *Exercise and Sport Sciences Reviews*, **10**, 120-159.

Dishman, R.K. (1983). Identity crises in North American sport psychology: Academics in professional issues. *Journal of Sport Psychology*, **5**, 123-134.

Dishman, R.K., Ickes, W.J., & Morgan, W.P. (1980). Self-motivation and adherence to habitual physical activity. *Journal of Applied Social Psychology*, **10**, 115-131.

Duval, S., & Wicklund, R.A. (1972). *A theory of objective self-awareness*. New York: Academic.

Easterbrook, J.A. (1959). The effect of emotion on cue utilization and the organization of behavior. *Psychological Review*, **66**, 183-201.

Ewing, M.E. (1981). *Achievement orientations and sport behavior of males and females*. Unpublished doctoral dissertation, University of Illinois, Urbana.

Feltz, D.L. (1982). Path analysis of the causal elements in Bandura's theory of self-efficacy and an anxiety-based model of avoidance behavior. *Journal of Personality and Social Psychology*, **42**, 764-781.

Feltz, D.L. (1988, May). Gender differences in the causal elements of Bandura's theory of self-efficacy on a high-avoidance motor task. *Journal of Sport and Exercise Psychology*, **10**, 151-166.

Feltz, D.L., & Albrecht, R.R. (1986). Psychological implications of competitive running. In M. Weiss & D. Gould (Eds.), *Sport for children and youths* (pp. 225-230). Champaign, IL: Human Kinetics.

Feltz, D.L., & Mugno, D.A. (1983). A replication of the path analysis of the causal elements in Bandura's theory of self-efficacy and the influence of autonomic perception. *Journal of Sport Psychology*, **5**, 263-277.

Feltz, D.L., & Petlichkoff, L. (1983). Perceived competence among interscholastic sport participants and dropouts. *Canadian Journal of Applied Sport Sciences*, **8**, 231-235.

Fisher, A.C. (1984). New directions in sport personality research. In J.M. Silva & R.S. Weinberg (Eds.), *Psychological foundations of sport* (pp. 70-80). Champaign, IL: Human Kinetics.

Fisher, A.C., & Zwart, E.F. (1982). Psychological analysis of athletes' anxiety responses. *Journal of Sport Psychology*, **4**, 139-158.

Gill, D.L. (1981). Current research and future prospects in sport psychology. In G.A. Brooks (Ed.), *Perspectives on the academic discipline of physical education* (pp. 342-378). Champaign, IL: Human Kinetics.

Gill, D.L., & Gross, J.B. (1979). The influence of group success-failure on selected interpersonal variables. In G.C. Roberts & K.M. Newell (Eds.), *Psychology of motor behavior and sport—1978* (pp. 61-71). Champaign, IL: Human Kinetics.

Gill, D.L. & Martens, R.C. (1977). The role of task type and success-failure in group competition. *International Journal of Sport Psychology*, **8**, 160-177.

Gould, D., Feltz, D., Horn, T., & Weiss, M. (1982). Reasons for attrition in competitive swimming. *Journal of Sport Behavior*, **5**, 155-165.

Griffin, N.S., Keogh, J.F., & Baybee, R. (1984). Performer perceptions of movement confidence. *Journal of Sport Psychology*, **6**, 395-407.

Haas, J., & Roberts, G.C. (1975). Effect of evaluative others upon learning and performance of a complex motor task. *Journal of Motor Behavior*, **7**, 81-90.

Harter, S. (1978). Effectance motivation reconsiderd: Toward a developmental model. *Human Development*, **21**, 34-64.

Hoffman, S.J. (1985). Specialization & fragmentation = extermination: A formula for the demise of graduate education. *Journal of Physical Education, Recreation, and Dance*, **56**(6), 19-22.

Houts, A.C., Cook, T.D., & Shadish, W.R. (1986). The person-situation debate: A critical multiplist perspective. *Journal of Personality*, **54**, 52-105.

Kane, J.E. (1978). Personality research: The current controversy and implications for sport studies. In W.F. Straub (Ed.), *Sport psychology: An analysis of athlete behavior* (pp. 340-352). Ithaca, NY: Mouvement.

Keller, E.F. (1985). *Reflections on gender and science*. New Haven, CT: Yale University Press.

Klavora, P. (1978). An attempt to derive inverted-U curves based on the relationship between anxiety and athletic performance. In D.M. Landers & R.W. Christina (Eds.), *Psychology of motor behavior and sport—1977* (pp. 369-377). Champaign, IL: Human Kinetics.

Kroll, W. (1970). Current strategies and problems in personality assessment of athletes. In L.E. Smith (Ed.), *Psychology of motor learning* (pp. 349-367). Chicago: Athletic Institute.

Lakatos, I. (1976). *The methodology of scientific research programs*. Cambridge: Cambridge University Press.

Landers, D.M. (1980). The arousal-performance relationship revisited. *Research Quarterly for Exercise and Sport*, **51**, 77-90.

Landers, D.M. (1983). Whatever happened to theory testing in sport psychology? *Journal of Sport Psychology*, **5**, 135-151.

Landers, D.M., Boutcher, S., & Wang, M.Q. (1986). A report on the research submitted to the *Journal of Sport Psychology*. *Journal of Sport Psychology*, **8**(3), 149-163.

Landers, D.M., Snyder-Bauer, R., & Feltz, D.L. (1978). Social facilitation during the initial stage of motor learning: A re-examination of Martens' audience study. *Journal of Motor Behavior*, **10**, 325-337.

Laudan, L. (1977). *Progress and its problems: Towards a theory of scientific growth*. Berkeley: University of California Press.

Light, R.J., & Pillemer, D.B. (1984). *Summing up: The science of reviewing research*. Cambridge, MA: Harvard University Press.

Lott, B. (1985). The potential enrichment of social/personality psychology through feminist research and vice versa. *American Psychologist*, **40**, 155-164.

Maehr, M.L., & Nicholls, J.G. (1980). Culture and achievement motivation: A second look. In N. Warren (Ed.), *Studies in cross-cultural psychology* (pp. 221-267). New York: Academic Press.

Mahoney, M.J. (1976). *Scientist as subject: The psychological imperative*. Cambridge, MA: Ballinger.

Mahoney, M.J. (1977). Publication prejudices: An experimental study of confirmatory bias in the peer review system. *Cognitive Therapy and Research*, **1**, 161-175.

Mahoney, M.J. (1985). Open exchange and epistemic progress. *American Psychologist*, **40**, 29-39.

Martens, R. (1969). Effect of an audience on learning and performance of a complex motor skill. *Journal of Personality and Social Psychology*, **12**, 252-260.

Martens, R. (1970). A social psychology of physical activity. *Quest*, **14**, 8-17.

Martens, R. (1975). The paradigmatic crisis in American sport personology. *Sportwissenschaft*, **5**, 9-24.

Martens, R. (1977). *Sport Competition Anxiety Test*. Champaign, IL: Human Kinetics.

Martens, R. (1980). From smocks to jocks: A new adventure for sport psychologists. In P. Klavora & K.A.W. Wipper (Eds.), *Psychological and sociological factors in sport* (pp. 20-26). Toronto: Publications Division, School of Physical and Health Education, University of Toronto.

Martens, R., Burton, D., Vealey, R., Smith, D., & Bump, L. (1982, May). *Cognitive and somatic dimensions of competitive anxiety*. Paper presented at the North American Society for the Psychology of Sport and Physical Activity annual conference, University of Maryland.

Martens, R., & Landers, D.M. (1970). Motor performance under stress: A test of the inverted-U hypothesis. *Journal of Personality and Social Psychology*, **16**, 29-37.

Morgan, W.P. (1980). The trait psychology controversy. *Research Quarterly for Exercise and Sport*, **51**, 50-76.

Passer, M.W. (1981). Children in sport: Participation motives and psychological stress. *Quest*, **33**, 231-244.

Platt, J.R. (1964). Strong inference. *Science*, **146**, 347-352.

Popper, K.R. (1959). *The logic of scientific discovery*. New York: Basic Books.

Popper, K.R. (1963). *Conjectures and refutations*. New York: Harper.

Rejeski, W.J., & Brawley, L.R. (1983). Attribution theory in sports: Current status and new perspectives. *Journal of Sport Psychology*, **5**, 77-99.

Roberts, G.C., Kleiber, D.A., & Duda, J.L. (1981). An analysis of motivation in children's sport: The role of a perceived competence in participation. *Journal of Sport Psychology,* **3**, 206-216.

Roberts, G.C., & Pascuzzi, D. (1979). Causal attributions in sport: Some theoretical implications. *Journal of Sport Psychology,* **1**, 203-211.

Sanders, G.S. (1981). Driven by distraction—An integrative review of social facilitation theory and research. *Journal of Experimental Social Psychology,* **40**, 1102-1117.

Scanlan, T., & Lewthwaite, R. (1986). Social psychological aspects of competition for male youth sport participants: IV. Predictors of enjoyment. *Journal of Sport Psychology,* **8**, 25-35.

Schurr, K.T., Ashley, M.A., & Joy, K.L. (1977). A multivariate analysis of male athletic characteristics: Sport type and success. *Multivariate Experimental Clinical Research,* **3**, 53-68.

Seefeldt, V., & Steig, P. (1986). Introduction to an interdisciplinary assessment of competition on elite young distance runners. In M. Weiss & D. Gould (Eds.), *Sport for children and youths* (pp. 213-217). Champaign, IL: Human Kinetics.

Shadish, W.R., Jr. (1985). Planned critical multiplism: Some elaborations. *Behavioral Assessment,* **8**, 75-103.

Spielberger, C.D., Gorsuch, R.L., & Luschene, R.E. (1970). *Manual for the state-trait anxiety inventory (self-evaluation questionnaire).* Palo Alto, CA: Consulting Psychologists Press.

Spink, K.S., & Roberts, G.C. (1980). Ambiguity of outcome and causal attributions. *Journal of Sport Psychology,* **2**, 237-244.

Tenenbaum, G., Furst, D., & Weingarten, G. (1984). Attribution of causality in sport events: Validation of the Wingate sport achievement responsibility scale. *Journal of Sport Psychology,* **6**, 430-439.

Vealey, R.S. (1986). *The conceptualization of sport-confidence and competitive orientation: Preliminary investigation and instrument development.* Manuscript submitted for publication.

Wankel, L.M. (1975). A new energy source for sport psychology research: Toward a conversion from D.C. (drive conceptualizations) to A.C. (attributional cognitions). In D.M. Landers (Ed.), *Psychology of sport and motor behavior II* (pp. 221-245). University Park: Pennsylvania State University.

Wankel, L.M. (1984). Audience effects in sport. In J.M. Silva & R.S. Weinberg (Eds.), *Psychological foundations of sport* (pp. 293-314). Champaign, IL: Human Kinetics.

Webb, E.J., Campbell, D.T., Schwartz, R.D., & Sechrest, L. (1966). *Unobtrusive measures.* Skokie, IL: Rand McNally.

Weimer, W.B. (1979). *Notes on the methodology of scientific research.* Hillsdale, NJ: Erlbaum.

Weiner, B. (1972). *Theories of motivation: From mechanism to cognition.* New York: Rand McNally.

Weiner, B. (1979). A theory of motivation for some classroom experiences. *Journal of Educational Psychology,* **71**, 3-25.

Weiss, M.R., Bredemeier, B.J., & Shewchuk, R.M. (1986). The dynamics of perceived competence, perceived control, and motivational orientation in youth sports. In M. Weiss & D. Gould (Eds.), *Sport for children and youth* (pp. 89-102). Champaign, IL: Human Kinetics.

Wiggins, D.K. (1984). The history of sport psychology in North America. In J.M. Silva & R.S. Weinberg (Eds.), *Psychological foundations of sport* (pp. 9-22). Champaign, IL: Human Kinetics.

Zajonc, R.B. (1965). Social facilitation. *Science,* **149**, 269-274.

Models From Behavioral Clinical Psychology for Sport Psychology

Richard M. Suinn

In the United States, the early history of sport psychology is attributed to the work of Coleman Griffith, at the University of Illinois, about 1918. As Director of the Athletic Research Laboratory, he conducted studies on reaction times of football players versus basketball players, psychomotor skills, and personality. During Griffith's interview with Red Grange after the 1924 Illinois-Michigan game, Grange revealed that he had no recall of his scoring four touchdowns in the first 12 min of the game. Griffith conceived of the idea of the *automatic skill response*—a concept still of interest to modern practitioners possibly as flow or peak experience and to researchers as cognitive states, information processing, or movement memory encoding (Kroll & Lewis, 1970). Still, most would agree that research moved slowly; in fact, one person criticized that some researchers not only were looking down the wrong end of the telescope, but also had one eye closed (Kroll, 1980). I hope that we have accomplished more since then, in terms of both the types of issues studied and the sophistication of the designs. I shall not attempt to be comprehensive, or even fair, in this presentation, because that would be an impossible task in the time available. I will first address the evidence that suggests that principles from behavioral clinical psychology can serve as conceptual models for applied sport psychology. Next, I will illustrate the systematic expansion of knowledge possible in sport research as seen in the work on visualization. Finally, I will address both general and specific recommendations for future research.

Behavioral Principles

The Use of Models

My first illustration comes from the behaviorists working with performance acquisition and improvement via vicarious learning. Bandura (Bandura, Ross, & Ross, 1963) and Meichenbaum (1971) showed that therapeutic changes in fear occurred through watching a model, and that the characteristics of the model were important in effecting such therapy gains. Kazdin (1974) systematically studied the impact of two such characteristics: the degree of similarity of the model to the observer, and the degree to which the model showed a mastery versus a coping style. As Figure 1 demonstrates, the approach behavior of previously phobic subjects was clearly affected in an orderly fashion: The least therapeutic results occurred with a dissimilar mastery model, the next highest came from the dissimilar coping model, the next from the similar mastery model, and the most gains from the similar coping model.

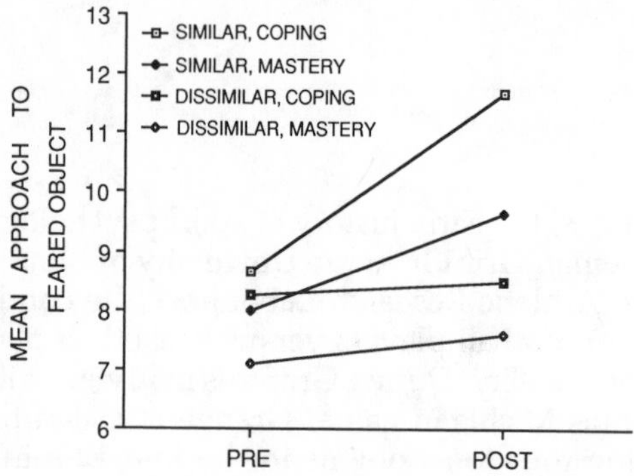

Figure 1. Effects of model similarity and coping characteristics on approach. *Note.* From "Covert Modeling, Model Similarity, and Reduction of Avoidance Behavior" by A. Kazdin, 1974, *Behavior Therapy*, **5**, p. 333. Copyright 1974 by *Behavior Therapy*. Reprinted by permission.

In sport psychology, Gould and Weiss (1981) studied the practical issue of how observing a model influences performance on a muscle endurance motor task. Model similarity and coping/mastery characteristics were manipulated akin to the Kazdin research reported nearly a decade earlier. The results were a startling confirmation of the therapy report on efficacy changes: The dissimilar mastery model was the lowest, then dissimilar coping, then similar mastery, and finally similar coping was the best (Figure 2). Also, both studies confirmed that model similarity was a more powerful influence than coping/mastery.

Self-Monitoring

A second illustration derives from the behavioral principle that having persons monitor their own behaviors (self-monitoring) can be a powerful mechanism for either increasing or decreasing behaviors. For instance, counting each time you achieve a desirable behavior (SM+) helps the furthering of such behaviors, whereas tallying the occurrences of undesirable behaviors (SM−) helps to diminish such actions. This principle has been applied successfully in behavior modification to smoking and weight

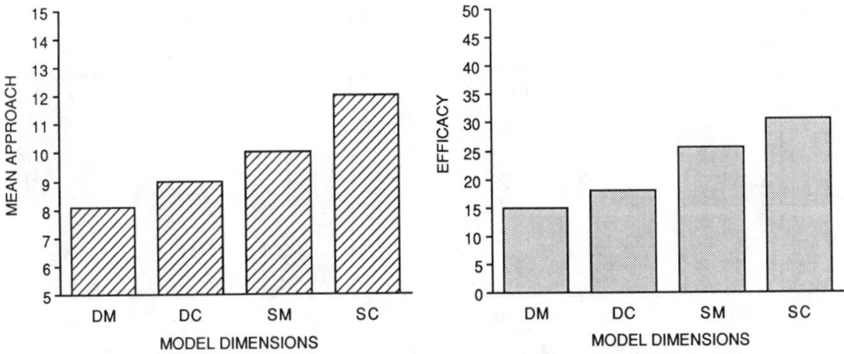

Figure 2. Results of two studies on model dimensions of similarity and coping characteristics. DM = dissimilar, mastery; DC = dissimilar, coping; SM = similar, mastery; SC = similar, coping. *Note.* From "The Effects of Model Similarity and Model Talk on Self-Efficacy and Muscular Endurance" by D. Gould and M. Weiss, 1981, *Journal of Sport Psychology*, **3**, p. 24. Copyright 1981 by *Journal of Sport Psychology*. Reprinted by permission. And from "Covert Modeling, Model Similarity, and Reduction of Avoidance Behavior" by A. Kazdin, 1974, *Behavior Therapy*, **5**, p. 333. Copyright 1974 by *Behavior Therapy*. Reprinted by permission.

control. Litrownik and Freitas (1980) studied retarded children to determine if positive self-monitoring (SM+) was equivalent to negative self-monitoring (SM−). It turns out that SM+ did strengthen the targeted behavior, whereas SM− was ineffective (Figures 3 and 4). In sport psychology, Kirschenbaum, Ordman, Tonarken, and Holtzbauer (1982) transferred the concept to bowlers with amazingly comparable results. Clearly positive self-monitoring of correct performance was superior to monitoring of errors.

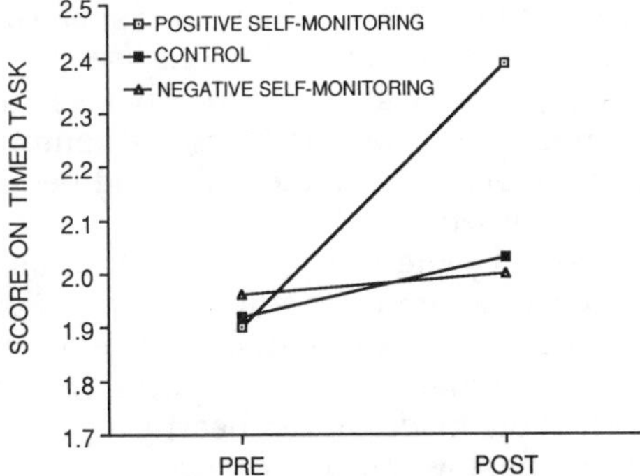

Figure 3. Effects of positive and negative self-monitoring on a timed task for retarded subjects. *Note.* From "Self-Monitoring in Moderately Retarded Adolescents: Reactivity and Accuracy as a Function of Valence" by A. Litrownik and J. Freitas, 1980, *Behavior Therapy*, **11**, p. 252. Copyright 1980 by *Behavior Therapy*. Reprinted by permission.

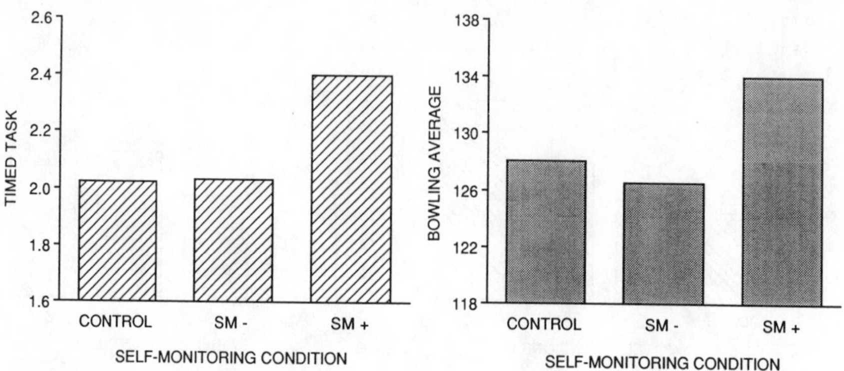

Figure 4. Comparison of two studies on positive and negative self-monitoring. *Note.* From "Self-Monitoring in Moderately Retarded Adolescents: Reactivity and Accuracy as a Function of Valence" by A. Litrownik and J. Freitas, 1980, *Behavior Therapy*, **11**, p. 252. Copyright 1980 by *Behavior Therapy*. Reprinted by permission. And from "Effects of Differential Self-Monitoring and Level of Mastery on Sports Performance: Brain Power Bowling" by D. Kirschenbaum, A. Ordman, A. Tonarken, and R. Holtzbauer, 1982, *Cognitive Therapy and Research*, **6**, p. 340. Copyright 1982 by *Cognitive Therapy and Research*. Reprinted by permission.

Physiological Variables

In behavior therapy, there has always been an interest in physiological variables. Today, researchers are still attempting to determine if desynchrony in physiological responses is diagnostic of prognosis in therapy. In 1973, Borkovec defined synchrony as the accurate agreement between a physiological measure of autonomic reactivity and the subjects' own self-assessment of their reactivity. Desynchrony essentially meant a mismatch, for example, the subjects thought themselves to be autonomically reactive but they were actually low on measures, or vice versa. When exposed to training for reducing fear behaviors of snake phobics, the synchronous phobics showed greater improvements (seen in pulse rate) than the desynchronous phobics (Figure 5). In what seems a fascinating parallel, Daniels, Landers, and Hatfield (personal communication, 1984) confirmed that synchronous rifle shooters showed better performances than desynchronous competitors.

I have been impressed by the research sophistication of Daniels and Landers (1981) in their programmatic studies, using biofeedback. They demonstrated the influence of physiological variables on the performance of elite rifle shooters. For some, pulse was important, in that lower scores were correlated with shots made on the heartbeat. For others, respiration was important, in that lower scores occurred when shots were fired after breath was held longer than an optimal period. Although many researchers would have ended their study at this point, Landers is now replicating such findings and planning the next stage in the program, that

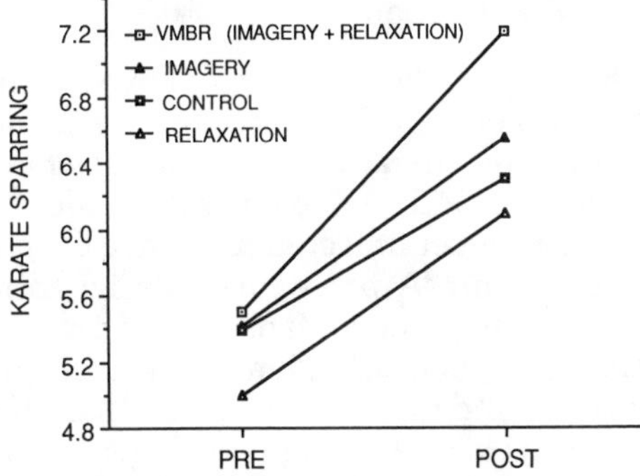

Figure 5. Comparison of two studies on synchronous (hi-hi, low-low) versus desynchronous (hi-low, low-hi) characteristics as effects on performance. *Note*. From "The Effects of Instructional Suggestion and Physiological Cues on Analogue Fear" by T. Borkovec, 1973, *Behavior Therapy*, **4**, p. 187. Copyright 1973 by *Behavior Therapy*. Reprinted by permission.

of determining whether biofeedback training will lead to performance improvements, when the training is made specific to the athlete's problem areas. Because biofeedback training in clinical problems has been proven effective in teaching clients physiological self-control, there is every reason to believe that sport performance will similarly be benefited. In a single case study, Suinn (1980) demonstrated that a biathlete's heart rate decreased during shooting, consistent with earlier training in physiological self-control.

There are numerous other examples of the transfer of principles or techniques derived from behavior modification or behavior therapy to the degree that I would argue for inclusion of a curriculum in behaviorism in sport psychology. Some of these examples of the crossover will now be discussed.

Behavioral Assessment

Behavorial assessment techniques have become much more situationally oriented and away from sole reliance on the general trait approach. For instance, instead of generalized anxiety testing, there are now state versions of the State-Trait Inventory, the Anxiety Differential, and the S-R Inventory, as well as specific measures including the Suinn Test Anxiety Behavior Scale (that assess behaviors under concrete situations) and the Mathematics Anxiety Rating Scale (Endler & Hunt, 1966; Husek & Alexander, 1963; Spielberger et al., 1979; Suinn, 1969, 1972). In sport psychology, situation-specific measures are available, such as the Sport Competition Anxiety Tests and the basketball revision of the S-R Inventory of Anxiety (Fisher & Zwart, 1982; Martens, 1977; Martens, Burton, Rivkin, & Simon, 1980). A colleague and I once put together an instrument for assessing "motivation," defined more concretely as ratings of incentives (Youngblood & Suinn, 1980).

Cognitive Behavior Modification

Cognitive behavior modification has been viewed both as a revolution in behavior therapy theory and practice and as a natural evolution (Mahoney, 1985). Cognitive therapy studies have examined applications to depression and anxiety (Beck, 1976; Ellis, 1962; Meichenbaum, 1977). In sport psychology, a number of techniques have been taken from cognitive behavior modification. A procedure I designed for treatment of anxiety disorders known as Anxiety Management Training (Suinn, 1983; Suinn & Richardson, 1971) is nearly identical to procedures tested with runners to reduce stress and increase cardiovascular efficiency (Ziegler, Klinzing, & Williamson, 1982). Although no longer considered a method of choice for therapy, the cognitive approach of thought-stopping is another example of cognitive methods applied to sport performance for thought management (Gravel, Lemieux, & Ladouceur, 1980; Suinn, 1986). Recently, I described other thought-control or conditioning methods (Seabourne, Weinberg, Jackson, & Suinn, 1986; Suinn, 1980). The research on Meichenbaum's Stress Inoculation Training for pain management in counseling psychology has also found a theoretical match to studies in sport psychology (Hackett & Horan, 1980). Specifically, cognitive strategies that were found useful for pain control seem similar to those identified by Morgan as helpful strategies among marathon runners (Morgan, 1984; Morgan, Horstman, Cymerman, & Stokes, 1983).

Research Design Methodologies

Behavioral research may be said to contribute in another way to research, and that is in terms of research design methodologies. Briefly, such researchers have described and defended the validity of various approaches such as reversal, multiple, and multi-element baseline designs (Hersen & Barlow, 1976; Kazdin, 1982). Subsequently, sport psychology researchers have adopted such approaches to provide more rigor in their studies (Allison & Ayllon, 1980; Buzas & Ayllon, 1981; Heward, 1978; Komacki & Barnett, 1977; McKenzie & Liskevych, personal communication, 1984; McKenzie & Rushall, 1980; Simek & O'Brien, 1982).

Relaxation Training

Although there is justification for arguing that certain applied techniques have had parallel developments in behavioral psychology and in physical education/motor learning, certainly behaviorism has systematized such methods and research analyses. Among these techniques that have had concurrent histories in both fields are relaxation training and approaches to mental rehearsal. Although most behavioral psychologists rely upon a relaxation training exercise frequently used by physical educators as well, the psychologist group has taken this procedure, Jacobson's (1938) deep muscle relaxation method, and extended its applications. For example, relaxation is the foundation for many stress management procedures, for some behavior therapies, and for clinical problems such as hypertension and tension headaches. It is interesting to note that relaxation training is now viewed as playing a significant role in mental rehearsal, and I'd like to now shift to that topic in the next section.

Mental Rehearsal

Earlier research on mental rehearsal compared the effects of physical practice (PP), mental practice (MP), and the combination on physical performance outcomes. Reviews of this literature (Corbin, 1972; Oxendine, 1968; Richardson, 1967a, 1967b; Suinn, 1982; Weinberg, 1985) offer several conclusions: Physical practice is better than mental practice; mental practice can lead to gains in motor performance, although such practice may not always produce gains; and mental practice alternated with physical practice appears to be the best combination for enhancing the value of mental practice. I would like to emphasize that the studies on mental practice have been inconsistent. Part of the difficulty has been in methodological issues: the failure to define what is involved in mental practice exercises, the differences across studies in tasks and in skill levels of the subjects, and even the differences in goals established (Suinn, 1982). In the 1970s, as a result of some work with clinical clients in behavior therapy, I became interested in two things: the combined effects of relaxation and visualization, and the application of such a combination to performance enhancement.

Among my earlier applications were training a management executive in oral presentations, aiding a musician in the preparation of solo performance, and helping an actress in the practice of a difficult role. I also had the good fortune to be invited to work with our university's Alpine ski team—an experience that escalated into an appointment with the U.S. Nordic Ski Team, assignment to the 1976 Winter Olympic Games for Biathlon and Nordic Teams, a later assignment to the 1980 Summer Olympic Games for Women's Track and Field, and my current role on the Sports Psychology Advisory Committee for the U.S. Olympic Committee—all because of relaxation and visualization. My approach to mental practice has been called visual motor behavior rehearsal (VMBR) to distinguish it from earlier versions of mental practice (Suinn, 1972). VMBR is systematic enough as a training procedure that a written description is now available (Suinn, 1984), and it has become the topic of several research studies by other sport psychologists.

VMBR research findings. A variety of studies of both group and single-case designs have demonstrated that VMBR does positively enhance motor performance, and consistently so, with performance tasks ranging from basketball to tennis and diving (Desiderato & Miller, 1979; Kolonay, 1977; Nideffer, 1971; Noel, 1980; Schleser, Meyers, & Montgomery, 1980). The early research either used wait-list control groups or multiple baselines; more recently Weinberg, Seabourne, and Jackson (1981) used a placebo control group and again confirmed the value of VMBR.

VMBR does appear to be an improved approach to mental practice because of the combined reliance on relaxation and mental rehearsal (imagery). As early as 1977, Kolonay did a component analysis, comparing VMBR against relaxation alone and mental rehearsal alone, and demonstrated that the combination of relaxation and visualization (i.e., VMBR) was superior. In the more sophisticated study of Weinberg cited earlier, this very same finding was replicated.

A new level of refinement in understanding the use of VMBR was reported by Noel (1980), who investigated the role of athlete characteristics on outcomes. Noel discovered that VMBR enhanced the accuracy of first serves for skilled tennis players; however, performance decrements were observed in novices. In understanding this effect, it should be stated that VMBR may be viewed as involving neuromuscular activity during the mental visualization, even though the motor activity might not be observable in gross motor movements. We have confirmed this in two cases. In one, the athlete's muscle involvement was measured through electromyographic (EMG) instrumentation. Results demonstrated not only the existence of motor activity, but also showed that the activity matched that required to ski the downhill race course that the athlete was experiencing through VMBR. A second case was conducted for ABC television for a special series on sport psychology. Once more, heart rate and muscle activities reflected the effort required by the jogger as she ran up the steeper section of her VMBR scene.

With reference to Noel's findings, what is being said is that VMBR involves real practice, that practice makes perfect, but that imperfect practicing leads to imperfection. In effect, without proper coaching regarding the proper movements, the novice may be simply rehearsing errors. Although this represents my explanation of Noel's results, there is some confirmatory evidence for my view. Woolfolk, Parrish, and Murphy (1985) conducted an investigation that illustrates the way in which research can continue to add to our understanding of our applied techniques. On the one hand, they instructed one group of golfers to use visualization in the usual way (i.e., to rehearse correct putting technique). On the other hand, they instructed a second group to visualize incorrect putting. In comparison with a control group, the correct-practice golfers improved in performance, whereas the incorrect-practice golfers showed performance deterioration below that of the control.

Application of VMBR to performance enhancement. VMBR is a systematic method about which enough is known for others to use it as a training technique, and a written description is now available given the research support for its value. It is a tool to achieve a variety of goals for different athletes; such goals are stated in my description, ranging from practicing new motor techniques (such as a gymnastic routine), to rehearsing mental skills (such as concentration), to error analysis and correction (through reexperiencing a prior performance), to preparation for an oncoming competitive event (rehearsing performance under various weather conditions).

The exact content of VMBR scenes must vary with the goals and take into account the skill level of the athlete. Recently, we had women athletes view videotapes of their afternoon's performance at a meet, with analyses being provided by a coach and kinesiologist. I then had the kinesiologist put the athlete through the range of movements needed for improvement and followed this with a VMBR session to rehearse the exact movements as they would occur on the competitive field. Such coaching expertise is important where the VMBR practice emphasizes physical skills; similary, where VMBR is used to improve on psychological/mental skills, then a sport psychologist is required. Clearly the ideal is a total team effort.

Finally, VMBR is in itself a type of skill, and training is important. As the athlete becomes more competent in the development of relaxation and the use of visualization, sessions can be shortened, VMBR can be self-directed, goals may be broadened, and VMBR rehearsal can be initiated on the competitive field or arena itself.

The Future of Applied Research

Research in sport psychology has been developing toward higher levels. Our sophistication about research designs has improved such that we no longer are restricting efforts to reporting on mean personality test scores for different groups of subjects. Where such a simple design is used, attempts are now being made to develop prediction formulas to test the validity and usability of such information. We are shifting to more work on performance enhancement procedures and are including performance data that includes outcomes regarding emotional states, physiological data, cognitive information, as well as the behavioral performance outcomes in terms of times, distances, scores, and so forth. Perhaps with the help of behavioral laws and principles, applied techniques are being investigated that have a basis in models for understanding performance. Factor analytic studies help to test conceptualizations regarding what an instrument is supposed to be measuring; meta-analyses are being applied to test the efficacy of training or intervention approaches.

What are the needs and directions for the future? Let me be brash enough to list my own personal views, with the recognition that many of you may have your own views.

General Recommendations

We simply must continue the trend for more rigorous research designs, and encourage journals to reject the simplistic report that raises more questions and provides little in the way of conclusive findings. Weak reports, by reason of being poorly conceptualized studies, involving poor sample selection, lack of control groups, reliance upon questionable instruments, or use of the looser "let's look at . . ." approach instead of a hypothesis-testing or one-tailed prediction approach to research design, should be discouraged. I do not argue for the complete exclusion of well-thought through, creative studies that may pilot new ideas, such as the interesting efforts at North Texas State in an in vivo field study of what athletes do when they engage in so-called psyching-up behaviors, and whether these indeed have any effects (Caudill, Weinberg, & Jackson, 1983).

We need to take known concepts from other fields and extend their implications and applications to sport psychology. Examples that are already proving promising include information processing and cognitive psychology, social psychological variables such as attributions and normative influences on expectations, and approaches to self-regulation. Naturally, my own feeling is that behavioral psychology will continue to be an important source of ideas because of its emphasis on behaviors and its acceptance of the concept of *skill* building, these being clearly transferable to athletic performance. As behavioral therapists who are also working within sport psychology, a number of us have already written conceptual overviews (Mahoney, 1979; Suinn, 1980).

We must provide standardized descriptions of sport psychology procedures similar to those available for relaxation training and VMBR. Many training approaches are more ambiguous than they seem on the surface. For example, we all know what is meant by stress management, yet there are many diverse activities imbedded in this term, ranging from cognitive training to biofeedback training to arousal techniques; and now more recently, even exercise appears to be a form of stress management. If we are to train persons in sport psychology procedures, and if we are to develop research to validate such procedures and identify the conditions under which such methods have value, then more written manuals or standardized descriptions are a must. What do sport psychologists provide when they indicate they provide biofeedback training, attention/concentration training, thought management, self-regulation, stress management, conflict resolution, goals clarification, team-cohesiveness building, communications training, or motivational sessions? From a consumer standpoint, teams have a right to know what they are buying into if they agree to participation in a program. From a research perspective, initial validation or replication is nearly impossible without precise descriptions. A manual I developed for mental training was recently tested, with and without the services of a sport psychologist. Initial results suggest that the training was equivalent (Seabourne, Weinberg, Jackson, & Suinn, 1985). This study now sets the stage for other research relying upon such standardized training in thought management, stress management, and visualization.

In the United States, we must begin to form research teams that model those in European countries, whereby sport institutes provide a wholistic approach to applied topics. Partly because psychology and physical education have separate curricula, separate departments, and separate faculty, cross-training and collaboration are not common. Indeed, within psychology departments, it is rare to see energies invested in sport psychology, and it is only the incautious assistant professor of psychology who devotes all of his or her research to this field, for tenure is not readily forthcoming. Although psychologist practitioners are crying for workshops and training experiences in sport psychology, these supporters tend not to be researchers. As head of a psychology department myself, I contribute to this dilemma because my department is not in a position to expand on its degree-granting curricula. Furthermore, I have been a collaborator with exercise physiologists on research only twice, and neither study was published! Still, the need exists and perhaps the demand will exist in the near future.

Specific Research Topics

Thus far, I have identified some broad recommendations, and will now cite some specific topics that either show promise for research from an applied standpoint, or deserve future attention.

The VMBR method. The basic work accomplished with VMBR should be expanded. It is safe to presume that visualization does have impact. Now we need to answer some specific questions.

Under what conditions does VMBR have its greatest efficiency? Are there different effects of massing versus distributed practice; are there interactions between such effects and whether the task involves acquisition or performance, or whether the subjects are novices at an early learning stage, reasonably athletically inclined persons at an intermediate stage, or elite performers adding new skills to an already strong base?

What factors aid in decision making about how to use VMBR? Is there an optimal sequence of alternating of VMBR rehearsal and physical practice; should the goals and therefore content of VMBR scenes be changed as the athlete nears the competition itself; should there be different sensory input modalities designed for athletes based upon different learning styles or differences in sports (e.g., emphasis on tactual elements with the VMBR scenes for athletes who are proprioceptively sensitive, or for sports where this sense provides important cues, such as for the wrestler who monitors his opponent's balance).

What are some of the scientific relationships involved between level of relaxation and control/clarity of visualization, or between clarity of visualization and performance outcomes, or between the internal orientation in imagery versus an external or observer orientation as such orientation affects learning or performance (there is some evidence that an internal orientation is better, but this comes from small and specialized samples)? Is it possible to speed up the pace at which athletes acquire skills in VMBR, or to identify those variables that prevent an athlete from effectively using this procedure? To the degree that VMBR practice leads to generalization from mental practice to physical performance, what variables enhance this generalization? Exactly what is the mechanism that explains the role of VMBR in performance enhancement: Is it, as I suggested, a different modality for practice involving neuromuscular rehearsal; are there central nervous system encoding and storage alterations that are the basic impacts of VMBR; and does the technique involve facilitating left-to-right brain acquisition (and does such hemispheric change have any role in performance enhancement anyway)? I might comment as an aside that although VMBR does reduce anxiety, the performance enhancement effects have been found to be attributable to factors additional to simple anxiety reduction (Weinberg et al., 1981).

Motivation. We still do not have a very useful comprehension of motivation, what it involves, or how to manage it, if it indeed is an "it." At times, motivation has been studied as a state of generalized arousal, which includes anxiety and muscle tension. At other times it has been viewed as only a state of positive emotion such as in the concept of achievement motivation, although the notion of fear of failure has sometimes been introduced. Other approaches include the concept of goal-directedness or incentive identification. And there is also the physiologically oriented perspective of level of autonomic regulation, and, of course, the subjective view expressed in the term *psyching up*. Rather than continuing in this seemingly endless exploration, research on motivation should do the following:

- Identify the fewest dependent variables that can be demonstrated to contribute the greatest amount to predicting performance outcomes, using multivariate statistics (i.e., multiple regression or discriminant functions) and cross-validations to confirm the validity of such variables;
- Develop assessment methods for such dependent variables that are objective in being answered and in scoring, which require the minimum of interpretation, and which are economical so as to be cost-effective.
- Determine whether such dependent variables are subject to change through training or interventions. If they are not, then the value for applied sport psychology is rather minimal in the United States. Here, elite level team members are all given equal opportunity to qualify through performance records. Preselection of members based upon predicted aptitude is considered unfair, at least for Olympic teams. However, if the motivational variables can be altered through training programs, then the identification of such variables will be a great stimulant to the development of new training techniques. The closest we have come are in areas such as goal setting, including the defining of behavioral subgoals; the control of interfering levels of arousal, such as the control of stress and anxiety; and the adoption of autonomic self-regulation, such as through versions of autogenic training.

Learning. We need to further transfer some of the principles of learning from operant and cognitive psychology. Some success has been reached in cases where coaches recognize the role of factors such as immediate feedback, use of shaping of skills, the operationalizing of behaviors that define steps toward goals, the use of prompting to facilitate errorless performance, the role of individually defined reinforcers, the loss of impact of feedback or reinforcers when these fail to provide new cognitive information, the role of learning styles in aiding encoding, the importance of strategies of learning to facilitate learning, and so on. Much of the information is available, but needs to be transferred to athletic performance to document its value to sport psychologists, coaches, and athletes.

Further, behavioral shaping principles tend to be applied to motor performance in sport psychology. What about their use in designing training programs for psychological skills, such as attentional control, thought management, pain management, or even teamwork? (I once used VMBR for rehearsing eye contact, verbal signals, word praise, and other body contact that I thought aided a volleyball team in developing a sense of teamwork or communication.) Finally, many are applying the techniques of cognitive behavior modification routinely, such as thought management techniques, cognitive restructuring, and self-affirmations for efficacy. Just as I question the routine reliance upon one method of coaching or learning applied slavishly to all athletes, so do I question the validity of assuming that cognitive methods are equally helpful for everyone. We need to know more about how to match such approaches to the athlete. I know of one elite fencer who was most responsive to cognitive training; my choice of such an approach was only after developing an understanding of her overall life approach to behavioral change and problem solving, which provided the clue to psychological training for competition.

Physiology. There is a need to combine brain-physiology-body research. Recently Hatfield and Landers (1983) decried the absence of models derived from psychophysiology and cited the program of research by Landers, Christina, Hatfield, Daniels, and Doyle (1980) as applications. There are numerous directions that might be pursued, all of which have either some theoretical justification or some preliminary research or casework.

We should investigate the possible role of synchrony/desynchrony in determining consistency of performance or peak performance, or in predicting response to training, where fine motor skills are involved or where intense, concentrated effort over a brief interval is characterized by the event. This topic was mentioned earlier in my review of research.

The possible role of right hemisphere influence in peak performance should also be investigated. Hatfield, Landers, and Ray (1984) discovered that marksmen showed left brain intellectual activity when preparing their weapons, but right brain activity appeared to become dominant during actual shooting for scores. Is this limited to riflery, where spatial dimensions are part of task demands, or might this be a more general condition for, let's say, automatic behaviors similar to the states of consciousness called flow? Does right brain dominance actually produce improved performance?

I have sometimes speculated that VMBR training is really accomplishing something other than a form of practice; that is, perhaps it is a method for facilitating left-right brain interactions. Occasionally it seems that motor skills rehearsed through VMBR, such as a new diving routine or even a running strategy under differing weather conditions, transfer from intellectual thought-directed rehearsing of the moves to the level of unconscious, automatic performance. Regrettably, there is so much conflicting data about left/right hemisphere influences on performance that my comments must be considered as sheer speculation.

While I'm speculating, another topic involves the possible use of VMBR for injury rehabilitation. I have certainly used it for eliminating the residual anxieties conditioned to an injury, in order to eliminate the athlete's holding back upon return to competition. What I mean, instead, is the use of VMBR to speed up bone healing. We know that electrical stimulation is used to prevent muscle atrophy and facilitate bone repair during recovery from fractures. Is it conceivable that VMBR might serve a similar function inasmuch as we have some data showing EMG activity? I recall one Alpine ski racer whom I put through VMBR involving racing scenes in order for him to retain his competitive edge. He was reported as having healed and returned to competition earlier than expected; of course, I have no way of telling what made the difference. Would there be a synergistic effect of VMBR paired with electrical stimulation?

There are a few studies that illustrate the ability of psychological training in affecting physiological outcomes, other than the biofeedback research. Two studies independently confirmed that visualization of desired running styles reduced stress and lowered $\dot{V}O_2$ consumption as measured by treadmill testing (Suinn, Morton, & Brammell, 1979; Ziegler et al., 1982). Future work might build on ways in which mental training techniques might further influence such physiological variables.

Consistency and slumps in performance. Consistency may well be associated with all of the usual rules about performance, including amount and quality of practice; practice under stimulus conditions matching those of competition; rules about transfer of practice; drive or arousal states; cue conditions that challenge the athlete to peak performance; perhaps efficacy; and naturally nutrition, sleep, training regime, and the like (Suinn, 1980). Similarly, Morgan (1985) has interpreted slumps and inconsistently poor performances as related to overtraining. I have interpreted slumps as being maintained because the athlete has observed poor results in competition, and not only loses self-efficacy, but also begins to randomly make adjustments to technique and focuses on negative self-thoughts. In retraining such individuals, I request that they work with their coach in systematically testing out technique revisions and viewing no improvement as positive information rather than cause for further depression, because this part of technique can now be ruled out as a contributing factor. However, in spite of these ideas, I am still not certain that we possess good *research* data on how to abort slumps or to produce peak performance, much less consistent peak performance. And what about flow or peak experience states? Are these truly altered states of consciousness, and can a person be trained to achieve this condition consistently; does flow cause peak performance or is it simply the subjective by-product of physical peak performance itself? Are the negative motor and psychological expressions of a slump entirely physiological and responsive only to purely physical interventions, or can cognitive and other psychological interventions promote motor and psychological changes? There is some evidence that some versions of severe depression are a reflection of neurotransmitter changes, as well as some evidence that such depression can be altered through behavioral or cognitive psychological procedures.

Arousal and performance. Arousal states are often considered as part of predicting performance. In the purely physical sense, the classic U-shaped curve is cited to demonstrate that level of activation influences level of performance. Procedures such as autogenic training for activation and stress management for decreased arousal have been described. In the psychological sense, arousal has been couched as psyching up (or down). Caudill, Weinberg, and Jackson (1983) have demonstrated that psyching up does seem to have performance outcomes, and they discovered that even religious thoughts can be helpful for some athletes. Related to these circumstances is the martial arts concept of energy control, including the conservation, building, and focusing of energy. Are these approaches, including autogenic and martial arts training, simply examples of autohypnosis, as some claim?

What about the recent information concerning the use of acupuncture to free up blocked energy pathways? It has always been a mystery to me how acupuncture can have effects such as anaesthetic, when the basis of Asian physiology is at such variance with that of Western medicine. According to Western understanding of nerve placements, acupuncture points should not work. I do not espouse that we be satisfied with adopting methods that appear to have results. Instead, it is important to seek to translate those results into a set of principles that can be cross-validated in our own environments, in order to seek improvements in efficiency. For instance, I would guess that some of the martial arts procedures, such as the sense of a lowered center of gravity, can be reproduced through breathing exercises without the lengthy training in Eastern martial arts philosophy. In fact, in training skiers, I have achieved some of these effects.

The concept of efficacy. Although the concept of efficacy has recently received intense support, I continue to view it as an area needing more clarification and study. On the one hand, Bandura's (1977, 1982) writings certainly provide powerful arguments in the area of clinical psychology. On the other hand, I am still unsure whether it is an epiphenomenon or by-product, or a salient, intervening variable directly influencing sport performance. Most important, we need to face the challenge of how to consistently and meaningfully alter an athlete's sense of efficacy. Mahoney (1979) mentions several methods for accomplishing such changes, methods derived more from Bandura's theory than from an empirical research literature in athletics. Such methods include response induction aids, visualization or modeling, reassurance from an authority, self-statements, and false feedback. My point is that it could be argued that several of those methods affect other variables, such as the strength of the motor skill, and therefore any self-efficacy changes might be no more than a by-product. For instance, response induction aids might include the use of a harness to help a diver or gymnast complete a new aerial movement with safety. Is it efficacy change that leads to future success in this routine, or is it the training aid leading to behavioral success, which in turn improves efficacy? I have been more impressed with Mahoney's research on what successful athletes do when faced with an error during competition (Mahoney & Avener, 1977). It was first determined that high- and low-success gymnasts both experienced equal nervousness about their competition, but the difference was in their responses to errors. The unsuccessful group worried and ruminated about the error; the successful refocused their attention on what had to be accomplished next. In training of athletes regarding negative thoughts, I have relied on Mahoney's findings and those of Morgan (1984). Morgan believes that experienced marathoners use information, such as bodily discomfort, as information to be processed for decision making. In both studies, the common element is the athlete's use of the negative experience as information for positive action. In training athletes, I have relied on this approach by having the athlete decide what adjustments they need to make, for instance, when they notice signs of cramping, then rehearsing these adjustments through visualization until it becomes second nature. One athlete commented that his level of confidence rose substantially because he now felt prepared to cope with any circumstance.

In effect, I'm suggesting that we need to know if efficacy is a primary and necessary inferential construct whose presence is required to improve performance, or whether it is a secondary by-product. Research is needed to identify the sequence of events, through a time-series design such as a path-analysis. Feltz's (1982) initial report using this approach provided only partial support for the early role of efficacy. Initially, efficacy had a strong influence on later performance; however, as practice trials proceeded, performance had a greater influence in determining efficacy than efficacy had in influencing performance. Certainly the next issue is the type of training or experiences that serves to raise or lower efficacy among athletes. Further, is efficacy no more than self-talk or expectations, or does efficacy describe a broader attitudinal state? If efficacy is responsive to behavioral experiences, such as recent success or positive feedback, what can we say about controlling such experiences? Take feedback, for instance: Under what conditions does feedback alter or confirm efficacy levels; is there an interaction with positive versus negative feedback and the time such feedback occurs prior to the day of competition; is feedback provided by another person superior to that obtained through videotape review; is there a delay between such personal experiences and changes in efficacy, and if so, what factors reduce this delay; is there any value to the technique attributed to boxing managers, whereby the opponents are chosen to provide opportunity for success experiences in the early career of the fighter? And finally, how do we understand the athlete for whom efficacy and performance are not positively correlated (i.e., the athlete who seems to lack confidence yet who is always a dependable performer or the one who seems confident but performs at a subpar level!).

Closing Remarks

I have attempted to provide some basis for the premise that principles and models of behavior from one area of psychology can serve as the foundation for sport psychology. In addition, in keeping with the goal of the conference, I have stretched my imagination to consider what might be the future directions in applied sport psychology research. However, I trust I haven't actually stretched too seriously, because some of my speculation derives from some pilot research, case experiences, and principles that lend some logic to my premises. I hope that by the year 2000, many of the questions I raise will have answers. Some of these may be a confirmation that these were important variables, whereas others may actually be in the direction of disproving their relevance. Whichever the results, the athletes in competition and those involved in health psychology actually wind up only being winners from better research.

This presentation first covers the current research in sport psychology through comparing such research against those models discovered in behavioral psychology. Comparisons cover results on use of modeling, on self-monitoring methods, and on physiological parameters. The applicability of behavioral research data to sport psychology is further illustrated through summaries on behavioral assessment, cognitive behavior modification, research design, and relaxation/mental rehearsal methods. Specific findings regarding developments in visualization as mental practice are cited to confirm the role of research in applied sport psychology.

In speculating on the future of applied research, I have discussed both general and specific issues. On the general level, the paper presents the need for rigor in research designs, extension of concepts from other findings in psychology, standardized descriptions of training techniques, and collaborative team efforts of persons with various professional expertise. On the level of specificity, some possible research questions or concepts are presented relating to visualization, motivation, operant and cognitive psychology applications, physiological brain-behavior issues, consistent/peak performances/slumps, activation and energy control, and self-efficacy. Although speculative, a number of the proposed topics derive either from preliminary research, from principles, or from case experiences.

References

Allison, M., & Ayllon, T. (1980). Behavioral coaching in the development of skills in football, gymnastics, and tennis. *Journal of Applied Behavior Analysis*, **13**, 297-314.

Bandura, A. (1977). *Social learning theory*. Englewood Cliffs, NJ: Prentice-Hall.

Bandura, A. (1982). Self-efficacy mechanism in human agency. *American Psychologist*, **37**, 122-147.

Bandura, A., Ross, D., & Ross, S. (1963). Imitation of film-mediated aggressive models. *Journal of Abnormal and Social Psychology*, **66**, 3-11.

Borkovec, T. (1973). The effects of instructional suggestion and phyisological cues on analogue fear. *Behavior Therapy*, **4**, 185-192.

Buzas, H., & Ayllon, T. (1981). Differential reinforcement in teaching tennis skills. *Behavior Modification*, **5**, 372-385.

Caudill, D., Weinberg, R., & Jackson, D. (1983). Psyching up and track athletes: A preliminary investigation. *Journal of Sport Psychology*, **5**, 231-235.

Corbin, C. (1972). Mental practice. In W. Morgan (Ed.), *Ergogenic aids and muscular performance* (pp. 93-118). New York: Academic Press.

Daniels, F., & Landers, D. (1981). Biofeedback and shooting performance: A test of disregulation and systems theory. *Journal of Sport Psychology*, **4**, 271-282.

Desiderato, O., & Miller, I. (1979). Improving tennis performance by cognitive behavior modification techniques. *The Behavior Therapist*, **2**, 19.

Endler, N., & Hunt, J. (1966). Sources of behavioral variance as measured by the S.R. Inventory of Anxiousness. *Psychological Bulletin*, **65**, 338-346.

Feltz, D. (1982). Path analysis of the causal elements in Bandura's theory of self-efficacy and an anxiety-based model of avoidance behavior. *Journal of Personality and Social Psychology*, **42**, 764-781.

Fisher, A., & Zwart, E. (1982). Psychological analysis of athletes' anxiety responses. *Journal of Sport Psychology*, **4**, 139-158.

Gould, D., & Weiss, M. (1981). The effects of model similarity and model talk on self-efficacy and muscular endurance. *Journal of Sport Psychology*, **3**, 17-29.

Gravel, R., Lemieux, G., & Ladouceur, R. (1980). Effectiveness of a cognitive behavioral treatment package for cross-country ski racers. *Cognitive Therapy and Research*, **4**, 83-90.

Hackett, G., & Horan, J. (1980). Stress inoculation for pain: What's really going on? *Journal of Counseling Psychology*, **27**, 107-116.

Hatfield, B., & Landers, D. (1983). Psychophysiology: A new direction for sport psychology. *Journal of Sport Psychology*, **5**, 243-259.

Hatfield, B., Landers, D., & Ray, W. (1984). Cognitive processes during self-paced motor performance: An electroencephalographic profile of skilled marksmen. *Journal of Sport Psychology*, **6**, 42-59.

Hersen, M., & Barlow, D. (1976). *Single case experimental designs: Strategies for studying behavior change*. New York: Pergamon Press.

Heward, W. (1978). Operant conditioning of a .300 hitter? The effect of reinforcement on the offensive efficiency of a barnstorming baseball team. *Behavior Modification*, **2**, 25-40.

Husek, T., & Alexander, S. (1963). The effectiveness of the anxiety differential in examination stress situations. *Educational and Psychological Measurement*, **23**, 309-318.

Jacobson, E. (1938). *Progressive relaxation*. Chicago, IL: University of Chicago Press.

Kazdin, A. (1974). Covert modeling, model similarity, and reduction of avoidance behavior. *Behavior Therapy*, **5**, 325-340.

Kazdin, A. (1982). *Single-case research designs: Methods for clinical and applied settings*. New York: Oxford University Press.

Kirschenbaum, D., Ordman, A., Tonarken, A., & Holtzbauer, R. (1982). Effects of differential self-monitoring and level of mastery on sports performance: Brain power bowling. *Cognitive Therapy and Research*, **6**, 335-342.

Kolonay, B. (1977). *The effects of visuo-motor behavior rehearsal on athletic performance*. Unpublished master's thesis, Hunter College, The City University of New York.

Komaki, J., & Barnett, F. (1977). A behavioral approach to coaching football: Improving the play execution of the offensive backfield on a youth football team. *Journal of Applied Behavior Analysis*, **10**, 657-664.

Kroll, W. (1980). Understanding skill: Is biomechanics or motor learning ahead? In P. Klavora & J. Flowers (Eds.), *Motor learning and biomechanical factors in physical performance* (pp. 211-219). Toronto: University of Toronto.

Kroll, W., & Lewis, G. (1970). America's first sport psychologist. *Quest*, **13**, 1-4.

Landers, D., Christina, R., Hatfield, B., Daniels, F., & Doyle, L. (1980). Moving competitive shooting into the scientist's lab. *American Rifleman*, **128**, 36-37, 76-77.

Litrownik, A., & Freitas, J. (1980). Self-monitoring in moderately retarded adolescents: Reactivity and accuracy as a function of valence. *Behavior Therapy*, **11**, 245-255.

Mahoney, M. (1979). Cognitive skills and athletic performance. In P. Kendall & S. Hollon (Eds.), *Cognitive-behavioral interventions: Theory, research and procedures* (pp. 423-443). New York: Academic Press.

Mahoney, M. (1985, November). *A cognitive revolution in behavior therapy: Conceptual and empirical issues*. In L. Reyna (Chair), Panel conducted at the meeting of the Association for the Advancement of Behavior Therapy, Houston, TX.

Mahoney, M., & Avener, M. (1977). Psychology of the elite athlete: An exploratory study. *Cognitive Therapy and Research*, **1**, 135-141.

Martens, R. (1977). *Sport Competition Anxiety Test*. Champaign, IL: Human Kinetics.

Martens, R., Burton, D., Rivkin, F., & Simon, J. (1980). Reliability and validity of the competitive state anxiety inventory. In C. Nadeau, W. Halliwell, K. Newell, & G. Roberts (Eds.), *Psychology of motor behavior and sport—1979* (pp. 91-99). Champaign, IL: Human Kinetics.

McKenzie, T., & Rushall, B. (1980). Controlling inappropriate behaviors in a competitive swimming environment. *Education and Treatment of Children*, **3**, 205-216.

Meichenbaum, D. (1971). Examination of model characteristics in reducing avoidance behavior. *Journal of Personality and Social Psychology*, **17**, 298-307.

Morgan, W. (1984). Mind over matter. In W. Straub & J. Williams (Eds.), *Cognitive sport psychology* (pp. 311-316). Lansing, NY: Sport Science Associations.

Morgan, W. (1985). *Overtraining*. Invited address to the Symposium on Sports Medicine, School of Medicine, University of Minnesota, Duluth, MN.

Morgan, W., Horstman, D. Cymerman, A., & Stokes, J. (1983). Facilitation of physical performance by means of a cognitive strategy. *Cognitive Therapy and Research*, **7**, 251-264.

Nideffer, R. (1971). Deep muscle relaxation: An aid to diving. *Coach and Athlete*, **24**, 38.

Noel, R.C. (1980). The effect of visuo-motor behavior rehearsal on tennis performance. *Journal of Sport Psychology*, **2**, 220-226.

Oxendine, J. (1968). *Psychology of motor learning*, New York: Meredith.

Richardson, A. (1967a). Mental practice: A review and discussion. Part 1. *Research Quarterly*, **38**, 95-107.

Richardson, A. (1967b). Mental practice: A review and discussion. Part 2. *Research Quarterly*, **38**, 263-273.

Seabourne, T., Weinberg, R., Jackson, A., & Suinn, R. (1985). Effect of individualized, nonindividualized, and package intervention strategies on karate performance. *Journal of Sport Psychology*, **7**, 40-50.

Schleser, R., Meyers, A.W., & Montgomery, T. (1980, November). *A cognitive behavioral intervention for improving basketball performance*. Paper presented at the 18th Annual Convention of the Association for the Advancement of Behavior Therapy, New York: NY.

Simek, T., & O'Brien, R. (1982, May). *A chaining-mastery, discrimination training program to teach little leaguers to hit a baseball: An unintentional between groups, multiple baseline study*. Paper presented at the Association for Behavior Analysis Convention, Milwaukee, WI.

Spielberger, C., Jacobs, G., Crane, R., Russell, S., Westberry, L., Barker, L., Johnson, E., Knight, J., & Marks, E. (1979). *Preliminary manual for the State-Trait Personality Inventory*. Tampa, FL: University of South Florida Human Resources Institute.

Suinn, R. (1969). The STABS, a measure of test anxiety for behavior therapy: Normative data. *Behaviour Research and Therapy*, **7**, 335-339.

Suinn, R. (1972). Behavior rehearsal training for ski racers. *Behavior Therapy*, **3**, 519.

Suinn, R. (1980). Psychology and sports performance: Principles and applications. In R. Suinn (Ed.), *Psychology in sports: Methods and applications* (pp. 26-36). Minneapolis, MN: Burgess.

Suinn, R. (1982). Imagery and sports. In A. Sheikh (Ed.), *Imagery, current theory, research and application* (pp. 507-534). New York: Wiley.

Suinn, R. (1983). *Manual: Anxiety management training* (rev. ed.). Fort Collins, CO: Rocky Mountain Behavioral Sciences Institute.

Suinn, R. (1984). Visual motor behavior rehearsal: The basic technique. *Scandinavian Journal of Behaviour Therapy*, **13**, 131-142.

Suinn, R. (1986). *The seven steps to peak performance: The mental training manual for athletes*. Toronto: Hans Huber.

Suinn, R., Morton, M., & Brammell, H. (1979). Psychological and mental training to increase efficiency in endurance athletes. In *Final report to U.S. Olympic Women's Athletics Developmental Subcommittee*. Fort Collins: Colorado State University.

Suinn, R., & Richardson, R. (1971). Anxiety management training: A nonspecific behavior therapy program for anxiety control. *Behavior Therapy*, **4**, 498.

Weinberg, R. (1985, November). Effect of mental preparation strategies and cognitive intervention techniques in enhancing motor performance. In A. Meyers (Chair), *Behavioral sports psychology: The current view*. Symposium conducted at the meeting of the Association for the Advancement of Behavior Therapy, Houston, TX.

Weinberg, R., Seabourne, T., & Jackson, A. (1981). Effects of visual-motor behavior rehearsal, relaxation, and imagery on karate performance. *Journal of Sport Psychology*, **3**, 228-238.

Woolfolk, R., Parrish, M., & Murphy, S. (1985). The effects of positive and negative imagery on motor skill performance. *Cognitive Therapy and Research*, **9**, 335-341.

Youngblood, D., & Suinn, R. (1980). A behavioral assessment of motivation. In R. Suinn (Ed.), *Psychology in sports: Methods and applications* (pp. 73-77). Minneapolis, MN: Burgess.

Ziegler, S., Klinzing, J., & Williamson, K. (1982). The effects of two stress management training programs on cardiorespiratory efficiency. *Journal of Sport Psychology*, **4**, 280-289.

Sport Psychology: A Commentary

Daniel M. Landers

In editing the motor learning/control and sport psychology papers delivered at the Gatorade conference I was impressed with many ideas presented by these authors. My charge as moderator for the session on "Future Direction in Exercise/Sport Research for Persons of Above-Average Health and Fitness" was to react to papers in the area of sport psychology, exercise physiology, and biomechanics. However, one paper wasn't received, and there was little that could be said about technological advances in biomechanics. Thus I considered a broader basis for my comments and have drawn from the areas of motor learning/control and sport psychology. Many of the points I wish to make deal with general scientific approaches that would apply to individuals who were below average, average, or above average in levels of performance, health, and fitness.

Given that my background is in sport psychology, the treatment of material from motor learning/control *and* sport psychology may be considered by some to be overambitious, or even presumptuous. However, many of the points I wish to make about sport psychology are contained in the motor learning/control papers and vice versa. This should not be too surprising because these two closely allied subdisciplines share a common interest in human behavior and mental operations governing this behavior. Generally, the techniques, methods, and theoretical approaches used to address this common interest have been different. Part of my premise, however, is that these fields have grown apart largely because they have become enamored with differences in methods, approaches, and techniques, and have lost sight of many common research problems.

My thesis is an old argument but one that I think we need to be reminded of from time to time; that is, we need to become more *problem-oriented* and less method/approach-oriented in our future research (Platt, 1964). There is a certain openness in regard to scientific inquiry presented in many of these papers that I find encouraging. I would like, therefore, to draw upon these ideas as I present some of the reasons why motor learning/control and sport psychology, in particular, have not become more problem oriented. I am uncomfortable trying to prophesy what the future directions of these fields will be because most predictions of past prophets have not been very accurate. I can, however, point out where I perceive problems have occurred in restricting a problem-oriented approach and ways in which these problems may be overcome. I will deal with four roadblocks, portrayed as inappropriate attitudes, limiting sport and exercise scientists from becoming more problem oriented. The first attitude perhaps explains why many sport psychologists in Morgan's terms may be perceived as "the most isolated of the isolates."

Roadblock 1: Ignore Science and Forget About Solving Problems

Morgan maintains that the contemporary *zeitgeist* in sport psychology calls for application, and he believes that future research in this field will be impaired if the applied movement continues to gain momentum. So as not to confuse this with the applied research that Christina characterizes as Levels 2 and 3, the term *applied* in sport psychology more often refers to service delivery to athletes and coaches. Thus the present-day characterization of the field of sport psychology would include basic and applied research (Levels 1-3 in Christina's categorization) as well as service delivery. The current interest in service delivery has been overwhelming, and it is Morgan's view that this movement will somehow dilute research efforts or lure budding young scientists away from research. According to Morgan and others (Landers, 1981), many sport psychologists are making applications for which they have no evidence and thus they are not sure if these applications will work. Some of those providing service evaluate the applications, but the vast majority do not. The techniques that they are using (e.g., imagery, relaxation, self-talk, goal setting) do have a research base, but as yet the research has not been conducted on athletes in practice or competitive settings. Thus many service providers are assuming that because it has been shown to work with Psychology 100 students, clinical patients, or businessmen, it should work as effectively in an athletic context.

I think that Morgan has some legitimate concerns here. However, before dealing with some of the problems that exist, I think it's important to point out that the applied or service delivery component of the field has helped to give sport psychology much greater visibility. It has resulted in more students desiring to enter this field and perhaps has contributed to the greater recognition given this field by organizations like the American Psychological Association, Biofeedback Society of America, and the U.S. Olympic Committee, to name a few.

Although this recognition is healthy for the field, there are some potential problems that must be dealt with in the future. For instance, there are some service providers that are either ill prepared or just disinterested in scientific research and, as a result, do not evaluate the applications they employ. Some even think that such an evaluation would be a waste of time for other scientists to undertake. In essence, they shun the scientific method and do not encourage attempts to apply it to Level 2 or 3 research aimed at testing the bread-and-butter techniques they employ. Some have even attempted to create an alternative method involving introspective methods and experiential knowledge (Martens, 1987).

This attitude is also associated with a separation from other scientific societies (e.g., North American Society for the Psychology of Sport and Physical Activity), and fear of aligning with major professional organizations in psychology (e.g., American Psychological Association). Many have created the illusion among PhD students, some of whom have little interest in scientific research, that they will find jobs in sport psychology. Six years ago it was predicted that there would be many new avenues of employment other than the conventional academic positions for PhDs in sport psychology. In universities with a strong research orientation, the PhD candidates with a primary service orientation did not make reasonable progress in the program. At other universities where research was not stressed as much, the service-oriented PhD candidates progressed quickly through these programs only to find few, if any, sport psychology jobs awaiting them when they were finished. Notwithstanding the full-time position at the Olympic Training Center, which requires research skills, the projected permanent positions in university athletic departments, industry, and professional or semiprofessional teams have not materialized. The limited consulting opportunities in sport psychology often go to the more experienced sport psychologists who have gained their reputations from their research efforts. I believe that many students are being given poor advice, and because of this are ill prepared as scientists to assume the only full-time jobs open to sport psychologists (i.e., academic positions for individuals with a PhD). There is also something basically wrong with permitting students, who are interested only in service and not scientific training, to pursue a terminal *research* degree like the PhD.

I do not think that those providing service should sit idle until scientific evidence has validated their particular application or technique. Until research is conducted, they should provide the best service possible based upon their informed opinion (or intuition perhaps) of worthwhile techniques. However, this source of knowledge should only be considered as a temporary state of affairs, and scientific research should be encouraged to eventually replace this relatively unreliable source of knowledge. It is this nonscientific attitude that is frightening, because it would greatly impair needed future applied research in sport psychology. It is as if those having this attitude were trying to escape responsibility by denying the importance of using the scientific method to evaluate the techniques they are using. To combat this nonscientific attitude, it is essential that a problem-oriented approach be encouraged in research efforts.

To minimize the formation of non-problem-solving attitudes, I would like to see professional associations/societies adopt guidelines for the training of sport psychologists that include scientific methodology in conducting applied research (Levels 2 and 3) in simulated or real sport and exercise settings. In fact, I would like to see prospective students selected foremost on their willingness to be involved in research rather than service activities. In other words, I would like them to be trained as scientists first before they are permitted to serve as interns providing service to athletes. In this way, individuals will not be allowed to shirk their responsibility of learning the rigorous, sometimes tedious, techniques for evaluating the applications they are using. Beyond this, new ways need to be sought to encourage those in the field to do evaluations of their techniques. They should be encouraged to attend workshops on evaluation research. This will at least allow them to have more flexible attitudes, so that if they do not do the evaluation, they will at least encourage others to evaluate the psychological skills for them. This would go a long way toward fostering open inquiry and a problem-solving approach in sport psychology, and help to bring sport psychologists more into the mainstream with other sport scientists who are providing applied research and service to coaches and athletes.

Roadblock 2: Everybody Should Use This Approach or Technique

Several of the papers in this volume (Feltz, Morgan, Schmidt) have provided a chronology of different approaches that have been in vogue over the years. The history of sport psychology and motor learning/control is full of trendy directions set forth by influential people in the field. In sport psychology the prevailing *zeitgeist* has gone from personality testing to social analysis (theory and data gathering), from mechanistic theories to field research and sport-specific questionnaires, and finally from cognitive psychology to psychological skills. In motor learning/control, Schmidt has characterized the field as going from a task-oriented approach to a process-oriented approach, and now he is advocating a return to the task-oriented approach. Feltz maintains that sport psychology, and it could be said motor learning/control as well, has had its respective leaders trying to influence their field in what they considered socially acceptable research.

There have been recent attempts to broaden the prevailing *zeitgeist* to allow consideration of alternative paradigms and techniques. Morgan (1985), for instance, has suggested a psychobiological approach, and Hatfield and Landers (1983) have similarly pointed out several methodological advantages in using a psychophysiological approach. They have also suggested research questions that would be difficult to address using behavioral or self-report methodologies. This natural science approach is not meant for everyone nor would it be of use in answering all of the research questions in sport psychology and motor learning/control. The key difference between recommending this approach and the other more trendy approaches that have been advocated is that psychophysiology is not viewed as the only approach for the field, or one that should necessarily take away from the other approaches. Thus it becomes one of many approaches that can be used if the research problem is such that it will lend itself to the techniques and theories that have been developed in this field. Morgan's suggested use of animal models may be quite foreign to sport psychologists, but it makes sense for a select few research problems that methodologically or ethically would be difficult to address with the conventional human model.

Understanding of psychophysiological theory enables investigators to examine some of the traditional interpretations that have been given to findings in the literature. For example, Feltz points out that the assessment of arousal has been problematic in social facilitation research. Some investigators were quick to suggest that physiological measures were troublesome and better results would be obtained from self-report measures of arousal. As more studies in this area have been conducted, however, it has become clear that the effect of audiences and coactors in these laboratory studies was so small as to be of trivial practical significance. It should be obvious that if the effect is very small (accounting for only 1–3% of the variance), there would be little change in physiological measures. This together with inappropriate psychophysiological measurement techniques (see Hatfield & Landers, 1987) makes it easy to understand why investigators have had trouble in assessing the suspected arousal believed to be associated with social facilitation research. Likewise, those who are interested in attention-distraction (Sanders, 1981), or objective self-awareness (Carver & Scheier, 1981; Duval & Wickland, 1972) explanations for social facilitation effects would benefit from psychophysiological theory (e.g., Lacey, Kagan, Lacey, & Moss, 1963, intake-rejection hypothesis) and the measures that have been shown to distinguish reliably between attention directed inward versus outward (e.g., beat-to-beat heart rate acceleration or deceleration). These performance problems together with the health-related problems outlined by Morgan are some of the areas in which a natural science approach should be considered.

In terms of motor learning/control, I think it would be a mistake if all researchers suddenly shifted to a strictly task-oriented approach and totally rejected the process approach. Again, if a better understanding of the problem being investigated would be provided by examining process as well as task factors, they by all means should be included in the design. As Stelmach points out, it is not the process-oriented research per se that was problematic; it was often the way the process-oriented approach was employed.

Stelmach goes on to argue that part of the problem with the process-oriented studies was that they created conditions in experiments that were molar and artificial, and did not typify real-life performance situations. This, of course, need not be the case. With some creative imagination and considerable pilot testing to refine procedures, it would be possible to examine real-world tasks and processes involved without sacrificing too much scientific control. I believe that some of the work conducted in our laboratory by Wang and Landers (1986) satisfies these requirements. Based upon previous research examining hemispheric asymmetries and cardiac deceleration among rifle shooters (Hatfield, Landers, & Ray, 1984, 1987), Wang and Landers (1986) extended this to a stimulus-response situation in the sport of archery. Psychophysiological measures of left and right hemisphere EEG and heart rate deceleration permitted inferences to be made regarding the degree and direction (internal vs. external) of attention in a 6-s period before the release of the arrow. We found that better archery performance was associated with greater attention being directed to the external environment, as inferred from measures of cardiac deceleration and hemispheric asymmetries. It should be clear that other types of measures of attention during task performance would have interfered with performance (e.g., evoked potentials or dual-task methodologies). The point needs to be made, however, that we do not need to restrict our process measures to the conventional measures employed in laboratory settings. Where appropriate, the newer techniques in electrophysiology and biomechanics should also be considered to examine process in many of the task-oriented studies.

I think the approach offered by Christina is in line with the problem-oriented approach that I am advocating. Although Christina develops his concept of three levels of relevance for the field of motor learning, it is also equally pertinent to sport psychology, and probably other fields as well. The basic point is that the type of research is directed by the question being asked. It is not that every study should ask basic questions or that finding immediate solutions to practical problems is the only way to go! It depends on how much direct relevance the investigator wishes to achieve, and this will dictate the task that should be employed.

A basic difference between sport psychology and motor learning/control is the amount of relevance that is attached to the research question posed by the investigator. In contemporary sport psychology, the problem often deals with real-world tasks (Christina's Levels 2 and 3), whereas in motor learning/control the tasks have often been artificial (Level 1). The unfortunate development of this rather uncompromising adherence to different levels of relevance has been that the people doing research in these two fields do not talk to one antoher. There are some signs of flexibility in the recent work of Robert Christina, John Shea, and Stephen Wallace because these motor learning/control investigators are beginning to stress more relevance (Level 2 studies). Likewise, I would like to see sport psychology studies conducted in the laboratory with artificial tasks or even animals (e.g., Rejeski, Brubaker, Herb, Kaplan, & Koritnik, 1988) if the research problem would be best answered by using such an approach. In short, I am arguing for less emphasis on the belief that everyone should adhere to what is considered to be the best method, technique, or theoretical approach.

An examination of the historical development of the fields of motor learning/control and sport psychology would reveal that the best approach at one time is not the best approach at a later time. I think Platt (1964) summed it up best when he said, "Beware of the man of one method or one instrument, either experimental or theoretical. He tends to become method-oriented rather than problem-oriented; the method-oriented man is shackled" (p. 351).

Roadblock 3: It Is a Sin to Borrow Theories From Other Disciplines

In Morgan's paper the point is made that the borrowing of theories from psychology has not met with much success and that these theories have usually been discarded in frustration because they didn't work. Feltz suggests a similar scenario for those who have not developed a "systematic plan of research." She adds, however, that they may not leave the area; instead, they may search for an explanation and attempt to modify methods, measures, or theories for sport. With the exception of applied behavior analysis areas mentioned in Richard Suinn's paper, there is little doubt that many, if not most, of the theories borrowed from social or personality psychology have not worked all that well in a performance or exercise context. This has led Morgan and others (Alderman, 1980; Dishman, 1983; Martens, 1980) to advocate the need to develop our own theories to gain a better understanding of sport behavior. In fact, Morgan does not believe that progress will be made until theoretical formulations are developed within the context of exercise and sport.

There is some merit to these suggestions. However, some clarification is in order because some people could interpret Morgan's ideas as license to abandon psychological theories. This may not be what Morgan intends: Later in his paper, he strongly advocates a multidisciplinary approach—an approach that suggests an understanding, and perhaps a use, of theory and methodology from other disciplines.

A case could be made that the borrowing of theories has been necessary for the development of sport psychology and motor learning/control. Feltz concedes that the borrowing of theories from psychology "has not been all that harmful." Likewise, Alderman (1980) has indicated that borrowing theories has provided initial understanding in the new areas of exercise and sport sciences, but he recognizes that it can only carry us so far in obtaining a complete understanding.

It is relatively easy to suggest that we develop our own unique theories, but in practice this is not an easy task. Upon closer examination, the "theories" that have been developed in our field involve constructs, assumptions, and empirical support from academic psychology (Griffin, Keogh, & Maybee, 1984; Scanlan, 1985; Vealey, 1985). In other homegrown theories (e.g., Martens's [1976] theory of competition) the scientific support for some of the borrowed assumptions has not held up over time. Even some of Morgan's own explanations for the euphoric or relaxed state following aerobic exercise (i.e., "the time-out hypothesis") bears many similarities to theoretical explanations in academic psychology (Gal & Lazarus, 1975).

The point is that theory can't be developed in a vacuum. Theories, methods, and approaches from academic psychology need to be borrowed and tested in original or modified form to determine if they work in a performance or exercise context. Rather than giving up and leaving the area if the application is unsuccessful, researchers should spend more time trying to reformulate the theoretical ideas into something that might be more meaningful.

Too often investigators in our field have constraining commitments to theories from academic psychology, and thus it is difficult for them to think about modifying the theory to make it fit the performance or exercise context. I have argued elsewhere (Landers, 1983) that we must give up such commitments to theories from academic psychology. They should be viewed as only a starting point and with an open-minded view toward modifying the theory in the event that it doesn't work.

I have suggested previously (Landers, 1983) that one way to avoid restraining commitments to particular theories is for investigators to use, where possible, the method of strong inference (Platt, 1964). This method lends itself to a problem-oriented approach because the basic premise is to test multiple theories, ideas, and hypotheses in a single or series of studies. In this way, the researcher can determine if one, none, or a combination of facets of each theory may best explain behavior in performance, health, and exercise contexts. Thus it is irrelevant where the theories come from; rather, the focus is on the critical assessment without premature commitments to any of them.

Feltz agrees with the idea of testing multiple theories. However, she points out the limitations imposed by the strong inference approach in that there is too much emphasis placed on science advancing by means of single disconfirmations. Although it is doubtful whether Platt (1964) would object to replication before concluding disproof of a theory, Feltz concludes that with such a heavy emphasis on falsification in strong inference there is a danger that the investigator may reject a hypothesis or theory prematurely.

In place of strong inference, Feltz recommends Shadish's (1985) approach of "planned critical multiplism." As part of a systematic research program, this method involves a critical examination of different biases in the multiple hypotheses, theories, or explanations tested so that a greater "scrutiny of inconsistencies" can be gleaned. I like the basic premise underlying this approach because it is clearly in line with a problem-oriented approach and incorporates much of what I had recommended (i.e., testing multiple theories, meta-analyses, etc.) in an earlier paper (Landers, 1983). However, this approach is fairly new and, unlike the strong inference approach (e.g., Feltz & Mugno's [1983] own work on self-efficacy), there are few good examples of its viability in advancing our understanding of health, performance, and exercise. This is not to say that we should not use it, only that lacking direction we need to carefully examine where it can be used and whether it is feasible. Until the full advantages of planned critical multiplism can be shown, I am not convinced that this approach will lead to relatively clear-cut answers to our problems. It remains to be seen if future research will benefit more from planned critical multiplism or from simply a more cautious approach to strong inference (i.e., less reliance on *single* disconfirmations).

Roadblock 4: Disciplinary Parochialism Should be the Model for the Field

In both the Feltz and Morgan papers there was encouragement for the field of sport psychology, and I would include motor learning/control as well, to conduct more interdisciplinary research. I would rephrase this slightly to suggest that if the research problem being addressed would benefit from interdisciplinary research, then by all means it should be conducted. This may involve investigators' retooling to learn the techniques or theories of another discipline, or it may necessitate forming collaborations with investigators in other disciplines.

Although this appears to be relatively logical and straightforward, it is not being practiced to any great extent in sport psychology. A parochial attitude is often conveyed by statements such as "they don't like exercise physiology," or that "biomechanics has no theory or ideas of its own, just a lot of techniques and instrumentation." It is also indicative of the isolation or marginality sport psychologists or motor learning/control investigators sometimes express in regard to other sport and exercise scientists on their own faculties. This attitude is also manifest in the meetings attended by sport psychologists. It is much more common to see people in motor learning/control attend meetings in academic psychology than it is for sport psychologists. However, it is rare for either of these groups to attend meetings with other exercise and sport scientists (e.g., American College of Sports Medicine). In addition, sport psychologists often choose their sabbatical leaves with some other motive in mind other than learning new methods, instrumentation, or theoretical approaches. Rarely do they ever stretch themselves and venture beyond the comfort zone of their own specific interest within sport psychology. Because I regard this as a generally correct characterization of the field of sport psychology, I would have to agree with Morgan that sport psychologists permit themselves to be "the most isolated of the isolates."

This parochial attitude is not conducive to the problem-oriented approach I am advocating. With more and more research questions necessitating a broader perspective of the myriad of psychological, biomechanical, and physiological factors affecting health, performance, and fitness, it is difficult to deny at present or in the future that a multidisciplinary approach will not be needed sometimes. The emphasis on this combined team approach has already been outlined in the U.S. Olympic Committee guidelines for research grants. As grant money becomes more and more a determinant as to who does research on college campuses, sport psychologists may need to undertake multidisciplinary research to improve their chances of obtaining research grants. Although I am not sympathetic to the pressure being created to obtain grants, the fact remains that to be on the frontiers of knowledge in any field often necessitates a multidisciplinary view to learning, and using new methods and techniques to address long-standing issues.

It is gratifying to see investigators like Morgan and Rejeski functioning as part of a research team to examine pertinent health-related questions using an animal model. Likewise, the use of psychophysiological theory and techniques by Hatfield, Landers, and Wang lends itself to a multidisciplinary approach. The interfacing of motor control with biomechanics to address research questions dealing with gait patterns is another area illustrating the mutual benefits of a multidisciplinary approach.

It is apparent that the multidisciplinary research approach needs to be encouraged among sport psychologists. At annual meetings of the North American Society for the Psychology of Sport and Physical Activity there should be workshops established to teach new methods, instrumentation, and theoretical approaches that are potentially useful for addressing research questions in sport psychology. I am not referring here to subtle variants of what sport psychologists are already doing (e.g., how to construct sport-specific questionnaires). Instead, I am referring to more complex techniques such as innovative multivariate design and analysis procedures, planned critical multiplism versus strong inference, procedures for conducting meta-analyses, and instrumentation (behavioral or electrophysiological) that can be used to make inferences to cognitive processes of interest to sport psychologists.

Finally, more has to be done to better educate aspiring young sport psychologists to become more multidisciplinary in their orientation. Having served on the same screening committee with Morgan, I will support his observation that the graduates of many sport psychology programs do not have graduate training in the parent discipline of psychology, nor do they have graduate course work in the sport sciences. I would like to see more emphasis placed on interdisciplinary research in our PhD programs. This can be accomplished in part by encouraging students to take independent study credits with faculty members with interests that border on the sport psychology area. Moreover, sponsoring occasional joint seminars to supplement discipline-specific seminars may help students become less isolated so they will be less afraid to ask more interesting and challenging questions involving cross-disciplinary interaction.

In summary, the subdisciplines of sport psychology, and to some extent motor learning/control, need to become more problem oriented by changing some pervasive attitudes that exist in these fields. If future research efforts are to show some improvement, investigators in these subdisciplines should not (a) ignore science as an important problem-solving method; (b) continue constraining commitments to one particular method, approach, or theory so that they lose sight of the problem and become method oriented (Platt, 1964); (c) limit the ways in which the problem can be addressed by restricting the search and use of relevant theory in the belief that we should not borrow theory from academic psychology; or (d) focus only on narrowly defined problems, involving singular methods, by thinking that we are somehow different from other scientists, and should remain relatively isolated from the mainstream scientific community in psychology or in exercise and sport science. I have argued that, if these attitudes are to change, new ways need to be devised to retool some investigators in the use of new technologies and theoretical developments. Likewise, I have echoed many of Morgan's assertions that basic changes need to be made in many of our PhD training programs. It is in this latter area of training future PhDs that Morgan contends is the single greatest challenge of all. Here again, I must agree!

References

Alderman, R.B. (1980). Sport psychology: Past, present, and future dilemmas. In P. Klavora & A.W. Wipper (Eds.), *Psychological and sociological factors in sport* (pp. 3-19). Toronto: Publications Division, School of Physical and Health Education, University of Toronto.

Carver, C.S., & Scheier, M.F. (1981). *Attention and self-regulation: A control theory approach to human behavior*. New York: Springer.

Dishman, R.K. (1983). Identity crisis in North American sport psychology: Academics in professional issues. *Journal of Sport Psychology*, **5**, 123-134.

Duval, S., & Wickland, R.A. (1972). *A theory of objective self-awareness*. New York: Academic Press.

Feltz, D.L., & Mugno, D.A. (1983). A replication of the path analysis of the causal elements in Bandura's theory of self-efficacy and the influence of autonomic perception. *Journal of Sport Psychology*, **5**, 263-277.

Gal, R., & Lazarus, R.S. (1975). The role of activity in anticipating and confronting stressful situations. *Journal of Human Stress*, **1**(4), 4-20.

Griffin, N.S., Keogh, J.F., & Maybee, R. (1984). Performer perceptions of movement confidence. *Journal of Sport Psychology*, **6**, 395-407.

Hatfield, B.D., & Landers, D.M. (1983). Psychophysiology—a new direction for sport psychology. *Journal of Sport Psychology*, **5**, 243-259.

Hatfield, B.D., & Landers, D.M. (1987). Psychophysiology within exercise and sport research: An overview. *Exercise and Sport Sciences Reviews*, **15**, 351-387.

Hatfield, B.D., Landers, D.M., & Ray, W.J. (1984). Cognitive processes during self-paced motor performance: An electroencephalographic profile of skilled marksmen. *Journal of Sport Psychology*, **6**, 42-59.

Hatfield, B.D., Landers, D.M., & Ray, W.J. (1987). Cardiovascular-CNS interactions during a self-paced, intentional attentive state: Elite marksmanship performance. *Psychophysiology*, **24**, 542-549.

Lacey, J.I., Kagan, J., Lacey, B.C., & Moss, H.A. (1963). The visceral level: Situational determinants and behavioral correlates of autonomic response patterns. In P.G. Knapp (Ed.), *Expression of emotions in man* (pp. 161-196). New York: International Universities Press.

Landers, D.M. (1981). Reflections on sport psychology and the Olympic athlete. In J. Segrave & D. Chu (Eds.), *Olympism* (pp. 189-200). Champaign, IL: Human Kinetics.

Landers, D.M. (1983). Whatever happened to theory testing in sport psychology? *Journal of Sport Psychology*, **5**, 135-151.

Martens, R. (1976). Competition: In need of a theory. In D. Landers (Ed.), *Social problems in athletics* (pp. 9-17). Champaign, IL: University of Illinois Press.

Martens, R. (1980). From smocks to jocks: A new adventure for sport psychologists. In P. Klavora & K.A.W. Wipper (Eds.), *Psychological and sociological factors in sport* (pp. 20-26). Toronto: Publications Division, School of Physical and Health Education, University of Toronto.

Martens, R. (1987). Science, knowledge, and sport psychology. *The Sport Psychologist*, **1**, 29-55.

Morgan, W.P. (1985). Affective beneficence of vigorous physical activity. *Medicine and Science in Sports and Exercise*, **17**, 94-100.

Platt, J.R. (1964). Strong inference. *Science*, **146**, 347-352.

Rejeski, W.J., Brubaker, P.H., Herb, R.A., Kaplan, J.R., & Koritnik, D. (1988). Anabolic steroids and aggressive behavior in cynomolgus monkeys. *Journal of Behavioral Medicine*, **11**, 95-105.

Sanders, G.S. (1981). Driven by distraction—An integrative review of social facilitation theory and research. *Journal of Experimental Social Psychology*, **40**, 1102-1117.

Scanlan, T. (1985). Social psychological aspects of competition for male youth sport participants: 4. Predictors of enjoyment. *Journal of Sport Psychology*, **8**, 25-35.

Shadish, W.R., Jr. (1985). Planned critical multiplism: Some elaborations. *Behavioral Assessment*, **8**, 74-103.

Vealey, R.S. (1985). Conceptualization of sport-confidence and competitive orientation: Preliminary investigation and instrument development. *Journal of Sport Psychology*, **8**, 221-246.

Wang, M.Q., & Landers, D.M. (1986). Cardiac response and hemispheric differentiation during archery performance: A psychophysiological investigation of attention [Abstract]. *Psychophysiology*, **23**, 469.